TABLE 3
Real GNP and prices

Year or Quarter	Real GNP 1972 Dollars	Implicit Price Deflator for Gross National Product	Consumer Price Index (CPI)	Annual Change in CPI (December—December)
1946	475.7	44.06	58.5	—
1947	468.3	49.70	66.9	—
1948	487.7	53.13	72.1	7.8
1949	490.7	52.59	71.4	−1.0
1950	533.5	53.64	72.1	1.0
1951	576.5	57.27	77.8	7.9
1952	598.5	58.00	79.5	2.2
1953	621.8	58.88	80.1	.8
1954	613.7	59.69	80.5	.5
1955	654.8	60.98	80.2	−.4
1956	668.8	62.90	81.4	1.5
1957	680.9	65.02	84.3	3.6
1958	679.5	66.06	86.6	2.7
1959	720.4	67.52	87.3	.8
1960	736.8	68.67	88.7	1.6
1961	755.3	69.28	89.6	1.0
1962	799.1	70.55	90.6	1.1
1963	830.7	71.59	91.7	1.2
1964	874.4	72.71	92.9	1.3
1965	925.9	74.32	94.5	1.7
1966	981.0	76.76	97.2	2.9
1967	1,007.7	79.02	100.0	2.9
1968	1,051.8	82.57	104.2	4.2
1969	1,078.8	86.72	109.8	5.4
1970	1,075.3	91.36	116.3	5.9
1971	1,107.5	96.02	121.3	4.3
1972	1,171.1	100.00	125.3	3.3
1973	1,233.4	105.92	133.1	6.2
1974	1,210.7	116.20	147.7	11.0
1975	1,186.4	126.35	161.2	9.1

TABLE 4
Population and employment

Year or Quarter	Total Population (thousands)	Civilian Labor Force (thousands)	Employed	Unemployed	Unemployment Rate (percent)
1946	141,389	—	—	—	3.9
1947	144,126	59,350	57,039	2,311	3.9
1948	146,631	60,621	58,344	2,276	3.8
1949	149,188	61,286	57,649	3,637	5.9
1950	152,271	62,208	58,920	3,288	5.3
1951	154,878	62,017	59,962	2,055	3.3
1952	157,553	62,138	60,254	1,883	3.0
1953	160,184	63,015	61,181	1,834	2.9
1954	163,026	63,643	60,110	3,532	5.5
1955	165,931	65,023	62,171	2,852	4.4
1956	168,903	66,552	63,802	2,750	4.1
1957	171,984	66,929	64,071	2,859	4.3
1958	174,882	67,639	63,036	4,602	6.8
1959	177,830	68,369	64,630	3,740	5.5
1960	180,671	69,528	65,778	3,852	5.5
1961	183,691	70,459	65,746	4,714	6.7
1962	186,538	70,614	66,702	3,911	5.5
1963	189,242	71,833	67,762	4,070	5.7
1964	191,889	73,091	69,305	3,786	5.2
1965	194,303	74,455	71,088	3,366	4.5
1966	196,560	75,770	72,895	2,875	3.8
1967	198,712	77,347	74,372	2,975	3.8
1968	200,706	78,737	75,920	2,817	3.6
1969	202,677	80,734	77,902	2,832	3.5
1970	204,878	82,715	78,627	4,088	4.9
1971	207,053	84,113	79,120	4,993	5.9
1972	208,846	86,542	81,702	4,840	5.6
1973	210,410	88,714	84,409	4,304	4.9
1974	211,894	91,011	85,936	5,076	5.6
1975	213,631	92,613	84,783	7,830	8.5

TABLE 5
Money and interest rates

Year or Quarter	M_1 (Currency plus Demand Deposits)	M_2 (M_1 plus Time Deposits at Commercial Banks Other than Large CD's)	3-month Treasury Bills	Moody's Aaa Corporate Bond Rate	Discount Rate Federal Reserve Bank of New York
1946			.375	2.53	1.00
1947	113.1		.594	2.61	1.00
1948	111.5		1.040	2.82	1.34
1949	111.2		1.102	2.66	1.50
1950	116.2		1.218	2.62	1.59
1951	122.7		1.552	2.86	1.75
1952	127.4		1.766	2.96	1.75
1953	128.8		1.931	3.20	1.99
1954	132.3		.953	2.90	1.60
1955	135.2		1.753	3.06	1.89
1956	136.9		2.658	3.36	2.77
1957	135.9		3.267	3.89	3.12
1958	141.1		1.839	3.79	2.15
1959	143.4	210.9	3.405	4.38	3.36
1960	144.2	217.1	2.928	4.41	3.53
1961	148.7	228.6	2.378	4.35	3.00
1962	150.9	242.9	2.778	4.33	3.00
1963	156.5	258.9	3.157	4.26	3.23
1964	163.7	277.1	3.549	4.40	3.55
1965	171.3	301.3	3.954	4.49	4.04
1966	175.4	317.8	4.881	5.13	4.50
1967	186.9	349.6	4.321	5.51	4.19
1968	201.7	382.3	5.339	6.18	5.17
1969	208.7	392.2	6.677	7.03	5.87
1970	221.4	425.3	6.458	8.04	5.95
1971	235.3	473.0	4.348	7.39	4.88
1972	255.8	525.7	4.071	7.21	4.50
1973	271.5	572.2	7.041	7.44	6.44
1974	284.4	613.5	7.886	8.57	7.83
1975	296.4	667.5	5.838	8.83	6.25

Basic Economics

Basic Economics

Edwin G. Dolan

*Assistant Professor of Economics, Dartmouth College
and Adjunct Professor of Economics, Royalton College*

with the collaboration of
David E. Lindsey

*Senior Economist
Division of Research and Statistics
Board of Governors of the Federal Reserve System*

THE DRYDEN PRESS
Hinsdale, Illinois

Copyright © 1977 by The Dryden Press.
A division of Holt, Rinehart and Winston, Publishers
All rights reserved
Library of Congress Catalog Card Number: 76-19363
ISBN: 0-03-089743-2
Printed in the United States of America
789   032   987654321

Editorial production services by Cobb/Dunlop, Publisher Services, Inc.
Picture research by Marcia Kelly
Cover and text design by Caliber
Typesetting by Applied Typographic Systems

Grateful acknowledgment is made to the following people and organizations for the use of
photographs:
Chase Ltd., Washington: Arthur Okun (p. 107)
Culver Pictures: Thomas Malthus (p. 523), David Ricardo (p. 551), and Adam Smith (p. 10)
Harvard University News Office, Cambridge: Joseph A. Schumpeter (p. 421)
Historical Pictures Service, Chicago: Samuel Gompers (p. 462), William Stanley Jevons
    (p. 304), John Maynard Keynes (p. 121), Alfred Marshall (p. 36), John Stuart Mill (p. 116)
Ramsey & Muspratt, Cambridge, England: Joan V. Robinson (p. 410)
Dan Thorburn, University of Guelph, Guelph, Canada: John Kenneth Galbraith (p. 322)
United Press International: Arthur F. Burns (p. 172), Milton Friedman (p. 206), Leonid V.
    Kantorovich (p. 365), Oskar Lange (p. 581), Friedrich A. von Hayek (p. 28)
Wiener Presse Bilddienst, Vienna, Austria: Ludwig von Mises (p. 587)

TO
EDWARD BASTIAN
and his tradition of excellence in teaching

EGD and DEL

Preface

Economics in Today's World

The economics profession, as we who pursue it know, is strongly counter-cyclical. Like suppliers of shoe repairs or intercity bus travel, suppliers of economic analysis enjoy a boom whenever the economy goes into a slump. In the sixties, students drifted away from economics in search of "relevance." Today we do not have to go around telling students that economics is relevant—our rising enrollments show that they already know it is. Our job now is not to disappoint them. They come to our principles courses with simple, practical concerns and questions. We must be equipped to address those concerns and questions. That is what this book is all about.

Inflation and Unemployment

The number one concern that draws students to the principles course is the problem of inflation and unemployment. When I first sat down to write this book, I had a survey at hand that showed inadequate treatment of inflation and unemployment to be the number one source of dissatisfaction with existing textbooks. To do the job right, it was clear that the macroeconomics section of the book had to be built from the ground up with the economic concerns of the seventies in mind. The traditional Keynesian income determination model, tried and tested through many editions of traditional textbooks, could serve as a starting point, but only that. You as an instructor had to be given a way to teach principles students the things that we in the profession have learned in the past few years about how our economy works—about the importance of inflationary expectations, about the role of money in the economy, about unemployment and the process of job search, and all the rest. These ideas are too important to be reserved for those few students who pursue economics into intermediate and advanced courses. Unfortunately, they are also too complex just to be tacked on to the traditional model by inserting a chapter on "contemporary macroeconomic issues." In this book, instead, the modern theories of inflation and unemployment are built right into the core of the macroeconomics section. The result is a text that is simpler, more straightforward, and easier to teach than anything you have ever seen.

Here is how it is done. First, Chapters 5 to 7 introduce the most important terms and concepts of macroeconomics, including the key concept of macroeconomic equilibrium. Chapters 8 to 13 then present conventional national income determination topics in a way that never muddles the key distinction between real and nominal values. That puts us in a position to ask the most important question of all: how is it determined what part of any change in nominal national income will take the form of a change in real income and employment, and what part will take the form of pure inflation?

This question is answered in a unique set of four chapters that builds on what the student has now learned. First, Chapter 14 discusses four traditional explanations of inflation and unemployment: the crude quantity theory, the Keynesian theory of inflationary gaps, the Phillips curve, and cost-push theories. It is shown how each of these ideas contains a part of the truth, but not the whole truth. Chapter 15 then takes up the economics of "the new unemployment," not neglecting the contribution that microeconomics has made to our understanding of unemployment in recent years. Next, Chapter 16 integrates the four incomplete theories of Chapter 14 into a whole. The four "crude" theories are seen to fit together almost like pieces of a jigsaw puzzle. This chapter uses a completely original graphical exposition of the theory of inflationary recession. It is this graphical presentation that brings this theory, often seen only in complex mathematical form, down to a level even simpler than the familiar "Keynesian cross" analysis that revolutionized the textbooks of a generation ago. Finally, Chapter 17 discusses contemporary controversies in macroeconomic policy, including wage and price controls, fine-tuning vs. policy rules, and indexing.

Chapter 17 also begins with a brief, entirely verbal and intuitive recap of what has gone on in Chapters 15 and 16. This gives the book a valuable two-track flexibility since Chapters 14 and 17 can be read as a coherent sequence by themselves if desired. The short track through this material makes it possible to cover the essentials of inflation and unemployment theory even in a one-semester course. But even if the short track is taken, this textbook still says more on these vital topics than anything previously available.

Economics and People

A second major theme of this book is that *economics is about people*. Important though this theme is, it is surprising how easy it is to neglect. The principles course, especially the microeconomics part, is in constant danger of degenerating into a course about criss-crossing curves and complex abbreviations. This leaves some students frustrated and disappointed, and wondering why they ever got into the course in the first place. Even worse, perhaps, it gives others a false sense of mastery. They leave the course with an "A" and a belief that they understand how the economy works, when all they have really done is demonstrated a knack for the mechanics of graphs.

This book makes a major effort to overcome this danger, by supplementing each step of the traditional neoclassical theory with broadly drawn pictures of the why's and how's of our economic system. Chapter 2, for example, precedes the next chapter's discussion of the mechanics of supply and demand with a discussion of markets as mechanisms for utilizing knowledge, as sources of incentives, and as windows on the future. Later, the chapter on consumer choice is supplemented by one on advertising and consumer sovereignty. The chapter on cost theory is supplemented by an extended discussion of the nature of the firm and by applications of economic thinking to practical business decision making. At all points, especially in the microeconomics section, much more than the usual emphasis is given to the role of the enterpreneur in the market economy. The entrepreneur is, after all, the flesh and blood individual who handles information, perceives new opportunities, and allocates real resources. It is always emphasized that the curves and graphs of traditional theory are only shorthand ways of representing what people are doing with their economic lives.

The Role of Government

A third way in which this book tries to meet the interests and concerns of today's students is the treatment of the role of government in the economy. In the changing political and economic climate of the seventies, Americans are taking a closer and more critical look at government than ever before. Economics textbooks of the past often reflected a bland acceptance of the way government performed its economic role, attributing dissenting views to an insignificant minority. Now it is the majority who are discontent. Today every aspect of the role of government—stabilization policy, welfare, defense, regulation, the administration of justice and all the rest—is the subject of turbulent national debate.

In this text, Washington is not treated as the home of philosopher kings (or economist kings), but rather as a place inhabited by fallible human beings, who sometimes make errors or succumb to selfish interests just as do the mere mortals who run the private sector. The student will learn why it is harder to achieve economic stability when politicians cannot see beyond the next elections; why the efforts made by federal regulatory agencies to improve resource allocation sometimes have effects opposite to those that are intended; and why Socialist and Communist planners stumble over many of the same economic problems that critics of capitalism identify as defects of our own system.

The Cases

No matter how well a textbook presents general principles, those principles by themselves are not enough. A time-honored doctrine tells us that each generalization should receive a specific illustration, just as each illustration should lead to a generalization. In this book, numerous short case studies are included to tie principles to reality. Many of these cases illustrate general statements about economic policy with specific policy episodes, such as the Kennedy tax cut or the Nixon wage-price controls. Other cases present empirical work to underline points of theory, for example, studies of the sources of U.S. economic growth, of demand elasticity for cotton, or of economies of scale in major industries.

If such illustrative material is to do its job, it must not interrupt proper concept flow. For that reason, the cases are short, to the point, and placed directly in the text just at the point they are needed. They thus appear not as digressions or interruptions, but as an integral part of the learning process.

Teaching and Learning Aids

This is a book from which students can and will learn. Some students come to college equipped with the study skills they would need to learn their economics by reading Marshall and Keynes in the original. Others, as we all know, come less well equipped. This book takes the realistic attitude that we must teach our students as they come to us and must help them develop good study skills as they go along.

Readability

For one thing, this book has a fully controlled reading level. It is designed to match the actual reading abilities of today's university freshmen and junior college students. Sad to say, the reading skills of many of them fall one, two, or even three years below established college standards. That puts the major competitive textbooks out of the reach of too many of the students who are asked to use them. This book, however, is designed to be fully readable even for students who read only at the 11th grade level. This combination of an accessible style of writing with sophisticated, up-to-date content makes the book unusually easy to teach and learn from.

As a further step toward readability, it should be added, this book discards the "alphabet soup" approach to teaching economics. When we talk about average variable cost or marginal propensity to consume, those are the very words we use, not AVC or MPC. It does not cost much in paper or ink to spell the words out in full. It does save students the unnecessary step of memorizing a whole bagful of abbreviations before they can even get down to learning economic principles.

Vocabulary

That brings us to another point—vocabulary. For many students, vocabulary is one of the big stumbling blocks in learning economics. This book uses a unique three-level reinforcement technique to handle the problem. First, each new term is printed in boldface at the point it is first used and defined. Next, the term and its definition are repeated on the same page in a marginal vocabulary note. Finally, there is a complete alphabetical glossary of all terms at the end of the book.

Working with Graphs

Another big obstacle for many students is working with graphs. For that reason, we have an appendix on working with graphs at the end of Chapter 1. This appendix does more than just explain techniques. It also addresses the most common student problems of working with graphs. One of these problems is the tendency to memorize graphs as meaningless pictures, with no understanding of their content. Another is the inability to draw original graphs when needed in note taking or on examinations. Our appendix carefully warns of the pitfalls and explains how they can be avoided.

Other Learning Aids

Other learning aids are provided for the student as well. A very important item is the Study Guide, a companion volume written by Thomas Anderson of Eastern Michigan University. In the textbook itself, students are provided with chapter previews and summaries, profiles of well-known economists, discussion questions, review suggestions, suggestions for further reading, and a complete index.

Teaching Aids

This book is also accompanied by a complete set of teaching aids for you, the instructor. First and foremost, there is an Instructor's Manual. This contains learning objectives, lecture notes, and answers to the end-of-chapter questions in the text. It also contains a section for each chapter entitled "What's Different Here, and Why." This section provides the information you need to convert your course to using this book from using whichever major competing textbook you had adopted in the past. A complete test bank and a set of transparency masters are also available to instructors, printed separately from the Instructor's Manual.

The Newsletter

As a final feature to help both you and your students, a twice-yearly newsletter is available to all instructors adopting this textbook. This newsletter serves a number of purposes. First, it contains fresh case studies of the same format as those included in the text. These can either be used as lecture material or be duplicated and distributed to students. Second, the newsletter updates the suggestions for further reading with mini-reviews of new books suitable for use in the principles course. Finally, the newsletter updates the most important statistical series used in the text.

Appendixes

Appendixes are used here and there in this book to cover those "can't please everyone" topics that some instructors like to include and others do not. One example is the appendix on indifference curves that follows Chapter 19. Another is the appendix on inflation and the money market after Chapter 16.

Two appendixes in particular deserve special comment. The appendixes to Chapters 10 and 13 present simple algebraic versions of the income determination model expounded verbally in the text. The text itself uses no algebra at all, and this approach will best serve the needs of most students and instructors. Even though a majority of students may never use them, however, the algebraic appendixes are valuable for two reasons. First, almost every university economics class contains a few students who are very good at mathematics and who can actually catch on faster to a set of equations than to a whole chapter of verbal exposition. Such students can read the appendixes on their own. Second, at schools that emphasize a technical curriculum, nearly all students may be well trained in mathematics. The appendixes can then be used as a regular part of the course.

Planning Your Course

This text is designed to give you the maximum possible flexibility in setting up your course, whatever the academic calendar employed by your particular school. Here, briefly, are suggested outlines for both one- and two-semester courses, microeconomics first or macroeconomics first outlines, and alternative application emphases. A more detailed discussion of course planning can be found in the Instructor's Manual that accompanies the textbook.

TWO-SEMESTER, MACROECONOMICS FIRST

	First Semester	*Second Semester*
Core	Parts 1 and 2	Parts 3 and 4
Applications	Part 5 or 6	Part 5 or 6, plus Part 7

TWO-SEMESTER, MICROECONOMICS FIRST

	First Semester	*Second Semester*
Core	Parts 1, 3, 4	Part 2
Applications	Part 5, 6, or 7	Part 5, 6, or 7

ONE-SEMESTER

Core	Chapters 1–5, 8–10, 12, 13, 17–19, 21, 22, 24, 26, 29 (approximately 40 percent of book)

Applications:

Option 1	Prebusiness emphasis. Select from Chapters 20, 23, 27, 28, 30
Option 2	Institutional emphasis. Select from Chapters 11, 25, 27, 30, 32, 38, 39
Option 3	Contemporary issues emphasis. Select from Chapters 14, 15, 32–35
Option 4	International and comparative emphasis. Select from Chapters 7, 34–39

A Word or Two of Thanks

I have been extremely fortunate in getting help of many kinds from many quarters while writing this book. It is a pleasure to acknowledge this help here.

I owe the greatest thanks to my collaborating author, David E. Lindsey. David, my longtime friend and professional colleague, provided the theoretical inspiration and technical details for the basic macroeconomics model presented in Part 2. The approach is one he developed over many years of teaching at Ohio State University and MacAllister College. Although the heavy commitments he has now as a senior research economist at the Federal Reserve Board of Governors prevented him from participating actively in the actual writing of this book, Part 2 is really as much his as mine. Of course, it must be made clear that the contributions he has made are his personally, and can in no way be construed as representing the official views of the Federal Reserve System on matters either of theory or of policy. It ought also to be added that any errors or shortcomings in Part 2 of this book are, just as much as elsewhere, entirely my own responsibility, not his.

Second, I would like to thank two people who helped me prepare the ancillary materials for this text. Tom Anderson, already mentioned as author of the Study Guide, did an excellent job. Bill Rushing of Georgia

State University also made a valuable contribution in the form of items for our test bank.

Next, I must thank the many reviewers who commented on various drafts of the text and suggested countless improvements. I was very fortunate in having an especially astute critic and reader as my neighbor in Vermont, Herbert Goertz of Royalton College. Professor Goertz did his job so diligently that at times his written comments and suggestions seemed longer than my draft chapters! I find it hard to imagine how I could have gotten the job done without his help.

Of course, I do not by any means wish to belittle the contributions of all the other people who read and commented on all or part of the manuscript. My thanks, in this regard, to

Dr. Thomas Anderson
Eastern Michigan University

Charles Britton
University of Arkansas

Steven G. Dworsky
Hudson Valley Community College

Dr. Upton Henderson
Central State University

John Gilliam
Texas Technical University

William Holahan
University of Wisconsin

David R. Kamerschen
University of Georgia

Randolph C. Martin
University of South Carolina

Kent W. Olson
Oklahoma State University

John Pisciotta
University of Southern Colorado

Robert Pollard
University of Texas

Francis W. Rushing
Georgia State University

Courtenay Stone
California State University—Northridge

Carl B. Turner
North Carolina State University—Raleigh

Raymond F. Turner
Anne Arundel Community College

Royce J. Watts
West Virginia University

Travis Wilson
DeKalb College—Central Campus

At two critical points in writing the text I was able to find specialized research help when I needed it. First, Chris Tame of the Institute for Economic Affairs in London researched the profiles of leading economists for me. Later, Russ Cappelle of Bethel, Vermont supplied me with the data on which the endpaper tables of this book are based. As always, of course, the credit is theirs and the blame for any errors is mine.

Last but not least I would like to recognize three very efficient and long-suffering typists: Maureen Bayman and Norma Scott of Belvedere, Kent, in England and Ellen Blanchard of Gaysville, Vermont. Among the three of them they produced literally thousands of pages, working most of the time under the pressure of overly tight deadlines.

Dozens of other people who go unnamed here—publishers, editors, consultants, and staff—have worked hard to make this book what it is. Remember, though, that all we have done is only half the job. The rest is up to you, the instructor.

South Royalton, Vermont   *Edwin G. Dolan*
November, 1976

Contents
in Brief

PART SIX
International Economics 547

PART SEVEN
Economic Systems Compared 575

Detailed Contents

PART TWO
National Income, Inflation, and Unemployment   69

PART THREE
Theory of Prices and Markets 287

PART FIVE
**The Economics of Life on a Very Small
Planet 503**

PART SIX
International Economics 547

PART ONE
An Overview of the Market Economy

Economics, as it is usually taught in the United States, is largely a study of how markets work. Economic activity is not entirely a matter of buying and selling things, but buying and selling are a central importance. In this part we shall learn that the buying and selling activities taking place in markets accomplish two important functions. The first function is to move goods and services around, passing them from people who value them less to people who value them more. The desire to move goods and services around is the main intended consequence of market activity. When people buy and sell, however, they also fulfill a second, unintended function; that is generating information that can be used in economic decision making. This information takes the form of market prices.

In Chapters 2 and 3, we shall look in some detail at how markets perform these two functions. First we shall take a general view, in order to learn how markets function as a mechanism for utilizing knowledge. After that, we shall develop some elementary theoretical tools for analyzing markets. These tools of supply and demand analysis will be put to work in every subsequent chapter of the book.

Although economics is largely the study of markets, markets are not the only mechanism used for moving resources around in our economy. Government also plays a major role. Government does some buying and selling just as private individuals do, but that is not all that government does. In addition, government has the power to move resources by nonvoluntary means. It can take a part of people's incomes through taxation. It can, to a limited extent, order people to perform specific economic tasks. And it can regulate much private economic activity.

In the United States, government is large, but not too large to prevent us from thinking of our economy as primarily a market economy. We thus study markets first, and then look at how the presence of government modifies the way they operate. Chapter 4 will introduce the role of government in the economy, and provide background for looking at particular problems of economic policy in later chapters.

CHAPTER 1
What Economics Is All About

What You Will Learn in This Chapter
Understanding economics means learning the economic way of thinking. Key ideas in the economic way of thinking are scarcity, choice, and division of labor. To make these abstract ideas easy to visualize, economists sometimes use diagrams such as the *production possibility frontier.* Economic science can contribute to the evaluation of economic policy, but economic policy decisions also require value judgments. Science and value judgments must stand in the proper relationship to one another if valid policy evaluations are to be made.

Understanding economics means learning how to think like an economist. So what is the economic way of thinking? Sometimes people call economics "the science of common sense," a definition that gives us a good start. To say that economics is common sense means that economists do not have some mysterious special logic all their own. There is no theory or concept in all of economics that cannot be expressed in a straightforward English sentence. Economists frequently draw pictures in the margins of their books in order to put their ideas across more vividly, but the pictures themselves are not economics. They are just learning aids. At other times (especially when exchanging ideas among themselves) economists write mathematical equations as a sort of shorthand, but that does not mean that economics is a branch of mathematics. You can read right through the main parts of this book without coming across a single algebraic equation, and besides, mathematicians tell us that their science is just common sense too.

If the economic way of thinking is not a special kind of logic, or graphs, or mathematics, then what is it? The key to the economic way of thinking lies not in the *way* economists think, but in the things they think *about.* Learning the economic way of thinking means developing a certain alertness or sensitivity to certain features of ordinary, everyday situations. The same can be said of other social sciences. When psychologists look at what is going on in the world around them, they are likely to be sensitive to how people's motivations and personalities shape their behavior toward one another. Political scientists might be alert to clues that signal certain kinds of power relationships. Economists have their own list of what to look for.

The purpose of this chapter will be to introduce a few signals that economists look for, as a sort of sensitivity training. This will give a big head start on understanding the economic way of thinking.

Scarcity and Opportunity Cost

Scarcity

The most basic concept of economics is **scarcity.** In economics, scarcity means not having as much of some thing as we want. Economic scarcity is not measured by any objective physical standard. A geologist might say that tin ore is scarce relative to iron ore, but an economist would say that both are scarce because we do not have as much of either one as we want. Because scarcity is subjective—part of the human condition—we cannot escape from it. **Ascetics** may try to escape from scarcity by limiting their desires, but even when they go out to look for twigs to build a fire to cook a bowl of rice, they come up against the fact that twigs are scarce. They have to take time off from meditation in order to gather them; so they would carefully build the fire in such a way as to boil the water with the least possible amount of fuel.

Scarcity As used in economics, not having enough to fill all subjective wants.

Ascetic A person who tries to achieve happiness by purposely limiting desires.

Choice

Because things are scarce, we must make choices. What is more, in economic life we are almost always closely constrained in the range of alternatives among which we must choose. We shall be talking a lot about constraints and choice in this book. We shall examine the choices that a shopper makes among items in a supermarket, when constrained by a weekly food budget. We shall look at the way a business firm chooses what to produce and what inputs to use when constrained by the actions of its competitors and its own past decisions. We shall look at economic policy decisions that governments make, at how political constraints affect their choices, and at how those choices, in turn, affect all of us.

Opportunity Cost

Because economists are so sensitive to choice and scarcity, they are very much concerned with costs. The most important kind of cost in economics is what is called **opportunity cost.** The opportunity cost of doing something is the loss of the opportunity of doing the next best thing instead with the same time or resources.

Opportunity Cost The cost of doing something as measured by the loss of the opportunity to do the next best thing instead with the same amount of time or resources.

Opportunity cost is everywhere, so we do not have to look far to find illustrations. In fact, we have already given one illustration without noticing it. For the ascetics of whom we just spoke, the opportunity cost of a bundle of twigs was the loss of an hour's meditation. The following case study provides an illustration somewhat closer to home.

CASE 1.1
The Opportunity Cost of a College Education

Susan, an average student, is enrolled at National Average University. If you ask her how much it is costing her to go to college, she will refer you to a little budget she has drawn up for her four years at NAU. It is shown in

EXHIBIT 1.1

The cost of a college education

Part a of this exhibit shows the out-of-pocket costs of a four-year college education for a typical student. Each entry in that table represents an actual cash payment that the student must make. Part b shows the opportunity cost of an education at the same college. Each entry there represents a sacrifice that the student must make in order to obtain an education. Note that room and board (Part a) is only an out-of-pocket cost, while foregone income (Part b) is only an opportunity cost.

a. Budget of out-of-pocket costs	
Tuition and fees	$12,000
Books, transportation to and from home, etc.	2,000
Room and board	10,000
Total out-of-pocket costs	$24,000
b. Budget in terms of opportunity costs	
Tuition and fees	$12,000
Books, transportation, etc.	2,000
Foregone income	32,000
Total opportunity cost	$46,000

Exhibit 1.1a. This budget bears the heading "out-of-pocket costs" because it includes all the items, and only those items, for which Susan actually makes a cash payment.

Your own out-of-pocket costs for a college education may be considerably higher or lower than these national average figures, but chances are that the items in this budget are the same ones that would come to your mind if you were asked about the matter. As soon as you start to learn the economic way of thinking, though, a different set of items will come to mind. Which of the items in Exhibit 1.1a represent opportunities foregone in order to go to college? Are there any foregone opportunities that are missing from the table? To see the answers, look at Exhibit 1.1b, which is an opportunity cost budget for Susan, our average student.

The first two items in the out-of-pocket budget show up again in the opportunity cost budget. In order to spend $14,000 on tuition, fees, books, and transportation, Susan has to give up the opportunity to consume an equivalent quantity of other goods, say, to buy a car, make a down payment on a house, or travel to Europe. Not so with the third item in the out-of-pocket budget. By spending $10,000 on room and board while she is in college, this student is not really giving up an opportunity to do something different than she could otherwise have done. Whether she went to college or not, she would have to eat something and live somewhere. Room and board is a cost that she would have to meet in any case and is not a specific opportunity cost of college.

Thinking about what Susan would have done had she not gone to college suggests an item that must be added to the opportunity cost account but that does not show up on the out-of-pocket account. Had she not gone to college, she very likely would have taken a job and begun earning money right after leaving school. Suppose that she had taken a job as, say, a clerk in a local shoe factory and earned $8,000 annually. This potential income—$32,000 over a four-year period—is something that she must give up to attend college. It is part of the opportunity cost of a college education.

Trade-offs[1]

Our discussion of opportunity cost gives us a good chance to show how economists use diagrams to put their ideas across more vividly. In the example we just looked at, we saw that a college education involves certain opportunity costs. That means that for the economy as a whole, there is a trade-off between producing education and producing other goods that people also desire. Let us see how a simple diagram can give us a visual image of what that trade-off is like. Look at Exhibit 1.2. The horizontal

[1]Readers who want a quick brush-up on how to work with graphs may wish to look at the appendix to this chapter (pp. 18–24) before proceeding.

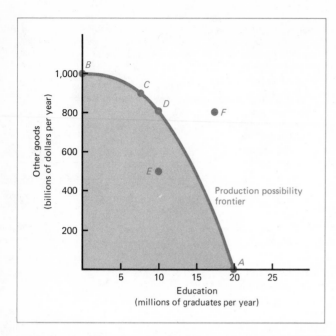

EXHIBIT 1.2
A production possibility frontier for education and other goods
This diagram shows a production possibility frontier for education and other goods. Point *A* represents the maximum production of education if no other goods are produced, and point *B* represents the maximum production of other goods if no education is produced. *A, B, C, D,* and all other points along the frontier, as well as points such as *E* in the shaded area under it, are possible. Points such as *F,* outside the frontier, are not possible given the quantity and quality of factors of production available.

axis of the figure measures the quantity of education produced in terms of the number of college graduates produced per year. The vertical axis measures the production of all other goods in billions of dollars per year. Any combination of education and other goods that were produced in the economy in some year can be shown as a point in the space between the two axes. For example, the production of 10 million college graduates and $500 billion worth of other goods would be represented by point *E* in Exhibit 1.2.

Production Possibility Frontier

Even if we all devoted all our time and all our resources to producing education, there would be a limit to the quantity of education that could be produced each year. For the sake of illustration, let us suppose this limit to be 20 million graduates per year. This extreme possibility of producing 20 million graduates and nothing else is shown by point *A* in Exhibit 1.2. Point *B* in the exhibit shows the maximum rate of output of other goods if no resources at all were put into education and $1,000 billion of other goods were produced. Between these two extreme cases, there is a whole range of possibilities for producing education and other goods in combination. Those intermediate possibilities are represented by points such as *C* and *D,* which

Production Possibility Frontier A curve showing the possible combinations of goods that can be produced by an economy, given the quantity and quality of factors of production available.

fall along the curve drawn in the diagram. Such a curve is called a **production possibility frontier.**

This curve is called a *frontier* because it is a boundary between those combinations of education and other goods that can be produced, and those that cannot possibly be produced. Points *A, B, C,* and *D,* which lie right on the curve, represent combinations of education and other goods that can be produced. A combination such as that represented by point *E* in the shaded area under the production possibility frontier can be produced without even making the maximum effort, or even if some resources are used wastefully. In contrast, a combination of education and other goods such as that represented by point F cannot possibly all be produced in one year. All the points outside the shaded area are impossible.

At any point along the production possibility frontier, there is a trade-off between education and other goods. More of one cannot be produced without giving up some of the other. For example, suppose that we began at point C, where 8 million students were graduating from college each year and $900 billion of other goods were being produced. If we wanted to increase the output of graduates to 10 million per year, we would have to give up some other goods and use those resources to build classrooms, print books, and staff lecture halls instead. That would move us to point D, which represents 10 million graduates and only $800 billion of other goods.

Now we can see how the production possibility curve allows us to visualize the concept of opportunity cost. In moving from C to D on the production possibility frontier, 2 million extra graduates are obtained at the opportunity cost of $100 billion in other goods. Putting this on a per student basis, we can say that the opportunity cost of college education (in the range between C and D) is approximately $50,000 per additional graduate. In geometric terms, we can say that the opportunity cost of education, in terms of other goods, is given by the slope of the production possibility frontier.

Factors of Production

It is important to point out that the limits on our range of choice imposed by the production possibility frontier apply only so long as available quantities of **factors of production** do not change. Factors of production are the basic inputs we use in the production of all goods. They include (1) **natural resources**—land with its original fertility and mineral deposits, (2) **labor**—the productive contributions made by people working with their minds and their muscles, and (3) **capital**—all manufactured productive resources, such as tools, industrial equipment, structures, and artificial improvements to land. As time passes and the available quantities of factors of production expand, the production possibility frontier expands too, as shown in Exhibit 1.3.

Improvements in the quality of factors also permit the expansion of production possibilities. The quality of labor done by a given population improves as people become healthier and better educated. The quality of capital increases dramatically as technological change improves equipment and brings new methods of production. Only natural resources do not undergo qualitative improvements; in fact, many actually decline in quality as they are depleted by use. So far, the increases in quantity and quality of other factors has more than made up for the depletion of natural resources. Whether this will continue to be possible is a matter we shall discuss in Chapters 7, 34, and 35 of this book.

Factors of Production The basic inputs of natural resources, labor, and capital used in the production of all goods.

Natural Resources As a factor of production, land with its original fertility and mineral deposits.

Labor As a factor of production, the contributions to production made by people working with their minds and their muscles.

Capital As a factor of production, all manufactured productive resources such as tools, industrial equipment, structures, and artificial improvements to land.

Specialization and the Margin

Specialization

You may have wondered why the production possibility frontier is a curve rather than a straight line. If it were a straight line, that would mean

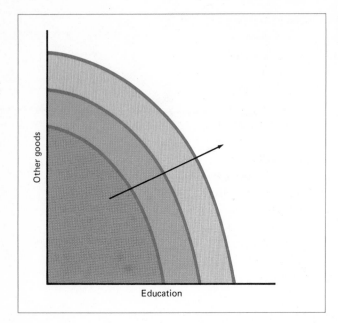

Other goods

Education

EXHIBIT 1.3
Expanding production possibility frontier
The position of the production possibility frontier at any point in time depends on the quantity and quality of the factors of production available. As time goes by, population grows, new capital is accumulated, and technological change takes place, permitting the production possibility frontier to shift outward, as indicated by the arrow in this diagram.

Homogeneous   Having the property that every unit is just like every other unit.

that the opportunity cost of educating an additional college graduate, in terms of other goods, would be the same no matter how people chose to divide their efforts and resources between the two possibilities of production. Why should this not be so?

The answer concerns specialization. Factors of production are not **homogeneous;** that is, the individual units of labor, capital, and natural resources that we have available are different from one another. Individual units of labor—individual people—are the most diverse of all. It is easy to see what this implies.

Imagine that starting today we wanted to increase the output of college graduates. The first thing we would need would be more teachers. The opportunity cost of getting the first few teachers would be low. We could call on professors who had just retired, or on their spouses who might be qualified but not currently working, or on graduate students who could combine teaching with learning. Few other goods would be lost by engaging these people. Next we might turn to industry, and hire chemists, engineers, or economists working there to staff additional classrooms. These people might make very productive teachers, but they would be sorely missed by the firms that had employed them, and there would be a noticeable drop in the output of other goods. The opportunity cost of education would rise, and the production possibility curve would begin to bend as we moved along it. Pretty soon we would have to start calling in people who were not even well qualified to be teachers, even though they might be doing a good job at something else. These people would not add much at all to the output of education, but a lot would be lost elsewhere. The production possibility frontier would bend still more sharply. In short, we see that differences of ability and specialization among people (and also differences among units of other factors) can be counted on to give the production possibility frontier its typical bowed-out shape.

The Division of Labor

People are not interchangeable parts, so we must pay careful attention to the division of labor if we are to do well in our struggle with the pervasive problem of scarcity. Once again let us use our handy tool, the production possibility frontier, to show why. Suppose that for some reason or other we chose to devote half the nation's labor power to producing education and half to producing other goods, but that we used the wrong half in each place. Skilled production workers would awkwardly mumble their way through lecture notes on Greek history, while professors got their thumbs jammed in delicate factory machinery. What would happen is that we would not produce as much as possible of either education or other goods. The economy would drop right off the production possibility frontier and end up at some interior point, such as point *A* in Exhibit 1.4. Just by using the proper division of labor, we could produce the output combination indicated by point *B* instead, and have more of both goods.

More than 200 years ago, Adam Smith began the most famous economics book of all time with an example emphasizing the importance of the division of labor. Smith had visited a pin factory and had seen how when one man specialized in putting heads on the pins, another in sharpening the points, another in placing them on cards, and so forth, they all together could produce 100 times more than could the same number of men working separately. Smith went on to show how free markets and private enterprise solve the problem of the division of labor. We shall spend many chapters doing the same ourselves (beginning with Chapter 2) and have time left over for a look at how governments sometimes try to improve on the market by substituting their own judgments concerning the division of labor.

EXHIBIT 1.4

Effects of a poorly organized division of labor

Poor organization of the division of labor can cause the economy to drop off the production possibility frontier and end up at an interior point such as *A* in this diagram. Just by getting the division of labor right, more of both goods could be produced, as at point *B.*

Adam Smith (1723–1790)

Adam Smith was born in Kirkaldy, on the east coast of Scotland. He studied first at Glasgow University, and then at Oxford. In those days, the universities of Scotland were greater centers of learning than those of England, so Smith returned to the north after finishing his studies at Oxford, and obtained a chair at Glasgow. It was not, of course, a chair in economics. Economics had not yet been invented as a distinct discipline, and besides, it was not yet Smith's major interest. His specialty was moral philosophy.

During his long career, Smith wrote just two books. It was his good fortune, however, to have both bring him immediate fame. Smith's first book was *The Theory of Moral Sentiments,* published in 1759. His second, *The Wealth of Nations,* appeared seventeen years later, in 1776. David Hume, a friend of Smith's, commented that "the reading of it necessarily requires so much attention, and the public is disposed to give so little, that I shall still doubt for some time of its being at first very popular." Hume, however, was wrong. The book sold well from the start.

The task Smith sets himself first of all is to explain the workings of the economic system, that is, the sources of the "wealth of nations." The greatest source, he discovers, is the division of labor. Chapter 1 opens with the observation that "the greatest improvement in the productive powers of labor, and the greater part of the skill, dexterity, and judgment with which it is anywhere directed, or applied, seem to have been the effects of the division of labor." He then goes on to give his famous pin factory example.

It is not enough for Smith to just describe the division of labor, however. He wants to explain how the division of labor comes about. His explanation is highly characteristic. "This division of labor, from which so many advantages are derived, is not originally the effect of any human wisdom, which foresees and intends that general opulence to which it gives occasion. It is the necessary, though very slow and gradual consequence of a certain propensity in human nature which has in view no such extensive utility; the propensity to truck, barter, and exchange one thing for another." Here, for the first time in the book, Smith emphasizes the importance of the unintended consequences of human action. Each person acting in the marketplace has only his narrow ends in mind, but the joint result of the actions of everyone is a general benefit that none intended.

As the *Wealth of Nations* progresses, Smith adds another theme, that of the benefits of economic liberty. The free, spontaneous interaction of people in the marketplace is not just one way to bring about the general benefit of mankind—it is the best way. Government attempts to guide or regulate the market end up doing more harm than good. Smith especially attacks the privileges of legally protected monopolies, the Poor Laws (which he saw as inhibiting the mobility of labor), and the apprenticeship system (which worked against free entry into occupations). All such restraints on the market tended to force trade into "unnatural" and less beneficial channels.

Smith's book has meant various things to various people. To some it has been a handbook of laissez-faire liberalism. To others, it has been the fountainhead of economic science. Still others have found it, not without reason, to be unoriginal and crammed with errors. Whatever its faults, it is a book that continues to be read and debated. In 1976, its bicentennial brought leading economists from all over the world to Glasgow to pay tribute to the absent-minded professor of moral philosophy who had lectured there so long before.

The Margin

Next we come to an element of the economic way of thinking that was not around in Adam Smith's day but that has become very important since.

That is the idea of the **margin.** Whenever economists talk about the margin or use the adjective "marginal," they are talking about the effects of making a small increase or decrease in some economic activity. "Margin" is an idea that is hard to define abstractly but easy to illustrate. When we talk about "the marginal cost" of producing cars at General Motors, we are referring to the added cost of producing one more car beyond the limit of the number currently being produced. When we speak of the "marginal benefit" of sewage treatment in a certain river basin, we mean the benefit of making a small increase in the effort put into sewage treatment in the area. These particular terms and quite a few more will be defined more precisely when we come to them in later chapters. For now, though, let us look at just one example that will give us a general idea of why thinking in terms of the margin is important.

Margin, Marginal Terms referring to the effects of making a small increase in any economic activity. See specific glossary entries under *marginal cost, marginal product,* etc.

CASE 1.2
The Marginal Cost of Oil

Ever since the oil crisis of 1974, we have all become very much concerned about the cost of oil. But what is "the" cost of producing oil? That depends on where you extract it. There are fields in the Middle East and in Texas and Oklahoma where getting oil out of the ground costs practically nothing. There are medium-cost fields, such as those where such secondary recovery methods as pumping live steam down the wells to make the oil more liquid are used. And there are high-cost fields, such as those in Alaska or under the North Sea, where oil is very expensive to extract, especially when the necessary environmental safeguards are taken. To repeat, then, of all this range of figures, what is "the" cost of oil?

The economist's answer to this question is that the cost that counts is the *marginal cost* of oil. The marginal cost of oil means the cost per barrel of getting a few additional tons of oil, given the efforts that are already being made. Because easy fields are usually exploited to capacity before the hard ones are tapped, the marginal cost of oil means the cost of getting it where it is hardest to get, say, in Alaska or the North Sea.

In the United States today, special price control laws keep the market price of oil below its marginal cost and close to its cost of production as averaged over good fields and bad fields alike. When important decisions are to be made, though, thinking in terms of the artificially low controlled price can lead to mistakes. Suppose, for instance, that a government economist were trying to decide whether to increase spending on solar energy research. Solar energy costs more than energy from the oil that is pumped from average fields, but with just a little more research and development, it is likely to cost less than energy from the most expensive Alaskan or North Sea oil. If the solar energy decision were made on the basis of the low, controlled price, solar power research might seem uneconomical, but that is wrong. Each extra barrel of oil burned has to be replaced not from average fields—those that are already running at capacity—but from the most difficult fields. As long as there is a hope that additional research can bring the cost of solar energy down to or below the *marginal* cost of oil, that research is worthwhile.

Economic Science and Economic Policy

A great part of what one reads about economics in the newspapers or hears about economics on television is focused on specific problems of economic policy. Should the federal government spend more money and run a larger budget deficit? Should price controls on oil be lifted in the hope of increasing production and decreasing consumption? Should the government encourage or discourage exports of American agricultural products? If we are to learn the economic way of thinking, we must learn how economists think about policy issues as well as how they think about pure theory.

The mention of economic policies such as price controls or budget deficits tends to set little lights labeled "hurrah" or "ugh" flashing in our minds. Sometimes our mental circuits work so fast that we do not notice that between the mention of the policy and the flashing of the lights, a chain of thinking somewhat like the following must occur:

1. If policy X is followed, outcome Y will result.
2. Outcome Y is a good (or a bad) thing.
3. Therefore, hurrah! (or ugh!) for policy X.

In order to understand the contents of this book and how to put what you learn to work as a citizen or in public life, it is very important to understand the logic of this three-step chain of thinking. Let us go through it one step at a time.

Positive Economics

Economic science cannot foretell the future, but it can offer predictions of the limited, "if . . . , then . . ." form: "If A occurs, then B will occur, other things being equal." An economist might, then, make the assertion: "If government spending were increased, then unemployment would decline, as long as no other changes in economic conditions occur in the meantime." Such a statement is sometimes called a **scientific prediction.** It is a statement of cause and effect, but one that is valid only under specified conditions. In making scientific predictions of the "If A, then B, other things being equal" form, economists rarely attempt to foretell whether or not A will actually occur or whether other things will actually remain constant.

Scientific Prediction A conditional prediction having the form "if A, then B, other things being equal."

When economists limit their attention to statements that are pure scientific predictions, they are said to be practicing **positive economics.** All sound analysis of economic policy must begin with positive economics as step number one.

Positive Economics That part of economics limited to making scientific predictions and purely descriptive statements.

Resolving Disagreements

Of course, economists sometimes disagree on whether a certain scientific prediction is valid. In fact, a great deal of the day-to-day work in which economists engage is directed toward resolving disagreements on matters of positive economics. Some scientific disagreements among economists concern matters of pure theory and are much like the disagreements among mathematicians concerning whether some unproved theorem is true or false. These disputes can, in time, be resolved by a process in which each party tries to state as carefully as possible the reasoning that seems to lead to a certain conclusion, while others try to verify the reasoning or to detect logical errors.

Very frequently, economists try to resolve disputes over matters of positive economics by looking carefully at past experience. Much of this work is done by specialists in the statistical analysis of economic data who are called **econometricians.** Suppose that the scientific prediction in dispute were one that said: "If government spending were to increase, then unemployment would decline, other things being equal." An econometrician might enter the debate with the announcement that according to a study of postwar data taken from the American economy, an increase in government expenditure has, in fact, been consistently associated with a decline in unemployment, taking into account the probable influence of other factors. Or the econometrician might, instead, assert that the data reveal no systematic association at all between government spending and unemployment when advanced statistical techniques are used to eliminate the influence of other changes in economic conditions. Questions of this sort are not usually resolved by a single econometric study, but repeated studies and the gradual accumulation of evidence serve to narrow areas of disagreement and contribute to scientific progress in economics.

Econometrician An expert in the statistical analysis of economic data.

Normative Economics

A positive economic statement of the type "if policy X, then outcome Y" cannot by itself resolve the issue of whether policy X is desirable. To come to a conclusion on the desirability of the policy, one must decide whether the outcome Y is good or bad. When economists make statements of the type "outcome Y is good," they are engaging in **normative economics.**

Most economists do not consider themselves experts in ethical theory, and few economists would be prepared to defend their normative statements with the same rigor and clarity as they would use to defend their positive economic analysis. Nonetheless, economists who wish to speak persuasively on the subject of economic policy should be able at least to point to some general ethical principles on which their normative conclusions might plausibly be based. Economists who base their liking or disliking of a particular policy on arbitrary whims are less likely to be listened to than are economists who speak in terms of consistent and well-thought-out values. With this in mind, let us look at a few basic ideas that frequently arise in discussions of normative economics.

Normative Economics That part of economics devoted to making value judgments about what economic policies or conditions are good or bad.

The Efficiency Standard

The standard of **efficiency** occupies a prominent place among those by which economists judge the performance of the systems they observe. In its most general sense, the word "efficiency" means the property of producing or acting with a minimum of expense, waste, and effort. We gave a good economic example of the difference between efficiency and inefficiency in Exhibit 1.4. That diagram showed how a badly organized division of labor could cause the economy to drop off the production possibility frontier and end up at an *inefficient* interior point. A better division of labor would have permitted the production of more output with the same quantities of inputs and thus would have been more efficient.

Efficiency The property of producing or acting with a minimum of expense, waste, and effort.

Efficiency and Equity

Most economists think that efficiency is, in itself, a good thing. This does not mean, however, that any economic policy that promotes efficiency is automatically a good policy. Other norms and values must be introduced into policy analysis to supplement the efficiency standard. Among the most important of these supplementary standards are those to which we refer in everyday speech as equity, merit, and justice.

The standard of equity has two roles to play in relation to that of efficiency. First, it may be used to supplement the efficiency standard in cases where the choice to be made is between policies that are equally efficient. Efficiency alone does not define a single, unique pattern of economic life but only a range of possible patterns. Different but equally efficient patterns often involve different distributions of welfare among specific individuals. In one efficient state of the world, Jones may be rich and Smith poor; in another, Smith may be rich and Jones poor; and in a third, Jones and Smith may be equally well off. When such alternatives confront us, we may be led to reason like this:

1. Policies X and Y produce equally efficient outcomes but imply different distributions of individual welfare.
2. The distributional outcome of policy X is more equitable.
3. Therefore, let us undertake policy X.

A second possible use for the criterion of equity is to override that of efficiency. For many people, efficiency is not a goal that should be pursued at the expense of equity but rather should, if needed, be sacrificed to the pursuit of equity. In such cases, our logic might run as follows:

1. Policy X would be bad for efficiency but would help achieve greater equity.
2. The loss of efficiency is unfortunate, but the gain in equity outweighs it.
3. Therefore, in the absence of a policy that will serve both goals at once, let us go ahead with policy X.

A Difficulty

Whichever way it is used, the concept of equity plays an important role in policy analysis. Using it involves a difficulty, however, that did not bother us in the case of efficiency. The difficulty is that equity has no universally agreed-upon meaning. It means different things to different people, depending on the values they hold and the ideologies they profess. Few things are more harmful to intelligent debate on questions of economic policy than for two parties to a discussion to use the same word to mean different things. The word "equity," and the associated terms "merit" and "justice," are possibly the cause of more misunderstanding than are any other terms in economics.

In the interest of avoiding such misunderstanding, we might wish to establish beyond doubt that one particular meaning of the term "equity" is the right one. But to attempt this would take us deep into details of philosophy and far from the main subject of this book. Instead we shall, more modestly, simply suggest two alternative meanings of the equity concept (or, rather, two classes of meanings within which there are many minor variations) without authoritatively choosing between them.

Distributive Justice The principle of distribution according to innate merit or, roughly, the principle of "from each according to his abilities, to each according to his needs."

Equity as Distributive Justice

The first meaning of "equity" makes equity equivalent to **distributive justice.** The popular phrase, "from each according to his abilities, to each according to his needs," gives us a rough idea of what the principle of distributive justice means. The concept of distributive justice is based on the idea of innate merit; that is, all people are presumed, solely by virtue of their birth, their existence, and their common humanity, to merit some share of the total stream of goods and services turned out by the economic system. We could improve the popular phrase by making it read "to each according to his innate merits."

Just what each person's innate merits are is a point that gives rise to many variations on the idea of distributive justice. For example, some people believe that all economic goods should be distributed equally among all members of society. This view is known as **egalitarianism.** Others think that a person's innate claims on economic goods ought to be limited to some minimum standard of living and would be willing to see any surplus above this minimum distributed according to other principles. Still others conceive of innate merits as being limited to certain specific types of goods. Each person might have, for example, an innate claim to a share of food, shelter, medical care, and education, but no such claim to even a minimum share of tobacco, imported wine, or manicuring services.

Egalitarianism The principle that economic goods should be distributed equally among all members of society.

Equity as Market Justice

The second meaning of the concept of equity makes equity equivalent to what we can call **market justice.** The justice of the marketplace is *value for value.* Market justice is based on the idea of acquired merit. Individuals have no innate claims to a share in the total economic output but merit only whatever share they acquire through production, exchange, or voluntary donation.

The idea of market justice gives a special significance to the concepts of property and contract. Suppose that the entire mass of economic goods is divided up as the properties of specific individuals (or voluntary associations of individuals), so that for every loaf of bread, some person stands ready to say "this bread is mine—my property to use and to exclude others from the use of." Then the central meaning of "market justice" becomes the movement of property from hand to hand only by fair contract (except for voluntary gifts). By "fair contract," we mean that each party must be satisfied that the value to him of the property he receives is at least as great as the value of the property he gives. Commutative justice may be summed up as the observance of property rights and the honoring of contracts.

Market Justice The principle of distribution according to acquired merit. The observance of property rights and the honoring of contracts. Roughly, the principle of "value for value."

Economic Ideology

Each person carries out the job of policy analysis, whether in a systematic or a casual way, within a personal framework of thought that, for lack of a better term, we might call an **economic ideology.** An economic ideology includes a person's judgments concerning the relative priority (and exact interpretation) of distributive justice and market justice and attitudes toward the relative importance of equity and efficiency as goals of economic policy. An economic ideology often also includes a set of prejudices and more or less rationally founded beliefs concerning matters of positive economics. Liberalism, Marxism, libertarianism, conservatism—these and many other "isms" are the labels we use to refer to economic ideologies.

Economic Ideology A set of judgements and beliefs concerning efficiency, market justice, and distributive justice as goals of economic policy, together with a set of prejudices or beliefs concerning matters of positive economics.

To deal with every policy issue from all possible ideological points of view would be too much for us to attempt in this book. Instead, we shall, for the most part, content ourselves with pointing out the implications of various policies in terms of the standards of efficiency and equity we have just discussed. Readers will have to reach their own conclusions on the ideological level.

Why Distinguish?

When policy analysis is broken down into a three-step process, in which positive and normative elements are clearly separated, orderly debate on important economic issues is made easier in several ways.

First, the breakdown of policy analysis into positive and normative components makes it clear that disagreements on policy questions can arise from two different sources. If you and I disagree as to whether policy X is good or bad, it may be either because we disagree on the positive issue of whether X will, in fact, result in outcome Y, or because we disagree on the normative issue of whether Y is good or bad. Our analysis also indicates that a particular sort of spurious agreement could arise between us: You might think that X will cause Y and that Y is good, whereas I think Y is bad but that X will not cause it! This sort of thing occurs surprisingly often. In any event, it is clear that intelligent policy analysis requires careful thinking.

Second, if a positive statement is associated with an unpopular normative position, it is less likely to gain acceptance. Critics must be persuaded that both are valid. We are less likely to pay serious attention to the claim that fluoridation of water harms our bodies when its opponents also claim that fluoridation is an evil communist plot. A positive statement divorced from any normative view is not disadvantaged in this way.

Third, when a positive statement is associated with a very popular normative position, it may be accepted too uncritically. Why? It is because reactions to value judgments are much more pronounced than are reactions to positive statements, so that value judgments surreptitiously tend to dominate our thought. We are all too likely to accept a "what is" statement from someone who agrees with us about "what ought to be." This natural reaction helps, for example, to explain the inability of economists to persuade politicians that increases in the legal minimum wage have worsened the employment opportunities of poor people.[2] Politicians say they want to help the poor and resent being informed that a method they support has not worked. Perhaps they even suspect that economists critical of minimum wages do not share their values. They mistakenly believe that minimum wage laws help the poor simply because they believe that the poor ought to be helped.

Conclusions

In a once-over fashion, we have tried to give some idea of the kinds of things to which economists are sensitive when they look at the world around them.

[2]Minimum wage laws are discussed in Chapter 15.

We have learned that economists think in terms of scarcity, choice, and trade-offs. We have seen some simple examples of how economists use diagrams to make it easier to visualize abstract concepts in a concrete form. We have seen how to distinguish between positive and normative economics and why that distinction is important. What can we say now to sum it all up?

If there is one single feature of overriding importance about the economic way of thinking, it is this: *Economics is about people.* Individual people are the units of analysis in all economic theory. Every economic principle that we develop in this book must be a statement about the way that individuals make choices, struggle with the problem of scarcity, and respond to changes in their environment. And all economic policies must be judged in terms of their impact on the welfare of individual people.

This does not mean that economists are all "rugged individualists," in the sense that they do not care about social issues, or that they are political know-nothings who do not care about the national interest. What it does mean is that economic science (and all valid social science, for that matter) is based on the recognition that "society" and "the nation" have no existence and no importance apart from the individual people of which they are composed. "Society" is not a super-being, and "the nation" is not a sentient creature capable of feeling pain when a pin is stuck in the national thumb. They are only the names of groups of which you, I, and all the rest of us are equally members. *We* are what economics is all about.

SUMMARY

1. The economic way of thinking is less a matter of the way economists think than a matter of the things they think about. In looking at ordinary situations in the world about them, economists are sensitive to the ways in which such considerations as scarcity and opportunity cost influence the ways in which people relate to one another.

2. The production possibility frontier shows which combinations of goods can be produced and which cannot. The slope of the production possibility frontier shows the opportunity cost of the good measured on the horizontal axis in terms of the good measured on the vertical axis. The position of the production possibility frontier depends on the quantity and quality of factors of production available to an economy. Over time, the production possibility frontier may expand and the economy may grow. If the division of labor is not organized efficiently, the economy may drop off the production possibility frontier and end up at an interior point.

3. Positive economics cannot foretell the future, but it can offer scientific predictions in the form "if A occurs, then B will occur, other things being equal." Disputes in positive economics can, in principle, be resolved by reasoned discussion or by the examination of statistical data.

4. Normative economics is concerned with statements about what ought to be. Most economists think that efficiency is, in itself, a worthy goal of economic policy. The efficiency standard must, however, be supplemented by considerations of equity when policy decisions are to be made. There is no universal agreement on what equity means. Some economists maintain that equity is primarily a matter of distributive justice. Others emphasize market justice. Partly because of such disagreements on the meaning of equity, economists try to distinguish carefully between their positive statements and their normative statements.

5. Economics is about people. All economic principles must be framed in terms of the way individuals make choices and respond to changes in their environment, and all economic policies must be judged in terms of their impact on the welfare of individual people.

DISCUSSION QUESTIONS

1. Suppose that you want to get as high a grade-point average as you can this term, yet your time and abilities are limited. Would it be possible to look at the way you spend your time as an economic problem? What is the opportunity cost of getting higher grades?
2. Suppose that you won a lottery prize of $20 million. Would this solve all of your personal economic problems? Explain.
3. Can you give some real-world examples of how the economy, a firm, or even an individual might be operating on the interior of its respective production possibilities curve?
4. Do you think it is possible to achieve both efficiency and equity in the real world? Or is this another economic problem in which it is necessary to sacrifice one for the other? Explain.
5. Could we say that economics is about money, or about goods and services, rather than about people? Explain.
6. Do the animals in a forest face an economic problem? What are their objectives, constraints, and alternatives? What has happened to their economic problems as people have impinged on their habitat? Is economics about nonpeople too?
7. Should we all be entitled to our fair share of the earth's produce? Would this question be better stated if we replaced the phrase, "the earth's produce," with "the goods and services that Smith and Jones and Jansen and M'Boye and Li Ha Ching and. . . (listing all the earth's 4 billion people by name) produce? To make it still easier, suppose that Smith and Jones are the only two people on earth. Is Smith entitled to a fair share of what Jones produces and vice versa?
8. List several problems that you think you will be better able to analyze after reading this book.

Appendix
Working with Graphs

How Economists Use Graphs

At one of our country's well-known colleges, the students have their own names for all the courses. They call the astronomy course "stars," the geology course "rocks," and the biology course "frogs." Their name for the economics course is "graphs and laughs." This choice of names indicates two things. First, it says that the students think the professor has a noteworthy sense of humor. Second, it shows that in the minds of students, economics is a matter of "learning about graphs" in the same sense that astronomy is a matter of learning about stars, or geology a matter of learning about rocks.

Let us begin, then, by saying that economics is not "about" graphs. Economics is about people. It is about the way that people make choices, use resources, and cooperate with one another in an effort to overcome the universal problem of scarcity. Economics is a social science, not an offshoot of analytic geometry.

Well, the skeptical reader may say, "If economics is not about graphs, why are there so many of them in this book?" The answer is that economists use graphs to illustrate the theories they develop about people's economic behavior in order to make them vivid, eye-catching, and easy to remember. Everything that can be said in the form of a graph can also be said in words, but saying something twice in two different ways is a proven aid to learning. The purpose of this appendix is to help you to be able to make maximum use of an important learning aid by explaining how to work with graphs.

Pairs of Numbers and Points

The first thing to learn is how to use points on a graph to represent pairs of numbers. Consider Exhibit 1.5. The small table in that exhibit presents six pairs of numbers. The two columns in the table are labeled x and y. The first number in each pair is called the x *value*, and the second is called the y *value*. Each *pair* of numbers is labeled with a capital letter A through E. Pair A has an x value of 2 and a y value of 3; pair B has an x value of 4 and a y value of 4, and so forth.

Next to the table in Exhibit 1.5 is a diagram. First look at the lines placed at right angles to one another along the bottom and the left-hand side of the diagram. These are called *coordinate axes*. The horizontal axis is marked off into units and is used for measuring the x value, while the vertical axis is marked off into units for measuring the y value. In the space between these axes, we can represent each lettered pair of numbers from the table as a lettered point. For example, to put point A in place we go two units to the right along the horizontal axis to represent the x value of 2, and then three units straight up, parallel to the vertical axis, to represent the y value of 3. The other points are placed the same way.

Very often the visual effect of a graph is improved by connecting the points we have located by a smooth line or curve. When this is done (as shown in the diagram) we can see at a glance that as the x value increases, the y value also tends to increase.

EXHIBIT 1.5

Pairs of numbers and points

Each lettered pair of numbers in the table corresponds to a lettered point on the graph. The x value of each point corresponds to the horizontal distance of the point from the vertical axis, and the y value to the vertical distance from the horizontal axis.

	x	y
A	2	3
B	4	4
C	6	5
D	8	6
E	10	7

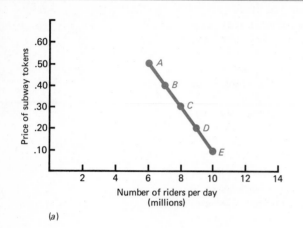

(a)

	Price of Tokens	Number of Riders (millions)
A	$.50	6
B	$.40	7
C	$.30	8
D	$.20	9
E	$.10	10

(b)

	Number of Hamburgers	Number of Milkshakes
A	5	0
B	4	1
C	3	2
D	2	3
E	1	4
F	0	5

Year	Railroad Investment (billions of dollars)
1950	1.18
1951	1.58
1952	1.50
1953	1.42
1954	.93
1955	1.02
1956	1.37
1957	1.58
1958	.86
1959	1.02

(c)

EXHIBIT 1.6

Three typical economic graphs

This exhibit shows three graphs typical of those used in economics. Part *a* shows the relationship between the price of tokens and the number of riders per day on a certain city subway system. When a graph shows the relationship between a price and a quantity, it is conventional to put the price on the vertical axis. Part *b* shows the possible choices open to a person who has $1 to spend on lunch, and can buy hamburgers at $.20 each or milkshakes at $.20 each. Part *c* shows how a graph can be used to represent change over time.

Source: (c) Economic Report of the President, 1976, Table B-38.

Common Economic Graphs

In economics, we are not interested in abstract relationships between x's and y's but, rather, in relationships concerning people and the things they do under various conditions. This means that graphs in economics are labeled in terms of the ideas used in putting together economic theories. Exhibit 1.6 shows three very common ways of labeling coordinate axes. Each of these will be encountered many times in this book.

In Exhibit 1.6a, we have represented the relationship between the price of subway tokens in some city and the number of people who would choose to ride the subway each day at any given price. The table shows that as the price of tokens goes up, fewer people choose to ride the subway. The graph shows the same thing. As a matter of tradition in economics, whenever we draw a graph where both money values and quantity units are involved, we use the vertical axis to measure the money values (in this case, the price of subway tokens) and the horizontal axis to measure the quantity units (in this case, the number of riders per day).

Exhibit 1.6b uses quantity units on both axes. Here our problem is to represent the various combinations of milkshakes and hamburgers that a student can buy at the local carry-out when milkshakes cost $.20 each, hamburgers cost $.20 each, and the student has exactly $1 to spend on her lunch. The table shows that she can buy five burgers and no shakes, four burgers and one shake, three burgers and two shakes, and so forth.

The graph gives us a visual picture of the "menu" the student has available to choose from, given the limited money she has to spend. The points from the table are drawn in and labeled. Our student can choose any of these. A diagonal line has been sketched in to connect these points, and if we allow the purchase of parts of hamburgers and milkshakes, the student can choose from among all the points along this line. (For example, she could buy $2\frac{1}{2}$ burgers and $2\frac{1}{2}$ shakes.) If she wanted to have some money left over, she could buy a lunch represented by a point within the shaded area, such as point G. (Point G stands for two hamburgers and one shake, and costs only $.60.) But unless she gets some more money, our student cannot choose from points outside the shaded area.

Exhibit 1.6c shows still another kind of graph frequently used in economics. Here we are interested in how some economic magnitude changes over time. The table gives data on railroad investment over a series of ten years. The graph is drawn using time on the horizontal axis and billions of dollars per year on the vertical axis to give a visual representation of the ups and downs of railroad investment.

Slopes

When we are talking about graphs, it is frequently convenient to describe lines or curves in terms of their *slopes*. The slope of a straight line drawn between two points is defined as the ratio of the change in the y value to the change in the x value between two points. In Exhibit 1.7, for example, the slope of the line drawn between points A and B is 2. The y value changes by six units between these two points, while the x value changes by only three units. The slope is the ratio $6/3 = 2$. When a line slants downward like the line between points C and D in Exhibit 1.7, the x value and the y value change in opposite directions. As we go from point C to point D, the y value changes by -2 (that is, it decreases by two units), while the x value changes by $+4$ (that is, it increases by four units). The slope of this line is the ratio $-2/4 = -1/2$. This type of a line is said to have a negative slope.

We can also speak of the slope of a curved line, but we must remember that the slope of a curved line varies from point to point. The slope of a curve at any given point is defined as the slope of a straight line drawn tangent to the curve at that point. (A tangent line is one just touching the curve without crossing it). Consider the curve in Exhibit 1.8. Applying our definition, we see that the slope of this line at point A is 1, and its slope at point B is -2.

EXHIBIT 1.7

Slopes of lines

The slope of a straight line drawn between two points is defined as the ratio of the change in the *y* value to the change in the *x* value between the two points. For example, the line drawn between points *A* and *B* in this exhibit has a slope of $+2$, whereas the line drawn between points *C* and *D* has a slope of $-\frac{1}{2}$.

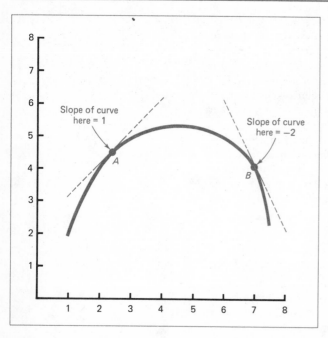

EXHIBIT 1.8

Slopes of curves

The slope of a curve at any given point is defined as the slope of a straight line drawn tangent to the curve at that point. A tangent line is one that just touches the curve without crossing it. In this exhibit, the slope of the curve at point *A* is 1, and the slope of the curve at point *B* is -2.

Abstract Graphs

In all our examples so far, we have had specific numbers to work with for the *x* and *y* values. Sometimes, though, we only know the general nature of the relationship between two economic magnitudes without knowing specific numbers. For example, we might know that when people's incomes rise, they tend to increase their consumption of meat rapidly at first, but then as very high incomes are reached, their meat consumption levels off. If we want to represent a relationship like this without getting specific about the numbers involved, we draw a graph

EXHIBIT 1.9

An abstract graph

When we know the general form of an economic relationship but do not know the exact numbers involved, we can draw an abstract graph. Here we know that as people's income rises, their consumption of meat increases rapidly at first, and then levels off. Because we do not know the exact numbers for meat consumption or income, we have not marked any units on the axes.

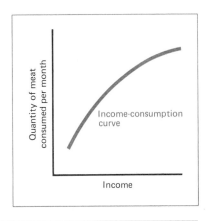

like that shown in Exhibit 1.9. The vertical axis is just labeled "income" without any units, and the horizontal axis "meat" without any units. The curve, which rises rapidly at first and then levels off, tells us the general nature of the relationship between income and meat consumption. We shall use abstract graphs like this one very frequently in this book. Abstract graphs are used to express general principles, whereas graphs with numbers on the axes are used to summarize specific known information.

Study Hints for Graphs

When you come to a chapter in this book that is full of graphs, how should you study it? The first and most important rule is *do not ever memorize graphs.* I have never taught economics without having at least one student come to me after failing an exam and say, "But I learned every one of those graphs! What happened?" I always tell those students that they should have learned the economics instead of learning the graphs, or else that they should have taken analytical geometry instead.

Here are some specific study hints for working with graphs. After you have read carefully through a chapter that uses graphs frequently, go back through the graphs one at a time. Put your hand over the explanatory note that appears beside each graph and try putting what the graph says into words. If you cannot say at least as much in words about the graph as the explanatory note says, read the text over again.

If you do all right going from graphs to words, half the battle is won. Next, try covering up the graph and, using the explanatory note as a guide, sketch the graph on a piece of scratch paper. If you understand what the words mean and can comfortably go back and forth between the words and the graphs, you will find out that the two together are much easier to remember and apply than either would be separately. If you "learn the graphs" as meaningless patterns of lines, you are lost.

Constructing Your Own Graphs

For some students, the hardest kind of question to answer on an exam is the kind that requires construction of an original graph as part of an essay answer. Here are some hints for constructing your own graphs.

1. Put down in words the answer to the question. If you cannot do that, you might as well skip on to the next question without wasting time on the graph. Try underlining the most important quantities in what you have written. The result might be something like: "The larger the *number of students* who attend a university, the lower the *cost per student* of providing them with an education."

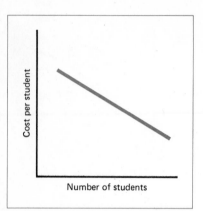

EXHIBIT 1.10
Constructing a graph
To construct a graph, first put down in words what you want to say: "The larger the *number of students* at a university, the lower the *cost per student* of providing them with an education." Next, label the coordinate axes.
Then, if you have exact numbers to work with, construct a table. Here we have no exact numbers, so we draw an abstract graph that slopes downward to show that cost goes down as numbers go up. For graphs with more than one curve, repeat these steps.

2. Decide how you are going to label the coordinate axes of your graph. In our example, because it is conventional to put money values on the vertical axis, we shall label the vertical axis "cost per student" and the horizontal axis "number of students."

3. Do you have exact numbers to work with? If you do, your next step should be to make a table showing what you know and then to use that to sketch your graph. If you do not have numbers, you will be drawing an abstract graph. In this case, all you know is that costs per student go down when the number of students goes up. Sketch in any convenient downward-sloping line (as in Exhibit 1.10), and you will have done as well as can be done.

4. If your graph involves more than one relationship between pairs of economic quantities, repeat steps 1–3 for each relationship that you want to represent by a line or curve. When sketching graphs with more than one curve, pay particular attention to points where you think two curves ought to intersect (which will happen whenever both the x and y values of the two relationships are equal) and to points where you think they ought to be tangent (which will happen whenever the slopes of two curves are equal).

5. After your graph is completed, try translating it back into words. Does it really say what you wanted it to say?

Conclusion

That is about all we can say about graphs in general. As you work through this book and are introduced to various specific kinds of graphs, turn back to this appendix now and then. Do not commit the fatal error of memorizing graphs as meaningless pictures. Do remember that if you can go back and forth between graphs and words, the underlying theory that both are trying to express will stay with you more vividly than if you rely on either graphs or words alone. Do remember that economics is about *people,* not graphs.

CHAPTER 2
The Price System and the Market Economy

What You Will Learn in This Chapter
Resource allocation means determining what will be produced, how it will be produced, who will produce it, and for whom it will be produced. In the American economy, most resource allocation decisions are made in markets. Markets perform three major functions. They act as mechanisms for utilizing knowledge, as sources of incentives, and as windows on the future.

When economists speak of the **allocation of resources,** they mean the determination of *what* will be produced, *how* it will be produced, *who* will produce it, and *for whom* it will be produced. Millions of people are involved in finding the answers to these questions, and the interaction of all that they do determines, in turn, the whole course of economic life.

In the American economy, most resource allocation decisions are made by people acting in **markets.** By "markets" we mean all of the various arrangements that people have for trading with one another. Markets may be very elaborately organized, like the New York Stock Exchange, with its computers and ticker-tape machines, or very informal, like the word-of-mouth network that puts teenage babysitters in touch with the people who need them.

However markets are organized, they play an important role in determining *what, how, who,* and *for whom.* Businesspeople look to markets for clues as to *what* can be sold and, accordingly, *what* to produce. They look at the markets where factors of production can be bought and decide *how* to make their products at the least cost, given the prices of those factors. The question of *who* is to produce what is decided by millions of working men and women who search on the job market for the opportunities best suited to their interests and abilities. And as to the matter of *for whom* it is all produced, the answer, for the most part, is for whoever is willing and able to buy things at the price for which they are put up for sale.

Because so many important economic decisions are made in the marketplace, it is a wise custom among writers of economic textbooks to devote a few early chapters to a general overview of the theory of prices and markets before proceeding to more specialized topics. We shall follow that custom here, in this chapter and the next.

Allocation The distribution or assignment of things to specific uses. In economics, the term *resource allocation* means determining what will be produced, how it will be produced, who will produce it, and for whom it will be produced.

Markets A general term referring to all of the various arrangements that people have for trading with one another.

Markets as Mechanisms for Utilizing Knowledge

The insight that markets are, first and foremost, *mechanisms for utilizing knowledge* comes to us from Friedrich von Hayek. Hayek saw that if any one person, or a small group of people, could possess *complete knowledge* of the economy, the economic problems of *what, how, who,* and *for whom* would be comparatively easy to solve. With *given* knowledge of resources available, *given* knowledge of production techniques, and *given* knowledge of the relative importance of various economic goals, all economic problems would be problems of pure logic. A computer (although it would take a rather large one) could be programmed to give the answers that would best satisfy human needs, given the available resources.

Time and Place

What puts the idea of a computer-controlled economy in the realm of fantasy is not any shortcoming of electronic technology. Instead, it is the fact that complete economic knowledge is not, and by its nature cannot be, possessed by any one or a few individuals. To be sure, some types of economic knowledge could be collected and sent to a single central point. We could compile a census of labor and natural resources. We could put together a library of the techniques of modern production engineering. We could conduct opinion surveys of consumer preferences. But when we had collected all this information, and expressed it in the form of general rules, trends, and regularities, it would not represent the totality of economic knowledge. There would still remain a vast amount of vital knowledge that, by its very nature, is always fragmented and widely spread among large numbers of individuals. That is the knowledge of *particular circumstances of time and place.*

The importance of the knowledge of particular circumstances of time and place can be clearly understood if we consider the extent to which day-to-day business decision making depends on it. A young management trainee straight out of business school earns less and contributes less to the firm for which he works than he will later on. In time, he will have supplemented his theoretical knowledge with a knowledge of the strengths and weaknesses of the particular individuals with whom he works, knowledge of the likes and dislikes of particular customers, and in general, knowledge of all the things that make his firm just a little different from its competitors. In addition to knowing that, as a general principle, a certain component part of his firm's product can be made out of either steel or plastic, he also will learn to be alert to any pending shortage of steel and know which particular supplier will be able most rapidly to fill his order for the plastic replacement.

The difference between success and bankruptcy for a firm hinges on how well such detailed, localized knowledge is utilized. So does the difference between a prosperous and a stagnant economy for a nation as a whole.

Centralization Not Possible

Because so many economic decisions depend on detailed knowledge of time and place, it is not possible to handle most economic problems by first communicating information to a central point, making decisions there, and then sending instructions back to someone at a particular spot. Yet leaving decisions up to someone on the spot does not in itself guarantee the effective use of economic knowledge. The person on the spot may know the ins and outs of the particular business, but also needs information about variations in general business conditions, about technological changes in other, different industries, perhaps even about shortages developing somewhere on the other side of the globe. The market plays a vital role as a mechanism for transmitting knowledge of such distant changes to the person who actually makes decisions on the spot. Here is an example that Hayek uses to make this point:

CASE 2.1
Knowledge and the Price System[1]

"Assume that somewhere in the world a new opportunity for the use of some raw material, say tin, has arisen, or that one of the sources of supply of tin has been eliminated. It does not matter for our purpose—and it is very significant that it does not matter—which of these two causes has made tin more scarce. All that the users of tin need to know is that some of the tin they used to consume is now more profitably employed elsewhere, and that in consequence they must economize tin. There is no need for the great majority of them even to know where the more urgent need has arisen, or in favor of what other needs they ought to husband the supply. If only some of them know directly of the new demand, and switch resources over to it, and if the people who are aware of the new gap thus created in turn fill it from still other sources, the effect will rapidly spread throughout the whole economic system and influence not only the uses of tin, but also those of its substitutes and the substitutes of these substitutes, the supply of all the things made of tin, and their substitutes, and so on; and all this without the great majority of those instrumental in bringing about these substitutions knowing anything at all about the original cause of these changes. The whole acts as one market, not because any of its members survey the whole field, but because their limited individual fields of vision sufficiently overlap so that through many intermediaries the relevant information is communicated to all."

[1] F. A. Hayek, "The Use of Knowledge in Society" *American Economic Review*, vol. XXXV, no. 4. (Sept. 1945), pp. 519–530.

The most remarkable thing about all this is how little each participant in the whole chain of events needs to know in order to play his part. The person on the spot needs only one scrap of information, namely, that the price of tin has risen. All the rest—shipping schedules, Bolivian politics, techniques of nonferrous metallurgy—need be known only by a few other people at other points in the chain. In short, prices are the market's telegraph signals—cryptic, abbreviated bits of information that allow general knowledge to be combined with particular knowledge of time and place and to be put to work when and where it is needed.

Markets as Sources of Economic Incentives

Markets transmit to economic decision makers the knowledge they need to put the resources they control to good use. At the same time, markets are

Friedrich August von Hayek
(1899–   )

In 1944, a slim volume entitled *The Road to Serfdom* burst onto the world's best-seller list. This book warned that an enthusiasm for economic planning and strong central government was leading Western democracies down a path that, if not checked, could end in Soviet- or Nazi-style totalitarianism. The author of the book was as surprised as anyone to find it a best seller. He was Friedrich von Hayek, then a Professor at the London School of Economics.

Hayek, born and educated in Vienna, by 1944 already had a first-class international reputation as an economic theorist. He had written widely on monetary theory and on the subject we now know as macroeconomics. In contrast to many of his contemporaries, he did not believe that the Great Depression of the 1930s signaled the final failure of the market economy. The market would and could work, he held, if it were freed of the distortions introduced by ill-advised government policies. Most of all, what the economies of the world did not need as a cure for their troubles was comprehensive economic planning. Planning could never replace the market as a method for utilizing knowledge and guiding the division of labor. The attempt to make it do so would lead only to a loss of political freedom, not greater economic prosperity.

In 1950, Hayek left London for the University of Chicago, where he taught for twelve years as professor of social and moral science. Much of his time he now spent writing on broad issues of law and social philosophy. His major work of the University of Chicago period was *The Constitution of Liberty*. In this book, he defended the classical liberal ideal of the limited state based on a free market economy and a written constitution.

In 1962, Hayek saw that the University of Chicago's mandatory retirement age was fast approaching. Retirement seemed such an impossible idea to him that he returned to Europe, where professors could serve for a lifetime. He is now Visiting Professor at the University of Salzburg in Austria, and Professor Emeritus of the University of Freiburg in Germany. In 1974, the name Friedrich von Hayek was back in the international headlines once again. The Swedish Academy of Science had awarded him the Nobel Memorial Prize in Economics—the highest professional distinction there is. A fitting time to retire from a distinguished career? Not for Hayek. The first volume of his new work, *Law, Legislation, and Liberty,* had just appeared the year before, and there were two more volumes to complete. Asked recently what he would do when that job had been finished, Hayek indicated that he would then, after a detour of many years, be ready to get back to some unfinished problems of economic theory.

also the sources of the incentives necessary to encourage decision makers to carry out the actions that are known to be the correct ones.

Profits

Every businessperson watches the market for one thing: an opportunity to buy low and sell high. To take a prosaic example, suppose that Smith is a used car dealer. He learns that a certain Ms. Jones owns a used VW microbus for which she will accept any offer over $300. From his experience, Smith judges that if he buys the car and puts it on his lot, some third party will come along who will be willing to pay $600 for the vehicle. It is clear how Smith can put his knowledge to work and earn a **profit** by buying low and selling high. It is also clear that the result of his action will be the right result: The car will be moved from Ms. Jones, who values it less, to the third party, who values it more.

Profit Income earned by buying low and selling high. Includes the case in which an entrepreneur buys factors of production and uses them to make something that can then be sold for more than the cost of obtaining the factor inputs.

In the example just given, the trading process involved one buyer, one seller, one commodity, and one middleman. This served to illustrate the general principles involved in the transaction, but simpler and more complex arrangements are also possible.

Trade takes a simpler form if the middleman is left out and the original owner sells directly to the final user. In that case, the gains from trade are split just two ways, so the share of the gains for each party can be larger. This being the case, we might wonder why trade would ever involve a middleman. The reason is that the middleman plays the role of a "communications specialist" in the economic system. The ultimate buyer and seller may be miles apart and totally unacquainted with each other's needs and resources. The middleman, in contrast, makes it his business to be well informed of the bidding and asking prices everywhere, and to initiate transactions that would never be noticed or carried out by the original owners and final users.

It is important to notice that the presence of a middleman in a transaction is not in any way wasteful or inefficient. The total gains from trade are the same whether he is there or not. If buyer and seller can get together directly and eliminate the middleman, that is fine for them, but it does nothing to improve resource allocation in general. On the other hand, if, for lack of a middleman, they fail to get together to do business, then efficiency suffers.

The Entrepreneur

Trade takes a more complex form when middlemen sell things in a form different from the one in which they buy them. When middlemen buy factors of production and organize them for the production of new goods before selling, they are called **entrepreneurs.** They still make their profits by buying inputs low and selling output high, but their role as "communication specialists" is more important than ever. Entrepreneurs must make it their business not only to keep informed of all bidding and asking prices of their customers and suppliers, but also to be aware of technical information about production processes as well. Their reward lies in the fact that if they know their business well, they can offer prices to their suppliers that are sufficiently high to induce them to sell, and prices to their customers that are sufficiently low to induce them to buy, and still have a margin of profit left over for themselves.

Entrepreneur In general, anyone who is alert to opportunities for buying low and selling high in order to make a profit. More particularly, someone who undertakes to buy factors of production and organizes them for the production of useful goods or services in the hope that those goods or services can be sold at a profit.

Other Incentives

Profits are not the only incentives that markets offer. There are particular kinds of incentives to encourage every economic decision maker to seek out and make the best use of the information that the price system provides. Consumers who shop the sales and pay careful attention to the way product prices vary from place to place and time to time find themselves rewarded by the satisfaction of more needs with a limited budget. Workers who know their way around the job market earn better wages and salaries by working where their productivity is highest. Markets for rental housing help match tenants to landlords in a mutually satisfactory way. In every case, the person who first learns a new bit of economic knowledge has an economic incentive to put that knowledge to work and not just to file it away.

Markets as Windows on the Future

There are many kinds of knowledge that can be turned to profit in the marketplace, but the most profitable of all to possess would be true knowledge of the future. To know next week's stock market quotations, or whether a drought that threatens Russia's wheat crop will be broken, or whether the Japanese will tighten their restrictions on textile imports, and to know these things with certainty, would be worth millions. Sadly, true knowledge of the future is beyond human reach.

Nonetheless, intelligent economic decisions cannot be made without taking the future into account. Everyone has to do some guessing and take some chances. In a market economy, this guessing is not completely random or undirected. It turns out that market prices provide a *window on the future* because they reflect, in summary form, the guesses of all the people whose business leads them to trade in any particular market. Let us see how this works in a variety of cases.

Commodity Future Markets

For many basic **commodities,** the necessary window is provided by special markets called **future markets.** In future markets, people meet and agree to deliver or take delivery of some commodity at some specified *future* date, and at a price *currently* agreed on. The agreed future prices are published in the business pages of most major daily newspapers. For example, if you had read *The New York Times* of October 14, 1975, you would have found the table reproduced here in Exhibit 2.1. Reading down that table to the line we have marked, we can see that at the opening of that trading day, you could have placed an order for 5,000 bushels of wheat to be delivered the next March and found someone to agree to sell it for a payment of $4.20 per bushel on the day of delivery. Reading across the line, we see that the price at which such a contract could have been made fluctuated during the day, touching a high of $4.31 at one point, reaching a low of $4.16 at another, and ending up at $4.27 per bushel when the market closed in the afternoon. If you had been interested in placing an order for wheat to be delivered in December, May, July, or September, other lines of the table would have told you what you needed to know. Traders in gold, orange juice, soybeans, or hogs would have looked at still other parts of the table.

Clearly, the kind of information future markets provide is very useful. Suppose that you were a farmer who was planning to plant wheat to be harvested in July. You could agree to a selling price before you even planted, and then spend the next eight months worrying about the technical details of farming rather than about the ups and downs of market prices. Or if you were a manufacturer planning a production run of 50,000

Commodity (1) In a general sense, any good or service produced to be sold in any market; (2) in a more particular sense, any of a number of basic industrial raw materials and agricultural products, such as gold, silver, wheat, corn, cattle, or hogs, that are traded in organized future markets.

Future Markets A market in which buyers and sellers agree to deliver or take delivery of some commodity at a specified future date and at a price currently agreed on.

Listing of Prices of Commodity Futures

Thursday, July 15, 1976

WHEAT

	Open	High	Low	Close	Prev
Jul	3.71	3.71	3.58	3.61½	3.73
Sep	3.75	3.76	3.63	3.67	3.79
Dec	3.92	3.92	3.77½	3.81½	3.92
Mar	4.03	4.03	3.90	3.95	4.05
May	4.08	4.08	3.96	3.99½	4.11
Jul	4.10	4.11	4.00	4.02	4.13

CORN

Jul	3.06	3.10	3.01	3.05¼	3.09
Sep	3.06	3.06	2.96¾	3.00	3.06¾
Dec	2.91	2.94¾	2.85	2.90	2.95
Mar	3.00	3.03¼	2.94	2.99	3.04
May	3.05	3.09	2.99	3.03	3.08
Jul	3.08	3.12	3.03½	3.08	3.13

OATS

Jul	1.96	1.96½	1.91	1.91	1.96¾
Sep	1.89	1.90½	1.84	1.85	1.90
Dec	1.88	1.89½	1.83½	1.84½	1.89¼
Mar	1.87½	1.88½	1.82½	1.82¾	1.88½
May	1.85½	1.86	1.80½	1.80½	1.86

SOYBEANS

Jul	7.43	7.43	7.13½	7.13½	7.33½
Aug	7.46	7.46	7.14	7.14	7.34
Sep	7.49	7.52	7.18	7.18	7.38
Nov	7.58	7.58	7.27	7.27	7.47
Jan	7.60	7.65	7.32	7.32	7.52
Mar	7.68	7.68	7.36½	7.36½	7.56½
May	7.66	7.67	7.36½	7.36½	7.56½
Jul	7.65	7.65	7.35½	7.35½	7.55½

SOYBEAN OIL

Jul	24.00	24.00	22.30	22.70	22.75
Aug	24.00	24.05	22.48	22.60	23.48
Sep	24.15	24.30	22.60	22.70	23.60
Oct	24.45	24.55	22.70	2.80	.70323
Oct	24.45	24.55	22.70	22.80	23.70
Dec	24.50	24.60	22.95	23.00	23.95
Jan	24.50	24.55	23.00	23.05	24.00
Mar	24.55	24.60	22.98	23.05	23.98
May	24.65	24.65	23.10	23.15	24.10
Jul	24.65	24.65	23.10	23.20	24.10

SOYBEAN MEAL

Jul	214.00	214.00	199.50	20.000	212.50
Aug	215.00	21)00	203.20	203.20	2 0.00
Sep	214.00	215.00	204.00	204.00	214.00
Oct	216.00	216.00	204.80	204.80	214.50
Dec	216.00	217.00	206.20	206.20	216.00
Jan	217.00	217.00	237.00	207.00	217.00
Mar	217.00	218.00	208.20	208.20	218.00
May	217.00	218.50	208.00	210.00	218.00
Jul	220.00	220.00	211.00	213.00	221.00

KANSAS CITY WHEAT

July	3.75	3.77	3.67½	3.68½	3.80
Sept.	3.87	3.87	3.73¾	3.75½	3.88
Dec.	3.95	3.96	3.84½	3.86¾	3.98½
Mar.	4.06	4.06¼	3.96	3.97½	4.08
May	4.10	4.10	4.03	4.03	4.12½

SUGAR

Contract No. 12

Raw sugar spot 14.65 nominal.

Contract No. 11

Sep	14.00	14.00	13.10	13.20	14.04
Oct	14.32	14.35	13.60	13.65	14.45
Jan	14.70	14.70	13.75	13.75	14.75
Mar	14.80	14.86	14.18	14.20	14.87
May	14.72	14.78	14.10	14.20	14.77
Jul	14.70	14.70	14.05	14.05	14.65
Sep	14.45	14.45	13.85	13.85	n14.49
Oct	14.35	14.35	13.70	13.75	n14.42

Sales 8,429.
n-nominal.

COCOA

	Open	High	Low	Close	Prev.
Jul	94.35	94.35	94.25	93.85s	95.35
Sep	94.50	94.75	91.00	91.75s	92.65
Dec	91.25	91.25	88.00	88.85s	89.35
Mar	87.69	87.75	84.40	85.40s	86.05
May	84.75	84.10	80.40	80.65s	83.55
Jul	82.25	82.25	78.95	80.00s	81.25
Sep	79.50	79.50	79.25	77.40s	78.50
Dec	75.50	75.50	72.50	73.65s	74.75

Sales: 1,941.
Spot Accra 106½.
s-Settling.

EGGS (Shell)

Chicago Mercantile Exchange

Jul	57.50	57.50	57.15	a57.15	57.50
Aug	57.30	57.35	56.75	57.35	57.20
Sep	60.55	60.85	59.50	59.50	60.45

Oct	58.00	58.00	58.00	58.00	57.75
Nov	61.75	61.90	60.90	61.00	a61.50
Dec	63.80	63.95	62.50	62.50	63.30

Sales: Jul 7; Aug 12; Sep 324; Oct 1;
Nov 16; Dec 164.
Open interest: Jul 47; Aug 120; Sep
1494; Oct 12; Nov 458; Dec 1012.

FROZEN PORK BELLIES

Jul	67.70	68.80	67.25	68.10	67.70
Aug	65.50	66.75	65.05	66.00	65.60
Feb	61.60	62.95	61.60	62.80	61.60
Mar	61.52	62.85	61.52	b62.65	61.70
May	62.25	63.30	62.10	a63.05	62.10
Jul	63.05	63.05	62.50	a62.50	a62.00

Sales: July 337; Aug 4074; Feb 924;
March 38; May 8; July 5.
Open interest: July 7007; Aug 5050; Feb
2484; March 754; May 273; July 26.
b—Bid; a—Asked; n—Nominal.

POTATOES

N.Y. Mercantile Exchange

	Open	High	Low	Close	Prev.
Nov	5.55	5.63	5.47	5.47	b5.50
Mar	6.80	6.88	6.64	6.70	6.74
Apr	7.72	7.85	7.60	7.64	6.72
May	8.40	8.40	8.40	a8.35	8.25

Sales 815.
a-asked.

PLATINUM

New York Mercantile Exchange

Oct.	182.0	182.70	179.20	179.30	183.00
Jan.	185.90	186.10	182.50	182.50	186.50
Apr.	189.50	189.50	186.10	186.10	189.50
July	192.70	193.20	191.50	191.50	190.20
Oct.	197.00	197.00	197.00	197.00	190.20

Sales, 798 contracts.

PALLADIUM

New York Mercantile Exchange

Sept.	61.50	61.70	61.10	61.70	61.90
Dec.	63.00	63.20	61.70	62.85	62.70
Mar.	63.00	63.25	62.80	63.20	63.20

Sales, 62 contracts.

U.S. SILVER COINS (In Dollars)

New York Mercantile Exchange

Oct.	3,507	3,507	3,415	3,415	3,505
Jan.	3,500	3,500	3,460	3,460	3,587
Apr.	3,575	3,575	3,575	3,575	3,625
July	....	....	....	3,575b	
Oct.	....	....	....	3,635b	3,737

CSales, 12 contracts.

COPPER

New York Commodity Exchange

	Open	High	Low	Close	Prev.
Jul	76.70	76.70	74.90	74.90s	76.50
Sep	77.50	77.70	75.40	75.70s	77.30
Dec	79.40	79.80	77.40	77.60s	79.20
Jan	79.90	80.20	78.10	78.10s	79.70
Mar	81.00	81.40	79.30	79.30s	80.80
May	81.90	82.20	80.20	80.20s	81.70
Jul	82.50	83.00	81.00	81.00s	82.40

Sales: estimated 6.500.
s-settling.

GOLD

New York Commodity Exchange
100 troy ounce contracts

	Open	High	Low	Close	Prev.
Aug	122.10	122.20	120.10	117.50s	123.10
Sep	122.40	122.40	120.10	118.10s	123.70
Oct	123.50	123.50	121.60	118.70s	124.40
Dec	124.50	124.70	121.03	120.00s	125.70
Feb	126.80	126.80	124.20	121.50s	127.20
Apr	128.00	128.00	125.30	123.00s	128.70
Jun	130.00	130.00	127.60	124.50s	130.20
Aug	131.50	131.50	128.80	126.00s	131.70
Oct	133.00	133.10	132.40	127.60s	133.20

Sales 1,651.
s-settling

N.Y. SILVER (5,000 troy oz.)

	Open	High	Low	Close	Prev.
Jul	501.00	501.00	493.50	483.80s	500.00
Sep	504.50	505.90	487.00	487.50s	503.60
Dec	511.00	511.10	491.00	492.80s	509.00
Jan	512.50	512.50	494.50	494.50s	511.20
Mar	517.50	517.50	499.00	499.40s	515.70
May	521.50	522.00	505.00	504.10s	520.40
Jul	526.50	526.50	510.00	508.80s	525.10
Sep	527.50	527.50	514.00	513.50s	529.80

Sales estimated 10,035.
s-settling

ORANGE JUICE (Frozen Concentrated)

Jul	54.80	54.85	54.50	b54.30	54.75
Sep	54.70	54.70	54.10	b54.10	54.60
Nov	56.20	56.20	55.30	b5.30	5.06
Jan	57.10	57.10	56.40	b56.40	56.90
Mar	57.90	57.90	57.90	b57.50	b57.85
May	58.70	58.70	58.70	b58.60	b58.90

Sales 150.
b-bid

WOOL

	Open	High	Low	Close	Prev.

No trades.

COFFEE

	Open	High	Low	Close	Prev.
Jul	131.00	131.50	128.50	128.50	n133.90
Sep	132.30	131.00	129.35	a129.35	132.15
Dec	130.50	131.00	127.15	127.15	130.15
Mar	128.20	128.30	124.30	124.30	127.10
May	128.50	128.50	124.05	a124.05	b127.05
Jul	127.80	127.80	124.00	a124.00	127.00

Sales: 603.
Parana spot 1.43.
a-Asked, n-Nominal.

LIVE BEEF CATTLE

Aug	40.25	40.82	40.05	40.45	40.45
Oct	43.85	44.40	43.85	44.00	43.97
Dec	45.60	46.00	45.55	45.70	45.55
Feb	45.20	45.95	45.30	b45.70	45.45
Apr	45.30	45.80	45.30	45.65	b45.40
Jun	46.35	46.75	46.35	b46.60	46.40
Aug				b45.60	n46.15

Sales: Aug 4540; Oct 2366; Dec 1926;
Feb 225; April 15; June 16; Aug 0.
Open interest: Aug 14619; Oct 9223; Dec
5792; Feb 3090; April 666; June 267; Aug
42.

FEEDER CATTLE

Aug	39.67	40.22	39.65	40.05	39.65
Sep	40.25	40.50	40.25	40.50	a40.35
Oct	39.80	40.65	39.80	40.55	40.65
Nov	40.15	40.70	40.15	40.50	40.30
Mar				n43.25	43.25
Apr				n43.10	a43.10
May	42.75	42.75	42.75	42.75	43.10

Sales Aug 48; Sep 4; Oct 71; Nov 11;
March 0; April 0; May 1; .
Open interest: Aug 371; Sep 148; Oct
1421; Nov 331; March 43; April 21; May
55; .

LIVE HOGS

Jul	49.10	49.30	48.75	48.82	48.95
Jul	48.85	49.00	48.35	48.62	43.82
Aug	45.50	45.52	44.90	45.15	45.15
Oct	41.50	41.97	41.30	41.60	41.50
Dec	41.50	41.90	41.25	41.50	41.10
Feb	41.55	42.05	41.55	41.82	41.60
Apr	40.60	40.75	40.52	a40.60	40.50
Jun	41.65	41.90	41.65	b41.90	41.90
Jul	42.00	42.20	41.55	42.00	41.90
Aug	41.10	41.10	40.60	40.90	40.70

Sales: July 844; Aug 1860; Oct 714; Dec
287; Feb 86; April 21; June 18; July 1;
Aug 1.
Open interest: July 1434; Aug 4250; Oct
2245; Dec 1489; Feb 756; April 403; June
143; July 100; Aug 3.

ICED BROILERS

Chicago Board of Trade

Jul	42.40	42.40	42.20	42.35	42.45
Aug	41.75	41.80	41.37	41.50	41.70
Sep	40.65	40.65	40.45	40.55	40.75
Nov	40.10	40.20	39.60	39.60	40.00
Jan	41.50	41.57	41.15	41.30	41.45

b-Bid; a-Asked; n-Nominal.

LUMBER

Chicago Mercantile Exchange

Jul	152.10	154.30	151.10	152.90	152.10
Sep	151.80	153.90	151.10	151.53	152.00
Nov	153.50	155.20	152.00	152.40	154.00
Jan	160.00	160.90	158.00	158.00	160.00
Mar	165.90	166.00	163.50	163.50	166.00

Sales: July 192; Sep 978; Nov 325; Jan
155; March 33.
Open interest: July 251; Sep 2278; Nov
1462; J an930; March 181.

PLYWOOD

Chicago Board of Trade

Jul	147.00	14.700	144.50	144.60	147.00
Sep	147.80	148.20	145.20	146.20	147.80
Nov	150.50	151.00	148.00	149.00	150.20
Jan	152.50	152.80	150.00	151.00	152.30
Mar	154.00	154.30	153.00	153.00	154.00
May	155.25	156.0	0154.50	155.00	155.00
Jul	157.00	157.00	155.50	155.50	156.90

EXHIBIT 2.1

Future market prices for selected commodities

Future markets allow people to meet and agree to deliver or take delivery of some commodity at some specified future date, and at a price currently agreed on. This daily table of commodity future prices was published in *The New York Times* on July 16, 1976. The table shows, for example, that on June 15, at the opening of the trading day, an agreement could have been made to buy or sell wheat at $4.03 per bushel in March 1977.

Source: The New York Times, July 16, 1976. © 1976 by The New York Times Company. Reprinted by permission.

gold-plated cigarette lighters next February, you could place a firm order for the gold now, and not have to worry that a change in the price of gold would upset your cost calculations in the meantime.

Other Windows

Not all goods and services have organized future markets, but there are also other ways in which people's judgments and guesses about the future are conveyed to us by the price system. For one thing, the stock market serves to transmit much information about what people think future business conditions will be like. If people think that the automobile industry will be hard-hit by the energy crisis, the stocks of automobile firms will fall in price. At the same time, the stocks of firms that have invested in, say, solar power technology are likely to rise. These stock price movements give investors a clue to which kinds of businesses are worth expanding and which others will not need to grow as much.

Real estate prices also reflect people's judgments about the future. Today's prices for land just outside the boundaries of a city reflect not just the value that the land has in its present use, but also the value the land is likely to have in the future, based on guesses of how fast the city will grow. Present prices of Vermont woodland are based not just on the value of the timber now standing on it, but also on guesses about whether Vermont will retain its popularity among New Yorkers as a site for weekend cottages.

Speculation

How can we be sure that the information that prices give us about the future is a summary of the *best* guesses people are capable of making? Why is it not just as likely to be true that the market will give us false signals, based on the guesses of the ignorant or of people with chronically bad judgment? A large part of the answer has to do with the incentives that the market provides and, especially, on the incentives that it provides to **speculators.**

Speculator A person who buys something now at a low price, hoping to be able to sell it later at a high price.

A speculator is a person who buys something now at a low price, hoping to be able to sell it later at a high price. To make money, a speculator must be able to make better guesses about the future than the average of other traders in the market. Suppose, for instance, that you have the ability to make shrewd guesses about future residential patterns. You buy land in places that you think people will be moving into. Later, you will sell it at a great profit. (Meanwhile, although it is no part of your intention, your speculative buying will signal other people that land values are changing in that area, and they can plan accordingly. For example, farmers will know that the area you are buying in will not be a good one for them to move into.) The market thus gives you an incentive to put your ability to make shrewd guesses to work and not just keep the information to yourself.

Survivorship

Survivorship Principle The principle that business decisions are more often made by people with good judgment than by people with bad judgment, because those with good judgment make profits and survive, while the incompetents soon loose their decision-making positions.

There is a further guarantee that prices will reflect the guesses of those best able to judge the future and not the guesses of incompetents. This guarantee is provided by what economists call the **survivorship principle.** This principle simply tells us that people with consistently good business judgment survive and prosper and achieve positions of great influence in the market economy, while people with chronically bad judgment or faulty sources of information lose money and eventually go out of business. It follows that, on the average, the people who have the most money at their disposal (and, hence, have the greatest impact on market prices when they decide to buy or sell) are the survivors, whose judgment has been tested and found reliable. Those whose judgment is faulty do cause the price system to send out false signals for a while, but not for long, because they soon go bankrupt.

Conclusions

In a modern economy, efficient resource allocation requires a very complex division of labor. Millions of different people are involved every day in the crucial decisions of *what, how, who,* and *for whom.* Somehow, their activities must all be coordinated. In a market economy, the price system is the most important coordinating force. The price system makes information about what is happening far away available to the person on the spot, so that the information can be combined with that person's own special knowledge of time and place. The price system provides an incentive for people to put their knowledge to work earning profits, and although that is not their intention, their buying and selling activities send useful signals to others. The price system even provides information about the future, because prices reflect the guesses that everyone makes about future patterns of resource use. Having said this much in general about *what* markets do, let us turn to a more detailed analysis of *how* they work. That will require a separate chapter.

SUMMARY

1. Resource allocation means determining *what* will be produced, *how* it will be produced, *who* will produce it, and *for whom* it will be produced. In the American economy, most resource allocation decisions are made in markets.
2. Markets play an important role as mechanisms for utilizing knowledge. They transmit general information in the form of prices from distant sources to the people on the spot. These individuals in turn combine the general information with their own particular knowledge of time and place and make decisions that utilize both kinds of information.
3. Markets also are a source of incentives. Entrepreneurs earn profits by buying low and selling high. Often this means buying factors of production and combining them to make goods and services that have a higher market value than the factors themselves did when purchased separately. Consumers and workers also have an incentive to make use of the information with which market prices provide them.
4. Finally, markets act as windows on the future. For some commodities, there are specially organized future markets to serve this purpose. For other goods, present prices reflect not only the uses to which the goods can now be put, but also people's judgments and guesses about what the future will bring. The incentives offered by the market to speculators, combined with the survivorship principle, guarantee that market prices reflect a summary of the *best* guesses that people make about the future.

DISCUSSION QUESTIONS

1. In your opinion, do the salaries and employment possibilities of different occupations have a very strong influence on people's decisions as to whether to go to college and what to major in? Justify your position. Explain how this is another example of the market system operating to determine *what, how, who,* and *for whom.*

2. If you were the manager of a division of a major automobile manufacturer and you noticed that the price of steel had been going up relative to the prices of other materials used in the manufacturing of automobiles, how would you react? What would you do and have others do to make adjustments? How would you expect your competitors to react? Explain.

3. Is it possible to have a market system without money? How important is money in the efficient operation of the market system? What advantages and disadvantages does it have over barter?

4. Often you can get more for something (say, a home or a car) if you sell it yourself rather than selling it through a dealer. Why is it, then, that everyone doesn't sell everything themselves, in view of the fact that dealers charge commissions? What is the dealer providing? Is it logical for the individual to settle for less money?

5. When you purchase something, are you improving your economic situation or not? Under what circumstances would you be being exploited? If you think someone is exploiting you whenever you buy something, are you also exploiting someone whenever you sell something?

6. There have been times when the government has stepped in and prevented the market system from functioning fully, as during wars, the oil embargo of the early 1970s, or the wage-price controls period of the Nixon administration. Why doesn't the government let the price system function all of the time? What are the advantages and disadvantages (the benefits and costs) of this government interference?

7. Is it possible that the market might give business firms the wrong signal as to what will happen in the future? Explain.

CHAPTER 3
Supply and Demand— The Basics

What You Will Learn in This Chapter
People tend to be more eager to buy when prices are low and more eager to sell when prices are high. That is the basis of supply and demand analysis. This useful tool of economics explains how shortages and surpluses of goods are related to changes in market prices and under what conditions markets can be in equilibrium. Thinking in terms of supply and demand also gives additional insight into the role of markets as mechanisms for utilizing knowledge.

For Review
Here are some important terms and concepts that will be put to use in this chapter. Be certain that you understand them, or review them before proceeding.
Opportunity cost (Chapter 1)
Working with graphs (Appendix to Chapter 1)

The number of markets in our economy is as large as the number of different kinds of goods and services produced—and that is very large. These markets differ enormously from one another in all sorts of details. Despite the great diversity of markets, though, there are some economic principles so powerful that they are useful in understanding all of them. The principles of supply and demand fall in this category.

The fundamental ideas of supply and demand have been known to merchants and traders of all ages. As long as there have been markets, sellers have realized that one way to encourage people to buy more of their product is to offer it at a lower price, and buyers have known that one way to get more of the goods they want is to offer to pay more for them. It is really only about 100 years, though, since economists began to make systematic use of the principles of supply and demand as a central basis of their science. In the English-speaking world, Alfred Marshall deserves much of the credit for showing how widely useful the ideas of supply and demand can be. This chapter—and the corresponding chapters in all modern textbooks—is little more than a rewrite of the principles as he taught them in his own famous *Principles of Economics*.

Alfred Marshall (1842–1924)

Alfred Marshall was born in London in 1842, the son of a Bank of England cashier. His father hoped that he would enter the ministry, but young Marshall had other ideas. He turned down a theological scholarship at Oxford to study mathematics instead. He received an M.A. in mathematics from Cambridge in 1865.

While at Cambridge, he joined a philosophical discussion group. There, he became interested in promoting the wide development of the human mind. He was soon told, however, that harsh economic reality would prevent his ideas from being carried out. Britain's productive resources, it was said, could never allow the mass of the people sufficient leisure for education. This disillusioning episode appears to have first turned Marshall's attention to economics.

At the time, British economics was dominated by the so-called classical school. Marshall had great respect for the classical writers. Initially, we saw his own work as simply one of using his mathematical training to strengthen and systematize the classical system. It was not long, however, before he was breaking new ground and developing a system of his own. By 1890, when he brought out his famous *Principles of Economics,* he had laid the foundation of what we now call the *neoclassical* school.

Attempting to explain the essence of his approach, Marshall included this passage in the second edition of his *Principles:*

> In spite of a great variety in detail, nearly all the chief problems of economics agree in that they have a kernel of the same kind. This kernel is an inquiry as to the balancing of two opposed classes of motives, the one consisting of desires to acquire certain new goods, and thus satisfy wants; while the other consists of desires to avoid certain efforts or retain certain immediate enjoyment . . . in other words, it is an inquiry into the balancing of the forces of demand and supply.

Marshall's influence on economics, at least in the English-speaking world, was enormous. His *Principles* was the leading text for decades, and the modern student can still learn much from reading it. As a professor at Cambridge, he taught a great many of the next generation of leading economists. Today the neoclassical school he founded continues to dominate the profession. It has received many challenges, but so far, has weathered them all.

The Law of Demand

Law of Demand The quantity of a good demanded by buyers tends to increase as the price of the good decreases, and tends to decrease as the price increases, others things being equal.

Our analysis begins with the **law of demand.** The law of demand says simply that in the market for any good, the quantity of that good demanded by buyers tends to increase as the price of the good decreases and tends to decrease as the price increases, other things being equal. This law corresponds so closely to what common sense tells us about the way markets work that we might, perhaps, simply state it without further elaboration. To make sure that it is properly understood, though, we shall add a few explanatory comments.

Effective Demand

Effective Demand The quantity of a good that purchasers are willing and able to buy at a particular price.

First, what do we mean by quantity demanded? It is important to understand that by the quantity demanded at a given price we mean **effective demand,** that is, the quantity that purchasers are *willing and able* to buy at that price. The effective demand at a particular price may be different than the quantity that consumers *want* or *need.* I may *want* a new Rolls Royce, but given my limited financial resources, I am not willing actually to offer to buy such a car at its current price of $30,000. My want does not count as part of the quantity demanded in the market for Rolls

Royces. Similarly, a poor man might *need* corrective dental surgery to avoid premature loss of his teeth, but if he is unable to pay, and no other person or agency is willing to pay, his need it not counted as part of the quantity demanded in the market for dental services.

Other Things Equal

Second, why do we attach the phrase "other things being equal" to the law of demand? The reason is that a change in the price of a product is not the only thing that will affect the quantity of that product demanded. If people's incomes go up, they are likely to increase the quantities they demand of a great many goods, even if prices do not change. If the price of beef rises, the effective demand for soy-protein meat substitute is likely to rise, even if the price of soy-protein does not change. And if people *expect* the price of sugar to rise soon, they are likely to increase the quantity of sugar they demand even before the price actually changes. When we state the law of demand, which says that the quantity of a good demanded changes when its price changes, we place incomes, prices of other goods, and expectations about future price changes in a box labeled "other things being equal" simply in order to be able to study one thing at a time. In a moment, we shall come back to the effects of changes in some of these "other things."

Why?

Now that we have made the meaning of the law of demand clear, we may ask why it works. Three particular explanations are worth considering.

First, when the price of a good falls while the prices of other goods remain unchanged, it is likely that we shall *substitute* some of that good for other things. For example, if the price of fish falls while the price of meat remains the same, we are likely to put fish into our menu a few days a month where we would have put meat had the price of fish not changed.

Second, when the price of a good changes, other things being equal, our effective purchasing power changes even though our income, measured in money terms, does not. For example, if the price of clothing rises while nothing else changes, we shall feel poorer, very much as if a few dollars a year had been trimmed from our paycheck or allowance. Feeling poorer, it is likely that we shall buy a bit less of many things, including clothing.

Third—and this reason is not quite distinct from the other two—when the price of a good falls, new buyers who did not use a product at all before are drawn into a market. There was a time, for example, when tape recorders were playthings for the rich, or technical tools for business uses only. Now tape recorders can be bought very cheaply. Rich people do not now buy ten or twenty tape recorders, but sales have gone up ten- or twentyfold because many people now buy them who never entered that market at all before.

Exceptions to the Law

Are there exceptions to the law of demand? Are there cases in which an increase in the price of a good causes us to use more of it? Theoretically, such exceptions are possible, although in practice they are quite rare. One possible kind of exception can occur if the change in the price of a good has such a strong impact on effective purchasing power that it causes a radical change in people's whole pattern of consumption. Imagine a family that lives in Minnesota, and habitually spends January each year vacationing in Florida. One year the price of home heating fuel jumps dramatically. The family reacts by turning down their thermostat a little, but their fuel bills for September through December still go up so much that they cannot afford to take their Florida vacation in January. Yet staying at home, even though it is cheaper than going to Florida, requires them to burn more fuel than during previous winters, when they left the house unheated for that month. The total effect of the rise in fuel price is thus to cause an *increase* in their consumption of the product.

Perhaps other rare kinds of exceptions to the law of demand are also possible. The point is, though, that we have to think so hard to come up with examples that we end up being more convinced than ever of the widespread validity of the law.

Demand Schedules and Curves

The law of demand, like so many other economic ideas, can usefully be illustrated with numerical tables and graphs. Suppose, for example, that we wished to study the operation of the law of demand in the market for widgets.[1] One way to express the relationship between the price of widgets and the quantity of widgets demanded by all buyers in the market is in the form of a table like that given in Exhibit 3.1.

First reading column (1) of this table, we learn that when the price of widgets is $1.50, the quantity demanded will be 200,000 units per year. Reading further, we find that as the price decreases, the quantity demanded increases. At $1.40 per widget, buyers would be willing and able to purchase 240,000 units per year; at $1.30 it would be 280,000 units, and so forth. This complete table is called the **demand schedule** for widgets.

Demand Schedule A table showing the quantity of a good demanded at various prices.

The information given by the demand schedule can be expressed just as easily in graphical form. This is also done in Exhibit 3.1. The diagonal line drawn in the graph is called the **demand curve** for widgets. Suppose that we want to use the demand curve to determine what the quantity demanded will be when the price is $1.20 per unit. Beginning at $1.20 on the vertical axis, we follow across as shown by the arrow until we reach the demand curve, and then down from that point to the horizontal axis, where we read off the answer. This answer, 320,000 widgets per year, is, of course, the same one given in the tabular demand schedule.

Demand Curve A graphical representation of the relationship between the price of a good and the quantity of that good demanded.

Shifts in the Curve

At the risk of being overly repetitive, let us say again that the demand curve shows how the quantity demanded changes in response to price changes, *other things being equal*. When a change in the quantity of widgets demanded occurs as a result of a change in the price of widgets acting

---

[1]Why widgets, and not some real product, such as wheat or haircuts? Our reason for using widgets is to emphasize that we are studying the workings of supply and demand under *idealized* conditions. No real-world market quite corresponds to the theoretical ideal. We shall say more on this point as we go along.

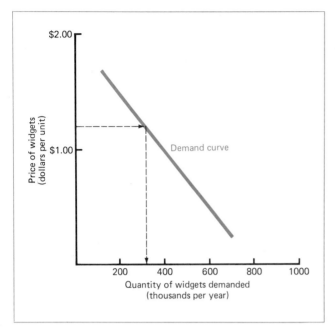

Demand Schedule	
(1) Price of Widgets (dollars)	(2) Quantity of Widgets Demanded (thousands of units per year)
1.50	200
1.40	240
1.30	280
1.20	320
1.10	360
1.00	400
.90	440
.80	480
.70	520
.60	560
.50	600
.40	640

EXHIBIT 3.1
The demand curve and demand schedule for widgets
Both the demand schedule and the demand curve show the quantity of widgets demanded at various possible prices. Either the demand curve or demand schedule tell us, for example, that when the price is $1.20 per unit, the quantity demanded will be 320,000 units per year.

alone, that change is represented graphically as a *movement along* the demand curve for widgets. If the quantity demanded changes for some reason other than price, the graphical representation of the change is different.

Consider Exhibit 3.2. The demand curve labeled D_1 in that figure is the same as that shown in Exhibit 3.1. It is drawn on certain assumptions about household income, the prices of other goods, and buyers' expectations about future changes in price. Given those assumptions, the quantity demanded at a price of $1.00 per unit would be 400,000 units per year, as at point A on the demand curve D_1. A fall in the price from $1.00 per unit to $.50 per unit, other things being equal, would cause the quantity demanded to increase to 600,000 units per year. This change in price would be represented by a movement along the demand curve D_1 from point A to point B.

Return now to point A. Suppose that the price does not change, but that something else changes—say, household income rises. A sufficiently large increase in household income could cause the quantity of widgets demanded to increase by 200,000 units per year, even without a change in the price of widgets. This change would be represented by a movement from point A to point C in the diagram, a movement *off* the demand curve D_1 rather than along it. With household income established at its new, higher level, changes in *price* would now cause movements up or down along the new demand curve D_2, which passes through point C, and lies

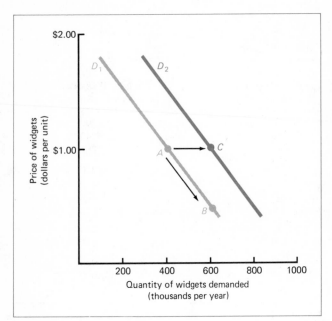

EXHIBIT 3.2
A shift in the demand curve for widgets
The effect of a change in the price of widgets, other things being equal, is represented by a movement along the demand curve for widgets, as from point *A* to point *B* along the demand curve D_1. When the quantity of widgets demanded changes for some reason other than a change in the price of widgets (say, because of a change in household income), the change must be represented by a shift in the entire demand curve, as from the position D_1 to the position D_2.

everywhere to the right of the old demand curve D_1. The new demand curve indicates that whatever the price of widgets, the quantity demanded, given the new, higher level of household income, will be larger than it would have been at the same price, given the old level of income.

We could have told a similar story if it had been the prices of other goods or buyers' expectations that had changed rather than income. The general point we wish to establish is this: When the quantity of some good demanded changes for a reason *other* than a change in the price of that product itself, the change is represented graphically by a *shift* in the entire demand curve to a new position.

Normal and Inferior Goods

Economists have some special terms that are used in discussing the sources of shifts in demand curves. Changes in income are one source of such shifts. When a rise in buyers' income causes the demand curve for a good to shift to the right (as happened in Exhibit 3.2) the good is called a **normal good.** People tend to reduce their consumption of some goods when their incomes go up. Such goods are called **inferior goods.** Inferior goods are those for which there are more desirable, but more costly substitutes. Hamburger and intercity bus travel are often cited as examples. An increase in buyers' income causes the demand curve for an inferior good to shift to the left.

Normal Good A good for which an increase in the income of buyers causes a rightward shift in the demand curve.

Inferior Good A good for which an increase in the income of buyers causes a leftward shift in the demand curve.

Substitutes and Complements

The position of the demand curve for a good may also be affected by changes in the prices of other, closely related goods. For example, salads can be made either from lettuce or from cabbage. As a result, an increase in the price of lettuce is likely to cause not only a decrease in the quantity of lettuce demanded (represented graphically by a movement up and to the left along the lettuce demand curve) but also an increase in the quantity of cabbage demanded (represented graphically by a shift to the right in the entire cabbage demand curve). When an increase in the price of one good causes an increase in the quantity demanded of another good, those two goods are said to be **substitutes** for one another. Other goods, such as photographic film and flashbulbs, tend to be used together. If the price of film were to rise, we would expect not only a decrease in the quantity of film sold, but a decrease in the quantity of flashbulbs sold also. The effect of the change in the price of film would be represented graphically as a movement along the film demand curve, but as a leftward shift in the flashbulb demand curve. When an increase in the price of one good causes a decrease in the quantity demanded of another good, the two goods are said to be **complements.**

> **Substitutes** A pair of goods for which an increase in the price of one good causes an increase in the quantity demanded of the other, other things being equal.

> **Complements** A pair of goods for which an increase in the price of one good causes a decrease in the quantity demanded of the other, other things being equal.

Supply

The next step in our analysis of markets will be to examine the relationship between the price of a good and the quantity of that good that suppliers are willing and able to provide for sale. The relationship between product price and quantity supplied does not conform quite so closely to one simple rule as does the relationship between price and quantity demanded. We shall not state any general "law of supply." Instead, we shall simply look at some important cases.

The Upward-Sloping Supply Curve

Among the possible variations of the relationship between product price and the quantity supplied, there is a very important class of cases for which increases in the quantity supplied are associated with increases in price. In particular, this will be true when the cost per unit of producing some good or service increases as the quantity supplied increases. Then, producers will usually be willing to increase the quantity supplied to the market only if offered a sufficient increase in price at least to cover the increased cost of producing the additional units. Imagine that the production of widgets takes place under these conditions. We would then expect the **supply schedule** and **supply curve** for widgets to look something like those shown in Exhibit 3.3. Unless there is some special reason to think that the supply curve for a product has some different shape, economists usually draw supply curves with an upward slope, like the one in Exhibit 3.3.

> **Supply Schedule** A table showing the quantity of a good supplied at various prices.

> **Supply Curve** A graphical representation of the relationship between the price of a good and the quantity of that good supplied.

Other Supply Curves

Sometimes special conditions are encountered, and the supply curve loses its upward slope. Other possible shapes of supply curves are shown in Exhibit 3.4.

The supply of some goods cannot be increased at all, at any cost. Original drawings by Picasso are an example, so the supply curve for Picasso drawings is a vertical line, as shown in Exhibit 3.4a. The total number of such drawings in existence corresponds to the point on the horizontal axis

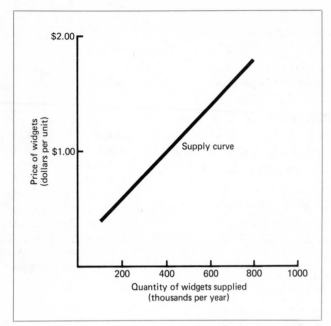

Supply Schedule	
Price of Widgets (dollars per unit)	Quantity Supplied (thousands of units per year)
1.50	650
1.40	600
1.30	550
1.20	500
1.10	450
1.00	400
.90	350
.80	300
.70	250
.60	200
.50	150
.40	100

EXHIBIT 3.3

The supply curve and supply schedule for widgets

Upward sloping supply curves are produced when the cost per unit of making some good increases as the quantity supplied increases. In that case, producers will be willing to increase the quantity supplied to the market only if offered a sufficient increase in price at least to cover the increased cost of producing additional units. Unless there is some special reason to do otherwise, economists usually draw supply curves with upward slopes like this one.

from which the supply curve begins. This number stays the same regardless of the price that owners of such drawings might be offered by enthusiastic buyers.

There are some markets in which producers can be persuaded to increase the quantity supplied without requiring an increase in price. The local market for Campbell's cream of tomato soup in Ithaca, New York, might provide an example. Within any reasonable range, whatever quantity Ithaca's consumers desire can be supplied at no more and no less than $.21 per can. The shape of the supply curve in a market like this is a horizontal line, as shown in Exhibit 3.4b.

Finally, there are some products for which the cost of production decreases as the quantity of the product produced increases. Automobiles are often cited as an example. The more cars of a given model a plant produces, the more it can take advantage of mass-production techniques to reduce the cost per unit. The result can be a downward-sloping supply curve like that shown in Exhibit 3.4c.

The assumptions underlying each of these various shapes of supply curves will be discussed in detail in Part Three of this book. For the moment, it is enough simply to know that the various possibilities exist.

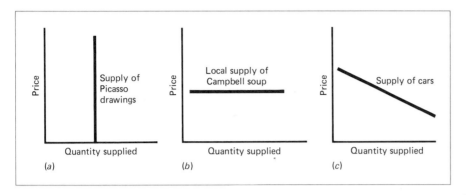

EXHIBIT 3.4
Other possible supply curves
Supply curves do not always have upward slopes. Part *a* of this exhibit shows the vertical supply curve for a good, such as original Picasso drawings, which cannot be increased in supply at any price. Part *b* shows a horizontal supply curve, typical of the local market for a widely distributed good such as Campbell's soup. Part *c* shows that the supply curve for a mass-produced product such as automobiles can have a downward slope.

Shifts in Supply Curves

Supply curves, like demand curves, are drawn on the basis of an "other things being equal" assumption. Other things being equal, changes in the price of a good are reflected in movements up or down along a given supply curve. When underlying conditions change, supply curves may shift their position.

The sources of shifts in supply curves are another subject that will be treated in detail in Part Three. For now, we need only comment that the most important of the conditions underlying the position of the supply curve for a good is the cost of producing it. Any change in the price of the factors of production used in making a good, or any change in technology that affects the quantity of inputs used per unit of output, will cause the supply curve of the good to shift. A reduction in cost will cause a downward or rightward shift, and an increase in cost will cause an upward or leftward shift. Some examples of shifting supply curves will be given later in this chapter.

Supply and Demand

Market Equilibrium

In Chapter 2 we saw how the market transmits information in the form of prices to the people who are potential buyers and sellers of any good. Taking the price of the good into account, together with the other knowledge that they possess, these buyers and sellers form plans. Each one decides to enter the market and buy or sell a certain number of units of the good.

Commonly, large numbers of buyers and sellers formulate their market plans independently of one another. When buyers and sellers of some particular good actually meet and engage in the process of exchange, some of them may find it impossible to carry out their plans. Perhaps the total quantity of planned purchases will exceed the total quantity of planned sales at the expected price. Some of the would-be buyers will find their plans frustrated, and will have to modify them. Perhaps, instead, it is planned sales that exceed planned purchases. Then some would-be sellers will be unable to sell all they had expected to, and will have to change their plans.

Sometimes no one will be disappointed, and, given the information that market prices have conveyed, the total quantity of the good that buyers plan to purchase will exactly equal the quantity that suppliers plan to sell. The separately formulated plans of all market participants turn out to mesh exactly when tested in the marketplace, and no one has frustrated expectations or is forced to modify plans. When this happens, the market is said to be in **equilibrium.**

Market Equilibrium A condition in which the separately formulated plans of buyers and sellers of some good exactly mesh when tested in the market place, so that the quantity supplied is exactly equal to the quantity demanded at the prevailing price.

If we have supply and demand schedules for a market, we can describe more exactly the conditions under which that market will be in equilibrium. Let us take the market for widgets as an example. In Exhibit 3.5, columns (1)–(3) give the supply and demand schedules. Reading down column (2), we see how many widgets producers will plan to sell at each price. Reading down column (3), we see how many widgets buyers will plan to purchase at each price. Comparing the two, it does not take long to dis-

EXHIBIT 3.5
Supply and demand in the market for widgets
When the quantity demanded of a product exceeds the quantity supplied, there is an excess quantity demanded, or shortage, of the product. A shortage puts upward pressure on the price of the product. When the quantity supplied exceeds the quantity demanded, there is an excess quantity supplied, or surplus of the product. A surplus puts downward pressure on the price. Only when the price of this product is $1.00 is their no shortage or surplus, and no upward or downward pressure on price. At that price, the market is in equilibrium.

(1) Price	(2) Quantity Supplied	(3) Quantity Demanded	(4) Shortage	(5) Surplus	(6) Direction of Pressure on Price
$1.50	650	200	. . .	450	Downward
1.40	600	240	. . .	360	Downward
1.30	550	280	. . .	270	Downward
1.20	500	320	. . .	180	Downward
1.10	450	360	. . .	90	Downward
1.00	400	400	. . .	. . .	Equilibrium
.90	350	440	90	. . .	Upward
.80	300	480	180	. . .	Upward
.70	250	520	270	. . .	Upward
.60	200	560	360	. . .	Upward
.50	150	600	450	. . .	Upward
.40	100	640	540	. . .	Upward

cover that only when the price is $1.00 do the separately formulated plans of buyers and sellers exactly mesh. The price for which this market is in equilibrium is $1.00 per unit. If both buyers and sellers make their market plans in the expectation that the price will be $1.00, none of them will be disappointed, and none of them will have to change their plans.

Shortages

What if, for some reason, buyers and sellers expect the market price to be something different than $1.00? Suppose, for example, that a price of $.50 per unit somehow became established in the market. Column (2) of Exhibit 3.5 tells us that at this price, producers would plan to supply widgets to the market at a rate of 150,000 per year. Column (3) tells us that buyers would plan to purchase at a rate of 600,000 per year. When the quantity demanded exceeds the quantity supplied, the difference between the two is called an **excess quantity demanded** or, more simply, a **shortage.**[2] In the case of widgets, the shortage [shown in Column (4) of the exhibit] is 450,000 units per year when the price is $.50 per unit.

When there is a shortage, some buyers will be disappointed. Suppliers will run out of the product before all buyers are able to make their planned purchases. What happens next may vary in detail from one market to another. Perhaps some producers will take advantage of the shortage to raise their price, hoping for greater profits. Perhaps buyers will take the initiative, and offer a premium price in order to get at least some of the good. Whatever happens, one generalization can be made fairly safely: A shortage puts upward pressure on the product price.

As the price of the product rises, producers begin to plan to sell more, and buyers begin to plan to purchase less. The higher the price, the smaller the shortage. When the price reaches $1.00 per unit, shortage is entirely eliminated. With the elimination of the shortage, there is no further upward pressure on prices. The market is in equilibrium.

Surpluses

Suppose now that, for some reason, the price of widgets were to become established at a price higher than the equilibrium price, say at $1.50. At this price, Exhibit 3.5 tells us, producers would plan to sell 650,000 units per year, but buyers would plan to purchase only 200,000. When the quantity supplied exceeds the quantity demanded, we say that there is an **excess quantity supplied** or a **surplus.** As column (5) of the exhibit shows, the surplus of widgets is 450,000 units per year when the price is $1.50.

When there is a surplus of the product, some producers will be disappointed and not be able actually to make all their planned sales at the expected price. Although again the details may vary from market to market, the generalization can be made that a surplus puts downward pressure

Excess Quantity Demanded The amount by which the quantity demanded of a good exceeds the quantity supplied when the price of the good is below the equilibrium level.

Shortage In technical economic terminology, an excess quantity demanded.

Excess Quantity Supplied The amount by which the quantity supplied of a good exceeds the quantity demanded when the price of the good is above the equilibrium level.

Surplus In technical economic terminology, an excess quantity supplied.

[2]We introduced two equivalent terms, "shortage" and "excess quantity demanded," in order to make it clear that economists use the term shortage in a different and somewhat narrower sense than it is used in everyday speech. In this book we shall use the word "shortage" most of the time, when it is clear that the economic meaning is intended, but sometimes, to avoid possible ambiguity, we shall use the more precise term "excess quantity demanded" instead. The same considerations apply to the terms "surplus" and "excess quantity supplied" defined below.

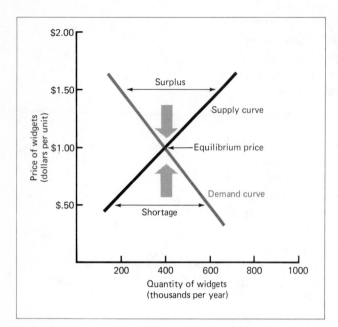

EXHIBIT 3.6
Supply and demand in the market for widgets
In this diagram, a surplus or shortage is indicated by the horizontal distance between the supply and demand curves. A surplus puts downward pressure on price, and a shortage upward pressure, as indicated by the large arrows. The market is in equilibrium at the price where the supply and demand curves intersect. Compare this diagram with the table in Exhibit 3.5.

on the product price. The table shows that as the price falls, the quantity supplied decreases and the quantity demanded increases. Gradually, the surplus is eliminated, until, when the price reaches $1.00 per unit, the market returns to equilibrium.

Graphical Presentation

It is so important to understand the principles of supply, demand, and market equilibrium clearly that we shall go back again over the ground we have just covered, this time making a graphical presentation. Look at Exhibit 3.6. In the diagram presented there, we have drawn both the demand curve for widgets (taken from Exhibit 3.1) and the supply curve for widgets (taken from Exhibit 3.3). With both curves on the same diagram, we can directly compare the quantity demanded and the quantity supplied at any price. The distance from the vertical axis to the demand curve measures the quantity demanded, and the distance from the vertical axis to the supply curve measures the quantity supplied. It follows that the horizontal gap between the two curves measures the surplus or shortage at any price. The surplus at a price of $1.50 and the shortage at a price of $.50 are indicated in the exhibit.

As we saw when working through our numerical example for this market, a surplus tends to put downward pressure on the price, and a shortage tends to put upward pressure on it. These "pressures" result from the actions of frustrated buyers and sellers, who must change their plans when they find that they cannot buy or sell the quantities they had intended at the price they had expected. The pressures are indicated by large arrows in the diagram.

There is only one price where neither upward nor downward pressure is in force. That is the price of $1.00 per unit, where the supply and demand curves intersect. There is neither shortage nor surplus at that point. The quantity that buyers plan to purchase exactly equals the quantity that suppliers plan to sell. Everyone can carry out his or her plans exactly as intended, and the market is in equilibrium.

Changing Economic Conditions

When underlying economic conditions change, supply and demand curves can shift to new positions. These shifts upset the plans of buyers and sellers who may have adjusted to some previous market equilibrium, and they bring about changes in prices and quantities. The following example describes an episode that is typical of the way that markets work every day. In reading through the example, pay particular attention to the distinction between the kinds of changes that cause shifts in supply or demand curves and the kinds of changes that cause movements along curves.

CASE 3.1
Supply and Demand in the Soybean Market[3]

In the second quarter of 1976, the market for soybeans experienced a virtual explosion of prices. Between April and July, the price shot up from less than $5 a bushel to more than $7. Writing for *The New York Times*, market analyst H. J. Mainenberg attributed the price rise directly to supply and demand factors.

On the demand side, a major factor in the price rise was the appearance of the Soviet Union as a big buyer of soybeans. Previously, the Soviet Union had not been active in the international soybean market, relying on other sources of edible oils and high-protein livestock feed. Now they were forced to change this policy. Bad Soviet harvests the previous year had created a serious shortage of livestock feed of all kinds. What is more, in July 1976, Peru announced a ban on the export of fishmeal and fish oil. The disappearance of these substitutes from the international market further increased the Soviet demand for soybeans.

Exhibit 3.7a gives a graphical interpretation of the Soviet entry into the soybean market. The immediate result is shown as a rightward shift in the demand curve, from its initial position D_1 to a new position D_2. Before this shift occurred, the market equilibrium price would have been p_1. After the shift, there would be a shortage of soybeans as long as the price remained at its previous level. The shortage would cause the market price to be bid up. As the price rose, suppliers would move up and to the right along the supply curve S_1. When the price had risen to p_2, the shortage would be eliminated, and if no further changes in economic conditions occurred, p_2 would be the new equilibrium price.

Other economic conditions did not remain unchanged, however. At the same time the demand shift occurred, conditions were also changing on the supply side of the market. Soybeans, it seems, are favored as an alternate crop by cotton growers. If the weather is poor for cotton, or the cotton price is low, these farmers grow lots of soybeans. In 1976, though, the weather favored cotton and cotton prices were quite high. As a result, farmers shifted from soybeans to cotton, cutting the bean crop from 1.5 million bushels in 1975 to an estimated 1.3 million in 1976. We can represent the effect of these supply-side changes as an upward shift of the supply curve, from its original position S_1 to a new position S_2, as shown in Exhibit 3.7b. With the supply

[3]Based on H. J. Maidenberg, "Why Prices of Soybeans are Soaring," *The New York Times*, July 13, 1976, p. 47.

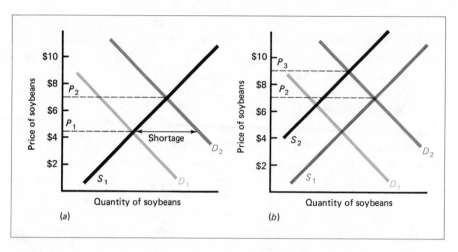

EXHIBIT 3.7
The effects of changing economic conditions of the price of soybeans
Part a shows the effects of a demand shift resulting from the entry of the Soviet Union
into the soybean market as a new major buyer. The demand curve is shifted to the
right, from D_1 to D_2. The resulting shortage of soybeans drives the price up from
p_1 to p_2. Part b shows the effects of a reduction in soybean supply, as farmers shifted
partially from soybeans to cotton. Now the supply curve shifts too, from S_1 to S_2.
Together, the shift of both curves requires an increase in price to p_3 in order to restore
equilibrium.

curve shifting at the same time as the demand curve shifted, a rise in price
from p_1 to p_2 would no longer be sufficient to eliminate the entire shortage
of soybeans. Instead, the price would have to rise all the way to p_3. In comparison to the equilibrium shown in part a of the exhibit, we can see that the
shift in the supply curve requires a movement of consumers along their new
demand curve D_2, until equilibrium is finally reached at the point where S_2
and D_2 intersect. The simultaneous shifts in the supply and demand curves
reinforced one another and caused the rise in the price of soybeans to
be much sharper than it would have been had only one of the changes
occurred.

Markets in Disequilibrium

We have seen that when a market is not in equilibrium, an excess quantity demanded or excess quantity supplied will put upward or downward
pressure on the price. If the price is free to respond to this pressure, a new
equilibrium will be established at a higher or lower price. Sometimes,
though, market prices are not free to fluctuate. The forces of supply and
demand must then work themselves out in some other way, as the following
example shows.

CASE 3.2
The Gasoline Shortage of 1974

In the winter of 1974, a significant gasoline shortage struck the United States.
Arab countries, trying to gain political advantage in the Middle East conflict,
drastically cut the supply of imported oil. Because there was no immediate

EXHIBIT 3.8

The gasoline shortage of 1974

During the gasoline shortage of 1974, government price controls prevented gasoline prices from rising to the equilibrium level, here estimated as $1.00 per gallon. Instead of causing the price to rise, the shortage of gasoline caused long lines to form at gas stations, until the opportunity cost of waiting in line became great enough roughly to fill the gap between the official ceiling price and the true equilibrium price.

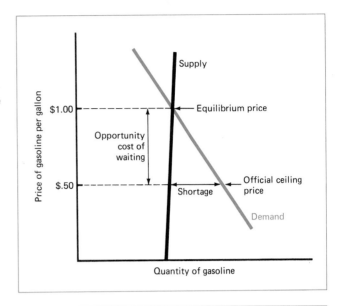

alternative source to which to turn, the supply curve for gasoline could be considered almost vertical, as shown in Exhibit 3.8.

This exhibit shows that a sufficiently high price ($1.00 per gallon as the graph is drawn, but this is only a guess) would have put the gasoline market in equilibrium. However, government price controls in force at the time kept the price from rising much above $.50 per gallon. There was a substantial excess quantity demanded that, instead of making itself visible in terms of rising prices, made itself visible in the form of long lines at gas stations.

People who waited in line for gasoline had lots of time to think, and anyone who had studied a little economics could have figured out that the forces of supply and demand were still at work in a roundabout way. There were opportunity costs of waiting in line. Some people actually missed work. Others sacrificed valuable leisure hours. As the lines grew, the opportunity cost of waiting in them grew also, until at some point the *total* cost of gasoline—the money cost plus the opportunity cost of waiting—was at least roughly equal to the price of $1.00 to which gasoline would have risen without controls. At that point, the lines stopped growing longer, and a sort of rough-and-ready equilibrium was established.

Who benefited from the fact that long lines, rather than high prices, were used to ration scarce gas among users? Who was harmed? Consumers in general did not gain, because what they saved in money, they lost in time. But some consumers—those for whom the opportunity cost of time spent in line was low—were hurt less severely than they would have been by a price rise, whereas those for whom time was particularly precious were hurt more.

Conclusions

This completes our presentation of the basics of supply and demand analysis. To conclude the chapter, we shall make a few remarks relating supply and demand to the role of markets as a mechanism for utilizing knowledge, and a few remarks also concerning the scope of applicability of supply and demand analysis.

Knowledge and Equilibrium

There is a simple connection between the idea of equilibrium and the idea of the market as a mechanism for utilizing knowledge. The connection is found in the fact that the market can be in equilibrium when, and only when, it has entirely completed its job of distributing knowledge among buyers and sellers.

It is easy to see why this is true. First, if buyers and sellers have incomplete knowledge of prices, and of other economic conditions, it is very unlikely that their separately formulated market plans will exactly mesh. It may be that both buyers and sellers expect the price tomorrow to be higher (or lower) than it actually will be. It may be that buyers have one idea about what price will be, and sellers another. Whatever the case, someone is bound to be disappointed, and disappointed plans are the stuff of which disequilibrium is made.

On the other hand, if both buyers and sellers had complete and accurate knowledge of both present and future prices and market conditions, how could their plans fail to mesh? No one would plan to buy at a certain price knowing that there would be no one willing to sell, or plan to sell knowing that there would be no one to buy. With perfect knowledge, people would formulate only such market plans as they knew could be carried out on the expected terms, and that is what we mean by equilibrium.

Saying that markets are in equilibrium only when all buyers and sellers have perfect knowledge leads us to a conclusion that perhaps seems strange. The conclusion is that in the real world, we can hardly ever expect to find a market that is in equilibrium! To paraphrase a famous saying, all people know something all of the time, and some people may know a great deal all of the time, but everybody does not know everything all of the time. In real markets, prices are always being pushed this way or that by changes in underlying economic conditions. Some people learn of these changes right away, and the buying and selling they do telegraphs that information, via the price system, to others. But the market telegraph does not work with the speed of light. Before everyone who is directly or indirectly interested in what goes on in a particular market learns of some change, other changes have occurred. The whirling stream of human knowledge never quite catches up with an even more fluid reality.

Applicability

The fact that markets are never really in equilibrium is, in a sense, a limitation on the applicability of supply and demand analysis. There are other limitations too. We shall see in Part Three of this book that supply and demand analysis applies in its pure form only to markets where the numbers of buyers and sellers are very large, and where the products offered by one seller differ very little from those offered by another. Our imaginary market for widgets perfectly fitted these conditions—that is why we made it up. Some real-world markets fit the conditions fairly well. The markets for agricultural products are an example. But the markets for many other products do not look exactly like the idealized markets of economic theory.

For now, though, we do not need to be overly concerned with differences between the real and the ideal. The theory of supply and demand may not *exactly* fit any market at any particular moment in time, yet in a general sense, thinking in terms of supply and demand can give us extremely useful insights into the way that almost all markets work. The usefulness of these tools will be proved in application as we work through this book. Fine points can be left for more advanced courses.

SUMMARY

1. The law of demand tells us that the quantity of a good demanded by buyers tends to change in a direction opposite to any change in price, other things being equal. By quantity demanded, economists mean effective demand, as distinguished from wants or needs not backed up by willingness and ability to buy. By other things being equal, we have in mind such things as buyer's incomes, the prices of other goods, and buyers' expectations concerning future price changes.
2. When the quantity demanded of a good changes solely because of a change in the price of that good, the change is represented graphically as a movement along a demand curve. When the quantity demanded of a good changes because something other than its price changes (for example, buyer's incomes, the prices of substitutes or complements, or buyers' expectations), the change is represented graphically as a shift in the entire demand curve.
3. A supply curve shows us the relationship between the price of a good and the quantity of that good supplied, other things being equal. Unless there is some particular reason to do otherwise, economists usually draw supply curves with upward slopes. Exceptions to the rule of upward-sloping supply curves are much more common, though, than are exceptions to the rule of downward-sloping demand curves. It is easy to find illustrations of vertical, horizontal, or downward-sloping supply curves.
4. A change in the quantity of some good supplied caused solely by a change in the price of that good is represented graphically as a movement along the supply curve. A change in the quantity supplied brought about by some other cause— for example, by a change in the cost of production—is represented by a shift in the supply curve.
5. Market equilibrium is a condition in which the separately formulated plans of buyers and sellers exactly mesh, so that the quantity supplied is equal to the quantity demanded. If the price of a product is too high for equilibrium, there will be a surplus of the good, which, in turn, will tend to push the price down. If the price is below the equilibrium level, there will be a shortage, which will tend to drive the price up. Equilibrium is possible only when the market has completely carried out its job of distributing information among buyers and sellers.

DISCUSSION QUESTIONS

1. The text notes that the "law" of demand states that there is an inverse relationship between the price of a good and the quantity that people will be willing and able to pay for. How is this "law" like the law of gravity? How is it different? Explain.
2. Illustrate the supply of McDonald's hamburgers to an individual consumer. What is the slope of the supply curve?
3. Suppose that there were a drought in the Midwest, where much of the nation's wheat is grown. What would be the impact of the drought on the demand and supply of wheat? What would happen to the price of wheat? Why? How would this be likely to affect the individual consumers of products containing wheat?
4. If you drop a marble in a bowl it will eventually come to rest at the bottom. We could say the marble is at equilibrium at the bottom of the bowl. What is

meant by equilibrium? In what ways is equilibrium in a market similar and in what ways is it different from the equilibrium of the marble?

5. If you were a wholesaler and you could see sooner than your competitors when a market was going to be in disequilibrium, how could you use this advance knowledge to make money? Would you be benefiting anyone besides yourself in getting rid of the disequilibrium? Explain.

6. Suppose that you read the following news item in the daily paper: "Frost in Brazil has caused a severe shortage of coffee, which has driven the price well above normal levels. The shortage is expected to persist for several years until new coffee bushes can be planted and reach maturity." Do you think the newswriter is using the word "shortage" in the same sense as we have used it in this chapter?

7. Suppose that the opportunity cost of time spent waiting in line to buy gasoline were uniformly $5 per hour for all consumers. Would imposing price controls on gasoline to deal with a sudden decrease in supply then benefit anyone at all? Would it make anyone worse off than if the price were simply allowed to rise to a higher equilibrium level? Should the owners of gas stations and oil companies be counted as "anyone" in answering this question?

CHAPTER 4
The Role
~~~vernment
~~ Economy

~Will Learn in This Chapter

arkets are the most important mechanisms for allocates in the American economy, government is too large
red. Just how big is government in the United States,
solute terms and in comparison to the governments of
ntries? How does decision making in government differ
sion making in the private sector? What economic func-
es government perform, and who pays the bill? It is im-
o know answers to all of these questions as background
for later topics taken up in this book.

For Review
Here are some important terms and concepts that will be put to
use in this chapter. Be certain that you understand them, or review
them before proceeding.

Resource allocation (Chapter 2)
Supply and demand (Chapter 3)

Understanding markets gives the most important single key to the way
the basic questions of *what, how, who,* and *for whom* are answered in the
American economy. The forces of supply and demand, acting through markets, affect every economic decision of significance. Still, ours is not a pure
market economy. There are other economic forces at work as well that
affect resource allocation. By far the most important of these nonmarket
forces is that of government.

How Big is Government
in the United States?

Before getting into a discussion of how government works, it is important
to get some idea of just how big government is in economic terms. Exhibit
4.1 gives three alternative measures of the size of government in the United
States.

EXHIBIT 4.1

The size of government in the United States, (1974 figures)

This table provides three different measures of the size of government in the United States. The first item tells how big government is as a buyer in all markets. The second item shows what share of Gross National Product passes through government hands in the form of taxes. The third shows government as a source of income for individuals.

1. Government purchases of goods and services as a percent of gross national product	Federal	8.4%
	State and local	13.7%
	Total	22.1%
2. Taxes as a percent of gross national product	Federal	20.8%
	State and local	14.8%
	Total	35.6%
3. Government-derived and private income as a percent of all personal income	Wages and salaries of government employees, including military	13.7%
	Transfer payments to individuals by all levels of government	11.8%
	Total government-derived, income	25.5%
	Wages, salaries, and other labor income paid in private sector	56.0%
	Property income of private individuals	18.5%
	Total personal income	100.0%

Government Purchases

The first group of figures in Exhibit 4.1 tells us how large government is as a buyer of goods and services from private individuals and business firms. The term **government purchases of goods and services** (or just *government purchases,* for short) includes all the finished products purchased by government (everything from submarines to typewriter ribbons) plus the cost of hiring the services of all government employees (everyone from the President right down to the courthouse janitor). Government purchases are compared with gross national product (GNP), a measure of the economy's total output of goods and services.[1] We see that in 1974, 22.1 percent of all goods and services produced by the American economy were purchased by federal state, and local governments.

Taxes and Transfers

Government purchases, although a useful measure of the size of government, do not tell the whole story. Looking at government purchases alone somewhat understates the size of the public sector, because governments do more than just buy things. They give money away, too. More precisely, a large portion of the money that governments at all levels take in as taxes are distributed to individuals in the form of **transfer payments.** Transfers are all payments made to individuals that are not made in return

Government Purchases of Goods and Services (government purchases) Expenditures made by federal, state, and local governments to purchase goods from private firms and to hire the services of government employees.

Transfer Payments All payments made by government to individuals that are not made in return for goods or factor services currently supplied. Social security benefits, welfare payments, and unemployment compensation are major forms of transfers.

[1]Gross national product will be given a precise definition in Chapter 6.

for goods or factor services currently supplied. They include such things as social security benefits, welfare payments, and unemployment compensation. The second item in Exhibit 4.1, which shows total taxes as a percentage of gross national product, reflects the size of transfer payments as well as purchases of goods and services. We see that in 1974 approximately $.36 in taxes were paid for every dollar's worth of goods and services produced in the economy.

Government-Derived Income

A third way to gauge the size of government in the economy is to look at the extent to which individuals depend on government for their income. The third item in Exhibit 4.1 shows how total personal income can be broken down into income derived from government, wages and salaries paid in the private sector, and property income (rents, interest, dividends, and so forth) earned in the private sector. It shows that somewhat more than a quarter of all personal income arrives in the form of a check from some agency of federal, state, or local government.

Growth of Government

These figures can be put in perspective by looking at what has happened to the size of government over time. Exhibit 4.2 shows the growth of government purchases as a percentage of GNP from 1909 to the present. In the early part of the century, government expenditures amounted to less

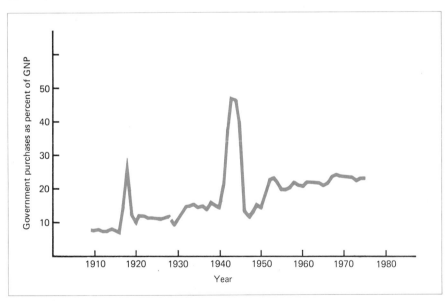

EXHIBIT 4.2
Growth of government purchases in the United States
The percentage of total government purchases in GNP has grown substantially over time. In the early years of the century, government purchases averaged less than 10 percent of GNP. Except for peaks during the war years, this figure did not grow very much until the 1950s. Government purchases now average over 20 percent of GNP, and they may still be growing.

Source: Data from Bureau of the Census, *Historical Statistics of the United States: Colonial Times to 1970* (Washington, D.C.: U.S. Government Printing Office, 1975).

than 10 percent of GNP, and grew only very slowly, except for brief peaks during World War I and World War II. After World War II, government purchases dropped back to their prewar levels, falling to 11 percent of GNP by 1947. The 1950s saw a steady growth of this figure, and by 1959, a level of 20 percent was reached. Since then, the figure has fluctuated from year to year, averaging around 20 percent. It is too early to tell whether the new highs reached in the mid 1970s represent the start of a new upward trend.

International Comparisons

Some international comparisons can give us additional perspective on the size of government in the United States. Using government purchases as our measure, the public sector of the American economy is neither remarkably large nor remarkably small by Western standards. In the early 1970s, countries like Sweden and Denmark spent 2 or 3 percent more of their GNP on government purchases than did the United States. France and Switzerland, on the other hand, had substantially smaller public sectors, with government purchases taking only about 12 percent of their GNP.[2]

Still another way to get a perspective on the size of the American government is to ask how large the public sector of an economy could possibly get. There is no purely theoretical way to answer this question, but again, some international comparisons can help. Perhaps unexpectedly, the largest public sectors among developed economies are not to be found in the communist countries. It is true that in those countries, the government plays a much larger role in directing industry than does the American government, but if a comparison is made in terms of government purchases and transfers, the governments of communist countries are only three or four percentage points larger than that of the United States.[3] A better indication of where the economic limits to the size of government lie is provided by the example of Britain, as the following account shows.

CASE 4.1
The Growth of Government Expenditure in Britain

During the 1970s, the British economy has experienced a virtual explosion in the size of the public sector. In the early 1960s, total government expenditures, including both purchases of goods and services and transfer payments, averaged about 43 percent of GNP. By 1975, as we see from Exhibit 4.3, this figure had reached a remarkable 65 percent.

It appears that this figure of 65 percent marks the limit, or even exceeds the limit, of the size a government can attain without severe economic disruption. In order to channel two-thirds of GNP through the public sector, taxes must be raised so high that work incentives are seriously distorted. This is true not just for the wealthy classes, who have long borne a very heavy burden of taxation in Britain, but also now for the average worker, and even

---

[2]These comparisons are based on data given in the UN Statistical Yearbook, 1974, Table 182.

[3]F. L. Pryor has done some very careful work adjusting U.S. and Soviet data on public expenditure to make them as closely comparable as possible. He calculates that "adjusted budget expenditure" in 1962 was 23 percent of GNP for the United States, and 27 percent for the Soviet Union. With defense excluded, the figures were 15 percent and 18 percent, respectively. See F. L. Pryor, *Public Expenditures in Communist and Capitalist Nations* (London: Allen & Unwin, 1968).

EXHIBIT 4.3

The growth of public expenditure in Britain, 1960–1975
Since the early 1960s, total public expenditure in Britain has grown from approximately 43 percent of GNP to approximately 65 percent. The data on which this chart is based include both government purchases of goods and services and transfer payments.

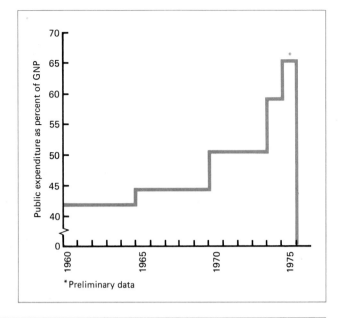

* Preliminary data

Source: Official figures as reported in the London *Times,* February 16, 1976.

the poor. In fact, the British now speak of a "poverty trap" produced by high taxation—a person who gets a low-paying job and leaves the welfare roles is immediately hit with such high rates of income taxes that he may be worse off working than he was while on public assistance.

Because taxes just cannot be raised high enough to pay for all that expenditure, the British government has had to borrow enormous sums of money from the public. This huge government borrowing robs industry of investment funds needed for expansion and modernization, and this deepens the general economic crisis.

There is a sobering lesson to be learned from the British experience. This lesson lies in the fact that the growth of the British public sector does not seem to have resulted from conscious policy decisions by any government. Expenditures grew both under Labour Party and Conservative administrations. In every year, expenditures grew faster than policy makers intended them to grow. Among the major sources of unplanned expenditure growth were (1) increased subsidies to nationalized industries, which were supposed to pay their own way but in fact ran increasing losses; (2) rising levels of transfer payments, including unemployment compensation, brought about by business recession; (3) poor cost-control practices, especially in local government; and (4) a tendency to use public service jobs as a buffer against unemployment in periods of business downturn.

It appears that in a country with a democratic political system, government expenditure tends to grow to its natural maximum even if political authorities do not actively encourage that growth. Instead, active political effort seems to be required simply to prevent expenditures from spontaneously running out of control.

Government and the Market

Clearly, however we measure it, government is too big to be ignored in any thorough discussion of what goes on in the American economy. The public sector requires special treatment in economic analysis because governments play the game of *what, how, who,* and *for whom* according to one set of rules, while the private individuals and firms who make up the market sector play according to another. Three characteristics in particular distinguish the economic behavior of government from that of most private persons and firms.

Distinguishing Characteristics of Governments

First, governments at all levels engage in the systematic and legitimate use of force in economic affairs. In the private sector, firms and households are limited by law and custom to peaceable means of production and exchange requiring the voluntary consent of everyone involved. Governments, on the other hand, are able to employ force, coercion, and involuntary expropriation in pursuit of their economic goals. When the government taxes incomes, regulates prices, drafts soldiers, or outlaws gambling it does not require the immediate, explicit consent of the individuals thus taxed, regulated, conscripted, or outlawed. Although in a democracy these uses of government power are supposed to rest, at least indirectly, on the consent of a majority of voters, they are binding on minorities and nonvoters as well. Without the use or threat of force, government could do very few of the things it does.

A second characteristic setting governments apart from other economic agents is the fact that the great bulk of goods and services that governments produce are provided to users without charge. In most cases, people do not have to pay for the defense services, highway use, education, or police protection that they receive. Instead, they pay for these things indirectly, through taxes. Only in a few cases do the taxes paid vary according to the quantity of public service consumed. The fact that governments do not charge users for most of their services has important implications for measuring the total contribution of government to the national product, and for the degree of efficiency with which government services are utilized. More on this in later chapters.

A third way governments differ from other economic agents is in the methods by which they arrive at economic decisions. The system of voting and bargaining by which public decisions are made is very much more complex and hard to analyze than the decision processes of private business firms and consumers. As a result, economists have not gotten as far in formulating simple rules or theories to explain resource allocation in the public sector. In the past, economists have traditionally treated government decisions as "givens" for purposes of economic analysis, and not tried to explain why one governmental decision rather than another is made at a particular time. In recent years, though, some progress has been made in formulating an economic theory of "public choice" to parallel the theory of private choice with which economists have traditionally worked.

Market Influences on Government

Despite the pecularities of government, market forces of supply and demand do make themselves felt to a degree even within the public sector of the economy. The principal reason is that governments have to purchase most of the inputs they require on the open market. The U.S. Department of Justice cannot hire a new clerk unless it pays the wage determined by supply and demand for workers with that particular skill. The city of Chicago cannot buy police cars unless it pays something pretty close to what private individuals would pay for the same vehicles. The necessity of purchasing inputs at market prices makes government aware of the relative cost of various programs and helps constrain total public spending.

Of course, sometimes particular government agencies ignore the messages the market sends to them via the price system. Corrupt bidding practices sometimes result in government purchases from politically favored firms at higher than market prices. Sometimes devices such as eminent domain or the draft are used to obtain resources without paying their full market value. In such instances, the degree of market influence on government is less than usual.

The Economic Functions of Government

We have talked about how large government is, and how governments differ from households and private firms. Next we turn to the subject of what governments do with our money once they have collected it as taxes. First we shall analyze government programs in terms of five general economic functions. Then, in the next section, we shall look at government spending in terms of specific programs and agencies.

Public Goods

The first function of government is to provide what economists call **public goods.** Public goods are goods or services having the two properties that (1) they cannot be provided to one citizen without being supplied also to his neighbors, and (2) once provided for one citizen, the cost of providing them to others is zero. Perhaps the best example of a public good is national defense. One citizen cannot very well be protected against foreign invasion or atomic attack without having the protection "spill over" on his neighbors. Also, it costs no more to protect a single resident of a given area from invasion or nuclear holocaust than to protect an entire city.

Public Goods Goods or services having the two properties that (1) they cannot be provided to one citizen without being supplied also to his neighbors, and (2) once they are provided for one citizen, the cost of providing them to others is zero.

Public goods are traditionally provided by government because their special properties make it hard for private business to market them profitably. Imagine what would happen if someone tried to set up a commercially operated ballistic missile defense system. If my neighbor subscribed, I would have no reason to subscribe too, but would instead play the "free rider," relying on the spillover effect for my protection. But he would not subscribe, hoping that I would, so that he could be the free rider. The missile defense company would soon go bankrupt.

The Transfer Function

The second function of government consists of making transfers of income and wealth from one citizen to another. Income or wealth is usually taken from citizens by means of taxation but sometimes, as in the case of the military draft or jury duty, it is taken by conscription of services. Benefits are distributed either in the form of direct cash payments or in the form of the free or below-cost provision of goods and services. Among the more familiar types of cash transfers are social security payments, welfare benefits, and unemployment compensation. Goods and services used for transfers include public education, public housing, fire protection, and subsidized mass-transit systems. These are provided at low or zero cost on the basis of political decisons rather than at market prices on the basis of ability to pay.

From the viewpoint of economic theory, the subsidized services that serve as vehicles for income transfers are different from the true public goods discussed above. They are consumed individually by selected citizens, and do not share the two special properties of public goods. It sometimes happens, though, that services provided primarily as transfers may be public goods in part. For example, consider the fraction of fire protection devoted to preventing general conflagration as opposed to putting out fires in individual private buildings, or the fraction of public health services devoted to controlling epidemic diseases as opposed to treating individual patients. We shall discuss a variety of transfer programs in detail in our chapter on the problem of poverty.

Stabilization

Economic stabilization is a third major economic function of government. By economic stabilization policies we mean all those aimed at controlling unemployment, inflation, and economic growth. The Employment Act of 1946 defines the federal government's responsibility for economic stabilization in these terms:

> The Congress hereby declares that it is the continuing policy and responsibility of the federal government to use all practicable means consistent with its needs and obligations and other essential considerations of national policy, with assitance, and co-operation of industry, agriculture, labor and state and local governments, to coordinate and utilize all its plans, functions, and resources for the purpose of creating and maintaining, in a manner calculated to foster and promote free competitive enterprise and the general welfare, conditions under which will be afforded useful employment opportunities, including self-employment, for those able, willing and seeking to work and to promote maximum employment, production and purchasing power.

We shall spend almost all of Part Two of this book talking about economic stabilization policy and developing the economic theory necessary to understand that policy.

Regulation

A fourth major function of government is the regulation of private business. Regulatory control is exercised through a network of dozens of specialized agencies. Regulation takes a variety of specific forms. Some agencies, such as the Federal Power Commission, set maximum prices at which certain products can be sold, whereas others, such as the Civil Aeronautics Board, set minimum prices. The Food and Drug Administration and the Federal Communications Commission exercise considerable control over *what* can be produced by the firms they regulate. Agencies such as the Occupational Health and Safety Administration and the Environmental

Protection Agency regulate *how* things are produced. Finally, the Equal Employment Opportunity Commission exercises a major say over *who* shall produce which goods.

Over the years, the federal regulatory establishment has grown into a virtual "fourth branch of government," alongside the legislative, executive, and judicial branches set up by the Constitution. Regulation is a subject of widespread research and controversy. In Chapter 28 we shall take a look at some major issues in the economics of regulation.

Administration of Justice

The fifth major economic function of government is the administration of justice. Usually we do not think of the police and courts as part of the *economic* branch of government, but their activities do, in fact, have important economic consequences.

Consider what happens, for example, when a judge makes a decision in a case involving an unsafe product, a breach of contract, or an automobile accident. The decision will have an immediate effect on resource allocation in the particular case, because one party will have to pay damages to the other, or make some other form of compensation. More importantly, other people will observe the outcome of the decision, and may change the way they do things as a result. If the courts say that buyers can collect damages from the makers of unsafe products, firms are likely to design their products differently. If certain standards are set for liability in automobile accidents, car makers, road builders, and insurance companies will take notice.

In recent years, an entire field of research has opened up in the "law and economics" area. Unfortunately, space will not permit us to say much about this field in this book, but readers interested in practical applications of economic thinking may wish to pursue this area on their own or in advanced courses.[4]

One further area of economic policy combines the judicial and regulatory functions of government. That is the field of antitrust policy and the control of monopoly. Chapter 27 in Part Three of this book will take up the problem of public policy toward monopoly.

Overlapping Functions

This five-way classification of government activities by functions helps give us a theoretical understanding of the role of governments in the economy, but it does not correspond very well to any breakdown of government activities by program or agency. Particular programs and agencies often perform a number of different functions at the same time. For example, the main business of the Defense Department would appear to be the provision of a public good, national defense, but it performs other functions as well. In wartime it performs a transfer function by shifting part of the cost of wars from the general taxpayer to young lower-class males via the draft. In peacetime it provides an instrument of economic stabilization through the way its huge budget for the purchase of goods and services is administered.

---

[4]A good place to start is with Richard Posner, *The Economics of Law* (Boston: Little, Brown, 1972).

To get a full picture of the role of government, then, we should look not only at a breakdown of its activities by function, but also a breakdown by levels of government, agencies, and programs. We shall do this in the next section.

The Composition of Government Budgets

Federal Receipts and Outlays

Exhibit 4.4 shows the percentage distribution of receipts and outlays of the federal government for 1975. Total federal outlays in that year were $313 billion, and total receipts were $279 billion.

Looking first at outlays, we see that the biggest single category was income security. This category includes the social security program, unemployment compensation, public assistance (welfare), and federal employee retirement and disability benefits   Income security began to take the largest share of the federal budget only in 1974. Before that, defense had been the largest category. Throughout the 1960s, defense spending consistently took over 40 percent of the budget, peaking at 45 percent in 1968, at the height of the Vietnam war. The other items on the outlay side of the budget are largely self-explanatory.

The biggest single source of receipts for the federal government was the individual income tax. This accounted for some 42 percent of all federal revenues in 1975. Next in line were social insurance taxes and contributions, with 31 percent of the total. This item has been growing rapidly in recent years. In third place were corporate income taxes. These used to be the second biggest revenue source, but are now much less significant than formerly. A number of smaller items make up the balance. All these revenues together were sufficient to pay for only 89 percent of all federal expenditure in 1975. The remainder, some $35 billion, was made up by government borrowing.

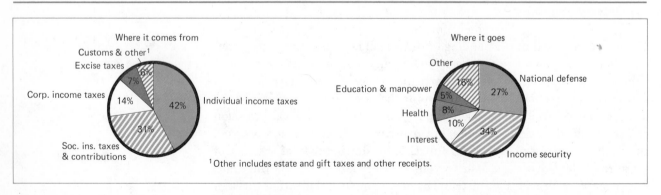

EXHIBIT 4.4
The federal budget, 1975

Source: Chart prepared by U.S. Bureau of the Census. Data from U.S. Office of Management and Budget.

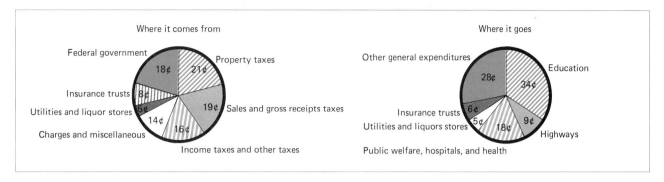

EXHIBIT 4.5
The state and local government dollar, 1973
Source: U.S. Bureau of the Census.

State and Local Receipts and Outlays

Exhibit 4.5 shows how the receipts and outlays of state and local government were distributed in 1973. Total state and local expenditures in that year were $205 billion. Of this amount, local government took about two-thirds, and state government one-third. State and local government spending together made up just over 47 percent of all government spending. State and local government have both grown more rapidly than the federal government in recent years. Twenty years ago, state and local spending accounted only for 37 percent of the total.

The biggest single item in state and local expenditure was education. A little more than three-quarters of this figure went for elementary and secondary education, and a little less than a quarter for higher education. Public welfare, hospitals, and health (18 percent), and highways (9 percent) were the other really large categories. The item "other general expenditures" includes a large number of things, including police and fire protection, sanitation, parks and recreation, and housing, which do not amount to very much separately.

The revenue side of the state and local government budget is quite different from that of the federal budget. State and local income taxes bring in only 16 percent of total revenue, and a few states do not use the income tax at all. Instead, the major sources of revenue are property taxes and sales taxes. Property taxes are used more by local government, and sales taxes by state governments. The federal government provides some 18 percent of all state and local revenues, and a variety of smaller sources make up the balance.

Who Pays the Taxes?

Tax Incidence

Exhibits 4.4 and 4.5 tell us what kinds of taxes are paid to support federal, state, and local governments, but not who pays them. Economists refer to the question of who bears the burden of taxation as the problem of **tax incidence.**

Tax Incidence The matter of who bears the economic burden of taxation.

The problem of tax incidence is not at all an easy one to solve. It is not enough just to look up the tax records of federal, state, and local governments. That would reveal only who had actually handed over the tax money to the authorities, not who actually bore the economic burden of the taxes. What makes tax incidence a difficult problem is the fact that the party who is obligated by law to pay the tax can often shift the burden of the tax to someone else.

For a simple example, suppose that a law is passed that asks all retailers to turn over a tax payment of $.10 to the government for each pack of cigarettes they sell. Who will bear the economic burden of this tax? We can use simple supply and demand analysis to find an answer.

Look at the supply and demand curves drawn in Exhibit 4.6. We see that without the tax, the equilibrium price of cigarettes would be $.20 per pack and 200 million packs per day would be sold. Next we have to figure out how the equilibrium price and quantity will change when the tax is imposed. We know that in the new, aftertax equilibrium, two things must be true. First, the price paid by buyers, including the tax, must be $.10 greater than the price received by sellers, net of the tax. Second, at the new equilibrium price, there must be neither an excess quantity of cigarettes

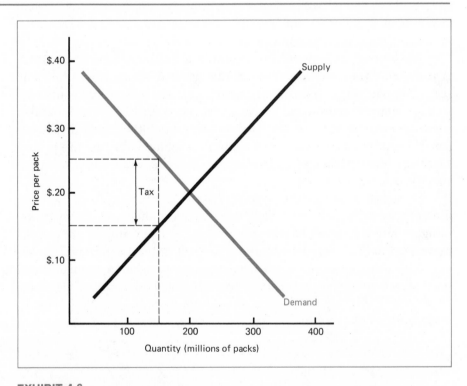

EXHIBIT 4.6

Effects of a sales tax on cigarettes

Before imposition of a tax of $.10 per pack, the market equilibrium price is $.20 per pack, and the quantity sold is 200 million packs. After imposition of the tax, a new equilibrium will be established in which buyers pay $.25 per pack, sellers receive $.15 per pack, and $.10 per pack goes to the government. The burden of the tax is divided equally between buyers and sellers.

supplied nor an excess quantity demanded. From the diagram we see that there is only one position at which *both* of these things are true. This is an output of 150 million packs, which corresponds to the place where the vertical gap between the supply and demand curves is exactly $.10. In this new equilibrium, consumers must pay $.25 per pack, and sellers receive only $.15 per pack after tax.

Comparing the before-tax with the after-tax equilibrium, we see that although retailers must hand over $.10 to the government for each pack they sell, half of the burden of this tax is shifted to buyers. Sellers actually end up receiving only $.05 less per pack than before ($.15 instead of $.20), while buyers must pay $.05 more ($.25 instead of $.20). We can say that, in this case, the *incidence* of the cigarette tax falls half on buyers and half on sellers.

In our example, the economic burden of the tax was divided equally between buyers and sellers, but the division need not always work out that way. If the demand curve we drew had happened to be a little steeper and the supply curve a little flatter, the major share of the burden would have fallen on buyers. If the supply curve had been steeper than the demand curve, sellers would have borne the bigger part of the incidence of the tax. A large part of solving the puzzle of tax incidence, then, is determining just what the shapes of supply and demand curves really are for the important goods and services on which taxes are placed.

The Incidence of Major Taxes

This is not the place to treat each kind of tax in detail, but we ought to take a moment to compare some of the major kinds of taxes in terms of their incidence. Economists usually assume that the burden of the personal income tax is not shifted, and remains to be borne by the taxpayers themselves. Sales taxes, in contrast, are believed to be shifted to consumers to a very substantial degree. Property taxes are more difficult to analyze. Probably property taxes on owner-occupied houses are largely borne by the owner-occupant, while property taxes on rental housing seem to be shifted, at least in part, to tenants.

Sometimes the analysis of tax incidence can have important implications for economic policy. A few pages back, we noted the growing importance of social insurance contributions as a source of federal revenue. By law, employees pay a tax of 5.2 percent on their wages to support social insurance programs, while employers contribute an additional 5.2 percent. Analysis of the incidence of payroll taxes shows, however, that the economic burden of both the employer and employee share rests entirely on the employee. Because of the legal fiction of having half the tax paid by employers, wage earners do not always realize how burdensome the tax is. Many economists now believe that social insurance taxes are inequitable, and that less reliance should be placed on them as a source of federal revenue.

In some cases, it is not possible to come to any firm conclusion about the incidence of a tax. The most puzzling case of all is the corporate income tax. The most obvious conclusion would be that the owners of corporations bear the burden. A closer look, however, seems to indicate that part of the burden of the corporate income tax may be shifted to owners of noncorporate businesses. Some of the corporate income tax may also be shifted to consumers through higher prices, but there is wide disagreement about how much is shifted in this way.

Overall Tax Incidence

Taxes can be classified, in terms of their incidence, as **progressive** or **regressive.** A progressive tax takes a larger percentage of income from people whose incomes are high, and a regressive tax takes a larger percentage of income from people whose incomes are low. One of the most interesting questions in the economics of taxation is whether the overall effect of federal, state, and local taxes are progressive, regressive, or somewhere between.

In a recent study, Joseph Pechman and Benjamin Okner of the Brookings Institution tried to bring together all of the available evidence in order to answer this question. They came up with a range of estimates differing according to the exact assumptions made about the incidence of various taxes. Exhibit 4.7 summarizes their results in terms of two variants. The "most progressive" variant assumes in all cases of doubt that the rich are unable to shift taxes to the poor (for example, that landlords cannot shift the property tax to tenants, and that corporations cannot shift the cor-

Progressive Tax   One that takes a larger percentage of income from people whose incomes are high.

Regressive Tax   One that takes a larger percentage of income from people whose income is low.

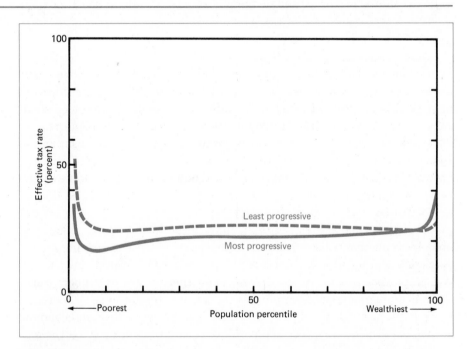

EXHIBIT 4.7
Effective rates of federal, state, and local taxes under the most and least progressive incidence variants, by population percentile, 1966
Pechman and Okner's study of tax incidence shows that the U.S. tax system is neither notably progressive nor notably regressive. To the extent that it accomplishes any redistribution at all, it seems to take from both extremes, thus easing the burden on middle-income groups.

Source: Joseph A. Pechman and Benjamin Okner, *Who Bears the Tax Burden?,* (Washington, D.C.: Brookings Institution. 1974), Fig. 1–2, p. 5. © 1974 by the Brookings Institution, Washington, D.C.

porate income tax to consumers of their products). The "least progressive" variant decides all cases in doubt as if the rich *could* shift the tax burden to the poor.

Two things are particularly interesting about the results shown in the exhibit. First, whichever variant is considered, the broad middle range of the population, excluding only the richest 5 percent and the lowest quarter, all pay very nearly the same portion of their total income in taxes. Second, the *very* rich and the *very* poor *both* pay much more of their income in taxes than do those in the middle. The tax systems of federal, state, and local government do not, taken all together, accomplish very much by way of redistribution of income. They are neither notably progressive nor notably regressive. To the extent that taxes redistribute income at all, they seem to take from both extremes and make things easy for those in the middle.

Conclusions

We have learned now that government plays a very big role in allocating resources in the American economy. Nearly a quarter of all goods and services produced are purchased by government and over a third of all income passes through the government budget in the form of taxes. If we take the regulatory function of government into account, its role appears even bigger.

One major question that we have not asked is *how well* all this vast machinery of government does its job. This is an important question and involves both normative and positive economics. The normative element comes in deciding what goals the government ought to pursue, and the positive element in measuring how closely it comes to meeting those goals. This question of *how well* is one to which we shall return repeatedly throughout the book.

Readers who proceed immediately to Part Two of this book will begin to learn the analytical tools needed to determine how well the government performs its function of economic stabilization. This is one of the most important applications of economics, and in some respects one of the most controversial. The high rates of inflation and unemployment that the American economy has experienced in the 1970s have given rise to some important new theories, and also to some important new doubts about how well the government has been doing its job.

Those other readers who will go from here directly to Part Three will soon encounter other parts of the question of how well government does its job. Part Three begins with a more detailed look at the tools of supply and demand analysis, and the theory of prices and markets that stands behind it. This theory will then be applied to evaluating government performance in the areas of agricultural policy, policy toward monopoly, the production of public goods, and the regulation of private business.

In still later parts of the book, more questions of the *how well* variety will be raised. A chapter on the problem of poverty will examine how well government performs its transfer function. Other chapters will deal with the problems of pollution, economic growth, and international trade. Finally, two chapters will examine the important question of how well a capitalist economy works in comparison with a socialist economy, where the government takes on even a more comprehensive range of functions.

Until we get to all these later chapters we shall at least have the preliminary conclusion that government is there, and that it is important. In our theorizing, we may often speak of how markets work, as if the public sector were not there, but we shall always come back to questions of government policy.

SUMMARY

1. The American economy has a large and important government sector. Government purchases are nearly a quarter of gross national product, and taxes take over a third of GNP. The American government is neither remarkably large nor remarkably small by world standards, but it appears to have a tendency to grow.
2. Government differs from private households and firms in several ways. Government can use force in pursuit of its economic goals, while private individuals cannot. Government gives away most of the services it produces without charge. Also, political decision making processes differ substantially from those of the private sector. Still, because government must go to markets to buy most of what it needs, market forces do exercise some influence over the public sector.
3. Five major economic functions of government are the provision of public goods, the carrying out of transfers, the stabilization of the economy, the regulation of the private sector, and the administration of justice.
4. The determination of the incidence of various kinds of taxes is a difficult problem of applied economics. The burden of many taxes can be shifted from those who bear the legal obligation of paying the tax to other parties. When all kinds of shifting are taken into account, it appears that the combined federal, state, and local tax systems are neither progressive nor regressive overall. Instead, the burden of taxes is shifted to some degree from middle-income groups to both the very rich and the very poor.

DISCUSSION QUESTIONS

1. What would happen to our society if we completely did away with the federal government? Could state and local governments fill in? In which cases could they or could they not?
2. List the major goods and services that are provided by the government at different levels. Then determine the extent to which these goods are public goods. Which level of government tends to supply relatively more "public" goods? Which one the least? Can you determine which?
3. How can a government respond to changes in the relative prices of the goods and services that it buys and provides for its constituents? How is it subject to the same forces as a business? How not?
4. Transfer payments obviously affect the question of *for whom*. Do you think government tax and transfer programs also affect the economy's *who, what,* and *how?*
5. Would you prefer living where income taxes are very progressive or regressive? Why?
6. When a tax is imposed on cigarettes, the price paid by consumers goes up and the price received by sellers goes down. The government benefits by the amount of the difference on each pack sold. There is also a second effect of the tax. Fewer packs are sold. Who benefits and who is hurt by the fact that fewer packs are sold? Does the fact that cigarettes are harmful to people influence your answer? What if they were good for people?

PART TWO
National Income, Inflation, and Unemployment

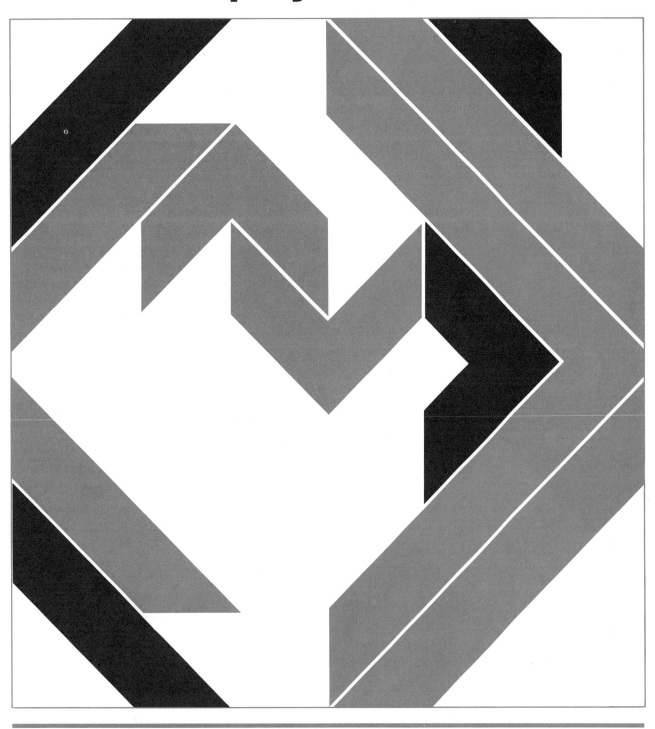

Economic science is traditionally divided into two branches, called *macroeconomics* and *microeconomics.* The prefix *macro* comes from a Greek word meaning *big,* and *micro* from a Greek word meaning *small.* Macroeconomics deals primarily with issues relating to the operation of the economy as a whole, and microeconomics with issues relating to individual people, firms, and markets.

For example, the study of inflation (by which we mean a rise in the average price of all goods and services) is a part of macroeconomics, whereas the study of relative prices (by which we mean the study of such things as why a pair of socks costs the same as a dozen eggs, but only a third as much as a haircut) is a part of microeconomics. Likewise, the study of rising and falling levels of unemployment, measured as a percentage of the national labor force, is part of macroeconomics, and the study of the reasons why there are more unemployed engineers than unemployed lawyers is a part of microeconomics.

In this book, as in most contemporary texts, macroeconomics is treated first. But there is no real reason that the two branches of economics must be studied in this order. In fact, there are some good reasons why microeconomics should be studied first. For example, to study inflation, we must know something about the individual factors causing the prices of each separate item in the consumer's market basket to rise. To understand unemployment, we must know something about the microeconomic forces acting to produce relatively higher or lower rates of unemployment in various sectors. To understand the determination of national income as a whole, we must have some idea of how the individuals and firms who make cheese, automobiles, movies, and so forth decide how much to pay each separate individual who contributes resources to the production process.

You may, then, want to read Parts Three and Four of this book before going on the Part Two. Others who read the parts in the order they are set forth here, however, will not be handicapped. Many of the most important microeconomic principles have already been sketched in Chapters 2, 3, and 4. Other microeconomic principles will be introduced as they are needed in the next several chapters. By the time both micro and macroeconomics have been studied, the distinction between the two branches will seem less sharp, and the common principles and methods that underlie them will become evident.

CHAPTER 5
The Circular Flow of Income and Product

What You Will Learn in This Chapter
The circular flow of income and product sends goods moving from firms to households, and factor services moving from households to firms. At the same time, payments for these goods and services flow in the other direction through the economy. The idea of the circular flow serves two purposes in economic analysis. First, it provides a framework for a set of important definitions and equalities. Second, it shows how the concepts of supply, demand, and equilibrium can be applied in a macroeconomic context.

For Review
Here are some important terms and concepts that will be put to use in this chapter. Be certain that you understand them, or review them before proceeding.

    Factors of production (Chapter 1)
    Equilibrium (Chapter 3)
    Government purchases and transfers (Chapter 4)

The Structure of the Circular Flow
With this chapter, we begin to put together a theory that will explain unemployment, inflation, and economic growth, and that will give us a framework for thinking about the major issues of economic stabilization policy. Because it will take several chapters to complete this theory, it will help to have a clear idea of the lay of the land before we start. The best way to get an overview of the economic system we shall be discussing is to represent it in terms of a **circular flow of income and product.**

The idea of the circular flow is based on two simple principles. First, each time anything is bought or sold in any market, the payment received by the seller must equal the amount paid out by the buyer. Second, every market transaction takes the form of money passing in one direction while goods or services pass in the other.

A Simple Economy
To see the circular flow in its most basic form, we shall begin by imagining an economy made up only of households and firms—an economy with no public sector at all. To make things simpler still, we shall suppose that

Circular Flow of Income and Product The flow of goods from firms to households and factor services from households to firms, counterbalanced by the flow of expenditures from households to firms and factor payments from firms to households.

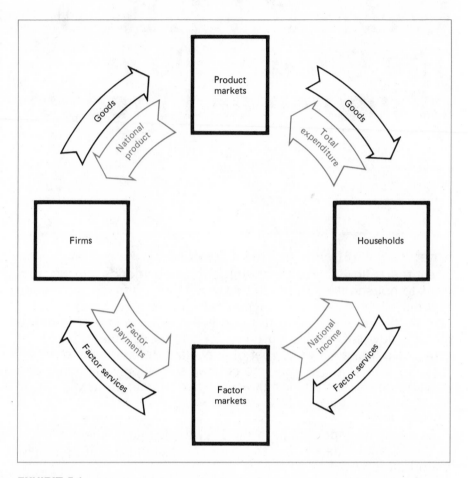

EXHIBIT 5.1
The circular flow in a simple economy
In this simple economy, households spend all their income on consumer goods as soon as they receive it, and firms sell all their output to households as soon as they produce it. Physical goods and factor services flow clockwise, while corresponding money payments flow counterclockwise.

our households live entirely from hand to mouth, spending all of their income on consumer goods as soon as that income is received, while firms sell their entire output to consumers as soon as it is produced.

The circular flow of income and product for this ultrasimple economy is shown in Exhibit 5.1. In the diagram, physical goods and services flow clockwise. Goods are produced by firms and sold to households through product markets. Factor services provided by people who work for the firms (or who supply them with capital and natural resources) flow from households to firms through factor markets. This clockwise flow of goods and services generates a corresponding counterclockwise flow of money payments. At the top of the diagram, we see the stream of money payments made by households to firms in exchange for the consumer goods they buy in product markets. At the bottom, we see a stream of money payments made by firms to households in exchange for the productive inputs that firms buy in factor markets.

Stocks and Flows

Having said this much, we should pause for a moment to comment on a word we have been using in almost every sentence. Economists call all of the things shown in Exhibit 5.1 **flows** because they are processes that occur continuously through time. Flows are measured in units per time period, for example, in dollars per year, gallons per minute, or tons per month. Measurments of flows are measurements of rates at which things are happening. In the technical language of economics we always distinguish carefully between flows and **stocks.** A stock is an accumulated quantity of something existing at a particular time. (The word stock in this general sense has nothing to do with the stockmarket kind of stocks that are bought and sold on Wall Street.)

For a homely example of the difference between stocks and flows, think of a bathtub filling. When we talk about how fast the water is running, we are talking about a *flow,* measured in gallons per minute, and when we talk about how much water there is in the tub at a given moment, we are talking about a *stock* measured just in gallons. Similarly, in the world of economics, we might talk about the rate of housing construction in Buffalo, New York, in terms of new units per month (a *flow*) as distinct from the housing *stock* in Buffalo as of January 1, 1977, meaning the actual number of houses standing on that date.

National Income and Product

Two of the flows in Exhibit 5.1 deserve special attention and have special names. The first is **national income,** which is the total of all wages, rents, interest payments, and profits received by households. National income is shown in our diagram as an arrow passing into the box representing households. The second important flow is **national product,** which is a measure of the total value of the goods and services supplied. In the diagram, national product is shown as an arrow passing from the box representing firms into the product markets.

In this simple economy, national income and national product are equal, simply because of the way that they are defined.[1] We can verify this equality in either of two ways. First, consider household expenditures as a link between national income and national product. Households are assumed to spend *all* of their income on consumer goods as soon as they receive them, and firms are assumed to sell *all* of their output to consumers as soon as it is produced. The payments made by buyers must equal the payments received by sellers, so national product must equal national income.

Alternatively, consider factor payments as a link between national income and national product. When firms receive money for the goods they sell, they use part of it to pay the workers, natural resource owners, and others who contributed factors of production to make the goods. Anything

Flows Processes occurring continuously through time, measured in units per time period.

Stocks Accumulated quantities existing at a particular time, measured in terms of simple units.

National Income The total of all incomes, including wages, rents, interest payments, and profits, received by households.

National Product The total value of all goods and services supplied in the economy.

[1]In Chapter 6 we shall see that the equality between national income and product does not hold precisely as these concepts are actually measured by the official statisticians of the U.S. government. It would be pointless, though, to let this statistical detail complicate all our theoretical discussions. Everywhere in this chapter, and everywhere from Chapter 7 onward, we make the necessary simplifying assumption so that national income and product *are* equal.

left over is profit. Factor payments, including profits,[2] account for all the money received by firms, so total factor payments must be equal to national product. Factor payments also account for all of the income received by households, so total factor payments must be equal to national income. It again follows that national income and national product must be equal.

Saving and Investment

The circular flow shown in Exhibit 5.1 is so simple that there is not really very much of interest to be said about it. To build a theory that will be useful for understanding the real-world economy, we have to introduce a few complications.

Our first change will be to drop the requirement that households immediately spend all of their income to purchase consumer goods, and instead permit them to save part of what they earn. The rate of saving by households, under this assumption, is simply the difference between national income and household consumption expenditures.

The second change we shall make is to drop the requirement that firms immediately sell all of their product to consumers. Instead, we shall now allow them to sell some products to other firms, and let some accumulate in inventory before they are sold to anyone. When firms buy newly produced capital goods (for example, production machinery, newly built structures, or office equipment) from other firms, they are said to engage in **fixed investment.** When firms increase the stock of finished products or raw materials that they keep on hand, they are said to engage in **inventory investment.** The rate of inventory investment can be less than zero in periods when firms are decreasing their stocks of goods or raw materials goods on hand. The sum of fixed investment and inventory investment will be called simply **investment.**

Circular Flow with Saving and Investment

Exhibit 5.2 shows how the circular flow of income and expenditure looks when saving and investment are added. (The clockwise arrows showing the flows of goods and services have been omitted to simplify the diagram.) There are now two pathways along which expenditures can travel on their way from households to product markets. Some household income is used for consumption expenditure, reaching product markets directly. Other household income is diverted to saving, which supplies a source of funds for firms to use in making investment expenditure, thus reaching product markets indirectly.

On the way from households to firms, the flow of saving passes through a set of markets called **credit markets.** These markets are made up of a great variety of financial institutions, including commercial banks, savings and loan associations, the stock and bond markets, insurance companies, and others that act as intermediaries between households which save and

Fixed Investment Purchases by firms of newly produced capital goods, such as production machinery, newly built structures, office equipment, and so forth.

Inventory Investment Changes in the stocks of finished products and raw materials firms keep on hand. If stocks are increasing, inventory investment is positive; if they are decreasing, it is negative.

Investment The sum of fixed investment and inventory investment.

Credit Markets A general term for the complex of financial institutions, including commercial banks, savings and loan associations, the stock and bond markets, insurance companies, and others that act as intermediaries between households which save and firms which invest.

[2]In macroeconomic theory, it is traditional to consider profits to be a part of factor payments, along with the wages, interest payments, and rentals received by workers and the owners of capital and natural resources. In contrast, microeconomic theory traditionally draws a distinction betwween profits on the one hand and factor payments on the other. Throughout Part Two we shall use factor payments in the macroeconomic sense, that is, including profits. Elsewhere, profits are not counted as factor payments. Chapter 31 explains in detail why the distinction is necessary in microeconomics.

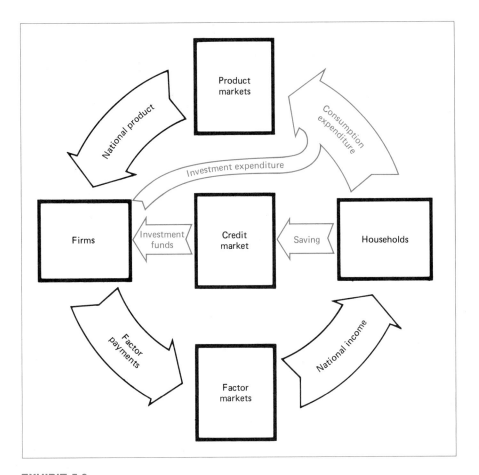

EXHIBIT 5.2
The circular flow with saving and investment
When saving and investment are added to the circular flow, there are two
pathways by which expenditures can travel on their way from households to
product markets. Some income is spent directly on consumer goods. The
rest is saved, and passes to firms via credit markets. The firms then use the
investment funds to make investment expenditures in the product markets.

firms which make investment expenditures. Households supply funds to
the credit markets (for example, by depositing money in their bank accounts). Firms can then borrow from credit markets to obtain the funds
they need to make investment expenditures.

Equilibrium and Disequilibrium
in the Circular Flow

Adding saving and investment to the circular flow raises an entirely new
issue. The issue is, can we still count on total expenditure to provide an
equalizing link between national income and national product? We now
have two entirely different sets of people making expenditure decisions.
Households decide how much to spend on consumption, and firms decide
how much to spend on investment. How can we be sure that when these

two kinds of expenditure are added together, the total will just equal the total value of all goods produced? A new way of applying supply and demand analysis will help us find the answers we need.

Aggregate Supply and Demand

Aggregate An adjective used in economics to describe any quantity that is a grand total for the whole economy.

Aggregate Supply The total value of all goods and services supplied in the economy; identical to national product.

Aggregate Demand The total value of all planned expenditures of all buyers in the economy.

Economists use the term **aggregate** to describe any quantity that is a grand total for the entire economy. **Aggregate supply,** then, means the grand total of all goods supplied by all firms in the entire economy. We already have another term for the same thing: national product. Aggregate supply and national product are just two different names for the total value of goods and services supplied by all firms. Following the same terminology, we can use the term **aggregate demand** to mean the grand total of all goods demanded for the whole economy. In defining aggregate demand this way, though, we have to be very careful just what we mean by "demand." The precise way of defining aggregate demand is to say that it means the total *planned* expenditures of all buyers in the economy.

In discussing ordinary markets (such as the market for wheat, or cars, or widgets), our next step after defining the terms supply and demand was to explain what we meant by equilibrium. Let us do the same now, and show how aggregate supply and aggregate demand can be used to explain the ideas of equilibrium and disequilibrium in the circular flow.

A Numerical Example

We shall use a numerical example to make our point. Imagine an economy in which only three goods are produced: apples, milling machines, and widgets. Looking at this economy, we find that various firms have plans to produce apples at a rate of $30,000 worth per year, milling machines at a rate of $40,000 worth per year, and widgets at a rate of $30,000 worth per year. All firms are busy carrying out their plans. The result is a flow of output at a rate of $100,000 per year. This output flow, which we can call either national product or aggregate supply, is detailed in lines 1–4 of Exhibit 5.3.

While producers are busy carrying out their plans, various buyers make plans too. Consumers plan to buy apples at a rate of $25,000 worth per year and to buy widgets at a rate of $30,000 worth per year. Also, the firms that make widgets are planning to buy milling machines at a rate of $30,000 worth per year, in order to increase their widget-producing capacity for the future. No one is planning either to increase or to decrease the stocks of finished products that are held in inventory, so planned inventory investment is zero. All these buying plans are expressed in lines 5–11 of Exhibit 5.3. The total of all planned expenditures (consumption plus planned investment) is listed in line 11 with the label *aggregate demand.*

Comparing line 1 with line 11, we see that the plans of producers and the plans of buyers do not mesh. Aggregate supply is not equal to aggregate demand. There is nothing very surprising about that. After all, there were no direct consultations between the various buyers and sellers when plans were being made. Each acted on the basis of what knowledge was available from the price system, plus private judgments about future trends or changes. What happens is just that things do not always work out for

EXHIBIT 5.3

A numerical example of the circular flow for a simple economy

National product must always be equal to total expenditure even when the circular flow is not in equilibrium. In the example shown here, national product (aggregate supply) exceeds total planned expenditure (aggregate demand), so unplanned inventory investment makes up the difference.

Output resulting from producers' plans		
1 Total national product (aggregate supply):		100
2 Apples	30	
3 Widgets	30	
4 Milling machines	40	
Expenditures resulting from buyers' plans		
5 Total consumption expenditure:		55
6 Apples	25	
7 Widgets	30	
8 Total planned investment expenditure:		35
9 Fixed investment	35	
10 Planned inventory investment	0	
11 Total planned expenditure (aggregate demand)		90
Other expenditure		
12 Total unplanned inventory investment:		10
13 Unsold apples	5	
14 Unsold milling machines	5	
Summary		
15 Total national product		100
16 Total national expenditure:		100
17 Planned	90	
18 Unplanned	10	

everyone according to plan. The apples, widgets, and milling machines are all produced, but not all of them are sold. After buyers have bought all they planned to, $5,000 worth of apples are left over and so are $5,000 worth of milling machines. These products cannot simply vanish into thin air. The firms that made them put them into inventory, even though they had not planned to, and hope to sell them at some time in the future. The result is unplanned inventory investment of $10,000, as shown in lines 12–14 of Exhibit 5.3.

An Important Equality

Because aggregate buying plans do not mesh with aggregate production plans, we say that the circular flow is in disequilibrium. Aggregate supply and aggregate demand are not equal. National product and total planned expenditure are not equal. One crucial equality still *does* hold, though. National product is still equal to total expenditure *when both planned and unplanned expenditure are taken into account*. The reason is that goods that are produced and not sold *must* be added to inventories, whether firms planned to put them there or not. To repeat, they cannot simply vanish into thin air. As long as we count unplanned inventory investment as a part of total expenditure—and we do—total expenditure is by definition equal to national product. In equation form, we can write

$$\text{National Product} = \text{Total Planned Expenditure} + \text{Unplanned Inventory Investment} = \text{Total Expenditure}$$

Another way to write exactly the same thing is

$$\text{Aggregate Supply} = \text{Aggregate Demand} + \text{Unplanned Inventory Investment}$$

Reactions to Disequilibrium

In our numerical example, outlines in Exhibit 5.3, aggregate demand fell short of aggregate supply. Because buyers' and sellers' plans failed to mesh, there was an unplanned accumulation of inventories. Firms would not want this unplanned rise in inventories to go on and on. In order to stop it, they would reduce their rate of output, or lower prices in order to stimulate sales, or both. These reactions would amount to a reduction in aggregate supply. The size of the circular flow would begin to shrink as the number of dollars received by firms for their products and the number of dollars paid out to workers fell.

It might be that at another time, aggregate demand would exceed aggregate supply. With total planned expenditures greater than national product, unplanned inventory depletion would take place. Firms would react in a way opposite to their reaction to an excess of aggregate supply over aggregate demand. Either they would increase output to rebuild inventories, or they would take advantage of the high level of demand to raise prices, or both. Whichever they did, the size of the circular flow would grow as incomes and expenditures rose.

Finally, it is entirely possible that when the plans of buyers and sellers were tested in the market, they would turn out just to mesh. In that case, with production and planned expenditure equal, no unplanned inventory investment would occur, and no corrections would be necessary. The circular flow would be in equilibrium.

Income and Expenditure

We have not yet said anything about national income. Let us go back for a moment to the situation shown in Exhibit 5.3. Firms are shown to be producing $100,000 worth of goods a year. To produce those goods requires them to make factor payments (including profits, if any) of $100,000 to households, which means that national income is $100,000 too. The households receiving this income planned to buy consumer goods at a rate of $55,000 per year, which meant that they planned to save at a rate of $45,000 per year. (Remember that saving plus consumption exhaust income in this simple economy.)

Now, household saving plans do not mesh with firms' investment plans, as shown in line 8 of Exhibit 5.3. As things actually turned out, though, firms invested more than they had planned to. The actual total of investment, including unplanned inventory investment, *was* exactly equal to saving. It had to be. Once again, goods cannot vanish into thin air once produced, and unplanned inventory investment acts as the balancing item.

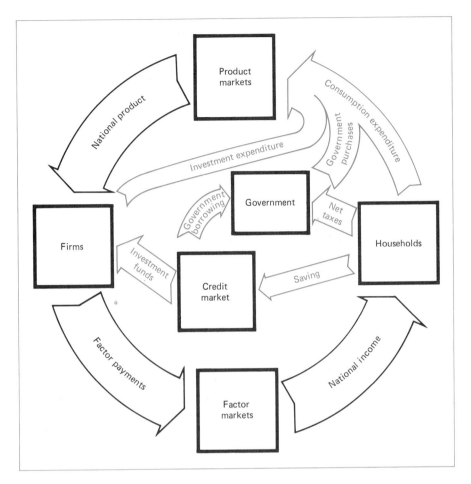

EXHIBIT 5.4
The circular flow with government included

With government added to the circular flow of income and product, there are two new channels along which funds can flow from households to product markets. Some income is diverted to government in the form of net taxes, and then used to finance government purchases. Alternatively, if the government runs a budget deficit, it may borrow from the public via credit markets and use the borrowed funds to finance its expenditures. If the government runs a budget surplus, the flow of funds along this pathway may be reversed, in which case the arrow from government to the credit market would point in the opposite direction from that shown.

The Place of Government
in the Circular Flow

When government enters the circular flow of income, expenditure, and product, things become slightly more complicated. Exhibit 5.4 shows how the circular flow looks when government is added. Two new pathways are opened up along which expenditures can flow from households to the product markets.

First, governments take in money from taxes that they levy on households. Some of that money, as we saw in Chapter 4, is immediately returned to households in the form of transfer payments. The difference between

Net Taxes Total tax revenues collected by government at all levels minus total transfer payments disbursed.

Deficit (of the government budget) An excess of government purchases over net taxes.

Surplus (of the government budget) An excess of net taxes over government purchases.

what governments take in as tax revenue and what they pay out in the form of transfer payments is called **net taxes.** Funds thus flow from households to government as net taxes and then from government to product markets as government purchases.

Second, if government purchases of goods and services exceed net taxes, the government may need to borrow money from the public through credit markets. In this case, the government budget is said to be in **deficit.** When the government runs a deficit, funds flow from households to the credit market as savings, then from credit markets to the government as government borrowing, and finally from government to the product markets as government purchases.

Sometimes the government budget is in **surplus** rather than in deficit. In that case, government borrowing from the public is less than its repayment of past debts. The net flow of funds between government and the credit market would be the reverse of what is shown in Exhibit 5.4.

Numerical Example with Government

Another numerical example will show that a government surplus or deficit does not disturb the basic equalities of the circular flow of income, expenditure, and product. Exhibit 5.5 shows an economy in which firms are again producing output at a rate of $100,000 per year, so national product is $100,000. Total expenditure is made up of consumer purchases at a rate of $60,000 per year, investment (planned and unplanned) at a rate of $25,000 per year, and government purchases of goods and services at a rate of $15,000 per year. Total expenditure is, as always, equal to national product because it includes unplanned inventory investment as a balancing item in case the planned expenditures of households, firms, and government do not exactly add up to current production.

Production of the national product of $100,000 per year generates a national income flow of the same amount. Households are making consumption expenditures out of this at a rate of $60,000 per year, as already noted. Part of the rest, $10,000 per year to be exact, is taken by government in net taxes. What is not spent or taxed away is saved, at a rate of $30,000 per year.

The government in this example has not balanced its budget. It is running a deficit of $5,000 per year. This does not disturb the equality of national income and total expenditure, however, because there is an offsetting surplus of saving over investment of $5,000 per year. The government can use this excess saving to finance its deficit by borrowing it from households via the credit market.

It is not just chance, of course, that the difference between saving and investment is exactly equal to the government deficit. The equality is maintained exactly because investment includes unplanned inventory investment. Suppose that the government suddenly reduced its expenditures by $1,000 per year, without giving time for any planned adjustments on the part of firms or households. The result would be that firms that produced the type of goods the government usually bought would find their inventories unexpectedly increasing at a rate $1,000 per year faster than previously. Now total investment would be $26,000 rather than $25,000, and the difference between saving and investment, now $4,000, will automatically have adjusted to the reduced size of the budget deficit.

EXHIBIT 5.5

A numerical example of the circular flow with government

When government is added to the circular flow, national product, total expenditure, and national income must still all be equal. If government purchases are not equal to net taxes, the difference will be offset by an equal difference between saving and investment. Another way to put this is to say that saving plus taxes must equal government purchases plus investment. As always, unplanned inventory investment acts as a balancing item, so that these equalities hold whether the circular flow is in equilibrium or not.

1	National product	100
2	Total expenditure:	100
3	Consumption	60
4	Investment	25
5	Government purchases	15
6	National income allocated to:	100
7	Consumption	60
8	Net taxes	10
9	Saving	30

We can put what we have learned from this example into an important new equality. If the difference between saving and investment is always equal to the goverment deficit (or surplus), then it must also be true that

$$\text{Saving} + \text{Net Taxes} = \text{Investment} + \text{Government Purchases}$$

Conclusions

Key Equalities

We have put some very big ideas into this short chapter. For one thing, we have used the circular flow to show how various parts of the economy fit together. First we established that national product must be equal to total expenditure, and that total expenditure, in turn, is made up of consumption plus investment plus government expenditure. In equation form,

$$\text{National Product} = \text{Total Expenditure}$$
$$= \text{Consumption} + \text{Investment} + \text{Government Purchases}$$

We then saw that national income can be broken down into three components representing the three different things people can do with their money: spend it, save it, or pay taxes. In equation form, this means that

$$\text{National Income} = \text{Consumption} + \text{Saving} + \text{Net Taxes}$$

Finally, we discovered that saving plus taxes must always equal investment plus government purchases, with the difference between saving and investment exactly offsetting any government deficit or surplus. This crucial relationship provides a link between the two equations we have just written. Our final conclusion, summarized in Exhibit 5.6, is that national income is equal to national product.

The conclusion that national product and national income are equal was trivial and obvious for the simplified economy shown in Exhibit 5.1. With saving, investment, taxes, and government purchases added, it is not so trivial or obvious, but it is no less true.

Equilibrium

Up to that point in this chapter we used the circular flow simply as a descriptive device, a set of pegs on which to hang some important definitions. At the same time as we were establishing these definitions and equal-

EXHIBIT 5.6
Key equalities in the circular flow

Three key equalities

National Product = Total Expenditure = Consumption + Investment + Government Purchases   (1)

National Income = Consumption + Saving + Net Taxes   (2)

Saving + Net Taxes = Investment + Government Purchases   (3)

Fit together to make a fourth equality

National Income = Consumption + Saving + Net Taxes = Investment + Government Purchases + Consumption = National Product   (4)

---

ities, though, we used the circular flow in a different way. As soon as we introduced the terms aggregate supply and aggregate demand, the circular flow was no longer just dollars chasing goods around in a circle. Instead, it became a living, active market economy in which buyers met and tested their plans and encountered success or disappointment.

We saw that the idea of equilibrium could be applied to the circular flow to describe a situation in which the plans of buyers and sellers exactly meshed. More than that, we saw what happens when plans do not mesh, so that the circular flow is not in equilibrium. If buyers do not demand as much as firms supply, the excess products go on the shelf, whether firms had planned to put them in inventory or not. To correct the unplanned inventory accumulation, firms must cut output or reduce prices to boost sales. Either action causes the circular flow to shrink, when this flow is measured in terms of dollars spent on products or earned in incomes. If buyers demand more than firms currently produce, goods come off the shelf, even if firms had not planned to run their inventories down. This unplanned inventory depletion causes firms to raise prices or increase output, either of which causes the volume of the circular flow to grow.

If you have mastered this chapter, do not put down the book thinking that you know everything there is to know about macroeconomic theory. Still, you have made a pretty good start.

SUMMARY

1. Two of the most important elements of the circular flow are national income and national product. These two elements are linked on one side by factor payments and on the other by total expenditures. National income and national product are equal.
2. Saving and investment can be added to the circular flow without disturbing the equality between national product and total expenditure. If total *planned* expenditure is not exactly equal to national product, unplanned inventory investment (positive or negative) will make up the difference between the two.
3. Aggregate supply is another term for national product, and aggregate demand another term for total planned expenditure. When aggregate supply is equal to aggregate demand, unplanned inventory investment must be zero, and the circular flow is said to be in equilibrium. When aggregate supply and demand are not equal, unplanned inventory investment (positive or negative) must take place. The circular flow is then said to be in disequilibrium.

4. Adding government to the economy does not disturb the basic equalities of national product, total expenditure, and national income. If government purchases are not equal to net taxes, the surplus or deficit will be offset by the difference between saving and investment, with unplanned inventory investment acting as a balancing item if necessary. It follows that saving plus net taxes must be equal to investment plus government purchases.

DISCUSSION QUESTIONS

1. Contrast the flow of money you put into your bank account each payday with the stock of money indicated by the balance in your passbook. How are the flow and stock related? Why is one referred to as a flow and the other as a stock?

2. In the real world, who are the savers and who are the investors? Are they the same people all of the time? Some of the time? Can you provide examples of when a person can be both the saver and the investor? Give examples where someone is a saver but not an investor; an investor but not a saver.

3. In what sense is the owner of a grocery store chain "investing" when his inventories increase? How is this similar to investment in new display freezers for his stores? How is it different?

4. Because savers and investors are not always the same people, why is it that after the fact savings must always equal investment? Or must they? Is this relationship true in the real world or only under certain restrictive assumptions? What assumptions?

5. Suppose that you bought a dollar's worth of gasoline. Trace through the route this dollar might take, in fact several different ways it might take, to go through the whole circular flow.

6. Use the circular flow diagram to analyze each of the following:
   (a) The interest rate falls and businesses borrow more money and do more investing.
   (b) People decide to work less; they prefer more time off to watch ball games or some other leisure activity.
   (c) Governments in the economy raise their taxes.
   (d) Firms decide to lower their inventories, so they lay off 10 percent of their work force.
   (e) The government increases its flow of both taxes and government spending.

7. How would the circular flow model change if there were no money in the system, that is, if all exchanges had to be barter exchanges?

8. How do unemployed or unproductive workers fit into the circular flow diagram? What flows are connected to them?

CHAPTER 6
Measuring National Income and Product

What You Will Learn in This Chapter
National income accounting means attaching numbers to the elements of the circular flow of income and product. By providing a statistical record of what has happened in the economy in the past, national income accountants help economists to refine and develop their theories, and help give decision makers in business and government a basis on which to formulate plans for the future. National income accounting is not an exact science, and published measurements of saving, investment, expenditure, income, and output are always estimates or approximations that fall short of the theoretical ideal. But despite their imperfections, these measures are so widely publicized and so frequently mentioned in economic discussions that it is important to learn how the basic national accounts are put together, and how to read them.

For Review
Here is an important concept that will be put to use in this chapter. Be certain that you know it, or review it before proceeding.
    Basic equalities of the circular flow (Chapter 5)

Introduction

Measurement Problems

In Chapter 5 we cut the circular flow of income and product into convenient pieces, and gave them names like "national income," "investment," "saving," and so forth. These are the concepts on which much economic theory is based. Because they are so central to our theory, it is useful to be able to measure them, in order to see how well our theory fits the real world.

Unfortunately, measurement is not a completely straightforward job. National income, investment, and saving do not run around out there with labels tied around their necks. At least three important measurement problems face national income accountants.

First, there are problems of fitting concepts to reality. Things that are distinct in economic theory turn out to be mixed up in the real world. Consider factor payments as an example. When the owner-operator of a one-man gas station earns a net income of $8,000 per year, how can anyone tell what part of that money is wages he deserves for manning the pumps, what part is rent he deserves as owner of the corner lot where the station stands, and what part is interest he earns as the man who put up the capital to get the business started? Not only are we unable to identify things our theory says should be out there in the real world, we keep running into things that theoreticians wish would just go away. Sales taxes and business property taxes are good examples of complications in the national accounts that, for the sake of theory, we would like to ignore.

Second, measuring national income and product gets us into problems with recording and sampling. Statisticians cannot take the time to check up on what everyone does, so they sample the economic activities of some households and firms and hope that these more or less represent the rest. There is also the problem that when things like tax returns are used as a source of data, people may have turned in false information.

Nominal and Real Values

Third, and this is perhaps the greatest single problem of national income accounting, we have to worry about changing prices. Changing prices make it necessary to keep two entirely separate sets of accounts, one in **nominal** terms and one in **real** terms. Nominal measurements are those made in terms of actual market prices at which goods are sold. Real measurements are those that include adjustments for changes in prices from one year to another. Nominal measurements are fine for some purposes. If we wished to compare the incomes of white workers in Los Angeles in 1975 with the incomes of nonwhite workers in the same city during the same year, a nominal measurement would be appropriate. In other cases, though, nominal measurements can be highly misleading. If we said that the nominal starting salary for economics professors at Dartmouth College had gone up by $1,000 between 1970 and 1975, we would be drawing attention away from the fact that the cost of living had risen so much that the 1975 salary actually bought less than the 1970 salary did. Comparisons over time require real measurements.

Nominal Values Measurements of economic values made in terms of actual market prices at which goods are sold.

Real Values Measurements of economic values that include adjustments for changes in prices between one year and another.

Personal consumption expenditure		973.2
Durable goods	131.7	
Nondurable goods	409.1	
Services	432.4	
Plus: Gross private domestic investment		183.7
Producers durable equipment	96.4	
New construction	101.8	
Change in business inventories	−14.6	
Plus: Government purchases of goods and services		339.0
Federal	124.4	
State and local	214.5	
Plus: Net exports of goods and services		20.5
Exports	148.1	
Less imports	−127.6	
Equals: Gross national product (GNP)		1,516.4
Less: Capital consumption allowance	−161.4	
Equals: Net national product (NNP)		1,355.0

EXHIBIT 6.1

Nominal gross national product by type of expenditure, 1975

Gross national product is officially estimated by the expenditure approach. This means adding together the values of expenditures on newly produced goods and services made by all economic units to get a measure of aggregate economic activity. Net national product is derived from gross national product by excluding the value of investment expenditures that merely replace worn out or obsolete capital equipment.

The national income accountants who keep the country's official economic statistics deserve a lot of credit for doing their very best to overcome all these difficulties. National income accounting is a relatively young branch of economics. Forty-five years ago, when the Great Depression was hitting the country, national economic statistics were very bad. So bad, in fact, that policy makers in Washington literally did not know what was going on. By comparison, today's still far from perfect statistics make life much easier for policy makers and economic theorists alike.

In the remainder of this chapter we shall take a brief tour through some of the mechanics of national income accounting. We shall start with nominal measures, then turn to the problem of prices and real measures, and finally end with an evaluation of the validity of national income statistics as a whole.

Measuring Nominal Income and Product

Gross National Product

Of all economic statistics, perhaps the most widely publicized is the measure of an economy's level of total production called the **gross national product,** or GNP. This statistic represents the dollar value at current market prices (that is, the nominal value) of all final goods and services produced annually by the nation's economy.

In principle, gross national product could be measured directly, by constructing a table showing the quantity of each final good and service produced—massages, apples, submarines, housing units, and all the rest—multiplying these quantities by the prices at which they were sold, and adding the resulting column of figures. That is not, of course, what national income accountants actually do. Instead, they take a shortcut based on the equality of national product and total expenditure. In practice, then, GNP is measured by summing the nominal expenditure of all economic units on domestically produced final goods and services. This way of measuring aggregate economic activity is known as the **expenditure approach.** Exhibit 6.1 provides an illustration of how it works, using actual 1975 data.

Consumption

Consumption expenditures by households and unattached persons fall into three categories: durable goods, nondurable goods, and services. In principle, goods that do not wear out entirely in one year, such as automobiles, furniture, or household appliances, are considered durable, and goods that are used up in less than a year, such as soap, food, or gasoline, are considered nondurable. (In practice, the classifications actually used are often arbitrary. All clothing, for example, is considered nondurable, whether it is a pair of stockings, which wears out in a matter of weeks, or a woolen overcoat, which may be used for a decade.) The remaining item, services, includes things such as haircuts, legal advice, or education, which are not embodied in any physical object when sold. No distinction is made between services that are durable and nondurable in their effects.

Both the goods and the services components of consumption contain items that are produced but do not actually pass through the marketplace

Gross National Product (GNP) The dollar value at current market prices of all final goods and services produced annually by the nation's economy.

Expenditure Approach A method of estimating aggregate economic activity by adding together the nominal expenditure of all economic units on newly produced final goods and services.

on their way to consumers. One of these is an estimate of the food produced and directly consumed on farms. Another is an estimate of the rental value of owner-occupied homes. Rental payments on tenant-occupied housing are included automatically.

Investment

The item called gross private domestic investment is the sum of all firms' purchases of newly produced capital goods—fixed investment—plus changes in business inventories. Fixed investment, in turn, is broken down into the durable equipment of producers (such as machine tools, trucks, and office equipment) and new construction (including both business structures and residential housing).

When thinking about investment, keep in mind the phrase "newly produced capital goods." The businessperson who buys a used machine is not engaging in an investment expenditure according to the national income accountants' definition. The machine was already counted in some previous year. Also, anyone who says that he just made an "investment" of $2,000 when he means he paid that much for a plot of land or a corporate bond is not using the word "investment" in the national income accountants' sense. Real estate or securities are not capital goods. In fact, they are not even part of the more general category, goods and services, with which the measure GNP is concerned.

Government Purchases and Net Exports

Government purchases of goods and services are the next item to be added in. Transfer payments are not included in GNP because they do not represent expenditures made to purchase newly produced products.

The final item in GNP is **net exports.** This is the difference between the nominal value of goods and services exported to foreigners and the nominal value of goods and services imported from abroad. Exported goods must be added in because they are products produced in the United States, even though they are bought by foreigners. Imports are subtracted because some of the expenditures on consumer goods, investment goods, and government purchases, which we have already added in, were purchases of goods made abroad, and we do not want to count these as part of *national* product. When we add *net* exports into GNP, then, what we are doing is first adding all expenditures by Americans on goods and services regardless of where they were produced, then adding the total of American goods purchased by foreigners, and finally deducting purchases by Americans of goods made abroad.

Net Exports The value of all domestically produced goods and services sold to foreigners less the value of all goods and services bought from foreigners; exports minus imports.

Net National Product

What makes gross national product "gross"? It is the fact that gross private domestic investment is not a measure of the actual change in capital assets and business inventories for a particular year. In the process of production, existing buildings and equipment and other capital assets wear out. Other capital goods do not wear out, but lose their value through obsolescence. Accountants say that this part of the nation's capital stock existing at the beginning of the year *depreciates* by the year's end. It follows, then, that the actual increase in the stocks of capital goods and business inventories each year, which we call net private domestic investment, differs from gross private domestic investment by an allowance for the capital assets that depreciate each year. This allowance is called the capital consumption allowance.

Investment that merely replaces plant and equipment that has worn out during the year does not move the economy ahead, but only keeps it standing in the same place. Gross national product is thus, in a sense, an overstatement of how much we are getting out of the economy. To arrive at a measure of national product that includes only the actual net increase in capital goods and business inventories, the capital consumption allowance is subtracted from GNP. The resulting figure is called **net national product** (NNP). All told, net national product is the sum of personal consumption expenditure, net private domestic investment, government purchases of goods and services, and net exports of goods and services.

Income Approach

So much for gross national product, as measured by the expenditure approach. Let us turn now to a rather different way of measuring what goes on in the circular flow: the **income approach** to national accounting.

As the name implies, the income approach measures the overall nominal rate of the circular flow by adding up all the different kinds of income earned by households. This is done as shown in Exhibit 6.2. The categories of income used by national income accountants differ somewhat from the theoretical classification of incomes into wages, rent, interest, and profit, and deserve some explanation.

Compensation of employees includes not only wages and salaries, but two other items as well. One is employer contributions for social insurance. In Chapter 4 we argued that the economic burden of these taxes was borne by employees even though employers actually made the payments. The second is "other labor income," which includes various fringe benefits received by employees.

Rental income of persons includes all income in the form of rent and royalties received by owners of property. Net interest includes only interest payments from firms to households or government, on the grounds that interest payments made by consumers or government do not represent part of the cost of producing current output.

Net National Product (NNP) A measure of national product adjusted to exclude the value of investment expenditures that merely replace worn out or obsolete capital goods. Officially, NNP equals GNP minus the capital consumption allowance.

Income Approach A method of estimating aggregate economic activity by adding together the incomes earned by all households.

EXHIBIT 6.2

Nominal national income, 1975

National income is officially estimated by the income approach. This means adding together the values of all income earned by households. Note that some items of income, such as the portion of corporate profits that go to pay corporate profits taxes, are counted as "earned" by households even though households never actually receive the income.

Compensation of employees		928.8
Wages and salaries	806.7	
Employer contributions for social insurance	59.7	
Other labor income	62.5	
Rental income of persons		22.4
Net interest		74.6
Corporate profits		91.6
Dividends	32.1	
Corporate profits taxes	49.2	
Undistributed corporate profits	10.3	
Proprietors income		90.2
National income		1,207.6

Corporate profits include all income earned by the owners (that is, the stockholders) of corporations, whether the owners actually receive that income or not. Dividends are the part of that income that the owners actually receive. Another part goes to pay corporate profits taxes, and a third part, "undistributed corporate profits," is retained by the corporations to use for investment purposes.

The final component of national income, proprietors' income, is a sort of grab-bag including all income earned by owners of unincorporated businesses and self-employed professionals. National income accountants make no attempt to sort out what parts of this income ought theoretically to be classified as wages, rent, interest, or profit.

National Income and GNP

In our theoretical circular flow of Chapter 6, national income and national product were defined in such a way that they were exactly equal. In the real world, things do not work out quite so neatly. Some adjustments must be made to make national income, as measured by the income approach, fit GNP, as measured by the expenditure approach. These adjustments are shown in Exhibit 6.3.

For one thing, in the real world we must distinguish between net and gross national product, a difference we ignore in elementary theoretical discussions. The investment expenditures made to replace worn-out or obsolete equipment are counted as part of the business expenses of firms, so that they do not show up either in corporate profits or in proprietors' income. The first step in going from GNP to national income, then, is to subtract the capital consumption allowance, leaving us with net national product.

Next an adjustment must be made to reflect the fact that some of the money that firms receive from sales of their product is not "earned" by owners of the firms. Instead, it is taken directly by government in payment of indirect business taxes. These include sales taxes, excise taxes, and business property taxes paid to federal, state, and local governments. These taxes are treated differently from the corporate income tax, which is considered to be earned by owners, and then taken by government out of corporate profits. Indirect business taxes are included in the prices of goods and services, so they count as part of net national product, but they are not

Gross national product	1,516.4
Less: Capital consumption allowance	−161.4
Equals: Net national product	1,355.0
Less: Indirect business taxes*	−143.0
Less: Statistical discrepancy	−4.4
Equals: National income	1,207.6

*Includes minor adjustments for business transfer payments and net subsidies to government enterprises.

EXHIBIT 6.3
Relation of national income to GNP, 1975
In the simple world of elementary economic theory, national product and national income are equal by definition. In the real world, certain adjustments must be made to get GNP and national income to "fit." First the capital consumption allowance is subtracted from GNP to get NNP. Then indirect business taxes and the statistical discrepancy are subtracted from NNP to get national income.

included in income, so they must be subtracted when going from NNP to national income, as shown in Exhibit 6.3.

In principle, subtracting the capital consumption allowance and indirect business taxes from GNP ought to give us national income, but in practice there is one further difficulty. GNP is estimated by the expenditure approach, using one set of data, and national income is measured by the income approach, using an entirely different set of data. Inevitably, no matter how carefully the work is done, there are some errors and omissions so that the two sets of figures do not quite fit. The difference between NNP less indirect business taxes, on the one hand, and national income, on the other, is called the statistical discrepancy. It has no theoretical significance; it is simply a "fudge factor" that makes things balance.

Personal Income

National income, as we have mentioned several times, is a measure of income earned by households, whether those households ever actually get their hands on the income or not. For some purposes, it is more important to measure what households actually receive, instead of what they earn. The total of income actually received by households is called **personal income.**

Exhibit 6.4 shows the steps required to translate national income into personal income. First we subtract three items that are earned by households but not received by them. These are contributions for social insurance (both employer and employee), corporate profits taxes, and undistributed corporate profits. Next we add transfer payments, which represent money received by households although it is not earned by them. The result is personal income.

One further income measure is shown at the bottom of Exhibit 6.4. This is **disposable personal income** (or just **disposable income,** for short). Disposable income is what households have left of their personal income after they pay personal income taxes.

This completes our discussion of the nominal side of national income accounting. In the next section, we turn to the problem of making adjustments for changing prices.

Personal Income   The total of all income, including transfer payments, actually received by households before payment of personal income taxes.

Disposable Personal Income (disposable income)   Personal income minus personal income taxes.

EXHIBIT 6.4

National income and personal income, 1975

National income is a measure of all income earned by households, while personal income is a measure of the income they actually receive. To go from national income to personal income, we subtract payroll taxes, corporate profits taxes, and undistributed corporate profits, and then add transfer payments. If we subtract personal income taxes from this, we get disposable personal income.

National Income		1,207.6
Less: Contributions for social insurance		−109.6
Employer contributions	59.7	
Employee contributions	50.0	
Less: Corporate profits taxes		−49.2
Less: Undistributed corporate profits		−10.3
Plus: Transfer payments*		211.2
Equals: Personal income		1,249.7
Less: Personal income taxes		−168.8
Equals: Disposable personal income		1,080.9

*Includes government and consumer interest payments and business transfer payments.

Measuring Real Income and Prices

A Simple Economy

Let us begin our investigation of real income and prices by looking at an economy much simpler than that of the United States. This will permit us to present the essentials in the clearest possible way, before getting into practical details.

Exhibit 6.5 shows nominal GNP accounts for two years in a simple economy where only three goods are produced: movies, apples, and shirts. The tables show us that nominal GNP grew from $400 in 1972 to $1,000 in 1977. But how are we to interpret these figures? Do they mean that people really had more of the things they wanted in 1977 than in 1972? More exactly, do the figures mean that they had $2\frac{1}{2}$ times as much? We need to take a closer look.

A line-by-line comparison of the two tables in Exhibit 6.5 shows that the figures on nominal income do not tell the whole story. The problem is that prices went up sharply between 1972 and 1977. Movies cost twice what they used to, apples three times as much, and shirts half again as much. So how much more was *really* produced in the second year than in the first?

We could try looking directly at the quantities of individual goods and services produced, but if we do so, we get conflicting indications. We see that twice as many movies and shirts were produced in 1977 as in 1972 but only half as many apples. Instead, it might occur to us to approach the matter in another way, by asking how much the total value of output would have changed from 1972 to 1977 if prices had not changed.

This approach to the problem gives us the results shown in Exhibit 6.6. There, we see that the 1977 output of 100 movies, 500 apples, and 20 shirts, which had a value of $1,000 in terms of the prices at which the goods and services were actually sold, would have had a value of only $500 in terms of the prices that prevailed in 1972. This figure of $500, which eliminates the effect of changing prices, is the one we should compare with the 1972 GNP of $400 if we want to know what really happened to physical production in the economy between the two years. Much of the apparent growth of the economy appears to have been due to higher prices. It seems that instead of having 250 percent more in 1977 than in 1972, the people in our simple economy had only about 25 percent more.

	Quantity	Price	Value
		1972	
Movies	50	$ 2.00	$ 100
Apples	1,000	.20	200
Shirts	10	10.00	100
1972 nominal GNP			$ 400
		1977	
Movies	100	$ 4.00	$ 400
Apples	500	.60	300
Shirts	20	15.00	300
1977 nominal GNP			$1,000

EXHIBIT 6.5

Nominal GNP in selected years for a simple economy
In this simple economy, where only three goods are produced, nominal national income grew from $400 in 1972 to $1,000 in 1977. Prices also went up between the two years, though, so people did not really have two and a half times as much of the things they wanted in 1977.

EXHIBIT 6.6

Nominal and real GNP in 1977 for a simple economy

This exhibit shows how the numbers from Exhibit 6.5 can be adjusted to take changing prices into account. The 1977 quantities are multiplied by 1972 prices, to get the value of 1977 GNP as it would have been had prices not changed. The total of 1977 quantities valued at 1972 prices is called the real GNP for 1977.

	1977 Quantity	1977 Price	Value at 1977 Price	1972 Price	Value of 1977 Output at 1972 Prices
Movies	100	$ 4.00	$ 400	$ 2.00	$200
Apples	500	.60	300	.20	100
Shirts	20	15.00	300	10.00	200
Totals		1977 nominal GNP = $1,000		1977 real GNP = $500	

Real GNP and the Price Index

Let us put the ideas we have gotten from this example into a convenient definition. When we make a comparison of GNP between a given current year and some other year (called the **base year**), we shall use the term **real GNP** to mean the total value of current-year quantities of final output evaluated in terms of base-year prices.

This definition of real GNP immediately suggests a simple way of measuring the change in prices between the base year and the current year. Look once again at the example summarized in Exhibits 6.5 and 6.6. We saw that nominal GNP grew from $400 to $1,000 from 1972 (the base year in our example) to 1977 (the current year). Real GNP, in contrast, rose only from $400 to $500. The difference between the nominal and real GNP figures for 1977 is attributable to rising prices. As a measure of the change in prices between the two years, then, it seems natural to use the ratio of nominal to real GNP in the current year. To make another definition, we say that the **price index** for any current year, measured in relation to any given base year, is given by the formula

$$\text{Price Index} = \frac{\text{Current-Year Nominal GNP}}{\text{Current-Year Real GNP}}$$

or, alternatively,

$$\text{Price Index} = \frac{\text{Current-Year Quantities Evaluated in Terms of Current-Year Prices}}{\text{Current-Year Quantities Evaluated in Terms of Base-Year Prices}}$$

If we use the data from our example to compute the price index for 1977 in terms of the 1972 base year, we get

$$\text{Price Index} = \frac{\$1,000}{\$500} = 2.0$$

We can think of this figure as meaning that, on the average, goods and services were twice as expensive in 1977 as in 1972. Alternatively, we could interpret the price index as indicating a decline in the purchasing power of our simple economy's dollar. We could say that the 1977 dollar was worth only half as much as the 1972 dollar.

Base Year For measurement of real GNP, the year from which prices are used in evaluating both base-year and current-year outputs.

Real GNP A measure of aggregate economic activity obtained by evaluating current-year quantities in terms of the prices of some base year.

Price Index In the most general sense, the ratio of current-year nominal GNP to current-year real GNP. See also *consumer* and *wholesale price indexes*.

Consumer Price Index A price index based on a "representative market basket" of about 400 goods and services purchased by urban wage earners and clerical workers. This index is calculated using base-year quantities.

Wholesale Price Index A price index based on a sample of about 2,500 goods purchased in large quantities in transactions between firms. This index is calculated using base-year quantities.

Price Indexes in the American Economy

Official government statisticians calculate not just one, but several price indexes for the American economy. The underlying principle is the same for all these indexes, but because first one and then another may come to our attention in the news, it is useful to understand how they differ.

The broadest measure of price changes is an index called the implicit price deflator of the GNP. It is exactly the kind of index defined above, and can be interpreted as showing the "average" or "general" price level of all final goods and services. It is called "deflator" because dividing (deflating) nominal GNP by this price index gives real GNP. The U.S. Department of Commerce currently uses 1972 as the base year for its GNP deflator.

Two other important measures of prices are the **consumer price index** (CPI) and the **wholesale price index** (WPI), which differ from the implicit deflator both in the products that are included in calculating them and in the way they are constructed. The consumer price index measures the average prices of all major categories of goods and services purchased by urban wage earners and clerical workers. A "representative market basket" has been chosen from studies of actual expenditures by such individuals. The prices of approximately 400 different goods and services are currently included in this index. The wholesale price index, in contrast, excludes prices paid by household consumers, and measures the average prices of commodities purchased in large quantities in transactions between firms. Currently, the constituent price quotations are obtained on a sample of about 2,500 items from manufacturers or other producers; no services are included in the wholesale price index. At the time this book is being written, the CPI and WPI are using 1967 as their base year. The U.S. Bureau of Labor Statistics, which constructs these indexes, changes the base year once a decade or so.

Both the consumer price index and the wholesale price index are constructed using base-year quantities rather than current-year quantities. They are found by the formula

$$\text{Price Index} = \frac{\text{Value of Base-Year Quantities at Current-Year Prices}}{\text{Value of Base-Year Quantities at Base-Year Prices}}$$

Using base-year rather than current-year quantities provides an important practical advantage. It means that in order to recalculate the index it is necessary to collect new data only on prices, which are easily available, and not on quantities, which are not quite so readily measured. Consequently, the Bureau of Labor Statistics is able to issue up-to-date computations of the consumer price index and the wholesale price index every month, before data on the implicit deflator of the GNP are issued.

Exhibit 6.7 shows how the wholesale price index and the consumer price index have moved over the last decade. As everyone knows, having studied economics or not, the price levels have risen sharply over this period. Later, in Chapter 14–17, we shall discuss the causes of these price increases at some length. Now, though, we need to add a few cautionary words about interpreting the indexes.

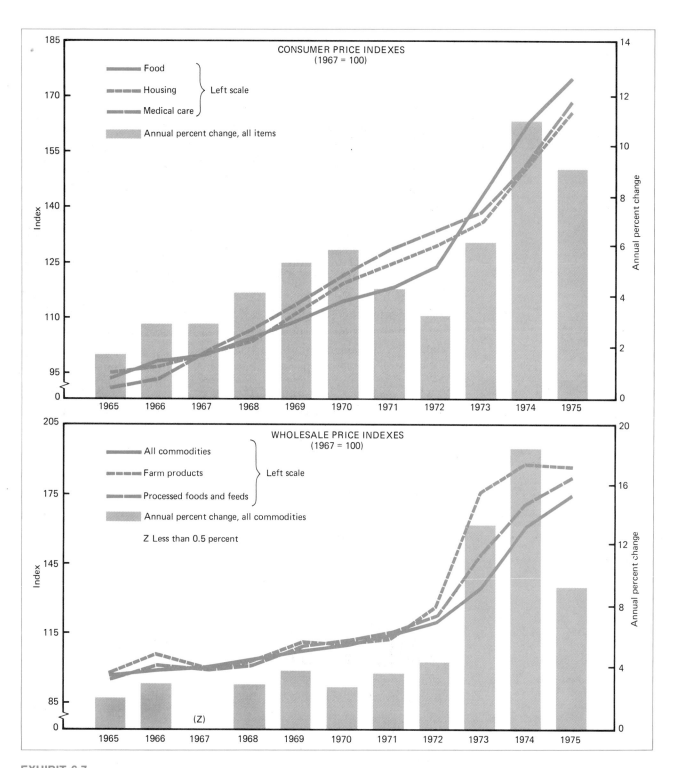

EXHIBIT 6.7

Prices indexes, 1965–1975

The CPI is based on a "representative market basket" of goods and services purchased by urban wage earners. The WPI is based on a sample of about 2,500 items purchased in large quantities in transactions between firms. Both indexes have risen sharply in recent years.

Source: Charts prepared by U.S. Bureau of the Census; data from U.S. Bureau of Labor Statistics. 1975 data from *Economic Report of the President*, 1976.

Biases in Price Indexes

Two important problems affect the accuracy of price indexes as measures of price change. One stems from buyers' reactions to price changes and the other from quality improvements and new products.

In the simple three-good economy which we looked at earlier, the prices of movies and apples rose relative to the price of shirts between 1972 and 1977. The law of demand would lead us to expect buyers to react to these changes by stepping up their purchases of the relatively lower-priced shirts. By using the 1977 quantities, the implicit price deflator places too much weight on the relatively lower-priced shirts and too little weight on the relatively higher-priced movies and apples in comparison to the quantities actually bought in 1972. For this reason it understates the amount of inflation, or as we say, it has a downward bias.

The consumer and wholesale price indexes, on the other hand, use base-year quantities. In so doing, they put too little weight on lower-priced goods, which are now purchased in greater quantities, and too much weight on higher-priced ones, which are now purchased less. For this reason, the consumer and wholesale price indexes tend to overstate the amount of inflation, or to have an upward bias.

A second problem imparts an upward bias to all three indexes and probably outweighs the first in importance. Economists would not want to attribute to "inflation" those price increases that arise solely from improvements in the quality of goods and services. Government statisticians attempt to hold "quality" constant in constructing the price indexes. They also attempt to substitute new products for obsolete ones in making up the price indexes. But careful studies indicate that quality improvements and new products are not adequately accounted for. Unfortunately, the actual magnitude of this upward bias cannot be determined very accurately.

Conclusions

We have now looked at length at the ways nominal and real GNP are measured. In most cases, we have given the benefit of the doubt to the national income accountants who put our official statistics together. They do, in fact, do quite a competent job, given the imperfect nature of the materials with which they have to work. Still, we would not want to give more credit than is due, and above all, we would not want to leave the reader thinking that national income statistics have more significance than they really have. We shall conclude this chapter, then, by listing all the things that GNP is not.

GNP and Output

Gross national product tries only to be a measure of the value of all goods and services produced in the economy. A number of technical difficulties keep it from doing even this in a very satisfactory way. We have already discussed some of these technical difficulties. One is the problem that GNP statistics are only estimates of actual economic activity, based on an incomplete sample of the activities of firms and individuals. Another is the problem that when nominal GNP figures are converted into real terms, they pick up a further source of error from the biases inherent in price indexes.

GNP does not measure perfectly the things it tries to measure, and there are some things that it does not measure at all. Nonmarket goods are one example of omitted items. Two kinds of nonmarket goods are included in GNP (the rental value of owner-occupied housing and the food produced and consumeed on farms), but many others are left out. All do-it-yourself activities are left out, and these include such very large items as the domestic services of housewives. The man who marries his former housekeeper causes a decline in GNP by the amount of her former salary even though her workload and productive services stay the same (or even rise).

Not only are many nonmarket goods left out, but a great many goods and services that *are* bought and sold in market transactions do not show up in GNP. The most important are those arising from illegal activities. Prostitution, bootlegging, narcotics, and gambling are industries whose multibillion-dollar sales go unreported, despite the fact that producers engaged in these lines yield real services to their customers. Some legal economic activity also goes unreported for purposes of income tax evasion, such as part of the cash income of professionals.

GNP Not a Measure of Welfare

Even if real GNP did measure output accurately, a measure of output is not the same thing as a measure of welfare or human satisfaction. There are a number of factors that affect human satisfaction but are not reflected in the real GNP measure. These factors can change, and would alter welfare even if real GNP remains constant.

First, the size of the population may affect the satisfaction derived from a given level of real GNP. The adjustment of real GNP to a per capita figure by dividing by population is a crude allowance for this factor.

Second, the way income is distributed may affect the level of satisfaction. The level of real GNP per capita does not directly reflect the number of families in poverty or the relative income status of upper- and lower-income groups. This situation is as it must be, because positive economics as a science cannot compare the relative satisfactions of different people. It cannot say what effect a redistribution of income has on "total" satisfaction. Do the recipients of government transfers gain more welfare than the taxpayers lose? There is no scientific way to tell.

Third, fewer and fewer labor-hours per worker are devoted to producing real GNP as the years go by. It seems plausible to think that more leisure would cause satisfaction to rise. Leisure is evidently a scarce economic good valued by workers. However, the substantial increase in the leisure of the American worker in this century is not explicitly reflected in GNP calculations.

Fourth, real GNP is a measure only of currently produced goods and services. Satisfaction is also provided by durable consumer goods produced in the past that are still providing services. Surely, the larger the present stock of consumer durables, the higher is satisfaction.

Fifth, the market prices at which goods are sold do not reflect costs or benefits affecting third parties not directly involved in the exchange. For example, environmental pollution caused by productive activities detracts from welfare. Pollution adversely affects people who are neither buyers nor sellers of the goods whose production created it. Like several of the nonmarketed goods discussed above that affect satisfaction, pollution is not entered into GNP calculations. Unlike those goods, though, pollution is a "bad"—a kind of output with a negative value. Annual additions to the amount of pollution should, in principle, be subtracted from GNP, but practical problems make this adjustment impossible.

Sixth on the list, an increase in output would not necessarily imply an increase in welfare, even if none of the problems yet mentioned were there. An unseasonably cold winter, for example, or an epidemic of infectious disease could cause the purchases of heating fuel or medical services to rise dramatically. Yet the resulting increases in real GNP would hardly represent an increase in satisfaction! Wartime defense expenditures provide another example of the lack of direct correspondence between output and welfare. We could argue that in principle these kinds of expenditures are for the maintenance of the stock of human beings, and should be treated just like investment expenditures that offset depreciation of the capital stock; that is, they should be subtracted from real GNP to get real NNP. Putting this idea into practice, however, would be quite difficult.

Finally, it should be pointed out that many aspects of human welfare are not related at all to the flow of economic goods and services or to the economic satisfaction obtained from them. Everyone would agree that people do not live by bread alone, although obtaining agreement about exactly what personal and social attributes are important, and how much each contributes, would not be easy. How important are unspoiled natural areas, unalienating work, loving human contact, space exploration, social justice, income equality, economic growth, or freedom? These are normative questions that each person may answer individually. The positive economist could never hope to lump these social and economic conditions into an objective measure of social welfare.

For all these reasons, then, real GNP should never be interpreted as a measure of social welfare. Still, it is not completely worthless. Real GNP provides a roughly accurate picture of the economy's annual production of final goods and services, which, of course, is all that it was ever intended to do. As we shall see, it is valuable for several purposes even given its limitations.

SUMMARY

1. Official measurements of national product are made using the expenditure approach. Gross national product is obtained by adding together the values of all expenditures on newly produced goods and services. Net national product is derived from gross national product by excluding the value of investment expenditures that merely replace worn-out or obsolete capital equipment.
2. National income is officially estimated by the income approach. This means adding together the values of all income earned by households. In the real world, certain adjustments must be made to get GNP and national income to fit, even though for elementary theoretical purposes, we consider the two to be equal. The difference between GNP and national income is equal to the capital consumption allowance plus indirect business taxes plus the statistical discrepancy.
3. National income measures all income earned by households, while personal income measures all the income they actually receive. To go from national income to personal income, we subtract payroll taxes, corporate profits taxes, and

undistributed corporate profits, and then add transfer payments. If we subtract personal income taxes from personal income, we get disposable personal income.

4. Measurements of aggregate economic activity can be made in real terms in order to adjust for changes in prices. Real GNP means the total value of current-year quantities of output evaluated in terms of the prices of some base year. The price index (GNP deflator) is defined as the ratio of current-year nominal GNP to current-year real GNP.

5. Real GNP does not attempt to be a measure of welfare or satisfaction, but only a measure of the output of goods and services. It does not do even that job perfectly because of sampling error, omitted items, and biases in price indexes. It is important to remember that a great many things contribute to overall human welfare that are not in any way measured by GNP.

DISCUSSION QUESTIONS

1. During this past year I received a raise of 5 percent, but the cost of living (the prices of all the goods and services I buy) went up 10 percent. Explain what happened to my nominal and real income.

2. If all mothers in the United States traded off housework with their neighbors, received a wage for doing their neighbor's work, and hence did none of their own housework, what would happen to GNP as measured by national income accountants? Would society be better off with a situation where everyone got paid? Explain.

3. Do you think transfer payments should be included in the measure of GNP? Justify your answer.

4. Is it possible that net private domestic investment could be negative? Show how this could happen by providing an example.

5. A firm gets rid of its inventory of $10,000 worth of shoes by having a sale to the public. What happens to GNP in this case? What happens to each of its components?

6. If the government increased the social security payroll deduction from 6 to 10 percent, what would happen to GNP, national income, and personal income?

7. Determine whether each of the following expenditures of my own earnings is consumption, saving, investment, or something else:
   (a) Purchase of a new home
   (b) Purchase of an automobile for cash
   (c) Payment of a monthly installment on a loan
   (d) Purchase of an item of $4.00 plus $.20 sales tax
   (e) Purchase of common stock
   (f) Giving my children a weekly allowance
   (g) Payment of tuition for additional education
   (h) A tip at a restaurant

8. What would happen to GNP and national income if an attorney married her secretary and she no longer paid him a wage? Has real production or the economic well-being of the nation changed as a result?

CHAPTER 7
Economic Growth and Living Standards

What You Will Learn in This Chapter
The high American standard of living is built on a long record of past economic growth. The American economy is still growing at a respectable rate, although some other industrialized countries are catching up through even more rapid growth. In the short run, the rate of growth can vary substantially from year to year because of changes in the share of available resources that are actually employed. In the long run, growth of output depends on advances in knowledge, education, increases in the amount of work done, and the accumulation of capital. In recent years, many people have begun to doubt that further economic growth is possible or desirable. These doubts are not groundless, but extreme pessimism does not seem to be justified.

For Review
Here are some important terms and concepts that will be put to use in this chapter. Be certain that you understand them, or review them before proceeding.

Production possibility frontier (Chapter 1)
Real GNP (Chapter 6)
GNP not a measure of welfare (Chapter 6)

American Economic Growth
Economic growth means the growth of opportunities to satisfy economic wants. At any one time, economic opportunities are limited. Labor, natural resources, and capital are scarce. Their scarcity, together with the state of our technological knowledge, limit production possibilities. Not all the useful goods and services we want can be produced at once.

As time passes, though, the range of possibilities among which we may choose expands. Capital accumulates and new resources are found. New methods of production make it possible to get more output from each unit of input. We still will not be able to have everything at once, but we can have more things at once than before.

The Growth Record
Economic growth is commonly measured in terms of real gross national product. Although real GNP is not a perfect measure of our ability to satisfy wants, or even of output, it is the best measure we have. Exhibit 7.1

EXHIBIT 7.1

The American economy has a long record of economic growth At the time of the Civil War, per capita GNP appears to have been roughly what it is in Brazil today. Since then per capita GNP has increased by nearly a factor of ten. The growth of total real GNP has been even more impressive. Aided by population growth, it is nearly forty times higher now than a century ago.

Source: 1869–1946, *Historical Statistics of the United States.* 1946–1975, *Economic Report of the President, 1976.*

shows what has happened to real GNP in the United States from 1869 to the present, both in total and per capita terms. The per capita figures give us a better idea of how individual economic welfare has changed. The total

EXHIBIT 7.2

Economic growth in selected developed and less developed countries during the 1960s

This table shows the growth rate for a selection of countries during the 1960s, about half of which grew faster than the United States in per capita terms, and half more slowly. U.S. growth was a little on the low side by Western standards. Per capita growth in many less developed countries was seriously reduced by rapid population growth. This is shown by big differences between total and per capita growth rates for those countries.

Country	Total Growth Rate of GNP	Per Capita Growth Rate of GNP
Developed Countries		
Japan	10.5	9.3
Italy	5.3	4.8
France	5.7	4.6
Canada	5.6	3.7
West Germany	4.6	3.5
Sweden	4.2	3.5
Australia	5.4	3.4
United States	4.6	3.3
United Kingdom	2.8	2.1
Switzerland	3.2	2.0
Less Developed Countries		
South Korea	8.9	6.3
Thailand	8.3	5.0
Turkey	6.0	3.5
Kenya	6.9	3.3
Sudan	6.3	3.0
Guatemala	5.6	2.5
Pakistan	5.4	1.9
Peru	4.8	1.7
Indonesia	3.0	0.4
Haiti	0.7	−1.3

Source: U.N. Statistical Yearbook.

figures, on the other hand, tell us more about the growth of national economic power or military power.

International Comparisons

American economic growth has been respectable but not really outstanding compared with that of other nations. Exhibit 7.2 shows average annual growth rates for a selected group of countries during the 1960s. About half of these are countries that did better than the United States in per capita terms, and half are countries that did worse.

The champion of the growth league, as the table shows, is Japan. Not only did it benefit from a high absolute rate of growth, but also from a fairly stable population, so that per capita growth was high too. Some less developed countries such as Thailand and South Korea, had absolute growth rates nearly as high as Japan. However, their populations grew rapidly so that per capita income did not grow as fast.

Among the fully industrialized countries on our list, the United States ranks a bit lower than most in terms of the growth of per capita GNP. The differences in growth rates were sufficient to bring living standards in most of these countries gradually closer to those in the United States.

The range of growth rates is much wider among the less developed countries than among the industrialized countries. Some of the poor nations did quite respectably in the decade covered by the table, but most dropped farther behind the rich. In every country on the list, population growth was more rapid than in the developed countries. This shows up in the dif-

Country	Per Capita Income in Terms of Purchasing Power, Percent of U.S. Level, 1970
Kenya	5.7
India	7.1
Colombia	15.9
Hungary	40.3
Italy	45.8
Great Britain	60.3
Japan	61.5
West Germany	74.7
France	75.0
United States	100.00

Source: Irving B. Kravis et al., *A System of International Comparisons of Gross Product and Purchasing Power* (Baltimore: Johns Hopkins, 1975). Published for the World Bank by The Johns Hopkins University Press, © 1975.

EXHIBIT 7.3

International comparisons of living standards

Direct comparisons of per capita GNP show living standards in many Western countries and Japan to be very close to those in the United States. This set of figures attempts to correct GNP comparisons by taking the actual purchasing power of income in various countries into account. In terms of real purchasing power, the United States still appeared to have a lead over other wealthy countries in 1970.

ference between the good absolute rates of growth and the disappointing per capita rates. We shall discuss the special problems of economic growth in the less developed countries in Chapter 35 of this book.

Comparing Living Standards

Americans are used to thinking of themselves as the richest people in the world. Is this still the case, even though other nations have been growing faster in recent years? One set of figures suggests that the American lead in living standards has greatly diminished, if not disappeared completely. Direct comparisons of GNP per capita show West Germany at 94 percent of the United States, France at 81 percent, and Japan at 64 percent (an increase from just 40 percent five years earlier).

The trouble with figures like this is that GNP is not a very accurate guide to living standards. Recently, a group of economists at the University of Pennsylvania did a study comparing living standards in terms of the things people really consume.[1] They used a "market basket" of goods rather like that used in drawing up the consumer price index as a basis for their comparisons. The results are shown in Exhibit 7.3.

The University of Pennsylvania study contained a few surprises for people who were used to thinking in terms of GNP. For one thing, the study shows living standards in the most advanced Western European countries, such as France and West Germany, to still be much below those in the United States. For another, the new figures appear to put living standards in Japan equal to or even a little ahead of those in Great Britain. (As recently as 1950, they were something like a fourth of the British level.) Finally, the new figures make the poorest countries shown in Exhibit 7.3, Kenya and India, look a little less poor than do straight GNP comparisons. On a GNP basis, 1970 living standards in Kenya would have been only 3.2 percent of those in the United States instead of 5.7 percent. Those in India would have been only 2.3 percent instead of 7.1 percent.

[1]Irving B. Kravis et al., *A System of International Comparisons of Gross Product and Purchasing Power* (Baltimore: Johns Hopkins, 1975).

EXHIBIT 7.4

The process of economic growth

Economic growth can be represented as an outward expansion of the production possibilities frontier. In any one year, getting more "guns" means giving up some "butter," as in a movement from B to A. Over time, however, growth could give us more of both "guns" and "butter," as in a movement from A to C, D, and E.

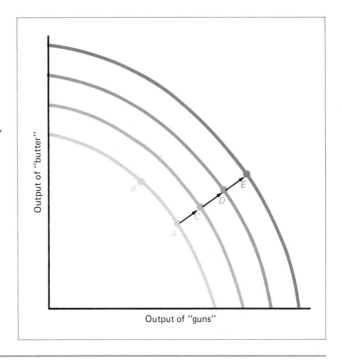

Actual and Potential Growth

Growth and Production Possibilities

The production possibilities frontier can give us some important insights into economic growth. Resources and technology limit production possibilities at any one time. Once this year's production possibilities are fully exploited, we must give up some of one thing to get more of another. Over time, though, resources and technology change. The frontier expands and we can have a little more of everything if we wish.

Exhibit 7.4 shows how the process of economic growth looks in these terms. We imagine an economy in which only two goods are produced: "guns" and "butter." In any one year, more of one good can be produced only at the opportunity cost of producing less of the other. Economic choice is limited to movements along the frontier, as from point A to point B. Over time, though, economic growth moves the frontier outward. New technology and new productive resources provide the opportunity to produce more of one good while also expanding output of the other. As growth proceeds, we might move, if we wished, from point A to C, and eventually to D and E and beyond.

Actual and Potential Output

There is just one hitch. In order actually to be on the production possibilities frontier in any year, all available resources must by fully used. If some go to waste, output will be less than it could be. The economy will fall below the frontier.

This creates a problem for measuring the rate of economic growth. It turns out that we have two reasons why real GNP could change from one year to the next. One reason is that the production possibilities frontier

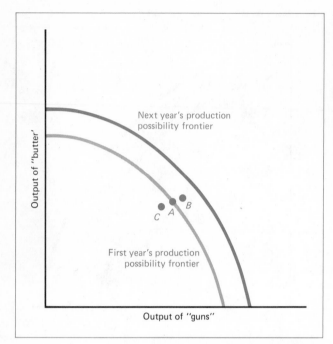

EXHIBIT 7.5
Growth and resource utilization
In order actually to be on the production possibility frontier in any year, all available resources must be put to efficient use. This figure shows that growth of potential output (represented by the outward shift of the frontier) need not bring an equivalent growth of actual output. The economy could move from A only to B, or even to C as the frontier expanded if at the same time the proportion of resources actually employed fell.

could expand. The other is that the proportion of available resources that are put to efficient use could change.

Consider Exhibit 7.5. In one year, the economy might be at point A, with all production possibilities fully utilized. In the next year, investment, new technology, or new resource discoveries might shift the production possibilities frontier outward as shown, but at the same time, actual use of resources might decline. With many resources idle, the economy could end up at point B, with only a little real growth, or even at point C, with a fall in real output.

Economists call the level of output that the economy would achieve if it were on its production possibility frontier **potential output** to distinguish it from the actual level of real output as measured in the national income accounts. As Exhibit 7.5 shows, potential output can grow faster than actual output. Potential and actual output can even move in opposite directions. In the long run, changes in potential output determine the rate of economic growth, but this need not be true in the short run.

Okun's Law

We learned how actual real output was measured in Chapter 6. For many purposes, it is useful to be able to measure potential output too. The standard way of measuring potential output is to use a simple rule of thumb called **Okun's law.** Okun's law tells us that the difference between actual and potential output in any year depends on how fully the economy's labor resources are employed. If labor is not fully employed, there is said to be an **output gap** between actual and potential GNP. In numerical terms, Okun's law says that for each percentage point by which the unemployment rate differs from full employment, there will be an output gap of 3.2 percent.

Potential Output (potential real GNP) The level of output that the economy could in principle achieve if it were operating on the production possibilities frontier. Potential output can be estimated from actual real output using Okun's law.

Okun's Law A rule of thumb that says that for each percentage point by which the unemployment rate rises above the "full employment" benchmark (traditionally taken to be 4 percent measured unemployment), actual output will fall below potential output by about 3 percent.

Output Gap The difference between actual real GNP and potential real GNP in any year.

Arthur Okun is one of the best known of a generation of "new economists" who dominated economic policy making during the Kennedy and Johnson administrations of the 1960s. In 1961, the young Associate Professor left Yale to join the "New Frontier" as a staff economist on the President's Council of Economic Advisors. In 1964, he became a full member of the Council, and eventually, in 1968–9, was its chairman. When Johnson left office, Okun stayed in Washington as a Senior Fellow of the Brookings Institution, a position that permitted him to combine research with active public affairs involvement.

Okun's name is perhaps most widely heard in connection with his famous "law" relating changes in unemployment to changes in real national product. This noteworthy empirical generalization was first formulated in a paper, "Potential GNP, Its Measurement and Significance," written for the American Statistical Association in 1962. In this paper, Okun tried to answer the question of how much output the economy could produce under conditions of full employment. Because of his concern for "the enormous social cost of idle resources," he found this question a central one for economic policy.

At the time Okun was on the Council of Economic Advisors, "growthmanship" was at its height in the economics profession. Okun saw rapid economic growth as crucial to avoiding the "waste and extravagance" of unemployment. "The economy loses ground if it stands still," he wrote. "Unless the growth of output keeps pace with our ever-expanding potential, the unemployment rate tends to rise. The nation needs continually to set new records in production and sales. Its economy needs to grow bigger and better than ever before—because its labor force, capital stock, technology, and managerial and organizational resources are always getting bigger and better."

Are Okun's words the echo of a naively optimistic era now past, or do they represent a lesson yet to be learned? The issue is far from settled, and Okun himself is still vigorously involved in the debate.

Arthur Okun (1928–)

The original formulation of Okun's law used a measured unemployment rate of 4 percent as its "full employment" benchmark. That means that for an unemployment rate of 5 percent, actual output would be 3.2 percent below its potential, for an unemployment rate of 6 percent it would be 6.4 percent below potential, and so forth. Knowing actual real GNP and the unemployment rate for any year, then, we can calculate potential GNP. Exhibit 7.6 shows actual GNP, potential GNP, and the output gap for the American economy from 1950 to 1975.

There are some difficulties in using 4 percent unemployment as the "full employment" benchmark. On the one hand, it seems more logical for zero unemployment to be the benchmark. That would avoid the awkward matter of having actual GNP being higher than potential GNP in years when unemployment is less than 4 percent, so that the output gap is negative. On the other hand, many economists now argue that 4 percent is too low a level to use as a benchmark. For various reasons, it is said, unemployment tends to be around 5 percent even when the economy is functioning as well as we can normally expect it to. The whole issue of just what "full employment" means will be taken up in some detail in Chapter 15. For now, we can stick with Okun's original 4 percent benchmark, for the sake of tradition if nothing else.

One peculiarity of Okun's law needs additional explanation. Why is it that output is so sensitive to unemployment? If 1 percent more people go to work, why should output rise by more than 1 percent?

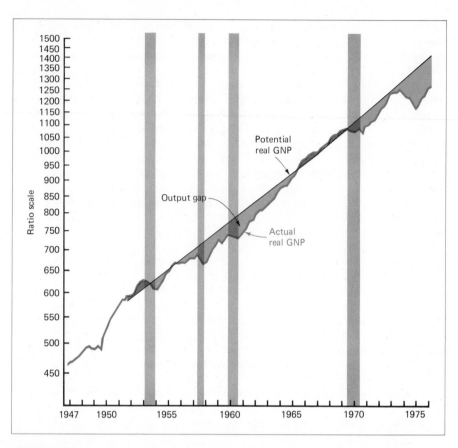

EXHIBIT 7.6

Growth of actual and potential GNP in the American economy

According to Okun's law, there is an output gap between actual and potential real GNP whenever the unemployment rate is above its "full employment" benchmark. In drawing this figure, full employment is considered to mean 4 percent measured unemployment. In some years unemployment was below 4 percent, so the output gap was negative.

The easy answer is that that is just the way it happens. Okun's law is not based on any deep economic theory. It is just a rule of thumb based on what has usually been seen to happen in the past.

A slightly closer look, though, shows us a little of what lies behind the high-powered effect of a change in unemployment. For one thing, the unemployment rate is measured as a percentage of people who are "in the labor force." Roughly speaking, the labor force means those people who have a job or who are looking for one.[2] When times are bad, some people do not even bother to look. They withdraw from the labor force. When things begin to look up, then, we find not only that the employed percentage of the labor force grows, but that the labor force itself grows as formerly discouraged workers reenter the market. The number of employed persons thus grows faster than the measured unemployment rate falls.

A further reason for the high-powered effect of changes in unemployment is "labor hoarding." When business turns down, firms do not always

[2]See Chapter 15 for a full discussion of how unemployment and the labor force are measured.

lay off every nonessential worker. Instead, they cut back overtime work, or let workers double up on jobs, or keep them on to do odd bits of work that do not have very high priority. That way, the firms know that when business turns up again, the workers they need will be right at hand. Output can be expanded without new hiring just by putting the existing labor force back to work more productively. Because productivity per worker rises during an upturn, output expands more than in proportion to the expansion of number of people at work.

Sources of Potential Economic Growth

Actual economic growth from year to year, we have seen, need not reflect changes in real economic potential. Over the long run, though, it is growth of potential that counts. Putting year-to-year changes in employment aside, then, what are the sources of the long-run growth of potential output?

Population and Productivity

As a start, we can identify two major sources of long-run economic growth. These are growth of the working population and growth of output per worker.

If we want to talk about the growth of per capita income, it is growth of output per worker that really counts. Some per capita gains can be realized by putting a higher percentage of the population to work, but sooner or later this reaches a limit. Normally, increasing the absolute size of the population without changing the proportion of people who work will not improve per capita income. In fact, many less developed countries of the world are so short on capital and natural resources that population growth actually detracts from the growth of per capita income. Let us put population growth aside, then, and look at the sources of the growth of output per worker.

Growth of Knowledge

The growth of knowledge is the greatest source of economic growth in the long run. We often tend to think of whole periods of growth in terms of one or two key inventions. When we think of the Industrial Revolution in England, we think of the steam engine. When we think of growth in nineteenth-century America, the railroad comes to mind. In the twentieth century, first the automobile and then the computer have led the way.

New technology is not the only important form of new knowledge. Changes in business organization also play a big role. The modern corporation and the assembly line are cases in point. Future growth will very likely see still more organizational changes, for example, the spread of worker participation in business decisions.

Capital Accumulation

Another leading source of economic growth is capital accumulation. More tools and equipment enable each worker to produce more per hour. Drainage and fencing allow farmers to grow more on each acre of land. What is more, most new knowledge needs to be embodied in new capital goods before it can be put to work.

Growth by capital accumulation involves a trade-off between present and future living standards. We know that gross national product is composed of consumption, investment, and government purchases. To raise the rate of capital accumulation, we must save and invest more. That means that there will be less left over for private consumption and government purchases. In return for giving those things up now, though, the added investment will make output grow faster. In the future, we can have more consumption and government purchases than we could have if we saved less now.

We can be grateful to our ancestors that they saved and invested as much as they did. The high living standards we enjoy today are built in large part on the capital they piled up for us. Does this mean that we should make an effort now to save more than we do for the sake of future generations? That is not an easy question to answer. Some economists point out that Americans invest only a very small part of national product compared with other advanced countries. This is one reason for our slightly slower rate of growth. Others argue, though, that building more machines and factories just means that we shall run out of natural resources sooner, and have more future pollution. According to this view, we should create less new capital, not more. We shall return to this complex issue later in the chapter.

Human Capital

Output also grows when education and job training raise the quality of the labor force. Economists refer to this source of growth as the accumulation of **human capital.** In what way is education or job training like building new tools or factories? The main point of similarity is that education and job training involve the same sort of trade-off between the present and the future as does investment in physical capital. People who stay off the job market in the present to finish school or learn new job skills give up earning power or consumption in the present. In return, they hope to earn more and have a higher standard of living in the future.

Human Capital A name for the productive potential of an individual person. The term calls attention to the fact that this productive potential can be increased by "investing" in education or job training.

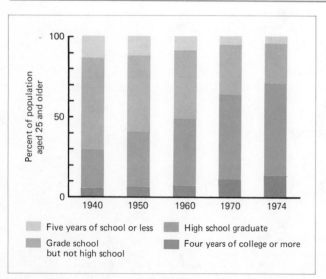

Education as an indicator of the growth of human capital in the American economy

Formal education is a very important part of investment in human capital. Since 1940, the average education level attained in the United States has increased very substantially. The proportion of the population with a high school education or better has increased two-and-a-half-fold, and the proportion with four years of college or more has tripled.

Source: Statistical Abstract of the United States, 1975.

The amount of investment in human capital in the American economy has been enormous. Exhibit 7.7 gives an idea of what has been achieved since 1940.

Relative Importance of Sources of Growth

With so many sources of economic growth available, there is more than one way to grow. In some countries, growth has been built largely on the discovery of new natural resources and the cultivation of new land. Other countries have grown by the sheer effort of investing an enormous proportion of current output. The following case study gives an idea of the relative importance of various sources of growth for our own economy.

CASE 7.1
Sources of U.S. Economic Growth[3]

The best-known attempt to measure the sources of U.S. economic growth is that of Edward F. Denison. His study covers the period 1929 to 1969. The American economy grew at an average annual rate of 3.3 percent during these years. In the second half of the period, 1948–1969, the rate of growth was a bit faster, at 3.85 percent per year. Exhibit 7.8 presents Denison's estimates of the relative importance of various sources of economic growth for the time span his study covered.

The most important source of growth throughout the period was the growth of knowledge. Denison was not able to measure this item directly. He made direct measurements of the other sources of growth and assumed that all growth that could not otherwise be explained came from advances in knowledge.

The first of the items that could be measured directly is what Denison calls "more work done." This includes the effects of population growth, changes in hours worked per week, and changes in the composition of the work force by age and sex. Next comes the accumulation of capital. Some people find the contribution of new capital to be surprisingly small in view of the importance sometimes given to this source of growth in theoretical discussions. The growth of human capital was almost as important as that of physical capital when the whole forty years are taken into account. Since World War II, though, this item has been less important.

These four items together can be said to have brought about an outward shift of the production possibility frontier. The rest of the economic growth during the period under study came from two sources. One was the more efficient use of available factors of production. A major shift of surplus labor from agriculture to industry played a big role here. The other source of growth from 1929 to 1969 was a small reduction in the unemployment rate.

[3]Based on Edward F. Denison, *Accounting for U.S. Economic Growth, 1929–69* (Washington, D.C.: Brookings Institution, 1974).

EXHIBIT 7.8
Sources of U.S. economic growth
This table shows the relative importance of various souces of economic growth for the American economy. The first four items can be considered to account for the expansion of the production possibility frontier. The remaining part of economic growth comes from fuller and more efficient use of resources, which has moved the economy closer to the frontier.

Source	Percent of Growth Rate 1929–1969	Percent of Growth Rate 1948–1969
Advances in knowledge	31.1	34.1
More work done	28.7	23.9
Capital accumulation	15.8	21.6
Increased education	14.1	11.9
Other	10.3	8.5
Total	100.0	100.0

Source: Edward F. Denison, *Accounting for U.S. Economic Growth, 1929–69* (Washington, D.C.: Brookings Institution, 1974) © 1974 by the Brookings Institution, Washington, D.C.

Limits to Growth?

For many years, everyone thought economic growth was a good thing. The only debates about growth took place between people who thought that the present pace was good enough and those who wanted government action to increase the growth rate. Now things are different.

Today, the people who are satisfied with our record of growth and those who would like to step up the pace have been forced into a defensive alliance. On the other side are two groups. One is made up of people who think that further economic growth is impossible, or will soon be so. The other is made up of those who think that further growth may be possible, but who do not want it. Of course, some people belong to both groups, thinking that no significant future growth is possible, and also that to keep trying to grow anyway will just make things worse.

The growth debate raises some rather technical issues. Some of these will be discussed later in this book, in the chapters on pollution, resources, and economic development. The matter is important enough, so that it is worth giving at least an outline of the main issues here.

Growth Undesirable

Let us look first at the claim that we ought not to want further economic growth, whether it is possible or not. The heart of this argument is the perfectly valid proposition that GNP is not a measure of human welfare. The trouble, it is said, is that growth of GNP can be offset by a decline in the "quality of life." These fears can be expressed in the form of a parable:

Imagine a peaceful little country with a per capita GNP of $100. All of this is produced by the women, who work the fields in the morning and gossip in the afternoon. The men do nothing at all but sit around and play cards and drink tea all day. Suppose now that an enterprising foreign businessperson sets up a soap factory and puts all of the men to work. Each man can make $40 worth of soap per year. Previously there was no market for soap in this pastoral nation, but now the soap factory belches black coal smoke from its boilers and this soils everyone's curtains. The entire output of the soap factory is sold to local housewives who now spend all of their afternoons at the laundromat.

Question: What has happened to the GNP of this country? As any economist will tell you, it has gone up by 20 percent, to $120 per capita. Farm output has not fallen, and industrial production of $20 per capita has been added. Question: What has happened to the level of well-being of the people of this country? They have no more to eat than before. Their curtains are no cleaner than before. Yet they are working four times as long. They are, let us say, about one-quarter as well off as before.

Many people believe that this parable applies to the American economy. They are worried not only about pollution, but about other values as well that they think tend to be lost as growth continues. Rapid economic growth makes skills, and hence people, obsolete before their working lives are over. Economic growth crowds out green places and covers them with asphalt. It replaces the community life of the town with the anonymity of the city. In all these ways, growth is said to make life less worth living in ways for which more cars and toaster ovens do not fully compensate.

EXHIBIT 7.9

Pollution and economic growth

In any one year, there is a trade-off between cars and clean air. More cars make the air dirtier, whereas having fewer cars makes cleaner air possible. As the production possibility frontier moves outward, we can choose between two kinds of growth. We can make as many dirty new cars as possible, moving from *A* to *B*, if that is what we want. Alternatively, we can spend more on each car to make it run cleaner, and move from *A* to *C* instead.

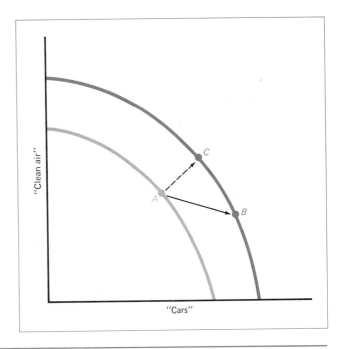

Separating the Issues

How valid is this "quality of life" argument? Are we really becoming worse off year by year, or is that just romanticism? It cannot be denied that economic growth is a *potential* threat to the quality of life. As it stands, though, the argument we have given is misleading because it confuses two issues. One issue has to do with the size of gross national product, and the other with its composition.

In Exhibit 7.9, we have used the production possibility frontier to help separate these two issues. The diagram shows an economy in which the two goods produced are called "clean air" and "cars" rather than "guns" and "butter." In any one year, there is a trade-off between the two goods. More cars make the air less clean. Making fewer cars (or spending more money on each car to make them run cleaner) allows us to have better air.

As technology improves and as we accumulate more capital, the production possibility frontier shifts outward. If the actual growth path of the economy is from point *A* to point *B*, people will complain that the quality of life has deteriorated. It is not really economic growth that is to blame though. Instead, the problem is the composition of output that has been chosen. Instead of moving from *A* to *B* by producing as many new dirty cars as possible, we could have grown along the path from *A* to *C*. That would mean fewer cars, each more carefully built to cause less pollution. Growth *could* bring us more cars *and* more clean air if we chose to go that way.

Pollution is a serious problem. It cannot be brushed aside. Still, it is wrong to blame pollution on economic growth. To stop growth in order to stop pollution would be to throw out the baby with the bath water. Controlling pollution requires policies to encourage the correct composition of national product, not policies to control its size. We shall take a look at a number of such policies in Chapter 33.

Growth Impossible

There is little point in arguing about the direction of growth if growth is impossible. Is it? Exhibit 7.8, which gave us the sources of past growth, can help us to think about future growth too. Turn back to it for a moment.

Let us begin with some optimistic observations. The greatest source of growth in the past has been the growth of knowledge. We can be pretty certain that the growth of knowledge will continue in the future. Now and then, of course, someone denies this. It is said that at the end of the last century, someone suggested that we close the patent office, because all the important inventions seemed by then to have been made.

Next in order of optimism, we turn to human capital. The growth of human capital does not use up any nonrenewable natural resources, and it is hard to see why it should not continue. It may be, though, that further increases in educational levels will not add as much as before to measured economic output. There may always be some jobs that people cannot do any better with a college degree than they can without one. Perhaps we should put more faith in education as a way of improving the quality of life than as a source of future growth of GNP.

For the moment, let us ignore the "more work done" and "other" categories as sources of future economic growth. We cannot be sure that they will continue to contribute to growth, but there is no real reason to think that they pose limits to growth either. We shall assume that they are neutral.

Resource Depletion

Now we come to the strong point of the growth pessimists. This is the depletion of nonrenewable sources of energy and raw materials. Notice that Denison did not list discoveries of new resources as a major source of growth in the past. In the future, say the pessimists, we shall have to start putting a "natural resources" line in the sources-of-growth table. The entry we put on that line will be a big fat minus, and eventually it will be big enough to cancel out all the pluses.

There are two reasons why the depletion of resources is said to limit growth. First, as the best mines and oil fields are exhausted, more and more work, research, and investment is needed to keep a steady supply of raw materials coming out. Second, it is said that resource depletion puts a brake on capital accumulation. There will not be enough of the right metals to build more machines, or enough energy to dig deeper mines, or enough oil to produce plastic substitutes for the metals we run out of. Without the ability to build new capital equipment, it is said, new knowledge cannot be put to use, and the whole growth machine will grind to a halt.

Separating the Issues Again

There is no doubt some truth to the argument that depletion of resources will make problems for future economic growth. The question is whether we shall be able to get around those problems. We cannot come up with a proper answer to that question unless we once again separate the issue of the growth of output from that of the composition of output.

The great weakness in the argument of the growth pessimists is that

EXHIBIT 7.10
Growth and resource depletion
In this diagram, "cars" stand for all goods that use up large amounts of nonrenewable resources, and "watches" stand for goods that pack a lot of value into a small physical package. As the production possibility frontier expands, growth can continue in value terms even though growth measured in tons of output might fall.

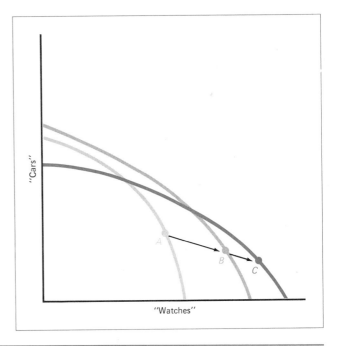

they think of growth in physical rather than economic terms. Resource depletion does place a limit on physical growth. If airplanes are made out of aluminum, and if we run out of aluminum, then we just cannot build any more aluminum airplanes. But economic growth is not measured in tons of aluminum or numbers of airplanes. It is measured in terms of value. The way to beat the physical limits to growth, then, is to switch the composition of output in favor of things that pack a lot of value into small physical packages.

Let us once again use a production possibility frontier to show what we mean. In Exhibit 7.10, we consider an economy with two goods called "cars" and "watches." "Cars" stand for the kind of goods that do face real resource limits. "Watches" stand for goods that face no serious physical resource constraint.

As this car-watch economy expands over the years its production possibility frontier shifts. When the frontier reaches the third position shown, we see that resource depletion actually cuts the maximum potential output of cars. All the time, though, GNP continues to grow as measured in value terms. The economy moves from A to B to C, with the composition of output shifting away from "cars" in favor of "watches."

What is true of consumer goods like cars and watches is also true of capital goods. Resource depletion may at some time stop us from building, say, any new uranium-fueled power stations. In other areas, though, the growth of knowledge shows us how to put more and more capital into smaller and smaller physical packages. The development of electronic computers is a striking case in point. It could well be that, say, putting special computer-controlled thermostats in our houses will make it possible to get along with fewer atomic power stations.

John Stuart Mill (1806–1873)

John Stuart Mill was in every respect one of the most brilliant and remarkable figures of the nineteenth century. Eldest son of the prominent economist and philosopher James Mill, John Stuart lived an extraordinary childhood. He began his study of classical Greek at the age of three. By eight, he was reading Plato's dialogues in the original, and teaching Latin to the younger members of the Mill family. His education in economics began at thirteen, under his father's tutorship, with a study of Adam Smith and the other classics.

This unusual upbringing was bound to produce a strong reaction sooner or later. In his early twenties, young Mill went through a spiritual crisis that led him to reject many of his father's ideas. About that time, he met Mrs. Harriet Taylor and began a long association with her. (Years later, after her husband's death, they were married.) Her ideas on feminism and socialism powerfully influenced Mill's thinking.

John Stuart Mill published his *Principles of Political Economy* in 1848. This work can be seen today as the high-water mark of the classical school, founded by Adam Smith three generations before. As a textbook and authority on economic questions, Mill's *Principles* stood unchallenged until Alfred Marshall transformed "political economy" into "economics" at the end of the century.

Mill's *Principles* is a work by no means limited to the narrowly technical side of economics. Mill always faced the broad social implications of economic theory squarely wherever they arose. For example, like other economists of the classical school, Mill believed there were not-too-distant limits to the process of economic growth. "At the end of the progressive state," he wrote, "lies the stationary state. All progress in wealth is but a postponement of this and all advance is an approach to it." Mill was not content, however, simply to describe the mechanics of growth and the technical properties of the stationary state. He wondered what a world without progress would really be like. His conclusions so clearly address the concerns of our own age that they are worth quoting at length:

> I cannot . . . regard the stationary state of capital and wealth with the unaffected aversion so generally manifested towards it by political economists of the old school. I am inclined to believe that it would be, on the whole, a very considerable improvement on our present condition. I confess I am not charmed with the ideal of life held out by those who think that the normal state of human beings is that of struggling to get on; that the trampling, crushing, elbowing, and treading on each other's heels, which form the existing type of social life, are the most desirable lot of human kind, or anything but the disagreeable symptoms of one of the phases of our industrial progress. . . .
>
> If the earth must lose that great portion of its pleasantries which it owes to things that the unlimited increase of wealth and population would extirpate from it, for the mere purpose of enabling it to support a larger, but not a better or happier population, I sincerely hope, for the sake of posterity, that they will be content to be stationary long before necessity compels them to.

Conclusions

What we have said should not be interpreted as establishing a case for unbounded optimism. Continued growth, we have claimed, is possible *if* the proper shifts in the composition of output are made, and made in time. We may even have to stretch our concept of the "composition of output" to include the way future growth is split between producing more human beings and producing higher living standards for a smaller total population. It is not hard to imagine ways that things *could* go wrong. In fact, the publicity that the prophets of doom get does a great service by calling such possibilities to our attention.

The interlocking issues of economic growth, population, resources, and environment are important ones, and we shall return to them in Part Five. We have said enough for the moment, though, to fit economic growth into our discussion of macroeconomics.

SUMMARY

1. Over the past century, the American economy has grown by nearly a factor of forty in terms of total real GNP, and nearly a factor of ten in terms of per capita GNP. American economic growth is still proceeding at a good rate, although many other economies are growing more rapidly still.

2. If resources are not fully employed, actual output is less than potential output. Okun's law is a simple rule of thumb that lets us put the relationship between unemployment and output more exactly. The law says that for each percentage point by which unemployment rises above its "full employment" benchmark, real GNP will decline by about 3 percent.

3. The major sources of economic growth, in order of their past importance in the American economy, are growth of knowledge, more work done, accumulation of capital, and increases in education. In other countries or at other times, the relative importance of these sources of growth may be quite different.

4. Many people now doubt that further economic growth is either possible or desirable. These growth pessimists base their arguments on some perfectly valid points. Many antigrowth arguments, however, involve a confusion between growth in the size of output and changes in the composition of output. Once these two issues are separated, it is open to us to conclude that further growth can still be a good thing, provided that such growth proceeds in the right direction.

DISCUSSION QUESTIONS

1. Is it possible with increased knowledge and technological know-how for an economy to be better off even if it does not produce any more goods and services? Explain.

2. Suppose that an economy were operating on its production possibilities frontier. What changes could be made to operate inside the frontier and still have full employment? Or is this impossible?

3. In what sense can you say that the education you are getting is an investment in human capital? What is meant by human capital?

4. What has human capital and investment in human capital got to do with the quality of life?

5. How would you go about comparing your standard of living with that of someone in a foreign country? With someone in another state? Can you simply compare incomes?

6. If people are to become better off, is it necessary that they become more productive? Explain.

7. If we were almost out of a particular resource, what would happen to the price of that resource? How might firms and consumers adjust to this increased scarcity?

CHAPTER 8
The Determinants of Planned Expenditure

What You Will Learn in This Chapter

The British economist John Maynard Keynes made aggregate demand a key element of his economic theory. Following his approach, our theory building begins by looking at the determinants of each separate component of aggregate demand. Consumption expenditure depends to a substantial extent on the level of national income. Planned investment expenditure depends on the rate of interest and on business expectations concerning the profitability of investment projects. Government purchases and net exports are determined by forces outside the scope of elementary economic theory, so they are treated as "givens" in our analysis.

For Review

Here are some important terms and concepts that will be put to use in this chapter. Be certain that you know them, or review them before proceeding.

Aggregate demand (Chapter 5)

Planned and unplanned investment (Chapter 5)

Relationships among gross national product, national income, personal income, and disposable income (Chapter 6)

In Chapter 5 we introduced the circular flow and the ideas of aggregate supply and demand. In Chapter 6 we saw how national income accountants go about measuring the elements of the circular flow. We discovered how gross national product can be broken down into its separate components of consumption, investment, government purchases, and net exports. In Chapter 7 we saw how all these have grown with time. Now, finally, we are ready to put all these preliminary concepts and definitions to work and begin developing a *theory*. This theory will explain why national income and product are at one level rather than another in any particular year, and why they have their ups and downs over time.

Some Simplifications

In economics, theory building always begins by making some simplifications so that we may concentrate on essentials. One simplification that we shall employ throughout our discussion of macroeconomic theory is the assumption that there are no indirect business taxes, capital consumption allowance, or statistical discrepancy. Getting rid of these elements of the national income accounts greatly simplifies our discussion. Gross national product, net national product, and national income once again become equal by definition, as they were in the simplified circular flow diagrams of Chapter 5.

A second useful simplification that we shall use throughout our discussion is to omit undistributed corporate profits. With neither indirect business taxes nor undistributed corporate profits, personal income will be equal to national income minus net taxes. The term *net taxes,* as in Chapter 5, means all taxes (personal income tax, social insurance contributions, and corporate profits tax) minus all transfer payments.

Nominal and Real Values

Another way in which we shall simplify our theory building is to begin by concentrating our attention on *nominal* values of national income, consumption, and so forth. This is simply a matter of taking one thing at a time. In this chapter and the next five, we shall be trying to understand why nominal national income is, say, $1.5 billion in some year rather than some other value. Then, in Chapters 14–17, we shall turn to the question of why changes in nominal income sometimes take the form of changes in prices rather than changes in real output.

In these early chapters, in which our discussion will be entirely in terms of nominal values, we shall not repeat the term "nominal" every time we mention consumption, investment, income, or whatever. You should keep in mind, though, that we mean nominal values in every case unless we explicitly say something to the contrary.

Keynesian Economics

As we begin our discussion of macroeconomic theory, we are entering the heartland of what is known as Keynesian economics, named after the British economist John Maynard Keynes. It is no exaggeration to say that his writings revolutionized macroeconomic thought. Although many of Keynes' particular conclusions have been challenged by contemporary economists, the fact that these challenges occur within his basic theoretical framework attests to his lasting influence. Keynes' ideas underlie all of modern macroeconomic theory as well as the contents of this book, even in places where we do not pause to acknowledge them specifically.

Keynes made the concept of *aggregate demand* a key element of his theory. He taught that macroeconomic analysis should begin by asking what determines each of the separate types of planned expenditure that make up aggregate demand: consumption, planned investment, government purchases, and net exports. Let us follow his plan by discussing each of these in turn.

Consumption

Consumption and Income

Keynes' theory of consumption expenditure was novel and very simple. Both common sense and experience, he said, suggest that in general and on

John Maynard Keynes was born into economics. His father, John Neville Keynes, was a lecturer in economics and logic at Cambridge University. John Maynard began his own studies at Cambridge with an emphasis on mathematics and philosophy. His abilities soon so impressed Alfred Marshall, however, that the distinguished teacher urged him to concentrate on economics. In 1908, after Keynes had finished his studies and done a brief stint in the civil service, Marshall offered him a lectureship in economics at Cambridge, which he accepted.

Keynes is remembered above all for his *General Theory of Employment, Interest, and Money,* published in 1936, although that was by no means his first important work. Keynes' reputation as the outstanding economist of his generation lay in the departure from classical and neoclassical theory he made there. It is hardly necessary to say much about the substance of Keynes' *General Theory* in these paragraphs, because they are extensively discussed in every modern textbook on economics. It will be enough to say that its major features were a theory boldly drawn in terms of broad macroeconomic aggregates, and a policy position tending toward activism and interventionism.

Keynes was no "narrow" economist. He was an honored member not only of the British academic upper class, but also of Britain's highest financial, political, diplomatic, administrative, and even artistic circles. He was intimately involved with the colorful "Bloomsbury set" of London's literary-Bohemian world. He was a friend of Virginia Woolf, E. M. Forster, and Lytton Strachey, and in 1925, married the ballerina Lydia Lopokovia. He was a dazzling success at whatever he turned his hand to, from mountain climbing to financial speculation. As a speculator, he made an enormous fortune for himself, and as Bursar of Kings College, he turned an endowment of £30,000 into one of £380,000.

In even the briefest discussion of Keynes, it would be unforgivable not to give his most famous quotation. Writing in the *General Theory,* he pronounced that "the ideas of economists and political philosophers, both when they are right and when they are wrong, are more powerful than is commonly understood. Indeed the world is ruled by little else. Practical men, who believe themselves to be quite exempt from any intellectual influences, are usually the slaves of some defunct economist. Madmen in authority, who hear voices in the air, are distilling their frenzy from some academic scribbler of a few years back. . . . There are not many who are influenced by new theories after they are twenty-five or thirty years of age, so that the ideas which civil servants and politicians and even agitators apply to current events are not likely to be the newest."

Was Keynes issuing a warning here? Whether he had any such thing in mind or not, his words, forty years later, have become one of the great ironies of the history of economic ideas.

John Maynard Keynes
(1883–1946)

---

the average, people increase their consumption as their income increases, but not by as much as the full increase in their income.

A look at the historical record of consumption and income in the United States does in fact reveal this pattern. In Exhibit 8.1, consumption is measured on the vertical axis and disposable income on the horizontal axis. The points on the graph show levels of consumption and disposable income for years from 1929 to 1975. By passing a straight line through as many points as possible, we can see how the level of consumption expenditure varied on average as the level of disposable income varied. Notice that the straight line passes above the points representing war years because rationing and unavailability of certain consumer goods made consumption artificially low.

To make Exhibit 8.1 easier to read, we have drawn in a 45° reference line. The point for any year when consumption and income are equal will

EXHIBIT 8.1

Income and consumption in the United States

The figure shows that since 1929, consumption has increased as disposable income has increased. The 45° reference line helps in interpreting the figure. The points for years when income and consumption were exactly equal fall on the 45° line. In years when the consumption point was below the reference line, the distance between the point and the reference line equals saving.

fall exactly on this line. Since 1939, the points showing actual consumption lie below the reference line. The vertical gap between the reference line and the consumption points is equal to the difference between disposable income and consumption. As we saw in Chapter 5, this difference is saving. In some years in the 1930s the consumption points lie slightly above the 45° reference line. In those years negative saving, or **dissaving,** occurred. Households consumed more than their disposable income either by using up past savings or by borrowing. The illustration shows that since 1929, as disposable income has risen, both consumption and saving have risen.

Consumption Schedule

Keynes suggested that the relationship between income and consumption was deeply rooted in human nature. We shall give the name **consumption schedule** to any table or graph showing the way nominal consumption expenditure varies when nominal income varies, other things being equal.[1] The straight line drawn through the various points in Exhibit 8.1 can be referred to as a historical consumption schedule for the American economy. In our theory building, we shall use a simplified numerical example instead of actual historical data. This simplified consumption schedule is shown in Exhibit 8.2.

Autonomous Consumption

According to Exhibit 8.2, when disposable income is zero, consumption is $150. This indicates that people plan to consume some minimum quantity of goods and services regardless of their disposable income. We shall call this minimum level of planned consumption expenditure ($150 in our example) **autonomous consumption.** In the graphical representation of the consumption schedule, autonomous consumption is equal to the height of the point at which the consumption schedule intersects the vertical axis. Even if people do not have enough current income to finance the autonomous consumption they plan to undertake, they will consume anyway by drawing on past savings or borrowing.

It should be emphasized that autonomous consumption is autonomous only in the sense that it does not depend on the level of disposable income. This does not mean that the level of autonomous consumption is independent of other economic influences. The consumption schedule includes an "other things being equal" clause, and changes in these other things can change autonomous consumption. More on this shortly.

Marginal Propensity to Consume

Look now at columns (3), (4), and (5) in the Exhibit 8.2a. The numbers in these columns show that whenever household income increases, some of the additional income is devoted to additional consumption above and beyond autonomous consumption. The fraction of each added dollar of disposable income that goes to added consumption is called the **marginal propensity to consume.**

We see, for example, that a $100 increase in income, from $500 to $600, raises consumption by $50, from $400 to $450. The ratio 50/100 = 0.5 is the value of the marginal propensity to consume for this numerical example.

In geometric terms, the marginal propensity to consume is equal to the slope of the consumption schedule. In Exhibit 8.2b, a horizontal movement

Dissaving Negative saving; the difference between disposable income and consumption expenditure when consumption exceeds disposable income.

Consumption Schedule A graphical or numerical representation of the way in which nominal consumption expenditure varies as nominal income varies, other things being equal.

Autonomous Consumption The level of consumption shown by a consumption schedule for a zero disposable income level.

Marginal Propensity to Consume The fraction of each added dollar of disposable income that goes to added consumption.

---

[1]The term "consumption function" is also widely used, especially in mathematically oriented writings.

Exhibit 8.2a

(1) Nominal Disposable Income	(2) Nominal Consumption Expenditure	(3) Change in Income	(4) Change in Consumption	(5) Marginal Propensity to Consume
$ 0	$150			
		$100	$50	0.5
100	200			
		100	50	0.5
200	250			
		100	50	0.5
300	300			
		100	50	0.5
400	350			
		100	50	0.5
500	400			
		100	50	0.5
600	450			
		100	50	0.5
700	500			
		100	50	0.5
800	550			
		100	50	0.5
900	600			
		100	50	0.5
1,000	650			
		100	50	0.5
1,100	700			
		100	50	0.5
1,200	750			
		100	50	0.5
1,300	800			
		100	50	0.5
1,400	850			

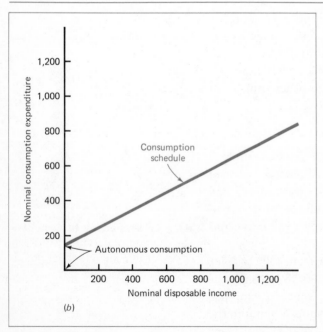

(b)

EXHIBIT 8.2

The consumption schedule (simplified example)

The table and graph both show a simple numerical example of the relationship between disposable income and consumption. The level of autonomous consumption is shown on the graph by the height of the intersection of the consumption schedule with the vertical axis. The slope of the consumption schedule is equal to the marginal propensity to consume.

Exhibit 8.3a

(1) Nominal Disposable Income	(2) Nominal Consumption Expenditure	(3) Nominal Saving
$ 0	$150	$ −150
100	200	−100
200	250	− 50
300	300	0
400	350	50
500	400	100
600	450	150
700	500	200
800	550	250
900	600	300
1,000	650	350
1,100	700	400
1,200	750	450
1,300	800	500
1,400	850	550

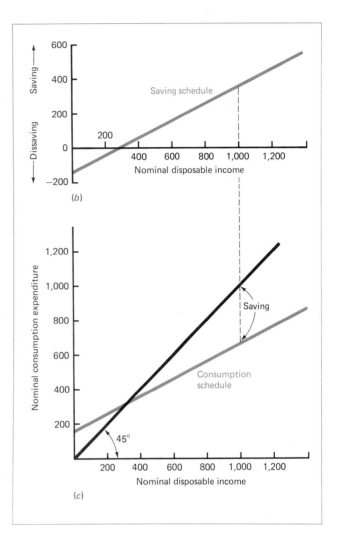

EXHIBIT 8.3

The saving schedule

The saving schedule shows the relationship between saving and income. In the table, saving is found by subtracting consumption from disposable income. In part b of the exhibit, the saving schedule is given in graphical form. It could be constructed directly from the numbers in column (3) of the table, or alternatively, from the consumption schedule shown in part c.

of $100 in disposable income corresponds to a vertical movement of $50 in planned consumption as we move along the consumption schedule. The slope of the consumption schedule is thus 50/100 = 0.5, the same as the marginal propensity to consume.

Saving Schedule

Once we know the level of consumption corresponding to each level of disposable income, we can easily calculate the level of saving that corresponds to each level of disposable income. The relationship between saving and income is called the **saving schedule.** The saving schedule is given in numerical form in Exhibit 8.3a. The numbers in this table are calculated by subtracting consumption from disposable income.

The saving schedule is shown in geometric form in Exhibit 8.3b. This figure can be constructed simply by plotting the numbers from column (3) of the table. Alternatively, the saving schedule can be derived directly from the consumption schedule, which is reproduced as Exhibit 8.3c. The level

Saving Schedule A graphical or numerical representation of the way in which nominal saving varies as nominal income varies, other things being equal.

of saving corresponding to each level of disposable income is equal to the vertical distance between the consumption schedule and the 45° reference line.

In our numerical example, a dissaving of $150 occurs when disposable income is zero. Saving at zero disposable income is the negative of autonomous consumption. At a $300 level of disposable income there is a "break-even point" at which neither saving nor dissaving occurs. Below that point, consumption exceeds disposable income, and above that point, consumption falls short of disposable income.

Marginal Propensity to Save

Marginal Propensity to Save The fraction of each added dollar of disposable income that is not consumed.

We use the term **marginal propensity to save** to mean the fraction of each additional dollar of disposable income that is not consumed. Because all disposable income is, by definition, either saved or consumed, it follows that the marginal propensity to save (MPS) is equal to one minus the marginal propensity to consume (MPC):

$$MPS = 1 - MPC$$

In geometric terms, the marginal propensity to save is equal to the slope of the saving schedule.

Long and Short Run

Now let us compare the hypothetical consumption schedule of Exhibit 8.2 with the observed historical record of income and consumption shown in Exhibit 8.1. Both of these diagrams are reproduced in Exhibit 8.4 for easy comparison. In Exhibit 8.4a we have drawn a straight line through most of the consumption points given by United States data. This line has constant slope of about 0.9, indicating that on the average, about 90 percent of each year's increase in disposable income went into consumption. This implies a marginal propensity to consume of about 0.9. Furthermore, we notice that this line passes through the origin of the graph. If income were to fall to zero, it appears that planned consumption would also fall to zero. The historical data do not seem to include any allowance for autonomous consumption.

The relationship between income and consumption indicated by historical data is quite different from the relationship indicated by the hypothetical consumption schedule shown in Exhibit 8.4b. The latter displays a much lower marginal propensity to consume and a substantial positive level of autonomous consumption. Which type of relationship should we use in constructing our theories?

It turns our that one type of relationship is appropriate when dealing with long-run changes in disposable income, and the other when dealing with short-run changes. We have already seen that plotting historical data over a forty-year period creates a steep line passing through the origin. In contrast, if we were to look at data describing consumption behavior over short periods—say changes in consumption within a year, as revealed by quarterly data—we would observe a flatter consumption function and substantial autonomous consumption. (This latter type of relationship is also revealed by so-called *cross-sectional data,* where the level of income of different individual households is measured for a particular year and associated with the level of consumption expenditure of each household.)

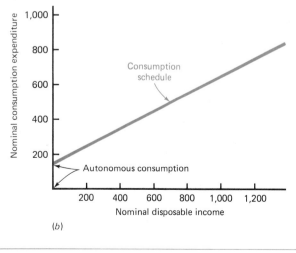

EXHIBIT 8.4

Long- and short-run consumption schedules

Actual U.S. data on income and consumption expenditures since 1929 indicate a long-run marginal propensity to consume of about .9, as shown in part *a* of this exhibit. The short-run consumption schedule for the U.S. economy has a lower marginal propensity to consume and a higher level of autonomous consumption, more like the hypothetical consumption schedule of part *b*, taken from our simplified numerical example.

Permanent Income

How can we account for the observed differences in consumption behavior as revealed by long- and short-run data? One ingenious explanation is known as the **permanent income hypothesis.** By *permanent income* we mean the average income that a person expects to receive in the intermediate future. The hypothesis is that people plan to increase their consumption by about $.90 for each $1.00 of additional permanent income they receive. In the short run, though, when people receive additional income they do not always know whether or not to consider the increase permanent. For example, if a person earned $200 more in the first quarter of 1974 than in the fourth quarter of 1973, $100 of that might be regarded as a permanent improvement in earning expectations but the other $100 might be considered a transitory increase in income, which was not likely to be repeated. The permanent income hypothesis assumes that people are not as likely to consume out of transitory increases in income, but instead tend to save all of such income for a "rainy day," when their income may temporarily be lower than their permanent income.

In addition to reconciling the differences between short-run and long-run behavior, the permanent income hypothesis also explains why cross-sectional observations of consumption behavior look more like short-run than long-run observations. Many households with a high measured income in a given year are fortunate in having a high transitory income, and their low consumption expenditure relative to measured income is really based on their lower levels of permanent income. At the same time, the relatively high consumption levels of households with low measured incomes can be explained by the fact that many households with low income in a given year actually have higher permanent income.

Because much of our discussion in later chapters will focus on short-run policies for economic stabilization, we shall use the short-run rather than the long-run consumption schedule in building our theory. There is no magic number that gives "the" proper marginal propensity to consume for all circumstances, but we shall use a value of 0.5 for the short-run marginal propensity to consume in our numerical examples.

Other Factors Affecting Consumption

The consumption schedule shows the relationship between nominal consumption expenditures and nominal income, other things being equal. If any of the "other things" change, the proportion of any given level of income that people devote to consumption can change. Among the other factors of possible importance to consumption are the following:

1. A change in the value of people's accumulated savings or wealth may have an influence on their consumption expenditure. It is thought that, other things being equal, people with a comfortable cushion of accumulated savings may spend more in relation to their current income than people with few financial reserves.
2. The state of consumer expectations can have a strong influence on consumer spending, especially in the short run. If people expect good times, they may spend more freely. If they are pessimistic about the immediate future, they may postpone major spending decisions, and save more than usual.

Permanent Income Hypothesis A hypothesis that reconciles a high long-run marginal propensity to consume with a low short-run marginal propensity to consume, by saying that people are likely to consume less out of transitory increases in income than out of those increases that they consider to be permanent.

3. Changes in the price level can affect the level of nominal expenditure associated with a given level of nominal income. Here we must distinguish between long-run and short-run effects. In the long run, a change in the price level will produce a proportional change in the nominal value of autonomous consumption. For example, in 1975 the purchasing power of the dollar was about half what it was in 1945. If people's consumption behavior had called for $150 of nominal autonomous consumption in 1945, they would have had to increase that to $300 in 1975 in order to maintain the real value of that level of autonomous consumption. In graphical terms, the price change would have produced an upward shift in the consumption schedule, so that it would intersect the vertical axis at $300 of nominal expenditure in 1975 if it had intersected at $150 in 1945.

In the short run, the relationship between price changes and consumption expenditure is far less certain. The problem is that inflation, and changes in the rate of inflation, may strongly affect consumer expectations. Inflation can also erode the real value of people's accumulated savings. The uncertain short-run effects of price changes may thus cause the consumption schedule to shift either upward or downward by an unpredictable amount.

With all of these factors at work affecting consumption, we cannot consider the exact shape or position of the consumption schedule to be unchanging. In an elementary discussion like the present one, where we put all the inconvenient features of reality out of sight in an "other things being equal" box, we run the risk of making consumer behavior seem more dependable and predictable than it really is.

Adjusting for Taxes

One more step is needed to get our consumption schedule completely ready for use in theory building. We must make an adjustment for taxes so that the consumption schedule can be expressed in terms of national income rather than in terms of disposable income. Remember that throughout our theoretical discussion, we are assuming that there are no indirect business taxes or undistributed corporate profits. That means that national income is simply equal to disposable personal income plus net taxes.

In adjusting the consumption schedule for taxes, we shall consider two separate cases. In the first case, illustrated by Exhibit 8.5, all taxes and transfers are of the **lump sum** form. That means that they do not change as income changes. Columns (3) and (4) of the table give the familiar consumption schedule in terms of disposable income, while columns (1) and (4) show the relationship between national income and consumption expenditure.

In the second case, illustrated in Exhibit 8.6, the government employs a personal income tax. Now the amount of tax collected does change as the level of national income changes. In constructing the table, we have assumed that everyone pays a straight 20 percent income tax, regardless of the amount of earnings. (The actual income tax is much more complicated, of course.) Again, columns (3) and (4) give the consumption schedule in terms of disposable income, and columns (1) and (4) give the consumption schedule in terms of national income.

Lump Sum Taxes   Taxes that do not vary as income varies.

EXHIBIT 8.5

National income and consumption with lump sum taxes

Lump sum taxes are taxes that do not change when the level of income changes. This table shows how the consumption schedule can be expressed either in terms of disposable income [columns (3) and (4)] or in terms of national income [columns (1) and (4)] for an economy where all taxes are of the lump sum variety. In the simple economy on which the table is based, there are no undistributed corporate profits or indirect business taxes, so that national income is equal to disposable personal income plus net taxes.

(1) Nominal National Income	(2) Nominal Net Taxes	(3) Nominal Disposable Income	(4) Nominal Consumption Expenditure	(5) Nominal Saving
$ 100	$100	$ 0	$150	$ −150
200	100	100	200	−100
300	100	200	250	− 50
400	100	300	300	0
500	100	400	350	50
600	100	500	400	100
700	100	600	450	150
800	100	700	500	200
900	100	800	550	250
1,000	100	900	600	300
1,100	100	1,000	650	350
1,200	100	1,100	700	400
1,300	100	1,200	750	450
1,400	100	1,300	800	500

Compare the two cases. With lump sum taxes, an additional dollar of national income results in an additional $.50 of consumption expenditure and an additional $.50 in saving. With an income tax, the additional dollar of national income results in an additional $.40 of consumption, an additional $.40 of saving, and an additional $.20 of net taxes. We might say that in the second case, there are two different marginal propensities to consume. The marginal propensity to consume national income (0.4) is lower than the marginal propensity to consume disposable income (0.5).

The U.S. government does make heavy use of the personal income tax, so the second of the two cases considered here is the more realistic. On the other hand, lump sum taxes simplify our job of theory building. In the chapters that follow, we shall use the simplifying assumption of lump sum taxes whenever possible. When it is important for questions of policy, though, we shall also discuss the effects of an income tax.

Investment Expenditure

Planned Investment and Aggregate Demand

The second major component of aggregate demand is planned investment expenditure. Planned investment, we recall, includes both fixed investment and planned inventory investment. Total investment, as measured in the national income accounts, includes planned investment plus

EXHIBIT 8.6

National income and consumption with a 20 percent income tax

With an income tax, net taxes rise as income increases. Each additional dollar of national income results in an additional $.40 of consumption, an additional $.40 of saving, and an additional $.20 of net taxes. Half of each added dollar of disposable income goes to consumption, but only 40 percent of each added dollar of national income goes to consumption.

(1) Nominal National Income	(2) Nominal Net Taxes	(3) Nominal Disposable Income	(4) Nominal Consumption Expenditure	(5) Nominal Saving
$ 100	$ 20	$ 80	$190	$−110
200	40	160	230	−70
300	60	240	270	−30
400	80	320	310	10
500	100	400	350	50
600	120	480	390	90
700	140	560	430	130
800	160	640	470	170
900	180	720	510	210
1,000	200	800	550	250
1,100	220	880	590	290
1,200	240	960	630	330
1,300	260	1,040	670	370
1,400	280	1,120	710	410

unplanned inventory investment. Our immediate interest is to explain what determines aggregate demand, so we ignore unplanned inventory investment for the moment.

Determinants of Planned Investment[2]

The rate of planned investment expenditure depends on two things. First, it depends on the **expected rate of return** on investment. By the expected rate of return we mean the net annual improvement in a firm's cost or revenue that it expects to obtain by making an investment, expressed as a percentage of the sum invested. Second, the rate of planned investment expenditure depends on the rate of interest. By the rate of interest we mean the cost to the firm of borrowing funds from outside sources, or the opportunity cost to the firm of using its own funds. A simple example will show how these two factors enter into the decision to invest.

Suppose that you are the manager of a small factory. You are worried about the rising cost of energy, so you hire a consultant who is a specialist in energy conservation. The consultant tells you that if you insulate the roof of your warehouse, you will save $1,200 per year in heating and cooling costs. The insulation will cost $10,000 to install. How do you decide whether to undertake this investment project?

First, you must calculate the rate of return on the investment. Twelve hundred dollars per year means saving $.12 per year for each dollar invested

Expected Rate of Return The annual net improvement in a firm's cost or revenue that it expects to obtain by making an investment, expressed as a percentage of the sum invested.

---

[2]Only the bare outlines of investment decision making are covered in this section. The reader will find a more complete treatment in Chapter 23, under the heading of "Capital Budgeting."

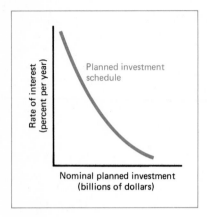

EXHIBIT 8.7
Planned investment schedule
The planned investment schedule shows how the rate of planned investment for the economy as a whole varies as the rate of interest varies, other things being equal. The downward slope of the schedule indicates that decreases in the rate of interest tend to cause increases in the rate of planned investment.

Planned Investment Schedule
A graphical representation of the way in which the rate of planned investment for the economy as a whole varies as the rate of interest varies, other things being equal.

Accelerator Effect The tendency of increases in national income to induce new investments, which in turn fuel further increases in national income.

to install the insulation, so the rate of return is 12 percent per year. Next you find out what the rate of interest is. You call your banker, who says that the money is available at 10 percent per year. That means that you will have to pay $1,000 per year in interest charges. Even after paying the interest, you will have $200 in pure profit left out of your $1,200 saving in energy cost. The investment is worthwhile, so you go ahead with it.

Perhaps you do not need to borrow money to make the investment. Instead, your firm has $10,000 or more in uncommitted cash balances left over from last year's profits. In that case, the interest rate you must use for your investment decision is the rate those funds are now earning for you. Let us say that your uncommitted cash is invested in U.S. government bonds, which pay interest of 10 percent per year. Taking $10,000 out of bonds has an opportunity cost to you of $1,000 per year in foregone interest payments, but the $1,200 saving in energy cost will more than make up for that. You still decide to put in the insulation.

This very simple example provides the basis for an important generalization. A firm will find it profitable to undertake an investment project if, and only if, the rate of return on that investment project is higher than the rate of interest. If the rate of return is equal to the rate of interest, the project will just break even, and it is a matter of indifference whether it is undertaken or not. If the rate of interest exceeds the rate of return, the project will involve a loss, and will not be undertaken.

Planned Investment Schedule

Our analysis of the determinants of planned investment suggests a general relationship between the rate of interest and the rate of planned investment for the economy as a whole. The lower the rate of interest, the greater will be the number of profitable investment projects. Other things being equal, then, the rate of planned investment will be higher, the lower the rate of interest. This relationship between interest and planned investment is shown graphically in the form of a **planned investment schedule** in Exhibit 8.7.

Changes in Expectations

The rate of planned investment depends on the rate of interest and the expected rate of return on investment. The planned investment schedule shows the relationship between the first two items, investment and the interest rate, other things being equal. We know, then, that the "other things being equal" box must in this case be filled by all the things that affect the expected rate of return on investment. What are those things? A complete list would go on and on, but here are some of the most important ones.

1. Technological developments may add new items to the list of projects that are expected to be profitable. Major technological developments such as railways or computers can have an economy-wide impact on expected rates of return.
2. Changes in the level of business activity can affect firms' expectations regarding the profitability of investment. The tendency of increases in national income to induce new investments, which in turn fuel further increases in national income, is sometimes known as the **accelerator effect**.

3. Analysis of business trends and forecasts of future trends can strongly affect expected rates of return. Numerous specialized private firms and government agencies feed business decision makers a constant stream of estimates and forecasts concerning consumer demand, inflation, foreign trade developments, and anything else anyone thinks significant. Pessimistic forecasts cause firms to postpone investment decisions; optimistic forecasts induce them to take projects "off the shelf" and get them under way.

4. Changes in government policy, and uncertainty about possible future changes in government policy, can strongly affect expected rates of return. The fear of an adverse change in policy can be as effective as the policy itself in discouraging private investment.

5. Beyond all these more or less tangible influences on expected rates of return, there is an imponderable element of "business psychology." Sometimes optimistic or pessimistic moods having relatively small initial causes can become self-reinforcing and bring about significant changes in investment plans.

Whatever the source of changes in expected rates of return, the effect of such changes can be represented as a shift in the planned investment schedule. Consider Exhibit 8.8, which shows the effects of, say, a government announcement of new tax credits for business firms. The announcement immediately raises the expected aftertax profitability of many investment projects, so the entire planned investment schedule shifts to the right. Whatever the rate of interest, the rate of planned investment will be higher after the announcement than before.

Instability of Investment Expenditure

Because the rate of planned investment depends so heavily on expectations, and because expectations can sometimes change quickly, planned investment expenditure can vary considerably from year to year. As Exhibit 8.9 shows, there have been periods in American economic history when investment has been very unstable, undergoing wide swings over short periods.

Inventory investment is a particularly unstable component of total investment expenditure as Exhibit 8.9b shows. Unfortunately, it is impossible to distinguish statistically between year-to-year changes in *planned* inventory investment, and year-to-year changes in *unplanned* inventory investment. As we shall understand more fully when our theory building is complete, changes in planned inventory investment can be considered a *cause* of instability for the economy as a whole, while changes in unplanned inventory investment are a *consequence* of disequilibrium originating elsewhere in the economy. Exhibit 8.9b lumps planned and unplanned inventory investment together.

Other Types of Expenditure

Government Purchases

The third major component of aggregate demand, after consumption and planned investment, is government purchases of goods and services. In macroeconomic analysis, the level of government purchases traditionally

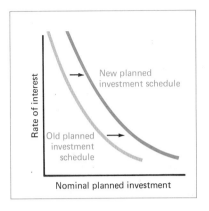

EXHIBIT 8.8
Shift in planned investment schedule
A change in the interest rate, other things being equal, causes a movement along a given planned investment schedule. A change in the expected rate of return on investment causes a shift in the entire planned investment schedule. Here we show the effects of an increase in business optimism caused, say, by a government announcement of new tax credits for private firms.

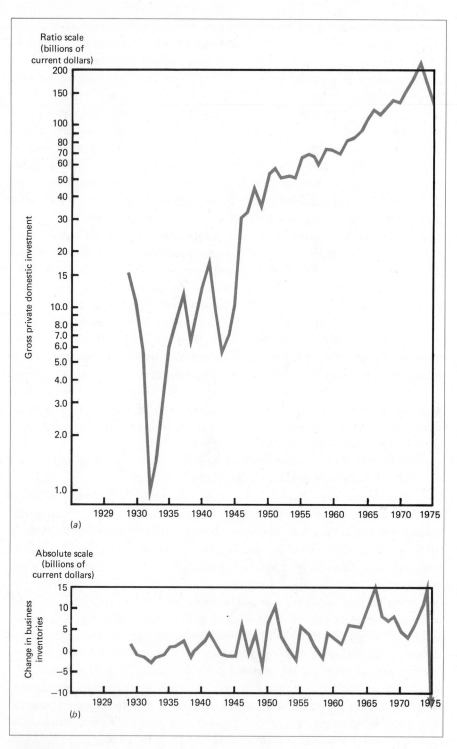

EXHIBIT 8.9

Investment expenditures in the U.S. economy, 1929–1975

Investment expenditure in the American economy has often changed sharply from year to year. The changes shown here were caused partly by changes in interest rates and partly by changes in expected rates of return. The inventory component of total investment expenditure is particularly unstable. The data on inventory investment shown here lump planned and unplanned inventory expenditure together.

is considered to be determined by political decision processes that are "outside" the economic system. In adhering to that tradition here, we do not mean to pretend that the legislators and executives who make spending decisions at various levels of government are wholly uninfluenced by economic considerations, such as the level of national income or the rate of unemployment. It is only that these relationships, whatever they are, are too indirect and complex to put into a simple theory.

Net Exports

Net exports are the fourth and final component of aggregate demand. Much work has been done to develop theories of net export expenditures. However, in the American economy, net exports are a relatively small part of total expenditure. In 1975, net exports were only $20.5 billion, less than 2 percent of a $1,516.3 billion GNP. So, rather than complicate our theory of aggregate demand at this point by taking the small effect of the foreign sector into account, we shall ignore net exports altogether and put off discussion of that part of economic theory until Chapter 37. We shall mention in passing, though, that an increase in nominal income tends to reduce net exports because of its tendency to stimulate spending on imports. This effect can be quite important in the economies of other countries, which depend much more on foreign trade than does the United States.

Conclusions

Aggregate Demand Schedule

Our objective in this chapter has been to look at the determinants of each kind of planned expenditure in order to understand how aggregate demand as a whole is determined. We have discovered that consumption depends on disposable income, that planned investment depends on the interest rate (among other things), that government spending depends on the political process, and that net exports are small enough to be ignored in an introductory discussion. Now we are ready to put together a complete **aggregate demand schedule** for the economy. This will be a schedule that shows what the nominal level of total planned expenditure will be for each possible level of nominal national income. Exhibit 8.10 shows the schedule as both a table and a graph.

To construct the graphical form of the aggregate demand schedule, we first draw a set of axes that shows national income on the horizontal axis and planned expenditure on the vertical axis. We then draw in the consumption schedule, stated in terms of national income using the numbers in columns (1) and (2) of Exhibit 8.10a [based on columns (1) and (4) of Exhibit 8.5]. This schedule is labeled C in Exhibit 8.10b.

Next we add planned investment expenditure. Given the shape and position of the planned investment schedule, and given the rate of interest, planned investment is fixed and does not change as national income changes. We thus draw a line parallel to the consumption schedule, separated from it by a distance equal to the level of planned investment, and label it $C + I$.

Aggregate Demand Schedule A schedule showing what the nominal level of total planned expenditure (aggregate demand) will be at each possible level of nominal national income.

Exhibit 8.10a

(1) Nominal National Income	(2) Nominal Consumption Expenditure	(3) Nominal Planned Investment	(4) Nominal Government Purchases	(5) Nominal Total Planned Expenditure (Aggregate Demand)
$ 100	$150	$100	$100	$ 350
200	200	100	100	400
300	250	100	100	450
400	300	100	100	500
500	350	100	100	550
600	400	100	100	600
700	450	100	100	650
800	500	100	100	700
900	550	100	100	750
1,000	600	100	100	800
1,100	650	100	100	850
1,200	700	100	100	900
1,300	750	100	100	950
1,400	800	100	100	1,000

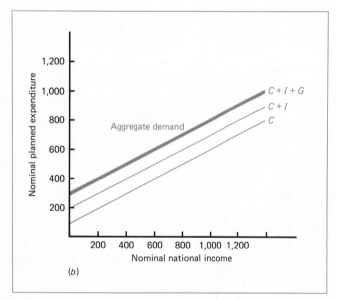

(b)

EXHIBIT 8.10

The aggregate demand schedule

To construct the aggregate demand schedule, we begin by drawing the consumption schedule, adjusted for net taxes. We then add investment, getting the line labeled $C + I$. Finally, layer-cake fashion, we add government purchases. This results in $C + I + G$, the aggregate demand schedule.

Finally, we add government purchases of goods and services in layer-cake fashion. We have assumed that government expenditure does not depend directly on national income, so we draw another line parallel to the first two, and raised above the $C + I$ line by an amount equal to government purchases. This line is labeled $C + I + G$, and is also labeled as the aggregate demand schedule, because it shows the sum of all three components of planned expenditure, as given in column (5) of Exhibit 8.10a.

This completes our discussion of the determinants of planned expenditure and aggregate demand. In the next chapter we shall use what we have learned to carry our theory building one step further.

SUMMARY

1. Following the tradition of Keynesian economics, our theory building begins by looking at what determines each separate component of aggregate demand: consumption, planned investment, government purchases, and net exports.
2. The consumption schedule shows that as income increases, consumption expenditure increases, but not by as much as the increase in income. The fraction of each added dollar of income that is devoted to consumption is called the marginal propensity to consume. That part of disposable income that is not consumed is saved. The marginal propensity to save is equal to one minus the marginal propensity to consume.
3. Planned investment expenditure depends on the rate of interest and the expected rate of return on investment projects. The planned investment schedule represents the way that planned investment varies as the rate of interest varies, other things being equal. Changes in the expected rate of return on investment are represented graphically as shifts in the planned investment schedule.
4. For purposes of elementary theory, we consider government purchases to be determined by forces outside the scope of economic analysis. We also ignore the effect of net exports, because these play a relatively small part in determining aggregate demand in the American economy.
5. The aggregate demand schedule shows the relationship between total planned expenditure and national income. Once we know the determinants of each separate component of aggregate demand, we can put the aggregate demand schedule together like a layer cake.

DISCUSSION QUESTIONS

1. "Marginal" is a term used many times and in many circumstances in economics, yet other terms could be used. What alternative expressions might be used for "marginal propensity to consume" without using the word marginal?
2. Autonomous consumption is the level of consumption that would occur if national income were zero. Because national income will never be zero, why do we talk about autonomous consumption? In other words, what does it really mean? And how does it affect the consumption schedule? What word or expression might you use in place of "autonomous" when talking about autonomous consumption?
3. Because saving and consumption are related, is there an autonomous saving that would be related to autonomous consumption? How would you find "autonomous saving"?
4. What if there were a decrease in the rate of interest and as a result firms planned to invest more. What would happen: Would there be a shift in the investment schedule or a movement along the curve?
5. What if consumers became pessimistic about the future and decided that they had better put more of their money away for a rainy day. What would happen to the consumption and saving schedules?
6. In what sense might the planned expenditure schedule be considered a demand curve? Is demand in this case a function of price, or of some other variable? Explain.
7. If you were a business executive, would you take the rate of interest into account when deciding how large an inventory of your product to keep on hand? How would a change in the rate of interest affect the stock of inventory you keep? How would it affect your flow of inventory investment?

CHAPTER 9
The Multiplier Theory of National Income Determination

What You Will Learn in This Chapter
Knowing the determinants of planned expenditure allows us to determine the exact level of national income for which the circular flow will be in equilibrium. Any shifts in the components of the aggregate demand schedule—the consumption schedule, planned investment, or government purchases—will result in changes in the equilibrium level of national income. In fact, a $1 shift in the planned expenditure schedule causes equilibrium national income to change by *more* than $1. This is known as the multiplier effect.

For Review
Here is an important concept that will be put to use in this chapter. Be certain that you understand it, or review it before proceeding.
Equilibrium and disequilibrium in the circular flow (Chapter 5)

Determining the Equilibrium Level of National Income
In Chapter 5 we learned that the circular flow could be in equilibrium only when aggregate demand was equal to aggregate supply, that is, only when the total of planned expenditures was equal to total national product. If planned expenditures exceeded national product, the attempt of buyers to purchase more than was currently being produced would lead to unplanned decreases in business inventories. Firms would react to these unplanned decreases in inventories by increasing output or by raising prices, causing the level of the circular flow, as measured in nominal terms, to increase. If planned expenditures fell short of national product, business inventories would accumulate at a rate faster than planned, and firms would react by cutting production or lowering prices, so that the nominal level of the circular flow would drop.

These are the ideas on which the Keynesian theory of national income determination are based. All we need to do now is add a bit more precision by making use of the detailed analysis of planned expenditure that we developed in the last chapter.

EXHIBIT 9.1
The aggregate supply schedule
The aggregate supply schedule shows the level of nominal national product (aggregate supply) associated with each level of nominal national income. In our simplified economy, national product and national income are equal whatever the level of national income, so the aggregate supply schedule is simply a straight line extending from the origin at an angle of 45°.

The Aggregate Supply Schedule

In Chapter 8 we showed how to draw an aggregate demand schedule. That schedule showed what the nominal level of total planned expenditure would be for each possible level of nominal national income, given certain unchanging assumptions regarding the nonincome factors affecting consumption, investment, and government purchases. As the next step in our theory building, we need an **aggregate supply schedule** to show the level of nominal national product associated with each level of nominal national income.

In the simplified economy we are now using, there are no indirect business taxes, capital consumption allowance, or statistical discrepancy. As a result, there is no distinction between gross and net national product, and national product is equal by definition to national income. That means that our aggregate supply schedule is extremely easy to draw. Because the level of nominal national product associated with any given level of nominal national income is *equal* to that level of nominal national income, the aggregate supply schedule is simply a straight 45° line. Such an aggregate supply schedule is drawn in Exhibit 9.1. The reader can easily check that each point on the schedule is equally far from the horizontal axis (national income) and the vertical axis (national product).

Aggregate Supply Schedule A table or graph showing the level of nominal national product (aggregate supply) associated with each level of nominal national income.

Keynesian Cross

If we draw both the aggregate supply and aggregate demand schedule on one diagram, as in Exhibit 9.2, we get a figure often called the **Keynesian cross.** A diagram much like this was used by Keynes in his *General Theory* to show how the equilibrium level of national income is determined. From Chapter 5, we know that the circular flow will be in equilibrium only when total planned expenditure (aggregate demand) is equal to national

Keynesian Cross A graph that shows how the equilibrium level of nominal national income is determined. The "cross" is formed by the intersection of the aggregate demand and aggregate supply schedules.

EXHIBIT 9.2
The Keynesian cross
In this Keynesian cross diagram, the aggregate demand and aggregate supply schedules are drawn together. The intersection of the two marks the level of national income for which total planned expenditure is equal to national product. That is the equilibrium level of nominal national income, where no unplanned inventory investment occurs.

product (aggregate supply). The point of intersection of the two schedules that comprise the Keynesian cross shows us exactly which level of national income permits aggregate supply and demand to be equal. That point, which corresponds to a nominal national income of $600 in Exhibit 9.2, is the equilibrium point.

It is easy to see that no other level of nominal national income can represent equilibrium in the circular flow. If national income were lower than the equilibrium level, say $400, planned expenditure (aggregate demand) would exceed national product (aggregate supply). There would be unplanned depletion of business inventories equal to the vertical distance between the aggregate demand schedule and aggregate supply schedule, as shown in Exhibit 9.2. Firms would try to restore inventories to their planned levels by increasing production and/or prices. That in turn would cause nominal national income to rise until equilibrium were reached.

If, on the other hand, nominal national income were to be higher than the equilibrium level, say $800, then planned expenditures would fall short of national product. The unsold goods would go to unplanned inventory investment equal to the gap between the aggregate demand schedule and the aggregate supply schedule. Firms would react to the unplanned buildup in inventories by cutting production and/or prices. The cutback in production would cause nominal national income to fall until equilibrium was restored.

Numerical Example

The same story is told with numbers in Exhibit 9.3. This table gives numerical values for nominal national income, planned expenditure, and other variables that correspond to the Keynesian cross diagram of Exhibit 9.2. The table confirms that $600 is the only level of national income that

EXHIBIT 9.3

Determination of equilibrium national income

The table gives a numerical example of national income determination corresponding exactly to the Keynesian cross of Exhibit 9.2. If planned expenditure does not equal national product, unplanned inventory change occurs which in turn pushes national income in the direction of equilibrium.

(1) Nominal National Income	(2) Nominal Planned Expenditure* (Aggregate Demand)	(3) Nominal National Product (Aggregate Supply)	(4) Unplanned Inventory Change	(5) Tendency of Change in National Income
$ 100	$350	$ 100	$−250	Increase
200	400	200	−200	Increase
300	450	300	−150	Increase
400	500	400	−100	Increase
500	550	500	−50	Increase
600	600	600	0	Equilibrium
700	650	700	+50	Decrease
800	700	800	+100	Decrease
900	750	900	+150	Decrease
1,000	800	1,000	+200	Decrease
1,100	850	1,100	+250	Decrease
1,200	900	1,200	+300	Decrease

*Planned expenditure based on government purchases of $100, planned investment of $100, autonomous consumption of $150, and marginal propensity to consume of 0.5. See Exhibit 8.10 for details.

allows equilibrium in the circular flow. Column (5) of the table shows that there is a tendency of national income to move toward equilibrium whenever it is at any level other than $600.

Saving Approach

There is an alternative approach to the determination of equilibrium nominal national income that uses the saving schedule rather than the consumption schedule as its starting point. We shall refer to this as the *saving approach* to income determination.

Consider Exhibit 9.4*a*. Columns (1)–(5) show how national income is divided into net taxes (the lump sum tax assumption is used here), consumption, and saving. In Exhibit 9.4*b*, we have drawn two diagonal lines to indicate how the part of national income *that is not consumed by households* varies as national income varies. The lower diagonal, labeled *S*, is the saving schedule, based on column (5) of the table. The diagonal labeled *S* + *T* adds the amount of net taxes to saving, and thus shows the total nonconsumed portion of national income.

Columns (6) and (7) of the table show the parts of planned expenditure that are not spent by households, that is, planned investment and government purchases. Neither of these change as national income changes, so they are represented by horizontal lines in the figure. The point in the diagram where the *S* + *T* line intersects the *I* + *G* line is the level of national income at which the portion of income not spent by households is exactly equal to the planned expenditures made outside the household

2146

Business Reply Card
No postage necessary if mailed in the United States

Postage will be paid by

College Store Service Bureau
National Association of College Stores
Oberlin, Ohio 44074

1/2 Price for Students

U.S.News & World Report

18¢ per week

☐ 26 weekly issues for $4.50   ☐ 1 year for $9.00 (regularly $18.00 per year)

☐ "Build your own" subscription at 18¢ a week. _____ issues for $_____
(26 week minimum, 1 year maximum)

☐ Payment enclosed.   ☐ Bill me.

Name _____

Address _____

City _____ State _____ Zip _____

Student at (college) _____ Year of Graduation _____

☐ Undergraduate Student   ☐ Graduate Student   478

Exhibit 9.4a

(1) Nominal National	(2) Net Taxes	(3) Disposable Income	(4) Consumption Expenditure	(5) Saving	(6) Planned Investment	(7) Government Purchases
$ 100	$100	$ 0	$150	$ − 150	$100	$100
200	100	100	200	− 100	100	100
300	100	200	250	− 50	100	100
400	100	300	300	0	100	100
500	100	400	350	50	100	100
600	100	500	400	100	100	100
700	100	600	450	150	100	100
800	100	700	500	200	100	100
900	100	800	550	250	100	100
1,000	100	900	600	300	100	100
1,100	100	1,000	650	350	100	100
1,200	100	1,100	700	400	100	100

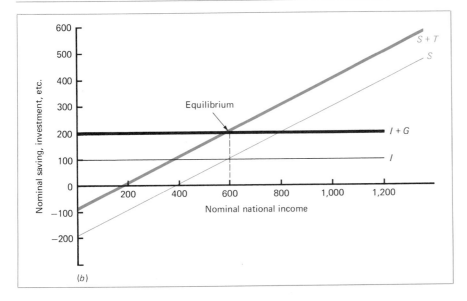

(b)

EXHIBIT 9.4

The saving approach to national income determination

The table and diagram show that the part of national income that consumers do not spend (saving plus net taxes) must equal the planned expenditures of nonconsumers (planned investment plus government purchases) in order for the circular flow to be in equilibrium.

sector of the economy. At this point, and only at this point, total expenditures equal total national income. The saving approach tells us, then, that the circular flow is in equilibrium when, and only when, saving plus net taxes equal planned investment plus government purchases.

A careful comparison of Exhibits 9.4 and 9.2 will reveal that the gap between the $S + T$ and $I + G$ lines at any level of national income is exactly equal to the gap between the aggregate demand and supply schedules at the same level of national income. It is easy to understand why. If the part of national income that consumers do not spend ($S + T$) is greater than the planned expenditures of nonconsumers ($I + G$), some goods that were produced will end up in unplanned inventories rather than being sold. The plans of buyers and sellers do not mesh. The part of total output left over after household consumption exceeds the investment demands of firms plus government purchases. On the other hand, if firms and government plan to spend more than consumers set aside in taxes and saving, the difference will have to be made up by unplanned depletion of business inventories. The two approaches are thus entirely equivalent.

Changes in Nominal National Income and the Multiplier Effect

Expenditure Changes

A great many economic factors can affect the level of planned expenditure. When we draw an aggregate demand schedule, we single out the effects of changes in national income on planned expenditure. The effects of changes in national income on planned expenditure are represented by *movements along* a given aggregate demand schedule.

Other factors besides income also influence planned expenditure. Changes in consumer expectations, in wealth, or in prices cause the level of autonomous consumption to change. Changes in the interest rate or in business expectations cause the level of planned investment to change. Changes in policy cause the government purchases component of planned expenditure to change. All of these changes in planned expenditure that arise from reasons other than changes in national income must be represented by shifts in the aggregate demand schedule.

Consider Exhibit 9.5, which shows the effects of a $100 increase in planned expenditure at all levels of income. For the moment, we shall not worry about whether this increase originates in the consumption, invest-

EXHIBIT 9.5

The multiplier effect

If a $100 increase in consumption, planned investment, or government purchases shifts the aggregate demand schedule from AD_1 to AD_2, equilibrium nominal national income will rise from $600 to $800. The ability of a given shift in planned expenditure to induce a larger increase in nominal national income is known as the multiplier effect.

In 1970, the Swedish Academy of Sciences awarded its Nobel Memorial Prize in Economics to MIT Professor Paul Samuelson. In doing so, the Academy announced that "Professor Samuelson's extensive production, covering nearly all areas of economic theory, is characterized by an outstanding ability to derive important new theorems and to find new applications for existing ones. By his contributions, Samuelson has done more than any other contemporary economist to raise the level of scientific analysis in economic theory." The multiplier theory of national income determination is just one of dozens that has been refined, restated, and sharpened by Samuelson's penetrating mind.

Samuelson began his task of raising the level of scientific analysis in economic theory early in his career. His doctoral dissertation at Harvard, written when he was just 26, was boldly entitled *Foundations of Economic Analysis.* (Contrast this with the narrow, ultraspecialized topics of most dissertations!) Published in 1947, the *Foundations* immediately became, and to a great extent remains, the definitive statement in modern mathematical dress of much of neoclassical economics.

In the nineteenth century, leading economists had seen their major theoretical statements go on to become textbooks to future generations. Alas, Samuelson's *Foundations* could not serve that purpose. One must already be well educated in economics and mathematics even to read it! Something had to be done to bring the advances in economic theory made during the 1930s and 1940s into the college classroom. Samuelson solved the problem with his famous *Principles of Economics.* That book was based on the simple assumption that beginning students did not need to be taught a different *kind* of economics than the kind economists wrote in their own professional journals. What they needed was a lucid, step-by-step presentation. The formula was so successful that Samuelson's *Principles* sold millions on millions of copies as it went through a total of ten editions.

On policy issues Samuelson ranks as a liberal and an activist. He derides the laissez-faire market economy as a "system of coercion by dollar votes." Unlike many like-minded colleagues, however, Samuelson did not move to Washington during the Kennedy-Johnson years. He was called on frequently for his opinions and advice, but he resisted service on the Council of Economic Advisors. Although much sought as a lecturer and writer of popular articles, Samuelson remains fundamentally an economist's economist. "In the long run," he has said, "the economic scholar works for the only coin worth having—our own applause."

Paul Anthony Samuelson (1915–   )

ment, or government purchases component of aggregate demand. The effect in any case is to shift the aggregate schedule upward by $100, from the position AD_1 to the position AD_2.

The Multiplier Effect

What happens to the equilibrium level of national income when the planned expenditure schedule shifts upward by $100? The immediate effect is that planned expenditures exceed national product, so that inventories start to be depleted at a rate of $100 per year. Firms react to this unplanned inventory depletion by increasing output and/or prices. Nominal national income rises to its new equilibrium level of $800.

Notice what has happened: A $100 upward shift in the aggregate demand schedule has induced a $200 increase in equilibrium nominal income. This ability of a given shift in aggregate demand to create a larger increase

Multiplier Effect The ability of a $1 shift in the aggregate demand schedule to induce more than a $1 change in the equilibrium level of nominal national income.

in equilibrium national income is the famous **multiplier effect,** a central pillar of Keynesian macroeconomics. Let us look closely at the multiplier effect, to see where it comes from.

Round by Round

One way to view the multiplier effect is to imagine the effects of the initial upward shift in aggregate demand percolating down through the economy, "round by round." Suppose that the original shift were caused by a $100 per year increase in the rate of autonomous consumption expenditure. In response to the $100 increase in demand, firms would raise their prices and/or output enough to cause a $100 increase in nominal national product. The increase in national product would result in $100 of additional nominal *income* for some people, in the form of higher profits, wages, rents, or interest payments. Let us call all of what has happened so far the first-round effect of the shift in aggregate demand.

The second round consists in tracing the effects of the $100 in new income generated by the first round. Given an assumed marginal propensity to consume of 0.5, the people who receive this income will spend $50 of it on consumer goods and services. This, in turn, will cause firms to step up output by $50 more and generate $50 in new factor payments and income.

In the third round, half of this $50 is spent, generating $25 more of nominal national product, factor payments, and income. In the fourth round, $12.50 is added, then $6.25 in the fifth round, and so forth until the increments become too small to worry about. When we add together the sum of all the increments to income induced by the original $100 upward shift in the aggregate nominal demand function, we get a total of $100 + $50 + $25 + $12.50 + . . . = $200, just as we expected.

This round-by-round version of the multiplier effect is summarized in Exhibit 9.6.

The Multiplier

Looking at Exhibit 9.6. we see quite clearly that as income increases in response to the original upward shift in the aggregate demand schedule, national income "catches up" with planned expenditure. For each $1 increase in nominal national income, output increases by $1 but expenditure increases by only a fraction of a dollar. The fraction is equal to the marginal propensity to consume. At the new equilibrium, the difference between planned expenditure and national income is eliminated.

Multiplier (Simple) The ratio of an induced change in the equilibrium level of national income to an initial change in planned expenditure. Later known as the simple multiplier, to distinguish it from other specialized terms. The value of the multiplier is given by the formula $M = 1/(1 - \text{MPC})$.

The ratio of the induced increase in national income to the original increase in planned expenditure is called the **multiplier.** The value of the multiplier depends on the fraction of each added dollar of income that goes to added planned expenditure. More precisely, the multiplier M is given by the formula

$$M = \frac{1}{1 - \text{MPC}}$$

where MPC stands for the marginal propensity to consume.

Because we know that the marginal propensity to save is equal to one minus the marginal propensity to consume, we can, alternatively, write the formula for the multiplier as

Exhibit 9.6a

Round	Change in Aggregate Demand	Change in Income
First	$100.00	$100.00
Second	50.00	50.00
Third	25.00	25.00
Fourth	12.50	12.50
Fifth	6.25	6.25
. . . . .	. . . . .	
All later rounds	6.25	6.25
Totals	$200.00	$200.00

EXHIBIT 9.6

The multiplier effect viewed round by round

A spontaneous $100 increase in planned expenditure (first round) generates $100 in new income. With a marginal propensity to consume of 0.5, half of that is spent, giving a second-round boost of $50 to income. Half of that is spent in the third round, and so forth, until income rises by an eventual total of $200.

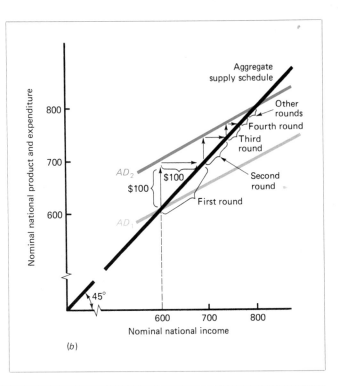

(b)

$$M = \frac{1}{\text{MPS}}$$

where MPS stands for the marginal propensity to save. Whichever way we write the formula, we see that the multiplier is larger the larger the marginal propensity to consume, and smaller the larger the marginal propensity to save.

Conclusions

The multiplier effect plays a central role in Keynesian economic theory and economic policy analysis. The central implication of the multiplier is that even small changes in planned expenditure will have magnified effects on the national economy. Remember how unstable planned investment expenditure can sometimes be. Early Keynesian economists saw the instability of investment, magnified by the multiplier effect, as an explanation of the cycle of boom and bust that had plagued capitalist economies since the nineteenth century. They also saw in the multiplier effect the key to a new policy for economic stabilization. That part of their analysis is important enough for us to devote a separate chapter to it.

SUMMARY

1. *Equilibrium nominal national income.* For a given aggregate demand schedule, the circular flow can be in equilibrium at only one level of nominal national income. The equilibrium condition is that planned expenditure and national product must be equal. If planned expenditure exceeds national product, there will be unplanned depletion of inventories and upward pressure on income.

If national product exceeds planned expenditure, there will be unplanned accumulation of inventories and downward pressure on national income.

2. *Saving approach.* The saving approach to the determination of the equilibrium level of nominal national income shows that equilibrium can occur only when the part of nominal national income that consumers do not spend $(S + T)$ is equal to the planned expenditure of nonconsumers $(I + G)$.

3. *Multiplier effect.* A shift in the aggregate demand schedule changes the equilibrium level of nominal national income. According to the multiplier effect, the induced change in equilibrium nominal national income will be larger than the initial shift in planned expenditure. The ratio of the change in income to the shift in planned expenditure is known as the multiplier.

DISCUSSION QUESTIONS

1. It is possible to analyze the determinants of national income and product with either the circular flow or the Keynesian cross. Which do you prefer? Why? Does each contribute some insights of its own?

2. Explain the "round by round" effect of the multiplier by using the circular flow model.

3. If you expected a depression in the near future, would it be to your advantage to save in order to prepare for it? What would happen if we all tried to save a larger fraction of our income than usual to prepare for an expected depression?

4. If planned saving exceeds planned investment, will gross national product increase or decrease? Suppose you know that the government's budget is exactly in balance. Now can you answer the question?

5. What would be the size of the multiplier if the marginal propensity to consume were 0.5, 0.75, 0.8, 0.9, 0.95?

6. In what ways are the Keynesian cross and the supply and demand diagram of previous chapters similar, and in what ways are they different?

7. What changes in the economy would force a movement along the aggregate demand curve, and what changes would result in a shift of the curve?

8. Suppose that consumers suddenly increase their marginal propensity to consume from 0.5 to 0.75. What effect will this have on the aggregate demand curve? Trace the impact of this change using the Keynesian cross diagram.

CHAPTER 10
Fiscal Policy and the Multiplier Theory

What You Will Learn in This Chapter
Early followers of Keynes believed that the multiplier theory gave them the key to economic stabilization policy. If private investment or consumer spending were not great enough to guarantee full employment of the nation's resources, increased government purchases or tax cuts could be used to fill the gap. When John Kennedy was elected President, he brought economic advisors to Washington who believed that any desired level of national income could be chosen as a target, and any target hit given the political will to apply known policies. Those policies are described here.

For Review
Here are some important terms and concepts that will be put to use in this chapter. Be certain that you understand them, or review them before proceeding.

Potential real gross national product (Chapter 7)
The multiplier theory (Chapter 9)

Early Keynesian economists believed the multiplier theory to have far-reaching significance for economic policy. During the 1930s and 1940s, investment expenditure had been particularly unstable. Now their new theory suggested that year-to-year changes in planned investment would have multiplied effects on national income and product.

What is more, early Keynesians had not distinguished carefully between long- and short-run consumption schedules. If, as they thought, the short-run marginal propensity to consume were close to its long-run level of 0.9, the multiplier would be not 2, as in our examples, but 10. If this were true, a $100 million change in planned investment expenditure would cause a $1 billion change in national income. Their assumption of such a large value for the multiplier reinforced their belief that the instability of investment was the major cause of the historical instability of the economy as a whole.

At the same time that the multiplier theory gave the Keynesians a diagnosis for economic instability, it also suggested a cure. What was needed was a way to manipulate government purchases and consumption spending so that changes in these could be used to offset potentially destabilizing changes in planned investment. Government spending could be controlled directly by policy makers, given the political will to do so. Consumption expenditure is not under direct government control, but it can be manipulated indirectly by raising or lowering taxes. Taken together, the policies that determine the levels of government purchases and taxes are known as **fiscal policy.** We shall devote this chapter to explaining the fiscal policy cure for economic instability.

Fiscal Policy The policies that determine the levels of government purchases and taxes.

Fiscal Policy and the Target Level of National Income

The Income Target

The first step in applying the multiplier theory to fiscal policy is to specify a **target level of national income.** Traditionally, policy makers set a target that they hope will bring about full employment, and that will allow the economy to reach its full potential for real output. We state the income target in nominal terms. It is perfectly possible, of course, for different people to have different ideas about just what target should be chosen, as a result of different ideas about the exact meaning of "full employment" or "potential real gross national product." Considerations of price stability, economic growth, and the balance of payments may also lead to disagreements about where the target should be set. All that is important at the moment, though, is that *some* specific target be chosen that we can use as a reference point.

Target Level of National Income The level of nominal income that policy makers think will permit their main economic goals (full employment, price stability, economic growth, or whatever) to be best realized.

A Contractionary Gap

The second step in applying the multiplier theory to fiscal policy is to determine the relationship between the *target* level of nominal national income and the *equilibrium* level of nominal national income. Consider Exhibit 10.1. In that figure we have drawn an aggregate demand schedule

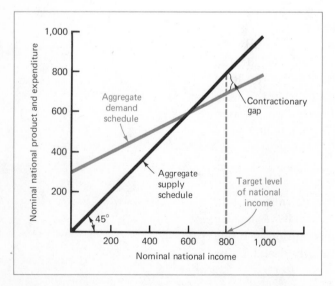

EXHIBIT 10.1
A contractionary gap
A contractionary gap is said to occur whenever planned expenditure (aggregate demand) at the target level of national income is less than national product (aggregate supply) at the target level of national income. Under these conditions, the equilibrium level of nominal national income is below the target level. If national income were at the target level, unplanned inventory accumulation would put downward pressure on the level of income and cause the circular flow to contract.

that gives an equilibrium nominal national income of $600. The underlying data for this schedule are the same as those given in Exhibit 9.3.

Let us suppose that policy makers consider $600 too low a level for nominal income, and set their target instead at $800. With the planned expenditure schedule shown, $800 cannot be the equilibrium level of income, because planned expenditures would fall short of national product by $100. We shall call this crucial $100 a **contractionary gap.** A contractionary gap occurs whenever planned expenditure is less than national product at the target level of income. The size of the gap measures the rate of unplanned inventory accumulation that would take place at the target level of income with the given aggregate demand schedule. The word "contractionary" refers to the fact that unplanned inventory accumulation would put *downward* pressure on the level of nominal national income if income were at the target level.

Contractionary Gap   The gap between planned expenditures and national product at the target level of national income when aggregate supply exceeds aggregate demand at that level.

An Expansionary Gap

Sometimes the equilibrium level of national income can be higher than the target level. Such a case is shown in Exhibit 10.2. In that figure, the aggregate demand schedule yields $200 more expenditure at each level of income than the one shown in Exhibit 10.1. Now planned expenditures would *exceed* national income at the target level of national income. Instead of unplanned inventory accumulation and a contractionary gap at the target income, there is unplanned inventory depletion and an **expansionary gap.**

When there is an expansionary gap, nominal national income will again not be in equilibrium at the target level. If national income were to be at the target level, unplanned inventory depletion would cause the circular flow, measured in nominal terms, to expand. Depending on circumstances, the expansion of nominal income could take the form of an increase in real output, an increase in the price level, or a combination of the two. In later chapters we shall explain just how an expansion in nom-

Expansionary Gap   The gap between planned expenditures and national product at the target level of national income when aggregate demand exceeds aggregate supply at that level.

EXHIBIT 10.2

An expansionary gap

An expansionary gap is said to occur whenever planned expenditure (aggregate demand) at the target level of national income is greater than national product (aggregate supply) at the target level of national income. Under these conditions, the equilibrium level of nominal national income is above the target level. If national income were at the target level, unplanned inventory depletion would put upward pressure on the level of income and cause the circular flow to expand.

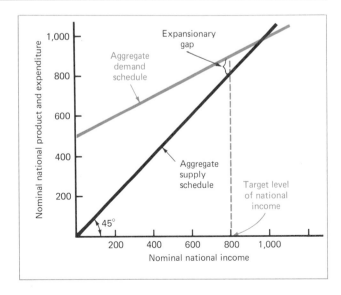

inal national income will be divided between increases in prices and increases in real output. For the moment, though, it does not matter which form a given change in nominal income takes.

Filling the Gap

When there is an expansionary or contractionary gap in the economy, fiscal policy can be used to fill it. In the case of a contractionary gap, consumption plus planned investment plus government purchases are not great enough to add up to national income at the target level. Policy makers can either try to fill the gap directly, by increasing government purchases, or indirectly, by stimulating consumption through reduced taxes. In the case of an expansionary gap, consumption plus planned investment plus government purchases are so great that they exceed national income at the target level. Policy makers then try to eliminate the gap by cutting government purchases or discouraging consumption with a tax increase.

Saving Approach

In Chapter 9 we discussed an alternative approach to national income determination called the saving approach. The saving approach sheds additional light on the process of eliminating expansionary and contractionary gaps. The saving approach tells us that saving plus net taxes must be equal to planned investment plus government purchases in equilibrium. When there is a contractionary gap, households put more income aside in saving and taxes at the target level of income than planned investment and government purchases can soak up. Unless fiscal policy intervenes, the difference will be taken up by unplanned inventory investment, which will then drive nominal income below the target level. Government can step in to buy the goods that would otherwise have gone unsold, or it can reduce taxes to get consumers to buy them. That will keep income at the target level.

When there is an expansionary gap, the saving approach tells us that planned investment plus government purchases exceed saving plus taxes at the target level of income. That means that firms and government are planning to spend more money than households put aside in saving and taxes. Not enough product is left over after household consumption expenditures to meet the planned needs of investment and government purchases. If nothing is done, the planned investment expenditures and government purchases can be carried out only at the expense of an unplanned depletion of business inventories. Fiscal policy can eliminate the gap. It can force consumers to set aside more in taxes, or it can reduce planned government expenditures.

In outline, that is how fiscal policy works, according to the multiplier theory. Now we turn to an examination of details.

Government Purchases Policy

Let us begin with the simplest case: the government fills a contractionary gap by increasing government spending. In Exhibit 10.3, we begin with the state of affairs shown in Exhibit 10.1. The consumption schedule is the same as the one used in Chapter 9 (see Exhibit 9.4). Planned investment is

EXHIBIT 10.3

Filling a contractionary gap with increased government purchases

Increased government purchases can be used to fill a contractionary gap. Initially, government purchases were at the level G_1, putting the aggregate demand schedule at $C + I + G_1$. An additional $100 of government purchases shifted the aggregate demand schedule up to $C + I + G_2$, bringing equilibrium nominal national income up to the target level. Part b of the exhibit shows the same process from the point of view of the saving approach to nominal income determination.

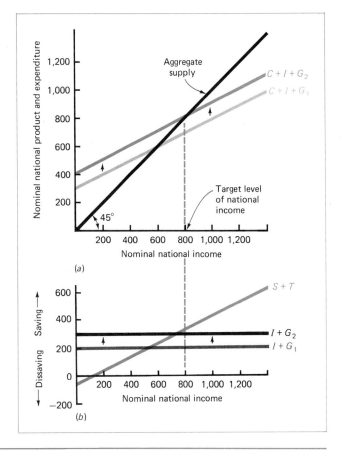

$100 and government purchases are $100. The resulting planned expenditure schedule is labeled $C + I + G_1$. This gives an equilibrium level of national income $200 below the target level, with a contractionary gap of $100. (Remember that this gap is always measured vertically at the target level of national income.) The lower part of the diagram shows the same initial situation from the point of view of the saving approach. (Compare this to Exhibit 9.4b.)

To bring income up to the target level, the makers of fiscal policy decide to increase government purchases by an amount just equal to the contractionary gap. To be specific, let us suppose that they authorize spending an extra $100 to accelerate the completion of a stretch of interstate highway. If their policy is to work, this added spending *must not* be paid for by increased taxes. Bills for the construction work must be paid either by borrowing from the public or by creating new money. Let us look now at the consequences of this increased spending from three viewpoints.

Round by Round

First, we can take a round-by-round approach. Spending $100 on the highway project creates $100 in new incomes for construction workers. This raises total national income, in the first round, from $600 to $700. Given a propensity to consume of 0.5, the workers save half of this money and spend half of it on, say, clothing. This generates $50 new income for clothing workers and retailers, raising total income to $750 in the second round. In the third round, clothing workers spend half of their new income on something else, adding $25 more to the stream of income and expenditures, so that national total creeps up to $775. As further rounds progress, the target level of $800 national income is approached more and more closely.

Aggregate Supply and Demand Approach

Instead of taking the round-by-round approach, we can refer to Exhibit 10.3a, which shows the effects of the increased government purchases in terms of aggregate supply and demand. The decision to spend $100 on the highway project shifts the aggregate demand schedule upward by $100 to the position labeled $C + I + G_2$. At the initial level of national income ($600), we see that planned expenditures exceed national income, and hence national product, by $100. This tells us that the construction workers' expenditures must initially cause inventories to decline by an unexpected $50. Efforts to replenish these inventories generate $50 in second-round incomes and start national income and product moving upward. The unplanned depletion of inventories will not be eliminated entirely until the new equilibrium level of nominal national income is reached, at the point where the new aggregate demand schedule intersects the aggregate supply schedule. This new equilibrium is, of course, at the target income of $800.

Saving Approach

Finally, let us look at the effects of the increased government purchases in terms of the saving approach. In Exhibit 10.3b, increased government purchases shift the line representing nonhousehold expenditure up by $100 to the position $I + G_2$. Investors and government now spend more at the $600 income level than households set aside in saving and taxes. Inventories are unexpectedly depleted, and income begins to rise as explained above. With a marginal propensity to save of 0.5, $.50 in new saving results from each $1.00 rise in income. By the time national income reaches $800, saving plus taxes have risen enough to cover the total of planned investment plus government purchases.

Notice that in the new equilibrium, planned investment plus government purchases equals saving plus net taxes, as required, but the individual components no longer match up. Saving now exceeds planned investment, and government purchases now exceed net taxes. This *has* to be true, for after all, the whole purpose of the increased government expenditure was to "soak up" the deflationary gap of $100 excess saving that would otherwise have existed at the target level of income.

Multiplier

Whichever approach we use, we come to the same conclusion: *When government purchases are increased while taxes, planned investment, and the consumption schedule remain unchanged, equilibrium nominal national income will change by an amount equal to the change in government purchases times the multiplier.* In this case, where the change in government purchases was $100 and the multiplier was 2, the change in equilibrium income was 2 × $100 = $200.

Politics

The "government policy makers" of textbook economics are able to make decisions and push the appropriate curves and schedules around without worrying about practical politics. Life is not so easy for real policy makers in Washington. Different political interest groups may operate on different assumptions about what economic targets ought to be, and may receive conflicting estimates about how far away from any given target the economy is or will be in the immediate future. Furthermore, policy proposals may be put forward as much with an eye to their effect on the next election as to their effect on national income. The following case study gives a minor, but very typical instance of the kind of political conflict that occurs continually in the actual conduct of fiscal policy.

CASE 10.1
A Job Program Gets a Veto

Throughout most of 1975, President Gerald Ford and the Congress were at odds on the issue of fiscal policy. Looking ahead to 1976, the President and his advisors saw continuing inflationary pressures, and insisted that government purchases should not be allowed to exceed net taxes by more than $60 billion. Congress, on the other hand, was under pressure to spend more federal money to create more jobs, even if the result were a much larger budget deficit.

In May, Congress passed a bill that would have called for spending $5.3 billion of federal money on programs designed to create 900,000 new jobs. The emphasis was on government purchase of services. The bill included money for public service jobs, summer youth jobs, construction and repair of federal buildings, and flood control projects.

The response was a Presidential veto. The bill "would exacerbate budgetary and economic pressures," said President Ford in his veto message. What is more, much of the money would not actually be spent until 1977. By then, according to his advisors' forecasts, the economy's current deflationary gap would already have disappeared without this additional stimulus. The small skirmish in the extended battle over fiscal policy ended this time in victory for the President's point of view.

Tax Policy and the Net Tax Multiplier

Let us go back to the starting point of our previous example, with national income $200 below the target level and a contractionary gap of $100. Suppose now that the fiscal policy authorities decide to stimulate the economy by lowering taxes rather than by raising government spending. To make comparison with the the previous section easier, let us say that they cut net taxes by a lump sum amount of $100. This is a bit extreme, perhaps, because net taxes were only $100 to begin with, but it simplifies the numbers and diagrams and helps clearly establish the principles in which we are interested. Once again, we can look at the effects of this fiscal policy from three points of view.

Round by Round

The $100 tax cut gives households $100 in added disposable income. We cannot add this $100 into the multiplier process directly, though, because it is not *newly generated* income. There has been no increase in production, and no increase in factor payments. All that has happened is that $100 of the original $600 total income has been shifted from government to households.

The multiplier process starts when households spend the money—or more precisely, when they spend half of it, because their marginal propensity to consume is 0.5. Let us say that they spend it on haircuts. That generates $50 of new income for barbers, and national income rises to $650. The first round is complete. When the barbers spend half of their new earnings, they provide the basis for a second-round income increase of $25 in whatever sector they direct their money to. Subsequent rounds add $12.50, $6.25, $3.12½, and so forth until national income has risen to a new equilibrium at $700.

It turns out that although $100 of government purchases caused equilibrium income to rise by $200, a $100 tax cut causes equilibrium income to rise by only $100. Let us check this result.

Aggregate Supply and Demand Approach

Turn now to Exhibit 10.4a, which shows the effect of our tax cut in terms of aggregate supply and demand. The initial position of the aggregate demand schedule is $C_1 + I + G$. When taxes are cut, the consumption schedule shifts *to the left* by $100. The reason for the leftward shift is that disposable income of households is $100 higher at each level of national income than before. Originally, when national income was, say, $600, consumers would have a disposable income of $500 and would have spent accordingly. Now, after the tax cut, consumers would have a disposable income of $500 when national income was only $500. With $100 less tax burden, they would thus spend as much at $500 as they used to at $600, as much at $600 as they used to at $700, and so forth.

The tax cut does not change planned investment or government spending, so when the consumption schedule shifts leftward by $100, it carries the whole aggregate demand schedule with it just the same distance, until it reaches the new position labeled $C_2 + I + G$. Without going through the whole story of what happens after that, we can see that this new aggregate demand schedule intersects the aggregate supply schedule at $700. That will be the new equilibrium level of national income, confirming the result we got by the round-by-round approach.

Saving Approach

Exhibit 10.4b shows how the tax cut works in terms of the saving approach. Here things are very simple indeed, because the tax cut has eliminated the T component of the $S + T$ schedule altogether. Disposable income rises by $100, shifting the saving schedule to its new position S_2. All we have to do to find the new equilibrium is look for the point where the savings schedule S_2 intersects the $I + G$ schedule. That intersection is at the $700 level of national income, just as we expect.

Transfers

Remember that when we talk about net taxes, we mean taxes paid in to the Treasury minus government transfer payments. It might have been, for example, that our original $100 level of lump sum net taxes was com-

EXHIBIT 10.4
Expansionary tax policy

A tax cut has an expansionary effect on the economy. Here, with the aggregate demand schedule at $C_1 + I + G$, there was a $100 contractionary gap. A tax cut of $100 shifted the aggregate demand schedule to $C_2 + I + G$, as consumers received more disposable income. A new equilibrium was reached at $700 nominal income, still below the target but closer than before. Part *b* shows the same events in terms of the saving approach. Because taxes were assumed to be only $100 to begin with, the tax cut entirely eliminated the T component of the $S + T$ schedule.

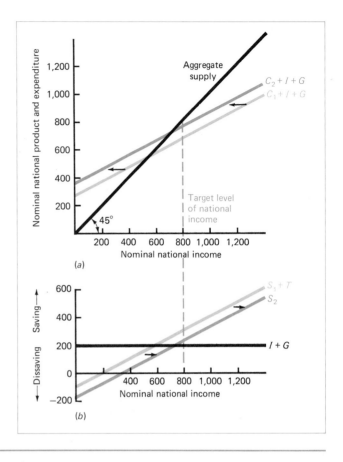

posed of $150 property taxes on homeowners, and $50 in disability benefits to Vietnam veterans. The $100 decrease in net taxes which we have been discussing could have been brought about by cutting property taxes to $50, or by increasing veterans' benefits to $150. Either policy, or a mixture, would bring the level of *net* taxes down from $100 to zero. An increase in transfer payments has, dollar for dollar, the same macroeconomic effects as a cut in the amount of taxes paid into the Treasury.

Net Tax Multiplier

We have seen that the multiplier effect works less powerfully in the case of a tax cut than in the case of an increase in government purchases. Just how much less powerfully depends on the marginal propensity to consume. If the government borrows enough or creates enough new money to add $100 to its budget for purchases of goods and services, it can guarantee that all $100 will be spent. When it adds $100 to household budgets through a cut in net taxes, households will *not* spend all the money directly. They will spend only the portion that their marginal propensity to consume says they will, and they will save the rest.

We now know that a tax cut is less effective than an increase in government purchases exactly in proportion to the marginal propensity to consume. This fact allows us to define a new concept: the **net tax multiplier.** The net tax multiplier is defined by the formula

Net Tax Multiplier A multiplier showing how much equilibrium nominal national income will change in response to a change in net taxes. The formula for the net tax multiplier is $M_T = MPC/MPS$.

$$M_T = \frac{\text{MPC}}{\text{MPS}}$$

where M_T stands for the net tax multiplier, MPS for the marginal propensity to save, and MPC for the marginal propensity to consume.

Using this new definition, we can summarize our analysis of tax policy as follows: *When net taxes are changed while government purchases, planned investment, autonomous consumption, and the marginal propensity to consume remain unchanged, equilibrium nominal national income will change in the direction opposite to the change in taxes by an amount equal to the change in net taxes times the net tax multiplier.* In the case we have examined, where the change in net taxes was $100 and the net tax multiplier was 1, the change in equilibrium income was $1 \times \$100 = \$100$.

CASE 10.2
The Kennedy Tax Cut

Probably the most famous episode in the history of fiscal policy was the Kennedy tax cut. John F. Kennedy assumed the office of President in January 1961 in the middle of a business recession. He had been elected on a promise to "get the country moving again," and he brought to Washington a group of economic advisors firmly committed to the active use of fiscal policy.

At first, the emphasis of the new administration was primarily on the spending side of fiscal policy. The President issued orders aimed at stepping up federal expenditures by speeding highway fund allocations and accelerating procurement activities. He also submitted a package of new spending proposals to Congress.

By the next year, the economy seemed to be making considerable progress. Presidential advisors thought that the administration's national income target, aimed high enough to ensure full employment, would be achieved by the end of 1963. But contrary to these forecasts, the expansion slowed. By June 1962, the President decided on more stimulus. On June 7, 1962, he announced that he favored a tax cut of some $10 billion.

Kennedy's tax cut proposal did not get quick treatment from Congress. Long delays resulted from Congressional demands to couple the tax cut to reforms in tax structure and changes in expenditure policy. As it turned out, Kennedy did not live to see his great tax cut enacted. But in February 1964, his successor, President Lyndon Johnson, finally signed the Kennedy tax cut into law. This tax cut is now considered a famous test case of fiscal policy, and we shall return to a consideration of its effectiveness in later chapters.

The Balanced Budget Multiplier

In both of the examples we have looked at so far, fiscal policy makers began with a balanced budget and then tried to plug a contractionary gap by **deficit spending.** That means that they set a policy course under which government purchases would purposely exceed net taxes, the difference being made up by borrowing from the public or creating new money. Now we shall see that deficit spending is not strictly necessary in order for fiscal policy to be effective.

No special diagram or lengthy analysis is required to show this. Suppose simply that we begin again with a contractionary gap of $100 and an equilibrium national income $200 below the target level. As before, government purchases are initially $100 and net taxes also initially $100, so the budget is balanced. Now suppose that fiscal policy makers raise govern-

Deficit Spending A policy of purposely allowing government purchases to exceed net taxes, with the difference being made up by borrowing from the public or creating new money.

ment spending by \$100, and at the same time *raise* net taxes by \$100. What happens?

We know from our first example that the effect of a \$100 increase in government purchases, taken in isolation, is to raise equilibrium national income by \$200. We also know that the effect of a \$100 change in net taxes is a \$100 change in equilibrium national income in the opposite direction of the tax change. The combined policy we have proposed, then, must raise equilibrium national income by \$200 and at the same time lower it by \$100, for a net *upward* effect of \$100. If the fiscal authorities were to raise both government purchases and net taxes by \$200, they could bring equilibrium national income all the way up to the target level without running a deficit at all.

Balanced Budget Multiplier

This example suggests still another kind of multiplier, the **balanced budget multiplier.** The balanced budget multiplier is equal to the simple multiplier *minus* the net tax multiplier. In algebraic terms, we could express the balanced budget multiplier this way:

$$M_B = M - M_T = \frac{1}{\text{MPS}} - \frac{\text{MPC}}{\text{MPS}} = \frac{1 - \text{MPC}}{\text{MPS}}$$

where M_B stands for the balanced budget multiplier, and all other symbols have the same meaning as before. The expression on the extreme right-hand side can be simplified if we remember that $\text{MPC} = 1 - \text{MPS}$. We get

$$M_B = \frac{1 - (1 - \text{MPS})}{\text{MPS}} = \frac{\text{MPS}}{\text{MPS}} = 1$$

It turns out that the value of the balanced budget multiplier is just 1, no matter what is the value of the marginal propensity to consume or save. In short, *an increase in government spending, accompanied by an equal increase in net taxes, with planned investment, autonomous consumption, and the marginal propensity to consume unchanged, produces a dollar-for-dollar increase in equilibrium nominal national income.*

Balanced Budget Multiplier A multiplier showing how much equilibrium nominal national income will change in response to a change in government purchases matched dollar for dollar by an offsetting change in net taxes. The value of the balanced budget multiplier is always exactly 1.

CASE 10.3
Ford's Balanced Budget Proposal of 1975

After skirmishing for a year with Congress over details of fiscal policy, President Gerald Ford undertook an offensive. On October 6, 1975, he went on national television with a major speech on economic policy.

The country, he said, was at a crossroads. The decision before the nation was whether or not to continue in the direction of recent years toward higher taxes, and higher spending by "a massive, overzealous bureaucracy which has become too involved in trying to run too much of your daily life." To put a halt to what he saw as this excessive growth of government, he proposed to cut \$28 billion from projected federal spending in the next year. This spending cut was to be matched by a \$28 billion reduction in taxes. "For every dollar that we return to the American taxpayer, we must also cut our projected spending by the same amount."

As several commentators on the President's proposals pointed out, this policy, if enacted, would have provided a textbook illustration of the balanced budget multiplier in action. Although equal amounts would have been cut from taxes and spending, the commentators feared that the net effect would be contractionary. As a result, the proposal found little favor with Congress, which still believed that the economy would need more, not less stimulus from fiscal policy in the coming year.

The Multipliers Compared

We now have three multipliers, corresponding to three types of fiscal policy. These are the simple multiplier, the net tax multiplier, and the balanced budget multiplier. The simple multiplier is always larger than the net tax multiplier, and the balanced budget multiplier is always equal to 1.

In the cases we have looked at, the balanced budget multiplier and the net tax multiplier were equal, but that was just a coincidence arising from the fact that we used 0.5 for the value of the marginal propensity to consume. If the value of the marginal propensity to consume is between 0.5 and 1.0, the net tax multiplier is between the balanced budget multiplier and the simple multiplier. For example, if the marginal propensity to consume were 0.75, we would get these values for our three multipliers:

$$M = 4.0 \qquad M_T = 3.0 \qquad M_B = 1.0$$

We should caution against an unwarranted interpretation of these multipliers. A change in government spending is the "most powerful" tool of fiscal policy, in the sense that it takes advantage of the full value of the simple multiplier. That does not mean, though, that a change in government spending is necessarily the *best* way to eliminate an expansionary or contractionary gap.

Any one of the three policies is equally good from a macroeconomic point of view, so long as a big enough change in taxes or the balanced budget is used. The important differences between the policies are of a micro-economic nature.

In particular, the policies differ in terms of the proportion of national income devoted to government purchases in the new equilibrium. Let us go back to our example where the initial level of income was $600, the target level $800, and the initial level of both taxes and government purchases $100. If the contractionary gap were filled by only raising government purchases, the new equilibrium level of government purchases would be $200. If the gap were filled entirely by reducing net taxes, the target income could be reached without increasing government purchases at all. (This would require cutting net taxes to *minus* $100; that is, it would require government transfer payments to be $100 greater than tax collections in the new equilibrium.) Finally, if the gap were filled while maintaining a balanced budget, the new equilibrium level of government purchases would have to be $300.

Which is better, a level of government purchases of $100, $200, or $300? It depends on whether the actual government expenditure projects undertaken are judged to be worthwhile *on their own merits,* without looking at their macroeconomic effects. To take an extreme case, suppose that all the government can think of to spend money on is putting men to work digging holes and then filling the holes back in again. If this were the case, filling a contractionary gap with added government purchases would be silly, and a balanced budget policy would be doubly silly. It would be better to cut taxes, even if they had to be cut a lot, and put the men to work producing something that consumers found worthwhile to spend their money on. On the other hand, if the government has a big backlog of projects that give taxpayers more for their money, in terms of real benefits, than they get from the money they spend in the consumer sector, then raising government spending makes sense.

Educated at Harvard, James Tobin has spent most of his professional career at Yale. Tobin is widely recognized for his work in macroeconomic theory. In particular, he has made fundamental contributions to the "portfolio balance" theory of the demand for money, to be discussed in Chapter 12 of this book. He has received many awards and honorary degrees, and in 1971, served as President of the American Economic Association.

Together with his great accomplishments as a theorist, Tobin has long had a very active interest in economic policy. This interest took him to Washington in 1961 as a member of President Kennedy's Council of Economic Advisors. His views at that time appear to have been typical of the economics profession in the Kennedy era. It was an era when economists were confident of their theories and Presidents confident of the power of government to solve social problems.

Writing for the *New Republic* in 1960, just before going to Washington, Tobin summarized his views in these terms: "If the overwhelming problem of democratic capitalism in the 30's and even the 50's was to bring the business cycle under social control, the challenge of the 60's is to bring under public decision the broad allocation of national output. Fortunately, the means are at hand. They are techniques well within the peacetime scope of government. We can do the job without the direct controls of wartime—priorities, rationing, price and wage controls. . . . The means are at hand; to use them we will need to muster more wisdom, maturity, leadership, and sense of national purpose than we displayed in the 1950's."

James Tobin (1918–   )

Tobin stayed on the Council of Economic Advisors only briefly, but by no means lost his active interest in public policy. When George McGovern campaigned for the Presidency in 1972, Tobin was on hand as his most influential economic advisor.

Tobin's most recent book, *The New Economics One Decade Older* (1974), looks back on the policy experiences of the 1960s. His earlier confidence in the infallibility of economic theory plus government power as a means to overcome social injustice is perhaps a bit tempered now, but only a bit. Despite mistakes that may have been made, it is clear that Tobin continues to believe that the means are at hand to solve economic problems, and all that is needed is the political will to use them.

We can put this in terms of a provisional guideline: *Set the level of government purchases by looking at the actual economic merit of spending projects, without considering macroeconomic effects. Then, if the resulting budget does not provide the right amount of macroeconomic stimulus, aim for the target level of national income by adjusting net taxes upward or downward, as required.* This is not an ironclad law that gives the indisputable answer to every problem of fiscal policy. It is just a common sense rule of thumb.

Conclusion

In the decades since Keynes wrote his treatise, thousands of economists and policy makers have seen an exciting picture in the multiplier theory of income determination. Put simply, the Keynesian theory carries the message that *any desired level of national income can be chosen as a target, and any target can be hit given the political will to apply known policies.* The only limits are the physical productive capacity and resource base of the economy.

Does It Work?

Despite the confidence of statements issued from the highest level of the economics profession, you must want to ask, does it work? Do the economic events of the 1970s reflect intelligently chosen targets accurately arrived at by enlightened policy? Were the simultaneous presence of unprecedented peacetime inflation and the highest unemployment since the 1930s the result of careful fine tuning of planned expenditure? From the record, it looks as if either the policies outlined here had not been tried (but we know they have been!) or that there is something more to good economic policy than juggling contractionary and expansionary gaps.

Perhaps the fact that there is more to be learned than we yet know about the intelligent conduct of macroeconomic policy makes economics an even more exciting picture today than a decade ago, when the men at the top thought that they knew all the answers. In this book, too, we have a long way to go, but by the end of seven more chapters we promise that you will at least be in sight of the frontiers of macroeconomic science.

SUMMARY

1. If the equilibrium level of nominal national income is different from the target level, there will be a gap between total planned expenditure and national product measured at the target level of income. If the equilibrium level of income is lower than policy makers want it to be, a contractionary gap is said to exist. If the equilibrium level of nominal income is too high, the gap is said to be expansionary.
2. One way to fill a contractionary gap is by increasing government purchases without increasing net taxes. When government purchases are increased while net taxes, planned investment, and the consumption schedule remain unchanged, equilibrium nominal national income will change by an amount equal to the change in government purchases times the multiplier.
3. A contractionary gap can also be filled by cutting net taxes without changing government purchases. When net taxes are changed while government purchases, planned investment, autonomous consumption, and the marginal propensity to consume remain unchanged, equilibrium nominal national income will change in the direction opposite to the change in taxes by an amount equal to the change in net taxes times the net tax multiplier.
4. An increase in government spending, accompanied by an equal increase in net taxes, with planned investment, autonomous consumption, and the marginal propensity to consume unchanged, produces a dollar-for-dollar increase in equilibrium nominal national income. The balanced budget multiplier is thus equal to 1.
5. A provisional guideline for fiscal policy is to set the level of government purchases by looking at the actual economic merit of spending projects without considering macroeconomic effects. Then, if the resulting budget does not provide the right amount of macroeconomic stimulus, aim for the target level of national income by adjusting net taxes upward or downward as required.
6. Recent experiences tend to cast doubt on the original Keynesian faith that any desired level of national income can be chosen as a target, and that any target can be hit given the political will to apply known policies. There is more to economic policy than juggling expansionary and contractionary gaps.

DISCUSSION QUESTIONS

1. Is the target level of national income always that level of national income at which there will be equilibrium?
2. Do you think that the major tool of fiscal policy should be changes in government spending or changes in taxation? Justify your position.

3. Use the circular flow to trace the effect of government spending in closing a contractionary gap.
4. What importance does the size of the marginal propensity to consume have on the effectiveness of fiscal policy in closing both inflationary and deflationary gaps?
5. Explain why a given change in government spending has a greater impact on the economy than the same change in taxation.
6. If there were a contractionary gap, would there be some advantage to simply paying workers to dig ditches and then fill them in? Under what circumstances would this policy be beneficial?
7. Who pays the cost and who receives the benefits of (a) increased government spending and (b) increased taxes. Does your answer to this question differ now from what it would have been just after you read Chapter 4?
8. Do you think that there is an expansionary gap in the economy right now (as you are taking this course)? A contractionary gap? How can you tell? What is the government doing about the gap if there is one?
9. Do you think the current President and his economic advisors are confident of their ability to make the economy do what they think it ought to? Are you confident of their ability? Why or why not?

Appendix
An Algebraic Approach to Income Determination and the Multiplier

All of the theoretical propositions we have illustrated with graphs and numerical examples in the last three chapters can be expressed equally well in terms of elementary algebraic equations. Let us begin with the consumption schedule. Using **a** to represent autonomous consumption, **b** for the marginal propensity to consume, C for consumption, T for net taxes, and Y for nominal national income, the consumption schedule can be written

$$C = \mathbf{a} + \mathbf{b}(Y - T) \qquad (1)$$

Note that the expression $(Y - T)$ that appears in the right-hand side of this equation represents disposable income.

Next we put together the aggregate demand schedule. Using AD for total planned expenditure, I for planned investment, G for government purchases, and other symbols as before, we can write the aggregate demand schedule as

$$AD = C + I + G \qquad (2)$$

Substituting for C on the basis of Eq. (1), this becomes

$$AD = \mathbf{a} + \mathbf{b}(Y - T) + I + G \qquad (3)$$

Our theory tells us that national income must be equal to planned expenditure in order for the circular flow to be in equilibrium. This equilibrium condition can be written as

$$Y = AD \qquad (4)$$

Using Eq. (3) to substitute for AD, the equilibrium condition becomes

$$Y = \mathbf{a} + \mathbf{b}(Y - T) + I + G \qquad (5)$$

Solving Eq. (5) for Y gives us this formula for the equilibrium value of nominal national income:

$$Y^* = \frac{1}{1 - \mathbf{b}}(\mathbf{a} - \mathbf{b}T + I + G) \qquad (6)$$

The asterisk (*) after the Y in this formula reminds us that the equation holds only for the *equilibrium* value of nominal national income.

Notice that the first term of the right-hand side of Eq. (6), $1/(1 - \mathbf{b})$, gives the value of the simple multiplier.

Let us use this formula to solve some simple problems in the theory of income determination and fiscal policy.

Problem 1: Suppose that $\mathbf{a} = 150$, $\mathbf{b} = 0.5$, $I = 100$, $G = 100$, and $T = 100$. What is the value of equilibrium national income?

Solution: Insert the given values in Eq. (6). This gives

$$Y^* = \frac{1}{1 - 0.5}[150 - 0.5(100) + 100 + 100]$$
$$= 2(300)$$
$$= 600$$

Compare this solution with Exhibits 9.1 and 9.2 in order to see the parallel between the graphical, numerical, and algebraic solutions to this income determination problem.

Problem 2: Suppose that, initially, all variables have the values given in Problem 1, but that the government adopts a target value for nominal national income of $900. Assuming no change in taxes, how much will government purchases have to be in order for the national income target to be reached?

Solution: Insert the known values for $\mathbf{a}$, $\mathbf{b}$, I, and T in Eq. (6). Use the target value of nominal national income, $900, in place of Y^*, and leave G as the unknown. This gives

$$900 = 2[150 - 0.5(100) + 100 + G]$$

Solve this equation for G:

$$900 = 400 + 2G$$
$$2G = 500$$
$$G = 250$$

We see that government purchases must be raised from $100 to $250 in order to raise national income from $600 to $900. This accords with the principle that, other things being equal, the change in equilibrium nominal national income resulting from a given change in government purchases is equal to the simple multiplier times the change in government purchases.

Problem 3: According to the formula given in the text, when the marginal propensity to consume is 0.75, the net tax multiplier must be 3. Confirm this by showing that a $100 tax cut will result in a $300 increase in equilibrium national income if the marginal propensity to consume is 0.75.

Solution: Use Y_0 for the initial equilibrium level of national income, Y_1 for the equilibrium level of national income after the tax cut, T_0 for the initial level of net taxes, a value of 0.75 for $\mathbf{b}$, and the usual letters for the other unknown values. First we get

$$Y_0 = \frac{1}{1 - 0.75}[\mathbf{a} - 0.75(T_0) + I + G]$$

Which simplifies to

$$Y_0 = 4[\mathbf{a} - 0.75(T_0) + I + G]$$

Next find the expression for Y_1 by using $T_0 - 100$ for the new level of net taxes. This gives

$$Y_1 = 4[\mathbf{a} - 0.75(T_0 - 100) + I + G]$$

Which can be rewritten as

$$Y_1 = 4[\mathbf{a} - 0.75(T_0) + I + G] + 300$$

Substituting the expression for Y_0 that we obtained earlier into the right-hand side of this last equation gives

$$Y_1 = Y_0 + 300$$

which is just what we wanted to know. The $100 tax cut does raise the equilibrium level of national income by $300, as we expect from application of the net tax multiplier.

CHAPTER 11
The Banking System and the Supply of Money

What You Will Learn in This Chapter
Money plays a big role in economic life. We use it every day as a means of payment and a store of value. In the American economy, checking accounts in commercial banks are the most common form of money. The commercial banks that create checking accounts for use as money are closely regulated by the Federal Reserve System. These regulations allow the Federal Reserve to control the total quantity of money supplied in the economy. Later, we shall see that this control of the money supply is a powerful tool of economic stabilization policy.

For Review
Here is an important term that will be put to use in this chapter. Be certain that you understand it, or review it before proceeding.
    Opportunity cost (Chapter 1)

There is still a big piece missing from our theory of nominal national income and the multiplier. The missing piece is money. In this chapter and the next two, we fill in what we need to know about money and the banking system. By doing so, we shall add greatly to our understanding of stabilization policy. Once again, our familiar tools of supply and demand will come into use. In the present chapter we shall explain how the banking system controls the supply of money. In Chapter 12 we shall look at the demand for money, and then put supply and demand together. Finally, in Chapter 13 we shall show how the multiplier theory can be modified to take money into account.

The Nature and Functions of Money

Money has three functions. It serves as a unit of account, a medium of exchange, and a store of purchasing power.

Unit of Account

As a unit of account, money serves as a convenient "common denominator" for measuring the value of all goods and services. We have seen how national income accountants use money prices to measure things such as national product and national income. On a smaller scale, we all use money as a unit of account in our day-to-day household budgeting.

Medium of Exchange

In saying that money serves as a medium of exchange, we mean that it is accepted as a means of payment in all market transactions. Without some generally accepted medium of exchange, we would have to trade by barter. Barter sometimes works on a very small scale, as when two farmers swap a ton of hay for a cord of firewood, or on a very large scale, as when the Soviet Union trades a train load of machine tools for a million tons of Polish coal. Most of the time, though, when we go to the grocery store or to our stockbroker it is easier to take along money than a bale of hay or a bag of grain. Needless to say, payment in money is also more likely to be acceptable to grocers and stockbrokers.

Store of Purchasing Power

The third function of money is to act as a temporary store of purchasing power. Money is one of several forms in which we can keep wealth until we need it to make transactions. This function of money is quite important from the point of view of economic theory. It will pay us to look at it in somewhat more detail than the first two functions.

Money is not the only thing that can function as a store of purchasing power. Wealth can be held as real estate, bonds, stocks, consumer durables, precious gems and metals, works of art, and any of a long list of other forms. Why might someone choose money as a store of purchasing power rather than one of these other assets?

Liquidity

Liquidity A property that an asset is said to have if it can be acquired and disposed of quickly and easily without the danger of a loss in nominal value.

Bonds Certificates issued by a borrower that entitle the lender (called the bondholder) to receive fixed periodic payments of interest, plus a larger final payment when the bond "matures" after a set number of years.

The outstanding attraction of money as an asset is **liquidity.** An asset is said to be liquid if it can be acquired and disposed of quickly and easily, without the danger of a loss in nominal value. Compare money in this respect to **bonds,** for example. To buy or sell a bond, you have to visit a broker. This takes time, may be done only during business hours, and means paying a small commission to the broker. Furthermore, there is the danger that when you go to your broker to sell a bond, it may be worth less than when you bought it. If you paid $100 for a bond and its price has gone down to $90, you are in a dilemma. Should you sell it now, suffering a capital loss of $10 on top of paying the brokerage fee? Or should you keep it in the hope that its market price will go back up, even though you really would prefer to change it for some other type of asset? Keeping assets in the form of money makes disposing of them much easier. Almost anyone will take money, night or day. What is more, there is no danger of capital loss on money. The nominal value of a dollar is always a dollar, no more and no less.

Opportunity Costs

There are major opportunity costs to holding money, which must be balanced against the advantage of its liquidity. The biggest opportunity cost is that most forms of money earn no interest return. Stocks and bonds are superior in this respect. Other less liquid assets, such as consumer durables and owner-occupied real estate, do not pay an explicit return, but do provide useful material services to their owners.

Moreover, although holding money avoids the danger of a loss in the nominal value of one's assets, it does involve some risk. The major risk is that of a loss in real purchasing power in the event of inflation. If prices double, all those dollar bills under your mattress will buy only half as many beefsteaks or movie tickets when you pull them out to spend them. In contrast, owning physical assets such as works of art, useful commodities, or real estate gives some protection against inflation, because the prices of these things can be expected to rise in step with other prices. We shall return to a discussion of money as a store of purchasing power in the next chapter.

Types of Money

In modern economies, there are two things that perform all three of the basic functions of money: currency and demand deposits. By **currency** we mean coins and paper money. **Demand deposits** are the accounts in commercial banks that we commonly call checking accounts. By conventional definition, money is held only by households and firms other than banks. No currency or demand deposits that belong to the Treasury, Federal Reserve, or commercial banks are included in the definition of money. When we speak of the economy's stock of money in this book, this is what we mean: the total currency outside banks plus the nonbank public's holdings of demand deposits. This total is called M_1.

Some other assets closely resemble money. Of these, the most important are **time deposits** in commercial banks. By time deposits we mean savings accounts and certificates of deposits. Some economists think that when we total up the economy's money stock we should add these in too. When this is done, the total is called M_2. Exhibit 11.1 shows us the total amount of each component of the money stock for the United States, according to recent data.

Currency Outside Banks

Currency is issued by two institutions of the government: the Federal Reserve System and the Treasury. It represents their monetary obligations

Currency Coins and paper money.

Demand Deposits Deposits at commercial banks that permit the depositor to make payments to others by writing a check against the deposit. Demand deposits are what we commonly call checking accounts.

M_1 The money supply defined as currency plus demand deposits.

Time Deposits Interest-paying accounts at commercial banks against which it is not ordinarily possible to write checks. Both passbook savings accounts and certificates of deposits are included, except for certain very large certificates of deposit used by corporate depositors.

M_2 The money supply defined as M_1 plus time deposits at commercial banks.

EXHIBIT 11.1
Components of money and near money, September 1975 (billions of current dollars)
Money takes several forms in the American economy. Currency and demand deposits fully perform all three of the major functions of money. Together they are called M_1. Time deposits in commercial banks act as stores of value, but not as means of payment. M_1 plus time deposits in commercial banks is called M_2.

Type	Amount in Circulation
Currency outside banks*	71.9
Demand deposits†	220.9
Money supply M_1	292.8
Time deposits‡	359.9
Money supply plus time deposits M_2	652.7

*Excludes currency in the vaults of commercial banks, the Federal Reserve banks, and the U.S. Treasury.

†Includes (1) demand deposits at all commercial banks other than those due to domestic commercial banks and the U.S. government, less cash items in process of collection and Federal Reserve float, and (2) foreign demand deposits at Federal Reserve banks.

‡Excludes negotiable time certificates of deposit issued in denominations of $100,000 or more by large banks.

Source: *Federal Reserve Bulletin,* November 1975.

or IOUs to the public. Today, currency consists almost entirely of Federal Reserve notes and Treasury coins.

Paper money and coins are no longer backed by any intrinsically valuable commodity. Neither the Federal Reserve nor the Treasury will now give anything in exchange for a $10 bill or a dime other than another $10 bill or dime—another promise to pay. Up until 1934, the government issued gold coins and paper currency redeemable in gold. Until the mid-1960s one could readily obtain silver coins and "silver certificates" (dollar bills redeemable in silver), but these were gradually phased out. The few remaining silver certificates in circulation can no longer be turned in for metallic silver, and the remaining silver coins are mostly lodged in collections. We now have a currency whose value is based purely on the public's faith in its ability to exchange it for all kinds of goods and services.

Demand Deposits

Demand deposits are bookkeeping entries of commercial banks. They represent obligations of these banks to their depositors. As shown in Exhibit 11.1, demand deposits account for some 75 percent of the money supply, but this figure actually understates their importance. Demand deposits turn out to be used to conduct some 95 percent of the dollar volume of all transactions in the economy. Although demand deposits are issued by private commerical banks, there are limits on the volume of such deposits that banks can create. We shall discuss these limits shortly.

Near Money

Time deposits in commercial banks are also included in Exhibit 11.1. In contrast to demand deposits, time deposits pay interest to depositors. The reason they have not traditionally been considered to be true money is that they could not be used directly as a means of payment. In recent years, though, the distinction between money and near money has begun to blur. A major step in this direction is the introduction of **NOW accounts,** which permit depositors to write checks on interest-bearing savings accounts. Also, recent changes in regulations have made it possible, in some cases, for depositors to transfer money from a savings to a checking account by telephone. That also has the effect of making savings deposits more liquid.

Although they are not mentioned in Exhibit 11.1, we should note that savings deposits at nonbank financial institutions, such as savings and loan institutions, hardly differ from savings deposits in commercial banks. Securities such as government bonds, commercial paper, and Treasury bills are also very liquid.

NOW Accounts Accounts that permit checks to be written on interest-bearing time deposits. NOW stands for "negotiable orders of withdrawal."

The Federal Reserve System[1]

On December 23, 1913, President Woodrow Wilson signed the Federal Reserve Act, which established the **Federal Reserve System,** or **Fed** for

Federal Reserve System (Fed) The central banking system of the United States, which provides banking services to government and commercial banks, and regulates the activities of commercial banks.

[1]This section and the following one give a very concise description of the structure and functioning of the Federal Reserve System and the U.S. commercial banking system. Readers who wish to learn additional details may consult Colin and Rosemary Campbell, *An Introduction to Money and Banking* (New York: Holt, Rinehart and Winston, 1972). For a somewhat more advanced treatment, see Thomas D. Simpson, *Money, Banking, and Economic Analysis* (Englewood Cliffs, N.J.: Prentice-Hall, 1976).

short. The Fed functions as the central bank of the United States. It is the government bank where commercial banks and the Treasury do their banking. It regulates the commercial banking system. It controls the supply of money. By exercising its powers, as we shall see, the Fed can have a major effect on the level of prices of all goods and services, on the level of employment and output in the economy, and on the nation's balance of payments.

By law, the Federal Reserve is an "independent agency" of the federal government, not under the direction of the executive branch. The original intent of making the Fed independent was to prevent the Treasury Department from manipulating monetary conditions for political ends. In practice, the monetary actions of the Fed and the fiscal actions of the Treasury are usually coordinated. The Chairman of the Federal Reserve Board of Governors, the Secretary of the Treasury, and the Chairman of the President's Council of Economic Advisors meet weekly to discuss national policy. It would be more accurate to say that the Fed serves as an equal partner in determining government policy than to say that it acts as an independent agent.

Structure

The overall organizational structure of the Federal Reserve System is shown in Exhibit 11.2. At the heart of the structure are the twelve District Federal Reserve Banks. Ten of these banks have branches, a total of

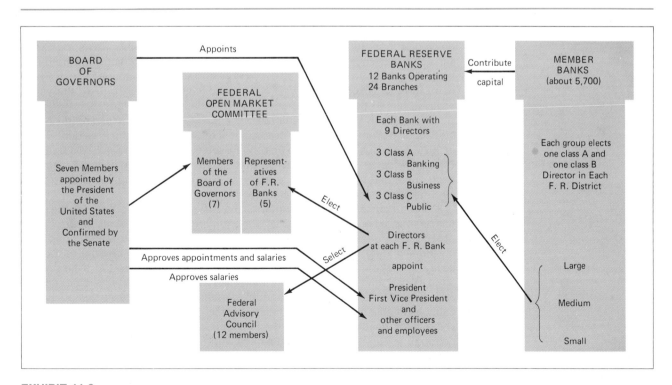

EXHIBIT 11.2
Organization of the Federal Reserve System
The Federal Reserve system, or Fed, acts as the central bank for the United States. It provides banking services to commercial banks and government, and regulates the activities of commercial banks.

twenty-four branches in all. Each of the twelve regional banks is a separate corporation chartered by the federal government and owned by its stockholders, who are the member commercial banks of the district. Although the Federal Reserve banks are owned by their stockholders, they are not typical of privately owned corporations because profit seeking is not one of their goals. Any extra earnings of a Federal Reserve bank over and above operating expenses and the fixed dividends that go to member banks are passed on to the Treasury.

Primary control of each district bank lies with a nine-member board. Of these nine, six are elected by the member bank stockholders, and the remaining three are appointed by the Fed's own Board of Governors. Each board is responsible for the policies of its own bank and for appointing bank officers.

The Federal Reserve banks perform several important functions in the banking system. They carry out policy decisions, examine and supervise the member banks in their district, and provide banking services for the

Arthur Frank Burns (1904–   )

Arthur Burns is among those many distinguished economists born in Austria, but his education and training were entirely American. He moved to America with his parents as a boy, and went on to study at Columbia University, where he earned his doctorate in 1934. During the 1930s and 1940s, Burns taught at Rutgers University and then at Columbia. Early in this period, he began a long association with the National Bureau of Economic Research. His research on business cycles at the Bureau earned him a solid reputation among his professional colleagues. In 1959, they honored him with the Presidency of the American Economic Association.

When Dwight Eisenhower became President of the United States, he appointed Arthur Burns Chairman of his Council of Economic Advisors. Burns served in that capacity until 1956. Perhaps the most important thing he did in those years was to establish a friendship with the ambitious young Vice President, Richard Nixon. He maintained an association with Nixon over the years, advising him in both his 1960 and 1968 Presidential campaigns.

Predictably, when Nixon entered office Burns returned to Washington. Nixon first appointed him to the newly created post of Counselor to the President. Then, in 1970, a job opened up at the Federal Reserve. Members of the Fed's Board of Governors serve 14-year terms, so that by 1970, a majority of the Board had been appointed by Democratic presidents. Nixon naturally wanted his own man as Chairman, and gave Burns the job.

Burns has served as Chairman of the Board of Governors under the most difficult circumstances imaginable. For one thing, the years of his tenure in that post have seen the worst economic instability since the 1930s. Many economists lay the blame for a large share of that instability squarely at the door of the Fed itself. To make matters even more difficult, Burns has served at a time when "monetarist" and "Keynesian" economists have been locked in a furious theoretical debate over the proper conduct of monetary policy. Burns has pursued a cautious middle course that has made no one entirely happy. He has introduced some much-needed changes in the Fed's operating procedures, but these have not gone as far as the monetarists have wanted. At the same time, the Keynesians, many allied politically with the Democrats, have scored Burns for keeping monetary conditions too tight, and thus worsening unemployment.

Publicly, Burns takes all this criticism in stride. He is by nature independent-minded, and did not hesitate even to disagree openly on matters of policy with Nixon. His office is a natural lightning rod for criticism, and that is a role that he seems at times almost to relish.

U.S. Treasury and other governmental agencies. They provide banking services to their member banks, such as clearing checks, handling commercial banks' reserve deposit accounts, making loans to member banks, and providing currency for member banks. In addition, they issue Federal Reserve notes, which form a major part of the stock of currency.

The Board of Governors

The highest policy-making body of the entire Federal Reserve System is its Board of Governors. The board acts as a supervisor of the twelve Federal Reserve banks. The board has seven members who are appointed by the President and confirmed by the Senate. Each governor serves a single fourteen-year term, and devotes full-time service to the business of the Federal Reserve System. One term expires every other year. The present chairman of the board is Arthur F. Burns. Like most recent appointees to the board, he was a professional economist and active in public affairs before his appointment.

The Federal Open Market Committee

A special Fed committee decides when and how open market operations—which, as we shall see, are a powerful instrument of monetary policy—will be used. The Federal Open Market Committee is composed of the seven members of the board of governors, plus five District Reserve bank presidents. It meets every month to decide on changes to be made in the Fed's security holdings. Actual transactions are carried out through the Federal Reserve Bank of New York.

The Commercial Banking System

As of June 30, 1975, there were 14,573 commercial banks in the United States. Among this group of banks, those that have obtained charters from the federal government are called national banks. National banks are required to belong to the Federal Reserve System, which means that they must own stock in the system and be governed by its regulations. In addition to national banks, there are also state-chartered banks, which may choose to join the Federal Reserve System if they wish. Exhibit 11.3 shows the number of each type of bank and their total assets.

Fed Membership

Banks belonging to the Federal Reserve System are entitled to certain privileges of membership. Member banks can acquire loans, currency, and financial advice from their district Federal Reserve bank. They can use the Fed's check-clearing facilities and transfer funds over its teletype wires. They earn a fixed dividend on the stock they are required to own in the system.

There are some disadvantages to membership, though. Member banks are required by the Federal Reserve to keep a larger fraction of their assets in the form of non-interest-bearing reserves than are nonmember banks in most states. They are also subject to more stringent regulations regarding capital, assets, mergers, branches, holding companies, and officers than are nonmember banks.

EXHIBIT 11.3

Number of banks and total assets, June 1975

Commercial banks in the United States may be chartered either by the federal government (national banks) or the individual states. National banks must belong to the Federal Reserve System, but state banks need not be members. Only a minority of all banks are members, but member banks are larger on the average. Member banks hold nearly four-fifths of all bank assets.

	Number of Banks	Percent of Total	Total Assets (in billions of dollars)	Percent of Total
National banks	4,730	32.5	536.8	57.6
State member banks	1,064	7.3	179.7	19.3
Total member banks	5,794		716.5	
Nonmember banks	8,779	60.2	214.4	23.0
Total banks	14,573	100.0	930.7	100.0

Note: Totals may not agree because of rounding.

Source: *Federal Reserve Bulletin*, November 1975.

Nonmember banks use large city banks to provide many of the services that the Federal Reserve system affords member banks.

Balance Sheet

What exactly do commercial banks do? The easiest way to find out is to look at a commercial bank balance sheet. A balance sheet is an accounting statement that describes the financial position of a bank at a particular date in terms of two columns of figures, one describing the bank's assets and the other describing its liabilities and net worth. By assets we mean everything that the bank owns. By liabilities we mean all claims against the bank's assets held by individuals, firms, or institutions other than the bank's owners. A bank's net worth is obtained by subtracting its liabilities from its assets. This figure gives the value of the assets not claimed by outsiders; it is the part of the bank's assets claimed by the bank's owners. Because of the way assets, liabilities, and net worth are defined, the following relationship among balance sheet entries must always hold:

$$Assets = Liabilities + Net\ Worth$$

Whenever a bank increases its total assets, its liabilities plus its net worth must by definition rise by an equal amount.

Exhibit 11.4 is a consolidated balance sheet for all member banks, with the principal balance sheet items listed as of June 30, 1975. The balance sheet shows that most of the assets held by banks are financial claims against others. These claims are mostly loans granted to individuals and businesses, and securities issued by business and by federal, state, and local governments. On the liability side of the balance sheet, the biggest items are demand and time deposits, which are claims against the bank owned by depositors. The net worth figure represents what would be left to the owners of the bank if they were to sell all their assets and pay off all their liabilities at "book" values.

EXHIBIT 11.4

Consolidated balance sheet of member banks, June 30, 1975
(in billions of dollars)

This table shows the consolidated balance sheet for all member banks of the Federal Reserves. Listed as assets are everything that the bank owns. Liabilities are all claims against the bank's assets held by individuals, firms, or institutions other than the bank's owners. The bank's net worth is obtained by subtracting liabilities form assets.

Assets			Liabilities and Net Worth	
Total reserves		34.4	Demand deposits	243.2
On deposit with Fed	26.9			
Held as currency	7.5		Time deposits	330.4
Loans		384.2	Borrowings from Fed	.1
Securities		149.7	Other liabilities	85.4
Other assets		182.7	Net worth	57.6
Total		716.6	Total	716.6

Source: *Federal Reserve Bulletin*, November 1975.

Reserves

The **reserves** item on the asset side of the balance sheet deserves some further explanation. Historically, the reason that banks hold some of their assets in the form of reserves is that at any moment depositors may want to withdraw their money from the bank, either by writing a check to someone who will deposit it in another bank, or by walking up to the teller's window and asking for currency. In the U.S. commercial banking system today, the quantity of reserves that banks hold is not left up to the judgment of individual bankers. Instead, the Fed sets certain reserve requirements for member banks. These take the form of fixed percentages of deposits that banks must hold as reserves. These percentages are called **required reserve ratios.** They vary according to the type and size of deposit, as shown in Exhibit 11.5. The Fed permits banks to hold reserves

Reserves (of Commercial Banks) Money held by commercial banks as cash or non-interest-bearing deposits with the Federal Reserve.

Required Reserve Ratios Legally required minimum quantities of reserves, expressed as ratios of reserves to various types of deposits.

EXHIBIT 11.5

Required reserve ratios (October 31, 1975)*

Historically, banks held some of their assets as reserves in order to pay depositors who wanted to withdraw their money. Today reserves still perform that function, but more important, they are a tool of the Fed's regulation of the banking system. Minimum reserves for member banks are set by the Fed. Nonmember banks have reserve requirements set by individual states. These may differ from those shown here.

Demand Deposits					Time Deposits	
0–2	1–10	10–100	100–400	Over 400	*Savings*	*Other Time Deposits†*
7.5%	10%	12%	13%	16.5%	3%	1–6%

*Deposit intervals are in millions of dollars. Requirement schedules are graduated, and each deposit interval applies to that part of the deposits of each bank.

†Varies according to maturity date.

Source: *Federal Reserve Bulletin*, November 1975.

either in the form of currency in their own vaults or in the form of non-interest-bearing deposits in the district Federal Reserve bank. As Exhibit 11.4 shows, the latter option is the most heavily used.

Excess Reserves

The law does not prevent commercial banks from holding more of their assets in the form of reserves than the Fed requires. Any reserves above the required level are referred to as **excess reserves.** However, banks generally try to keep their excess reserves low because reserves earn no interest. They tend to acquire more earning assets, either by making loans or buying securities, whenever they have large excess reserves. As a result, of the $34,706 million total reserves held by member banks on June 25, 1975, fully $34,615 million were required reserves. Excess reserves were only $91 million.

The Supply of Money

Deposits and Reserves

The authority of the Federal Reserve to set required reserve ratios is very important from the point of view of economic theory. That is because a close relationship exists between the level of total reserves and the level of demand deposits, which in turn are the major component of the economy's supply of money. The basic principles of this relationship are quite easy to understand. Let us begin with a numerical example.

For this example, we need to make some simplifications in the banking system. First, we assume that demand deposits are banks' only liabilities, that reserves and loans are their only assets, and that each bank's net worth is zero. Second, we assume that banks always try to keep their level of excess reserves at zero. Third, we assume that the required reserve ratio is a uniform 20 percent for all demand deposits.

Excess Reserves Commercial bank reserves in excess of the minimum legally required levels.

EXHIBIT 11.6

Consolidated balance sheet for a simplified banking system, showing the expansion of deposits

In this simplified banking system, demand deposits are banks' only liabilities, reserves and loans their only assets, and net worth is zero. All deposits are subject to a uniform required reserve ratio of 20 percent. An injection of $100 into this system has the effect of increasing the money supply by $500 by the time banks once again reduce their excess reserves to zero.

	Assets				Liabilities and Net Worth		
	Initial Position	Intermediate Position	Final Position		Initial Position	Intermediate Position	Final Position
Total reserves	100	200	200	Demand deposits	500	600	1,000
(Required reserves)	(100)	(120)	(200)				
(Excess reserves)	(0)	(80)	(0)				
Loans	400	400	800				
Total	500	600	1,000	Total	500	600	1,000

Suppose that initially the consolidated balance sheet of this simplified banking system showed total assets of $500, including $100 in total reserves and $400 in loans, and total liabilities of $500, composed entirely of demand deposits. With a required reserve ratio of 20 percent, required reserves are $100 and excess reserves are zero. These figures are shown in the columns labeled "initial position" in Exhibit 11.6.

Now suppose that some depositor comes along with a check, drawn not on one of the commercial banks in our system, but on one of the Federal Reserve banks. When this check is deposited, the commercial bank receiving it credits $100 to the account of the depositor. This appears on the bank's own balance sheet as an addition to liabilities. The bank, in turn, deposits the check in its own account at the district Federal Reserve bank. This action adds $100 in new reserves to the asset side of its balance sheet.

It is important that the original check be drawn on the Federal Reserve System. If it were drawn on another commercial bank, the bank on which it were drawn would lose $100 in reserves when the bank receiving the deposit cashed the check, and the two entries would cancel each other out on the consolidated balance sheet of all commercial banks. Why would the Fed system issue one of its own checks to a private citizen in the first place? Possibly because the citizen presented newly mined gold or foreign currency to a Federal Reserve bank, or possibly, as we shall discuss below, because the citizen sold $100 worth of securities to the Federal Reserve.

Deposit of the Federal Reserve check brings total reserves up to $200. Of this, $120 must now be held as required reserves, because total deposits have risen to $600. This leaves the banking system $80 in excess reserves. The balance sheet of the banking system as it looks at this point is shown in the column of Exhibit 11.6 labeled "intermediate position."

Individual banks are not satisfied with this intermediate position, because they do not like to hold excess reserves. Instead, they want to acquire additional earning assets. They do this by making loans. In exchange for an IOU, a lending bank will credit a borrower's checking account with the amount of the loan. The borrower need not leave the money on deposit, but when he writes checks on his account, those checks will end up in the accounts of other people in other banks. The total level of deposits as shown on the consolidated balance sheet rises by the exact amount of the loan in any event.

How far will the process of deposit expansion go? The limit is determined by the original change in total reserves (which caused the original change in excess reserves) and by the required reserve ratio. Suppose, for example, that banks make $200 worth of new loans on the basis of their $80 in excess reserves. This would raise total assets and demand deposits to $800 and hence raise required reserves to $160. There would still be $40 of excess reserves remaining somewhere in the banking system, and expansion could continue. Not until total deposits reach $1,000 will excess reserves be entirely eliminated. This requires a total of $400 in new loans by the banking system. After this quantity of loans has been made, the consolidated balance sheet looks like the columns labeled "final position" in Exhibit 11.6.

General Principles

Some important general principles can be seen at work in this example. In the banking system we have just looked at, there is a very simple relationship between the total quantity of demand deposits and the level of bank reserves. After the money expansion process is complete and excess reserves have been reduced to zero, the total quantity of demand deposits is equal to total reserves divided by the required reserves ratio.

In the numerical example, the required ratio is 20 percent, so the quantity of demand deposits is five times the quantity of total reserves. An injection into the banking system of $100 in new reserves results in an increase of $500 in the money supply.

Money Multiplier

In the real world, things are a bit more complicated than in our example. For one thing, money includes currency as well as demand deposits. What is more, the ratio of demand deposits to total reserves is not a simple constant. It varies over time, and its variations are not perfectly predictable.

Variations in the ratio of demand deposits to total reserves come from several sources. Partly they result from differing required reserve ratios on different classes of deposits at member banks. Partly they result from different reserve requirements for nonmember banks; these requirements vary considerably from state to state. Finally, the ratio of demand deposits to reserves can be affected by changes in the public's demand for time deposits, and changes in the willingness of banks to hold excess reserves.

Even with all these complications, the general principles of our simplified example carry over at least roughly to the real world. There is still an approximately proportional relationship between the money supply and total reserves. We shall call the ratio of the money supply (M_1) to total reserves the **money multiplier.** It must be remembered, though, that this multiplier is not a constant. Exhibit 11.7 shows that the money multiplier has varied over a range of 7.4 to 8.5 since 1969. About a third of the time, the multiplier has changed by 2 percent or more from one quarter to the next. This variability creates some problems for monetary policy, as the next section will make clear.

Money Multiplier The ratio of the money supply (M_1) to total reserves.

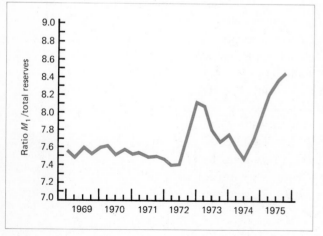

EXHIBIT 11.7
Recent variations in the money multiplier
The money multiplier is subject to significant variations from quarter to quarter. These result from variations in reserve requirements on different types of deposits, changes in the demand for money, and changes in the willingness of banks to hold excess reserves. The data shown here are corrected for statutory changes in required reserve ratios.

Source: Board of Governors, Federal Reserve System, unpublished.

The Instruments of Monetary Policy

Fed's Balance Sheet

We have seen now how the level of total reserves affects the level of demand deposits and the money supply. Next we turn to a discussion of the balance sheet of the Federal Reserve banks, and how the Fed manipulates them to control the level of total reserves.

Exhibit 11.8 is a consolidated balance sheet for the twelve Federal Reserve banks. Looking first at the liabilities side, we see that Federal Reserve notes in circulation are the largest single liability of these banks. The second major type of liability is member banks reserve deposits. Other liabilities include deposits of the Treasury and foreign central banks, and a number of miscellaneous items. The small net worth of the Reserve banks represents member banks' direct ownership claims on the assets of the Federal Reserve System.

On the assets side of the balance sheet, we see that holdings of U.S. government securities are the largest single item. Loans to member banks also appear. These are usually extended on request to help the member banks avoid falling short of their required reserve levels.

Instruments

There are three major instruments by which the Federal Reserve conducts monetary policy. These are **open market operations** (sales and purchases of government securities in the open market), changes in the **discount rate** (the interest rate paid by commercial banks to borrow reserve funds from the Fed), and changes in the *required reserve ratios* for member banks. Let us look at each of these in turn.

Open Market Operations

Open market operations are the Fed's most important policy instrument. The effect of open market operations on monetary conditions is easy to understand now that we have looked at the relationship between commercial bank reserves and the money supply. Once again, let us work through a numerical example.

Open Market Operations Purchases or sales of government securities between the Fed and the public, used as an instrument of monetary policy.

EXHIBIT 11.8

Consolidated balance sheet of the twelve Federal Reserve Banks, October 31, 1975 (in billions of dollars)

The Federal Reserve banks have liabilities to the general public, in the form of Federal Reserve notes, and to member banks, in the form of reserve deposits. Their main assets are government securities.

Assets		Liabilities and Net Worth	
Securities	87.1	Federal Reserve notes	73.0
Loans to member banks	.1	Member bank reserve deposits	26.3
Other assets	29.6	Other liabilities	15.1
Total	116.8	Total	116.8

Note: Subtotals may not add to totals due to rounding.

Source: Federal Reserve Bulletin, November 1975.

EXHIBIT 11.9

The effects of a $100 open market purchase on the consolidated balance sheets of Federal Reserve banks and commercial banks

If the Fed buys $100 worth of securities on the open market, its assets go up by $100, and its liabilities, in the form of member bank reserve deposits, go up by the same amount. In the commercial banking system, the $100 in new reserves show up on the assets side of the balance sheet. These new assets are initially balanced by new deposits of only $100. The position shown here as "after" is not the final one, for commercial banks now have excess reserves. They will proceed to expand deposits further by making new loans until they reach the required reserve ratio.

Before

| Federal Reserve | | | | Commercial Banks | | | |
Assets		Liabilities		Assets		Liabilities	
Securities	$ 500	Currency	$ 900	Reserves	$100	Deposits	$500
Other assets	$ 500	Reserve deposits	$ 100	Loans	$400		
Total	$1,000	Total	$1,000	Total	$500	Total	$500

After

| Federal Reserve | | | | Commercial Banks | | | |
Assets		Liabilities		Assets		Liabilities	
Securities	$ 600	Currency	$ 900	Reserves	$200	Deposits	$600
Other assets	$ 500	Reserve deposits	$ 200	Loans	$400		
Total	$1,100	Total	$1,100	Total	$600	Total	$600

Exhibit 11.9 illustrates the effects of an open market purchase of $100 in U.S. government securities from a member of the public. The effects are shown as they would occur in the simplified banking system described in our earlier numerical example. In that example, we saw what the effects of such a purchase looked like from the point of view of the commercial banking system. Now we see it from the points of view of both the commercial banking system and the Fed.

The first part of the table shows the consolidated balance sheets of both parts of the banking system before the open market operation. Beginning from there, suppose that the Federal Open Market Committee authorizes the purchase of $100 in government bonds from a private party. It pays with one of its own checks.

This gives the Federal Reserve banks $100 in new assets. The seller of the bond deposits the check in his own commerical bank. That gives the bank $100 in new liabilities, in the form of an increase in the original seller's demand deposits. Finally, the commerical bank deposits the check with its District Federal Reserve Bank, giving the commercial bank $100 in additional assets and the Federal Reserve $100 in additional liabilities, both in the form of increased member bank reserve deposits. The result of all this is shown in the lower portion of Exhibit 11.9. Assets and liabilities are each up $100 for the Federal Reserve banks and each up $100 for the commercial banking system.

This is still not the end of the story. The commercial banking system now has excess reserves. The open market operation is the starting point for a process of deposit expansion of the sort we described earlier. Commercial banks will continue to acquire earning assets until their deposits have risen by the full amount of the money multiplier times the added $100 in reserves.

The Discount Rate

A second policy instrument that the Fed can use is the discount rate. A rise in the discount rate, other things being equal, has the effect of discouraging commercial banks from borrowing to augment their reserves. A decline in the discount rate has the opposite impact.

Discount Rate (in the Banking System) The interest rate paid by commercial banks to borrow reserve funds from the Fed.

Changes in the discount rate are initiated by the District banks, but they must be approved by the Board of Governors. The managers of the District banks usually adjust the discount rate to keep it in line with other interest rates charged in the market. If the discount rate were substantially above prevailing market rates, member banks might not borrow at all from the Federal Reserve, finding other sources of funds when necessary. If the discount rate were too far below market rates, commercial banks would be tempted to borrow too readily from the Federal Reserve simply to finance new loans, or to purchase securities with higher interest rates. The discount rate is changed frequently to prevent either circumstance from arising.

The Required Reserve Ratios

The third instrument of monetary policy, changing required reserve ratios, is the most powerful. It is not used as often as other instruments, but recently it has been used more than in the past. Any change in required reserve ratios has a very large impact on total demand deposits because it directly affects the money multiplier. In the simplified case, this multiplier is simply the reciprocal of the required reserve ratio. With total reserves of, say $100 million, an increase in the required reserve ratio from 20 to 25 percent would reduce total demand deposits from $500 million to $400 million. The impact would be the same as the impact of $20 million of open market sales, without a change in the required reserve ratio.

The Board of Governors of the Federal Reserve has sole authority to change required reserve ratios. Such changes are usually made only when very large changes in the money supply are desired. For day-to-day policy purposes, the flexibility of open market operations is preferred. These can be made in any desired magnitude and reversed or adjusted immediately if necessary, without fanfare.

Conclusions

The conclusion to which our analysis of the banking system leads is that the Fed can control at will the quantity of money supplied. It can change total reserves when it wants by using open market operations and the discount rate. It can affect the money multiplier through changes in reserve ratios. Together, these determine the money supply.

In our theoretical discussions in the following chapters, we shall consider the Fed's control over the money supply to be absolute. The quantity of money supplied will be treated as something that changes only in response to changes in policy, and not in response to other economic conditions. In reality, though, the money supply is not under perfect control. We have already seen that the money multiplier can fluctuate sharply even over short periods. Nonmember banks, which hold a fifth of deposits now, are not under the Fed's direct control. As the demand of the public for money changes, people shift from one type of deposit to another, and different types of deposits have different reserve requirements. Finally, banks sometimes choose to hold excess reserves. Even though excess reserves are low on the average, they can sometimes change on short notice.

All of these things complicate the Fed's job of managing the money supply. Federal Reserve Board Chairman Burns takes the position that it would be a mistake even to try to control the money supply too closely. To do so, he believes, would cause many sudden short-term variations in interest rates in the face of short-run, temporary shifts in demand. These would disturb credit markets more seriously than the variability of the money supply does.

Current Fed practice is to announce in each quarter rather broad targets for money supply growth over the next twelve months. As this is written, for example, targets are set at 5 to 7½ percent growth for M_1 and 7½ to 10 percent growth for M_2. Given the political and economic pressures under which it works, the Fed does not always hit even these targets accurately.

All told, the relationships between the Fed's policy, economic conditions, and the money supply are still far from being understood. They are currently the subject of very active economic research by economists both inside and outside the banking system. In sticking with our assumption of a perfectly controlled money supply, then, we are leaving a great many interesting issues to other, more specialized books than this.

SUMMARY

1. Money performs three major functions in our economy. These are the functions of a unit of account, a medium of exchange, and a store of value. Only currency and demand deposits perform all three functions fully. Some other assets are close substitutes for money, notably time deposits at commercial banks.
2. The Federal Reserve System acts as the central bank of the United States. It provides banking services for commercial banks and the government, and also regulates the commercial banking system. Its regulatory powers allow it to control the money supply.
3. Demand deposits, the most common form of money, are created by the commercial banking system. The quantity of demand deposits created is limited by required reserve ratios. These are set by the Fed for member banks, and by the various states for nonmember banks. An injection of new reserves into the banking system causes a multiple expansion of demand deposits and the money supply. Under simplified conditions, the ratio of money to reserves (known as the money multiplier) is just the reciprocal of the required reserve ratio. In reality, the money multiplier is determined by more complex considerations, and it can vary from time to time in an unpredictable way.
4. The Fed has three major instruments of monetary policy. These are open market operations, changes in the discount rate, and changes in required reserve ratios. Open market operations are the most flexible instrument, and the one used for day-to-day policy purposes. For theoretical purposes, we can consider the Fed's control over the money supply to be absolute, but in practice it is imperfect.

DISCUSSION QUESTIONS

1. List the functions that money performs in the economy and illustrate how you have used money for each of these purposes. Then give an example of an occasion on which you have used something other than money for each of these purposes.
2. In what type of bank do you have an account? What type of account? Is the balance in your account part of M_1 or M_2?
3. If a commercial bank is not meeting the reserve requirement, what does it have to do? What changes are possible to make sure it meets its reserve requirement?
4. Over time we have switched from using currency to using demand deposits as money. Why do you think this has occurred?
5. It is possible that with increased use of credit cards we shall eventually do away with currency and demand deposits. Would we then be doing away with money? In what sense "yes" and what sense "no"?
6. Suppose that you put your artistic talents to good use, and print up $10,000 worth of counterfeit $20 bills, which go into circulation and are never detected as counterfeit. Trace the effects of your action through the banking system, and explain what happens to the economy's money supply. Do you think that undetected counterfeiting is a "victimless" crime?
7. Do you think that commercial banks should have required reserves? Would they have reserves if they were not required to do so? Explain.
8. If the Federal Reserve Board wanted to increase the money supply, what are the ways it could go about doing it? How could it decrease the money supply? Is it as easy for it to create money as it is for it to contract the money supply?

CHAPTER 12
The Demand for Money and the Money Market

What You Will Learn in This Chapter
The theory of money demand deals with the question of how much money people want under various circumstances. The quantity of money demanded depends on the interest rate and the level of nominal income. The theory of supply and demand and the concept of equilibrium can be applied to the money market in order to show what happens to the interest rate when the quantity of money supplied or the level of nominal income changes.

For Review
Here are some important terms and concepts that will be put to use in this chapter. Be certain that you understand them, or review them before proceeding.
Supply and demand (Chapter 3)
Money multiplier (Chapter 11)

In the last chapter we found that, as a general matter, people desire to hold part of their wealth in the form of money because money is highly liquid. Now we are ready to take up the more specific question of just *how much* money people want, and how changing economic conditions affect their need for money. This means developing a theory of the demand for money.

The Demand for Money

Portfolio Balance

Money demand theory is most easily explained in terms of the concept of **portfolio balance.** We say that people hold their wealth in the form of "portfolios" containing a variety of different kinds of assets. For example, moderately well-to-do individuals might include in their portfolios some real estate (their homes), some consumer durables (car, television, and refrigerator), some corporate stocks, some government bonds, and a certain amount of money in the form of currency and demand deposits. They each would have their own particular reasons for owning some of each of these types of assets and for maintaining a certain balance among them.

Portfolio Balance The idea that people try to maintain a balance among the various kinds of assets they own, including money, consumer durables, stocks, and bonds, shifting from one kind of asset to another as economic conditions change.

In order to understand how portfolios are balanced, let us begin by looking at just two types of financial assets, money and bonds. Each of these offers certain advantages that the other does not.

Bonds

Bonds come into existence when business firms or government agencies borrow money and, in exchange, give the lender a certificate representing their promise to pay. The certificate entitles its owner (who is called a bond-holder) to receive an annual interest payment of a fixed number of dollars, plus a larger final payment at the end of a set number of years when the bond "matures." The privilege of receiving the stream of interest payments is, of course, the main reason for holding part of one's wealth in the form of bonds.

A well-defined relationship exists between the rate of return from a bond, expressed as a percentage per year, and the price of the bond. For a very simple example, consider a bond that pays its holder $1 per year, year after year without limit. If investors pay $20 for such a bond, they receive a 5 percent rate of return–$1 per year divided by the $20 purchase price. If they could buy the same bond for $10, they would instead earn a 10 percent rate of return, and so forth. The price of a bond and its rate of return are thus logically linked, and must move in opposite directions.

Exhibit 12.1 gives a short table of the relationship between the rate of interest and the price of a bond paying $1 per year in perpetuity. For bonds that have a fixed maturity date, somewhat more complicated arithmetic is needed to determine the rate of return, given the bond's price. The logic of the relationship is the same for all bonds, though. A high price means a low rate of return, and a low price means a high rate of return.

Money

People who hold part of their wealth in the form of money bear an opportunity cost equal to the interest they could have earned by holding bonds instead. In explaining the reasons that people do hold part of their portfolios in the form of money, despite the opportunity cost of doing so, economists distinguish between the **transactions demand** for money and the **speculative demand** for money.

There is a transactions demand for money because money is acceptable to everyone as a medium of exchange. Holding money makes it easy to

Transactions Demand (for Money) The part of money demand arising from the usefulness of money as a generally acceptable medium of exchange.

Speculative Demand (for Money) The part of money demand arising from the advantages of money as an asset with a fixed nominal value, which offers protection against the danger of capital loss in periods when it is feared that the prices of other assets may fall.

Price	Rate of Return
$100	1%
50	2
20	5
10	10
5	20

EXHIBIT 12.1
Price and rate of return for a bond paying $1 per year in perpetuity
This table shows the relationship between the price and rate of return for a bond paying $1 per year in perpetuity. The rate of return is equal to the annual payment divided by the price. For bonds with a fixed maturity date, the arithmetic of translating a bond's price into its rate of return is somewhat more difficult, but the basic logic is the same. For all bonds, a high price means a low rate of return and a low price a high rate of return.

conduct market transactions—that is, to buy goods and services or financial assets quickly and conveniently, when and where one wants. There is a speculative demand for money because money has a fixed nominal value. Money is an especially attractive store of value in periods when people are afraid that the market price of other assets may fall.

Interest and Portfolio Balance

People balance their portfolios by adjusting the proportion of bonds and money they contain. Just what is a proper balance depends on all the factors that affect the relative attractiveness of different assets.

A major factor affecting the relative attractiveness of bonds and money is the rate of interest. The higher the rate of interest, the more income is earned on each dollar invested in bonds, and consequently, the higher the opportunity cost of holding money. For this reason, the higher the rate of interest, the lower the proportion of their portfolios that people will want to hold in bonds, other things being equal.

The rate of interest affects the demand for money in a second way, which reinforces the first. If at some particular time the interest rate is high relative to some "normal" rate experienced in the past, bond prices will necessarily be low relative to their "normal" level. If people expect the interest rate to return to normal, they will convert money into bonds in the hope of making a capital gain. When interest rates are "abnormally" low, people are likely to avoid bonds and raise the proportion of their portfolios held in the form of money. They will fear that a return to normal will send bond prices down, causing capital losses. Once again, then, we conclude that the demand for money varies inversely with the interest rate.

Income

An additional major factor affecting the relative demand for money and bonds is the level of nominal income. The higher a person's income, the larger and more frequent the purchases he or she will plan to make. More purchases mean a higher transactions demand for money. Also, over a long period, increases in income are accompanied by increases in wealth. People's portfolios get bigger, so the quantity of money demanded goes up even if they hold the same proportion of their wealth in the form of money.

Money Demand Schedule

The quantity of money demanded increases as the interest rate falls, and increases as nominal income increases. The relationship among the quantity of money demanded, the interest rate, and the level of nominal income that prevails in a given economy in a given period is known as that economy's **money demand schedule.** Exhibit 12.2 shows what the money demand schedule might look like for the kind of economy we have represented in our numerical examples during the last few chapters. The entries in Exhibit 12.2a show the quantity of money demanded when the interest rate is that shown at the left-hand border of the table and the level of nominal national income is that shown at the top of the table. We see, for example, that when the interest rate is 5 percent per year and the level of nominal national income is $600, the quantity of money demanded is $72.

Exhibit 12.2b gives the money demand schedule in graphical form. At

Money Demand Schedule A schedule showing the quantity of money that people desire to hold in their portfolios given various values for the interest rate and the level of nominal income.

Exhibit 12.2a

Interest Rate (%)	Level of Nominal National Income					
	200	400	600	800	1,000	1,200
1	120	240	360	480	600	720
2	60	120	180	240	300	360
3	40	80	120	160	200	240
4	30	60	90	120	150	180
5	24	48	72	96	120	144
6	20	40	60	80	100	120
7	17	34	51	68	85	102
8	15	30	45	60	75	90

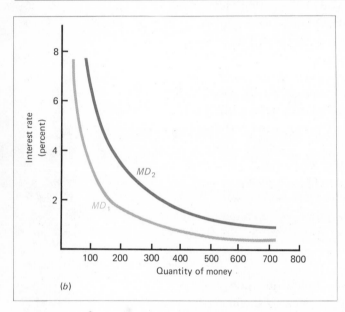

(b)

EXHIBIT 12.2

Money demand schedule for a hypothetical economy
The table and diagram show how money demand varies as the interest rate and the level of nominal income vary in a simplified economy like the one we have used in our numerical examples. The entries in the body of the table show the quantity of money demanded at the interest rate corresponding to the row and the nominal income corresponding to the column. Each column of the table can be graphed to get a money demand curve like that shown in part b of the exhibit. The curve MD_1 assumes income to be fixed at $600. A rise in income to $1,200 would shift the money demand curve to the position MD_2.

any given level of income, the relationship between the quantity of money demanded and the interest rate can be shown by a downward-sloping curve, which looks much like an ordinary demand curve. For example, the curve labeled MD_1 shows the way money demand varies as the interest rate varies when income is $600. This curve is drawn from the data in the $600 column of the table above it. A change in the level of income would produce a shift in the money demand curve. For example, if income were to increase to $1,200, the money demand curve would shift to the position labeled MD_2 in the figure. Checking the data given in the last column of the table, we see that when income doubles, the quantity of money demanded at any particular level of the interest rate doubles.

Proportionality

As Exhibit 12.2 is constructed, the *ratio* of money demanded to income, at each given interest rate, is constant for all levels of income. When the interest rate is 3 percent, for example, the quantity of money demanded is one-fifth of nominal national income at all levels of income. (Check this by reading across the third row of the table.) Let us check the realism of this proportionality assumption by using recent U.S. experience as a case study.

CASE 12.1
The Money-to-Income Ratio and Interest Rates in Recent U.S. Experience

Exhibit 12.3 traces the record of money, income, and interest rates for the postwar American economy. The horizontal axis in this figure measures the ratio of the quantity of money (M_1) to nominal gross national product. The vertical axis measures the corporate Aaa bond rate, that is, the rate of return earned by holders of bonds issued by the most financially sound American corporations. We note that the points representing various years fall rather closely along a curve of the same general shape as the money demand curves drawn for the imaginary economy represented by Exhibit 12.2.

Exhibit 12.3 can be thought of as a crude approximation of the money demand schedule for the American economy. With more sophisticated statistical techniques, we could construct a closer approximation, but even this diagram appears to bear out our two chief assumptions, namely, that the quantity of money demanded is inversely related to the interest rate and directly proportional to the level of nominal income.

It must be emphasized, though, that the relationships among money demand, nominal income, and interest rates are sometimes subject to unpredictable short-run variation. In the last two quarters of 1975, for example, nominal income rose very rapidly while interest rates fell, yet the quantity of money showed virtually no increase. That meant that the point for 1975 in Exhibit 12.3 fell significantly farther to the left than expected. (It should have moved down and slightly to the right compared with the 1974 point.)

In the 1976 Economic Report of the President, the Council of Economic Advisers advanced two possible explanations of the unexpected decline in money demand. Perhaps, they suggested, it was just a temporary deviation from normal, which would soon correct itself. On the other hand, it might indicate the beginning of a permanent shift to the left of the whole money demand schedule. In support of the second interpretation, they noted several

EXHIBIT 12.3
interest rates and the money/income ratio in the postwar American economy
This exhibit traces the relationship among money, income, and interest rates for the postwar American economy. The horizontal axis measures the ratio of the quantity of money (M_1) to gross national product, and the vertical axis measures the corporate Aaa bond interest rate. In general, the figure bears out the assumptions that the quantity of money demanded is inversely related to the interest rate and directly proportional to the level of nominal income. In some years, however, there have been short-run deviations from the general pattern.

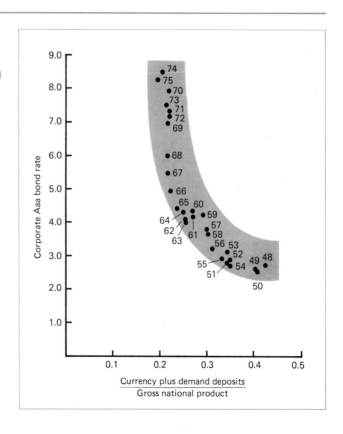

important innovations in banking institutions. These included the increased use of NOW accounts, the recently granted permission to make savings account withdrawals by telephone, and changes in regulations that now permit state and local governments and corporations to hold savings deposits at member banks of the Federal Reserve. It will be at least a year or two before it will be possible to tell if the suspected shift is permanent. Meanwhile, policy makers will find their work complicated by serious uncertainties.

Equilibrium and Disequilibrium in the Money Market

Now we have analyzed both the supply and the demand for money. Our next step will be to put the two together and investigate the nature of equilibrium and disequilibrium in what is called the *money market*. Exhibit 12.4 shows the basic diagram we shall use to do this. It contains a downward-sloping demand curve for money, taken from Exhibit 12.2, using an assumed national income of $1,200. It also contains a money supply curve. This is simply a vertical line, in accordance with our assumption that the money supply is determined solely by Federal Reserve policy and is not directly affected by changes in economic conditions. In this case, the quantity of money supplied is assumed to be $180. It is important to remember that both the demand for money and the supply of money are measured in terms of stocks, not flows. The supply represents the stock in existence at a given time, and the demand represents the stock that people desire to hold in their portfolios under given conditions.

Equilibrium

It is apparent from the diagram that there is only one rate of interest, 4 percent, at which the stock of money that people want to hold is equal to the stock of money supplied by the banking system in accordance with Federal Reserve policy. At any higher rate of interest, there would be an

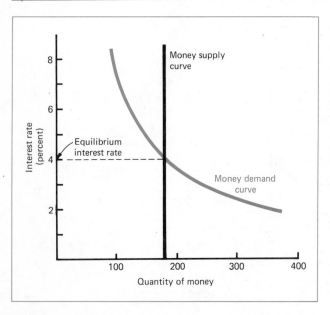

EXHIBIT 12.4
Equilibrium in the money market
The money demand curve in this diagram is based on the data given in Exhibit 12.2, using an assumed nominal national income of $1,200. The money supply curve assumes a quantity of money supplied of $180. The equilibrium interest rate is 4 percent. At any higher interest rate, an excess quantity of money supplied would put downward pressure on the interest rate. If the interest rate were below equilibrium, there would be an excess quantity of money demanded, and upward pressure. Both money supply and demand are measured in stock terms.

excess quantity of money supplied. At an interest rate of 6 percent, for example, the excess quantity supplied would be $60. The excess quantity supplied reflects the fact that people do not want to hold as much money in their portfolios as the Federal Reserve has caused the banking system to put into circulation.

Individual asset holders react to an excess quantity of money supplied by using their excess money to buy other assets. Given the high interest rate, they will be particularly attracted to the idea of replacing some of the money in their portfolios with bonds. However, although some individual asset holders can successfully reduce the quantity of money in their portfolios by buying bonds, not all asset holders can do so at once. Every time someone takes money out of his or her portfolio to buy a bond from someone else, that money ends up in the portfolio of the seller.

No matter how much the money is churned around from portfolio to portfolio in pursuit of bonds, every cent of the fixed stock of money supplied by the banking system always has to be in someone's portfolio at each moment. What occurs as a result of all this churning is not a fall in the money stock, but a rise in the price of bonds. This is just what is needed to restore equilibrium. A rise in the price of bonds means a fall in the percentage rate of interest return on bonds. As the interest rate falls, the excess quantity of money supplied is reduced not because the extra money disappears, but because the amount of money that people desire to keep in their portfolios rises until it catches up with the quantity of money supplied. Soon the interest rate reaches it equilibrium level, and the excess demand is entirely eliminated.

Opposite Process

If the interest rate were for some reason below the equilibrium level, there would be an excess quantity of money demanded and a process opposite to that just described would occur. People would want to sell bonds in order to get the greater quantity of money they would prefer to hold at the low interest rate. This would not increase the total supply of money available in the system, but it would depress the price of bonds. This in turn would raise the interest rate until equilibrium were restored.

This is the nature of equilibrium and disequilibrium in the money market. We can apply what we have learned by seeing how the money market reacts to two important types of disturbances.

Change in Money Supply

First, let us examine the effects of an increase in the money supply resulting from an open market purchase of securities by the Federal Reserve. Suppose that initially the money supply is $180 as shown by the money supply curve MS_1 in Exhibit 12.5. A nominal national income of $1,200 gives the money demand curve MD. The equilibrium interest rate is 4 percent.

Let the money multiplier be 9.0. Now imagine that the Federal Reserve makes an open market purchase of $20 worth of government securities, paying for the purchase with one of its own checks. The immediate effect of this open market purchase is to increase the supply by $20 and to raise bond prices slightly and lower the rate of interest slightly.

EXHIBIT 12.5

Effects of an increase in the money supply

Initially a money supply of $180 puts the money supply curve in the position MS_1. An open market purchase of $20 by the Federal Reserve has the immediate effect of moving the money supply curve to MS_2. That is not the end of the story, however. With a money multiplier of 9.0, the money supply reaches $360 ($MS_3$) before the deposit expansion process works itself out completely. The new equilibrium interest rate is 2 percent.

If this were the end of the story, it would put the money supply curve in the position indicated as MS_2, and it would put the market in a new equilibrium at the intersection of that curve with the money demand curve. But, of course, this is not the end of the story. As soon as the original Federal Reserve check is deposited in the bondseller's bank, total reserves of the banking system go up by $20. This sets off the process of deposit expansion, which we described in detail earlier, and by the time the reserves-to-money multiplier has worked itself out, the money supply will reach $360. This will shift the money supply curve all the way to the position MS_3.

New Equilibrium

Now there will be a large excess quantity of money supplied. Asset holders will not desire to hold the new money at the old interest rate, and will try to reduce their money holdings. It is likely that some excess money balances will be spent on physical assets, including consumer durables, and it is certain that some will be spent on bonds. As we have seen before, the actions of portfolio holders would bid up bond prices and lower interest rates. When the interest rate falls low enough (to 2 percent as our example is constructed), the demand for money would rise sufficiently to reestablish equilibrium. In the new equilibrium, total money balances outstanding would be larger than initially, and the interest rate would be lower.

Increase in Income

When we looked at the effects of an increase in the money supply on equilibrium in the money market, we assumed that nominal income remained unchanged throughout. Now let us look at the effects of a change in nominal income, assuming the money supply to remain fixed. When we have done this, we shall be ready for the next chapter, where we shall want to consider the two types of changes in combination.

Exhibit 12.6 sets the scene for exploring the effects of a change in nom-

EXHIBIT 12.6

Effects of an increase in national income

Initially, a nominal income of $600 puts the money demand curve at MD_1. The equilibrium interest rate is 2 percent with the money supply at $180. If an increase in nominal income to $1,200 shifts the money demand curve to MD_2, the interest rate will have to rise to 4 percent to restore equilibrium.

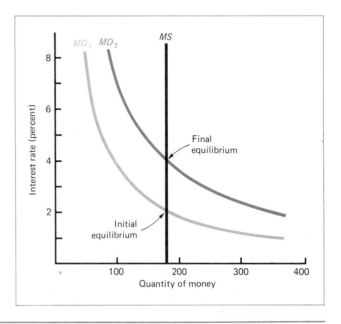

inal income. Suppose that initially the economy is in equilibrium with a money supply of $180 ($MS$), a nominal income of $600 ($MD_1$), and an interest rate of 2 percent. At an interest rate of 2 percent, the desired quantity of money holdings is $180, just equal to the money supply, as of course it must be in equilibrium.

Now let us suppose that for some reason or another, nominal income were to rise to $1,200. The increase in income would cause the money demand curve to shift to the new position MD_2. With the money supply still at $180, this would mean a very substantial excess quantity of money demanded. To meet their increased demand for money, portfolio holders would have to sell some of their earning assets, especially bonds. This would depress the price of bonds and raise the interest rate.

New Equilibrium

As the interest rate rose, the desired ratio of money to income would fall as the higher interest rate raised the implicit cost of holding money balances and weakened the speculative demand for money. When the interest rate rose high enough, the desired quantity of money would fall to $180, entirely eliminating the excess quantity of money demanded. This happens at an interest rate of 4 percent as our example is constructed. Four percent is therefore the new equilibrium rate of interest.

Conclusions

Our theory of the supply and demand for money is now complete. The important next step is to apply this theory to the problem of national income determination. This will be the aim of our next chapter. In it, we shall see that inclusion of the money market in the analysis of national income determination leads to some important modifications of the multiplier theory, and sets the stage for our discussion of inflation and unemployment.

SUMMARY

1. The collection of various assets a person owns (money, real estate, consumer durables, bonds, stocks, or whatever) is called a portfolio. Portfolio holders try to maintain a balance among the various kinds of assets they own, shifting from one to another as economic conditions change. As nominal income rises, people tend to want more money in their portfolios to satisfy their transactions demand. As the rate of interest rises, people tend to want less money in their portfolios, because the opportunity cost of holding money increases, and because their speculative demand for money decreases.

2. To show the money demand schedule in graphical form, we draw a downward-sloping curve showing how the quantity of money demanded changes as the interest rate changes, given some level of nominal income. An increase in the level of nominal income shifts this curve to the right, and a decrease in nominal income shifts it to the left.

3. The money supply curve can be represented by a vertical line, following our assumption that the money supply is fully controlled by Federal Reserve policy. Together the money supply and money demand curves determine the equilibrium rate of interest. With nominal income unchanged, an increase in the money supply causes the equilibrium interest rate to fall. With the money supply unchanged, an increase in nominal income causes the equilibrium interest rate to rise.

DISCUSSION QUESTIONS

1. List the items that you might consider part of your portfolio. Is it basically similar to the portfolio discussed in the text? In what ways is it similar? How is it different?

2. Which is more important in determining your own demand for money: the transactions demand or the speculative demand? Explain.

3. If the interest rate paid on savings deposits were increased, would you change your portfolio? Would you invest more or less in a savings account? Why or why not?

4. What is the average balance in your checkbook (during a typical month)? How much currency do you carry on a typical day? Finding the sum of these two figures gives a quantity of money demanded. In order to get a point on your demand for money schedule, we need a price. What price should we use?

5. Evaluate the following statement: "It is at best a mere metaphor, and at worst seriously misleading to speak of the money 'market.' Money cannot be bought and sold—it is just the means of payment we use in buying and selling everything else. Since it cannot be bought and sold, it cannot have a true market."

6. Do you know what Moody's corporate Aaa bond interest rate is at the time you are reading this chapter? Try to find out.

CHAPTER 13
The Interaction of Money and the Multiplier

What You Will Learn in This Chapter
To understand the major issues of economic stabilization, we must understand how monetary and fiscal policy interact to determine the equilibrium level of nominal national income. When we take monetary factors into account, we have to make some important modifications in the simple multiplier theory. These modifications give rise to a controversy over how effective fiscal policy really is as a tool of economic stabilization.

For Review
Here are some important terms and concepts that will be put to use in this chapter. Be certain that you understand them, or review them before proceeding.
 Fiscal policy and the multiplier theory (Chapter 10)
 Instruments and effects of monetary policy
  (Chapters 11 and 12)

General Equilibrium and National Income

General Equilibrium

In applying the theory of supply and demand, economists make an important distinction between **partial equilibrium analysis** and **general equilibrium analysis.** The difference between the two lies in the role played by the "other things being equal" assumption. In partial equilibrium analysis, we say "if such-and-such an event occurs, the effect on the market for good X will be so-and-so, *provided that other markets are not disturbed from equilibrium.*" In general equilibrium analysis, in contrast, we say "if such-and-such an event occurs, the effect on the market for good X will be so-and-so, *provided that other markets also adjust fully to the event in question.*"

So far we have looked at the multiplier theory and the theory of money only from the partial equilibrium point of view. In Chapter 10, for example, we analyzed the effect of a change in fiscal policy on the equilibrium level of the circular flow, without considering the possible effects that the change in fiscal policy might have on the demand for money, the interest rate, or

Partial Equilibrium Analysis An approach to the study of markets in which we say 'if such-and-such an event occurs, the effect on the market for good X will be so-and-so, provided that other markets are not disturbed from equilibrium."

General Equilibrium Analysis An approach to the study of markets in which we say "if such-and-such an event occurs, the effect on the market for good X will be so-and-so, provided that other markets also adjust fully to the event in question."

the level of planned investment. Similarly, in Chapter 12 we looked at what effect a change in the money supply would have on the equilibrium interest rate, without considering the possible effect of such an act of monetary policy on the level of nominal national income, or the position of the money demand curve.

Interactions

Our aim in this chapter will be to look again at fiscal and monetary policy, this time using the general equilibrium approach. That means taking into account the interactions between what goes on in the money market and what goes on in the circular flow.

Consider Exhibit 13.1. This figure shows two main channels of interaction between money and the level of nominal national income. The channels are represented by the large arrows. One of these interactions runs from the interest rate, determined in the money market, to the position of the aggregate demand schedule, by way of the effect of the interest rate on the level of planned investment. The other runs from the level of nominal national income, as determined by the intersection of the aggregate supply and demand curves, to the position of the money demand curve.

These interactions mean that we can no longer consider equilibrium of the circular flow and of the money market one at a time. We have to know the equilibrium rate of interest in order to know how much planned investment there will be. Otherwise we cannot put the aggregate demand schedule in its proper position. At the same time, we have to know the equilibrium level of nominal national income in order to put the money demand schedule in its proper position.

Equilibrium Conditions

The money market and the circular flow can both be in equilibrium simultaneously only if a certain pair of values for the interest rate and nominal national income prevail. Let us call the required level of national income Y and the required level of the interest rate r. Then the value of r must be just right to induce the planned investment needed to put equilibrium national income exactly at the level Y, and the value of Y must be just right to put the money demand curve in the position needed to keep the equilibrium interest rate at r.

As Exhibit 13.1 is drawn, an interest rate of 4 percent and a national income of $600 are what we need. The aggregate demand schedule is drawn on the assumptions that autonomous consumption is $150, the marginal propensity to consume is 0.5, government purchases are $100, and net taxes are $100. That means that planned investment must be $100 in order for equilibrium national income to be $600. Checking the planned investment schedule, we see that an interest rate of 4 percent is needed to encourage such an amount of planned investment.

Now turn to the money market, where we have assumed a money supply of $90. We see that for the equilibrium rate of interest to be 4 percent, the money demand curve must be in just the position we have drawn it. This is the position that corresponds to a nominal national income of $600. This verifies that $r = 4$ percent and $Y = \$600$ are an equilibrium pair for the interest rate and national income.

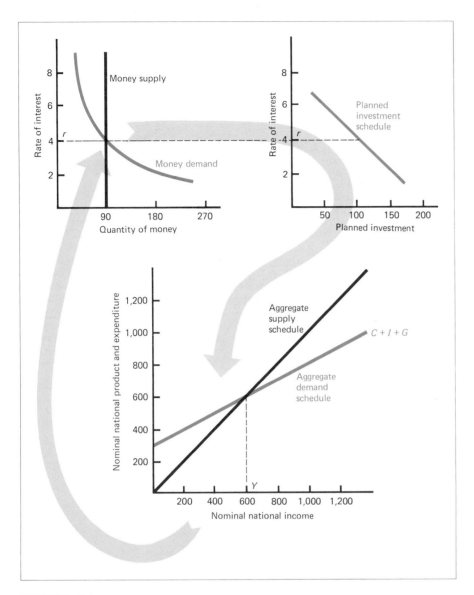

EXHIBIT 13.1

A general equilibrium view of national income determination

The money market and the circular flow can both be in equilibrium at once only if a certain pair of values for the interest rate and nominal income prevail. The large arrows in this figure show how the interest rate and nominal national income interact. The equilibrium interest rate *r* helps determine the position of the aggregate demand curve via its effect on planned investment spending. The level of nominal national income *Y* helps determine the interest rate via its effect on the position of the money demand curve.

The Equilibrium Is Unique

For any given set of assumptions about autonomous consumption, the marginal propensity to consume, government purchases, net taxes, the money supply, and the position of the planned investment schedule, there is just one pair of values for the interest rate and nominal national income that permits both the money market and the circular flow to be in equilibrium. We thus say that equilibrium values of nominal national income and the interest rate are *unique*.

To show this, all we have to do is momentarily assume that one of the values is different, and then show that this does not permit both markets to be in equilibrium. Suppose, for example, that the interest rate were only 2 percent, while all the underlying economic conditions were the same as before. The planned expenditure schedule in Exhibit 13.1 shows that a 2 percent interest rate would cause planned investment to rise to $150. With planned expenditure $50 higher than before, equilibrium national income would rise by $100 to $700 under the impact of the multiplier effect. We see, then, that an interest rate of 2 percent requires an equilibrium nominal national income of $700.

Turning to the money market part of Exhibit 13.1, we see that 2 percent cannot be the equilibrium rate of interest when money demand curve is in the position shown and the money supply is $90. The money demand curve would have to shift to the left to make 2 percent the equilibrium rate of interest. But an increase in national income from $600 to $700 would shift the money demand curve not to the left, but to the right. There is no way that 2 percent can be an equilibrium rate of interest when the level of national income is $700, given the assumed money supply. There is also no way that the equilibrium level of nominal national income can be anything but $700 when the rate of interest is 2 percent. Given the underlying economic conditions we have supposed, we are forced to conclude that when the interest rate is 2 percent, there is *no* value of national income that permits *both* the money market and the circular flow to be in equilibrium

The same reasoning could be repeated for any value of r other than 4 percent and any value of Y other than $600. This pair of equilibrium values for nominal national income and the interest rate is unique.

A Revised Look at the Effects of Fiscal Policy

Government Purchases

In Chapter 10 we studied the effects of three kinds of changes in fiscal policy: changes in government purchases, changes in net taxes, and matched changes in government purchases and taxes under a balanced budget policy. Now let us reconsider the first of these kinds of fiscal policy from the point of view of general equilibrium analysis. For purposes of comparison with what follows, we should recall the conclusion that we reached in Chapter 10 concerning the effects of a change in government purchases: When government purchases are increased while taxes, planned investment, and the consumption schedule remain unchanged, equilibrium national income will change by an amount equal to the change in government purchases times the multiplier.

Initial Effects

First, assume that the economy is in equilibrium with an interest rate r and a nominal national income Y. Now assume that fiscal policy makers decide that government purchases should be increased by $100, with no accompanying change in taxes. Let us trace the effects of this fiscal policy action as they work their way through the economy. The increase in government purchases shifts the aggregate demand schedule upward by $100.

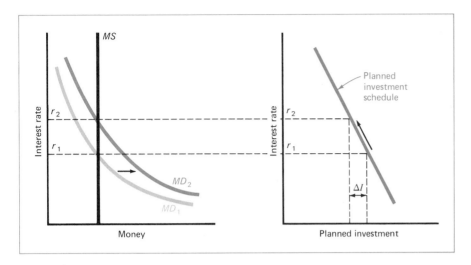

EXHIBIT 13.2
The crowding out effect
An increase in government purchases causes nominal national income to rise via the multiplier effect. The increase in income shifts the money demand curve from its initial position MD_1 to the new position MD_2. The equilibrium interest rate rises from r_1 to r_2. An amount of private investment equal to ΔI is "crowded out."

Planned expenditure now exceeds national product at the initial income level. This causes unplanned depletion of business inventories, to which firms respond by increasing output and/or raising prices. The level of nominal national income begins to rise.

Money Market Effect

As national income rises, the change in fiscal policy begins to affect the money market. The increase in nominal national income causes the money demand curve to shift rightward. In Exhibit 13.2, this is shown as a shift from the initial position MD_1 of the money demand curve toward a new position MD_2. The money demand curve shifts because when incomes rise, people tend to want more money in their portfolios. Because the money supply does not increase, these people's attempts to get more money by selling bonds simply drives down the price of bonds and drives up the rate of interest. Looking at all this together, we see that the effect on the money market of the increase in government purchases is to push up the rate of interest.

Crowding Out

Now let us shift our attention from the money market to the planned investment schedule, also shown in Exhibit 13.2. As the interest rate rises, firms find it more costly to undertake fixed investment projects and more costly to hold large inventories of raw materials or finished goods. They therefore reduce their planned investment expenditures, moving upward and to the left along the planned investment schedule. This decrease in planned investment expenditures, as an indirect effect of an increase in government purchases, is called the **crowding out effect.** The amount of investment crowded out is labeled ΔI in the exhibit.

Crowding Out Effect The tendency of expansionary fiscal policy to cause a drop in private planned investment expenditure as a result of a rise in the interest rate.

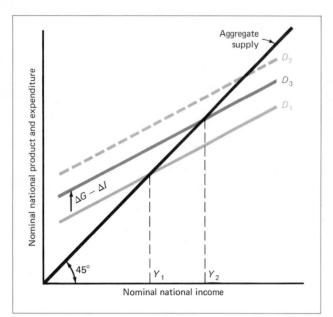

EXHIBIT 13.3
The crowding out effect in terms of aggregate supply and demand
Here the crowding out effect is shown from the perspective of aggregate supply and demand. Taken by itself, the increase in government purchases (ΔG) would have pushed the aggregate demand curve from D_1 to D_2. The crowding out effect chops ΔI off private investment, however, so the actual shift is only from D_1 to D_3, a distance equal to $\Delta G - \Delta I$.

Let us look at what has happened now in terms of aggregate supply and demand. The original position of the aggregate demand curve is shown as D_1 in Exhibit 13.3. Considered in isolation, the increase in government spending would have pushed the schedule all the way up to the position D_2. When we take crowding out into effect, though, it is apparent that the upward shift in aggregate demand is less than the amount of increase in government purchases. If we use ΔG to stand for the increase in government purchases and ΔI to stand for the amount of investment crowded out, the upward shift is reduced to $\Delta G - \Delta I$. This puts the final position of the aggregate demand curve at D_3.

Looking at Exhibits 13.2 and 13.3 together, now, we see that both income and the interest rate have changed. The new equilibrium interest rate r_2 and the new equilibrium nominal national income Y_2 are both higher than they were to begin with.

Crowding Out and the Multiplier

Because an increase in government purchases crowds out some private investment, national income does not rise by the full amount of the multiplier times the increase in government purchases. This fact does not, however, directly contradict the conclusion we reached in Chapter 10 and repeated at the beginning of this section. The trouble is that the earlier conclusion, which was based on partial equilibrium analysis, included the assumption that planned investment would not change when national income changed. The general equilibrium approach taken here shows that it is invalid to make that assumption. This means that we must modify the way we apply the multiplier theory to the analysis of fiscal policy. The multiplier must now be applied not just to the change in government purchases, but to the change in government purchases *minus* the induced change in private planned investment expenditure.

This new way of applying the multiplier theory to the analysis of fiscal policy can be put in the form of a simple equation. Using the symbol ΔY to represent the change in nominal national income resulting from a change ΔG in government purchases, we can write

$$\Delta Y = M(\Delta G - \Delta I)$$

M in this equation stands for the simple multiplier, as in Chapter 9.

Other Fiscal Policies

The crowding out effect applies to other types of fiscal policy as well as to changes in government purchases. When taxes are lowered, or when the level of government purchases is increased while the budget is kept in balance, nominal national income rises. This pushes the interest rate up, and crowds out some investment. That means that the overall effectiveness of these fiscal policies is somewhat less than would be predicted by the simple applications of the tax multiplier or balanced budget multiplier as outlined in Chapter 10.

It must also be remembered that when taxes are raised or government purchases lowered, as might be done to eliminate an expansionary gap from the economy, the crowding out effect works in reverse. The contractionary impact of fiscal policy is somewhat diminished, because as incomes fall, the demand for money and the interest rate fall too. These effects stimulate new private investment expenditure, somewhat offsetting the downward shift in the aggregate demand schedule that the contractionary policy produces.

Now let us look at the crowding out effect in a real-world situation.

CASE 13.1
The Wall Street Journal Looks at Crowding Out[1]

For American businessmen, the crowding out effect is not just an esoteric piece of economic theory, but a matter of serious practical concern. In 1975, the editors of *The Wall Street Journal* became concerned over the growth of the federal budget deficit, which was reaching record levels. They discussed the possibility that government borrowing to cover huge deficits "would force private borrowers out of the credit markets, reducing capital investment and offsetting or even reversing the supposedly stimulative effects of deficit spending."

By the spring of 1976, the editors concluded that their fears had at least in part been justified. In 1975, gross private domestic investment fell to 12.2 percent of GNP, the lowest rate in the postwar period. Fixed nonresidential investment (that is, investment in factories and machines) fell to 9.9 percent of GNP, well below the 12 percent rate the the Department of Commerce says is needed to meet legally established antipollution and energy independence goals, and still provide full employment in 1980. *The Journal* cited several items of evidence that the drop in investment was not just a coincidence, but was at least in substantial part a direct result of crowding out.

The editors summarized their fears for the future in these terms. "It is all very well for the Keynesians to tell us that the way to make up the shortfall in investment is to stimulate the economy and return to full employment rapidly. But how? Not by their standard prescription of a bigger deficit, if the above numbers have any meaning. Assuming for the moment that deficits can stimulate to begin with, the numbers suggest that they can stimulate only to the extent they fill in a naturally occurring fall in investment. Otherwise, they not only fail to stimulate, but detract from investment and future growth."

[1]Based on an editorial, "Crowding Out, Revisited," *The Wall Street Journal*, Tuesday, April 6, 1975, p. 22.

Monetary Policy and National Income

In Chapter 12 we looked at the effects of a change in the money supply from a partial equilibrium point of view, taking into account only what happens in the money market. Now we shall reconsider the effects of changes in the money supply in a general equilibrium context, taking into account the interaction of money and the multiplier theory of income determination.

To be specific, let us suppose that the Federal Reserve initiates an expansion of the money supply via an open market purchase of bonds. We need not give separate consideration to the expansion of the money supply by the use of other instruments of monetary policy because the effects are very little different than the effects of an open market operation.

Initial Effects

We have already analyzed initial effects of the open market purchase in Chapters 11 and 12. The open market purchase creates an increase in commercial bank reserves, and banks are induced to begin the process of deposit expansion. When the expansion is complete the money supply will have increased by an amount equal to the expansion in the reserves times the money multiplier. This is indicated in Exhibit 13.4 by the shift in the money supply curve from the position MS_1 to the position MS_2.

As the money supply expands, people find that they have more money than they want to hold in their portfolios at the original rate of interest.

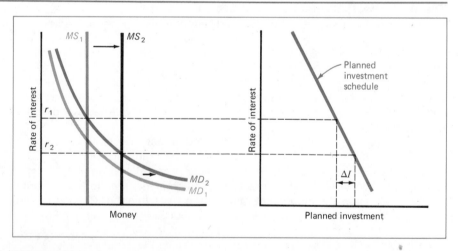

EXHIBIT 13.4

Money market and investment effects of an increase in the money supply
An increase in the money supply shifts the money supply curve from MS_1 to MS_2. The immediate effect of this is to cause a movement down along the money demand curve MD_1 toward its intersection with the new money supply curve. The interest rate then falls, and planned investment expenditure rises. That stimulates nominal national income via the multiplier effect. The rise in income in turn shifts the money demand schedule to a new position MD_2. That cuts short the fall in the interest rate, and a new equilibrium is established.

EXHIBIT 13.5

The effect of an increase in the money supply on aggregate demand and nominal national income

An increase in planned investment spending, caused by an increase in the money supply, shifts the aggregate demand curve upward. The amount of the shift is equal to the change in investment, ΔI. A new equilibrium is established with nominal national income increasing from Y_1 to Y_2.

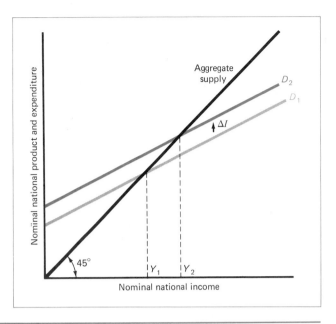

Income and Expenditure Effects

They attempt to reduce their money holdings by buying other assets, among them, bonds. This tends to push the price of bonds up and the interest rate down. In the diagram, this process is represented by a movement along the original money demand curve MD_1 toward its intersection with the new money supply curve.

Income and Expenditure Effects

As the interest rate begins to fall, business executives are encouraged to increase their level of planned investment, moving down and to the right along their planned investment schedule. The increase in investment expenditure shifts the aggregate demand schedule upward, as shown in Exhibit 13.5. Planned expenditure now temporarily exceeds national income, and by the familiar multiplier process, nominal national income begins to increase.

As national income increases, the money market is once again affected. Now the money demand curve begins to shift to the right, moving toward the position marked as MD_2 in Exhibit 13.4. This shift in the money demand curve cuts off the fall in the interest rate, and a new equilibrium interest rate is established where MD_2 and MS_2 intersect.

Once this equilibrium interest rate is established, planned investment stops expanding. The aggregate demand schedule comes to rest at a new equilibrium position D_2 in Exhibit 13.5. That means that the new equilibrium level of nominal national income will be higher than it was before the increase in the money supply.

In short, our general equilibrium analysis tells us that an increase in the money supply will result in new equilibrium values for both the interest rate and nominal national income. The interest rate will be lower than before the monetary expansion took place, and the level of nominal national income will be higher.

Transmission Mechanism   The whole set of ways in which monetary policy exerts an impact on the economy.

Transmission Mechanism

The ways in which monetary policy exerts an impact on the economy are together known as the **transmission mechanism.** Up to this point, our whole emphasis has been on one aspect of the transmission mechanism, namely, the tendency of expansionary monetary policy to lower interest rates, which in turn stimulates business investment. That is not quite the whole story. One or two other elements of the transmission mechanism also deserve to be mentioned.

For one thing, the effect of expansionary monetary policy on investment spending does not act solely through changes in the interest rate. When the money supply is tightly controlled, and banks have few if any excess reserves, individuals and businesses may find it difficult to borrow any money at all. Under such conditions, for example, banks may continue to post an interest rate of 9 percent for home mortgages, but potential home buyers may get the brush-off when they apply for money, or be told that there is a long waiting list. At another time, when easier monetary policy leaves banks with ample reserves, the waiting lists shorten and the standards by which the creditworthiness of borrowers is judged may be slackened a little. As a result, more loans may be made, and more construction and other types of investment may take place, even though the interest rates actually charged to borrowers do not change much.

Still another part of the transmission mechanism can help stimulate planned expenditure without directly affecting interest rates. When expansionary monetary policy puts excess money in people's portfolios, they will not necessarily try to exchange all of the excess for bonds, especially after the price of bonds rises and their yield becomes less attractive. They may also spend money to buy goods, including consumer durables, raw materials, and the like.

Economists are far from complete agreement over the nature of the transmission mechanism by which monetary policy affects the level of national income. For our limited purposes, we have concentrated on the interest rate-investment part of the mechanism. The reader should keep in mind, though, that this is only a convenient simplification.

Monetary Versus Fiscal Policy

Because both fiscal and monetary policy affect the level of nominal national income, they are to some extent substitutes. If policy makers believe that there is an expansionary or contractionary gap to get rid of, which policy should they use? The question of monetary versus fiscal policy turns out to be one of the most debated issues in modern economics.

A Historical Note

Keynes' *General Theory of Employment, Interest and Money* was intended to be "general" in the sense that it would take both monetary and fiscal influences on the economy into account. However, in the first years after the publication of Keynes' book, it was not the general theory as a whole that dominated the thinking of the economics profession. Instead, some followers of Keynes tended to place a somewhat one-sided emphasis on planned expenditure, and to downplay the role of money in the economy. Early followers of Keynes interpreted the experience of the Great Depression as justifying the view that "money doesn't matter." They attributed the fact that monetary policy had failed to prevent both the 46 percent decline in nominal income and the increase in the unemployment rate to 25 percent of the labor force, which occurred between 1929 and 1933, not to poor conduct of monetary policy, but to its ineffectiveness. The fact that the Great Depression did not end until World War II brought on a massive increase in government spending appeared to support this view.

After the war, many of the early Keynesians forecast a new depression and economic stagnation. They thought that private investment opportunities would "dry up" with the disappearance of wartime government spending. Experience proved them wrong. Instead, the United States and the countries of Western Europe experienced rapid postwar recovery. Central banks in most of the major economies pursued "easy" monetary policies during these years, and inflation was a more widespread problem than depression. In fact, inflationary pressures were kept under control only by "orthodox" monetary policies. Economists began to wonder if perhaps "money mattered" after all and to look once again at the general theory as a whole.

The Monetarists

The reaction against the one-sided theories of the early Keynesians received major support from the empirical research of the **monetarists** led by Milton Friedman of the University of Chicago. Friedman's reinterpretation of the historical record led him to think that the primary causes of ups and downs in business activity are movements in the money supply. It seemed possible to explain even the Great Depression in this way.

Monetarists Economists who believe that movements in the money supply are the primary causes of ups and downs in business activity.

The New Economists

The economics profession did not become converted to monetarism, at least not in its extreme "only money matters" form. But out of the debate between the monetarists and the old Keynesians there developed a "new economics," an updated Keynesian economics that assigns important roles to both monetary and fiscal policy. This modern Keynesianism finally came into its own during the Kennedy and Johnson administrations. Then, for the first time, the actual conduct of economic policy began to be based on Keynesian economic theory as interpreted by a group of economists associated with the President's Council of Economic Advisors, including Walter Heller, James Tobin, and Gardner Ackley. Paul Samuelson of MIT, although not a member of the Council, was another outspoken proponent of the new economics brand of governmental activism in economic stabilization. The successful economic resurgence of the Kennedy and Johnson years added considerably to their prestige.

Today it is hard to find an economist who would take either an extreme "money doesn't matter" or an "only money matters" position. Instead, the question is how much money matters. There is a great deal of common ground between Keynesian economists and monetarists. Virtually all of what we have said in these chapters belongs to this common ground. Still, within the common theoretical framework, there is room for debate on the relative effectiveness of monetary versus fiscal policy.

Milton Friedman (1912–   )

In October 1976, Milton Friedman received the Nobel Memorial Prize in economics, becoming the sixth American to win or share in that prize. Few were surprised. The main surprise was that this most original and influential of economists had had to wait in line so long! The explanation is that Friedman has built his career outside the economics establishment—built it, in fact, by challenging virtually every major establishment doctrine.

Friedman was born in New York in 1912, the son of immigrant garment workers. His hard-working parents sent him across the river to Rutgers University in New Jersey, where Friedman came under the influence of Arthur Burns, then a young Assistant Professor. From Burns, Friedman learned the importance of empirical work in economics. Statistical testing of all theory and policy prescriptions became a key characteristic of Friedman's later work. From Rutgers, Friedman went to the University of Chicago for an M.A., and then East again to Columbia University, where he got his Ph.D. in 1946. With his degree in hand, he returned to Chicago to teach. There, he became the leading member of the "Chicago School," which provides the main intellectual counterweight to the Eastern Establishment in American economics today.

If we were to single out one single theme that underlies all of Friedman's work, it would be his conviction that the market economy works, and works best when left alone. This can be seen in his best-known work, *A Monetary History of the United States.* Written with Anna Schwartz, this work challenges two major tenets of orthodox Keynesian economics. These are, first, the idea that the market economy is inherently unstable without the guiding hand of government, and second, that monetary policy had been tried and found useless as a cure for the Great Depression. Friedman and Schwartz found both beliefs to be the opposite of the truth. "The Great Depression," Friedman later wrote, "far from being a sign of the inherent instability of the private enterprise system, is a testament to how much harm can be done by mistakes on the part of a few men when they wield vast power over the monetary system of the country."

Friedman strongly favors a "hands-off" policy by governments in almost every area, not just in monetary matters. The trouble, in his view, is not that government is evil by nature, but rather that so many policies end up having the opposite of their intended effects. "The social reformers who seek through politics to do nothing but serve the public interest invariably end up serving some private interest that was no part of their intention to serve. They are led by an invisible hand to serve a private interest." Transport regulation, the income tax, public education, agricultural subsidies, and housing programs are among the many policy areas where Friedman believes the government has done more harm than good, and where a free competitive market would do better.

Today, Friedman continues to take on new challenges. He promotes his ideas before Congressional committees, in professional journals, in his *Newsweek* column, and in face-to-face debate with his colleagues. Economics has never had a more respected heretic.

Part of the debate concerns the size of the crowding out effect. The size of the crowding out effect depends critically on the exact shapes of the money demand curve and the planned investment schedule. Exhibit 13.6 shows why. Suppose that the money demand curve has the shape shown by MD_1, indicating that the demand for money is not very sensitive to changes in the interest rate. If this is the case, the portfolio adjustments required when the money demand curve shifts relative to the money supply curve (as when nominal income changes) or when the money supply curve shifts relative to the money demand curve (as in the conduct of monetary policy) will bring about large changes in the rate of interest. Suppose that at the same time the planned investment schedule is relatively flat, like

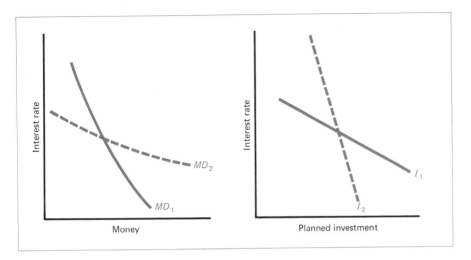

EXHIBIT 13.6
Alternative views of monetary and fiscal policy effectiveness.
If the money demand curve has a shape like MD_1 while the planned
investment schedule is shaped like I_1, monetary policy will tend to be more
effective than fiscal policy. A change in the money supply will have a big
impact on planned expenditure, while fiscal policy will be severely hampered
by the crowding out effect. On the other hand, a money demand schedule
like MD_2 with a planned investment schedule like I_2 would give the advantage
to fiscal policy. Changes in the money supply would have little impact on
investment spending, and the crowding out effect would be small.

the curve I_1, so that a change in the rate of interest will induce a large
change in planned investment expenditure. Taken together, the curves
MD_1 and I_1 would tend to give the sort of results expected by monetarists.
An expansion of government purchases would lead to a large increase in
the rate of interest, a large drop in private investment spending, and hence
a large crowding out effect. Also, an increase in the money supply would
lead to a large decline in the rate of interest and a large increase in investment spending. Therefore, given curves of these shapes, fiscal policy would
tend to be relatively ineffective and monetary policy would be relatively
effective.

On the other hand, if the money demand curve had the shape MD_2
and the planned investment schedule the shape I_2, the situation would be
just reversed. Fiscal policy would have relatively little impact on interest
rates, and interest rates, in turn, would have relatively little impact on
private investment. Changes in taxes or government purchases would then
operate on aggregate nominal demand without much hindrance from the
crowding out effect. At the same time, the economy would become much
less sensitive to changes in the money supply. The world would behave
more like a Keynesian would expect it to.

Transmission Mechanism

Another consideration bearing on the relative strength of fiscal and
monetary policy is the nature of the transmission mechanism. If the transmission mechanism does not operate solely through interest rate changes,
but instead allows monetary effects to bypass interest rate changes in some

cases, then monetarist conclusions about the importance of monetary policy would tend to follow. If interest rate changes were the only mechanism by which monetary policy can affect expenditure, then money would matter less.

Interpretation

Why were these controversies not settled long ago by simply looking at the evidence? The reason is that there are problems in interpreting available data, some of which are quite technical, but others of which are not difficult to understand.

One difference in interpretation concerns the changes in the money supply that accompany economic downturns. For example, monetarists interpret the 25 percent decrease in the money supply that occurred from 1929 to 1933 as a major cause of the Great Depression. Some new economists disagree. They say instead that it was the Depression that caused the decline in the money supply. Their reasoning is that, in periods of depression, banks may be unwilling to make use of excess reserves in ways that will expand the money supply, because it will not appear attractive to them either to make new loans or to buy securities. The excess reserves of commercial banks did indeed grow substantially during the Great Depression. According to the new economists, this is evidence that trying to use expansionary monetary policy in a depression would be like "pushing on a string." New reserves pumped into the banking system would simply lie idle as excess reserves. Instead of the money supply changing, only the total reserves to money supply multiplier would change.

Counter Interpretation

Monetarists hotly deny this interpretation. They argue that the money multiplier has been quite stable, at least recently, and also that any fall in this multiplier can be offset by still greater expansion of reserves through open market purchases. They turn right around and argue that it is the new economists who have misinterpreted the historical record regarding the relative strength of monetary and fiscal policy. To be sure, they say, there has tended to be a correspondence between the size of the stimulus provided by the federal government budget surplus or deficit and the rate of growth of aggregate nominal demand. Yet they argue that much of this correspondence stems not from the effectiveness of fiscal policy, but from the tendency of the Federal Reserve to pursue what is called an **accommodating monetary policy.** When the government runs a large deficit, the Treasury needs to make heavy sales of bonds to the public. That puts upward pressure on interest rates. The Federal Reserve has often acted to offset such upward pressure on interest rates by making open market purchases of bonds. To the extent that this is done, the money supply grows faster as the deficit grows larger. According to monetarists, it is this monetary expansion, not the deficit itself, that provides the major part of the supposed stimulus of deficit spending.

Accommodating Monetary Policy
A policy under which the Federal Reserve expands the money supply in an attempt to keep interest rates from rising when the Treasury sells bonds to cover a budget deficit.

Evidence

How can this debate be settled? Two possible ways of bringing evidence to bear on the issue of monetary versus fiscal policy are discussed in the following case studies. One approach, discussed in Case 13.2, is to look at critical policy episodes when monetary and fiscal policy move in opposite directions. Unfortunately, this happens too infrequently to provide conclusive answers. The alternative approach, discussed in Case 13.3, is to use modern econometric techniques to sort out monetary from fiscal influences in periods when the two policies have worked in the same direction.

CASE 13.2
Critical Episodes in Recent Economic Policy

During the 1960s there were two important policy episodes in which monetary and fiscal policy moved in opposite directions. Both of these episodes have been interpreted as favoring the monetarist position. Both are easily identified in Exhibit 13.7.

The first episode occurred in the second half of 1966. In that year, the Federal Reserve became worried about possible overheating of the economy and suddenly cut the growth of the money supply from 6.4 percent per year to zero.

During the same period, the federal budget swung from surplus to deficit. President Johnson, who did not believe in the need for restraint, was angered by the Federal Reserve's policy. He called William McChesney Martin, then the Federal Reserve Board Chairman, down to the LBJ Ranch for consultation, but to no avail. Champions of the Federal Reserve's independence from political control have picturesquely dubbed this episode "the Fed's finest hour." The outcome of the Fed's finest hour was the "mini-recession" of early 1967, apparently indicating that the restrictive monetary policy outweighed the effect of the rising federal deficit.

The second episode also occurred during the Johnson administration, but this time the lineup of forces was reversed. In mid-1968, Congress, at the request of the administration, passed a 10 percent income tax surcharge to cool off the economy. Exhibit 13.7 shows that this swung the federal budget very sharply from a strong deficit position to a strong surplus position. This time, the Federal Reserve feared "fiscal overkill" and continued through the end of 1968 to maintain a very rapid rate of monetary expansion. The outcome of this episode was that the tax surcharge failed to have its intended restraining effect on the economy. The growth of nominal GNP did not decline. This too is cited by monetarists as a demonstration of the relative strength of monetary and fiscal policy.

CASE 13.3
A Monetarist Analysis of the 1964 Tax Cut[2]

In Case 10.2, we recounted the history of the Kennedy tax cut of 1964. More than any other single episode of macroeconomic policy, the expansion that followed this tax cut bolstered the reputation of the new generation of Keynesian economists. Arthur Okun has written that the post-1964 expansion is an "insoluble mystery" unless one attributes it to the tax cut.[3] Another writer concluded that "the tax cut of 1964 should have convinced the last remaining skeptics that discretionary fiscal policy can be effective."[4]

Yet the skeptics have remained unconvinced. One of the unconvinced skeptics is Richard T. Froyen of the University of North Carolina. In 1974 he published an article challenging Okun's conclusion that the expansion of 1964 and 1965 could be explained only by the tax cut. Froyen points to the fact that monetary policy was also expansionary in the period surrounding the tax cut. In one statistical test, he shows that some 92 percent of the growth

[2]Richard T. Froyen "Monetarist Econometric Models and the 1964 Tax Cut," *Economic Inquiry*, Vol. XII, No. 2 (June 1974).

[3]A. M. Okun, "Measuring the Impact of the 1964 Tax Reduction," in W. W. Heller, (Ed.), *Perspectives on Economic Growth* (New York: 1968), as quoted in Froyen.

[4]M. K. Evans, *Macroeconomic Activity* (New York: 1969), as quoted in Froyen.

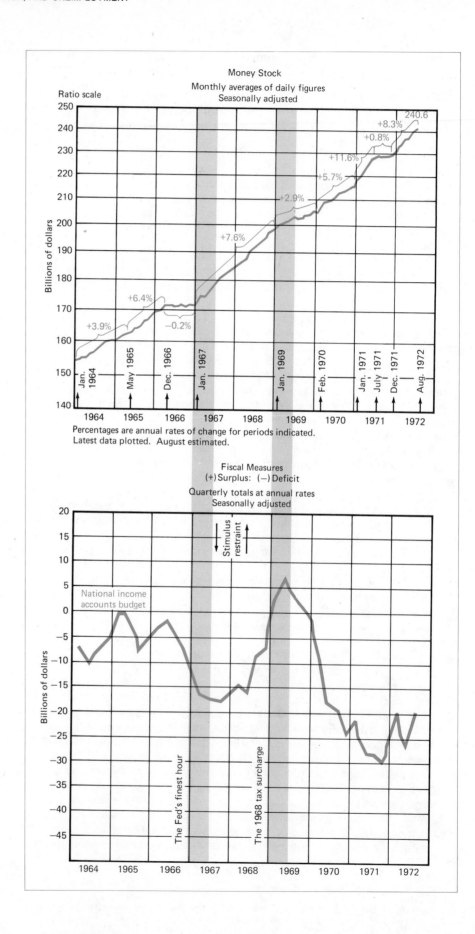

Money Stock
Monthly averages of daily figures
Seasonally adjusted

Percentages are annual rates of change for periods indicated.
Latest data plotted. August estimated.

Fiscal Measures
(+) Surplus: (−) Deficit
Quarterly totals at annual rates
Seasonally adjusted

EXHIBIT 13.7
Recent experience with monetary and fiscal policy
Twice during the 1960s fiscal and monetary policy moved in opposite directions. During the "Fed's finest hour" of 1966, monetary restraint was applied while the budget deficit grew. During the 1968 tax surcharge, in contrast, the money supply continued to expand while the budget swung from deficit to surplus. On both occasions, monetary policy appeared to dominate the outcome.
Source: U.S. Department of Commerce, Council of Economic Advisors and Federal Reserve Bank of St. Louis. Latest data plotted: third quarter preliminary.

in GNP from January 1964 to mid-1965 could be explained by looking at monetary policy and government purchases alone, without taking taxes into account at all.

In another test, he compares his monetarist approach with two of the most elaborate Keynesian studies, to see which would have best predicted the effects of the tax cut if predictions had been made at the end of 1963 using all three methods. He finds that one of the Keynesian studies does a slightly better job than his monetarist approach, and that the other one does much worse.

Froyen concludes that accelerating rates of monetary growth provide a plausible alternative explanation of the expansion that followed the tax cut. It would be wrong, in his view, to interpret this dramatic episode as confirming the Keynesian view of how the economy works. Instead, it seems to offer little conclusive evidence one way or the other. The debate goes on.

Conclusion

This brings us to the end of our long discussion of the determination of nominal national income and product. Much ground remains to be covered, though. In particular, we need to raise the issue of how a given change in nominal GNP is split up between a change in prices and a change in real output. Until we have a theory that can handle the split-up, we cannot take up the highly important policy issues of inflation and unemployment. It is quite likely that inflation and unemployment are the very issues that got the reader interested in studying economics in the first place. Let us turn to them, then, in the next four chapters.[5]

SUMMARY

1. In order to understand the interaction of money and the multiplier, we must move from partial equilibrium analysis to general equilibrium analysis. What happens in the money market affects aggregate demand because any change in the interest rate changes planned investment expenditure. What happens to aggregate demand affects the money market, because movements in nominal national income shift the money demand curve.
2. The money market and the circular flow can both be in equilibrium at once only if a certain pair of values for the interest rate and nominal income prevail. With the money supply, autonomous consumption, the marginal propensity to consume, net taxes, and the position of the planned investment schedule given,

---

[5]On a first reading, Chapters 14 and 17 can be read as a sequence without loss of continuity. Chapters 15 and 16 add much important detail on the theory of unemployment and inflation.

the equilibrium values for nominal national income and the interest rate are unique.

3. An increase in government purchases has a somewhat weaker impact on the equilibrium level of nominal national income than a simple application of the multiplier theory predicts. The reason is that any growth in nominal income shifts the money demand curve and pushes up the interest rate. This in turn crowds out some private investment, partially offsetting the increase in government purchases.

4. An increase in the money supply has the initial effect of depressing the interest rate. This stimulates planned investment, and aggregate demand increases. As nominal national income rises, the money demand schedule shifts to the right, limiting but not completely cancelling out the fall in the interest rate. In the new equilibrium position, the interest rate will be lower and the level of nominal national income higher than before the monetary expansion.

5. Because monetary and fiscal policies both affect the equilibrium level of nominal national income, they are to some extent substitutes. Which type of policy is more effective is a matter of considerable debate, and has been for many years. The debate is not entirely resolved. Some evidence points one way and some the other.

DISCUSSION QUESTIONS

1. Suppose that you wanted to study the effect of variation in rainfall on the prices of three agricultural products: corn, soybeans, and hogs. Do you think a general equilibrium approach or a partial equilibrium approach would give you more insight into the problem?

2. Use the theory presented in this chapter to trace the effects of a tax increase through the economy. What happens to national income, the interest rate, investment, and consumption?

3. Use the theory presented in this chapter to trace the effects of an increase in required reserve ratios on demand deposits. What happens to national income, the interest rate, investment, and consumption?

4. Suppose that there is a contractionary gap in the economy. For the sake of discussion, let us assume that the government could with equal ease bring national income up to its target level by using expansionary monetary policy or by increasing government purchases. If the government also had a long-term goal of promoting rapid economic growth, can you think of any reason for them to use one policy rather than the other?

5. Would you say that Fed Chairman Arthur Burns is one of the four most powerful men in the United States? Would your opinion have been the same before you read this chapter? Before you started this course?

6. Suppose that the Fed decided on a policy of "pegging" the interest rate at some level r by smoothly expanding or contracting the money supply. (This policy could be represented graphically by drawing a horizontal rather than a vertical money supply curve.) How would this affect the effectiveness of fiscal policy? What would happen to the crowding out effect?

Appendix
The Elementary Algebra
of Money and
Income Determination

This appendix is a continuation of the appendix to Chapter 10, in which we developed a simple algebraic version of the multiplier theory. It adds no new theory to what has been presented in the body of Chapter 13. Nonetheless, those readers who feel comfortable with elementary algebra may find the approach presented here useful in consolidating their understanding of the general theory of income determination.

Aggregate Demand

The basic equation for aggregate demand is

$$AD = C + I + G \qquad (1)$$

In the appendix to Chapter 10, we replaced the C in this equation with a consumption schedule, which we wrote as

$$C = \mathbf{a} + \mathbf{b}(Y - T) \qquad (2)$$

where $\mathbf{a}$ and $\mathbf{b}$ were constants representing autonomous consumption and the marginal propensity to consume. Now we shall also replace I in Eq. (1) with a simple planned investment schedule:

$$I = \mathbf{c} + \mathbf{d}r \qquad (3)$$

where I stands for planned investment, r for the interest rate, and $\mathbf{c}$ and $\mathbf{d}$ are constants. The constant $\mathbf{d}$ will have a negative value, because planned investment increases as the rate of interest falls.

Putting Eq. (1), (2), and (3) together, we get the following general expression for the aggregate demand schedule:

$$AD = \mathbf{a} + \mathbf{c} + \mathbf{b}(Y - T) + \mathbf{d}r + G \qquad (4)$$

Money Demand

For a general equilibrium analysis of income determination, we also need a money demand schedule. The one used in Chapters 11 and 12 gave a money demand curve in the shape of a rectangular hyperbola. (Exhibit 12.2, for example, is based on the formula $MD = 0.6Y/r$.) To retain this kind of money demand schedule would involve us in quadratic equations and unnecessarily complicate our arithmetic, so we shall replace it with a linearized money demand schedule written as

$$MD = \mathbf{e}Y + \mathbf{f}r \qquad (5)$$

where MD stands for the quantity of money demanded, r for the interest rate, Y for income, and $\mathbf{e}$ and $\mathbf{f}$ are constants. The constant $\mathbf{f}$ will be negative, because money demand decreases when the interest rate rises.

The reader is cautioned that this linear formulation of the money demand function has certain drawbacks. One is that, except for a certain central range of the variables, algebraic solution of the equilibrium equations (to be presented below) may produce negative values for income or the interest rate. Such negative values have no reasonable economic meaning. We shall be careful to stay within the safe range of values in the examples we give.

Numerical Values

Let us replace the constants in these equations with representative numerical values and see how our algebraic formulations of planned expenditures and money demand can be put to work. Using $\mathbf{a} = 150$, $\mathbf{b} = 0.5$, $\mathbf{c} = 200$, $\mathbf{d} = -2500$, $\mathbf{e} = 0.25$, and $\mathbf{f} = -1,250$, Eqs. (4) and (5) can be rewritten as

$$AD = 350 + 0.5(Y - T) - 2,500r + G \tag{6}$$

and

$$MD = 0.25Y - 1,250r \tag{7}$$

Equilibrium Conditions

As we saw in the text of Chapter 12, the economy as a whole can be in equilibrium only when both the money market and the circular flow are in equilibrium. Money market equilibrium requires that money demand equal money supply, and equilibrium in the circular flow requires that national product be equal to planned expenditure. These equilibrium conditions can be written as

$$MS = MD \tag{8}$$

for the money market, where MS stands for the money supply, and

$$Y = AD \tag{9}$$

for the circular flow.

Substituting Eqs. (6) and (7) into Eqs. (8) and (9), we get

$$MS = 0.25Y - 1,250r \tag{10}$$

and

$$Y = 350 + 0.5(Y - T) - 2,500r + G \tag{11}$$

which simplifies to

$$Y = 700 - T + 2G - 5,000r \tag{12}$$

Equilibrium in the economy is possible only for pairs of values of r and Y that simultaneously satisfy Eqs. (10) and (12).

Policy Variables

Policy Variables Those elements of the economy that are under the direct control of the government.

Besides r and Y, there are three variables in Eqs. (10) and (11) for which we have not yet specified numerical values. These are G (government purchases), T (net taxes), and MS (the money supply). These variables are collectively referred to as **policy variables,** because they stand for those elements of the economy that are under the direct control of the government. Let us turn to some problems now, to see how manipulation of these variables can be used by policy makers in their attempts to hit their economic targets.

Problem 1: Government policy makers set their policy variables at the values $G = 100$, $T = 100$, and $MS = 100$. Apply Eqs. (10) and (12) to determine the equilibrium values of r and Y.

Solution: Equation (10) becomes

$$100 = 0.25Y - 1,250r$$

and Eq. (12) becomes

$$Y = 700 - 100 + 200 = 5,000r$$

Simplifying and setting the equations equal to zero, we get

$$100 - 0.25Y + 1,250r = 0$$
$$800 - Y \quad\ - 5,000r = 0$$

The usual methods for solution of simultaneous equations give the pair of values $r = 0.04$ and $Y = 600$ as the equilibrium levels for the interest rate and national income.

Problem 2: Using the solution to Problem 1 as a starting point, assume that the authorities want to raise the equilibrium level of national income to a target level of $700, using monetary policy alone. How much will the money supply have to be increased to accomplish this objective?

Solution: Substitute $Y = 700$, $G = 100$, and $T = 100$ into Eq. (12) in order to find the required equilibrium value for r.

The substitutions give

$$700 = 700 - 100 + 200 - 5,000r$$

which simplifies to

$$100 - 5,000r = 0$$

The solution to this last equation is $r = 0.02$.

Next substitute the equilibrium values $Y = 700$ and $r = 0.02$ into Eq. (10) in order to determine the money supply necessary to give a 0.02 rate of interest when national income is 700. This gives

$$MS = 0.25(700) - 2,500(0.02) = 150$$

The solution to the problem, then, is that the money supply must be increased by $50, from $100 to $150, in order to raise national income to $700.

Problem 3: Using the solution to Problem 1 as a starting point, show that an increase of $100 in government purchases will be more effective in raising the equilibrium level of national income if the Fed pursues an accommodating monetary policy than if the Fed leaves the money supply unchanged.

Solution: An accommodating monetary policy is one that expands the money supply enough to keep the interest rate unchanged—in this case, equal to 0.04. Substitute the values $T = 100$, $G = 200$, and $r = 0.04$ into equation (12) to get the new value that equilibrium national income will reach if accommodating monetary policy is pursued. Without going into details, the new equilibrium Y with accommodating monetary policy is 800. [Further substitution of $Y = 800$ and $r = 0.04$ into Eq. (10) shows that the money supply would have to be increased to $150 to achieve this result.]

Without accommodating monetary policy, the new values of Y and r are found by going through the same steps outlined in the solution to Problem 1, using $G = 200$. Again without going into details, the solution turns out to be $Y = 700$ and $r = 0.06$. Substitution of the new, higher value of the interest rate into the investment schedule ($I = 200 - 2,500r$) shows us that $50 of the original $100 in private planned investment is crowded out by the $100 increase in government purchases. This accounts for the lower equilibrium value of Y when accommodating monetary policy is not used.

CHAPTER 14

Unemployment and Inflation: The Problem and Some Traditional Answers

What You Will Learn in This Chapter

The two most important goals of American economic policy have long been full employment and price stability. The record for achieving those goals over the past twenty-five years, however, is not very good. In all but four years, there has been either excessive inflation or excessive unemployment. Even more disturbing, in most years since 1970 there have been both excessive inflation and excessive unemployment. In the past, several theories have been developed to explain this not-too-good record. Each is worth looking at, although none contains the whole truth.

For Review

Here are some important terms and concepts that will be put to use in this chapter. Be certain that you understand them, or review them before proceeding.

Theory of money demand (Chapter 12)
Monetarism (Chapter 13)
Expansionary and contractionary gaps (Chapter 10)

Inflation and Unemployment in the Postwar American Economy

Goals and Targets

In the past several chapters, we have often referred to some particular level of nominal income as a target adopted by economic policy makers. Now the time has come to look behind this income target to the more fundamental goals of economic policy that cause a particular target to be chosen.

The two overriding goals of economic policy in the postwar American economy have been full employment and price stability. Those goals are the things that policy makers, and the rest of us for that matter, really want, just as their opposites, unemployment and inflation, are what we really want to avoid. A national income target, by comparison, is something secondary and derivative. If fiscal and monetary authorities pursue policies aimed at a nominal national income target of $1.5 trillion in some particular year, it is not because that number of dollars would, in itself, produce economic bliss. Rather, the income target is chosen in the hope that aiming for it will have favorable effects on unemployment and inflation.

One of our aims in these next four chapters will be to move from an analysis of economic policy conducted in terms of a target level of nominal national income to an analysis conducted in terms of the goals of full employment and price stability. This will require us to understand how the goals themselves can be defined, and how inflation and unemployment are affected when fiscal and monetary policy are employed to manipulate the equilibrium level of nominal national income.

The Employment Goal

"Full employment" is well established in the American political vocabulary as a major goal of policy, but from an economist's point of view, the term is an unfortunate one. Taken at face value, the term "full employment" would seem to indicate a total absence of unemployment, yet it is quite impossible that the level of unemployment, as officially measured, should ever drop to zero. As we shall see in Chapter 15, the structure of the economy and the methods used to prepare unemployment statistics mean that some portion of the labor force will always be unemployed.

The Employment Act of 1946 uses more sensible language in setting as a goal the *maximum* level of employment consistent with the pursuit of other important objectives of government. There is room for legitimate difference of opinion as to what this means in terms of numbers. The most we can safely say is that the vast majority of economists would consider the employment goal to be adequately met if the official unemployment rate were as low as 3 percent of the labor force. On the other hand, a substantial number would begin to complain if the measured rate were to rise above 5 percent.

The Unemployment Record

Exhibit 14.1 shows the record of unemployment in the United States since 1950. Inspection of this exhibit shows that the unemployment rate has been above the 3 to 5 percent range in twelve of the last twenty-five years. Those who still maintain an unemployment goal of 4 percent or below can look with satisfaction only to the years of the Korean and Vietnam wars.

True, even the peaks of postwar unemployment look moderate compared to the Great Depression of the 1930s. In some years then, more than a quarter of the labor force was out of work, and the unemployment rate stayed over 10 percent for an entire decade. By any standards but comparison with the 1930s, however, the American unemployment record of the last quarter century is less than brilliant.

The Price Stability Goal

Unlike "full employment," price stability is technically achievable, even when taken literally. There is nothing inherently impossible in having periods when prices, as measured by official indexes, show no change one way or the other. Years of declining prices are also possible. It ought to be remembered, though, that the price indexes most commonly used in the American economy, especially the consumer price index, have moderate upward biases. As a practical matter, most economists would consider the goal of price stability to be fulfilled in years when the consumer price index rose 1 percent or less. In light of recent experience, a majority would probably be quite happy with anything under 2 percent.

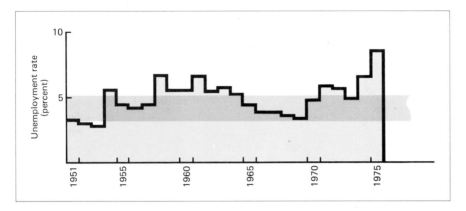

EXHIBIT 14.1
Unemployment in the United States since 1952
If the measured rate of unemployment could be kept in the range of 3 to 5 percent, most economists would accept that the full employment goal was being reasonably well served. As this exhibit shows, though, the unemployment rate has been above the 3 to 5 percent range in twelve of the last twenty-five years.
Source: Prepared by the Federal Reserve Bank of St. Louis.

The Inflation Record

Exhibit 14.2 shows the record of prices over the last twenty-five years in the American economy, as measured by the annual rate of change in the consumer price index. In comparison with the shaded 0 to 2 percent range, the record looks just slightly better than the unemployment record, but still, inflation exceeded 2 percent in more than half of these years.

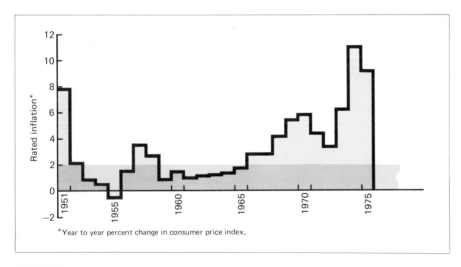

*Year to year percent change in consumer price index.

EXHIBIT 14.2
Inflation since 1948
Price stability, meaning a zero rate of change in official price indexes, is a technically possible goal. For practical purposes, however, most economists would say that the goal of price stability was being well served if inflation could be kept below 2 percent per year. In more than half of the last twenty-five years, inflation has been higher than the shaded 0 to 2 percent range.
Source: Economic Report of the President, 1976, Table B-46.

EXHIBIT 14.3
Combined inflation-unemployment record
As this exhibit shows, there have been only four years out of the last twenty-five when both the goal of price stability and the goal of full employment have been met within acceptable tolerances. What is more, in all but one year since 1971, neither goal has been achieved.

Combined Record

If we set the records on unemployment and inflation side by side, the picture is even less encouraging than when we look at either separately. Exhibit 14.3 gives a schematic representation of what has been achieved. This figure shows only four scattered years in which the goals of low unemployment and price stability were both achieved. The most ominous feature of Exhibit 14.3 is the almost unbroken string of years since 1971 in which neither goal was achieved. What is more, forecasts available at the time of this writing show this trend continuing at least into 1976 and 1977.

The economic problems of the 1970s have caused a considerable upheaval in macroeconomic theory. Before 1970, inflation and unemployment were conventionally thought of as problems that, although serious, at least came one at a time. Isolated bad years such as 1958 were thought only to represent ill-timed or badly handled transitions from one state to the other. Now much of earlier thinking is being reconsidered. Previously accepted explanations of unemployment and inflation are now seen to have been only partial truths.

Unfortunately, no completely worked out and generally accepted new theory of inflation and unemployment is yet available. That should not deter us, though, from following the rethinking process along as far as it has gone. With this in mind, we shall devote the remainder of this chapter to looking at some of the traditional theories of inflation and unemployment that provide the starting point for recent work. In Chapters 15 and 16 we shall look at some of the most fruitful new directions that macroeconomic thinking is now taking. Then, in Chapter 17 we shall discuss several important unresolved controversies of economic stabilization policy.

The Quantity Theory of Money

Velocity

The first theory of inflation we shall look at is also the oldest. The theory begins with the observation that in all modern economies, the quantity of money in existence at any time is less than a year's nominal national income for that economy. That does not mean that there is a shortage of money, however. The quantity of money is a stock and national income is a flow. As the circular flow of income and product churns around during the year, any given dollar, whether a dollar bill or an entry in a bank deposit, can be used again and again to conduct first one person's business and then another's.

It is easy to measure the average number of times each dollar is used for income-generating purposes during a year. All we need to do is divide gross national product, measured in nominal terms, by the quantity of money. The ratio of nominal GNP to the quantity of money is known as the **income velocity of money.** The income velocity of money is given by the formula

$$V = \frac{Y}{M}$$

where V stands for velocity, Y for nominal national income, and M for the quantity of money.

Exhibit 14.4 presents data on the income velocity of money in the United States over the last decade. The figure indicates that each dollar of currency and demand deposits now turns over about five times a year in the process of generating national income. The income velocity of money shows a gradual upward trend over this period, but no sharp year-to-year fluctuations.

Income Velocity of Money (Velocity) The ratio of nominal GNP to the quantity of money, hence, the average number of times per year each dollar of the money supply is used for income-generating purposes.

Quantity Theory

So far we have no theory of anything—just a definition of the concept velocity. Two steps are needed to turn this definition, and the equation on which it is based, into a theory of inflation.

The first step is to rewrite nominal national income as the product of two separate elements, real national income and the price level. In Chapter 7 we defined a price index as the ratio of nominal GNP to real GNP. Using this definition, together with the definition of velocity, we can now write

$$V = \frac{Py}{M}$$

where P stands for the price index, and lowercase y for real national income.

EXHIBIT 14.4
Income velocity of money, 1966–1975

The ratio of GNP to the money supply is known as the income velocity of money. As this exhibit shows, the income velocity of money has tended to rise over the last ten years, but is free of sudden year-to-year changes.

Year	Income Velocity*
1966	4.28
1967	4.26
1968	4.30
1969	4.47
1970	4.42
1971	4.48
1972	4.53
1973	4.76
1974	4.91
1975	5.11

*Ratio of GNP to M_1.

Source: Statistical Abstract of the United States.

The second step is to isolate the element of price on the left-hand side of the equation, and *then to assume that V is a constant*. This gives us the expression

$$P = \frac{MV}{y}$$

With *V* constant, this equation can now be interpreted as a theory that *explains* the price level in terms of the quantity of money. In a country with some predetermined level of real income, the price level is simply proportional to the quantity of money in circulation. The more money, the higher are prices; the less money, the lower are prices. This theory is called the **crude quantity theory of prices.**

Crude Quantity Theory of Prices (Quantity Theory) The theory that the price level in an economy is simply proportional to the quantity of money in circulation.

Does It Work?

The crude quantity theory of prices is an old idea. It was first suggested centuries ago, when prices rose in Europe following the great influx of Spanish silver and gold from the New World. Today, the crude quantity theory seems to fit the facts best in periods of very rapid inflation, called **hyperinflation,** as the following case study suggests.

Hyperinflation   Very rapid inflation.

CASE 14.1
Money and Inflation in Latin America[1]
Hyperinflation has been a chronic problem in many Latin American countries. Some have experienced inflation rates of up to 200 percent per year in the worst years, and even averaged over long periods, rates of price increase have been high.

The wide variation in inflation rates makes Latin American experience a good illustration of the applicability of the crude quantity theory. Economist Beryl W. Sprinkel assembled the data shown in Exhibit 14.5. These figures support the crude quantity theory prediction that the rate of change in the price level (*P*) should be equal to the rate of growth in the ratio of money to real national income (*M/y*), with velocity (*V*) approximately constant.

[1]Based on Beryl W. Sprinkel, *Money and Markets. A Monetarist View* (Homewood, Ill.: Richard D. Irwin, 1971).

Despite its intuitive appeal and its applicability in extreme cases, the crude quantity theory of prices has a very limited usefulness as a tool for short-run economic forecasting and policy making in a developed economy. The main trouble is that movements in prices do not occur instantly in response to changes in the money supply. Evidence from recent American experience suggests that the rate of price change in any year depends in a complex fashion on the trend of changes in the money supply and other economic variables in several preceding years.

In recent years, economists of the monetarist school, whose theories we referred to at the end of the last chapter, have been hard at work developing a "sophisticated" quantity theory to replace the crude quantity theory described here. One major difference between the crude quantity theory and its modern cousin is that the modern theory does not treat velocity as a constant. Instead, velocity changes as the interest rate and a few other

EXHIBIT 14.5

Rates of change in money and inflation in seven Latin American countries, 1955–1968

The crude quantity theory of prices appears to do rather well as an explanation of inflation when very wide ranges of price variation are involved. These data for seven Latin American countries show that the rate of increase in the consumer price index very closely matched the rate of growth of the money stock, measured in relation to real GNP.

Country	Compound Annual Rate of Change in	
	Money Supply / Real Gross National Production (%)	Consumer Price Index (%)
Brazil	35.3	37.9
Chile	29.0	27.6
Argentina	22.6	26.6
Colombia	11.2	10.4
Peru	7.7	9.0
Ecuador	4.4	2.3
Mexico	3.8	3.6

Source: Beryl W. Sprinkel, *Money and Markets. A Monetarist View* (Homewood, Ill.: Richard D. Irwin, 1971), p. 189.

key economic variables change. What is important, according to monetarists, is not that velocity is fixed, but that it changes in a fairly predictable way. The predictability of velocity, they believe, greatly enhances the effectiveness of monetary policy.

We should note that in Chapter 12, we said a great deal about velocity without actually using the word. The income velocity of money, Y/M, is, after all, just the reciprocal of the ratio money to GNP. By looking at the money demand schedule given in Exhibit 12.2, the reader can easily calculate the income velocity of money for various levels of the interest rate in the simplified economy of our examples. Similarly, data on velocity for the postwar American economy can be calculated from Exhibit 12.3. The data given in Exhibit 12.3 suggest that the variations in income velocity shown here in Exhibit 14.4 can largely be explained in terms of changes in the interest rate.

This is not the place, though, for a long discourse on modern theories of income velocity. For the moment, it is enough to conclude that the crude quantity theory contains a part of the key to the inflation-unemployment puzzle, but only a part, and turn to another theory.

Unemployment, Inflation, and the Keynesian Cross

Keynesian Theory

During the first two postwar decades, when periods of high unemployment alternated with periods of inflation, most economics textbooks featured a theory of unemployment and inflation that was based on simple Keynesian multiplier analysis. Let us look at this theory, which for want of a better term we shall call the "crude Keynesian theory."

Exhibit 14.6 contains a Keynesian cross diagram of the familiar kind. Notice, though, that we have made one significant change. One point on the horizontal axis has been marked "full employment national income." That replaces the indication of a "target" level of national income that some of our earlier diagrams contained.

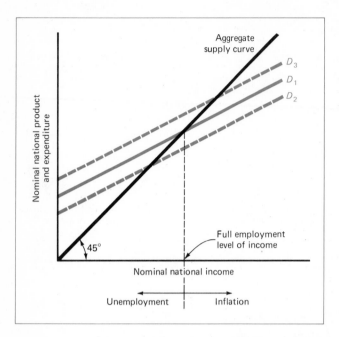

EXHIBIT 14.6
Inflation and the Keynesian cross
The crude Keynesian theory of inflation is based on this Keynesian cross diagram, plus some additional assumptions. When the aggregate demand curve is in position D_1, we assume that real GNP will be sufficient to keep everyone employed. If the aggregate demand curve shifts to D_2, it is assumed that the resulting fall in nominal GNP will all take the form of reduced real output and increased unemployment. If the aggregate demand curve shifts to D_3, it is assumed that all of the subsequent increase in nominal GNP will take the form of a price increase.

To get a theory of unemployment and inflation from this diagram, we reason like this: First, suppose that consumption, planned investment, and government spending are just sufficient to put the aggregate demand schedule at the level marked D_1. In this position, it intersects the aggregate supply schedule exactly at the "full employment" level of national income. By assumption, when equilibrium national income is at this level, just enough goods will be demanded to keep everyone busy who wants a job. (To put it less casually, just enough goods will be demanded to keep all but 4 or 5 percent of the labor force at work, as measured by official statistics.)

Next suppose that because of an error of policy, or some unexpected change in private consumption or planned investment, the aggregate demand schedule slips to the level marked D_2. This creates a contractionary gap. Applying the multiplier theory, we predict that this downward shift in planned expenditure will be followed by a downward movement of nominal national income. Now one more crucial assumption is added. That assumption is that in the short run, at least, all or most of the downward movement of nominal national income will take the form of a fall in real income and product, and not much if any will take the form of a decline in prices. Because the lower level of real output requires fewer workers to produce it, the economy will experience a period of relatively high unemployment and approximate price stability.

Finally, assume that for one reason or another, the aggregate demand schedule were to shift upward, reaching the position labeled D_3 in Exhibit 14.6. This high level of planned expenditure would produce an expansionary gap. In accordance with the multiplier theory, nominal national income would rise. Remember, though, that everyone, or almost everyone, who wants a job now has one. It is not physically possible to squeeze more than a little extra real output from the economy above the full employment level. The rise in nominal income that the multiplier theory requires can take place only in the form of an increase in the price level. As a result, the expansionary gap brings on a period of very low unemployment and inflation of the general price level.

Does It Work?

Like the crude quantity theory, the crude Keynesian theory has considerable intuitive appeal if applied in the proper time and place. In particular, the theory provides a fairly plausible reading of the American record of inflation and unemployment in the years 1951–1969. (See Exhibits 14.1–14.3.) Nonetheless, it cannot be judged to be entirely satisfactory, for several reasons.

First, proponents of this theory have always had difficulty explaining why downward movements in nominal income affected real output so much more strongly than prices, at least in the short run. A number of hypotheses were advanced by various authors, but no one of these was ever universally accepted. Also, it was sometimes difficult to rationalize the various hypotheses in terms of microeconomic theory.

Second, where expansionary gaps were involved, the crude Keynesian theory tells us at most how much prices will rise, but not how fast they will rise. Because inflation is by its nature a matter of the speed of change in the price level, the theory was incomplete here.

Finally, and clearly most serious of all, the crude Keynesian theory is altogether unable to explain how high (and even rising) unemployment can occur simultaneously with high (and even rising) rates of inflation. For this reason, the crude Keynesian theory has lost even its intuitive appeal as an explanation of unemployment and inflation in the 1970s.

As one would expect, Keynesian economists have not simply thrown up their hands in despair when faced with the lessons of recent experience. Instead, they are hard at work building sophisticated versions of Keynesian theory. These, it is hoped, will have superior explanatory powers.

The Phillips Curve

Early Empirical Work

Economists place a strong emphasis on empirical work—work based on real-world data—as well as on abstract theorizing. Sometimes a single empirical study can suggest a whole new direction for theory to take. A well-known research paper by the British economist A. W. Phillips, which we outline in the following case study, had such an impact.

CASE 14.2
A. W. H. Phillips and the Phillips Curve[2]
In 1958, A. W. H. Phillips published the results of some attempts he had made to test the simple hypothesis that wage rates tend to rise faster when unemployment is low than when it is high. The data he had available covered a very long period of the economic history of Britain, stretching from 1861 to

---

[2]A. W. H. Phillips, "The Relationship Between Unemployment and the Rate of Change of Money Wage Rates in the United Kingdom, 1861–1957," *Economica*, New Series Vol. 25 (Nov. 1958), pp. 283–299.

EXHIBIT 14.7
One of A. W. H. Phillips' original Phillips curves for the British economy
In 1958, A. W. H. Phillips published a very influential paper that looked at the relationship between unemployment and the rate of change in wages over a long period in Britain. He found that data from the period 1948 to 1957 fit rather closely a curve based on data from the period 1861 to 1913, as shown here. Curves like this have since come to be called *Phillips curves*.

Source: A. W. H. Phillips, "The Relationship between Unemployment and the Rate of Change of Money Wage Rates in the United Kingdom, 1861–1957," *Economica,* New Series Vol. 25 (Nov. 1958), pp. 283–299. Reprinted by permission.

1957. The statistical evidence he assembled seemed to support the idea that the rate of change in money wage rates can be explained by the level of unemployment.

Phillips presented his results in a series of charts, one of which is reproduced here as Exhibit 14.7. This diagram contains a curve that represents the average relationship between unemployment and the rate of change of wages during the period 1861 to 1913. The points scattered near the curve show wage and unemployment data for the years 1948 to 1957. The fit of the modern years in Phillips' study to the curve calculated on much earlier data is remarkably close.

Allan William H. Phillips
(1914–1975)

A. W. H. Phillips was an economist whose entire reputation was based on a single paper, published on the right topic at the right time. In the late 1950s, the relationship between inflation and unemployment ranked as the major unsolved problem of macroeconomic theory. The curves that Phillips drew in his famous article in *Economica* suggested a simple, stable relationship between inflation and unemployment. Phillips' paper offered little by way of a theoretical explanation of the relationship, but his curves became the peg on which all future discussion of the problem was hung. Almost immediately, every article on inflation and unemployment became a discussion of what was the shape of the "Phillips curve," what point on the Phillips curve was best as a policy target, how the Phillips curve could be shifted, and so forth. Today, the term is so well established that Phillips' name enjoys a sort of immortality even though his own interpretation of the famous curve has fallen into disrepute.

A. W. H. Phillips was born in New Zealand, but made London his base for most of his academic career. He taught at the London School of Economics during the 1950s and 1960s until moving to the Australian National University in 1967. Phillips was originally trained in electrical engineering, and this training seems to have influenced his approach to economic problems. This approach has been characterized as "scientistic." In the mid-1950s he was suggesting the use of an "electric analog machine or simulator" as an aid to the study of economic dynamics. This idea perhaps foreshadowed the intensive use of electronic computers in contemporary economic research.

Since the publication of Phillips' article, curves like the one in Exhibit 14.7 have come to be called **Phillips curves.** In recent years, the use of the term "Phillips curve" has been broadened to include similar curves drawn on diagrams where the vertical axis measures the rate of change of prices (that is, the rate of inflation) instead of the rate of change of wages. Recent data for the United States will be presented in a Phillips curve framework in Chapter 16.

Phillips Curve A curve showing the relationship between the rate of inflation and the level of unemployment. Inflation, usually placed on the vertical axis of such a figure, may be measured either in terms of the rate of change in wages or the rate of change in a price index.

A Menu

Like the crude quantity theory and the crude Keynesian theory we have already examined, the intuitively appealing concept of the Phillips curve is open to serious misinterpretation when applied to economic policy. A tempting but misleading interpretation is to regard the Phillips curve as a menu of alternatives from which policy makers can choose a preferred compromise between the evils of inflation and unemployment.

Suppose, for example, that the President and his Council of Economic Advisors were presented with data that suggested the Phillips curve shown in Exhibit 14.8. We might easily imagine that if the administration were a Democratic one, strongly influenced by union labor or sympathetic to the plight of the unemployed, it might pursue expansionary policies and aim for a point high up and to the left, such as the point marked *D* in the figure. In contrast, a Republican adminstration, dominated by conservative businesspeople and dour bankers, might aim for a point such as *R,* near the intersection of the Phillips curve and the horizontal axis.

Drift

The trouble with interpreting the Phillips curve as a policy menu is that it may not stand still while the diners enjoy their meal. As the 1960s progressed, economists in the United States began to notice that inflation-

---

EXHIBIT 14.8

The Phillips curve as a policy menu

The Phillips curve is sometimes misleadingly interpreted as a policy menu offering a fixed trade-off between inflation and unemployment. If the Phillips curve for the American economy had the shape shown here, we might imagine that Democrats would want to choose a point like *D,* where low unemployment would be "bought" at the price of high inflation, while Republicans might rather have a point like *R.* Unfortunately for this interpretation, the Phillips curve is not stable. Policies designed to produce movements along it can cause it to shift to a new position.

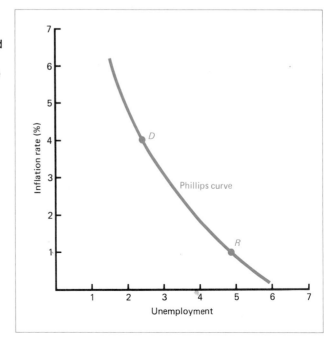

unemployment points for recent years did not fit the Phillips curves they had plotted using data from the 1950s. It became common to speak of an upward drift in the Phillips curve. The menu seemed to be getting less appetizing as time went by. If the upward drift had been entirely spontaneous, policy makers could simply have been told to make the best of disappointing circumstances, and still choose the point they liked best from the new, higher Phillips curve. If, however, it could be shown that shifts in the Phillips curve were caused by the particular policies chosen to move the economy *along* a supposedly fixed curve, the idea of the Phillips curve as a policy menu would have to be reevaluated altogether.

In fact, as we shall show in Chapter 16, it is now widely believed that the choice of particular inflation and unemployment goals does determine the position and rate of drift of the Phillips curve. The modern theory of inflation that economists are now developing does have a place in it for the Phillips curve, but the place is not quite the one that early interpreters envisaged.

Cost-Push Inflation

Demand-Pull

All three of the theories we have looked at so far share the common element that inflation is touched off by a rise in aggregate demand. In the quantity theory, the excessive aggregate demand results from an injection of new money into the economy. In the Keynesian theory it is represented by a shift in the aggregate demand schedule to a position high enough to produce an expansionary gap. And according to the Phillips curve analysis, inflation does not become serious until demand has risen enough to produce a shortage of labor. Because all these theories single out a rise in aggregate demand as the initial cause of a rise in the price level, they are collectively referred to as **demand-pull** theories of inflation.

Demand-Pull Inflation   Inflation that is initially touched off by an increase in aggregate demand.

Cost-Push

In the course of the 1950s and 1960s, economists began to realize that serious inflation could occur even when there was considerable slack in overall demand and a substantial level of unemployment. None of the demand-pull theories adequately explained this possibility, and it became increasingly popular to speak of a new kind of inflation, called **cost-push inflation.**

Cost-Push Inflation   Inflation that is initially touched off by a spontaneous rise in wages, profit margins, commodity prices, or other elements of cost during a period of slack aggregate demand.

The most commonly heard version of the cost-push theory runs something like this. Suppose that, initially, the economy is enjoying a period of approximate price stability and moderate, but not unusually low unemployment. Then imagine that it comes time for some powerful labor union in an important basic industry (let us call it the steel industry, for the sake of illustration) to renegotiate its contract with employers. Through aggressive bargaining, and perhaps the threat or actual occurrence of a strike, the union wins a very generous raise for all its members.

Suppose that the rise in wages is so big that it cannot be fully offset by increases in output per man hour. If so, the cost of making a ton of steel goes up. Citing the increase in cost as justification, the steel companies raise their prices. Steel is used to make cars, refrigerators, apartment buildings, and hundreds of other things, so costs rise in all those other industries. The makers of cars, refrigerators, and so forth all raise their prices, again citing the rise in costs as justification. The increase in the price of steel has now become a general increase in the price level.

As other union contracts expire, the bargaining becomes tougher and tougher. For one thing, the leaders of the auto workers, miners, teamsters, and so forth have their reputations on the line with their rank-and-file union members, who expect them to do as well as the steel workers did. On top of that, union negotiators are now able to point to the rise in the cost of living as additional justification for giving their workers a fat wage package. The cost-push mechanism is now in full swing, and the initial spark has touched off an inflationary wage-price spiral.

Adherents to the cost-push theory often point out that the process need not start with a rise in wages. Other powerful economic interests may fire the first shot. For example, it is often suggested that some large, highly concentrated industry like the automobile industry may initiate the cycle by unilaterally raising its prices simply to increase profits, even though there is no justification for such an increase in terms of rising costs or rising demand. The resulting inflation is then called **profit-push inflation** to distinguish it from the **wage-push inflation** of our first scenario.

Finally, the cost-push cycle may be touched off by a rise in the price of important basic commodities, such as oil or wheat. The initial source of commodity price rises may lie altogether outside the American economy, being found in such uncontrollable elements as Arab politics or the weather in Russia. Nonetheless, once under way, commodity price increases can spread throughout the economy by the cost-push mechanism, producing what can be called **commodity inflation.**

Does It Make Sense?

Does the cost-push theory of inflation make sense? The answer seems to be that, like the other theories we have examined, it contains an element of truth, but that element of truth is subject to strict qualifications. These qualifications are worth reviewing in detail.

The Cost-Push Illusion

The first qualification we must make is to distinguish between genuine cost-push inflation on the one hand, and the **cost-push illusion** on the other. Because of the cost-push illusion, ordinary demand-pull inflation may *look* like cost-push inflation to those who are actually caught up in it. Milton Friedman uses a vivid little example to illustrate the cost-push illusion. His story is based, in turn, on a much longer parable told by A. A. Alchian and W. R. Allen.

Profit-Push Inflation A variety of cost-push inflation in which a spontaneous increase in profit margins is the initial source of price increases.

Wage-Push Inflation A variety of cost-push inflation in which a spontaneous increase in nominal wage rates is the initial source of price increases.

Commodity Inflation A variety of cost-push inflation in which a spontaneous increase in commodity prices is the initial source of general price increases.

Cost-Push Illusion The phenomenon that demand-pull inflation often looks like cost-push inflation to those caught up in it, because inventories cushion the immediate impact of demand on prices at each link in the chain of distribution from producers to retailers.

CASE 14.3
The Cost-Push Illusion[3]
Let us suppose in a country in which everything else is fine all of a sudden there is a great craze for increasing the consumption of meat, and all the

[3]The story is quoted from Milton Friedman, "Unemployment versus Inflation?" Institute for Economic Affairs Occasional Paper No. 44 (London, 1975), pp. 34–35. Originally appeared in Armen A. Alchian and William R. Allen, *University Economics: Elements of Inquiry*, 2d ed., (Belmont, Calif.: Wadsworth, 1972).

housewives rush to the butchers to buy meat. The butchers are delighted to sell them the meat. They do not mark up the prices at all, they just sell out all the meat they have but they place additional orders with the wholesalers. The wholesalers are delighted to sell the meat. They clean out their inventories. They go back to the packing houses. The packing houses ship out their meat. The price is the same but the packing houses send orders to their buyers at the cattle market: "Buy more beef!" There is only a fixed amount of cattle available. And so the only thing that happens is that in the process of each packer trying to buy more beef, he bids up the price. Then a notice goes from the packer to the wholesaler. "We are very sorry, but due to an increase in our costs we are required to increase the price." A notice goes from the wholesaler to the retailer. And the retailer finally says to the customer when she comes in to complain that beef has gone up, "I'm terribly sorry, but my costs have gone up." He's right. But what started the increase in costs all the way up and down the line? It was the housewife rushing in to buy the meat.

The point of this example is that what is true for individual businesspeople is not necessarily true for the economy as a whole. All businesspeople may feel that they raise prices reluctantly, and only when placed under severe pressure by the rises of wages and costs. That may be true insofar as it goes. But where does the pressure come from? It comes from an increase in demand, say the critics of cost-push inflation.

What keeps the true cause of inflation from being obvious to everyone is the existence of inventories at every link in the chain from producer to consumer. The initial impact of an increase in demand is a decline in inventories, first at the retail level, then at the wholesale level, then at the factory level, and so forth. As businesspeople at each link in the chain increase their orders to replenish stocks, the process will eventually reach someone who cannot respond by pulling goods out of the inventories of the next person in line. This may be the packer who has to buy beef at auction, it may be the importer who has to bid for raw materials on world commodity markets, or it may be an employer who can find new workers only by bidding them away from other jobs. Sooner or later, the rise in demand encounters the inescapable fact of the scarcity of resources, and then a price rise starts to get passed back up the chain of distribution.

Monopoly Power

Monopoly Power A seller's power to raise the price of a product without losing all, or nearly all of his or her customers.

A second qualification to the cost-push theory of inflation hinges on the concept of **monopoly power.** Economists say that a firm has monopoly power whenever it is able to raise the price of its product without losing all, or nearly all of its customers to competitors. Applied to the labor market, a union can be said to have monopoly power if it is able to obtain a substantial increase in the wages of its members without a serious loss of jobs to nonunion workers.

Most accounts of cost-push inflation depend on monopoly power to set the cost-price spiral in motion. Clearly, a union or a firm would not make the initial push in wages or prices if it did not think it could gain an advantage by doing so. Without monopoly power, making such a push would only result in a loss of jobs or sales to competitors. About the only exception to the rule that cost-push inflation has to begin in a relatively monopolistic part of the economy would be commodity inflation set in motion by bad weather, which in turn might lead to rising prices in the agricultural sector.

Now, a well-established proposition of microeconomic theory[4] does tell us that, other things being equal, prices (or wages) will be higher in a market where sellers have substantial monopoly power than in a market where there is a high degree of competition. For any given degree of monopoly power, though, there will be a level beyond which prices cannot profitably be raised. In nontechnical language, this is a matter of "charging all that the market will bear." Once this profit-maximizing equilibrium price (or workers' welfare-maximizing wage) is reached, the prices (or wages) in a monopolistic market, although high, will stop rising.

Here, then, is the confusion that must be avoided. Monopoly power can cause *high* prices and wages, but there is no reason to expect it to cause *steadily rising* prices and wages. It follows that a firm or labor union with firmly established monopoly power is no more likely suddenly to push its prices or wages above the prevailing equilibrium level than one that operates in a fully competitive manner. Only a sudden *increase* in the degree of a firm's or union's monopoly power could cause the sudden *increase* in prices or wages needed to touch off the mechanism of cost-push inflation. No evidence has been found of any substantial increase in the monopoly power of either business or labor that could account for the steady acceleration of inflation over the last fifteen years.

Relative Prices

Even if we could identify a sudden increase in monopoly power as a source of cost-push inflation, one more qualification would still be needed. Let us grant, for the sake of discussion, that some major union (make it the steelworkers again) wins a sudden large rise in wages. Perhaps this is caused by the election of a new union leader, who is determined to bargain much more aggressively than the old one. The next question is why this should cause a general rise in prices and wages, and not just an increase in steel prices and steelworkers' wages relative to those in other sectors of the economy. Why will the increased prices and wages in the steel industry not be offset by lower prices and wages elsewhere?

Think of it this way. When the price of steel goes up, either the quantity of steel sold will be reduced, or the buyers of steel will have to spend more than before on the purchase of steel. Very probably both will happen. If the quantity of steel produced falls, some steel workers will be laid off. These will have to go hunt for work elsewhere, and the presence of these new job seekers will tend to depress wages outside the steel industry. If buyers of steel spend more to purchase steel, they will have less left over to purchase other things. The demand for other goods and the prices of other goods will thus tend to fall. Instead of a general wage-price spiral, then, all the economy would experience would be a shift in relative prices. The price of steel would go up and the prices of other things would go down. As measured by a price index, no significant inflation would occur.

[4]The issue of monopoly power is discussed at length in Chapter 26. The reader is referred to that chapter for details.

This argument suggests that in order to have true cost-push inflation, something must prevent the smooth adjustment of relative prices and wages. Suppose that prices and wages in other sectors did not fall when steel prices and wages went up. Other sectors of the economy would not be able to absorb the newly laid off steelworkers, so they would have to stay home and draw unemployment. Real output would drop, and unemployment would rise. Price indexes would go up because steel prices are higher and no other prices are lower.

Cost-Push Summary

All these qualifications together greatly narrow the range of circumstances in which the cost-push theory of inflation can be made to work. First, we must eliminate all those cases of demand-pull inflation that masquerade as cost-push inflation as a result of the cost-push illusion. Second, there must be some factor or combination of factors that touches off the wage-price spiral. A rise in international commodity prices might be sufficient, but the simple presence of monopoly power is not by itself enough. Third, there must be some reason for inflexibility of wages and prices in all sectors of the economy, so that wage and price rises in one sector are not simply offset by declines in wages and prices elsewhere. These qualifications do not entirely undermine the validity of the cost-push theory, but they do indicate that we have quite a bit more work to do before we know how to apply it properly.

Conclusions

Each of the four traditional theories of inflation and unemployment that we have presented in this chapter has something to recommend it. Each seems to fit the facts in some particular time or place. None of them is a completely general theory of inflation and unemployment, however. They are like the separate pieces of a puzzle that we have not yet put together.

Putting together the unemployment-inflation puzzle is perhaps the most important single job for economists today. The job is by no means finished, but little by little the outlines of a picture are beginning to emerge. Perhaps the most fascinating feature of the emerging picture is that it appears to have room for all of the pieces. As we develop the modern theories of unemployment and inflation in the next two chapters, we shall find that, properly qualified and interpreted, none of the four theories of this chapter directly contradicts any other. Taken together, there is reason to hope that they provide a theory that can help policy makers to guide our economy back toward "full employment" and price stability.

SUMMARY

1. Price stability and full employment are the two most important goals of economic stabilization policy. For practical purposes, we can think of full employment as being somewhere in the 3 to 5 percent range of measured unemployment, and price stability as being somewhere in the 0 to 2 percent range of inflation. By these standards, the postwar record of economic stabilization for the American economy has been poor and is apparently getting worse.

2. The crude quantity theory of inflation has a very long tradition in economic thought. It is based on the assumption that the velocity of money is a constant, so that prices are proportional to the money supply when real output is given. This theory appears to work fairly well during episodes of hyperinflation, but for practical short-run applications, a more sophisticated theory of velocity is needed.

3. The crude Keynesian theory of inflation and unemployment is based on the usual Keynesian nominal income determination theory, plus a few added assumptions. One assumption is that there is a particular level of nominal income that is associated with full employment. A second assumption is that below this level, movements in nominal income take the form only of movements in employment and real output, with prices unchanged. A third assumption is that above the full employment level, movements in nominal income take the form of pure price movements. The crude Keynesian theory does not allow for the possibility that high rates of inflation and unemployment might occur at the same time.

4. A Phillips curve shows the relationship between rates of inflation and unemployment for an economy. If the Phillips curve were stable, it would provide a "menu" from which policy makers could choose according to their tastes. However, the Phillips curve is not stable. It turns out that its position is partly determined by the very policies that government authorities pursue when they try to choose a particular point on the curve.

5. The idea of cost-push inflation was introduced to explain how prices could rise when there was substantial slack in employment and aggregate demand. According to the theory, inflation can be touched off by spontaneous increases in profits, prices, or wages. In applying the cost-push theory, it is very important to distinguish between genuine cost-push inflation and the cost-push illusion.

DISCUSSION QUESTIONS

1. In your own opinion, what levels of both inflation and unemployment would you consider to be excessive? Is either inflation or unemployment above your limit at the moment?

2. Milton Friedman writes, "long-continued inflation is always and everywhere a monetary phenomenon that arises from a more rapid expansion in the quantity of money than in the quantity of output." Why does he add the qualifying phrase "long-continued?" Can short-term inflation have other sources?

3. The crude Keynesian theory implies a sharply kinked, L-shaped Phillips curve. Can you explain why?

4. Some people maintain that unemployment is a painful human tragedy while inflation is just a matter of dollars chasing dollars. What sort of choice would such a person make if faced with a Phillips curve "menu" (assuming, for the sake of discussion, that the menu were a stable one)? Do you think that inflation, like unemployment, also affects *people?* If inflation is not "about people" but only "about dollars," why do we study it in an economics course?

5. Assume that in a country where everything else is fine, there is suddenly an outbreak of hoof and mouth disease that sharply decreases the supply of beef cattle. Would the resulting rise in the price of beef be true cost-push inflation? Trace this kind of inflation through the marketing chain for beef. At what points would it look different than demand-pull inflation? At what points would it be hard to tell the difference?

CHAPTER 15
A Closer Look at Unemployment

What You Will Learn in This Chapter

Most people think that "unemployed" means "not working" or "cannot find a job." It is not a simple matter, though, to translate those ideas into a single number, *the* unemployment rate, which can be used as a guide to policy. For some purposes, it is more interesting to look at the average duration of unemployment at a certain time. The duration of unemployment depends on how successful unemployed workers are in the process of job search. By looking at the impact of inflation on the process of job search, we get an important insight into the nature of the Phillips curve. Once unemployment is fully understood, we can begin to explore ways to reduce the unemployment rate to an acceptable level.

For Review

Here are some important terms and concepts that will be put to use in this chapter. Be certain that you understand them, or review them before proceeding.

The price system as a mechanism for utilizing knowledge (Chapter 2)

The Phillips curve (Chapter 14)

Measuring Unemployment

Unemployment statistics are perhaps the most closely watched numbers in the entire economy. The federal government is bound by law to keep unemployment at a low level. Newspapers and television make each monthly change of a fraction of a percentage point into headline news. Political careers can be made or broken by what happens to these magic numbers. The numbers are important enough, in fact, to make it worth knowing what they mean, and where they come from. We shall begin this chapter, then, by looking at how unemployment is measured.

What Is Unemployment?

Let us begin by looking not at what the Bureau of Labor Statistics officially means by "unemployment," but instead at two common sense meanings of the term. The first common sense meaning of "unemployed" is "not working," and the second is "cannot find a job."

Employed According to the official Bureau of Labor Statistics definition, a person who (a) works at least one hour a week for pay, or at least fifteen hours per week as an unpaid worker in a family business, or (b) normally works the required number of hours, but is temporarily not working because of bad weather, illness, vacation, or a labor dispute.

If unemployed means not working, then an astonishing 62 percent of the U.S. population were unemployed in 1974. By working, official statisticians mean someone who works at least one hour a week for pay, or at least fifteen hours a week as an unpaid worker in a family business. By that definition, only 80.6 million people out of a total population of 211.4 million were working in an average week of 1974. Another 5.3 million people had jobs from which they were temporarily absent as a result of illness, bad weather, labor disputes, or vacations. These people are referred to as **employed** even though they are not working. The other 130.1 million Americans were not employed in an average week of 1974, but as we shall see in a moment, most of them were not officially *un*employed either.

Our other common sense idea of unemployment—"cannot find a job"—turns out to fit a surprisingly small number of people. In the average week of 1974, just 3.5 million people, or 1.6 percent of the population, could not find a job even though they were actively looking for one. About half of those had been looking less than a month. However, some people who were not unable to find a job were counted as unemployed too.

The Unemployment Rate

The official unemployment rate falls somewhere between these two common sense measures of unemployment. In 1974, it stood at 5.6 percent. Exhibit 15.1 will help us understand where this number comes from.

Starting at the top, we first divide the total population into three large groups. One group includes people under 16, plus those who are institutionalized or in the armed forces. They are not considered to be potential workers at all. The second group consists of adults who could potentially be workers, but who for one reason or another did not have a job and were not actively looking for one. Well over half of these were women who cited home responsibilities as their reason for not looking for work, and most of the rest were retired, disabled, ill, or in school. The remaining group—91 million people or 43 percent of the population in 1974—make up the **civilian labor force.**

Civilian Labor Force All civilians aged 16 or over, who are either (a) employed, (b) actively looking for a job, (c) laid off from a job to which they expect to be recalled, or (d) waiting to start a new job that will begin within 30 days.

Unemployment Rate The percentage of the civilian labor force who are not employed.

The **unemployment rate** as officially measured is the percentage of the civilian labor force that is not employed. The Bureau of Labor Statistics in cooperation with the Bureau of the Census obtains the data needed to make unemployment measurements from a monthly sample of about 50,000 randomly selected households. Field agents go to preselected houses and ask a series of specific questions about the job status of each member of the household. The questions include such things as: Did anyone work last week? Did anyone look for work? How long have they been looking for work? How did they go about looking? The result is that one headline-making percentage, plus a large array of supplementary tables that receive much less public attention.

Gray Areas

Clearly, there are a lot of gray areas in the measurement of unemployment. The official unemployment rate can equally well be criticized for understating or for overstating the "true" number of the unemployed.

Many gray areas come to light when we compare "unemployment" with "cannot find a job." People are counted as unemployed even though

EXHIBIT 15.1

Employment and unemployment, 1974

The Bureau of Labor Statistics bases its official unemployment rate on a complex breakdown of the population according to age and unemployment status. The Bureau defines the unemployment rate as the percentage of the civilian labor force who are not employed. This definition of the unemployment rate can be thought of as a compromise between the two common sense definitions of "not working" and "cannot find a job."

Exhibit 15.1a
Millions of persons, 1974

Total population	211.4
Civilian labor force	91.0
Employed	85.9
Working	80.6
Not working	5.3
Unemployed	5.1
Lost last job	2.2
Left last job	0.8
Reentered labor force	1.4
Never worked before	0.7
Not in labor force	57.6
Home responsibilities	32.7
In school	7.2
Ill health and disability	5.4
Retirement and old age	7.4
All other	4.6
Under 16, institutionalized, and armed forces	62.8

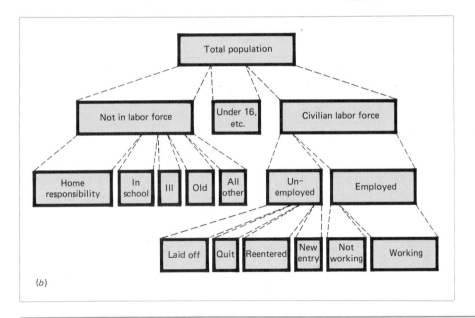

(b)

they are not looking for a job, if they are laid off from their job but expect to be recalled, or if they have found a job that they expect to start within thirty days. The label "cannot find a job" also does not seem very appropriate for a person who could have stayed on in his last job, but instead quit voluntarily, yet such people are counted as unemployed.

On the other hand, there are a certain number of people who really cannot find a job, and really would want one, but have become so discouraged with their prospects that they have gone a week or more without actively looking for one. Available data suggest that there is about one of these "discouraged workers" for every ten officially unemployed. Also, there are an unmeasured number of genuinely unemployed 14- and 15-year olds.

Some of these have been laid off from previous steady jobs and may even have dependents, but since 1967 they no longer count in the labor force so they cannot be unemployed. Finally, workers who want, need, and are actively looking for a *full-time* job are not counted as unemployed if they have worked even a single hour in the week before being surveyed. These workers are sometimes called "underemployed."

Unemployment Stocks and Flows

Wherever we draw the line between the employed and the unemployed, the unemployment rate measures a stock. The level of unemployment at any time, and changes in that level, depend on the size of the *flows* into and out of the stock of unemployed workers.

Exhibit 15.2 shows the relationships between the stock of unemployed workers and several key flows. Three ways to enter the stock of unemployed workers are shown. Employed workers can become unemployed either by quitting their jobs or by being laid off. Also, people not in the labor force can become officially unemployed if they begin seriously looking for work but do not find it immediately. Of course, some new entrants and reentrants find jobs right away, without going through a period of unemployment.

The exhibit also shows three ways for people to leave the stock of unemployed. They can be hired for a new job, or recalled to one from which they were laid off. Also, they can retire or withdraw from the labor force without ever having found a job.

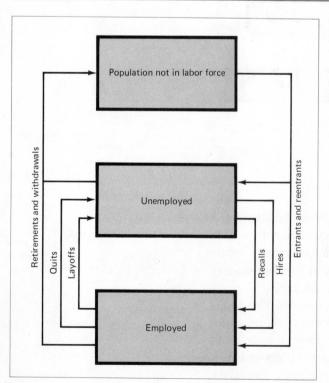

EXHIBIT 15.2

Labor market stocks and flows

The size of the stock of unemployed persons depends on the rates of flow of workers into and out of unemployed status. People can become unemployed by entering the labor force without finding a job immediately, or by quitting or being laid off from their last job and then looking for a new one. They can leave the stock of the unemployed by being hired for a new job or recalled to an old one, or by leaving the labor force in discouragement without ever having found a job.

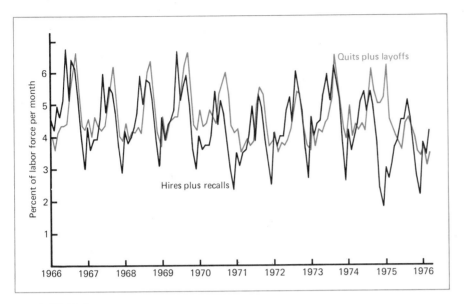

EXHIBIT 15.3
Quits, layoffs, hires, and recalls
The number of people unemployed at one time is fairly small compared to
the size of the flows into and out of unemployment. The monthly change in
the unemployment rate is equal to the difference between the rate of quits
plus layoffs, and the rate of hires plus recalls. Those flows are usually so
closely matched that the unemployment rate changes by less than half a
percentage point a month.

Balance

The number of workers actually unemployed at any time is rather
small compared to the size of the flows into and out of the stock of unemployed. This is clearly shown in Exhibit 15.3, which gives data on the major
flows identified in Exhibit 15.2. On the average, between 4 and 5 percent of
the labor force quit their jobs or are laid off each month, while a very nearly
equal number are hired or recalled to work.

Given these relatively large inflows and outflows, the unemployment
rate would fluctuate violently from month to month were it not for the fact
that the rate of quits plus layoffs and the rate of hires plus recalls is always
very nearly in balance. The rate of change in the unemployment rate is
equal to the difference between quits plus layoffs and hires plus recalls.
As Exhibit 15.3 shows, the difference is rarely as much as $\frac{1}{2}$ percent.

Frictional Unemployment

On the average, the total stock of unemployed workers "turns over"
every few weeks. That does not mean, of course, that every individual unemployed person in the stock is changed, but the picture of a quit or layoff,
followed by a brief stay among the unemployed, and then a hire or recall is
more the rule than the exception. Exhibit 15.4 gives figures on the average
duration of unemployment for selected years. In good years, well over half
the unemployed are out of work less than four weeks, and only one in

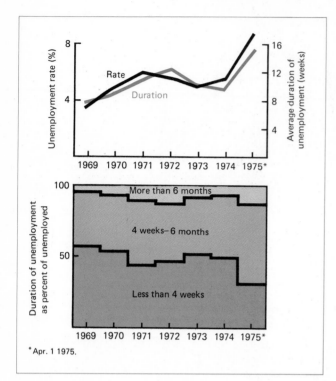

EXHIBIT 15.4
Duration and rate of unemployment
The unemployment picture is dominated by those spending a relatively short period between jobs. In a reasonably good year, well over half of the unemployed have been out of work less than four weeks. Even in a very bad year, only about one in eight of the unemployed has been out of work half a year or more. The average duration of unemployment closely follows the unemployment rate.

Source: U.S. Bureau of the Census, *Statistical Abstract of the United States, 1975* (Washington, D.C.: U.S. Government Printing Office, 1976).

twenty is out of work for more than six months. Even in years of high unemployment, the short-term unemployed dominate the picture.

Economists refer to that portion of unemployment accounted for by people spending relatively short periods between jobs as **frictional unemployment.** The presence of frictional unemployment is the major reason why the policy goal that we call "full employment" can never mean a zero measured rate of unemployment. Frictional unemployment is present in good times as well as bad, for the simple reason that as the economy picks up and layoffs are reduced, more people voluntarily quit their jobs to look for better ones. This tendency of people to switch jobs when times are good keeps the measured unemployment rate up, but it is nothing to worry about. Quite the contrary, a normal level of frictional unemployment is a sign of a healthy economy. It is the means by which each individual becomes matched with the best possible job.

Dual Labor Market

More serious policy problems are raised by that minority of workers who spend long periods in the ranks of the unemployed, or who become unemployed frequently. According to one often heard theory, these workers are victims of a **dual labor market.** The idea is that the primary sector of the labor market contains high-wage jobs with large, profitable firms. These jobs are likely to be unionized, to offer more opportunities for advancement, and to be less affected by ups and downs in business activity. The secondary sector of the labor market, in contrast, contains low-paying jobs with marginal firms, which are held by unorganized workers with unstable work

Frictional Unemployment That portion of unemployment accounted for by people spending relatively short periods between jobs.

Dual Labor Market The division of the labor market into a primary sector, containing good jobs with established firms, and a secondary sector, containing low-paid, unstable jobs with marginal firms.

patterns. These are largely "dead-end" jobs with few opportunities for advancement. They are heavily hit by cyclical swings in unemployment.

Because secondary-sector jobs are unattractive, workers who are not qualified for primary-sector jobs typically have short periods of employment often ending in quits rather than layoffs. These alternate with long periods of vainly trying to find something better. We shall return to the special policy problems raised by unemployment in the secondary labor market later in this chapter.

Unemployment and Job Search

We have seen that the unemployment rate depends on a delicate balance between flows of workers into and out of the stock of unemployed. We have also seen that these flows are large in relation to the number of workers unemployed at any time. It follows that anything that happens to change even slightly the average length of time a worker remains unemployed can have a very significant impact on the measured rate of unemployment.

For this reason, much recent work on the theory of unemployment has focused closely on the process of job search as a key to the average duration of unemployment, and hence to the measured unemployment rate. There are many variations of the job search theory of unemployment, and new ideas are still being put forth and tested. Certain basic assumptions, though, are shared by almost all economists working in this field.

Information

One basic assumption underlies all job search theories. That is the notion that workers looking for jobs and employers looking for workers operate without complete information of one another's needs or requirements, and without complete information about future economic trends. The job search process is essentially a matter of putting the labor market to work as a mechanism for obtaining knowledge.

Let us translate our discussion into more specific terms. Consider an individual unemployed worker who is looking for a new job. At the start of the job search, he or she knows that "somewhere out there" there are a number of employers looking for workers. The first necessity is to find out who and where these employers are, and what their jobs are like.

The jobs will not all be equally good. For one thing, some will pay better wages than others. In addition, some will offer pleasant surroundings and some not, some will be near and others far, and some will be stimulating, others dull. To keep things simple, we shall talk only about wage differences between different jobs, but the reader should remember that the job seeker will make mental adjustments in wage offers to allow for non-wage advantages and disadvantages of any job.

Our worker, then, sets out to sample the jobs available. Common sense tells us that people will not automatically take the first job offered. To play safe, even after getting one job offer, they would like to check a few more potential employers to see if something better turns up. On the average, the larger the number of jobs they include in their sample, the better will be the best wage offer they come across.

Reservation Wage   The wage (adjusted for nonmonetary advantages and disadvantages of a job) below which a person will not accept a job offer.

The Reservation Wage

There is a limit to the length of time a person will search for a job when jobs are available. That limit can be expressed in terms of the idea of a **reservation wage.** A person's reservation wage is the wage (adjusted for nonmonetary advantages of the job, as always) below which he or she will not accept an offer. A person who has a reservation wage of $150 per week, for example, will reject any offer of $149 a week or less, and take any job that comes along that offers $150 per week or more.

People's reservation wages tend to decline the longer their job search continues. There are at least two reasons for this. First, people may initially be very optimistic, overestimating their own worth in the eyes of potential employers, and then gradually they become more realistic as the hoped-for top-level offers do not materialize. Second, even if unemployment insurance is available, long periods without work tend to cut into people's savings, and financial pressure to get back to work increases. Case studies confirm the idea that reservation wages decline as the period of job search is lengthened.

CASE 15.1
Reservation Wages and the Duration of Unemployment

Several studies have been made of the effects of the duration of unemployment on the reservation wage. In one study,[1] Hirschel Kasper sampled 3,000 long-term unemployed workers in Minnesota during the 1961 recession. Their unemployment duration ranged from 0 to 20 months, with an average of 7.5 months. He found that workers initially asked for wages higher than their previous wages, but after about 6 months of unemployment they were willing to accept less. He also found that the faster the decline in the reservation wage, the sooner new employment was accepted.

Another study[2] was based on an incident in which the Boeing Company in Seattle laid off 7,700 workers when the Defense Department cancelled a big aerospace contract. Fourteen weeks after this huge layoff, some 69 percent of the former employees still had not found work. These were asked to respond to a questionnaire item saying "I need work that pays at least $_____ per month." The study revealed that, on the average, the reservation wage of these workers declined by 2.6 percent each month.

[1]Hirschel Kasper, "The Relation Between the Duration of Unemployment and the Asking Wage," unpublished Ph.D. dissertation, Department of Economics, University of Minnesota, 1963, and "The Asking Price of Labor and the Duration of Unemployment," *Review of Economics and Statistics* (May 1967). The data are used here as they are cited by Charles C. Holt in "Job Search, Phillips' Wage Relation, and Union Influence: Theory and Evidence," in Edmund S. Phelps (Ed.), *Microeconomic Foundations of Employment and Inflation Theory* (New York: W. W. Norton, 1970), p. 97.
[2]Data of the U.S. Arms Control and Disarmament Agency, as reported by Holt.

Duration of Unemployment

The idea of repeated sampling to find the best job offer plus the idea of a declining reservation wage gives us a simple theory of the duration of unemployment. Exhibit 15.5 gives a graphical presentation of the theory. An upward-sloping curve is drawn in the diagram to show that, on the average, a worker can find a better job offer by spending more time in job search. A downward-sloping curve is drawn to show how the worker's reservation wage falls as time goes by. The two curves come together the first time the worker gets a job offer that meets that worker's reservation wage. This

EXHIBIT 15.5

Determination of the average duration of unemployment
The longer people search for jobs, the better, on the average, will be the best wage offers they uncover. At the same time, the longer they search, the lower their reservation wages tend to fall. In this exhibit, the duration of unemployment is determined by the intersection of the reservation wage curve and the wage offer curve. That indicates the point at which people first receive job offers that meet their reservation wage.

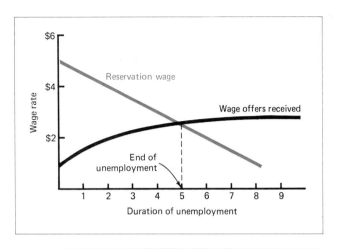

takes five weeks on the average as our figure is drawn. The worker takes the job, and the period of unemployment is at an end.

We should stress two things about this figure. First, the curves express averages for workers of similar skills and experience. Individual workers among them may, simply by good luck, find offers meeting their reservation wage on the first or second try. Others, less lucky, may have to look longer than average before they find something they will accept. Second, the positions of the curves, and hence the average length of job search, may be very different for workers at different skill levels. In particular, for workers in the secondary labor market, wage offers received are likely to be very low. At the same time, hope for something better, even if unrealistic, keeps the reservation wage from falling very rapidly. This can stretch out the period of unemployment to many months.

Job Search and Inflation

The job search theory we have just given, simple though it is, can give us some highly useful insights into what happens to unemployment when economic conditions change. In particular, the job search theory supplies a key piece to the unemployment-inflation puzzle that we introduced in Chapter 14. Let us see what happens to the job search process when inflation comes on the scene.

Imagine an economy in which neither prices nor wages have been changing in the recent past, and neither are expected to change in the immediate future. Suppose that under these initial conditions, the average duration of unemployment is five weeks, and the measured unemployment rate is 5 percent. Suddenly, out of the blue, all prices and nominal wages begin to rise. What will happen?

Let us look at things from the point of view of the unemployed job searchers. By assumption, they do not expect prices to go up. It does not occur to them that during the period they work at their new jobs, it will cost them more to live than before. Also by assumption, they do not know that wages *in general* have gone up, so they do not immediately reconsider their own estimates of their value to potential employers. Unexpected inflation thus has no effect on their reservation wages. What does happen is that before they have searched very long, they get nominal wage offers that look pretty good. Operating on their own, with incomplete information, job searchers are likely to consider such high wage offers to be isolated pieces of good luck. The jobs will quickly be accepted.

No individual job searcher realizes, of course, that many other job searchers are also experiencing "good luck" and taking less than five weeks, on the average, to find jobs. The decrease in the average duration of job search shows up as a drop in the measured unemployment rate. Our conclusion is that *unexpected* inflation causes unemployment to fall.

Expected Inflation

It will not take too long, of course, for workers to catch on to what is happening. Unexpected inflation then becomes expected inflation. The effect of expected inflation on unemployment is quite different.

Expected inflation does cause reservation wages to rise. If wages and prices begin rising by, say, 5 percent per year, and job searchers know it, it is easy to see what they will do. Expecting prices to be higher than before, they will reestimate the level of nominal wage they will need to keep up with the cost of living. Also, expecting wages to be higher than before, they will know that the first high nominal offer they get is not an isolated bit of good luck, but part of a general trend. They will not need to snap it up, because later offers may be even better.

In fact, if inflation is *fully* expected by all workers and employers, it will have no real impact on the labor market at all. Workers will know that by waiting, they will get better nominal wage offers, but that the cost of living will be going up just as fast. Employers will know that the higher nominal wages they have to pay each year will be entirely offset by the prices they will get for the products they sell. No one will be any better off or any worse off than if neither prices nor wages changed at all. Job searchers will behave no differently than they would if prices and wages were stable.

False Expectations

There is a third case to consider, that in which people *falsely* expect prices to rise when in fact they are stable. If wages and prices stopped rising, but workers still expected them to go up by 5 percent a year, their search for jobs would become more difficult. They would raise their reservation wages, thinking that they needed the extra money to cover a higher cost of living. They would expect nominal wage offers to rise also, but they would not. These workers, operating in isolation from one another, might well think that they were just having uncommonly bad luck. For a while, at least, they would keep looking and looking for jobs that met their expectations. Eventually, they would either really get lucky and find one, or become discouraged and lower their reservation wages to realistic levels. Meanwhile, though, the average duration of job search would have risen, and so would the measured unemployment rate.

The Natural Rate of Unemployment

Let us summarize what we have said now about inflation and unemployment. We have argued that unexpected inflation shortens the average duration of unemployment and lowers the unemployment rate. Falsely expected inflation, we said, lengthens the duration and raises the rate of unemployment. In the middle lie all cases where the expected rate of inflation and the actual rate are just equal. This middle ground includes the case where both the actual and expected rate of inflation are zero, that is, the case of price stability.

The case of price stability, when prices neither change nor are expected to, provides an important benchmark for economic policy. To emphasize its importance, we introduce a special term to refer to the rate of unemployment that prevails when prices are stable and expected inflation is zero. That rate is called the **natural rate of unemployment.** It is natural not, of course, in the sense that it is a God-given constant, beyond the influence of economic policy. Instead, it is natural in the sense that it is the rate of unemployment that prevails when everyone knows what is going on, and no one is fooled. Because it is the rate of unemployment that prevails when everyone has accurate knowledge of market conditions, we might alternatively call it the equilibrium rate of unemployment.

Natural Rate of Unemployment That rate of unemployment that would prevail if the expected rate of inflation were equal to the actual rate of inflation.

The Phillips Curve

In Chapter 14 we introduced the Phillips curve to represent the trade-off between inflation and unemployment. The Phillips curve contained an element of truth, we said, but the problem was that it seemed to drift over time. Now our job search theory of unemployment offers an explanation of why the Phillips curve can shift from one year to another.

Consider Exhibit 15.6. There we have sketched not one but three Phillips curves. Each of them represents the short-run trade-off between unemployment and inflation *for a given expected rate of inflation.* On each curve, unemployment is at the natural rate (here assumed to be 5 percent) when the actual rate of inflation and the expected rate are equal. If people expect the rate of inflation to be 2 percent, but in fact inflation accelerates

EXHIBIT 15.6
Expected inflation and the shifting Phillips' curve
The position of the Phillips curve depends on the rate of expected inflation, and the rate of unemployment depends on the relationship between the expected rate of inflation and the actual rate. With expected inflation at 2 percent, for example, an acceleration of actual inflation to 3½ percent would lower the unemployment rate, moving the economy from point *A* to point *B*. Unemployment is at the natural rate whenever actual and expected inflation are equal.

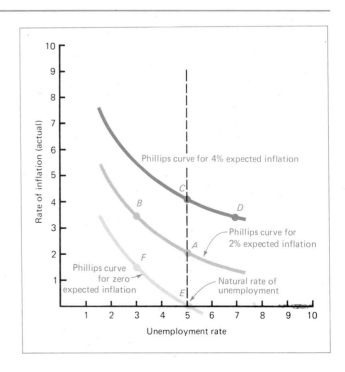

to $3\frac{1}{2}$ percent, the economy would move up and to the left along the middle Phillips curve, from point A to point B. If they expect the rate of inflation to be 4 percent but in fact it slows to $3\frac{1}{2}$ percent, they would move down and to the right along the top Phillips curve, from point C to point D.

Suppose that the economy had experienced a long period of price stability, so that actual and expected inflation were both zero. In that case, the bottom Phillips curve would provide a short-run "menu" from which policy makers might choose. If they wished, they might, for example, get unemployment down to 3 percent if they were willing to tolerate a bit of inflation, moving from point E to point F. They could do that only in the short run, however. After a while, people would notice that prices were going up. They would begin to expect them to continue to do so. As soon as that happened, the Phillips curve would begin to drift upward, and the policy menu would suddenly begin to look less appetizing.

By following this line of argument, we can construct a theory of inflation on the shoulders of our theory of unemployment. We shall do this in some detail in the next chapter. Before we leave our discussion of unemployment, though, there is one more important topic to cover. This is the question of what determines the natural rate of unemployment itself, and what, if anything, can be done to keep it down to an acceptable level.

Lowering the Natural Rate of Unemployment

To put the label "natural" on a rate of unemployment is not to say that such a level of unemployment is a good thing. During the 1960s, it was usual for economists to think of the natural rate as about 4 percent. That was the number used by Arthur Okun to represent full employment in his original formulation of Okun's law. For policy purposes, though, the Kennedy administration regarded even 4 percent as only an "interim" goal. It was to be bettered once it had been achieved.

Today 4 percent seems unrealistically low for the natural rate. Estimates based on the most recent data suggest that the natural rate may be as high as 5.36 percent. Certainly most guesses would now be closer to 5 than 4 percent. Yet 5 percent unemployment seems hard to accept as the best the American economy can do without runaway inflation. Must we live with such a high natural rate, and accept the social problems it may bring?

Unemployment as a Social Problem

To a considerable extent, the American fear of unemployment is a heritage of the Great Depression of the 1930s. In those days, when Keynes was writing his *General Theory,* unemployment meant millions upon millions of desperate people, thrown out of their jobs and into the breadlines where they waited hopelessly for work as months dragged into years.

The face of unemployment in the 1970s is no longer the same as in the Depression years. Now, even in a moderately poor year, some 90 percent of the unemployed are out or work less than six months. Well under half of the unemployed have been fired or laid off from their last job.

To understand unemployment as a social problem today, we have to look at it in terms of its impact on the specific types of people, or demo-

EXHIBIT 15.7

Unemployment by demographic categories

Unemployment is not distributed evenly among the population. Some demographic categories are hit harder than others. A high proportion of the members of hard-hit groups are locked into the secondary labor market. Statistical analysis suggests that unemployment among these groups would remain high even in a very tight labor market.

Demographic Category	Actual Unemployment Rate, 1971 (%)	Hypothetical Unemployment Rate with Tight Labor Market* (%)
Teenage[†] males	16.7	11.4
Teenage females	17.4	13.7
Teenage whites	15.2	10.8
Teenage nonwhites	31.8	24.5
Adult white males[‡]	4.0	1.7
Adult nonwhite males	7.3	3.3
Adult white females	5.3	3.2
Adult nonwhite females	8.7	6.1

*1.5 percent unemployed among white males 25 years and older.
[†]16 to 19 years.
[‡]Adult = 20 years and older.

Source: Martin S. Feldstein, "Lowering the Permanent Rate of Unemployment," (U.S. Congress, Joint Economic Committee, Sept. 18, 1973).

graphic categories, who are affected. Exhibit 15.7 shows the unemployment rate for 1971 broken down by demographic categories.

The first column of that table shows actual unemployment rates for 1971. We see that not many adult white males were unemployed that year, as their fathers may have been forty years before. Instead, unemployment was concentrated among females, nonwhites, and teenagers, with any group falling into two of those categories doubly hit. Teenage nonwhites were a real disaster area. One thing that makes these high unemployment rates a serious social problem is the fact that so many members of the hardest-hit groups are trapped in the secondary labor market. Secondary-sector unemployment tends not to fall as low as primary-sector unemployment even when the economy picks up. To show this, Harvard economist Martin Feldstein estimated the unemployment rate that would prevail for various groups in a "very tight" labor market. (Feldstein's idea of a tight labor market was one in which overall unemployment would be below the natural rate). His figures are given in the second column of Exhibit 15.7. They are rather distressing. Adult white females and nonwhite males seem to gain substantially from the tight labor market conditions, but unemployment among teenagers and nonwhite females remains at problem levels.

Policy and the Natural Rate

The high natural rate of unemployment in our economy poses a serious problem for policy makers. Part of the problem is that certain existing labor market policies act to increase the natural rate of unemployment. When the government pursues other policies designed to lower it, different government agencies end up working at cross purposes with one another. Another part of the problem is that most of the measures that could be taken to lower the natural rate of unemployment have unfortunate side effects. To get an idea of some of the problems and trade-offs, let us look first at some policies that tend to raise the natural rate, and then at some that might lower it.

Minimum Wage Laws

For years, economists have argued that minimum wage laws, rather than easing the plight of the poor, increase unemployment and throw more people into poverty. The usual explanation of this perverse effect is that some people may have reservation wages lower than the minimum wage rate, but cannot legally be offered jobs at such low wages. This is not the whole story concerning the effects of minimum wage laws, however. They have another effect as well, which is to discourage on-the-job training. This may help explain the particularly high rate of teenage unemployment.

To see how this works, consider a hypothetical example. John Jones, a 17-year-old high school dropout, approaches the Atlas Company looking for a job. Jones is completely untrained, but he still claims to be worth $2.25 an hour, and is in fact worth that much. The Atlas Company offers him his choice of two jobs, that of stock boy, paying $2.25 per hour, and that of a machinist's assistant. Unfortunately, the Atlas personnel manager explains, a lot of his time in the second position would be spent learning about machines and not really producing very much. The company can only afford to pay him $1.50 per hour for that job. Jones realizes the advantage of on-the-job training, and takes the lower-paying job. Within a year, he has been promoted to machinist first class and is earning $6 per hour.

Now introduce a legal minimum wage of $2 per hour. The Atlas Company can still offer him the stock boy job, but not the machinist assistantship. The company would lose money paying him $2 per hour in that position, and is legally barred from paying $1.50. Jones takes the stock boy job, but soon finds it to be boring and a dead end and quits to look again for something better.

This example shows us how minimum wage laws can contribute to a vicious cycle of teenage unemployment. Employers expect unstable work behavior from teenagers and tailor available jobs accordingly. The teenage workers themselves are turned off by the dead-end jobs thus created and shift aimlessly from one employer to another. One direction to move in lowering the natural rate of unemployment would be to get rid of minimum wage laws and replace them, if need be, with other types of income-assistance programs having a less serious disincentive effect.

Unemployment Compensation

Unemployment compensation is a second government program that, like minimum wage laws, keeps the natural rate of unemployment high. To understand the employment effects of unemployed compensation, it will be helpful to look at a detailed example constructed by Feldstein.[3]

CASE 15.2
Employment Effects of Unemployment Compensation

Consider a worker in Massachusetts in 1971 with a wife and two children. He earns $500 per month, or $6,000 per year if he experiences no unemployment. She earns $350 per month, or $4,200 per year if she experiences no unemployment. If he is unemployed for one month, he loses $500 in

---

[3]Martin S. Feldstein, "Lowering the Permanent Rated Unemployment" (U.S. Congress, Joint Economic Committee, Sept. 18, 1973).

gross earnings but less than $100 in net income. How does this occur? A reduction of $500 in annual earnings reduces his federal income tax by $83, his social security payroll tax by $26, and his Massachusetts income tax by $25. The total reduction in taxes is $134. Unemployment compensation consists of 50 percent of his wage plus dependents' allowances of $6 per week for each child. Total unemployment compensation is therefore $302. His net income therefore falls from $366 for the month if he is employed to the $302 paid as unemployment compensation.

If he returns to work after one month, his annual net income is only $128 higher than if he returns after three months. Moreover, part of the higher increase in income would be offset by the cost of transportation to work and other expenses associated with employment.

This case is by no means extreme. If his wife were to lose her job while he remained employed, the loss of income would be even less in relation to the loss in earnings. In fact, it is not difficult to construct examples in which a short period of unemployment will actually *increase* a family's annual income—not to mention providing an opportunity to do some work around the house! Small wonder some unions are now bargaining for "reverse seniority" clauses in their contracts, whereby long-term employees are laid off first, rather than last, if a temporary lull in production occurs.

How does the labor market react to the distinctive effects of unemployment compensation laws? One reaction is obvious. These laws greatly reduce the cost of job search. If the man from Massachusetts did not expect to be rehired at his old job, he could take his time looking for a new one, because the opportunity cost of job search to him would not be the $125 per week implied by his gross wage but in fact only about $15 per week.

A second reaction to unemployment compensation is less obvious but also very important. It provides a subsidy to seasonal, cyclical, and casual employment. Consider the construction industry, for example. Construction costs are lower in the summer than in the winter because of the weather, so firms have a natural incentive to employ seasonal labor. However, in the absence of unemployment compensation, there would be an offsetting disincentive. Workers would be reluctant to go into the building trades, where they would work fewer weeks per year, unless their hourly wage rate when employed were higher than for steady work. Thus, it might pay construction firms to hire on a steady-work basis at a lower wage, and absorb the added expense of the special equipment and materials needed for winter construction.

With unemployment compensation, the picture is different. Workers need not be paid such a high premium to enter a seasonal occupation if they will get supplemental benefits from the state during the months they are laid off. Hence, employers will not adapt their construction methods to year-round work.

The seasonal component of unemployment averages around three-quarters of a percentage point. When we consider that similar effects hold true with respect to the incentives firms have for scheduling work over the course of the business cycle, or over periods of temporary high demand, the impact of unemployment compensation on the rate of unemployment is even greater than this.

Job Placement

Let us turn now from policies that raise the natural rate of unemployment to policies designed to lower it. One way to attack unemployment is through job placement programs. An area where job placement programs might have particularly beneficial impact is that of teenage unemployment. In his testimony to Congress, which we have cited before, Martin Feldstein recommended a nationwide Youth Employment Service. British experience with such a program suggests that by improving the quality of first jobs taken by young people leaving school, the cycle of teenage unemployment might be broken before it begins.

For low-skilled adult workers, the prospects for reducing unemployment through job placement alone is not encouraging. An experimental program tried in Boston is a case in point. The idea of this program was to refer long-term unemployed adults to jobs for which they were qualified, which usually meant secondary-sector jobs. Seventy percent of the workers referred to potential employers were offered jobs, but 45 percent of the job offers were rejected. Of those who did accept work, less than half remained on the job for as long as one month. A very high proportion of the separations in this period were voluntary.[4]

Manpower Training

Such experiences have led many economists to recommend another approach to handling unemployment among low-skilled adult workers. Instead of simply sticking them in jobs corresponding to their current skills, the idea is to enroll them in *manpower training programs* designed to upgrade their skills to match those required by better jobs. Unfortunately, despite some ten years of experience with these programs and some $10 billion of federal expenditures on them, no one has a very clear idea of how well they work. We simply do not know whether unemployment rates are lower for those who have enrolled in manpower programs than for those with the same demographic characteristics who have not. Isolated evaluations of particular local experiences suggest that such programs have positive, but small effects. The general picture is clouded by the existence of some notable success and some spectacular failures.

Public Employment

Still another alternative for reducing unemployment is the proposal to make the government itself an "employer of last resort." The idea is that any person who is unemployed and wants work will be given a government job of some kind. Public employment programs were used on a large scale by the Roosevelt administration during the Great Depression, and a number of smaller-scale programs are in operation now. Because it is likely that the public employment concept will continue to find favor with Congress, it is worth mentioning two serious problems that this type of policy tends to encounter.

The first problem of public employment programs is, what should the new public employees do? The easy answer is that they should be put to work at the most productive jobs that can be devised for them, given their skills and experience. Unfortunately, there are certain drawbacks to put-

[4]*Ibid.*

ting this easy answer into effect. In the first place, the more necessary and productive the jobs public employment programs offer, the more likely it is that participants in these programs will simply displace existing workers, with no net impact on unemployment. A particularly serious problem is the tendency of federal public employment programs to displace public employment at the state and local level. In the second place, to put public employees to work in highly productive jobs usually requires investing public money in the tools, buildings, and other capital equipment needed to do the jobs. That makes public employment programs very expensive.

Consideration of these difficulties has led some policy makers to propose an alternative "easy answer" to the question of what public employment workers ought to do: They should do jobs that would otherwise go altogether undone, and that require an absolute minimum of capital equipment. The trouble with that approach, though, is that the jobs that result are often pure make-work. They produce little real benefit and give the workers involved no useful training or experience.

Perhaps an even more serious problem with making the government the employer of last resort lies in a "ratchet effect" from which such programs suffer. Workers who enter the public payroll when times are hard often do not return to the private sector when good times return. With each up and down of the cycle, the total number of public employees moves up a notch. This would not be so bad if the new public employees were doing work that was as useful or productive as that which they could be doing in the private sector, but for the reasons outlined above, their public-sector work is likely to be less productive.

Conclusions

Our discussion has not led us to a set of solutions for the problem of a high natural rate of unemployment, but instead, has left us with a set of open questions:

Do minimum wage laws provide sufficient benefit to any lower-income group to justify their effects on unemployment? This question is a bit less open than the others. Enough evidence is in to suggest a negative answer.

Can unemployment compensation be reformed in ways that would limit its disincentive effects? This question has not received the attention it deserves.

How much can improved job placement contribute to solving the unemployment problem? Under what conditions can manpower training programs yield benefits that justify their costs? It is troubling that experience to date in these areas has not provided more encouraging answers.

Are expanded public employment programs, including the employer-of-last-resort concept, compatible with an efficient allocation of resources between the public and private sectors? A study of British experience, which offers encouragement in the area of job placement, would indicate great caution in the area of public employment.

Living with Unemployment?

In sum, it appears that there are three broad directions that unemployment policy can take. None of the directions is costless, but it is hard to see how a choice among them can be avoided.

First, the government can use conventional macroeconomic policy in an attempt to keep unemployment as far below the natural rate as possible. This is the policy that has most frequently been chosen by successive administrations and Congresses in the United States since at least the 1960s. The entire next chapter will be devoted to an analysis of the costs and the chances for success of this very important option.

Second, the government can pursue the whole range of policies designed to lower the natural rate of unemployment. In some cases, such policies conflict with the goal of providing high living standards for unemployed and low-paid workers. In other cases, they conflict with the goal of efficient resource allocation, which means that they conflict with the goal of providing high living standards for the rest of us. To know just how great the costs of this option are, we must have more accurate answers to the "open questions" listed above.

Finally, the government can adopt a policy of living with unemployment. The cost of this option is abandoning "full employment" as a major goal of macroeconomic policy. The social problems associated with unemployment (especially those associated with the very high unemployment rates of some subsections of the labor force) would become problems of *micro*economic policy, to be treated by measures similar to those chosen to treat the social problems of disability or old age. *Macro*economic policy would then be left free to pursue the goals of price stability, economic growth, and international economic balance.

None of these policy options is costless, or free of serious disadvantages. In dealing with unemployment, as everywhere else in economic life, we must remember the old economic principle: There ain't no such thing as a free lunch.

SUMMARY

1. Unemployment, as measured by the Bureau of Labor Statistics, does not quite conform to the common sense notions of "not working" or "can't find a job." Instead, the unemployment rate measures the percentage of the civilian labor force that is not employed. The official unemployment rate can be criticized for having either an upward or a downward bias. Some who want a job and cannot find one are not counted, among them, so-called discouraged workers. Others who are not really unable to find a job are counted as unemployed, including workers who have voluntarily quit their jobs, or who have found a job but not started it yet.

2. The unemployment rate measures a stock. Changes in the unemployment rate depend on a rather close balance of flows into and out of the stock of unemployed persons. Turnover among the stock of unemployed persons is fairly rapid. In normal years, half of the unemployed have been out of work less than four weeks, and only in the worst years does the average duration of unemployment go above three months.

3. The unemployment rate is closely correlated with the average duration of unemployment. Anything that affects the process of job search thus has an important impact on the unemployment rate. Workers look for a job until they find one that meets their reservation wage—a process that takes several weeks on the average. In periods when inflation proceeds at a rate faster than people expect it, this period of job search tends to be shortened. In periods when inflation is slower than expected, the period of job search tends to stretch out. The rate of unemployment that prevails when no one is fooled by the rate of inflation is called the natural rate of unemployment.

4. The theory of job search helps us explain why the short-run Phillips curve shifts from time to time. The position of the Phillips curve depends on the expected rate of inflation, since unemployment equals the natural rate whenever actual and expected inflation are equal. The actual rate of unemployment at any time depends on the relationship between the actual and expected rates of inflation.

5. To call one particular rate of unemployment "natural" is not to say that it is a good thing. The natural rate for the U.S. economy in the 1970s appears to be 5 percent or more, high enough to be considered a significant social problem. Sometimes government efforts to help the poor and the unemployed have the side effect of keeping the natural rate of unemployment high. Minimum wage laws and unemployment compensation do this. Job placement programs, manpower training, and public employment have been tried as methods of lowering the natural rate, but none of these has yet proved entirely satisfactory. In the end, we are faced with the fact that lowering the natural rate of unemployment involves some very hard trade-offs.

DISCUSSION QUESTIONS

1. Some people say that we should change the way we measure unemployment so that the official unemployment figure includes all those and only those who are suffering genuine hardship because of their inability to find a job. What specific changes in measurement techniques would be necessary in order to put this suggestion into effect?

2. Some countries do not use the household survey method to measure unemployment. Instead, they just count people who show up at unemployment offices to claim compensation or to look for jobs. What difference do you think this technique would make for the measured level of unemployment?

3. In addition to keeping an unemployment index, the government also makes periodic surveys of job openings. Suppose that you looked at these data and found that the number of job openings was equal to or greater than the number of unemployed persons. Would you be justified in thinking that there was no unemployment *problem* in a human sense? In a political sense? In an economic sense?

4. Communist countries regularly claim that they have no unemployment at all. Is that claim believable? Do you think that it is just empty boasting, or do you think that it may largely reflect different ways of measuring unemployment?

5. If you like working with graphs, try using the wage offer curve and reservation wage curve to explain how inflation affects the measured level of unemployment. How does expected inflation affect each curve? How does unexpected inflation affect each curve?

6. What do you think determines people's expected rate of inflation? Do you think it is reasonable, as a rough rule of thumb, to say that people expect inflation this year to be just what it was last year? Why or why not? What do you expect the rate of inflation to be next year? Next month? Make a note of your answer, and check yourself a month or a year later.

7. Suppose that unemployment compensation were simply abolished. What would that do to measured unemployment? What would it do to the reservation wage curve in Exhibit 15.5? What would it do to the natural rate of unemployment? What would it do to the position of the short-run Phillips curves in Exhibit 15.6?

8. Feldstein's analysis implies that raising unemployment benefits would increase the rate of unemployment. Consider this plan, though: The level of unemployment payments for unemployed persons would remain exactly the same as it is now, but unemployment payments would *continue* for six weeks *after* a person began a new job. What do you think that would do to the unemployment rate? Why?

CHAPTER 16
A Closer Look at Inflation

What You Will Learn in This Chapter

A theory of inflation must explain how any change in nominal national product will be split up between change in real output and change in the price level. A theory that can do this can tell us what effect monetary and fiscal policy measures will have on inflation and unemployment. We already have all of the ingredients for such a theory. Now we need only to assemble the pieces and put them to use.

For Review

Here are some important terms and concepts that will be put to use in this chapter. Be certain that you understand them, or review them before proceeding.

Real and nominal values and the price index (Chapter 6)
Okun's law (Chapter 7)
Theory of nominal income determination (Chapters 8–13)
The Phillips curve (Chapters 14 and 15)

Ingredients

We now have all the ingredients we need for a theory of inflation. Let us review briefly what we have.

First, from Chapter 6 we have a way of measuring the price level for the economy. The price index for any year is equal to the ratio of nominal national product to real national product in that year.

Second, from Chapter 7 we have Okun's law. That law relates real output to unemployment. More precisely, it says that each percentage point change in the measured unemployment rate will produce roughly a 3 percent change in real national product.

Third, from Chapters 8 to 13 we have a theory to tell us what determines nominal national product. In that theory, nominal national product can be controlled by the use of monetary and fiscal policy. What we did not do in those earlier chapters was show how a given change in nominal national product would be split up between changes in prices and changes in real output. That is what we shall do here.

Fourth, from Chapter 14 we have a theory of unemployment. That theory makes unemployment depend, among other things, on the actual and expected rates of inflation. In graphical terms, the theory implies a short-run Phillips curve that shifts as the expected rate of inflation changes. Chapter 14 also gave us the idea of the natural rate of unemployment, an important benchmark for our discussion of inflation.

A Theory of Inflation

Inflation and Real Growth

All we really have to do now is put the pieces together. Our first step will be to establish a simple relationship between inflation and the growth of real national product. The price level in any year is the ratio of nominal to real national product in that year. It follows that the rate of change in the price level, that is, the rate of inflation, depends on the rate of growth of nominal national product and the rate of growth of real national product. For a given rate of growth of nominal national product, the rate of inflation will be less, the higher the rate of growth of real national product.

Consider some examples. If real national product grows at the same rate as nominal national product, there will be no inflation at all. At the other extreme, if nominal national product grows while real national product does not change, the rate of inflation will be equal to the rate of growth of nominal product. These two cases and all those in between fit a general rule. That rule tells us that the rate of inflation must be equal to the rate of growth of nominal national product minus the rate of growth of real national product. A 10 percent rate of growth of nominal product will produce 5 percent inflation if real product grows at 5 percent, 3 percent inflation if real product grows at 7 percent, and so forth.

Okun's Law

Our next step is to translate this relationship between inflation and real growth into a relationship between inflation and unemployment. Okun's law tells us that the rate of growth of real output from one year to the next depends on how much the unemployment rate changes.[1] For each percentage point drop in unemployment, we get approximately 3 percent growth of real output. It follows, then, that for a given rate of growth of nominal national product, each percentage point drop in unemployment will reduce the rate of inflation by about 3 percent.

Let us put this in the form of a graph. Consider Exhibit 16.1, where we have placed inflation on the vertical axis and unemployment on the horizontal axis. Suppose that initially unemployment is at its natural rate, which we take to be 5 percent. Now let nominal national product begin to grow at a rate of 6 percent. The amount of inflation produced by this rate of nominal growth depends on what happens to unemployment. If unemployment does not change, there must be 6 percent inflation, as at point A in the exhibit. To keep prices stable, real output would have to grow by 6 percent each year. Okun's law tells us that this can happen only if the unemployment rate drops 2 percentage points in the year. That would put the economy at point B, with no inflation and 3 percent unemployment.

[1]Throughout this chapter, we ignore the effects of growth in labor productivity or in the labor force. This simplifies presentation of the basic theory. Once the theory is clearly understood it is not hard to adjust it to allow for growth of potential output.

EXHIBIT 16.1

The inflationary pressure curve

For a given rate of growth of nominal GNP, the rate of inflation depends on what happens to real GNP. For a given initial rate of unemployment, the growth of real GNP depends on what happens to unemployment (Okun's law). Here we assume a 6 percent growth of nominal GNP and an initial rate of unemployment of 5 percent. If unemployment does not change, there will be 6 percent inflation, as at point A. Each percentage point decrease in unemployment adds 3 percent to real growth, and hence trims 3 percent from the rate of inflation.

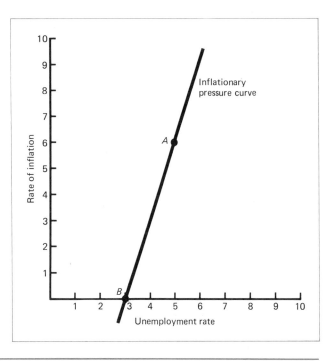

If unemployment decreased somewhat, but by less than 2 percentage points, there would be some amount of inflation between 0 and 6 percent.

The line drawn through points A and B in Exhibit 16.1 shows all the combinations of inflation and unemployment that are possible, given the assumed initial level of unemployment and the assumed rate of change in nominal national product. We shall call it an **inflationary pressure curve.** The inflationary pressure curve tells us that, other things being equal, each annual percentage point reduction in unemployment will trim about three percentage points from the annual rate of inflation.

An upward shift in the curve drawn in Exhibit 16.1 would indicate an increase in inflationary pressure. The position of the curve could change if either of two things happened. First, an increase in the rate of growth of nominal GNP would increase inflationary pressure. More real growth, and hence a bigger drop in unemployment, would be needed to hold inflation down to any given rate. Second, a lower initial rate of unemployment would also increase inflationary pressure. If the unemployment rate is high to begin with, there is a lot of room for improvement in real output. If it is already low, there is less room for further improvement. A drop in unemployment from 5 to 3 percent was enough to absorb a 6 percent growth of nominal GNP without inflation in Exhibit 16.1. If unemployment had been 3 percent to begin with, just keeping it at 3 percent would not have helped. Keeping inflation below 6 percent would have required cutting unemployment to an even lower level.

A simple rule makes it easy to sketch the correct inflationary pressure curve for any set of conditions. First find the point corresponding to the assumed initial level of unemployment and the assumed rate of growth of nominal national product (see point A in Exhibit 16.1). Then draw a line through that point with a slope of +3. That line will be the required inflationary pressure curve.

Inflationary Pressure Curve A graph, derived from Okun's law and the definition of the price level, that shows the amount of inflation associated with each rate of unemployment, given an initial unemployment rate and a rate of growth of nominal output.

Determining the Rate of Inflation

We have now almost finished putting the inflation-unemployment puzzle together. Our familiar multiplier theory tells us how monetary and fiscal policy affect nominal output. Given the growth of nominal output and the initial level of unemployment, the inflationary pressure curve sets out a possible range of rates of inflation. Each of these is tied to a certain level of unemployment. All we have left to do is show which of the points on the inflationary pressure curve will actually apply. The Phillips curve, as developed in Chapter 14, gives us this last missing piece.

Consider Exhibit 16.2. In drawing this exhibit, we have assumed that initially the economy is in a "standing start" position. By this we mean that in the immediate past, neither nominal nor real output has been growing, that there has been no inflation and no one expects any, and that unemployment is at the natural rate. Under these initial conditions, the inflationary pressure curve is in the position I_1, and the economy is at point A.

Next assume that the government applies a dose of fiscal or monetary policy big enough to start nominal output growing at 5 percent per year. Aggregate demand increases, and a familiar chain of events gets underway. Expenditures increase and firms unexpectedly find their inventories falling. Some respond by stepping up output, others by raising prices, and other by doing a little of both. Nominal national product rises, and pushes the inflationary pressure curve up to the position I_2 in Exhibit 16.2.

Now let us look at what happens in the labor market. Those firms that are stepping up their output go out to recruit new workers. Some will offer higher nominal wages, knowing that the rising level of demand will let them recoup these wages in higher prices and expanded sales volume. Job searchers will, on the average, be luckier in finding good offers. They

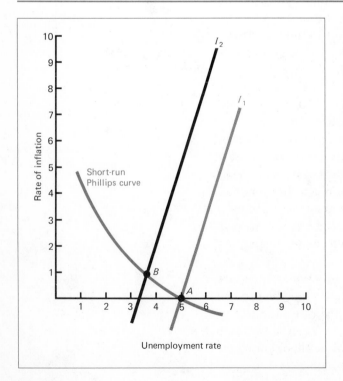

EXHIBIT 16.2

The determination of inflation and unemployment
Together, the Phillips curve and the inflationary pressure curve determine the rates of inflation and unemployment, given an initial level of unemployment and a rate of growth of nominal output. Here the economy begins from a "standing start" at A. There are no inflationary expectations, so the short-run Phillips curve is in the position shown. Raising the rate of nominal growth from 0 to 5 percent shifts the inflationary pressure curve from I_1 and I_2. Unemployment drops to just over 3½ percent, and inflation reaches a rate of just under 1 percent.

are not expecting any inflation, so they have not raised their reservation wages. The average duration of unemployment drops, and the economy begins to move away from point *A,* up and to the left along the short-run Phillips curve shown in Exhibit 16.2.

As the unemployment rate begins to drop, we have to watch what happens in terms of both the Phillips curve and the inflationary pressure curve at once. According to the Phillips curve, the more inflation there is, the less unemployment there will be. According to the inflationary pressure curve, the less unemployment there is, the less inflation there will be. *Together, the Phillips curve and the inflationary pressure curve determine both the level of unemployment and the rate of inflation.* The economy must end up at point *B,* where the inflationary pressure curve and Phillips curve intersect. As Exhibit 16.2 is drawn, this means just under 1 percent inflation and just over $3\frac{1}{2}$ percent unemployment.

No other combination of inflation and unemployment is possible under the conditions we have assumed. Suppose, for example, that inflation were only one-half of 1 percent. The Phillips curve shows us that that would barely get unemployment down by one percentage point. A 1 percent drop in unemployment means only a 3 percent rise in real output. But 5 percent nominal growth with only 3 percent real growth would mean 2 percent inflation, not $\frac{1}{2}$ percent. Assuming a $\frac{1}{2}$ percent rate of inflation thus leads to a contradiction.

By much the same reasoning, we can show that unemployment cannot be lower than what is shown by the intersection of our two curves. Suppose that we wanted unemployment to be 3 percent. The Phillips curve shows us that this would require inflation of about $1\frac{1}{2}$ percent. Three percent unemployment, though, would mean a 6 percent growth of real output. To have 6 percent growth of real output and 3 percent inflation, nominal output would have to grow not by 5 percent, but by 9 percent. Once again we have a contradiction.

To repeat, only one combination of inflation and unemployment is possible once the growth of nominal output and the initial unemployment rate are given. Our theory of inflation is complete.

Economic Policy and the Dynamics of Inflation

We now have a simple but powerful set of tools for determining the effects of economic policy. Chapters 8 through 13 gave us the theory we need to know how fiscal and monetary policy affect nominal national income and product. Now the Phillips curve and inflationary pressure curve tell us how any given change in nominal output will be split up between change in real output and change in the price level. In the remainder of this chapter, we shall use these new tools to explain how certain patterns of economic policy, extending over a period of years, can produce the dynamic swings of inflation and unemployment that take place in the economy around us.

Acceleration

The first pattern we shall examine is the repeated application of expansionary monetary or fiscal policy over a series of years. Let us go back to Exhibit 16.2. There we saw that, beginning from a standing start, a 5 percent expansion of nominal GNP produced a drop in unemployment of almost $1\frac{1}{2}$ percent at the cost of less than 1 percent inflation. Policy makers would have every reason to be very pleased with those results. They would be so pleased, in fact, that they would surely want to try another dose of the same medicine. In the second year, unfortunately, a further 5 percent expansion of nominal GNP would not be split up so favorably between inflationary and real output effects. There are two reasons for this.

First of all, to get continued growth of real output, it is not enough just to keep unemployment at a low level. We need a further drop in unemployment. Yet the farther to the left we go along the Phillips curve, the steeper the curve gets. This means that a bigger dose of unexpected inflation is needed to give each percentage point reduction in unemployment.

Also, in the second year of expansionary policy, the government no longer has the advantage of a standing start. People have experienced some inflation, even though mild, and some of them may be alert enough to realize that continued expansionary policy will bring more. Once people come to *expect* inflation, the short-run Phillips curve begins to shift upward. That too makes the inflation–unemployment trade-off less attractive than in the first year.

We see, then, that although a second year of expansionary policy is likely to produce some further gain in unemployment and real output, the cost in terms of inflation will be higher than before. In subsequent years, the trade-off will get less favorable still. Soon it will not be enough just to repeat the original policy of 5 percent growth of nominal output. Nominal output will have to expand faster and faster. The economy will then have reached the situation shown in Exhibit 16.3, where the inflationary pressure curve has to shift up each year just to keep even with the upward drift of the short-run Phillips curve.

EXHIBIT 16.3

The effects of prolonged acceleration

To keep unemployment below the natural rate for a sustained period requires a continuous acceleration of inflation. The actual rate of inflation must always be higher than the expected rate. Here, as rising inflationary expectations push the Phillips curves up from P_1 to P_2 to P_3, accelerating growth of nominal output shifts the inflationary pressure curve from I_1 to I_2 to I_3. A, B, and C are successive positions of the economy as acceleration continues.

EXHIBIT 16.4

The Kennedy-Johnson acceleration
During the Kennedy and Johnson administrations, the economy expanded almost without interruption. (Exceptions were the hesitation over Kennedy's tax cut in 1963, and the "Fed's finest hour" in 1966.) Accelerating inflation pulled unemployment well below the natural rate and kept it there for several years in a row.

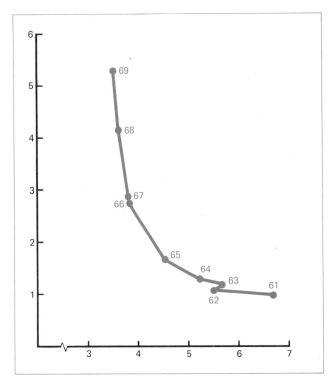

Source: Data from *Economic Report of the President* (Washington, D.C.: U.S. Government Printing Office, 1976).

We can put what we have learned in the form of an important generalization: *To keep unemployment below the natural rate for a sustained period requires a continuous acceleration of inflation.* A case study will show this principle in action.

CASE 16.1
Acceleration in the Kennedy-Johnson Era

As we have mentioned before, John Kennedy came to office in 1960 with the declared intention to "get the country moving again" after two recessions late in the Eisenhower administration. President Lyndon Johnson, who succeeded him, was equally determined to pursue an expansionary policy. Economists are still debating the relative importance of the Kennedy tax cut, heavy defense spending, and rapid monetary growth, but there is no doubt that in combination these policies were as expansionary as anyone could have wished. The result was what Johnson proudly called "the longest peacetime (*sic*) expansion in American history."

Exhibit 16.4 shows the unemployment-inflation record for the economy during the Kennedy-Johnson era. The pattern is much what our theory would lead us to expect. Expansionary policy at first produced substantial gains in employment with little inflation penalty. From the year of the Kennedy tax cut on, though, each successive reduction in unemployment was accompanied by a bigger jump in prices. By the end of Johnson's term in office, inflation was rising higher and higher each year just to keep unemployment where it was, substantially below what anyone would consider its natural rate.

Deceleration

In theory, there is no limit to the number of years that unemployment can be held below its natural rate by continued acceleration. In practice, though, political pressures eventually build up to "do something" about inflation. The most obvious thing to do is to put on the monetary and fiscal brakes, and decelerate the growth of aggregate demand. It is not necessary actually to cut aggregate demand in nominal terms—just to reduce its rate of growth.

As might be expected, the effects of deceleration are much like the initial effects of expansion, taken in reverse. As deceleration begins, aggregate demand will not grow as fast as firms have foreseen when making their production, pricing, and inventory plans. The result will be unplanned inventory accumulation. As stocks of unsold goods pile up, some firms will react by cutting prices (or at least raising them less than they had planned), while others will cut back production.

The production cutbacks will mean fewer job openings. They will also mean that those firms still taking on workers will be able to get the personnel they want without offering such high wages as they would otherwise have had to. Remember, though, that the deceleration is at first unexpected. Workers who have become used to low unemployment and steady inflation will set out to look for jobs with high reservation wages. At first, they will not realize that conditions in the labor market as a whole have changed. Each will attribute his difficulty in finding a job to individual bad luck. The average duration of job search will lengthen, and the unemployment rate will rise.

A word should be said about the unionized sector of the labor market. Inflationary expectations play an important role in labor-management negotiations. If, as deceleration begins, both parties expect prices to continue rising as before, they are likely to agree on nominal wage increases that fully reflect those expectations. To the extent that nominal wages in unionized industries continue to rise rapidly, however, job openings in these industries will become even scarcer than they otherwise would be, as demand falls off. High wage settlements in unionized industries will thus make the job search prospects of the unemployed that much more difficult.

Inflationary Recession

Inflationary Recession A period of rising unemployment during which the rate of inflation remains high, or even continues to rise.

What happens next can be called an **inflationary recession.**[2] Unemployment goes up, real output goes down, and prices continue to rise, perhaps temporarily even faster than before.

Exhibit 16.5 gives a graphical interpretation. This diagram starts where Exhibit 16.3 left off, at the end of a sustained acceleration. Expected inflation of 6 percent has pushed the short-run Phillips curve up to the position P_1. Policy makers have raised the rate of growth of nominal output to $7\frac{1}{2}$ percent, which puts the inflationary pressure curve at I_1. The economy is at point A. Actual inflation is still running ahead of expected inflation, and unemployment is a full two percentage points below its natural rate.

Then the brakes are applied. The next year, growth of aggregate demand is cut back to 3 percent, shifting the inflationary pressure curve to I_2. Inflationary expectations are still moving up. Last year people expected

---

[2]The phenomenon of inflationary recession is new enough that there is no single established name for it. News writers often employ such unpleasant-sounding hybrid words as "stagflation" or "slumpflation."

EXHIBIT 16.5
Inflationary recession
This exhibit begins where Exhibit 16.3 left off, at the end of a period of prolonged acceleration. Expected inflation is initially 6 percent with actual inflation even higher, 7½ percent, putting the economy at *A*. Then the rate of growth of nominal output is cut from 7½ percent to 3 percent, shifting the inflationary pressure curve to *I₂*. Inflationary expectations, based on last year's actual rate, push the Phillips curve up to *P₂*, so the economy moves from *A* to *B*, an inflationary recession.

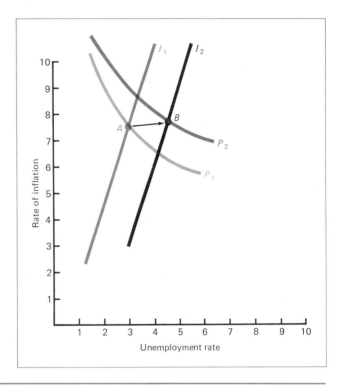

inflation to be only 6 percent when in fact it was 7½ percent. This year they expect inflation to be at least that high, which moves the Phillips curve up to the position *P₂*. The inflationary expectations are vindicated. The economy moves from point *A* to point *B*. Deceleration has brought on an inflationary recession.

Cost-Push Inflation

During an inflationary recession, cost-push inflation becomes important. In Chapter 14 we saw that two conditions must be met for true cost-push inflation (as distinct from the cost-push illusion) to occur. The first condition is that some force must be present that will touch off a rise in wages or prices when demand is not rising. The second is that something must prevent prices and wages in competitive markets from falling when wages or prices in more monopolistic markets rise.

During inflationary recession, just the conditions we need are present. In highly concentrated and highly unionized industries, inflationary expectations cause wages and prices to keep rising, even when demand begins to slow down. These wage and price increases mean fewer jobs in the sectors affected. We cannot count on falling wages in nonunionized sectors to take up the slack in employment. Any decline in wage offers that occurred while inflationary expectations continued to push up reservation wages would only lengthen the average period of job search and raise unemployment still further.

The cost-push theory of inflation comes into its own during an inflationary recession. In such a period, demand-pull and cost-push inflation are not conflicting interpretations of the same thing. Instead, the latter occurs as an aftereffect of the former.

Continued Deceleration

An inflationary recession is the worst of all possible worlds. It occurs when expected inflation rises while actual inflationary pressure is decreasing. Once people begin to realize that the brakes have been applied, things stop getting worse and start getting better. Once inflation peaks, the Phillips curve stops shifting upward, and begins to fall. Continued moderate growth of aggregate demand can then begin to slow inflation without making unemployment worse. In principle, by holding unemployment above the natural rate for an extended period, the economy could be brought to a "soft landing." Inflationary expectations could be reduced to zero, and then unemployment could be eased back to the natural rate with prices stable. Such a prolonged deceleration would be the downside equivalent of the continued acceleration we showed in Exhibit 16.3.

Reflation

Reflation An expansion of aggregate demand after a period of high unemployment and decelerating inflation. Reflation brings substantial short-term gains in employment with little or no inflationary penalty.

In the real world, though, a "soft landing" is difficult to achieve. Just as prolonged acceleration generates political pressure to "do something" about inflation, prolonged deceleration brings pressure to "do something" about unemployment. It is always politically tempting to respond to these pressures and **reflate.** In the first stages of a reflation, before inflationary expectations are rekindled, it is possible to get a big increase in real output with little penalty in terms of prices. In fact, if renewed expansion of aggregate demand starts while the Phillips curve is still drifting downward, it is perfectly possible to enjoy a few months when both inflation and unemployment are falling. Reflation is thus the mirror image of inflationary recession.

Stop-Go

Stop-Go Policy A cycle of acceleration, inflationary recession, deceleration, and reflation brought about by alternating political pressures to "do something" first about inflation and then about unemployment.

Although reflation brings the best of all possible economic worlds, its effects are only temporary. As soon as expectations adjust to what has happened, higher inflationary penalties will once again have to be paid, just to hold on to the gains in unemployment. We are back in familiar territory, having completed a cycle.

The cycle of acceleration, inflationary recession, deceleration, and reflation is popularly known as **stop-go** policy. Unlike the traditional business cycle, which economists have known about for more than a century, the origins of the stop-go cycle are more political than economic. Perhaps we can even say that the stop-go cycle is a peculiarity of democratic politics (little "d," not big "D"—Republicans are not immune). In an election year, it is particularly difficult to resist the short-run gains of reflation, or to take the initial steps to end run-away acceleration.

Inflationary Bias

To add the final touch to our discussion of stop-go, we must mention a possibility we have not yet considered. It may be that, on the average, the political system is more sensitive to the type of political pressures that arise from unemployment than to those arising from inflation. If this is the case, the symmetry of the stop-go pattern is destroyed. We shall not work through all the details of what happens when an inflationary bias is added to a policy of stop-go stabilization, but Exhibit 16.6 gives a sketch of the process. The economy goes into an upward spiral because the upward push

EXHIBIT 16.6

Stop-go with an inflationary bias

The so-called "stop-go" cycle means the alternation of acceleration, inflationary recession, deceleration, and reflation, as political pressure builds up first to "do something" about inflation and then to "do something" about unemployment. If the pressures to reduce unemployment are, on the average, stronger than the pressures to control inflation, the stop-go cycle may be given an upward bias. Each time around, the cycle spirals higher, as this sketch indicates.

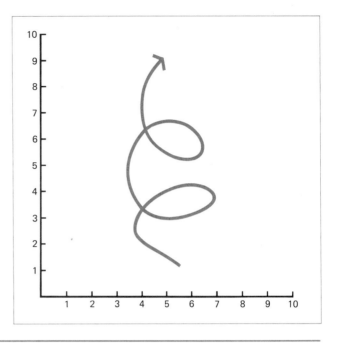

that the economy is given during the acceleration phase of the stop-go cycle is longer and more vigorous than the downward push it receives during the recessionary phase.

Conclusions

Sometimes economists construct theories purely for their own sake. The most interesting economic theories, though, are the ones that help us to interpret actual economic events. The theory of inflation presented in this chapter appears to be one of these. As simple as it is (lots of qualifications and elaborations would be added in an advanced course), it gives us some very useful insights, as one last case study will show.

CASE 16.2
Recent American Experience with
Unemployment and Inflation

Exhibit 16.7 presents actual data on inflation and unemployment in the American economy from 1954 to 1975. We have already examined one part of this record, the Kennedy-Johnson acceleration. Now let us look at some other features.

The overall impression one gets from the figure is that of a series of roughly triangular clockwise loops. Although the lengths and strengths of successive accelerations and decelerations are rather irregular, it does not take much imagination to see an upward spiral of sorts. There is at least a rough resemblance of this figure to the one we drew in Exhibit 16.6.

Although the rate of inflation has drifted up over the years, it has not moved up over every single cycle. Consider the period following the recession of 1957. The recovery from this recession was very weak. The vertical line drawn between the points for 1959 and 1960, which forms the upward side of the next triangular loop, is shorter and farther to the right than most. This weak recovery seems to have happened because Eisenhower had been

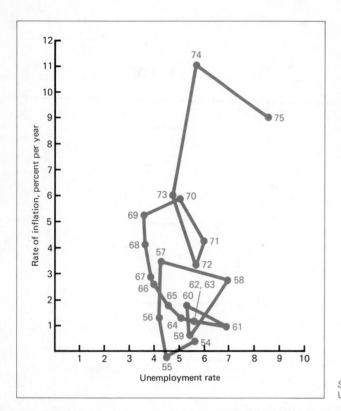

Source: Data from Economic Report of the President (Washington, D.C.: U.S. Government Printing Office, 1976).

EXHIBIT 16.7

Recent U.S. experience with inflation and unemployment Since 1954, inflation and unemployment have spiraled upward in a series of roughly triangular loops. One cycle, that which followed the 1957 recession, was cut off before the previous peak of inflation had been reached. In 1973–1974, inflation reached an especially high peak because internationally generated commodity inflation was added to domestic inflationary pressures. Inflation is given as year-to-year percentage increase In the consumer price index.

frightened by the inflation of 1956 and 1957, and did not want to repeat the experience. Tight monetary policy cut the recovery off before the previous peak of inflation was reached.

The last loop in the series, in contrast, is extraordinarily stretched out. In part, the new highs in the inflation can be blamed on the fact that the 1972 recession did not last long enough to purge inflationary expectations entirely. Reflation began from a higher level than it ever had before. That is not the whole story, however. In the years 1973 and 1974, some special cost-push elements must be taken into account.

First, 1973 and 1974 saw a "price bulge" as an aftereffect of Nixon's 1971–1972 price and wage controls. (These controls will be discussed more fully in the next chapter.) On top of this came two strong sources of commodity inflation. One of these was the fourfold rise in oil prices after 1974. The other was the near-doubling of food prices, also largely touched off by events outside U.S. borders. Finally, a decline in the exchange rate at which the dollar traded against foreign currencies added still more cost-push pressure. Exhibit 16.8 attempts to give some rough estimates of the importance of each of these cost-push elements. According to the numbers shown there, inflation would have been a little higher in 1971 and 1972 without controls. In 1973 and 1974, by comparison, inflation would have been considerably less if outside influences had not combined so forcefully.

SUMMARY

1. For a given rate of growth of nominal GNP, the rate of inflation depends on what happens to real GNP. For a given initial level of unemployment, the growth of real GNP depends on how unemployment moves (Okun's law).

EXHIBIT 16.8

Actual and estimated changes in percent rates of inflation*
Inflation in 1973 and 1974 was worse than it would otherwise
have been because of several special cost-push factors. One
was the "price bulge" following the end of Nixon's wage and
price controls. Another was the oil crisis. A third was devaluation of the dollar in international exchange markets, and a
fourth the rise in other commodity prices, especially food.
These figures should not be taken as exact, but they do
indicate the relative importance of the various special
influences.

	1971	1972	1973	1974	Total
	Actual Change				
	4.3	3.3	6.2	11.0	24.8%
	Change due to				Total Changes
Oil crisis	0	0	0	+2.0	+2.0%
Wage and price controls	−0.5	−2.0	+0.5	+2.0	0
Depreciation of exchange rates		+0.5	+2.0	+0.5	+3.0%
Internationally generated non-oil commodity price increases		+0.5	+1.0	+1.5	+3.0%
Total changes	−0.5	−1.0	+3.5	+6.0	+8.0%

*Calculated from annual averages of the consumer price index.

Putting these two propositions together gives us the inflationary pressure curve,
which relates inflation to unemployment, given the rate of nominal growth
and the initial unemployment rate. The inflationary pressure curve has a slope
of about + 3, indicating that each percentage point reduction in unemployment
cuts three points off the inflation rate. An increase in the rate of growth of
nominal output, or a reduction in the initial rate of unemployment, shifts
the inflationary pressure curve to the left. Opposite changes shift it to the right.

2. Together, the inflationary pressure curve and the Phillips curve determine the
rates of inflation and unemployment *given* (a) the rate of growth of nominal
national product, as determined by monetary and fiscal policy; (b) the initial
rate of unemployment; and (c) the level of inflationary expectations, which
determines the height of the Phillips curve. To assume levels of inflation or
unemployment other than those shown by the intersection of the two curves
must lead to a contradiction.

3. To keep unemployment below the natural rate requires that the actual rate
of inflation must be higher than the expected rate of inflation. Because people
tend to expect what has happened in the immediate past to continue to happen
in the future, inflationary expectations tend to catch up with the actual rate
of inflation. Only by continually accelerating the rate of inflation, so that expectations never catch up with actuality, can the unemployment rate be kept
below the natural rate for a prolonged period.

4. An inflationary recession is the worst of both worlds. Fiscal or monetary brakes
cut the rate of growth of nominal output, but past inflationary experience continues temporarily to push up inflationary expectations and the Phillips curve.
The result is a combination of rising unemployment and high or even increasing
inflation. Once people become aware that the brakes have been applied and
inflation has been checked, inflationary expectations will fall and eventually the
economy can be decelerated to a "soft landing."

5. During a prolonged period of acceleration, political pressures build up to "do
something" about inflation. Similarly, during a prolonged deceleration, pressures build up to take action on unemployment. The result can be a stop-go
cycle of alternating acceleration, inflationary recession, deceleration, and reflation. If the political system is, on the average, more sensitive to unemployment than to inflation, the stop-go cycle can be given an upward bias, sending
the rate of inflation spiraling upward over time.

DISCUSSION QUESTIONS

1. If after a long period of relatively steady prices there is an increase in aggregate demand, why would the initial increase in prices be strictly demand-pull inflation? Why would cost-push elements not appear right away?

2. In some periods and some countries, the government has used the acceleration technique to keep unemployment low for long periods. All the time they were doing it, however, they continually issued statements to the effect that they were keeping a watchful eye on prices, that they viewed price stability as an important goal, and so on. Do you think such statements might serve any actual economic purpose? Do you think it would make any difference if the government just announced, "OK, it is our policy to keep unemployment low, so we are going to let the rate of inflation climb each year by 2 percent above what it was the year before"?

3. Suppose that some private economic research organization discovered a 100 percent accurate and reliable method of forecasting next year's rate of inflation. Why might the government want to prevent this forecast from being published? What do you think would be the effect on the shape of the Phillips curve if the forecast were widely published, and were widely known to be accurate.

4. What effect do you think shortening the period between national elections would have on economic policy? What effect would lengthening the period have? What effect would there be if the government could call an election any time it wanted, as in some parliamentary systems? Under the last option, under what economic conditions do you think the government would most frequently decide to call an election?

5. Go to the newspaper, or to some government source such as the *Survey of Current Business* or the *Economic Report of the President,* and find inflation and unemployment statistics for 1976 and beyond. Include forecasts for the current year if you can find them. Plot these new data on Exhibit 16.7. Do they fall where you expect? Write a paragraph interpreting the newest data.

Appendix
Inflation and
the Money Market

This appendix is an extension of Chapters 11 through 13, where we discussed the role of money in the economy. It explains how our theory of money and aggregate demand can be modified to take inflation into account. Here, as throughout Chapters 15 and 16, inflationary expectations play an important part in the story.

Real and Nominal Rates of Interest

Let us begin by looking at a person who is about to lend $100 for one year. Suppose that he wants a 5 percent rate of return. If he receives $105 in principal plus interest at the end of the year, and there has been no inflation, he will be satisfied. But what if there has been 5 percent inflation? The $105 our lender is repaid would then be worth no more than the $100 he loaned. Although he would still have earned $5 measured in nominal terms, his *real* return would have been zero.

This example suggests that when there is inflation, we need to distinguish between real and nominal rates of interest. By the nominal rate of interest, we mean the rate of interest measured in current dollars, and by the real rate, we mean the nominal rate adjusted for inflation. There is a well-known theory to explain how the real and nominal rates are related. This theory was first set forth by Yale economist Irving Fisher at the turn of the century. In Fisher's theory, the nominal rate of interest will be approximately equal to the real rate of interest plus the expected rate of inflation.

This theory clearly makes sense. If a lender were willing to part with his money only if guaranteed a 5 percent rate of return when he expected no inflation, it stands to reason that he would ask for a 10 percent nominal return if he expected prices to rise by 5 percent. Experience seems to bear out the theory, at least roughly. Interest rates have been higher than ever before in recent years of record inflation. It is true that interest rates have not risen enough to protect real rates of return fully against increases in prices, and that in some years, actual real interest rates have been negative. Such facts, however, do not directly contradict Fisher's theory. It could simply be that in the worst years, inflation was higher than it was expected to be.

Interest and Investment

The theory of aggregate demand set forth in Chapter 13 did not use the distinction between real and nominal rates of interest. For periods of zero or low inflationary expectations, this does not make much difference, but the theory should be slightly modified to apply to inflationary periods.

First, the theory of money demand. The process of adjusting portfolios between bonds and money, which underlies the theory of the demand for money, works in terms of nominal rates of interest. It is the nominal rate that indicates the relative advantage of holding bonds rather than money.

Suppose that the nominal rate is 10 percent and inflation is zero. The real cost of holding money in such a case is the loss of an opportunity to earn a 10 percent real rate of return on bonds. Alternatively, suppose that the nominal rate is 10 percent, but expected inflation is 5 percent. In this case, the real cost of holding money is the loss of an opportunity to earn a 5 percent real rate of return on bonds, plus a second cost in the form of a 5 percent per year deterioration of the purchasing power of the money itself. Together the two costs total 10 percent. In either case, the relative attractiveness of bonds and money is the same. It follows that when we draw a money demand curve, we should label the vertical axis the nominal rate of interest.

In contrast, for planned investment, it is the real rate that counts. Suppose that a firm is willing to borrow $1,000 at 5 percent to buy a doughnut machine when the price of doughnuts (and of everything else) is expected to remain unchanged. Will the firm not then be willing to borrow $1,000 at a nominal 10 percent if it expects the price of the doughnuts it sells (and of everything else) to rise at 5 percent per year? Investment plans are made in terms of the real rate of interest, so it is the real rate that should go on the verticle axis when we draw a planned investment schedule.

In order to modify our theory of the determination of aggregate nominal demand to fit inflationary periods, then, we must use the nominal rate of interest in the money market and the real rate for the planned investment schedule. The reader can easily see how the diagrams of Chapter 13 could be changed to do this. All we would have to do would be to subtract the expected rate of inflation when numbering the vertical axis of the planned investment schedule.

Paradox

The distinction between the real and nominal rate of interest can be used to explain an apparent paradox of monetary policy. Our theory of Chapters 12 and 13 suggested that increasing the money supply would lower the rate of interest. Yet consider a period such as the late 1960s for the U.S. economy. From 1965 to 1970 the Federal Reserve allowed the money supply to grow at a rate of over 5 percent per year (contrasted to an average rate of growth from 1952 to 1964 of less than 2 percent). Nonetheless, the market yield on corporate bonds rose from under 5 percent to over 8 percent.

This "paradox," of course, has a simple resolution. The expansion of the money supply led to a rise in the rate of inflation from 1.9 percent per year in 1965 to 5.5 percent per year in 1970. The accelerating inflation widened the gap between the real and nominal rates of interest. With the real rate roughly steady during the period, the nominal rate went up. We see then that, in the long run, as inflationary expectations adjust to observed rates of inflation, expansionary monetary policy can actually cause the nominal rate of interest to rise rather than fall.

Error

Failure to keep in mind the distinction between real and nominal rates of interest can lead to serious errors in interpreting monetary policy. Traditionally people have tended to watch market rates of interest—that is, nominal rates—for an indication of the direction of monetary policy. A drop in rates was taken to indicate expansionary policy, and a rise to indicate restrictive policy.

This is all quite reasonable for a noninflationary world. In an inflationary period, though, market rates of interest do not give an accurate picture of monetary policy at all. In the late 1960s, for example, many people, apparently even including some at the Fed itself, were misled. They thought that because market interest rates were rising, monetary policy was taking a restrictive course and hence helping to combat inflation. In fact, exactly the opposite was true. The rapid growth in the money supply was helping to contribute to inflation. Because interest rates can be misleading in inflationary periods, it is now becoming more and more accepted to concentrate on rates of change of the money supply itself as an indicator of the direction of monetary policy, rather than to concentrate on market interest rates.

CHAPTER 17
The Future of Stabilization Policy

What You Will Learn in This Chapter

The postwar economic record has not been good. This has given rise to the charge that economic stabilization through the management of aggregate demand has failed. Our theory of inflation and unemployment helps us understand what truth there is to these charges. So does an understanding of lags in policy making. Now many economists are looking beyond demand management to new tools of economic stabilization. Two such tools are incomes policy and indexing.

For Review

Here are some important terms and concepts that will be put to use in this chapter. Be certain that you understand them, or review them before proceeding.

    Fiscal and monetary policy (Chapters 8–13)
    The Phillips curve (Chapter 14)
    Cost-push inflation (Chapter 14)

The Great Depression of the 1930s had many lasting effects on economic policy and economic thought. One of those effects was to give the government increased responsibility for economic stabilization. The Employment Act of 1946 made this the law of the land. Influenced by the work of Keynes, economists chose **demand management** as the key tool of stabilization policy. If the economy slumped and too many people were out of work, a boost to aggregate demand would plug the contractionary gap and fix things up. If a boom got too hot and prices rose too fast, putting the damper on demand would cool things off. Given the political will, there seemed reason to hope that the economy could be "fine-tuned" for prosperity without inflation.

    Sad to say, the postwar economic record has not been good. Perhaps we could forgive some early policy mistakes if there were a clear trend toward increasing stability, but there has been no such trend. By the 1970s, the economy was in worse shape than at any time for forty years. This experience has cast doubt on the whole idea of stability through demand management.

Demand Management A general term for the fiscal and monetary policies used to control aggregate demand for purposes of economic stabilization.

In this chapter we shall look at the source of those doubts, and at the new directions that economic thinking is taking in response to them. First we shall recap the theory we have developed in the last three chapters. Using that as a basis, we shall look at two competing philosophies of demand management: fine tuning and policy rules. Finally, we shall discuss some ideas that look beyond demand management for an answer to our problems.

Inflation, Unemployment, and Aggregate Demand—A Recap

To understand recent economic events, we must know how demand management policies affect inflation and unemployment. Let us begin, then, by restating what we have learned. The four traditional theories that we introduced in Chapter 14 will give us a framework for this brief recap.

Nominal Income Determination

The first two traditional theories we looked at were the crude quantity theory of inflation and the crude Keynesian theory. Neither of these theories gives a complete explanation of inflation and unemployment. Put together and brought up to date, though, they do give us a pretty good idea of how demand management policies determine nominal national income and product. That is an important first step.

Expectations and the Phillips Curve

The next traditional theory we looked at was the Phillips curve. The Phillips curve tells us that, in the short run at least, there is a trade-off between inflation and unemployment. Demand management can give us more jobs if we can stand a rise in prices, or it can cut the rate of inflation if we do not mind seeing a few more people out of work. In the long run, though, the Phillips curve does not give us a simple, stable trade-off. That is because it is not so much the rate of inflation that matters for unemployment as *changes* in the rate of inflation.

One idea more than any other helps us to understand how the Phillips curve really works. That is the idea that people make their plans for working and producing on the basis of what they *expect* to happen, not on the basis of what is actually happening. They must do this for the simple reason that they do not find out about what is actually happening until after it has happened.

Think of what goes on, then, when the rate of inflation changes. When inflation speeds up, employers offer workers fatter wage deals than they expected to get, and workers snap up the jobs. Unemployment goes down for a while, until people find out what prices are really doing. Higher prices mean that the workers' big new paychecks do not buy any more than before. Once workers come to expect inflation, they start shopping around for even better jobs, and unemployment rises again.

On the down side, something similar happens. When inflation first starts to drop, people will be caught unaware. Firms will still be willing to meet high wage demands because they expect to get the money back in higher prices. Instead, it turns out that they cannot sell as much as they had hoped at the higher prices, so they cut back output and lay workers off. Only when they come to expect the lower inflation will they get their plans straightened out and get production back to normal.

Cost-Push

This brings us to cost-push, our fourth traditional theory of inflation. The idea of expectations helps us see how cost-push fits into the picture. When inflation stops going up and starts coming down, workers and union negotiators will be taken by surprise at least for a while. They will keep demanding big pay increases to keep up with the inflation they think is going to get worse. Firms will grant those increases because they also think that inflation is still going up. Remember that true cost-push inflation requires that there be some force to push prices and wages up even when demand is not rising. Now we see that when expectations are slow in adjusting to an actual slowdown of inflation, just the right conditions for cost-push are created.[1]

Markets and the Use of Knowledge

This, then, is a rough outline of the theory of inflation and unemployment we have built in the last three chapters. Now that all the pieces are in place, we can see that this theory builds on the fundamental insight that markets are mechanisms for putting knowledge to use. In the best of times, we know that the plans of businesspeople, workers, and consumers do not always mesh. Some people make mistakes, while other lucky ones make windfall gains. Lots of little errors tend to cancel one another out.

Sudden changes in the rate of inflation, though, add something new to the picture. Such changes can mean that, for a while, *everyone will tend to make mistakes in the same direction at once.* When inflation speeds up, not just a few workers, but a great many will accept pay deals that turn out not to be so good after all. When inflation slows down, not just a few firms but many will find themselves stuck with wage bills and price lists that are higher than they ought to be. These widespread errors give rise to the changes in unemployment that are the familiar by-product of changes in the rate of inflation.

Are we saying, then, that people are fools? Not at all. People are smart. They learn from experience. All we are saying is that learning does not take place at the speed of light. A little time passes after actual events change their course before people adjust their plans and expectations to new conditions. In the meantime, people may be led to do things they would not do if they had complete knowledge of economic conditions.

Policy Implications

Our understanding of inflation and unemployment contains some important implications for economic policy. We discussed these in detail in Chapter 16, but it is worth listing three of them here again.

1. Unexpected increases in the rate of inflation pull the rate of unem-

---

[1]Another kind of cost-push inflation has also been important recently. That is commodity inflation brought about by increases in the international prices of oil, food, and some other goods. See Case 16.2 for a discussion of recent commodity inflation.

ployment below what it otherwise would be. It follows that if policy makers allow inflation to run faster and faster year after year, they can keep unemployment low for quite a while.

2. When inflation slows after a long period of acceleration, we end up in the worst of all possible worlds. Inflationary expectations generate cost-push inflation while the slowdown of demand pushes up unemployment. The worse the inflation, the more distasteful is the cure.

3. Recession cures inflation, but only slowly. After the cure is underway and prices are falling, a quick step-up of aggregate demand (reflation) temporarily brings the best of both worlds. Until expectations adjust to the reversal of policy, we get the best of all possible worlds: falling unemployment without rising inflation.

With these conclusions in mind, let us turn now to the debate over the future of demand management.

Fine Tuning Versus Policy Rules

When economists express a fear that demand management has failed, they do not mean that it has failed to have any effect on the economy. Everyone grants that the level of aggregate demand, measured in nominal terms, has a powerful influence on economic life. Disputes about the relative importance of monetary or fiscal tools of demand management should not obscure this agreement. Instead, doubts about demand management are doubts about whether the particular policies that have been pursued have had a *stabilizing* effect. The fear is that the powerful tools of demand management, if misused, can have results opposite to those intended.

Much of the debate over demand management revolves around two different philosophies of how such policies should be used. One group of economists takes an activist line. They think that the federal government should make frequent and vigorous use of both fiscal and monetary policy tools in order to *fine-tune* the economy. That way we can hope to get just the desired mix of high employment, high real growth, and price stability. Others argue that attempts to fine-tune usually do more harm than good. They should be replaced by a policy of "steady-as-you-go," governed by *rules* that remain unchanged over long periods.

The Case for Fine Tuning

The case for fine tuning is based on three beliefs about the economic and political system of a modern democracy like the United States. The first is the belief that, left to itself, the private economy is unstable. The second is the belief that the tools of demand management work fairly rapidly and predictably. The third belief is that, with careful scientific argument and patient persuasion, government authorities can be educated to use the tools of demand management in the best long-run interest of the public at large.

The belief that the private economy is unstable has a long history. For nearly two hundred years there have been alternating periods of boom and depression in market economies. By World War II, a whole branch of economic theory had grown up to support this view, under the name of business-cycle theory. The Great Depression reinforced the idea of instability in the minds of all those who lived through it.

The idea that fiscal and monetary policy are quick and predictable in their effects on the economy is part and parcel of the Keynesian tradition. It is supported by much of the theory presented in Chapters 8 through 13 of this book.

Then there is the idea that in a democratic nation political power will end up in the hands of politicians who will use the tools of policy wisely. This is an outgrowth of the American liberal tradition as it has developed from Franklin Roosevelt's New Deal to John Kennedy's New Frontier.

Experience

The fine-tuners came into their own in the Kennedy-Johnson era. Initially, their policies met with success. The years 1961 to 1969 saw the longest period of "peacetime" expansion in the history of the United States. Since that time something has gone wrong. Economic instability has increased. A stop-go policy cycle has pushed the economy into widening swings of unemployment and inflation. It looks, then, as if at least part of the fine-tuner's argument must be incorrect. Either the tools of activist monetary and fiscal policy do not work as quickly and predictably as they should, or else the tools have been badly mishandled. Let us see what the opponents of fine tuning have to say.

The Case Against Fine Tuning

Opponents of fine tuning challenge every aspect of the case we have just set forth. They claim that their historical studies show the private economy to be less unstable than is often thought. They are sceptical that politicians have the courage to keep long-run economic goals in mind when faced, in the short run, with the need for reelection. But the most telling point in the case against fine tuning is a challenge to the idea that the effects of demand management are either quick or predictable.

Lags

In recent years, economists have begun to worry more and more about lags and delays in the operation of fiscal and monetary policy. There are two major kinds of lags. First, there is the so-called **inside lag,** which is the delay between the time policy action is needed and the time action is taken. Second, there is the **outside lag,** which is the delay between the time policy action is taken and the time its effects on the economy are felt.

The inside lag has several sources. An important one is the time it takes to gather accurate economic statistics. During the famous episode of "the Fed's finest hour," President Johnson would probably have resisted tight monetary policy less if he had known how fast demand was already expanding. In late 1972 and early 1973, both monetary and fiscal policy might have been tighter if people in Washington had known in time of shortages that were developing in key industries. And in 1974, restrictive policy might have been relaxed earlier if it had been known how rapidly business inven-

Inside Lag The delay between the time a policy action is needed and the time policy action is taken.

Outside Lag The delay between the time policy action is taken and the time its effects on the economy are felt.

tories were piling up.[2] A second source of inside lag is the legislative process of Congress. This is particularly serious for fiscal policy. (Recall that the Kennedy tax cut took over two years to reach the statute books.) Because the Federal Reserve Board is independent of Congress, the inside lag for monetary policy is probably a little shorter than for fiscal policy.

The causes of the outside lag for fiscal and monetary policy are not really very well understood, but it is well established that the lag is a serious one. For monetary policy, it is likely to be at least six months before the first important effects of a policy change are felt, and perhaps two years before all the effects have worked through the system. It is sometimes thought that fiscal policy suffers from a shorter outside lag, although just how much shorter is not clear.

Destabilization

Lags make fine tuning very hard. You can understand this if you have ever stood under a shower when the water pressure changed. First you are scalded. When you try to adjust the taps, you find that there is a lag of a few seconds between the time you turn them and the time the water coming out changes in temperature. You overreact to the scalding and are next frozen. By the time you get the system fine-tuned again, the water pressure is probably back where it was in the first place anyway. You might just as well have stepped aside and waited.

The point is that when there are lags, policy actions can have a destabilizing rather than a stabilizing effect. A policy that is intended to speed recovery from a recession may take effect only in time to make inflation worse when recovery is already under way. An action intended to cool off a boom may take hold in the bottom of the next recession when it is least wanted.

Rules

What do the opponents of fine tuning offer in its place? Specific suggestions vary. A common theme, though, is that demand management should be made subject to explicit, long-term rules rather than being left to the discretion of policy makers.

Milton Friedman has for years tried to popularize the idea of a monetary policy rule. He suggests that the Fed should be required by law to keep money growth to the same steady pace year after year. Friedman thinks the constancy of the pace matters more than the specific rate, but suggests that a good target would be equal to the long-run growth of potential GNP. That would be somewhere in the neighborhood of 4 percent per year.

Full Employment Balanced Budget A rule under which tax and spending policy would be adjusted so that the federal budget would be in balance if the economy were at full employment.

The most often mentioned idea for a fiscal policy rule is the **full employment balanced budget.** Under such a rule, Congress and the President would decide the level of government purchases solely on the basis of the actual needs they see for defense, housing, health care, and so forth. No attention would be paid at this stage to the macroeconomic effects of

---

[2]These examples are given by Herbert Stein, who served as Chairman of the Council of Economic Advisors under President Nixon, in *Economic Planning and the Improvement of Economic Policy* (Washington: The American Enterprise Institute, 1975), p. 28.

these policies. Then, having made the spending decisions, they would adjust taxes so that the budget would be in balance if the economy were at full employment. Because actual net taxes change with the size of nominal income, there would still be actual budget deficits in times of recession and surpluses in times of exceptionally high employment. Fiscal policy of a sort of "automatic" variety would exist. This, it is hoped, would have a stabilizing effect on real output.

Discretionary Authority

Needless to say, fine-tuners think that the ideas of monetary rules and full employment balanced budgets are nonsense. Some think instead that more discretion and flexibility are needed, not less. For example, some recommend that the independence of the Federal Reserve be done away with, so that monetary and fiscal policy might be coordinated by the executive branch of government more closely than is now possible. Also, it has often been suggested that the President be given some degree of discretionary fiscal authority. The inside lag would be shortened by letting him order immediate tax cuts or surcharges, or increase or decrease government spending, without prior approval of Congress. But demands for more discretionary policy are heard less often now than they once were. Instead, one gets strong statements of what economic policy cannot do from the highest levels of the economics profession. A significant case study in changing attitudes is provided by this passage from the 1976 *Economic Report of the President:*

CASE 17.1
Humility Comes to the
Council of Economic Advisors

There is a lesson to be drawn from past policy mistakes. The history of monetary and fiscal policies demonstrates that we have a great deal to learn about implementing discretionary policy changes. Our ability to forecast is at best imperfect, especially in an increasingly complex and interdependent world, and the difficulties in forecasting grow larger as we extend the period for which the forecast is made. This is a significant problem because of the time lags involved in altering the pace of economic activity through discretionary monetary and fiscal actions. There is a perception lag in diagnosing the problem, a reaction lag in selecting the appropriate response, and an implementation lag in having the policy prescription accepted and put into effect through our political and administrative processes.

    We also lack reliable estimates of how long it takes before the economy responds to policies once they are undertaken and how large the response will be. This is especially true now because the high rates of inflation in recent years have made price expectations much more important . . . than they formerly were, but there has not been sufficient experience to pin down how inflationary processes affect key relationships within the economy. With respect to fiscal policy there is the additional complication that countercyclical increases in Government expenditures are difficult to check during later upswings. Because countercyclical policy changes may be slow to take hold and then hard to reverse, their effects may extend well past the time when they are most needed. Consequently a significant danger exists that, instead of smoothing economic fluctuations, discretionary changes in policy aimed at demand management may themselves become a source of economic instability. . . .

    The proper conclusion is not that we should forswear the use of discretionary policy. . . . Discretionary policies do have an important function in our economic system. But we must be mindful of the great difficulties in successfully executing countercyclical policies.

    What is called for in our judgment is a steadier course in macroeconomic policies than has been followed in the past. We should set policies broadly consistent with sustainable long-term noninflationary growth and try to limit the size and duration of any policy deviations that promise short-term benefits but risk interfering with our long-run goals.

Beyond Demand Management

In this section we turn our attention to two tools of stabilization policy that we have not yet discussed. These are incomes policies and indexing. The two have a common starting point in the assumption that demand management, at least as practiced in the past, has failed.

Incomes Policies

Incomes Policy   A policy of directly controlling wages, salaries, earnings, and prices in order to fight inflation.

By an **incomes policy,** we mean any policy that directly controls wages, salaries, and earnings for the purpose of fighting inflation. Ordinarily, such policies also include direct controls on wholesale and retail prices. The United States has experimented with incomes policies. Such policies have become a permanent feature of economic life in many Western European countries, Great Britain and Sweden being especially notable examples. It will be worth our while to look at how these policies work, and why they are highly controversial.

Theory of Controls

Let us begin by looking at policies that control prices and wages from a theoretical point of view. The case for controls is strongest as a temporary measure to fight inflationary recession. We have said that when policy makers put on the brakes after a long period of accelerating inflation, we are thrown for a time into the worst of all possible worlds. Workers and employers base their plans on the expectation of more inflation, yet aggregate demand is actually tailing off. Until expectations adjust to reality, wages, prices, and unemployment all rise at once.

Now enter the timely use of an incomes policy. Suppose that just at the moment the fiscal and monetary brakes are put on, the government announces a program of strict price and wage controls. This is done with great fanfare and a show of grim determination to lick inflation once and for all. What is hoped is that workers and businessmen will *believe* that controls are going to stop inflation. If they do, they will revise their inflationary expectations downward much more rapidly than if they had to wait to learn from experience. This revision of expectations will get rid of the cost-push element of the inflationary recession. Workers will know that they do not have to push for high wages to beat inflation, so they will accept the controls. Firms will know that they will not have to pay higher wages, so they will keep their prices in line and concentrate on increasing their sales. The readjustment to price stability and full employment will be more rapid and less painful than it would be without an incomes policy.

Problems with Controls

So much for theory. We may grant that controls are helpful in squeezing the cost-push element out of an inflationary recession. Does that mean that they are a cure-all for the economic problems of our time? Not really. The problem is that controls can be of help in correcting past mistakes in demand management policy, but they cannot work as a substitute for sound demand management. Unfortunate things can happen if we try to use an incomes policy to fight inflation without also slowing the growth of aggregate demand, or if we leave controls in force after a recession is over and a new boom gets underway.

If aggregate demand rises in nominal terms, one of three things must logically happen. First, national product (aggregate supply) could rise in real terms to meet the increased nominal demand without a rise in prices. Second, prices could rise to meet the increase in nominal demand without an increase in output. Finally, neither prices nor output might rise, in which case the aggregate quantity of goods demanded would exceed the aggregate quantity of goods supplied, and there would be an overall shortage of goods. A combination of these three alternatives may sometimes occur, but no fourth alternative is logically possible.

Naturally, the first alternative is the most attractive. That would mean real economic growth without inflation. Real economic growth can come from only two sources, however. One is an increase in potential GNP, which we can hope for at about 4 percent per year in the long run. The other is a fall in unemployment. This source of growth is temporary, because unemployment would soon reach a level below which it could fall no further. In the long run, then, *real growth without inflation or shortages is possible only if demand management limits the growth of nominal GNP to the long-term rate of growth of potential GNP.*

An incomes policy cannot buy us real growth without inflation or shortages if that rule of demand management is not followed. All it can do is determine which of the second two alternatives we get. If aggregate demand is allowed to run away without controls, we get runaway inflation. If controls are applied and demand still runs away, we get shortages, rationing, and black markets.

American Experience with Controls

There have been two major experiments with wage and price controls in the American economy. One was during World War II. Then huge wartime government spending made it impractical to control aggregate demand. The effects of controls in those conditions were as predicted. Rationing was introduced, and there were widespread shortages and black markets. All this was tolerated because people felt rationing to be the fairest way to distribute essentials during the emergency. As soon as the war had been won, controls were abandoned with a sigh of relief.

The other major experiment with an incomes policy took place during the Nixon administration. This case is much more relevant to future policy, and deserves a closer look.

CASE 17.2
Nixon's Wage and Price Controls

On August 15, 1971, President Richard Nixon announced a dramatic "new economic policy." The new policy was prompted as much by international as by domestic events, but the part of the program that got the most attention was domestic. That was a strict 90-day freeze on all prices and wages, announced to combat inflation.

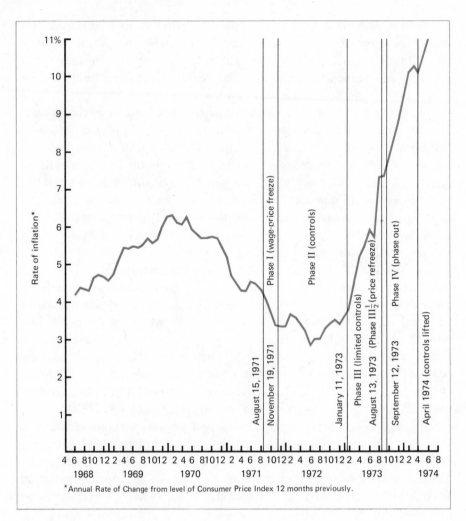

EXHIBIT 17.1
Inflation and price controls
Source: Federal Reserve Bank of St. Louis. Appeared in *Economic Report of the President* (Washington, D.C.: U.S. Government Printing Office, 1976).

The freeze later became known as Phase I of what proved to be a protracted experiment with controls. It was followed by Phase II, a full-fledged incomes policy lasting until January 11, 1973. Under Phase II, firms could raise prices to cover increases in costs, but could not increase their profit margins. Wage increases were limited to 5.5 percent except in special circumstances.

Phase I and II came at the sort of time when price controls can be expected to work best. As Exhibit 17.1 shows, inflation had been on the decline for almost two years. Phase I clearly speeded the fall of inflation while it lasted, although some of the gains were lost in a post-freeze "bulge." By mid-1972, the bulge had been overcome, and the rate of inflation had fallen further.

It is hard to say how much Phase I and Phase II actually speeded the decline of inflation. An eyeball interpretation of Exhibit 17.1 shows that what happened during the first year of controls was a steady continuation of what was already happening. There is no real way to tell whether inflation would have come down as fast without controls or not. At any rate, little harm had been done. There were a few isolated cases of shortages, mainly in lumber, but nothing alarming or widespread.

Believing that Phases I and II had done their job, Nixon wisely followed the orthodox prescription and began to put incomes policy back on the shelf. In January 1973, Phase II was replaced by Phase III. This imposed slightly looser standards and emphasized self-enforcement. Unfortunately, by the time Phase III came into effect, a strong recovery of aggregate demand was under way. Prices began to rise more rapidly, as Exhibit 17.1 clearly shows. Looking back on this period, it is now clear that the looser controls of Phase III did not *cause* this rise in prices, but at the time they were thought to have. Political pressure built up to "get tough." Nixon responded in August 1973 with a refreeze of prices and wages, which came to be called Phase III½.

Taken together, Phases III and III½ fit the principle that controls will not work when aggregate demand is not controlled. During Phase III, when controls were weak, inflation went up at a very rapid pace. During the re-freeze of Phase III½ inflation was temporarily halted, but serious shortages and distortions began to show up. Contractors could not build because they could not get reinforcing bars for their concrete. Miners could not mine because they could not get the bolts they needed to strengthen their mine-shafts. Publishers had to shift to expensive high-quality paper because cheap low-quality paper became hard to get. Firms began to hoard inventories of raw materials in fear of more shortages to come.

It was judged that the distortions of Phase III½ were too great a price to pay for artificially keeping inflation down. In September 1973, Nixon switched to Phase IV, which was a phase-out. By April 1974, controls were so unpopular that Congress let the authority for them expire, with little op-position from either party.

The Future of Controls

The Nixon experiment with controls was a mixed success at best. As long as inflation was falling anyway, the controls may have helped a little, and at least provided useful political window dressing. When inflation began to rise again, they proved useless and then worse than useless. Given the record shown in Exhibit 17.1, it seems likely that in the future, people will not even *expect* controls to do any good, so that even their psychological effect would be lost.

Not everyone is willing to give up yet on the idea of controls, though. A very bold British experiment with incomes policy, underway as of this writing, is being watched closely. The British incomes policy of 1976 has one novel feature. In return for accepting lower wage increases, the government has promised to cut taxes for wage earners. The idea is that this will protect workers' real incomes without making labor power so expensive that firms cannot afford to hire new workers. In combination, the wage controls and tax incentives are hoped to cut both inflation and unemployment at the same time. Arthur Okun has backed a similar scheme for the U.S. economy, which he calls "real wage insurance." Incomes policy is likely to be talked about and experimented with as long as inflation remains at its recent unacceptable levels.

Indexing

Let us turn now from controls to a very different kind of policy that also goes beyond demand management. That is the policy called **indexing.** Indexing means inflation-proofing wages, taxes, debts, savings, and a host of other things by using "escalator clauses" to adjust nominal values when prices change. Indexing is viewed partly as a way of combatting inflation, and partly as a way of easing some of its worst effects when it does occur

Indexing A policy under which wages, interest payments, taxes, and other things expressed in nominal terms are revalued up-ward to keep pace with inflation.

The best-known advocate of indexing has been Milton Friedman.[3] His program for indexation features five specific measures. The first three, which apply to government, would be compulsory. They are as follows:

1. Indexing income taxes. That means that if, say, the consumer price index went up 10 percent in a year, the personal exemption would automatically go up from $700 to $770, the $5,000–$6,000 income bracket would become the $5,500–$6,600 bracket, and so forth. Corporate income taxes would be indexed the same way.

2. Indexing capital gains for tax purposes. If you bought a house for $30,000 in 1976 and sold it for $40,000 in 1978, you now have to declare a capital gain of $10,000. If prices had gone up by 15 percent in the meantime, though, $4,500 of that would be only "paper" gain, not real capital gain. Under Friedman's plan, you would pay taxes only on the remaining $5,500.

3. Indexing government bonds. U.S. savings bonds would be written so that they would pay some fixed rate of interest (say 3 percent) *plus* the annual rate of inflation. If the consumer price index went up by 8 percent in a year, your bond would earn $3 + 8 = 11$ percent that year, and so forth.

In addition to these actions by government, Friedman would hope for additional voluntary actions in the private sector. These would include:

4. Indexing of private corporate bonds, mortgage loans, and perhaps even some savings deposits. This would work just like the indexing of government bonds.

5. Indexing of wages and salaries. Many union contracts already have "escalator clauses" that do this. If the consumer price index went up by 5 percent, wages would also rise by 5 percent under such a contract. Friedman hopes that these contracts become more widespread.

Effects of Indexation

How would indexation help? Proponents argue that there would be three beneficial effects.

First, indexation would, like wage and price controls, help squeeze the cost-push element out of inflationary recession. As things are now, when inflation slows down, workers want to keep pushing wages up because they fear that they will need the higher wages to offset expected inflation. With indexation, workers would no longer have to fear inflation. If prices went up, they would be protected by escalator clauses, and if they did not go up, the protection would not be needed. There would be no need to push wages up artificially.

Second, indexation would reduce the government's temptation to let aggregate demand run out of control. As things are now, the government gains enormously by inflation. People and corporations are pushed into higher tax brackets. People are taxed for capital gains that are really only "paper" gains. And the real cost of paying off the national debt goes down, which means that people who bought government bonds in the past are

[3]The following account of Friedman's indexing scheme is based on his pamphlet, "Monetary Correction," London: Institute for Economic Affairs Occasional Paper 41, 1974.

forced to pay an inflation "tax" too. Friedman estimates the government's revenue from such inflation "taxes" to be $25 billion in 1973 alone. With indexation, government could not get these huge windfall gains. Policy makers would thus have less incentive to pump up aggregate demand.

Finally, indexation would relieve some of the burdens of inflation even if it did not halt inflation altogether. Now, inflation robs people of the real value of their savings, and confers windfall gains on those lucky enough to be deep in debt. Wealthy people with clever accountants and financial advisors can already find ways to shelter their savings from inflation. People in lower and middle-income brackets now have no refuge. This is a special hardship on the old who have saved for retirement. Indexed government bonds would give them the protection they need.

Prospects for Indexation

Indexation is not a new or untried idea. In the United States, social security payments, federal retirement benefits, and wages of some government workers are already indexed. Many unions, including the huge auto workers union, have escalator clauses in their contracts. In Canada and Australia, the personal income tax is now indexed. In Brazil, almost everything in the economy is indexed. If inflation continues in the United States it is likely that indexation will become still more widespread here.

Indexation, like incomes policy, is no cure-all. Even its strongest supporters do not say it is. It is just one of a number of ideas that some economists think may make it easier to recover from the consequences of past errors of demand management, and escape a repetition of these errors.

Conclusions

The End of Macroeconomics?

Macroeconomics as we know it was born in the crisis of the Great Depression. Before that time, the distinction between what we now call macro- and microeconomics was not as sharp as it later became. Part of what made Keynes' ideas catch on was their *macro* quality. To the followers of Keynes, it seemed that the really important features of national economic life could be captured in a few key relationships between broad aggregate quantities. Macroeconomics meant building with big blocks, labeled "consumption," "investment," "aggregate supply," "money," and so forth. The demand management policies of the 1960s grew out of this macroeconomic approach.

Now, in the mid-1970s, there is not yet any one thing to replace macroeconomics. It is far from agreed, even, that the term should be given up. Yet one thing more than any other unites the critics of the theory and policy of the past. That is a belief in the great importance of understanding the detailed microstructure of economic life. This is as true of economists who are liberals as of those who are conservatives. It is as true of neo-Keynesians as it is of monetarists. And it is true of those who simply look for the truth with no labels attached. The exciting topics of macroeconomics today are such micro questions as these: How can we understand unemployment in terms of the job search decisions of individual workers?

How is cost-push inflation generated in concentrated as compared with competitive industries? Which particular sectors of the economy are affected first and which only after a long lag when new money is injected into the economy? How do individual workers, consumers, and businesspeople form their expectations and plans for the future?

We are back, it seems, to the theme with which we began this book. Economics is about people. It is not about aggregate demand, or expansionary gaps, or Phillips curves except when these things are understood as expressions of the way individual people think and act and plan. Macroeconomics is not yet dead and it need not die, but the more *people* are brought into it, the more the distinction between macro and micro will continue to blur.

SUMMARY

1. Modern theories of inflation and unemployment place major emphasis on the role of expectations in determining how demand management policies affect the economy. When there are unexpected changes in the rate of inflation, many workers and employers make mistakes, and do things they would not otherwise have done. These mistakes show up as changes in the unemployment rate.
2. If inflation gets faster and faster each year, unemployment can be kept low for a long period. When inflation does slow down, though, an inflationary recession is likely to be the result. Recession cures inflation, but only slowly. When aggregate demand first begins to grow again after a recession, unemployment may fall sharply with little increase in inflation.
3. There are important lags in the use of fiscal and monetary policy. There is an inside lag between the time a policy is needed and the time it is enacted, and an outside lag between that time and the time it takes effect. If lags are long enough, attempts to fine-tune the economy can have destabilizing rather than stabilizing effects. For this reason, some economists frown on fine tuning and advocate steady-as-you-go policy rules instead.
4. Incomes policies (wage and price controls) are one kind of stabilization policy that goes beyond demand management. There is good reason to believe that temporary controls may be helpful in easing the effects of inflationary recession. But an incomes policy cannot work as a substitute for good demand management.
5. Indexing seeks to fight inflation by tying the nominal values of taxes, bonds, mortgages, wages, and other things to the purchasing power of the dollar. Indexing is hoped to have three beneficial effects. It may, like wage-price controls, help squeeze the cost-push element out of inflationary recession. It may also lessen the incentive that government now has to inflate. And indexing may make it easier for retired and middle-class people to protect their savings against rising prices.

DISCUSSION QUESTIONS

1. In what sense does an abnormally high or low rate of unemployment indicate that the market is not performing its function of distributing knowledge very well?
2. What specific reforms in government can you think of that would slow the inside lag of economic policy? The outside lag?
3. Herbert Stein is a relatively conservative economist, who does not usually support spending large amounts of money to expand the federal bureaucracy. Yet he advocates spending large amounts of money to improve the quality

of economic statistics available to government, and the speed with which they are collected. Why does he think the data-gathering branch of government is so important?

4. If you feel ambitious, go to your library and see if you can find the *Economic Report of the President* for any of the years during President Kennedy's term of office. Do you think those reports generally reflect a confidence in the ability of policy makers to fine-tune the economy? Find some specific passage to contrast with the passage from the 1976 report quoted here as Case 17.1.

5. In 1975, Senators Hubert Humphrey and Jacob Javits introduced a bill called the "Balanced Growth and Planning Act." One of their reasons for introducing it was the belief that comprehensive economic planning would help avoid future errors of stabilization policy. Do you think they are right? What do you think "comprehensive economic planning" means?

PART THREE
The Theory of Prices and Markets

In the next 11 chapters, we enter into a detailed study of microeconomics. Traditionally, much of microeconomics consists of a detailed commentary on the laws of supply and demand. For that reason, we begin with a review of the principles of supply and demand in Chapter 18, and show how we can build on the basics as we learned them in Chapter 3.

Following that, our job will be to look at what lies behind the demand and supply curves. In Chapter 19, we shall discover how demand curves take on their characteristic shapes and positions as a result of the way consumers choose how to spend their limited budgets. In Chapter 20, we shall consider how consumer choices are modified by advertising. Next we shall turn to an analysis of what lies behind the supply curve. That is a job that will take several chapters, with short detours in between. We shall begin, in Chapter 21, by discussing the nature of the business firm, the organizational unit that supplies most goods and services in our economy. Then, in Chapters 22 through 26, we shall analyze how firms make supply decisions in various kinds of market situations.

Finally, in the last two chapters of Part Three, we shall turn once again to the role of government in the economy. In Chapter 27, we shall discuss government policy toward monopoly. Then, in Chapter 28, we shall look at the role of government as a regulator of private markets and a supplier of public goods.

These chapters on the role of government will raise questions of both positive and normative economics. We shall look both at how government actually behaves as a participant in the economy, and at how well it performs the roles it undertakes.

CHAPTER 18
Supply and Demand—Building on the Basics

What You Will Learn in This Chapter

The principles of supply and demand lie at the heart of microeconomics. The elements of supply and demand have already been applied many times in a macroeconomic context, but there is more to learn. The quantities supplied and demanded of various goods respond differently to changes in price. Sometimes small price changes induce large quantity changes. Sometimes large price changes have little effect on quantities. The concept of elasticity is important for measuring the responsiveness of supply and demand to changes in price. This concept must be defined, and methods for measuring it explained before proceeding further.

For Review

Here are some important terms and concepts that will be put to use in this chapter. Be certain that you understand them, or review them before proceeding.

    Market equilibrium (Chapter 3)
    Shortage and surplus (Chapter 3)
    Substitute and complementary goods (Chapter 3)

In Chapter 3 we introduced the basic principles of supply and demand. These principles found frequent application in our study of macroeconomics. As we move now into a detailed discussion of microeconomics, supply and demand become more important than ever. Before going further, it is appropriate that we review the basics, and then add some important new details to what we learned in Chapter 3.

Review of the Basics

Exhibit 18.1 sets the scene for our review. The diagram is based on the imaginary market for widgets. We have drawn a downward-sloping demand curve for widgets in accordance with the *law of demand*. That law tells us that as the price of a product decreases, the quantity demanded increases. The supply curve in Exhibit 18.1 is drawn with an upward slope. That indicates that sellers are willing to increase the quantity of widgets supplied

EXHIBIT 18.1
Equilibrium in the widget market
The equilibrium price is found at the point where the downward-sloping demand curve and the upward-sloping supply curve intersect. That is the only price where there is neither a shortage nor a surplus, so that no person has an incentive to change the price asked or offered.

only if offered the inducement of a higher price. (Later chapters in this part of the book will examine the assumptions behind the upward-sloping curve in more detail.)

Equilibrium

The price of $1 per unit is labeled as the *equilibrium price* in the exhibit. It is not hard to remember that the equilibrium is the point where the supply and demand curves intersect. What is more important is to understand *why* that intersection represents an equilibrium.

Simply put, the price of $1.00 is an equilibrium because that is the only one where no person has an incentive to change the price asked or offered for the product. Consider, by contrast, any price higher than $1.00. At a price of, say, $1.20, the quantity supplied would be 500 units and the quantity demanded only 320. There would be a surplus (an excess quantity supplied) of 180 units. Suppliers could not sell all they were willing to offer at that price. Suppliers who were unable to find buyers for their goods would then have an incentive to cut the price at which they offered widgets for sale. As they did so, the quantity demanded would increase and the quantity supplied would decrease. The surplus would gradually be eliminated, and equilibrium would be restored.

In much the same way, there would be an incentive for price changes if the price of widgets were below $1.00. As Exhibit 18.1 is drawn, for example, we see that a price of $.80 would produce a 180-unit shortage. Not all buyers would be able to get as many widgets as they wanted. Unsatisfied buyers would have an incentive to offer higher prices in order not to be left out altogether. Sellers would willingly accept these offers, and the price would rise toward equilibrium. Soon the shortage would disappear.

Changes in Equilibrium

As economic conditions change, the equilibrium price and quantity for the market change also. In analyzing changes in equilibrium, it is important to distinguish between *shifts* in supply or demand curves and movements *along* those curves.

When the quantity demanded of a good changes solely because of a change in the price of that good, the effect is seen as a movement along the good's demand curve. When the quantity demanded changes because something other than its price changes, the change is seen as a shift in the entire demand curve. Changes in buyers' incomes, the prices of substitute or complementary goods, or changes in tastes are all potential sources of shifts in demand curves.

Similarly, a change in the quantity supplied of some good that results solely from a change in the price of that good is shown as a movement along the supply curve. A change in the quantity supplied that is brought about by some other cause is represented as a shift in the supply curve. Changes in costs, as we shall see shortly, are an important source of supply-curve shifts.

These points regarding shifts in curves and movements along curves are illustrated in Exhibit 18.2. In Exhibit 18.2a, an increase in consumer incomes shifts the demand curve for widgets to the right. This creates a shortage of widgets, which in turn drives up the price. As the price rises, the market moves up along the supply curve to the new point of equilibrium. In Exhibit 18.2b, we see a price rise touched off by supply side changes. An increase in labor costs shifts the supply curve upward. This

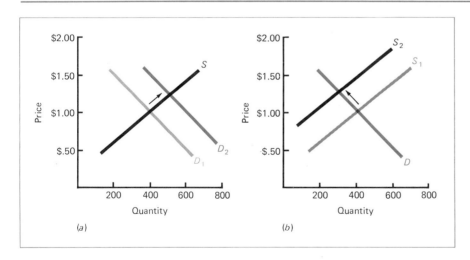

EXHIBIT 18.2

Changes in equilibrium

In Exhibit 18.2a, an increase in consumer incomes shifts the demand curve from the position D_1 to the new position D_2. A shortage is created, which in turn drives up the price. The market moves along the supply curve S to the new equilibrium. In Exhibit 18.2b, an increase in costs shifts the supply curve from S_1 to S_2. The resulting shortage drives up the price until the market has moved along the demand curve D to its new equilibrium.

creates a shortage of widgets at the initial price, which again pushes the price upward. As the price rises, the market moves along the demand curve to the new equilibrium.

Elasticity

We have now encountered many examples in which the quantity supplied or demanded of some good changes when its price changes. Up to now, in most cases we have been concerned only with the direction of the change and not its size. In many cases, though, it is useful to know *how much* quantities supplied or demanded change in response to price changes. Economists have developed measures for such changes. The measures are known as *elasticities*.

The first elasticity measure we shall define is the **price elasticity of demand** (or just **elasticity of demand,** for short). This is the percentage change in the quantity of a good demanded, divided by the percentage change in the price of the good. If, for example, a 10 percent increase in the price of eggs results in a 5 percent decrease in the quantity of eggs demanded, we would say that the price elasticity of demand for eggs is 0.5.

We can define the **price elasticity of supply** of a good in much the same way. It is the percentage change in the quantity of a good supplied, divided by the percentage change in the price of the good. If, for example, a 10 percent increase in the price of shampoo brought about a 25 percent increase in the quantity supplied, we would say that the elasticity of supply for shampoo was 2.5.

Price Elasticity of Demand (Elasticity of Demand) The percentage change in the quantity of a good demanded, divided by the percentage change in the price of the good.

Price Elasticity of Supply (Elasticity of Supply) The percentage change in the quantity of a good supplied, divided by the percentage change in the price of the good.

Elasticity Terminology

Economists use a number of standard terms to refer to various degrees of elasticity of supply and demand. First consider the case in which a 1 percent change in price causes more than a 1 percent change in the quantity supplied or demanded. Numerically, that means an elasticity greater than 1. When the elasticity of demand or supply is greater than 1, we say that demand or supply is **elastic.** An extreme case is possible in which the quantity of a good supplied or demanded can vary without a change in the price. In this case, we say that the supply or demand for the good is **perfectly elastic.** Perfectly elastic supply or demand means a perfectly horizontal supply or demand curve.

If a 1 percent change in price results in less than a 1 percent change in quantity, a good's elasticity of supply or demand will be numerically less than 1. In such a case, we say that supply or demand is **inelastic.** The extreme case occurs when the quantity supplied or demanded does not change at all when the price changes. We then say that supply or demand is **perfectly inelastic.** Perfect inelasticity of supply or demand means a perfectly vertical supply or demand curve.

Between the elastic and the inelastic range of possibilities, there is a case in which a 1 percent change in price results in exactly a 1 percent change in quantity. When the numerical elasticity is equal to 1, we say that supply or demand is **unit elastic.**

Elastic (Demand or Supply) An elasticity that is numerically greater than 1.

Perfectly Elastic (Demand or Supply) The situation where the quantity demanded or supplied can vary without a change in price. Corresponds to a horizontal demand or supply curve. Elasticity undefined numerically.

Inelastic (Demand or Supply) An elasticity numerically less than 1.

Perfectly Inelastic (Demand or Supply) An elasticity numerically equal to 0. No quantity change in response to a price change.

Unit Elastic (Demand or Supply) An elasticity numerically equal to 1.

Determinants of Elasticity

Why is the elasticity of supply or demand high for some goods and low for others? Let us look at the determinants of demand elasticity. The special factors determining supply elasticity will be discussed in later chapters.

One thing helping to determine the elasticity of demand for a good is the importance of substitutes or complements. If a good has close substitutes, demand for that good tends to be elastic. The demand for olive oil is more elastic than it would be if other salad oils were not available as substitutes. The demand for cars is less elastic than it would be if good public transport were available everywhere. If something is a minor complement to an important good, its demand tends to be inelastic. For example, the demand for motor oil tends to be inelastic, because it is a complement to the more important good, gasoline.

Elasticity of demand is also influenced by whether a good is a necessity or a luxury. For example, eating out is a luxury for most people. If restaurant prices go up, it is easy for them to respond by eating out less often. Medical or dental care, in contrast, are considered necessities by most people. Price changes have little effect on the quantity of care consumed.

Elasticity is further influenced by the portion of a person's budget spent on a good. Matches, for example, are no longer really a necessity, and good substitutes exist. Nonetheless, the demand for matches is thought to be very inelastic, just because people spend so little on them that they hardly notice a price change. In contrast, the demand for things like housing and transportation is not perfectly inelastic even though they are necessities. Since they occupy a large part of people's budgets, changes in prices just cannot be ignored.

Finally, elasticity of demand is influenced by the time perspective being considered. Demand is often less elastic in the short run than in the long run. Consider the demand for home heating fuel, for example. In the short run, people find it hard to cut back the quantity they use when the price goes up. They are used to living at a certain temperature, dressing a certain way, and so forth. Given time, though, they may find ways to economize. They can put better insulation in their homes, get in the habit of dressing more warmly, or even move to a warmer climate.

It should be stressed that all of the factors mentioned are only tendencies. Often the tendencies reinforce one another. The classic case of inelastic demand is salt, which has no good substitute, is a necessity, and takes a very small part of one's budget. Sometimes, though, the rules just do not seem to fit. Alcohol and tobacco, which are not necessities and do take a large share of many people's budgets, also are subject to notoriously inelastic demand. When all is said and done, each good is a case in itself.

An Elasticity Formula

One ambiguity needs to be cleared up before our concept of elasticity can be put to work. When prices or quantities change, should we use the value before the change, or the value after the change as a basis for calculating our percentages? If the price of strawberries goes up from $.75 a pint to $1.00 a pint, we normally say that there has been a 33 percent increase in the price. If the price falls from $1.00 to $.75 we usually call that a

25 percent decrease. This convention will not do for calculating elasticities, though. It would mean that the elasticity of supply or demand for berries would be different over the range from $.75 to $1.00 depending on which direction we were moving. That would lead to unnecessary confusion.

A simple compromise can resolve this ambiguity. Rather than using the higher or the lower end of the range, we use the average of the two. If P_1 and P_2 are the prices before and after a change, we calculate the percentage change as

$$\frac{P_1 - P_2}{(P_1 + P_2)/2}$$

In the example just given, the change in the price of strawberries would then be said to be 28.57 percent if the price rose from $.75 to $1.00, and the same if the price fell from $1.00 to $.75.

Defining percentage changes in this way allows us to write a practical formula for calculating elasticities. The formula can be applied to the elasticity of either supply or demand. Using P_1 and Q_1 to represent price and quantity before a change, and P_2 and Q_2 to represent price and quantity after the change, the formula is[1]

$$\text{Elasticity} = \frac{(Q_1 - Q_2)/(Q_1 + Q_2)}{(P_1 - P_2)/(P_1 + P_2)}$$

The reader will notice that when this formula is applied to a downward-sloping demand curve, it gives a negative number for the elasticity of demand. It will be our practice in this book to ignore the minus sign in such cases and to speak of the elasticity of demand for a good as being just two, or one-half, or whatever rather than as minus two or minus one-half. This convention of dropping the minus sign is widely used in economic writing, although it is not followed by all writers.

Varying and Constant Elasticities

A few examples will help familiarize us with the elasticity formula. First let us consider the demand curve shown in Exhibit 18.3. The exhibit shows elasticity measurements taken at two different points along the demand curve. Measured over the price range $8 to $9, the elasticity of demand is 5.66, and measured over the range $2 to $3, it is 0.33. This illustrates the general principle that elasticity declines as one moves down along a straight-line demand curve. It is easy to see why: With a straight-line demand curve, a $1 reduction in price always produces the same absolute increase in quantity demanded. At the upper end of the demand curve, though, a $1 change in price is a small percentage change, while the absolute change in quantity is large as a percentage of the small quantity already demanded. At the lower end of the curve, the situation is reversed. A

---

[1]Given our definition of percentage changes, we could write the elasticity formula as

$$\frac{\dfrac{Q_1 - Q_2}{(Q_1 + Q_2)/2}}{\dfrac{P_1 - P_2}{(P_1 + P_2)/2}}$$

This is unnecessarily complicated, however, because the 2's cancel out. The formula given in the text is the simplified equivalent of this one.

EXHIBIT 18.3

Elasticity on a straight-line demand curve

When the demand curve is a straight line, elasticity of demand falls as we move down along the curve. The calculations shown in the exhibit confirm this. Note that in applying the elasticity formula, we ignore the minus sign in the result.

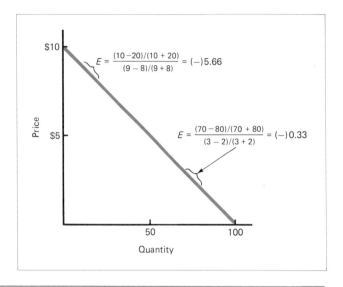

$$E = \frac{(10-20)/(10 + 20)}{(9 - 8)/(9 + 8)} = (-)5.66$$

$$E = \frac{(70-80)/(70 + 80)}{(3 - 2)/(3 + 2)} = (-)0.33$$

$1 change is now a large percentage of the price, while the constant absolute increase in quantity has become smaller in percentage terms. Because it is percentages, not absolute amounts, that count in elasticity calculations, elasticity is lower near the bottom of the curve than near the top. Because elasticity changes as we move along a straight-line demand curve, it makes sense to apply the formula only to small changes.

If the demand curve is not a straight line, though, this reasoning need not always apply. There is an important special case in which the demand curve has just the curvature needed to keep elasticity constant throughout its length. One such demand curve is shown in Exhibit 18.4. As the calculations in the exhibit show, elasticity is exactly 1.0 everywhere on this curve. It is possible to construct demand curves with constant elasticities of any desired value. Such demand curves are important in econometric work, as we shall see shortly.

EXHIBIT 18.4

A demand curve with constant elasticity

It is possible for a demand curve to have constant elasticity throughout its length. The calculations in the exhibit show that this curve has an elasticity of 1.0 wherever it is measured. This particular demand curve is a rectangular hyperbola with the formula $P \times Q = 100$.

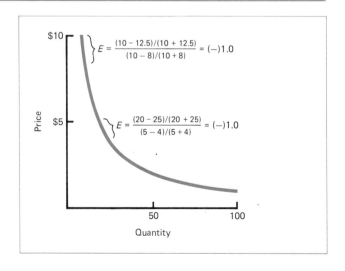

$$E = \frac{(10 - 12.5)/(10 + 12.5)}{(10 - 8)/(10 + 8)} = (-)1.0$$

$$E = \frac{(20 - 25)/(20 + 25)}{(5 - 4)/(5 + 4)} = (-)1.0$$

Elasticity and Revenue

There is an important relationship between the elasticity of demand and the way that total revenue changes as the price of a good changes. If you have ever had a job selling anything, you probably known of this relationship, whether you have ever thought of it in terms of elasticity or not. Let us say that you work for New York City, and want to find a way to raise more money for the city budget. One way to get more money might be to change the subway fare, but should it be raised or lowered? That depends on the elasticity of demand for subway rides. A 10 percent decrease in fares is sure to attract more riders, but unless there is more than a 10 percent increase in riders, total revenue will fall. A 10 percent increase in fares will bring in more money per rider, but if more than 10 percent of the riders are lost, revenue will fall. It is clear, then, that a price cut will increase revenue only if demand is elastic, and a price increase will raise revenue only if demand is inelastic. New York City officials seem to believe that the demand for subway rides is inelastic; they raise fares every time they need more money for the city budget.

Exhibit 18.5 gives a graphical demonstration of elasticity and revenue. Total revenue is always equal to price times quantity sold. That means that the total revenue earned at any point on a demand curve is equal to the area of a rectangle drawn between that point and the axes. In Exhibit 18.5a, for example, we see that the area of the rectangle drawn from point A is 12, while that drawn from point B is 15. Moving from A to B along the demand curve, revenue increases by 3 units. We see, then, that demand is elastic over the range A to B on this demand curve.

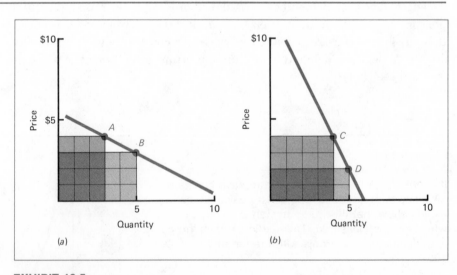

EXHIBIT 18.5

Revenue and elasticity of demand

When demand is elastic, revenue increases as price decreases. Exhibit 18.5a illustrates this case. Note how the revenue rectangle increases in area from point A to point B on the demand curve. When demand is inelastic, revenue decreases as price decreases. This is shown in Exhibit 18.5b, where the revenue rectangle decreases in area from C to D.

In contrast, look at Exhibit 18.5*b*. The rectangle under *C* has an area of 16, and that under *d* an area of only 10. Revenue falls as we move from *C* to *D* along this demand curve, so demand must be inelastic there.

Measuring Elasticity

Decision makers in business and government often would like to know what the elasticity of demand is for particular products. Sometimes econometricians are able to give them useful statistical estimates. The following case study illustrates the problems of measuring demand elasticity.

CASE 18.1
Measuring Elasticity of Demand
in the Cotton Market[2]

The market for cotton has tended to be relatively unstable in the postwar period. Price changes from one year to the next have often been very great. It is thought that one of the reasons for this instability is a very inelastic demand for cotton. With an inelastic demand, the price must fall a long way for producers to dispose of a relatively small surplus, and a considerable rise in price can occur when there is a shortage. Kenneth Lewis, an economist at Boston University, thought that it would be useful for those concerned with the cotton market to know just how inelastic demand was.

Lewis began by assembling data on the price of cotton and the quantity of cotton purchased in sixteen industrialized countries during the period from 1949 to 1964. To simplify his calculations, he followed a common econometric practice, and assumed that the cotton demand curve would have the shape needed to give constant elasticity throughout the normal range of prices. Next he had to deal with the problem of "other things being equal." A demand curve tells how the demand for cotton responds to the price for cotton when nothing else changes, but in the wide range of countries and years represented in Lewis's data, "other things" could hardly be expected to stand still. To deal with this problem, he used a statistical technique known as multiple regression analysis. This allowed an approximate correction for changes that had occurred over time in population, per capita consumer income, and the prices of other closely related products, particularly wool and synthetic fibers.

Lewis's statistical results confirmed that the demand for cotton was very inelastic—only 0.095, as nearly as he could estimate. This meant that more than a 10 percent change in price from one year to the next would be required to change the quantity demanded by 1 percent. Lewis suggested two reasons for the low elasticity of demand. One was that cotton is a raw material that often accounts for only a small portion of the value of a final product. For example, a 10 percent change in the price of cotton would have far less than a 10 percent effect on the price of a cotton shirt if the cost of manufacturing, labor, transportation, retailing, services, and the like remained unchanged. Second, the products made from cotton were themselves necessities rather than luxuries, for the most part, and hence they too could be expected to have low elasticities of demand.

[2]Based on Kenneth Lewis, "Multi-Market Demand Functions in the presence of Supply Constraints: International Demand for Cotton and Wool," *Southern Economic Journal*, vol. 38, no. 2.

It is important to recognize the limitations of statistical estimates of demand elasticity. To say that the elasticity of demand for cotton is 0.095 is not to measure any inherent quality of the good itself. Neither is the measured demand elasticity a true constant of consumer behavior. The actual measurement tells us only that over some range of particular times and places in the past, a 1 percent change in price appears to have been associated with approximately a 0.095 percent change in quantity demanded. Statistical estimates of demand elasticity are useful despite their limitations, however. Businesspeople and other economic decision makers must take past experience into account when planning for the future even though they know that market conditions in the future will not be *exactly* like the past.

Conclusions

In reviewing the basics of supply and demand, this chapter has set the stage for asking a great many questions. First, we need to ask what really lies behind the supply and demand curves. We have given these curves general common sense explanations, but now we need to see how they can be explained in terms of individual people's attempts to deal with the problems of scarcity and choice. That job will occupy us for the next seven chapters. Beyond that, though, we also need to know the limitations of supply and demand analysis. In the last three chapters of this part of the book, we shall enter territory where the law of supply and demand does not apply precisely. In particular, we shall find that in markets dominated by private monopolies or government regulators, our tools of supply and demand must be modified if they are to be of any help at all. We shall not discard them altogether by any means, though. Later, in Parts Four through Seven, we shall put them to work again and again.

SUMMARY

1. According to the law of demand, the quantity demanded of a product increases as its price decreases. It is also widely the case that sellers of a good are willing to increase the quantity supplied only if offered the inducement of a higher price. Where these conditions hold, there will be a market equilibrium price at the intersection of a good's supply and demand curves. That intersection represents the only price at which no one has an incentive to change the price asked or offered.
2. For some goods, a 1 percent change in price produces more than a 1 percent change in quantity supplied or demanded. Such goods are said to have elastic supply or demand. At the extreme, where supply or demand curves are horizontal, supply or demand is said to be perfectly elastic. For other goods, a 1 percent change in price will cause less than a 1 percent change in quantity supplied or demanded. Such goods are said to have inelastic demand or supply. Perfectly inelastic demand or supply means a vertical supply or demand curve.
3. The formula for calculating the elasticity of supply or demand between two points on a supply or demand curve is

$$\frac{(Q_1 - Q_2)/(Q_1 + Q_2)}{(P_1 - P_2)/(P_1 + P_2)}$$

In applying this formula to demand, it is conventional to drop the minus sign from the result, and consider elasticity to be a positive number.
4. For a good with elastic demand, revenue increases as the price decreases. For a good with inelastic demand, revenue increases as the price increases. If the demand for a good is unit elastic, a change in price will have no effect on revenue.

DISCUSSION QUESTIONS

1. How much of each of the following goods or services do you buy now in comparison with the quantity you bought a year ago?
   a. Clothing
   b. Movie tickets
   c. Gasoline
   d. Beer
   If the quantity you buy has changed for any of these, do you think the change is best described as a movement along your demand curve, a shift in your demand curve, or some combination of the two?
2. How do firms and consumers recognize market disequilibrium in the real world? What are the specific, tangible signs of a surplus or shortage?
3. If you were the president of a union bargaining for a new contract and asking for higher wages, would you prefer that the demand for your firm's product were relatively elastic or relatively inelastic? Why?
4. Suppose that again, as in 1974, Middle Eastern governments cut off imports of petroleum products into the United States, and that our government imposed a price ceiling. Do you think the lines that formed at gas stations would be longer if the demand for gasoline were relatively elastic, or if it were relatively inelastic? (You may wish to refer to Exhibit 3.8.)
5. Let us suppose that the supply of tobacco were relatively elastic and the demand relatively inelastic. Under these conditions, who do you think would protest an increase in the cigarette tax more strongly, consumers or producers? What if the elasticities were reversed? (You may wish to refer to Exhibit 4.6.)
6. The town manager of River City calls you in as a consultant to explain something he cannot understand. Last year, the city doubled fares on its downtown buses. For a few months, the bus line reported a strong increase in revenue, but then revenues began falling off and ended up lower than they had been to begin with. Does what you have learned about elasticity of demand and the determinants of elasticity of demand help you explain what happened?
7. Do you think it makes sense as a general principle to say that the demand for a broadly defined good, such as cars, clothing, or meat, will be less elastic than the demand for a corresponding narrowly defined good, such as Fords, Levi's, or pork chops? Why?
8. Why would the slope of a demand curve not be just as good a measure as elasticity for the responsiveness of demand to price changes? Can you formulate a simple generalization relating the slope of a demand curve to the way in which total revenue changes when the price changes?

CHAPTER 19
The Logic of Consumer Choice

What You Will Learn in This Chapter
The law of demand tells us that people tend to buy more of a good when its price goes down. This law can be justified by common sense and everyday experience, but for some purposes, a closer look is worthwhile. A study of the logic of consumer choice shows what lies behind the law of demand, and at the same time helps us to understand how consumers deal with the universal problem of scarcity.

For Review
Here are some important terms and concepts that will be put to use in this chapter. Be certain that you understand them, or review them before proceeding.

    Law of demand (Chapter 3)
    Normal and inferior goods (Chapter 19)

By now we are quite familiar with the law of demand. We are used to the idea that when the price of a good goes down, the quantity of that good demanded by consumers tends to go up. The law of demand is easy to accept, because our own common sense and everyday experience tell us that is the way things are.

Still, knowing that a thing is so does not keep us from asking *why* is it so. In Newton's day, everyone knew that when apples fell from trees, they fell down and not up. Nonetheless, Newton asked *why* they fell down and not up, and this led him to some valuable new insights about the laws of gravitation. In the same way, economists have often asked *why* people buy more of a good when its price falls. Trying to answer that question leads to some useful new insights too, as we shall see.

Consumption and Utility

The most basic question we might ask about the law of demand is why people have any demand at all for goods and services. The answer seems to be that people want material goods and services because they get pleasure and satisfaction from them. A loaf of bread to eat, a warm bed to sleep in,

Utility The economist's term for the pleasure, satisfaction, and need fulfillment that we get from the consumption of material goods and services.

or a book to read; each serves our needs or desires in one way or another. Economists have their own term for this sort of thing. They say that the use or consumption of material goods gives us **utility.**

Utility and Psychological Needs

To a psychologist, just saying that people want things because they get utility from them would sound like a very shallow answer. Some psychologists, at least, would want to go into detail about the nature and sources of human wants. Followers of Abraham Maslow, for example, find it useful to think in terms of five basic kinds of needs. These are (1) physiological needs, (2) safety and security needs, (3) affection and belongingness needs, (4) the need for self-esteem and the esteem of others, and (5) the need for "self-actualization" or self-fulfillment.[1] For each person the order of importance of these five needs is different.

This simple list of needs raises some important questions for psychologists. Is there a hierarchy among needs? Why is any given need more important to some people than to others? What factors in people's upbringing affect the needs they seek to satisfy in later life? Questions like these, however, get very little attention from economists. Smith may buy a tennis racket to satisfy a psychological need for exercise. Jones may buy one in order to gratify a belongingness need by joining a tennis club. Baker may buy a racket in order to gain the esteem of others by playing in tournaments. What is true of tennis rackets is true of other goods and services too. People with very different psychological hang-ups all have one thing in common. They get utility of one sort or another from material goods. Most economists feel that they do not really need to know any more psychology than that.

Diminishing Marginal Utility

Economists may not be interested in the origins of human wants, but they are interested in the intensity of those wants. What determines whether a person wants an apple strongly enough to pay $.25 for it, or a car strongly enough to pay $5,000 for it? The economist's answer to questions like these begins with something called the **principle of diminishing marginal utility.** This principle says simply that the greater the rate at which we consume some good, the smaller the increase in utility we get from a unit increase in our rate of consumption.

Diminishing Marginal Utility (principle of) The greater our rate of consumption of some good, the smaller the increase in utility we get from a unit increase in our rate of consumption.

For a simple illustration of diminishing marginal utility, imagine a boy in a blackberry patch eating berries by the handful. As he eats more and more berries, he gets more and more satisfaction, but at the same time, the satisfaction from each new handful diminishes. If he eats enough, he may even get to a point where more berries give him no additional utility at all. He then stops eating, at least until the next day.

Imagine that we could somehow tap into the boy's brain circuits and measure the amount of utility he gets from each handful of berries. That would allow us to construct tables and figures like those shown in Exhibit

[1]See Abraham Maslow, *Motivation and Personality,* (2nd ed). (New York: Harper & Row, 1970).

EXHIBIT 19.1

Diminishing marginal utility

As our rate of consumption of a product goes up, the utility we get from an added unit (marginal utility) declines. The table and figures here show that as the rate of consumption of berries increases, total utility increases, but at a decreasing rate. In *b,* a smooth curve is drawn through the stair-step total utility line, which is based on the table. Part *c* of this exhibit shows a marginal utility curve. The height of this curve at each point is equal to the slope of the smooth curve in *b.*

Exhibit 19.1*a*

Quantity of Berries (Handfuls per Day)	Total Utility ("Utils")	Marginal Utility (Utils per Handful)
1	3	
		2½
2	5½	
		2
3	7½	
		1½
4	9	
		1
5	10	
		½
6	10½	

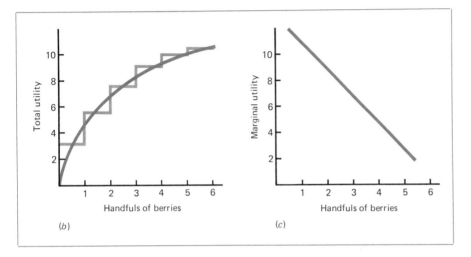

(b)   (c)

19.1. In these figures and tables, we use the "util" as an imaginary unit for measuring satisfaction. Both the table and the graphs show that as the quantity of berries consumed per day increases, total utility increases, but at a decreasing rate. Marginal utility, that is, the added utility obtained from each additional handful of berries, falls as the rate of consumption increases. We see, for example, that the third handful of berries increases utility by 2 units, from 5½ to 7½, while the fourth handful gives only 1½ utils more.

Consumer Equilibrium

For better or for worse, the world is not all one big blackberry patch, where we can eat as much as we want without making choices. To put the principle of diminishing marginal utility to work, we need a world a bit more like our own. More exactly, we need a world in which four things are true: First there are many different desirable goods. Second, consumers must pay fixed prices for everything they want. Third, consumers have limited budgets. And fourth, they try to get the greatest satisfaction they can from the limited budgets they have.

Consider some consumers in such a world who are deciding how to balance their spending between, say, food and clothing. If they spend an extra dollar a month on food, they get a certain added utility from doing so. At the same time, though, they must bear an opportunity cost equal to

William Stanley Jevons
(1835–1882)

The English economist William Stanley Jevons is generally credited with the first systematic exposition of the theory of marginal utility and with its first application to the problem of consumer equilibrium. Jevons was trained in mathematics and chemistry. With this background, it is not surprising that when his interest turned to economics, he would try to strengthen that science by restating its theories in mathematical form. It was this mathematical reworking of economics that led him to the theory of marginal utility.

Although Jevons wrote many books and papers, he is best remembered for his *Theory of Political Economy,* published in 1871. There he set forth the principle of diminishing marginal utility using this illustration:

> Let us imagine the whole quantity of food which a person consumes on an average during twenty-four hours to be divided into ten equal parts. If his food be reduced by the last part, he will suffer but little; if a second tenth part be deficient, he will feel the want distinctly; the subtraction of the third part will be decidedly injurious; with every subsequent subtraction of a tenth part his sufferings will be more and more serious, until at length he will be upon the verge of starvation. Now, if we call each of the tenth parts *an increment,* the meaning of these facts is, that each increment of food is less necessary, or possesses less utility, than the previous one.

Jevons was the first to put the new theory in print, but he must share credit for the "marginal revolution" in economics with at least three others who were working independently along the same lines at the same time. The Austrian Karl Menger published his version of marginal utility theory, also in 1871. Three years later the Swiss economist Leon Walras, who did not know of either Jevon's or Menger's work, came out with still another version. Finally, Alfred Marshall seems to have worked out the basics of marginal analysis about the same time, although his own major work was not published until 1890.

Jevons had a strong interest in applied economics as well as in pure theory. He wrote on Australian gold mining, on the problem of Britain's coal reserves, on monetary questions, and on issues of social reform. As a consultant to the British government, he successfully recommended the abolition of the import duty on corn. In 1880, he resigned his teaching position at the University of London to devote full time to research. Sadly for the science of economics, however, this prolific writer died in a boating accident just two years later, at the age of 47.

the utility they could have obtained by spending the dollar on clothing instead. Whether they actually spend the marginal dollar on food or clothing, then, depends on which utility is greater, that of an added dollar's worth of food, or that of an added dollar's worth of clothing.

Which is greater, the marginal utility of food or of clothing, depends on how much of each good is consumed. If people have relatively a lot of clothing and relatively little food, the marginal utility of clothing would tend to be low and that of food high. By shifting a dollar from clothing to food, they could give up a small marginal utility and gain a large one, thus increasing their total utility. If instead, they had relatively much food and little clothing, the marginal utilities might be reversed. They would get a lot of good from spending an extra dollar on clothing and lose little by giving up a dollar's worth of food. They could gain in total utility by redirecting their expenditures from food without spending any more over all.

We see, then, that if the marginal utility of a dollar's worth of clothing is different from that of a dollar's worth of food, consumers have an incentive to change their pattern of consumption. Only if the marginal utility per dollar's worth of the two goods is the same will people be getting the most possible total utility from their limited budgets. In that case, they will have no incentive to change their pattern of consumption. We can say that they are in **consumer equilibrium.**

Consumer Equilibrium A state of affairs in which consumers cannot increase the total utility they obtain from a given budget by shifting expenditure from one kind of good to another. In consumer equilibrium, the marginal utility of a dollar's worth of one good must be equal to the marginal utility of a dollar's worth of any other.

Alternate Statement

There is another, equivalent way to state the condition for consumer equilibrium. Suppose that the marginal utility of, say, a dollar's worth of butter is equal to that of a dollar's worth of bread. It must also be true, then, that the marginal utility of a pound of butter, divided by the price of butter per pound, is equal to the marginal utility of a loaf of bread, divided by the price of bread per loaf. In equation form, this comes out as

$$\frac{\text{Marginal Utility of Butter}}{\text{Price of Butter}} = \frac{\text{Marginal Utility of Bread}}{\text{Price of Bread}}$$

Suppose, for example, that butter costs $1.00 per pound and bread costs $.25 per loaf. If the equation just given holds, then we know that an extra pound of butter will give four times as much added utility to the consumer as an extra loaf of bread. That also means, of course, that the marginal utility of a dollar's worth (one pound) of butter is equal to the marginal utility of a dollar's worth (four loaves) of bread.

Our equation can be extended to a world with any number of goods and services. We use MU_a, MU_b, and so forth, to stand for the marginal utilities of goods A, B, and so forth. Likewise, P_a, P_b, and so forth, stand for the prices of the various goods. Our general expression for consumer equilibrium then becomes

$$\frac{MU_a}{P_a} = \frac{MU_b}{P_b} = \frac{MU_c}{P_c} = \frac{MU_d}{P_d} = \ldots$$

Consumer Equilibrium and Demand

The concept of consumer equilibrium can help us to understand the relationship between the principle of diminishing marginal utility and the law of demand. Suppose that a person is in consumer equilibrium with butter at $1.00 per pound and bread at $.25 per loaf. We know, then, that

$$\frac{MU_{\text{butter}}}{\$1.00} = \frac{MU_{\text{bread}}}{\$.25}$$

If the price of bread falls to $.20, this equality will be upset. Equilibrium can be restored, though, if the marginal utility of bread can be made to fall by the same proportion that the price of bread has fallen. The principle of diminishing marginal utility tells us that we can get the marginal utility of bread to go down by consuming more bread. The way back to equilibrium is clear. When the price of bread falls, one buys more bread until once again a dollar's worth of that good yields no more utility than a dollar's worth of any other.

Substitution Effect That part of the increase in quantity demanded of a good whose price has fallen that can be traced directly to the principle of diminishing marginal utility, not taking into account the change in real income resulting from the change in price.

Income Effect That part of the change in quantity demanded of a good whose price has fallen that can be traced directly to the change in real income resulting from the price change.

Substitution and Income Effect

Diminishing marginal utility tells us that when the price of a good drops, a person will tend to buy more of it in the course of restoring consumer equilibrium. This tendency is known as the **substitution effect,** because the cheaper good is substituted for those whose price has not fallen.

The substitution effect fits in well with what we know about the law of demand. It does not give quite the whole story, though. When the price of a good falls, there is another effect too. A drop in the price of one good, when the price of other goods remains unchanged, increases the real value of a consumer's income or budget. A change in income, as we already know, can also affect the quantity demanded of a good. How the quantity demanded of bread is affected by the rise in real income produced by a fall in the price of bread depends on whether bread is a normal or an inferior good. If bread is a normal good, the rise in income will cause a further increase in the quantity of bread demanded. If it is an inferior good, the rise in real income will tend to cause a decrease in the quantity demanded. In either case, the change in quantity demanded that results from the change in real income produced by a change in the price of bread is called the **income effect.**

Law of Demand

Now we can see the full scope of the relationship between diminishing marginal utility and the law of demand. When the price of a good falls, diminishing marginal utility, through the substitution effect, will tend to bring about an increase in the quantity of that good demanded. If we are dealing with a normal good, this tendency will be reinforced by the income effect, and the fall in price will produce an even stronger increase in the quantity demanded. If, on the other hand, we are dealing with an inferior good, the income effect will work in the opposite direction of the substitution effect, reducing the amount by which the quantity demanded goes up. Except in very unusual cases, the substitution effect will be strong enough to guarantee at least a small increase in the quantity demanded of an inferior good when the price of that good falls. Whatever kind of good we are dealing with, then, diminishing marginal utility reinforces our common sense faith in the law of demand. Exceptions to the law of demand must be so rare as to be of little practical importance.

Evidence

Much of the evidence we have concerning the theory set forth in this chapter is subjective. We found the principle of diminishing marginal utility, the substitution effect, and the law of demand plausible because we feel that they reflect the way we ourselves behave as consumers. Many economists are content to let the theory stand on a foundation of subjective evidence, but not all. Over the years, there have been repeated attempts to expose the theory to various empirical tests.

Most of these attempts at testing have used human subjects. Experimenters have set up games or artificial economies in which the subects "buy" goods or services with tokens, or something of the sort. The results of such experiments have always been clouded by certain difficulties, though. Human subjects are hard to use. It is impossible to find subjects free of past experience with a market economy. It is impossible for them not to know that they are only playing a game. It is difficult or very expensive to continue the experiments for long. And, it is hard to shut out all outside influences.

In an attempt to surmount these difficulties, a group of experimenters at Texas A & M and the State University of New York at Stony Brook recently took a dramatic new approach. Instead of using human subjects to test the theory of human behavior, they used ordinary laboratory rats! Their methods and some of their results are sketched in the following case study.

CASE 19.1
Testing Consumer Demand Theory with White Rats[2]

Two white male albino rats were placed in standard laboratory cages, with food and water freely available. At one end of each cage there were two levers that activated dipper cups. One dipper cup provided a measured quantity of root beer when the lever was depressed, and the other a measured quantity of collins mix. Previous experimentation had shown that rats prefer these beverages to water.

Within this setup, each rat could be given a fixed "income" of so many pushes on the levers per day. The pushes could be distributed in any way between the two levers. Experimenters could also control the "price" of root beer and collins mix by determining the number of pushes the rat had to "spend" to obtain 1 milliliter of liquid.

In an initial experimental run lasting 2 weeks, the rats were given an income of 300 pushes per day, and both beverages were priced at 20 pushes per milliliter. Under these conditions, rat 1 settled down to a pattern of drinking about 11 milliliters of root beer per day and about 4 milliliters of collins mix. Rat 2 preferred a diet of almost all root beer, averaging less than 1 milliliter of collins mix per day.

Next came the crucial test. By manipulating incomes and prices, could the rats be induced to shift their consumption patterns in the way economic theory predicts? To see if they would, the experimenters proceeded as follows. First, the price of root beer was doubled and the price of collins mix cut in half. At the same time, each subject's total income of pushes was adjusted to make it possible to afford to continue the previous consumption pattern if it should be chosen. (This adjustment in total income was made in order to eliminate any possible *income effect* of the price change, and concentrate solely on the *substitution effect*.) Economic theory predicts that under the new conditions, the rats would choose to consume more collins mix and less root beer than before, even though they would have the opportunity not to change their behavior.

The rats' behavior exactly fitted these predictions. In 2 weeks of living under the new conditions, rat 1 settled down to a new consumption pattern of about 8 milliliters of root beer and 17 milliliters of collins mixer per day. Rat 2, which had chosen root beer almost exclusively before, switched over to about 9 milliliters of root beer and 25 milliliters of collins mixer.

[2]Based on John H. Kagel, Raymond C. Battalio, Howard Rachlin, Leionard Green, Robert L. Basemann and W. R. Klemm, "Experimental Studies of Consumer Demand Behavior," *Economic Inquiry*, Vol. 8, No. 1 (March 1975), pp. 22–38. Reprinted by permission.

This fascinating experiment can hardly be taken as the ultimate proof of the economic theory of consumer choice. Further experiments carried out with the same rats pointed to possible limitations of the theory and suggested important directions for more research. In its way, though, the experiment gave more impressive evidence in favor of the theory than any experiment with human subjects could. The complete control over the environment of the subjects permitted the problem of consumer choice to be reduced to its absolute basics. The results of the experiments certainly correspond to our subjective feelings about what *we* would do if put in those cages.

Conclusions

In conclusion, it is fair to ask what good are these theories of marginal utility and consumer equilibrium. In terms of practical application, the answer must be that they are not very useful. The theories do not describe the way consumers actually think about the choices they make. They do not permit policy makers to help consumers make the right choices. If we could actually measure utility (perhaps by stitching a "utility meter" to each person's forehead), such practical applications might be possible. Without a utility meter, they are not.

The value of the theories of marginal utility and consumer equilibrium, then, lies elsewhere. Rather than producing practical applications, these theories produce insight and understanding. They help us understand how consumers deal with the universal economic problem of choosing among alternative uses for scarce resources. They give a deeper insight into the logic of our familiar law of demand. These things are important enough to keep the ideas of marginal utility and consumer equilibrium alive as a basic part of modern economics.

SUMMARY

1. People demand goods and services because they get utility from them. Psychologists are able to identify many different reasons why material goods and services give us utility. The same good may fulfill different needs for different people. Economists do not usually find it necessary to distinguish the various possible sources of utility. They are interested only in whether people want a good enough to pay for it, not in why they want it.
2. The increase in utility we get from a one-unit increase in our rate of consumption of some good is called the marginal utility of that good. As our rate of consumption of any good increases, the marginal utility of that good tends to decrease.
3. Consumer equilibrium is a state of affairs in which people cannot increase the utility they get from a given budget by shifting expenditure from one good to another. Consumer equilibrium requires that the marginal utility of a dollar's worth of any one good be equal to the marginal utility of a dollar's worth of any other. Alternatively, the condition for consumer equilibrium can be expressed in the form of the equation

$$\frac{MU_a}{P_a} = \frac{MU_b}{P_b} = \frac{MU_c}{P_c} = \frac{MU_d}{P_d} = \cdots$$

where the MU's stand for marginal utilities of various goods and the P's the prices of those goods.
4. The principle of diminishing marginal utility accounts for the substitution effect of a change in the price of a good. Because of the substitution effect,

the quantity demanded of a good tends to increase when its price decreases. In the case of inferior goods, though, this tendency is partially offset by the income effect of the price change.

DISCUSSION QUESTIONS

1. Is it true for all goods that more is always better than less? Or are there some situations in which marginal utility could become negative? Discuss.
2. Suppose that you have a room that will require 8 rolls of wallpaper to decorate. If someone gave you 7 rolls of wallpaper, you would not get much satisfaction. Roll number 8, however, would be very much appreciated. Do you think that this is a valid counterexample to the law of diminishing marginal utility?
3. Who is your favorite classical or popular musician? Do you think a concert by this person that lasted 30 minutes would give you more than ten times as much satisfaction as a concert lasting just 3 minutes? More than sixty times as much satisfaction as a concert lasting just 30 seconds? Would you even bother to go to a concert lasting just 30 seconds, even if it were free? What does all this have to do with diminishing marginal utility?
4. Martha Smith consumes 2 pounds of pork and 5 pounds of beef per month. She pays $1.50 per pound for the pork and $2.00 per pound for the beef. What inference can you draw about the ratio

$$\frac{\text{Martha's Marginal Utility per Pound of Pork}}{\text{Martha's Marginal Utility per Pound of Beef}}$$

Is this ratio equal to $\frac{3}{4}$, $\frac{4}{3}$, $\frac{5}{2}$, $\frac{2}{5}$, or none of those alternatives?
5. What would happen to the quantity you demanded of each of the following if its price rose while all other prices remained unchanged?
   a. The price of your favorite soft drink?
   b. The price of all forms of transportation?
   c. The price of Greyhound bus tickets?
   d. The price of Levi's (the genuine brand only)?
   In each case, how much of the change in quantity demanded would be attributable to the income effect and how much to the substitution effect?
6. In Chapter 3 we told this curious story: "A family who lives in Minnesota spends each January in Florida. One year the price of home heating fuel goes up sharply. They turn their thermostat down a little, but even so, their heating bill for September through December goes up so much that they cannot afford to go to Florida that year. Staying home in January means that they have to keep the house heated during that month instead of closing it down, so the total quantity of fuel they burn for the whole season actually increases as a result of the rise in the price of fuel." We said then that this example was a genuine exception to the law of demand. Analyze it in terms of the income effect and the substitution effect. Do you understand the example more fully now?
7. Imagine that you were the director of a slave-labor camp, and that you were a thick-skinned, antihumanitarian person with absolutely no regard whatsoever for the comfort or welfare of your charges. Do you think you could design an experiment to test the laws of consumer behavior using your prisoners as subjects? What possible pitfalls would you encounter that an experimenter using rats would not encounter? What advantages or disadvantages would you have compared with an experimenter who was restricted to the use of paid human volunteers?

Appendix
An Introduction to
Indifference Curves

Marginal utility gives us one way to approach the theory of consumer choice. There is also another way. The alternative approach is known as the method of indifference curves.

Indifference curves are not really among the minimum set of tools we need to understand economics. Nonetheless, they turn up very frequently in intermediate and advanced-level economic writings. Many students and teachers find it worthwhile to make their acquaintance as part of an introductory course. This appendix will serve the needs of interested readers.

Preference and Indifference

Suppose that we wish to study how a certain consumer feels about consuming various amounts of meat and cheese. Could we begin by offering him a basket containing 8 pounds of meat and 3 pounds of cheese and asking him how much utility he would get from it? No. This would not work, because people are not in the habit of thinking of utility in numerical terms. Besides, even if our subject told us that he would get 28 "utils" from basket *A*, we would not be much better off, because we do not know how big a unit of measurement a "util" represents for him.

A different way to proceed would be to offer him two baskets, *A* and *B*, at the same time. We would then ask him only to tell us whether he *preferred A* to *B, preferred B to A,* or was *indifferent between A* and *B.* The notions of preference and indifference are a good deal closer to the way that people really think about things than are ideas about measuring utility numerically. The chances are much better that we would get a sensible answer.

Indifference Sets

The first basket we offered (*A*) had 8 pounds of meat and 3 pounds of cheese. Suppose that the second basket (*B*) contained 6 pounds of meat and 4 pounds of cheese, and that our subject told us that he felt altogether indifferent between the two. He would be just as satisfied to have 8 pounds of meat and 3 pounds of cheese as to have 6 pounds of meat and 4 pounds of cheese. The extra pound of cheese in basket *B* would just make up for the fact that it had 2 fewer pounds of meat than *A.* This reply tells us that basket *A* and *B* belong to what we call an **indifference set.** This means a set of consumption alternatives each yielding the same amount of satisfaction, so that no member of the set is preferred to any other.

Exploring matters further, suppose we found that these additional consumption baskets also belonged to the indifference set containing *A* and *B:*

Indifference Set A set of consumption alternatives each yielding the same utility, so that no member of the set is preferred to any other.

Basket	Meat	Cheese
A	8	3
B	6	4
C	5	5
D	4	7

With this data in hand, we can draw a geometrical indifference curve. First we draw a set of coordinate axes as in Exhibit 19.2. Pounds of meat are measured on

EXHIBIT 19.2

An indifference curve

Each point in this diagram stands for a basket of meat and cheese. *A, B, C,* and *D* are all baskets among which a certain consumer is indifferent. All give him equal utility. Those points, and all the others on a smooth curve connecting them, constitute an indifference set. An indifference curve, such as the one shown here, is a graphical representation of an indifference set.

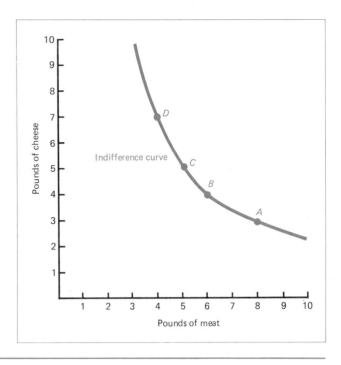

the horizontal axis and pounds of cheese on the vertical. Each basket of goods can be shown as a point in the area between the two axes. The points representing baskets *A* through *D* are shown in their proper spots in the diagram. These points and all the points in between them lying on the smooth curve that has been sketched in joining them are members of the same indifference set. The curve itself is an **indifference curve.** This we define as a curve composed entirely of points that are all members of a single indifference set.

Indifference Curve A graphical representation of an indifference set.

Some Properties of Indifference Curves

Indifference curves have properties that reflect certain basic regularities in patterns of consumer preferences. Five of these properties are of particular interest.

1. Indifference curves have downward (negative) slopes. For example, the curve sketched in Exhibit 19.3 is not a possible shape if both *X* and *Y* are desirable goods. The consumption basket shown by point *A* contains more of both goods than the one shown by point *B*. That implies that if greater quantities of goods *X* and *Y* give greater satisfaction, *A* must be *preferred* to *B*. It cannot then be a member of the same indifference set as *B*.

2. The absolute value of the slope of an indifference curve at any point represents the ratio of the marginal utility of the good on the horizontal axis to the marginal utility of the good on the vertical axis. For an example, refer back to Exhibit 19.2. Between *D* and *C*, the slope of the curve is approximately −2, or simply 2 when the minus sign is removed to give the absolute value. This tells us that the marginal utility of meat is approximately twice the marginal utility of cheese for this consumer, when the quantities consumed are in the area of baskets *C* and *D*. Because the marginal utility of meat is twice that of cheese in this region, the consumer would feel neither gain nor loss in total utility in trading basket *D* for basket *C*, which means giving up 2 pounds of cheese for 1 extra pound of meat. Because it tells us the rate at which meat can be substituted for cheese without gain or loss in satisfaction, the slope of the indifference curve is called the **marginal rate of substitution** of meat for cheese.

Marginal Rate of Substitution The rate at which one good can be substituted for another without gain or loss in satisfaction. Equal to the slope of an indifference curve at any point.

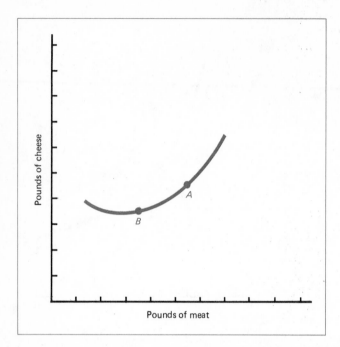

EXHIBIT 19.3
An "impossible" upward-sloping indifference curve
Indifference curves normally have negative slopes. The upward-sloping portion of the indifference curve shown here is impossible if both goods give increased satisfaction with increased quantity. A has more of both goods than B. Point A should thus be preferred to point B.

3. Indifference curves are convex; that is, their slope decreases as one moves down and to the right along them. The convexity results from diminishing marginal utility. Look once more at Exhibit 19.2. In the region between D and C, the slope of the curve is approximately -2, indicating that the ratio of the marginal utility of meat to that of cheese is approximately 2:1. By comparison, in the neighborhood between B and A, the slope is only about $-\frac{1}{2}$. This is because the consumer has more meat there, causing the marginal utility of meat to fall, and less cheese, causing the marginal utility of cheese to rise. The ratio of the decreased marginal utility of meat to the increased marginal utility of cheese is now approximately 1:2.

4. An indifference curve can be drawn through the point that represents any basket of goods whatsoever. Consider Exhibit 19.4. Here we have drawn the same indifference curve as in Exhibit 19.2, and labeled it I_1. Point E, representing a basket with 7 pounds of meat and 5 pounds of cheese, is not a member of the indifference set represented by this curve. Because it lies above and to the right of point B, and has more of both products than B, it must be preferred to B. There are other points, such as F and G, that have more cheese and less meat than E, and on balance, give the same satisfaction as E. The consumer is indifferent between E, F, G, and all other points on the curve I_2, and prefers all of these points to any of the points on I_1.

Any point taken at random, together with the other points that happen to be equally satisfactory, can form an indifference curve. Several other such curves, unlabeled, are sketched in Exhibit 19.4. If all possible curves were drawn in, they would be so close together that the ink of the lines would run into a solid sheet entirely filling the space between the axes. A representative selection of indifference curves, showing their general pattern but leaving enough space to make the diagram easy to read, is called an *indifference map*.

5. Indifference curves do not cross. This is because consumer preferences are **transitive.** By transitive, we mean that if a person prefers A to B, and B to C, he then prefers A to C. Looking at Exhibit 19.5, we can see that crossed indifference curves contradict this assumption of transitivity. Consider points A, B, and C. A and B both lie on the same indifference curve I_1, hence the consumer is indifferent between them. A and C both lie on I_2, hence the consumer is indif-

Transitivity The principle that tells us that if A is preferred to B, and B is preferred to C, then A must be preferred to C.

EXHIBIT 19.4

Multiple indifference curves

An indifference curve can be drawn through any point. Here the indifference curve I_1 represents an indifference set containing points A, B, C, and D, while I_2 represents a set containing the points E, F, and G. All points on I_2 are better than the points on I_1. A representative selection of indifference curves like the one shown here can be called an indifference map.

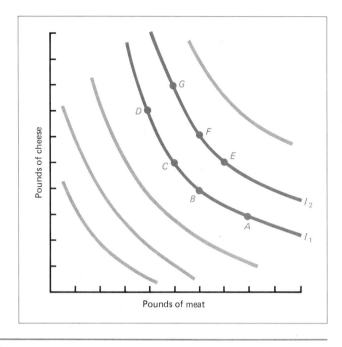

EXHIBIT 19.5

"Impossible" crossing indifference curves

Because consumer preferences are transitive, indifference curves do not cross. The impossible indifference curves shown here represent contradictory preferences. A and B are both on I_1, so the consumer must be indifferent between them. A and C both lie on I_2, so he must be indifferent between them too. By transitivity, this implies that he is indifferent between B and C, but this is impossible, because C contains more of both goods than B.

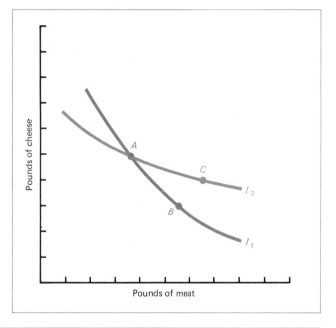

ferent between them also. From the property of transitivity, if B is as good as A, and A is as good as C, we can conclude that C is as good as B. But C lies above and to the right of B. It represents a combination of goods with more of both meat and cheese. If more is better, the consumer must prefer C to B. We see, then, that crossed indifference curves would imply a contradictory set of preferences, so we conclude that they cannot cross.

The Consumption Opportunity Line

The range of consumption opportunities open to a consumer, with a given budget and given prices can be shown on the same kind of graph as we have been using. Exhibit 19.6 shows how this is done. A certain consumer has a budget

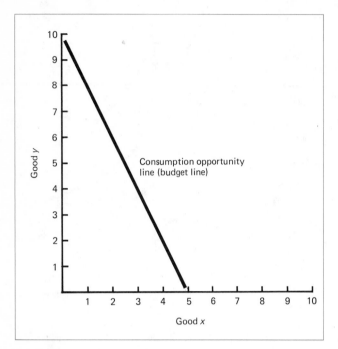

EXHIBIT 19.6

The consumption opportunity line (budget line)
A certain consumer has a budget of $1.00. He can spend his money on good x at $.20 per unit, or on good y at $.10 per unit, or on some combination of the two goods. The consumption opportunity line (budget line) shows all the possible combinations available to him, given these prices and his limited budget.

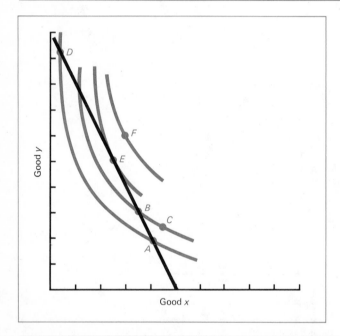

EXHIBIT 19.7

Graphical demonstration of consumer equilibrium
E is the point of consumer equilibrium, given the indifference curves and budget line shown. All points that are better than E (such as F) lie outside the boundary of the budget line. All other points that the consumer can afford to buy (such as A and D) lie on lower indifference curves than E, and are thus less preferred.

Consumption Opportunity Line (Budget Line) A line showing the various combinations of goods that can be purchased at given prices with a given budget.

of $1.00. The price of good x is $.20 per unit; that of Y is $.10 per unit. If the consumer spends all his money on x, he can have up to 5 units. If he spends it all on y, he can have up to 10 of that good. Combinations like 2x and 6y, 4x and 2y, and so forth, are also possible. These consumption opportunities are shown in the diagram by the diagonal line running from 10 on the y axis to 5 on the x axis. We call this the consumer's **consumption opportunity line,** or alternatively, the **budget line.**

Notice that the absolute value of the slope of the budget line is equal to the ratio of the price of good x to the price of good y. In this case, where the price of x is $.20 per unit and that of y is $.10 per unit, the slope is −2.

A Graphical Representation of Consumer Equilibrium

Now let us look at a graphical representation of consumer equilibrium. We draw both the consumer's indifference map, and his budget line on the same diagram, as in Exhibit 19.7. This diagram shows the relationship of preferences to opportunities at a glance. For example, we see that point *B* is preferred to point *A* because it lies on a "higher" indifference curve (that is, one that at some point like *C* passes above and to the right of *A*). By similar reasoning, we can see that point *D* is inferior to point *B*. Of all the points on or below the budget line, it is clear that point *E* is the most preferred, because all the other points on the budget line lie on lower indifference curves. Every point that, like *F*, is better still lies outside the range of consumption opportunities.

Because *E* is the point giving the highest possible satisfaction under the conditions we have set, it is the point of consumer equilibrium. Notice that at *E*, the relevent indifference curve is just tangent to the consumption opportunity line. Because their slopes are equal at the point of tangency, we know that in equilibrium the ratio of the marginal utility of *x* to the marginal utility of *y* (given by the slope of the indifference curve) is equal to the ratio of the price of *x* to the price of *y* (given by the slope of the consumption opportunity line).

CHAPTER 20
Advertising and the Consumer

What You Will Learn in This Chapter

Traditional theory pictures the consumer as an efficient, rational, well-informed utility maximizer. Useful insights into the nature of market equilibrium are gained by taking that approach. In reality, though, things are not so simple. In particular, different assumptions are required in order to understand the economics of advertising. Advertising, as we shall see, works only in a world where consumers are less than perfectly informed, and look for shortcuts in making decisions.

For Review

Here are some important terms and concepts that will be put to use in this chapter. Be certain that you understand them, or review them before proceeding.

Markets as mechanisms for using knowledge (Chapter 2)
Market equilibrium (Chapter 3)
Logic of consumer choice (Chapter 19)

Marketing and Consumer Theory

In the last chapter, we presented a well-established theory of consumer choice. This theory looks at consumer choice as a problem of pure logic. We are presented with certain "givens," namely, consumers' tastes, the characteristics of available goods, the prices of those goods, and the size of consumers' budgets. Using these givens, consumers must calculate the mix of purchases that will give them the maximum utility. This maximum is achieved by equalizing the marginal utilities per dollar's worth of all goods.

This very abstract picture of consumer choice is all that traditional economic theory needs. It was originally developed to bolster the theory of supply and demand by showing what lies behind the demand curve. The attempts of each consumer to reach consumer equilibrium determine the shape of the demand curve, and then the demand curve and supply curve together determine the market equilibrium.

There is little if any room in this picture for advertising. Instead, there is a great emphasis on equilibrium. In equilibrium, everyone knows all they need to know, and no opportunities for beneficial economic change exist. In such a world, how could advertising possibly be necessary or effective?

The World of Marketing

The world of advertising and marketing is very different from the world of traditional economic theory. It is, above all, a world of perpetual disequilibrium. Practical business managers do not ask their marketing researchers to calculate the equilibrium price and quantity for their firm's product. Instead, they ask the researchers to find new ways to make profits. The best profit opportunities do not lie in equilibrium, where supply and demand curves cross. They lie where a positive gap between supply and demand curves can be found or created.

Traditional economic theory tells us what the world would be like if consumers had given tastes, had complete knowledge of prices and products, and were able to make decisions quickly and at no cost. The activities of advertising and marketing proceed on directly opposite assumptions. In the world of marketing, consumer tastes are ever changing, people are widely ignorant of prices and product characteristics, and consumer decisions are costly and time consuming. Let us see how this alternative set of assumptions about consumer choice helps us to understand how advertising works.

Ignorance

On the simplest level, advertising works because consumers are ignorant. They have some idea how much eggs cost, but they do not automatically know whether this week eggs are cheaper at the A&P or at Safeway. They know that you buy beds in furniture stores, but they are not able to reel off a list of all the furniture stores in town, at least not if the town is very big. They know what a car is, but they do not always know which cars have front-wheel drive, or which cars this year have rear-window defrosters. Every firm can feel certain that there are consumers who would buy their product if they knew about it. By telling consumers of the price and characteristics of products, and the places where they can be bought, advertisements attract enough customers to pay for the resources spent to produce those advertisements.

Changing Tastes

Other kinds of advertisements are aimed not at informing consumers about prices and products, but at changing their tastes. If consumer tastes are changeable, firms can make profits by changing them. Making consumers like a firm's product more pushes the demand curve for its product to the right. Sales or prices or both can be increased, raising profits. To understand advertising, then, it is useful to know something about the mechanisms by which consumer tastes are produced and modified.

For one thing, people's tastes and preferences do not originate spontaneously within themselves. Instead, they are strongly influenced by the tastes and preferences of people around them. Some people are innovators, and take up new styles or products of their own accord, but more people are imitators, and change their buying patterns only after they see others change. The interaction of innovators and imitators in the consumer community keeps tastes and styles in flux. Through advertising, firms can hope to control the direction and pace of change. Controlled and predictable change is more profitable and less risky than random change. Such control can be worth the advertising resources invested to produce it.

Changing Perceptions

Changing tastes are not the whole story, though. Market researchers have found that advertising changes not only tastes, but also perceptions. It can influence not only which product people will like, but how well they will like a given, unchanged product. The following case study provides an interesting illustration.

CASE 20.1
Advertising and the Perceived Taste of Turkey Meat[1]

In 1965, James C. Makens of Michigan Technological University conducted an experiment to determine the effect of a well-known brand name on consumer's preferences for turkey meat. In Part I of the experiment, 150 subjects from Detroit were presented with two plates, each containing a slice of turkey meat. Although the two slices were actually from the same turkey, they were labeled differently, one bearing a brand name heavily advertised and well known in Detroit, and the other bearing an unfamiliar brand name. Of the 150 subjects, only 10 percent indicated that they thought the two samples tasted alike. Fifty-six percent expressed a definite preference for the known brand, and 34 percent preferred the unknown brand. Makens concluded that in the presence of brand name clues, the subjects perceived identical portions of turkey as being different, and that they tended to perfer the more familiar name.

In Part II of the experiment, 61 consumers were again presented with two plates. One of these had a slice of tender turkey meat, and the other a slice of tough turkey meat. This time, no brand names were used. The tender sample was marked (%) and the tough sample was marked (*). Forty-nine subjects said they preferred the tender meat, 4 preferred the tough meat, and 8 said they could not tell the difference. The conclusion was that, in the absence of brand name clues, consumers could perceive an actual difference in quality.

In the final part of the experiment, the 61 subjects who had tasted the samples marked (%) and (*) were asked to indicate which brand they thought each sample belonged to, after they had said which they preferred. Thirty-four subjects said that the turkey they preferred must have been the known brand. Eighteen identified the preferred turkey as probably the unknown brand, and one did not express an opinion. The conclusion was that consumers thought it likely that the high-quality product was the one with which they were familiar.

Makens summarized his results in these terms: "Brand preference for one well-known turkey brand was strong enough to influence the perceived taste for turkey meat among the subjects. . . .[Also] the consumers expect a well-known brand turkey to be of superior quality to an unknown brand."

[1]Based on James C. Makens, "Effect of Brand Preferences upon Consumers' Perceived Taste of Turkey Meat," *Journal of Applied Psychology*, Vol. 49 (Nov. 4, 1965).

Similar results have been reported elsewhere. These experiments leave us a long way from the idea that tastes and preferences are a "given" of the consumer choice process.

Brand Loyalty

In the idealized world of economic theory, the decisions consumers make are neither costly nor time-consuming. In the real world, it is not so. The shortcuts that consumers take to simplify the decisions they have to make sometimes create openings for advertisers. An example is the phenomenon of "brand loyalty."

A brand-loyal consumer keeps decision costs down by choosing the same brand again and again. Where does brand loyalty come from? Some degree of brand loyalty could perhaps be explained on the basis of innate differences in tastes among consumers. (Some people may just be born with a liking for Budweiser and others with a liking for Schlitz.) The following case study, though, shows that there is more to brand loyalty than just this.

CASE 20.2
An Experimental Study of Brand Loyalty[2]

In 1968, J. Douglass McConnell of the Stanford Research Institute reported the results of an experimental study of brand loyalty. The product chosen for the experiment was beer. It was chosen because people buy beer frequently, and because McConnell judged that the nature of the product would help motivate subjects to stay with the experiment over the 2 month period required. A random sample of sixty beer drinkers was drawn from Stanford University married student housing. The subjects were told that the experiment was part of a marketing test of three types of beer produced by a local brewer.

Once a week, the subjects were presented, in their homes, with an opportunity to choose one bottle from among three bottles labeled "M," "L," and "P." They were told that brand M was a high-price beer, brand L a medium-price beer, and brand P a bargain-price beer. The subjects did not actually have to pay for their beer, but to make the price difference seem realistic, the medium-price beer had a \$.02 "refund" taped to the bottle, and the low-price beer had a \$.05 "refund." The subjects could keep the refunds.

In point of fact, the three brands of beer were identical. They were all drawn from the same production run at the brewery, and differed only in terms of the labels added by the experimenter. This, however, did not prevent the development of fierce brand loyalties by many of the subjects. One measure of brand loyalty that McConnell used was the occurrence of four consecutive choices of the same label. Although at first the subjects experimented with different brands, by the end of 24 trials, 57 of the 60 had developed loyalty, as measured by the four-choice criterion. Of these 57, 26 chose brand M, 12 brand L, and 19 brand P.

Another measure of brand loyalty is the probability of making a switch in brands from one trial to the next. The lower the probability of switching, the more loyal. Exhibit 20.1 shows how the probability of switching decreased rapidly over the first 12 trials of the experiment.

Because the beer was actually all the same, these results could not be explained by any "given" differences in tastes. The results instead suggest that, by convincing themselves that one brand was better than another, the subjects avoided the painful task of having to make up their minds "from scratch" at each trial.

Given the nature of the choice the subjects were offered, it is remarkable how firmly set in their opinions some of the subjects became. One girl reported, "M is a good strong malty beer, but I like L because it is lighter.

[2]Based on J. Douglass McConnell, "The Development of Brand Loyalty, an Experimental Study," *Journal of Marketing Research*, Feb. 1968.

EXHIBIT 20.1
Effects of repeated tasting on brand loyalty
In the experiment, subjects were given a choice of three
bottles of beer on each trial. The bottles had different labels,
but the contents of the bottles were the same. At first, consumers experimented, switching from brand to brand to find
one they liked. Soon, though, the frequency of switching fell to
a low level as brand loyalty developed.

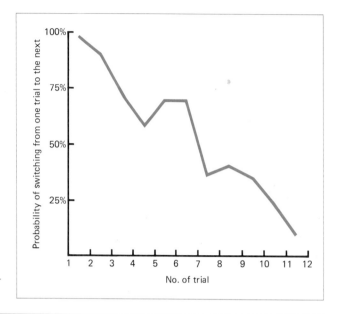

Source: J. Douglass McConnell, "The Development of Brand Loyalty, an
Experimental Study," *Journal of Marketing Research,* Feb. 1968. Table 3.
Reprinted from Journal of Marketing Research published by the
American Marketing Association.

Mmm!!! P would poison me—make me ill." Another subject, who developed
an enthusiasm for P, once deviated to experiment with a bottle of M and reported, "worst I've ever had; you couldn't give it away."

We see, then, that consumers look very different to the marketing re-
searcher than to the economist. To the one, they are fickle and ignorant.
To the other, they are consistent and well informed. For purposes of positive analysis, each way of looking at consumers has its uses. One viewpoint
is more useful if we want to sell people beer, and the other is more useful if
we want to understand equilibrium theory. Let us turn now from positive
to normative economics, and see what other issues are raised by these two
views of consumer behavior.

Advertising and Consumer Sovereignty: Some Normative Issues

Economists often use the term "consumer sovereignty" to get across the
idea that, in a market economy, consumers are the "kings." Everything
that is produced is, ultimately, destined to fulfill their needs. If new demands arise, firms will come forth with supplies of the proper products.
The simplest supply and demand analysis tells us this much.

When the idea of consumer sovereignty is used in a purely descriptive
sense, it is not a source of much controversy. Interesting issues begin to
arise, though, as soon as we try to use consumer sovereignty as a normative
standard by which to judge market institutions. These issues turn out to
revolve largely around the proper role of advertising in the economy.

The Case Against Advertising

It is not hard for opponents of advertising to get an audience. Anyone
who has ever been interrupted in the middle of his favorite Bogart film on
late-night television is an automatic convert. The case against advertising

John Kenneth Galbraith
(1908–　)

John Kenneth Galbraith enjoys a unique distinction among American economists today: His books regularly hit the best-seller list and stay there for long periods. Galbraith represents the opposite exteme from the economist who, like Paul Samuelson, writes primarily to gain the applause of other economists. On the contrary, his major books, *The Affluent Society* (1958) and *The New Industrial State* (1967), are all-out attacks on conventional economics, written to be read by the widest possible nonprofessional audience.

Galbraith lumps everything he dislikes about modern economics under the heading of the "conventional wisdom." By this phrase, he means all those ideas that he claims are widely believed not because they are true, but simply because they are so often repeated. He saves his sharpest barbs for two particular elements of the conventional wisdom: consumer sovereignty and the law of supply and demand.

Consumers are not sovereign, Galbraith says, because their tastes and preferences are heavily manipulated by advertising. The ability of business to manipulate consumers knocks the "demand" leg out from under supply and demand theory. The "supply" leg is then knocked out with a second deftly aimed kick. The supply curve is valid only in an economy where firms aim to maximize profits. In the American economy, says Galbraith, firms do not do this. How, then, can we say that supply and demand determine price? Instead, the kinds of goods that consumers are persuaded to buy and the prices at which these goods are sold are determined by the whims of the "technostructure," Galbraith's name for the managerial-professional-academic elite who run the country.

Galbraith is many other things than an economist. He is a political activist always found promoting liberal and ultraliberal causes. He has served as chairman of the Americans for Democratic Action, and he played a key role in securing the Democratic Presidential nomination for George McGovern. He is also a diplomat, having served as John Kennedy's ambassador to India. (At six feet eight inches, he towered almost comically over his local diplomatic counterparts.) In a burst of self-indulgence, he once even turned his hand to writing a novel (*The Triumph*).

Few economists take the complete Galbraithian system seriously, but many admit that he is a useful critic. Economics, like other social science disciplines, is in fact always in danger of becoming excessively abstract and formalistic. Economists who talk only to other economists, and then only in mathematical language, do indeed often end up saying things that are just plain silly. Galbraith is determined that they should not get away with it.

rests on much more, though, than merely the complaint that it is intrusive, annoying, ugly, and distracting. Let's review some of the most common *economic* objections to advertising.

Heading the list of arguments against advertising is the complaint that it violates consumer sovereignty. Producers, it is said, do not adjust their output to consumer preferences. Instead, they use advertising to force consumers to buy whatever it is that they feel like producing. John Kenneth Galbraith has been one of the most vocal proponents of this view. In his book, *The Affluent Society*, he put the matter this way:

> Were it so that a man arising each morning was assailed by demons which instilled in him a passion sometimes for silk shirts, sometimes for kitchen ware, sometimes for chamber pots, and sometimes for orange squash, there would be every reason to applaud the effort to find the goods, however odd, that quenched this flame. . . .
>
> Consumer wants can have bizarre, frivolous, or even immoral origins, and an admirable case can still be made for a society which seeks to satisfy

them. But the case cannot stand if it is the process of satisfying wants that creates the wants. For then the individual who urges the importance of production to satisfy those wants is precisely in the position of the onlooker who applauds the efforts of the squirrel to keep abreast of the wheel that is propelled by his own effort.[3]

Advertising is the chief method by which the people who satisfy the wants (that is, the economy's business firms) also create those wants. According to Galbraith, a distinction must be made between wants that are innate within the consumer and those that producers create through advertising. Consumer sovereignty means guiding production purely in accordance with wants of the first type. Advertising and all other means of want creation are a violation of that sovereignty.

Twenty years after the appearance of Galbraith's book, the ideas he expressed remain popular. Now they often take the form of the doctrine of "consumer alienation," to use a term favored by Marxist-oriented economists. The doctrine of consumer alienation is based on the idea that people have two sets of preferences. One set reflects their "true" wants and needs, the other "false" wants and needs created by advertising and other evils of modern capitalism. In this view, "consumer sovereignty" is a mockery unless preceded by consumer liberation from false needs and desires.

There are other kinds of arguments against advertising too. Many make the point that whether it distorts consumer preferences or not, much advertising is simply wasteful. Millions are spent by one company to win Marlboro smokers over to Winstons, while a rival spends millions to win them back. The net effect is to keep sales of both brands about where they would be without advertising. Meanwhile, millions of television viewers have their favorite programs broken into by obnoxious sloganeering, all to no avail.

Still another charge leveled against advertising is that it limits competition in the marketplace and promotes monopoly. We shall have to wait until Chapter 26 for some of the theoretical tools needed to evaluate this argument fully, but it deserves mention here because many economists think it to be among the most important objections to the high level of advertising expenditure in the American economy.

In Defense of Advertising

Of course, the controversy over advertising has two sides. Here are some common responses to each of the charges set forth above.

First, what about the charge that advertising is a violation of consumer sovereignty? The defenders of advertising begin by making the point that there are no such things as "natural," "given," or "innate" consumer preferences, at least not if one means by this preferences for specific kinds of goods and services. People may well be born with basic needs for food, security, affection, self-esteem, and the rest, but there is an infinite variety of particular goods that can satisfy these needs. If the advertisers of one generation persuade people that their need to keep their feet dry is best satisfied with pointed-toe boots, and those of the next that square-toed boots do

[3]John Kenneth Galbraith, *The Affluent Society* (Boston: Houghton Mifflin, 1958), pp. 153–154.

the job better, so what? We should not be silly enough to think that, left to their own devices, people's "true" tastes in boot-toes would magically emerge, making us all better off.

Some go so far as to say that the idea of "true" and "false" preferences itself poses a potential threat to consumer sovereignty. The argument is that the so-called true preferences are just the preferences of a cultural elite who do not like the "low-brow" lifestyles of their neighbors. Because the members of this elite prefer beaujolais to Budweiser, or camping in the High Sierra to snowmobiling in Iowa cornfields, or "tastefully" styled European cars to "tasteless" American cars, they think that everyone else ought to share their preferences. It is a short step from a policy of forbidding the advertising of Budweiser, snowmobiles, and Buicks to forbidding their production in the name of giving "the people" what they "really want." And then what becomes of consumer sovereignty?

Waste and Information

Next let us turn to the contention that advertising is wasteful. After all, with more than $26 billion being spent each year on advertising in the United States, it would be a serious matter if advertisers did nothing but bang heads in a futile battle for market shares that left them and their customers in much the same position from which they began.

For advertising to be productive, it must provide consumers with useful information about consumption opportunities. This information makes it easier for consumers to reach decisions, allows them to know what a wide range of competing sellers have to offer, and keeps them posted about changes in market prices. Just how much information does advertising really convey? The following case study provides an interesting indication.

CASE 20.3
The Information Content of *New Yorker* Advertising

The *New Yorker* magazine is an industry leader in terms of the amount of advertising it carries. The September 29, 1975, issue contained no fewer than 169 separate advertisements. We made an attempt to judge how much of this advertising was "informative," and how much was purely "persuasive" without being also informative.

Each separate advertisement was rated on a four-point scale. One point was given if it informed potential buyers of the advertised product's price. One point was given if it informed them of a specific location where the product could be purchased (not just the name of the manufacturer). One point was awarded if the advertisement described a product innovation of which consumers would be unlikely to know already. (For example, this point would be given for an advertisement that announced a newly published book or a dress of a new design, but was withheld in the case of an advertisement for a long-existing hotel, or a brand of whiskey that was unchanged from one year to the next). A final point was awarded, in addition to the others, if the advertisement offered readers a catalog or brochure providing further detailed information about the product.

Using this scale, the 169 advertisements contained an average of 2.3 useful items of information. Of the total, 31 scored 4 points, 52 scored 3 points, 39 scored 2 points, 33 just one point, and 14 scored zero.

It appears that there are indeed some advertisements that are "wasteful" in the sense of providing no information that could lead to consumer decisions being made more "wisely" in any objective sense of the word. Those advertisements, if they are effective at all, must work by inducing brand loyalty, by causing perceptual shifts, or by other nonrational mechanisms. In the sample studied, however, informative advertisements were in the majority.

Advertising and the Media

No defense of advertising would be complete without mentioning one further way in which advertising stimulates the flow of information in our economy. If you pick up any newspaper or magazine and flip through it, you will discover that here and there between the advertisements are stories and articles of a noncommercial nature. From the advertisers' point of view, all those long pieces about fishing and hunting one finds in *Field & Stream* serve only to attract an audience to whom rifle ammunition or deodorants can profitably be sold. From the readers' point of view, though, the text of a magazine or newspaper is full of information and entertainment valuable in its own right.

The $26 billion spent annually on advertising, then, is used to cover two very different kinds of expenses. The first is the expense of actually preparing and exhibiting the advertisements themselves. The second is the expense of preparing the printed text or programming that attracts readers or viewers to the advertising medium. Even though part of the first kind of expenditure may be wasteful (in the informational sense), this waste is offset by the effect of the second type of expenditure. The kinds of advertising that are richest in these informational by-products are advertising in newspapers ($7.9 billion), magazines ($1.5 billion), television ($4.8 billion), and radio ($1.7 billion). Expenditures on advertising that is poor in by-products (billboards, direct mail, and the like) accounts for only about a third of the total.

Eliminating advertising, then, would involve some heavy opportunity costs. For one thing, the genuine information in the advertisements themselves would be lost. More important, consumers would either have to pay more for newspapers, magazines, and television programming, or they would have to pay higher taxes to subsidize these media.

Conclusions

When all is said and done, advertising remains one of the most difficult aspects of business life for economists to deal with. The tools of equilibrium analysis on which we rely so often are of little use here, because advertising works only in markets that are in disequilibrium. In the past, economists have too frequently condemned advertising simply because it did not fit neatly into their world view. Some promising recent work goes beyond this naive reaction to advertising, but a complete economic theory of advertising is still not available. Our brief discussion of the subject here forms something of a disgression in our discussion of microeconomics. It is an important disgression, though, if only because it shows that there are some aspects of economic reality with which simple theories cannot adequately deal. More work is needed in many places to bridge the gap between theory and reality.

SUMMARY

1. The consumers of traditional economic theory are rational, well-informed calculators. They maximize total utility, given market prices and their budgets, by equalizing the marginal utility of a dollar's worth of each good. This picture of consumers leaves little room for advertising. Advertising works only in a world of disequilibrium, when consumers are less than perfectly informed and find decisions costly and time consuming to make.

2. Different kinds of advertisements work in different ways. Some simply inform consumers of prices and product characteristics. Others seek to alter tastes and perceptions. Still others offer consumers shortcuts to decision making, for example, by encouraging the formation of brand loyalties.

3. The term consumer sovereignty is sometimes used to indicate that consumers, through their effective demand for goods and services, exercise ultimate control over production. Whether advertising interferes with consumer sovereignty or not is a much-debated question of normative economics. Some people believe that advertising is wasteful, and alienates consumers from their true wants and needs. Others see advertising as a normal part of the entrepreneurial process, and a useful source of information.

DISCUSSION QUESTIONS

1. A cynic has said that everyone complains that advertising has too much power to manipulate people's tastes and behavior, yet no one will admit that his or her own tastes or behavior are shaped by such manipulation to any significant extent. Comment.

2. Suppose that you meet an attractive young man or woman at a friend's party. After sharing a few drinks and a dance or two, you learn that he or she works for a big Madison Avenue advertising agency. Your new aquaintance begins enthusiastically telling you how wonderful the work is, how much scope it gives for creativity, and so forth. How would you respond?

3. The XYZ distillery markets two brands of vodka. Brand A is heavily advertised, and the advertisements feature scenes of "beautiful people" in luxurious surroundings. Brand B is not advertised at all, and costs $1 less per bottle. About equal quantities of the two brands are sold. You yourself have always preferred brand A. One day you learn that, in point of fact, brand A and brand B are identical except for the labels—they both come out of the same vat. Do you think that XYZ has done anything unethical or immoral? Do you think that you would switch to brand B? Would you perhaps start buying brand B, but save one of your old A bottles, and pour out of that when guests come to your house?

4. Do you think the desire to smoke cigarettes is a "false want" created by manipulation of consumers through advertising? That the desire to smoke marijuana is a "false want" created through media glorification of the counter-culture? What is a "false want?"

5. Compare the advertising in the magazines *Ms.* and *Good Housekeeping.* Which do you think contains more "informative" advertising, and which more "persuasive" advertising? (Try scoring the ads according to the method explained in Case 20.3.) Do you find that because the readers of *Ms.* are known to be relatively well educated, sophisticated, and independent minded, advertisers do not bother to use the cruder forms of persuasive advertising in that magazine but, instead, stick to strictly informative ads?

6. Do you think that political campaigning and advertising raises the same sort of issues for "voter sovereignty" as commerical advertising raises for "consumer sovereignty"? Does making this comparison make you think that both kinds of advertising should be more strictly regulated than at present? That both should be equally unrestricted as a part of freedom of speech? Or is there a fundamental difference between the two? If so, what is the difference?

CHAPTER 21
The Nature of the Firm

What You Will Learn in This Chapter
The firm is the basic unit of production in a market economy. Firms play a vital role in organizing the division of labor. A firm's managers issue directives to coordinate the activities of those within the firm. The coordination of firms with one another is organized through the market. There are a number of different legal forms of organizations that firms can assume. Proprietorships, partnerships, and corporations each have their advantages and disadvantages. One special issue arises more strongly in the case of corporations than for other types of firms. That is the question of who exercises control—owners or managers? This continues to be a source of debate.

For Review
Here are some important terms and concepts that will be put to use in this chapter. Be certain that you understand them, or review them before proceeding.
    Entrepreneur, entrepreneurship (Chapter 2)

Throughout this book we have referred to "the firm" as the basic unit of business in a market economy. Up to now, though, we have not talked very much about what a firm really is or how it works. Firms, we know, come in a great variety of sizes and shapes. There are mom-and-pop corner stores, giant automobile and steel corporations, and powerful partnerships of lawyers or stockbrokers. What do all of these different firms have in common? Why are some firms organized one way rather than another? Who controls firms, and for what purposes is control exercised? These are a few of the questions we shall discuss in this chapter. Let us begin by looking at some of the things firms and their managers do.

Methods of Coordination

Coordination and the Division of Labor
Production in any modern economy is based on a vast division of labor. Each person makes his or her own individual contribution to the whole pattern. One person installs hubcaps on Ford station wagons. Another

maintains accounts in a New England branch of Woolworth's. Still another serves coffee, tea, or milk for Eastern Airlines. Somehow all of these different jobs have to be *coordinated*. When a team of Internal Revenue Service auditors want to pay a visit to that branch of Woolworth's, they must be sure that they will not run out of coffee on the airplane, that the rented Ford will not be missing a hubcap, and that the books they want to see will be balanced and ready when they arrive. How is it done?

There are two alternative means by which the division of labor can be coordinated: market coordination and managerial coordination.

The principle of *market coordination* uses the price system as a source of incentives. Coordination takes place without explicit central control. As Adam Smith wrote some 200 years ago,

> it is not from the benevolence of the butcher, the brewer, or the baker that we expect our dinner, but from their regard to their own interest. . . . Every individual is continually exerting himself to find out the most advantageous employment for whatever capital he can command. . . . By directing that industry in such a manner as its produce may be of the greater value, he intends only his own gain, and he is in this, as in many other cases, lead by an invisible hand to promote an end which was no part of his intention. . . .

There are large areas of the division of labor, however, which do not depend directly on the "invisible hand" of the market as a means of coordination. Hubcap fitters do not perform their job in response to market signals. It is not their business to judge that their skills are more profitably employed fitting hubcaps than running a milling machine in another part of the factory. Instead, they fit hubcaps because their immediate boss tells them that is what their job is today. Here we are in the realm of a different coordinating principle altogether, that of *managerial coordination*. Here the means of communication is that of direct instruction from manager to subordinate. Here the incentive that makes the instructions effective is the fact that subordinates have pledged obedience to the manager (at least within certain limits) as a condition of employment.

Coordination in the Firm

In a famous essay on the nature of the firm,[1] Ronald Coase posed a question about these two ways of coordinating the division of labor: If the market principle works as well as economists say it does, why is the managerial principle ever used at all?

Why do hubcap fitters have to be employees taking orders from a boss? If the market principle were applied everywhere, they would be self-employed, independent mechanics. Someone who wanted a car could hire them to put the hubcaps on for a standard fee, hire other people to attach the doors, still others to install the upholstery, and so forth. Changes in the rewards for hubcap fitting and upholstery fitting would keep the right number of workers at each job.

Coase found an answer to his question. He said that we do not use the market for every situation where coordination is required, because there are costs to using the market. There are costs of finding out what

---

[1]Ronald H. Coase, "The Nature of the Firm," *Economica*, n.s., Vol. IV (Nov. 1937).

Ronald Coase is the intellectual founder of the "new institutional economics." Through his own writings, his editorship of the *Journal of Law and Economics,* his famous workshops at the University of Chicago Law School, and his influence on many brilliant students, Coase has fostered a unification of institutional economics and analytical economics, once separate and even antagonistic branches of the discipline. The method of the new institutional economics is simple and productive of great insights. One selects an economic institution and poses two related questions: First, what are the effects of this particular institution on the allocation of resources? And second, how can we account for the evolution and continued existence of the institution *in terms of* our analysis of its effects on resource allocation?

Coase, born and educated in London, began his studies of economic institutions early in his career. In 1934, he published an analysis of the British postal system in the journal *Economica,* the first of several papers on this topic that he has written over the years. Comparing the performance of the British post office with the alternative of private messenger companies, Coase argued that the postal monopoly offered no inherent advantages in terms of the public interest.

Coase's famous paper on the nature of the firm followed in 1937 and first brought him international recognition. He came to the United States in 1951, to teach first at the University of Buffalo, then at the University of Virginia, and finally at the University of Chicago. In 1961, his most famous paper of all, "The Problem of Social Cost," appeared in the *Journal of Law and Economics.* At that time, the journal was new and the study of law and economics hardly existed as an independent specialty within either profession. Coase's probing analysis of the nature of the law as an economic institution sparked such enormous interest among both economists and lawyers that law and economics soon became one of the most exciting fields of study around. Within little over a decade, all leading law schools had economists on their staff and were offering courses in the new institutional economics as applied to legal institutions.

One subject on which the new institutional economics has had much to say is government regulation of industry. Coase himself has written extensively on the regulation of broadcasting, and articles on regulation of other industries appear regularly in his journal. Traditionally, the economics of regulation was largely concerned with how regulation ought to be conducted, and what beneficial effects would emerge from regulation under ideal conditions. Coase shifted the focus to an analysis of regulatory institutions as their structure and effects actually exist. The result, on balance, has been highly critical. Coase himself has recently gone so far as to write that "It is now generally accepted by all students of the subject that most (perhaps almost all) government regulation is anticompetitive and harmful in its effects."

Ronald H. Coase
(1910–)

prices are. There are costs of negotiating contracts, costs of writing bills and receipts, and costs of straightening things out when market contracts are not carried through. If a potential car buyer had to negotiate separately with each person who worked on the car, the costs of coordination would make the car too expensive to be worth it. If the buyer saved negotiating costs by having one or two local mechanics build the car all the way through from scratch, the advantages of mass production and the division of labor would be lost. The vehicle would still cost too much. But when Ford Motor Company acts as an intermediary between the buyer and the workers, thousands of market transactions are eliminated. Cars are sold on the market, but everything in between is coordinated by the managerial principle of simply giving orders and expecting them to be obeyed.

Coase realized, though, that in answering one question, he had just raised another. If managerial coordination works so well, why use the market at all? Why not run the entire economy as one big firm, with everyone as employees and a single, central manager running the whole show? Then it would not only be a matter of giving the auto workers orders about whether to fit hubcaps or doors that day, but also giving high school graduates orders about whether to be auto workers or accountants. Not only would the matter of how much coffee and how much tea to load on an airliner be handled by the managerial principle, but so would the matter of how many trains there should be in the national transport system.

The problem is that the managerial coordination has costs of its own as well as savings, compared with the market principle. Under the managerial system, the person actually doing a job does not need to know all the reasons behind the decision to do it, and that is a saving. Offsetting this is the fact that *managers* have to know all about all the different jobs they coordinate. That is a cost. Sometimes the costs of supplying knowledge to a manager or other central decision maker are greater than the costs of supplying the knowledge to people close to the job. When this is the case, managerial coordination loses its advantage over market coordination.

The Limits of the Firm

Coase saw that the two coordination principles give the key to understanding the nature of the firm and its role in the economy. A firm, he said, is an organization that uses the managerial principle of coordination internally, and uses the market to coordinate its activities with those of other firms and individuals. Each firm tends to grow until the cost of organizing one extra task within the firm becomes equal to the cost of organizing the same task outside the firm through the market. In some industries (as we shall see shortly), this rule dictates that firms grow to enormous size. In others, the limit to the growth of the firm occurs at a very small size. By allowing each firm to grow to its optimal size and leaving coordination between firms to the market, the total costs of organizing the division of labor are minimized.

Managerial Calculation and Entrepreneurship

Firms are run by managers who look at what is going on in the marketplace and make decisions for the firm on the basis of what they see there. There are two basic kinds of decisions to be made. Which kind of decision making comes into play depends largely on whether or not the markets where the firm operates are in equilibrium.

Managerial Calculation

Managerial Calculation The kind of decision making needed by a firm operating in markets that are in equilibrium, with given production methods, prices, and demand conditions.

One type of decision making we call **managerial calculation.** Managerial calculation involves doing what is needed to keep the firm on course when markets are in equilibrium, or approximately so. This part of decision making takes certain things as given. Among the givens are the technology of the firm's production processes, the prices of raw materials and factor services, and the demand conditions in the markets for the firm's product. Using these givens as a basis of calculation, a manager must decide which inputs the firm should hire, and what quantity of output it should produce. The success or failure of a firm depends on the ability of its management to make these calculations accurately, and to translate them efficiently into instructions to be relayed to the shop floor.

Entrepreneurship

The second kind of business decisions are those that exploit conditions of market disequilibrium. For the market to be in disequilibrium means that knowledge is not perfectly distributed among market participants. Entrepreneurship, then, is decision making in the presence of the unknown. It is *alertness* to new knowledge.

On the simplest level, that businessperson is being an entrepreneur who alertly catches the first signs of a shift in demand or supply conditions, and adjusts the operation of the firm to these changes before they become fully reflected in market prices. Beyond this, entrepreneurship consists in alertness to the appearance of entirely new methods of production, or potential markets for entirely new products. Entrepreneurs do not simply wait for things to happen; they make things happen.

Entrepreneurs hire the skills needed to translate scientific discoveries into practical production techniques, or to persuade consumers that new products are worth spending their money on. By these means, they gain a competitive edge for their firms over their rivals as the market adjusts to new conditions.

It can be difficult, or even impossible, for a firm to survive without entrepreneurship. Merely exploiting established markets and proven knowledge is not enough. The following case study illustrates this point quite clearly.

CASE 21.1
Conway-Stevens Misses the Point

The ballpoint pen was invented in 1888, but for fifty-seven years, there was no ballpoint pen market. Finally, in 1945, a Chicago manufacturer put together the old idea plus new precision grinding technology, which had been developed during the war, to make a marketable product. On October 29 of that year, 5,000 people stormed Gimbels in New York in search of the new writing sensation, and the ballpoint age was launched.

Not every manufacturer of writing instruments was headed by entrepreneurs ready to launch out into the unknown. The management of the prestigious Conway-Stevens Company in Britain preferred to deal with known technologies and established markets. Their main customers—the Post Office, the banks, the Ministry of Education—advised them that the ballpoint pen was a flash-in-the-pan, not worth getting tooled up for.

By 1963, the entrepreneurial phase had passed in the ballpoint pen market. The important original patents were expiring, the market was known and well established, and a merger brought Conway-Stevens into the ballpoint pen business. It was too late. In 1975, Conway-Stevens filed for bankruptcy. In writing the company's obituary, London's *Sunday Times* singled out the date of the beginning of the end: October 29, 1945.

Organization of the Firm

Business firms, which appear as well-defined, homogeneous units of analysis in economic theory, take on a very wide variety of forms in the real world. Some firms are tiny, consisting of a single individual doing all production and management jobs. At the other extreme are corporate giants like General Motors or ITT. These employ more people and dispose of more assets than the governments of all but the world's largest countries. Firms differ not only in size, but in their legal forms of organization as well. In the following three sections, we shall discuss the advantages and disadvantages of three main types of firm.[2]

The Sole Proprietorship

Sole Proprietorship A firm owned and usually managed by a single person, who receives all profits of the firm and who personally bears all of the firm's liabilities.

A **sole proprietorship** is a firm that is owned and usually managed by one person. In most cases this one person is also an operative employee. The responsibility for success or failure of the firm rests solely on the proprietor's shoulders. From a legal point of view, he or she owns all the assets and owes all the debts of the organization.

The following statement of financial position (balance sheet) exemplifies a sole proprietorship, that of Van Appelman, a grocery store owner. The property he owns, the debts he owes, and his equity in the business, aside from his personal assets, are shown in Exhibit 21.1.

Note that Van Appelman owns $34,000 worth of assets; he owes $5,500; his equity in the firm is $28,500, representing his ownership claim against the assets worth $34,000.

Advantages   One of the most important advantages of a sole proprietorship, from the owner's point of view, is the proprietor's ownership of all the assets and his or her rights to all the profits of the business. The sole proprietor is legally entitled to 100 percent of any rewards. This right to all the profits is a powerful incentive to the owner to invest money and to work harder to get the revenue from customers from whom profits are derived.

Another of the reasons the sole proprietorship legal form of ownership is so widely used is because it is relatively easy to organize. There are very few legal requirements to meet. Consequently, little or no costs of organization are involved. Practically anyone can develop an idea into a sole proprietorship form of organization. Of course, the firm may not succeed, but a sole proprietorship can be formed with little effort. To an owner of private property wishing to manage a business, the advantage of ease of organization may be a factor for choosing the sole proprietorship form of legal organization.

Still another factor in choosing the sole proprietorship may be the advantage of receiving a high degree of personal satisfaction from the management of the firm. People who like to have the freedom to exercise their personal judgment in management decisions and want to be able to make decisions promptly without consultation or approval of other owners or managers derive great personal satisfaction from the sole proprietorship of a firm. For people who do not work well with other managers or under supervision, the sole proprietorship form of legal organization may also be the most suitable.

Finally, ease of dissolution may become an important advantage of

---

[2]The material in this section is from Robert D. Hay, *Introduction to Business* (New York: Holt, Rinehart, and Winston, 1968), pp. 140–148. Reprinted by permission of the author.

EXHIBIT 21.1

Balance sheet of a sole proprietorship

In a sole proprietorship, all assets are owned by one person, and that person is solely liable for all debts. The difference between the firm's assets and its debts is the proprietor's equity, that is, the proprietor's own stake in the business.

Assets (Owns)		Debts (Owes)	
Cash	$ 2,000	Accounts payable	$ 500
Inventory on the shelves	10,000	Mortgage payable	5,000
Equipment	2,000	Total debts	$ 5,500
Land and buildings	20,000	Van Appelman, equity	28,500
Total assets	$34,000	Total debts plus equity	$34,000

the sole proprietorship. Just as there are few legal complications about going into business, there are very few in going out of business. Dissolution may simply mean selling the inventory, paying the debts, and locking the door. Ease of dissolution allows the owner to retire or enter another type of business quickly and easily.

Disadvantages The sole proprietorship form of organization also has some disadvantages. First and foremost is the disadvantage of unlimited financial liability, which means that the owner's personal property may be sold to pay the debts of the business. Because practically every piece of personal property an individual owns is subject to being used for the purpose of paying business debts, the unlimited feature of the sole proprietorship form of organization, people must consider the unpleasant fact that their business assets are not separate from their personal assets and therefore that their financial liability for any debts the business owes is unlimited.

Also, because the expansion of a proprietorship is limited by what the owner can contribute or borrow, he or she may find it difficult to expand. Difficulty of expansion is further magnified by the sole proprietor's inability to get into other lines of business because of a lack of capital or lack of managerial ability. Expansion often increases financial risks, and the owner's refusal or inability to bear these risks may make expansion impossible. If the minimum amount of capital required is more than one person can safely provide, the sole proprietorship will not work.

Finally, the death, injury, imprisonment, or bankruptcy of the owner may terminate the legal life of the firm. This lack of continuity stems from the legal fact that the individual and the business are one and the same in a sole proprietorship form of organization.

The Partnership

As defined by the Uniform Partnership Act, a **partnership** is an association of two or more persons who will carry on a business as co-owners by voluntary legal agreement (called the Articles of Co-Partnership). Instead of one person being the owner, there are at least two who own all the assets, owe all the liabilities, and who have an equity in the business.

Partnership A firm formed by two or more persons to carry on a business as co-owners. Each partner bears full legal liability for the debts of the firm.

EXHIBIT 21.2

Balance sheet of a partnership

In a partnership, all assets are owned jointly by the partners. Each partner is individually liable for all the firm's debts. The difference between the firm's assets and its debts is the owners' equity, shared between them as partners.

Assets (Owns)		Debts (Owes)	
Cash	$30,500	Accounts payable	$ 500
Inventory	10,000	Mortgage payable	5,000
Equipment	2,000	Total debts	$ 5,500
Land and building	20,000	Alice Appelman, equity	28,500
		Joe Kerwich, equity	28,500
Total assets	$62,500	Total debts plus equity	$62,500

For example, let us imagine that Joe Kerwich and Alice Appelman decide to go into business together. If Joe Kerwich and Alice Appelman both put $28,500 cash into the business, the balance sheet might look like Exhibit 21.2.

Note that both Appelman *and* Kerwich own $62,500 worth of assets; together they owe $5,500; they each have an equity of $28,500, or a total equity of $57,000.

Advantages Like the sole proprietorship, the partnership as a form of legal organization enjoys simplicity and ease in getting started and in some cases savings in income taxes.

The partnership is able to obtain more equity capital than the sole proprietorship, because the amount available is determined by the personal fortunes of two or more partners. One reason so many proprietorships evolve into partnerships is to raise more equity capital. For example, a person with a new idea may find another person who is willing to contribute a major share of the needed capital to turn the idea into a profitable business operation for both of them. Thus, the necessary amount of capital is acquired through the formation of a partnership.

An advantage closely related to raising equity capital is the enlarged credit standing, or ability to borrow capital, of the partnership. Because the personal wealth of all the partners is available to pay debts of the business organization, the partnership enjoys a higher credit standing than a sole proprietorship. If all other things were equal, we could expect a banker to be willing to lend more money to a partnership than to a sole proprietorship. Many partnerships are formed to take advantage of greater managerial ability. Because numerous functions are involved in the operation of a business, partners proficient in different functions may complement each other. This combined effort leads to greater managerial ability.

Disadvantages A partnership form of organization does not offer all the answers because it, too, has certain disadvantages. As in the sole proprietorship, the chief disadvantage is the unlimited financial liability. In the case of a partnership, the responsibility for the debts of the business is shared individually as well as jointly. Consequently, the unlimited financial liability could result in one partner being forced to pay not only his or her own share of the debts of the firm, but all of the debts of the firm.

Consider the Appelman and Kerwich partnership. Each person has invested $28,500. Now suppose that the firm subsequently incurred debts of $70,000, for all of which Appelman was responsible. After the investment of $57,000 has been paid to satisfy the debts of $70,000, Kerwich would be required to pay the remaining $23,000, because Appelman had no personal assets. Kerwich had unlimited financial liability (as did Appelman) and was required to delve into his personal assets to pay the debts.

Unlike the sole proprietorship, a partner cannot merely decide to sell the inventory and lock the door. A partner's investment is frozen because of the difficulty of transferring his or her interest to another partner. When partners wish to sell their interests, they must find other people with enough capital and who are acceptable to the other partners, or sell out to the remaining partners. Either course of action may be difficult to follow and can result in the partners' investments remaining frozen or being tied up for some time. A frozen investment is difficult to transfer and often occurs in the partnership form of organization.

In forming a partnership, you must accept your partners just as you accept a wife or a husband—for better or for worse. Although better decisions usually result from the combined judgments of the partners, such division of decision making can cause personal difficulties. More partnerships have been dissolved because of personal difficulties than for any other reason.

Because any change in the combination of partners automatically causes a dissolution of the firm, the partnership has limited life. Like the sole proprietorship, the death, incapacity, or withdrawal of one of the partners terminates the original partnership aggreement. The admission of a new partner or the sale of a partner's interest also ends the old partnership. Simply because there are more people involved, the limited life poses a larger problem in the partnership than in the sole proprietorship.

The Corporation

In 1819, Chief Justice John Marshall defined a **corporation** as "an artificial being, invisible, intangible, and existing in contemplation of law." A corporation is thus a legal entity separate and apart from its owners. The ownership of a corporation is divided into equal parts called shares of stock. Persons who own shares of stock are called shareowners, or shareholders, or stockholders. They elect officers who manage the business. Of course, if they own the majority of voting stock, they can and often do elect themselves as managers.

A major legal feature of the corporation is that it can be dealt with separately just like an individual. This means that the corporation serves as a buffer between the owners and the firm's customers, employees, suppliers, creditors, government, and community. The corporation can hold, buy, sell, and exchange property in the corporation's name. In a sole proprietorship or partnership, property must be held in the name of the individual owners.

Corporation A firm in which the ownership is divided into equal parts called shares, with each shareholder's liability limited to the amount of his or her investment in the firm.

EXHIBIT 21.3

Balance sheet of an incorporated firm

A corporation owns all of its assets in the name of the firm. Ownership of the firm's capital stock is their equity. Shareholders are liable for the firm's debts only to the extent that they have invested money in the firm.

Assets (Owns)		Debts (Owes)	
Cash	$30,500	Accounts payable	$ 500
Inventory	10,000	Mortgage payable	5,000
Equipment	2,000	Total debts	$ 5,500
Land and buildings	20,000	Capital stock	57,000
		Total debts plus	
Total assets	$62,500	capital stock	$62,500

Let us suppose that our partnership of Kerwich and Appelman decide to incorporate. They could transfer their owner's equity from a partnership interest to a stockholder's interest. Their balance sheet would appear as in Exhibit 21.3.

Notice that the $57,000 of owner's equity (in a sole proprietorship and partnership) is now called capital stock. The ownership remains essentially the same, but it is called something else. Why would an owner prefer a corporation as the legal form of organization?

Advantages The advantages of being a separate entity is that the owners carry only limited financial liability. This limited financial liability allows creditors to look only to the assets of the corporation for settlement of their claims. The creditors cannot hold the owners liable for the debts of the corporation. Should the corporation fail, the stockholders would lose the amount of their investment, but their personal assets could not be attached to pay the corporate debts.

This is not the case for a sole proprietorship or partnership, where the owners are held liable for all the debts and would be forced to pay them out of their personal assets. In a corporation, the owner's liability is limited only to their investment.

The corporation can grow to a larger size than a sole proprietorship or partnership. This is because it can attract capital from thousands of individuals. A corporation can expand or increase its size because the advantage of limited financial liability makes investors more willing to purchase additional shares of stock. It is easier for a corporation to raise $1 million by having a thousand people invest $1,000 each than it is to have one person invest $1 million in a sole proprietorship.

In addition, corporations may find it easier to borrow money from creditors because of their larger size. The larger size of most corporations in the United States is evidenced by the fact that more private capital is invested in corporations than in any other form of business organization.

A transfer of ownership is easily accomplished in the case of a corporation, especially those with capital stock listed and traded on the major stock exchanges and in the "over-the-counter" market. Millions of shares of capital stock change hands daily. As a general rule, corporations allow stockholders to transfer their ownership to anyone at any time (assuming that the price is agreeable to both buyer and seller) without the approval of the other stockholders.

Such an advantage of transferability of ownership also encourages continuity of the firm, although continuity depends on features other than transferability of capital stock. However, corporate life is not usually dependent on the life of an owner, as in the case of a partnership.

Disadvantages First among the disadvantages of the corporation is that it is subject to higher taxes than other forms of legal organizations. A corporation has to pay a tax to the state when it is incorporated. In addition to the franchise tax, the corporation is required to pay the federal corporate income tax on all earnings above $25,000.

In most states, the corporation is also required to pay a state income tax. In addition, the owners of a corporation must pay individual income taxes on all the dividends received from the corporation. The double taxation (on the corporate profits and on the dividends) is a major disadvantage of a corporation as far as owners are concerned. Corporations are also closely regulated. The regulations usually take the form of special reports, permits, and licenses. In large corporations, these reports require the services of at least one full-time employee or even a department. Close regulation can add to costs of doing business and can be a distinct disadvantage to the corporation form of organization.

Some Data on Business Organization

According to Coase's theory, described earlier this chapter, the firm exists because some tasks are more easily coordinated by managerial directive than by prices and markets. The theory predicts that each firm will grow until the cost of coordinating one more task within the firm exceeds the cost of coordinating one more task via the market. This limit to growth occurs at vastly different stages of development for different firms.

In 1972, there were almost 13 million firms in the United States, earning receipts totaling $2.5 trillion. Over 10 million of the firms were proprietorships, 1.8 million were corporations, and less than 1 million were partnerships. Exhibit 21.4 shows that the relatively small number of corporations accounted for the overwhelming share (86 percent) of business receipts. The reason is to be found in the advantages the proprietorship offers to small firms, and the corporation to large firms. Exhibit 21.5 confirms this impression. Some 76 percent of all proprietorships had receipts of less than $25,000 per year. Over half of all partnerships were below this same mark, but only about a quarter of all corporations. Corporations with $1 million or more in annual receipts numbered less than 2 percent of all firms, but accounted for nearly 80 percent of all business receipts. The relative advantages of the three types of firms vary greatly from one industry to another, as Exhibit 21.6 reveals.

The categories of manufacturing, mining, transportation and utilities, and finance and insurance are heavily dominated by corporations. Agriculture, at the other extreme, is dominated by the proprietorship— the family farm. Proprietorships are also very important in services (40 percent of receipts) and have a strong representation in wholesale

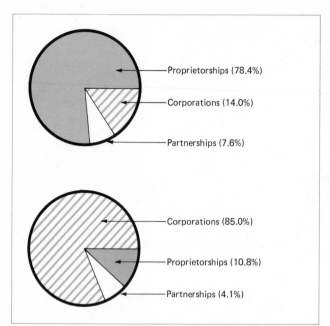

EXHIBIT 21.4

Distribution of firms by type of legal organization (1972 data)

In examining the various forms of legal organization available to the firm, we saw that the proprietorship had advantages for small firms and the corporation had advantages for large firms. The data given in these charts confirm this. Top figure shows that proprietorships constitute more than three-quarters of the number of all firms, but, as the bottom figure shows, only 4.1 percent of all business receipts accrue to proprietorships. The vast majority of receipts are earned by the relatively small number of corporations.

Source: U.S. Bureau of the Census, *Statistical Abstract of the United States, 1975* (Washington, D.C.: U.S. Government Printing Office, 1976).

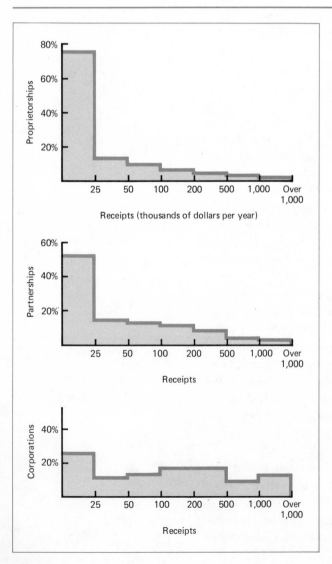

EXHIBIT 21.5

Size distribution of firms by type of organizational form (1972 data)

This exhibit presents further evidence that the proprietorship is favored as a form of legal organization predominantly by small firms. Note that the size profile of corporations is the reverse of that for proprietorships and partnerships.

Source: U.S. Bureau of the Census, *Statistical Abstract of the United States, 1975* (Washington, D.C.: U.S. Government Printing Office, 1976).

EXHIBIT 21.6

Distribution of types of firm in various industries

Firms of all types find their place in every industry, but some forms suit some industries better than others. The corporation dominates all major industrial groups except agriculture, where proprietorships dominate. Proprietorships are also important in services, trade, and construction. Only in the fields of finance, insurance, and real estate do partnerships hold a larger share of the industry than proprietorships.

Industry	Percentage of Receipts*		
	Proprietorships	Partnerships	Corporations
Agriculture, forestry, and fisheries	67	12	21
Mining	7	5	88
Construction	19	6	75
Manufacturing	1	1	98
Transportation, communication, electrical, gas, and sanitary services	4	1	95
Wholesale and retail trade	15	4	81
Finance, insurance, and real estate	4	7	89
Services	31	14	55

*1972 data.

Source: U.S. Bureau of the Census, *Statistical Abstract of the United States, 1975* (Washington, D.C.: U.S. Government Printing Office, 1976).

and retail trade (17 percent of receipts). Partnerships are the least common type of firm in every industry but finance, insurance, and real estate.

Ownership and Control of Corporations

Proprietorships are owned and controlled by their proprietors, and partnerships by their partners. Corporations are legally owned by their shareholders, but the matter of control is much less clearcut than for other types of firms. Because corporations do such a large part of America's business, no discussion of the nature of the firm would be complete without some mention of the controversy over control of the corporation.

Shareholder Rights

One of the advantages of the corporate form of business organization is that capital can be raised from many thousands of separate individuals, who need not invest a large share of their own portfolios in any one firm. Legally, those shareholders have the power to control the corporation. The principal channel for control is the shareholders' power to elect the corporation's board of directors, who decide company policy.

However, a great many, indeed most, shareholders do not actively exercise their ownership rights. Small shareholders are not really in a position to know what goes on inside "their" corporation, and why decisions are made as they are. They tend to accept the policies set by managers as all for the best. If they disapprove of management policies, it is easier for them to sell their stock and buy shares in a better-managed company than to try to throw their weight around at annual shareholder meetings. The result is a degree of separation of ownership from control unknown in proprietary firms or partnerships.

Shareholders Versus Managers

Why is the separation of ownership and control an important issue? The answer given by many economists is the interests of the shareholders. Most shareholders have only one interest in the corporation whose stock they own: that the corporation earn a maximum profit for them. Managers do not always think of their relationship to the corporation in such simple terms. For one thing, managers are naturally concerned about the security of their own jobs. They know that they must earn at least a respectable minimum of profits, or the shareholders may rebel and throw them out, but when it comes to delicate decisions involving marginal trade-offs between risk and profitability, their interests and those of stockholders may diverge. Shareholders do not normally put all their eggs in one basket. They hold diversified portfolios and if prudent risks can earn higher average returns, an occasional failure is no disaster. Because a manager's career is more closely tied up with the fate of a single corporation, or even a single project of a corporation, managers may tend to be excessively cautious from the shareholder's point of view.

Corporate growth is another possible area of conflict of interest. Shareholders are interested in growth to the extent that growth means more profit per share, but managers may sometimes favor growth purely for its own sake. The power and prestige of managers, the number of employees they have working under them, and even their salaries are enhanced by growth whether that growth increases profit per share or not.

Finally, it is claimed that managers who identify personally with their firms may be more willing than shareholders to spend money to improve their corporation's "image." Lavish headquarters, charitable contributions, community relations projects, and the like may in some cases attract customers and swell profits, but because they also swell managerial pride, there can be a temptation to carry them too far.

In short, the picture offered by some observers of the corporate scene is one of contrast between the traditional firm, single-mindedly pursuing the goal of profit maximization, and the modern management-controlled corporation, for which profits are only one goal among many, and not always the highest-ranking one.

Constraints on Managers

How much truth is there in this picture? The question cannot be regarded as altogether settled. Still, there are strong reasons to believe that managers cannot really act as independently of the profit-maximizing interests of owners as the preceding arguments might suggest.

For one thing, there are plans in existence in many corporations that permit management to share directly in company profits. One of the most important types of profit-sharing plans is the stock option. Managers benefit from stock options only if the quoted price of their corporation's stock rises. Stock prices, in turn, can be expected to reflect the degree of stockholder approval of management policies.

A second important constraint on the power of managers to slacken their pursuit of profits is the device of the takeover bid. It is true that when ordinary stockholders do not like a corporation's policy, they might simply sell out and buy other stocks rather than attempt to exercise their influence directly. But what if a great many shareholders do this? If they do, the price of the stock falls below the value it would have if the corporation were managed by profit maximizers. When this happens, an alert stock market entrepreneur can engineer a takeover bid. The takeover can be made by an individual, a group, or often another corporation. The idea is to buy a controlling percentage of the corporation's shares, and use the power thus gained to replace current managers with a more profit-minded team. If the gambit succeeds, the listed value of the stock's price will rise as the new management policies attract other buyers. Then the original takeover group reaps very handsome gains.

In practice, successful takeover bids do not occur with great frequency. This need not be interpreted, though, as meaning that they are ineffective in keeping management on the profit-maximizing track. Rather, the relative infrequency of takeovers probably indicates that few management groups neglect profits to a serious extent. The potential takeover is a powerful disciplinary device that can work its effect without being used every day.

Conclusions

In this chapter we have gotten just a glimpse of some of the complexities lying behind the simple concept of "the firm." In many branches of economic theory, we treat firms as simple, homogeneous building blocks. In reality, they are neither simple nor homogeneous. Except for the simplest one-person operations, each firm is an organization of separate individuals, united for a common purpose. The common purpose is to carry out more effectively the division of labor. Depending on circumstances, this purpose may best be served by the legal form of a proprietorship, partnership, or corporation. In the next few chapters we shall set aside most of these details and complexities. We shall treat firms as simple units devoted to the maximization of profits. This simplifying assumption may not be altogether appropriate in each individual case, however. What we have learned here may help us keep the firm in perspective, and help us to avoid thinking of the simplifications of theory as the whole picture.

SUMMARY

1. There are two major ways of coordinating the division of labor—market coordination and managerial coordination. Market coordination uses the price system for communication and the profit motive as a source of incentives. Managerial coordination proceeds through directives from superiors to subordinates. Managerial coordination is used to organize the division of labor within a firm, and market coordination to organize the division of labor among firms. Firms tend to grow until the cost of organizing one more task by managerial means exceeds the costs of organizing that task through the market.

2. The managers of a firm engage in two important types of decision making. Managerial calculation proceeds on the basis of given technology, prices, and demand conditions. Managerial calculation dominates when the firm is in equilibrium. Entrepreneurial decision making takes place in the unknown or uncertain conditions of market disequilibrium. It consists primarily of alertness to new profit making opportunities.

3. Firms may be organized as sole proprietorships, partnerships, or corporations. Proprietorships are very common for small firms. They are easy to set up, and have the advantage of giving the proprietor rights to all of the firm's profits. They have the disadvantage of unlimited liability. Partnerships also suffer from unlimited liability, but they can allow a firm to grow by bringing in new partners with new skills and new capital. Corporations protect their shareholders with limited liability, and permit huge sums of capital to be raised. They suffer the disadvantages of higher taxes and closer regulations than other kinds of businesses, however.

4. It is sometimes argued that managers, rather than shareholders, exercise effective control over corporations. This is an important issue, because the interests of managers and shareholders may sometimes conflict. Managers may be less willing than owners to take risks, and may sometimes pursue growth at the expense of profits. There are limits to the ability of managers to pursue policies opposed to shareholder interests, though. The most important single constraint is the threat of takeover if profits are too much neglected.

DISCUSSION QUESTIONS

1. Your college or university uses a type of managerial coordination to determine which courses should be offered and which professors should teach them. In principle, market coordination could be used instead. The college or university could limit itself to providing classrooms, dormitories, library facilities, and so forth. Professors would then be independent businesspeople, advertising that they would offer certain courses for so much per credit hour, and collecting fees directly from the students. Compare the advantages and disadvantages of each system. Why do you think the managerial system predominates? As far as you know, is the market system ever used in education?

2. The Dryden Press, publisher of this book, does not perform all of the operations necessary to bring out the book "in house." Instead, many particular jobs, such as manuscript typing, copy editing, drawing the artwork, composition, and printing are done on a subcontract basis by independent firms. How does Coase's theory of the firm help you understand why Dryden does not maintain all the necessary draftsmen, compositors, printers, and so forth on its own payroll?

3. John Day is playing around in the lab one day and produces a curious liquid. Accidentally, he spills it on the floor. His lab partner, Jane Ray, notices that when he has wiped up the spill, all the wax has been lifted from the floor in that spot. She suggests he market the mixture as a household wax remover. John finds out the prices of all the ingredients, the prices of existing wax removers, the size of the market for wax removers, and so forth. The project looks profitable, so he goes into business. Is John an entrepreneur? Is Jane? Do you think Jane, who contributes nothing to the project but the one suggestion, deserves a share of the profits?

4. On graduation, a classmate whom you barely know suggests that you go into business together selling sports equipment to students in your university town. He wants to make the business a partnership. "You supply the brains, I'll put up the money," he says. Do you think you might be better off if he set the business up as a sole proprietorship, with you as his employee? As a corporation, with the two of you each holding some of the stock? What would be the advantages and disadvantages to you of each alternative?

5. Why are corporations dominant in some lines of business, and not in others? As our economy becomes more service oriented, do you think the importance of the corporation will decline?

6. Corporation law varies from state to state in the United States. Sometimes states make changes in their corporation law in the hope of attracting new businesses into the state, and creating new jobs. Suppose the state where you lived wanted to change the law so that it would be almost impossible to make a successful takeover bid against a corporation located there. Do you think this would work as a means of attracting corporations, assuming that other states did not follow the move? Why and how would it work? Do you think it would be good for the economy as a whole if all states passed such legislation?

CHAPTER 22
The Theory of Cost

What You Will Learn in This Chapter
Further exploration of microeconomic theory requires a better understanding of what lies behind the supply curve. This, in turn, requires a theory of costs. What exactly do we mean by the term "cost"? How do costs vary as output varies for a typical firm? How do different time horizons affect our analysis of cost? These and other questions will be examined below.

For Review
Here are some important terms and concepts that will be put to use in this chapter. Be certain that you understand them, or review them before proceeding.

    Opportunity cost (Chapter 1)
    The margin (Chapter 1)

In earlier chapters, we have drawn many upward-sloping supply curves. These curves indicate that when prices are high, suppliers are willing to offer more of their product for sale then when prices are low. We suggested, in an offhand way, that the upward slope of such supply curves had something to do with costs of production. Now it is time to take up that suggestion in more detail, and develop a theory of costs. The theory of cost will later help us understand more precisely what lies behind the upward-sloping supply curve.

The Nature of Costs
Just what do we mean by the term "cost"? A cost means a sacrifice of some kind. If something is costly, we know that something else of value must be given up in order to get it. If we want to measure costs, we need to add up these sacrifices. Let us see how the costs of producing output can be added up for a typical business firm.

Explicit and Implicit Costs
The most obvious costs of production for a firm are the costs of buying the inputs it needs to operate. These include the labor and raw materials used in actual production operations, the services of managers, and sales-

people, insurance, legal advice, shipping services, and a great many other things. All of these things must be paid for. A firm's accountants can add up such outlays made to obtain these outputs. The total of all such outlays make up what we call the **explicit private costs** of production for the firm.

In addition to explicit costs, there are other costs that represent real sacrifices to the firm. These are what we call **implicit private costs.** Implicit private costs are the opportunity costs to the firm of using resources that the firm itself owns. When a firm occupies a building or uses machinery that it owns itself, it foregoes the opportunity of using that building or machinery in some other way. When the owner of a small proprietorship works alongside his employees, he foregoes the opportunity to work elsewhere. Firms do not normally note costs like these in their accounts, because no explicit payments are made to outsiders. That does not make the costs any less real, though. Income that could have been earned by selling or hiring out the firm's resources to others is sacrificed.

If we add together a firm's explicit and implicit costs of production, we get its **total private costs.** In economics, when we speak of a firm's *costs* with no modifiers attached, we always have in mind total private cost, that is, implicit and explicit costs together.

Private Cost and Opportunity Cost

How is this newly defined concept of total private cost related to that of opportunity cost? In a market economy, the two tend to be at least approximately equal. The reason is that firms must compete with one another for the inputs they purchase. Consider, for example, farmers who want to buy fuel and machinery to use in growing wheat. To get those inputs, they must compete with others who are trying to buy fuel and machinery to produce clothing, housing, cars, or other products. Each dollar of private cost for the farmers means a lost opportunity for some clothing producers, or housing contractors, or whatever to buy that dollar's worth of resources and use it in their own lines of production. Buying fuel or machinery to grow wheat, then, means not using those same resources to produce clothing or housing or cars. Private costs thus tend to correspond dollar for dollar with real opportunity costs when inputs are bought in the marketplace.

This tendency of private costs to reflect real opportunity costs is not without exceptions, however. Private costs are measured only from the point of view of a single firm, while opportunity costs are measured from the point of view of the economy as a whole. When a firm uses scarce resources without paying for them, the two kinds of costs need not correspond, as illustrated in the following case study.

CASE 22.1
Opportunity Costs of Coke Production[1]

In 1975, the United States Steel Corporation was operating a coke plant in Duluth, Minnesota. Total private costs of operating this plant, which produced 600,000 tons of coke a year, included expenditures for coal (the raw material), labor, and capital equipment. But raw material, labor, and capital are not the only resources the plant used. It also used the water of the St. Louis River

---

Explicit Private Costs All costs that a firm must cover by explicit payments to outsiders.

Implicit Private Costs The opportunity cost to a firm of using resources that the firm itself owns.

Total Private Costs Explicit plus implicit private costs.

---

[1]Based on an item in *The New York Times*, August 8, 1975.

and the air of the city of Duluth to dispose of thousands of tons of waste annually. The air and water were important and valuable inputs to the production process. U.S. Steel estimated that if the plant were forced to do without them, the costs of finding alternative methods of waste disposal that did not pollute the air and water around Duluth would be some $10 million.

Unlike the raw material, labor, and capital used by the plant, the air and water were not purchased in the marketplace. No fees or rentals were paid for their use, so no explicit or implicit private costs for them were entered on the company's books. Yet use of these resources *did* impose an opportunity cost on the local economy. Use of the air for disposal of gaseous wastes made it less suitable for breathing. Use of the river for the disposal of water-borne wastes preempted opportunities to use the river for fishing, drinking, or recreation. A complete reckoning of the opportunity cost of operating the coke plant would have to take these environmental costs into account. It would reveal that the opportunity cost of producing coke at this plant far exceeded the total private cost of production.

This example suggests that we must be cautious in interpreting private costs as opportunity costs. Sometimes there are imperfections in the market system that permit firms to use resources without paying for them. Then private costs fall short of opportunity costs. Other times market imperfections may force a firm to pay private costs for resources that exceed their opportunity costs. In later chapters, we shall discuss some policy problems that arise when private costs and opportunity costs do not match up properly. For the remainder of the present chapter, though, we shall set these issues aside and concentrate exclusively on private costs.

Costs in the Short Run

Now that we know clearly what we mean by cost, we can proceed to build a theory of cost. This theory answers the question, how do costs change as output changes? In developing this theory, we shall make use of two well-established conventions. One of these is the use of a simplified "typical" firm to illustrate the major features of the theory. (Later we shall compare this conventional "typical" firm with the kinds of firms that are found in the real-world economy). The second convention is a distinction between two different time perspectives, the long run and the short run. These deserve a bit of further explanation.

The Long Run and the Short Run

A firm uses many kinds of inputs to produce its outputs. By varying the quantities of inputs it uses, it can vary the quantity of output produced. Not all inputs can be varied as easily as others, though. The quantities of some things that a firm uses (say, raw materials, energy, and hourly labor) can often be adjusted very quickly. In contrast, inputs such as structures, basic capital equipment, and the services of salaried management are not so easy to adjust.

The distinction between inputs that are easily varied to meet changing production requirements and those that are not easily varied forms the basis of the distinction between the long-run and short-run perspectives in cost theory. We define the **short run** as any time perspective short enough that the quantities of at least some inputs cannot be changed. Those inputs

Short-Run Perspective Any time perspective short enough that the quantities of at least some of a firm's inputs cannot be varied.

Variable Inputs   Those inputs whose quantities can be varied in response to short-run changes in output.

Fixed Inputs   Those inputs whose quantities cannot be varied in response to short-run changes in output.

Long-Run Perspective   Any time perspective long enough that the quantities of all of a firm's inputs can be varied.

Diminishing Returns (Law of)   If the output of some good is increased by increasing the quantity of one variable input while the quantity of other inputs used remains fixed, then a point will eventually be reached beyond which the quantity of output produced by each additional unit of the variable input will diminish.

that can be varied in the short run are called **variable inputs,** and those that cannot be varied in the short run are called **fixed inputs.** The **long run,** in contrast, is a time perspective long enough that the quantities of all inputs can be varied.

Farming provides some good illustrations of the differences between fixed and variable inputs, and between the short- and long-run time perspectives. Suppose that a certain farmer raises wheat. In the short run, we can consider the farmer's land to be a fixed input. Even with a fixed quantity of land, though, he can vary the quantity of wheat he grows by devoting more or less labor to each acre. By double- or triple-plowing before the crop is sown, by greater efforts to control weeds and pests, or by greater care to avoid waste at harvest time, the yield per acre can be increased. In the long run, the farmer may also be able to vary the amount of land he uses. He can buy more land nearby, or clear some land previously not used for growing wheat. He can even move his whole farm to another area where more acreage is available. In the long run, there are no fixed inputs.

Diminishing Returns

The stage is now set to develop our short-run theory of cost. The theory is based on a well-known principle called the **law of diminishing returns.** According to the law of diminishing returns, if the output of some good is increased by increasing the quantity of one variable input while the quantity of other inputs used remains fixed, then a point will eventually be reached beyond which the quantity of output produced by each additional unit of the variable input will diminish.

The law of diminishing returns can be illustrated with the farming example we just gave. At one extreme, the farmer could use the least possible labor, simply scattering seeds on the bare ground and coming back later in the hope that something would have grown. Little wheat could be raised that way. Taking the time to plow the field before sowing would greatly increase the crop. A second plowing would increase the yield further, but not perhaps by as much as the first plowing. More and more work could be done to get more wheat from a given acre of land. Clearly, though, as more time were spent the farmer would move progressively to less and less essential operations. At the extreme of labor intensity, the farmer might hire dozens of workers to stand around the field frightening away birds so that not a single grain of wheat would be lost. By that point, though, the added output to be obtained from an added unit of labor input would have diminished to a very low level.

Exhibit 22.1 contains a sketch of what the relationship between output and labor input might be for a farmer growing wheat on 1 acre of land. Initially, there are great gains in output from using just a little labor. Soon, though, the output curve begins to bend downward. Output increases at a decreasing rate. As soon as the gain in output from each added unit of labor begins to decline, the principle of diminishing returns can be seen in operation.

Diminishing Returns and Cost

The law of diminishing returns has clear implications for cost theory. If a firm buys variable inputs at a constant price per unit, and if each unit of input contributes less to output than the previous one, the cost of pro-

EXHIBIT 22.1
Illustration of diminishing returns

According to the law of diminishing returns, if the output of some good is increased by increasing the quantity of one variable input while the quantity of other inputs remains constant, a point will eventually be reached beyond which the quantity of output produced by each additional unit of the variable input diminishes. This sketch shows the pattern of output of wheat when increasing amounts of labor are used on a fixed amount of land. The point of diminishing returns is reached where the curve begins to bend downward, so that output increases less than in proportion to labor input.

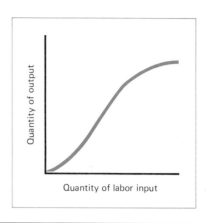

EXHIBIT 22.2
A typical short-run total cost curve

If input prices are constant, the law of diminishing returns implies that, beyond some point, short-run total costs will increase more than in proportion to output. In the case illustrated here, costs are not zero even when output is zero, because fixed inputs must still be paid for in the short run. For a while, costs increase less than in proportion to output, but beyond the point where the curve bends upward, they increase more than proportionately.

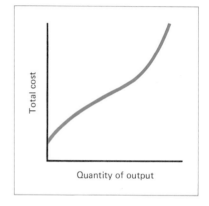

ducing each additional unit of output, in the short run, must rise. That in turn means that the total cost of production will rise more than in proportion to output in the short run. A typical short-run total cost curve will thus have roughly the shape shown in Exhibit 22.2. The firm's total costs are not zero even when output is zero, because some costs must be paid for fixed inputs regardless of how much output is produced. For a while, costs may rise less than in proportion to output, but eventually, the law of diminishing returns must come into effect. From that point, the short-run total cost curve begins to bend upward. Costs increase more than in proportion to output.

A Family of Short-Run Cost Curves

It is time now to introduce our typical firm, and a whole family of short-run cost curves for it. These curves are shown in the table and graphs of Exhibit 22.3.

The key to the whole family of cost curves is total cost. Total cost is shown numerically in column (2) of Exhibit 22.3a and graphically in Exhibit 22.3b. Total cost can be broken down into total fixed cost and total variable cost. Total fixed cost (here assumed to be $20) does not change, no matter what the level of output is. The graph of total fixed costs is a straight horizontal line, as shown in Exhibit 22.3b. Total variable cost is equal to total cost minus total fixed cost. The graph of total variable cost is symmetrical with the total cost curve, but lower by a distance just equal to total fixed cost.

EXHIBIT 22.3

A family of short-run cost schedules and curves

A whole family of short-run cost curves can be derived from the total cost data shown in part a of this exhibit. Three kinds of total cost curves are shown in part b, while average and marginal cost curves are shown in part c. Note that the marginal cost curve intersects the average total cost and average variable cost curves at their lowest points.

(a)

(1) Quantity of Output (Units)	(2) Total Cost ($)	(3) Total Fixed Cost ($)	(4) Total Variable Cost ($)	(5) Marginal Cost ($/Unit)	(6) Average Total Cost ($/Unit)	(7) Average Variable Cost ($/Unit)	(8) Average Fixed Cost ($/Unit)
0	20.00	20.00	0		0	0	—
1	23.80	20.00	3.80	3.80	23.80	3.80	20.00
2	27.20	20.00	7.20	3.40	13.60	3.60	10.00
3	30.25	20.00	10.25	3.05	10.09	3.42	6.67
4	33.00	20.00	13.00	2.75	8.25	3.25	5.00
5	35.00	20.00	15.50	2.50	7.10	3.10	4.00
6	37.80	20.00	17.80	2.30	6.29	2.96	3.33
7	39.95	20.00	19.95	2.15	5.71	2.85	2.86
8	42.00	20.00	22.00	2.05	5.25	2.75	2.50
9	44.00	20.00	24.00	2.00	4.88	2.66	2.22
10	46.05	20.00	26.05	2.05	4.60	2.60	2.00
11	48.20	20.00	28.20	2.15	4.37	.256	1.81
12	50.50	20.00	30.50	2.30	4.21	2.54	1.69
13	53.00	20.00	33.00	2.50	4.08	2.54	1.54
14	55.75	20.00	35.75	2.75	3.98	2.55	1.43
15	58.80	20.00	38.80	3.05	3.92	2.59	1.33
16	62.20	20.00	42.20	3.40	3.89	2.64	1.25
17	66.00	20.00	46.00	3.80	3.89	2.71	1.18
18	70.25	20.00	50.25	4.25	3.90	2.79	1.11
19	75.00	20.00	55.00	4.75	3.94	2.89	1.05
20	80.30	20.00	60.30	5.30	4.02	3.02	1.00
21	86.20	20.00	66.20	5.90	4.10	3.15	.95
22	92.75	20.00	72.75	6.55	4.22	3.31	.91
23	100.00	20.00	80.00	7.25	4.35	3.48	.87
24	108.00	20.00	88.00	8.00	4.50	3.67	.80

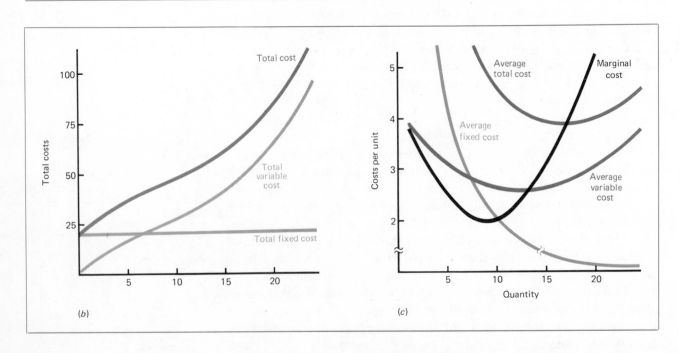

(b)

(c)

Next we turn to a variety of per-unit cost measures. These are shown numerically in columns (5)-(8) of Exhibit 22.3*a*, and graphically in Exhibit 22.3*c*. First we have the important item short-run **marginal cost.** The marginal cost of producing something means the rate at which total cost increases as output increases. (Alternately, think of marginal cost as the cost of producing one more unit.) Looking first at the table, we see that the numbers in the marginal cost column are equal to the differences between successive entries in the total variable cost column. For this firm, marginal cost falls for the first nine units of output, and then begins to rise again. That gives the short-run marginal cost curve drawn in Exhibit 22.3*c* its typical U shape.

The remaining three short-run cost concepts are all averages. Average total cost, average variable cost, and average fixed cost are each obtained by dividing the corresponding kind of total cost by the quantity of output. Average total cost and average variable cost produce U-shaped curves as shown in Exhibit 22.3*c*. The graph of average fixed cost is a smooth, downward-sloping curve with the shape known to mathematicians as a rectangular hyperbola.

The Marginal Average Rule

One feature of the cost curves drawn in Exhibit 22.3*c* deserves special comment. This is the fact that the marginal cost curve intersects both the average variable cost and average total cost curves exactly at their lowest points. This is not just coincidence. It is a consequence of a relationship that we can call the **marginal average rule.** This rule may be explained as follows: Beginning at any given point, ask what would be the cost of producing one more unit. The answer is given by marginal cost. Then ask whether this is more or less than the average cost of all units produced up to that point. If the next unit produced costs less than the average of previous units, then producing it will have the effect of "pulling down" the average. If the next unit costs more, it will "pull up" the average. It follows that whenever marginal cost is below average variable cost, the average variable cost curve must be downward sloping, and whenever marginal cost is above average variable cost, the average variable cost curve must be upward sloping. This in turn implies that the marginal cost curve cuts the average variable cost curve at its lowest point. All this is equally true of the relationship between marginal cost and average total cost.

Costs in the Long Run

Let us shift our perspective to the long run now, and take another look at the costs of production for our typical firm. In the long run, we recall, there are no fixed inputs. The firm is assumed to have time enough to adjust not just some, but all of its inputs to the rate of output it expects to maintain. Suppose that our typical firm uses just two inputs, labor and capital. In the short run, the quantity of output can be adjusted by varying the quantity of labor used. The amount of capital, that is, the size of the firm's physical plant, must remain fixed in the short run. In the long run, though, both the quantity of labor and the size of plant used can be varied.

Suppose you are an entrepreneur just in the process of establishing a

Marginal Cost The rate at which total cost increases as output increases. Alternately, the cost of producing one additional unit of output.

Marginal Average Rule The rule that marginal cost must be equal to average cost when average cost is at its minimum.

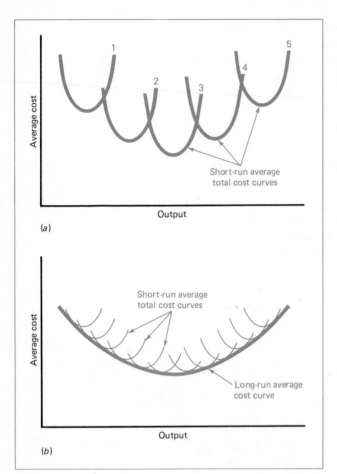

(a)

(b)

EXHIBIT 22.4
Derivation of the long-run average cost curve
In the long run, the firm has a choice of operating with any size plant it chooses. Each plant size can be represented by a different U-shaped short-run average total cost curve. Five such curves are shown in part *a* of the exhibit. By choosing the plant size best suited to each level of output, the firm can move along the long-run average cost curve. This curve, shown in part *b*, is the envelope of all possible short-run cost curves, including those shown in part *a*.

new firm. You think it wise to start with only a small plant, but you want to do some long-range planning too. You might, for example, calculate what your average total costs would be for several plants of larger size than the one with which you plan to start. As you build up the market for your firm's product, you can hope gradually to expand to larger and larger plants.

Exhibit 22.4*a* shows the framework for this long-range planning in terms of a series of short-run average total cost curves, each for a different-size plant. Each short-run average total cost curve is U shaped, as was the corresponding curve in Exhibit 22.3*c*. We see tht for the first few stages of expansion, moving up to a larger plant lowers the short-run average total cost curve. Beyond a point, though, further expansion of the plant begins to raise the short-run cost curve again.

The five short-run cost curves shown in Exhibit 22.4*a* represent only a sample of possible plant sizes. Intermediate poisitions are also possible. The size of plant a firm actually chooses to build depends, in the long run, on the quantity of output it expects to produce. For any given output, the firm will, in the long run, choose the size of plant that will permit that output to be produced at the lowest possible average total cost. As a firm gradually expands, it will move along a **long-run average cost** curve of the kind shown

Long-Run Average Cost   The cost per unit of producing a given output when the quantities of all inputs have been adjusted to reduce that cost to a minimum.

in Exhibit 22.4b. This curve is simply the "envelope" of all possible short-run average cost curves. The size of plant chosen in the long run for each output will be the one that produces a short-run average total cost curve just tangent to the long-run average total cost curve at that point.

Economies and Diseconomies of Scale

Economists have developed some special terminology to describe what happens to long-run average costs as output increases. In any range of output where long-run average cost *decreases* as output *increases,* the firm for which the cost curves are drawn is said to experience **economies of scale.** In any range of output where long-run average cost *increases* as output *increases,* the firm is said to experience **diseconomies of scale.** Finally, if there is any range of output for which long-run average cost does not change as output changes, the firm is said to experience **constant returns to scale** in that range.

Why do average costs change as the scale of output changes? Economies of scale can be attributed to two types of sources, managerial and technological. The managerial sources of economies of scale are those mentioned in the last chapter—the factors that, according to Coase's theory, explain why there are firms of any size at all. Technological sources of economies of scale are of many different kinds. Sometimes production of a good involves development costs or setup costs that do not need to be repeated, no matter how many units of output are produced. Sometimes large scale permits more efficient organization of inventories of inputs and products. Often increased scale permits greater specialization in labor or equipment. Finally, increased scale may permit several stages of production to be linked in an advantageous way.

Diseconomies of scale may occasionally be of a technological nature, but more often they are thought to be organizational or managerial. There would be obvious diseconomies of scale in a venture such as trying to run a single restaurant or barber shop big enough to serve all the people of New York City. That sort of thing is not quite the whole story, though. More subtle managerial diseconomies of scale may make it uneconomical for a single *firm* to run all the restaurant or barbering services in the city even if it operates as a network of individual outlets of normal size.

Constant returns to scale really require no special explanations. They can exist whenever economies of scale are exhausted before diseconomies set in, or perhaps in some cases where economies and diseconomies of scale exactly balance each other off over some range of output.

Real-World Economies of Scale

The economist's "typical" firm has a U-shaped long-run average cost curve. Such a curve shows first economies and then diseconomies of scale with no constant returns section between. In this pattern, so convenient for explaining elementary theory, really typical of real-world firms? Research suggests that it is not. Here is an example of empirical study that concluded that a wide range of industries have L-shaped long-run average cost curves.

Economies of Scale Said to be experienced whenever long-run average cost decreases as output increases.

Diseconomies of Scale Said to be experienced whenever long-run average cost increases as output increases.

Constant Returns to Scale Said to be experienced when there are neither economies nor diseconomies of scale.

CASE 22.2
Economies of Scale in Britain[2]

In 1972, Aubrey Silberston of St. John's College, Cambridge, published an analysis of economies of scale in thirty British industries. The data he used were gathered by his colleague, Cliff Pratten, using technical and engineering data submitted by industries themselves.

The data indicated that long-run average cost curves in the industries studies tended to be L shaped, with average costs falling at first, and then leveling out when the major sources of economies of scale were exhausted. (If it is true that diseconomies of scale arise from managerial rather than technical limitations, it is perhaps not surprising that a study based on engineering data had little to say about them.) Given the L-shaped pattern of the cost curves, Silberston developed two measures of the strength of economies of scale in each industry. One measure was the *minimum economic scale*—the scale of production at which the average cost curve substantially flattens out. The other measure is the increased average cost "penalty" that would result from operating at an output of one-half the minimum economic scale.

Silberston's findings for the thirty industries are recorded in Exhibit 22.5. In this exhibit, the industries are ranked in order of the significance of economies of scale. This is measured by the percentage of the total British market that could be supplied by one plant operating at the minimum economic scale. (For industries that ordinarily cater only to local markets— cement, bread, beer, and bricks—the size of the local rather than the national market was used as a basis for comparison.) The exhibit shows that for the industries where economies of scale are greatest, the British market by itself is not large enough for efficient operation. The minimum economic scale can be achieved only by producing for export as well as for the domestic market—which these industries of course do. For twenty of the industries, economies of scale were small enough to permit two or more efficient-sized plants even in the relatively small British market. For nine industries, ten or more firms could fit in the market.

The second measure of economies of scale ranks the industries in a somewhat different order. For some of the industries with very large minimum efficient scales—diesel engines, machine tools, and turbo-generators, in particular—the penalty for operating at half the efficient scale would be only a 10 percent increase in costs. In other industries, the penalty would be so great as to make production much below the minimum economic scale entirely impractical.

[2]Based on Aubrey Silberston, "Economies of Scale in Theory and Practice," *The Economic Journal*, March 1972.

Short-Run Costs in the Real World

Case 22.2 suggests that the long-run average cost curves for many real-world firms are L shaped, rather than U shaped like those of the theorist's "typical" firm. What about the short-run cost curves of real firms? Are short-run marginal and average cost curves really U shaped like those in Exhibit 23.3c?

Available data for the short run are less conclusive than for the long run. Many studies have indicated, though, that short-run marginal costs tend to be roughly constant, at least over some normal range of variation in output. This means that the short-run marginal cost curves of actual firms have extensive flat spots, even if they do perhaps fall at very low levels of output and rise at very high levels. Unfortunately, many of the studies in

EXHIBIT 22.5

Economies of scale in thirty British industries*

This exhibit ranks thirty British industries in terms of the importance to them of economies of scale. Column (2) shows one measure of economies of scale, namely, the minimum efficient scale of production (M.E.S.) as a percentage of the entire British market. Column (3) gives another measure of economies of sale, the cost penalty that would be incurred if the firm were to operate at half of the minimum efficient scale.

(1) Product†	(2) M.E.S. as Percent of British Market	(3) Percent Increase in Cost at 50 Percent M.E.S.‡
Aircraft	100	25
Diesel engines	100	10
Machine tools	100	10
Newspapers	100	40
Dyes	100	44
Turbo-generators	100	10
Computers, etc.	100	13
Steel rolling—plant	80	13
Polymer manufacture	66	23
Electric motors	60	20
Cars	50	13
Refrigerators, etc.	50	12
Oil refineries—plant	40	27
Cement§	40	17
Bulk steel production—plant	33	12–17
Bread—plant§	33	30
Polymer extrusion—plant	33	11
Sulphuric acid—plant	30	19
Cylinder blocks—plant	30	15
Ethylene—plant	25	30
Detergents—plant	20	20
Bicycles	10	(Small)
Beer—plant§	6	55
Bricks—plant§	5	30
Warp knitting—plant	3	(Small)
Cotton textiles—plant	2	(Small)
Book printing—plant	2	(Small)
Plastics—plant	1	(Small)
Engineering castings—plant	0.2	10
Footwear—plant	0.2	5

*Adapted from Aubrey Silberston, "Economies of Scale in Theory and Practice," *The Economic Journal*, March 1972, Table 2. Reprinted by permission.

†Unless plant is specified, "product" refers to one type, model, or range of models.

‡Increase in cost calculated as percentage of value added.

§M.E.S. calculated as a percentage of regional submarket.

question are open to criticism on various technical grounds. They do not mean that we need to discard the ideas of diminishing returns and increasing marginal costs from our theoretical discussions. They do indicate, though, that for practical business decisions one can often safely assume constant marginal costs.

Conclusions

In this chapter we have laid the groundwork for a theory of the supply curve. That groundwork consists of an analysis of the way that costs of production vary as the quantity of output produced by a firm varies. For the most part, our discussion has been framed in terms of a hypothetical "typical" firm. The typical firm traditionally discussed in economic theory is characterized by U-shaped average and marginal cost curves in both the short and long runs. Although this typical firm is very useful as a basis for explaining elementary theory, the reader must keep in mind that it is not necessarily typical in the sense of being the case most frequently encountered in the real world. Empirical studies of real-world firms have indicated that long-run cost curves may often be L shaped, and short-run cost curves may have extensive flat spots.

There are two directions in which we could proceed from here. One is to continue to develop a theory of the supply curve on the basis of the typical firm discussed in this chapter. This we shall do in Chapter 24. In the meanwhile, though, we invite the reader to take a short detour along an alternative path. There, in Chapter 23, we shall briefly explore some real-world problems related to cost and production from a managerial point of view. This should be of interest not only to those with a practical interest in management. The material will provide some important new theoretical insights too.

SUMMARY

1. A firm's costs of production include all of the sacrifices it must make in order to carry on production. Some of these take the form of explicit payments to outsiders, and are called explicit private costs. Others are opportunity costs of using resources owned by the firm itself. These are called implicit private costs. In some cases, total private costs may differ from opportunity costs, as calculated from the point of view of the economy as a whole. In particular, this will be the case when a firm uses scarce resources it does not own without paying for them.
2. The short run is a time period so short that not all of a firm's inputs can be varied in response to changes in output. In the short run, there must be some point beyond which the product of an extra unit of a variable input diminishes. Short-run average and marginal cost curves for the typical firm are U shaped. The marginal cost curve cuts the average variable cost and average total cost curves at their lowest points.
3. In the long run, a firm can adjust the quantities of all inputs in response to changes in output. A firm will choose the size of plant that will allow the expected long-run output to be produced at the minimum possible cost. A long-run average cost curve can be constructed as the envelope of a set of short-run average total cost curves, one for each possible size of plant.
4. A firm is said to experience economics of scale over any range of output where its long-run average cost curve slopes downward. Over any range of output where the long-run average cost curve slopes upward, it experiences diseconomies of scale. If there are flat spots on the long-run average cost curve, the firm is said to experience constant returns to scale there.
5. Empirical studies indicate that long-run average cost curves for many firms are L shaped rather than U shaped. Beyond some minimum efficient scale, constant returns to scale are experienced, at least over a wide range. Some evidence also exists to suggest that short-run marginal cost curves also have extensive flat spots, at least over the normal range of production.

DISCUSSION QUESTIONS

1. Consider the costs of owning and operating an automobile. Which of the costs are implicit private costs, and which are explicit private costs? Are there any economy-wide opportunity costs of operating an automobile that do not show up at all in your tally of private costs?

2. Now divide the costs of owning and operating an automobile into fixed costs and variable costs. Suppose that you were deciding whether to drive to a neighboring college to a football game or to take the bus instead. Would you take both fixed and variable costs into account? Suppose that you were deciding whether to buy a house in a neighborhood where you could walk to work, or a house located where you would have to buy a second car to drive to work every day. Would you then take both fixed and variable costs of the car into account?

3. It is sometimes said that "businesses plan in the long run but operate in the short run." Can you make any sense out of this aphorism?

4. What are the economies of scale and diseconomies of scale involved in running a university? Give specific examples.

5. Do you see any parallel between the law of diminishing returns and the principle of diminishing marginal utility? Do you think that both could be lumped together in a "law of diminishing marginal everything?" Try stating such a general law.

6. Take a piece of graph paper and draw, freehand, a typical reverse-S short-run total cost curve. Now, as accurately as you can, construct the corresponding average total cost, average variable cost, average fixed cost, and marginal cost curves. When you have mastered this, try something harder, just for fun. Draw some nontypical short-run total cost curves, say, with funny kinks or bends or perhaps bumps like a roller coaster. They will not make much economic sense, but trying to draw the average and marginal cost curves for them will be an excellent test of whether you can really understand a graph like Exhibit 22.3. If you cannot do this exercise successfully, you may need to review the appendix to Chapter 1 of this book.

7. Turn to Exhibit 22.4a. Copy this diagram onto a sheet of graph paper, drawing the long-run average cost curve and just one of the short-run average total cost curves. Use the curves you have drawn to construct the corresponding long-run and short-run total cost curves. The total cost curves you get should both be reverse-S shaped and should be tangent to one another at the same level of output at which the average cost curves are tangent.

CHAPTER 23
Cost and Production Problems of Business Management

What You Will Learn in This Chapter
Business decision making and pure economic theory are both places where the economic way of thinking can be applied. This can be illustrated with examples of both short-run and long-run decision making. Concepts such as fixed and variable costs, the production possibility frontier, and opportunity cost all find many practical applications.

For Review
Here are some important terms and concepts that will be put to use in this chapter. Be certain that you understand them, or review them before proceeding.
>   Production possibility frontier (Chapter 1)
>   Fixed and variable costs (Chapter 2)

Business administration and economic theory are closely related fields of study. What differences there are between the two stem for the most part from differences in the goals of business managers and economists. Economists look at how firms make decisions in order to gain insights into how markets work. With this goal in mind, they find such concepts as the "typical firm" or "market equilibrium" to be useful and productive. Business managers look at the economy with the more down-to-earth objective of learning how to maximize profits. Because no real-world manager ever sees a "typical firm" or a market that is truly in "equilibrium," such concepts are less used in the business world.

These differences should not be exaggerated, though. The principles of business administration are in a fundamental sense founded on economic theory. The economic way of thinking is common to both areas. Ideas such as margin and opportunity cost are as important for practical management as for pure theory. In this chapter we shall give some examples chosen to underline the connection between managerial economics and economic theory. We shall start by discussing some aspects of short-run decision making, and later move to the long-run and investment decisions.

Fixed costs:	
Copy editing and other editorial costs	$ 3,000
Preparation of illustrations	2,000
Typesetting	20,000
Total fixed costs	$25,000
Variable costs per copy:	
Printing and binding	$ 1.60
Bookstore discounts	2.40
Sales commissions	0.25
Author's royalties	1.60
General and administrative costs	1.15
Total variable costs per copy	$ 7.00
List price per copy	$12.00

Source: From *Managerial Economics* by Eugene F. Brigham and James L. Pappas (Hinsdale, Ill.: The Dryden Press, 1972), pp. 224–225. Copyright © 1972 by The Dryden Press, Inc., A Division of Holt, Rinehart and Winston. Adapted by permission of Holt, Rinehart and Winston.

EXHIBIT 23.1

Data for breakeven analysis of a new textbook

This exhibit lists the major fixed and variable costs of bringing out a typical new college textbook. The data given here can be used to construct the breakeven chart shown in Exhibit 23.2.

Business Decisions in the Short Run

Breakeven Analysis

Breakeven Analysis A business decision-making technique that relates fixed and variable costs to revenue per unit in order to identify the minimum level of output needed to break even on a project.

Let us begin with a very simple kind of problem. A firm needs to decide whether or not to introduce some new product. In the simplest case, the decision depends on just three things. First, it depends on the initial fixed costs of bringing the product out. Second, it depends on the variable cost of producing it. And third, the decision depends on the revenue that can be earned by selling the product. A technique called **breakeven analysis** gives an easy way of bringing these three factors together and arriving at a decision. An example will show how it works.[1]

The New Product Decision

The new product decision is a very common one for textbook publishers. Let us suppose that a firm is considering a new title that it expects to sell for $12 per copy. The fixed costs of bringing the book out consist of things like editing, original artwork, and typesetting. Variable costs include paper, printing and binding, bookstore discounts, sales commissions, and author's royalties. These can be treated as roughly constant over a wide range of output. For a typical new college textbook, the various costs might be those shown in Exhibit 23.1.

To make a breakeven analysis, we construct the chart shown in Exhibit 23.2. Here the vertical axis of measures total costs and revenue, while the horizontal axis measures the number of copies sold. Three lines are drawn on the chart. A diagonal line from the origin shows the way that total revenue grows as sales increase. The slope of this line is equal to the price per copy of $12. A horizontal line representing fixed costs is drawn at a height equal to the total fixed cost of $25,000. Finally, a diagonal line with a slope equal to the variable cost per copy ($7) is drawn beginning from the point where the fixed cost line intercepts the vertical axis. The height of this line at any point gives the total cost (fixed and variable together) of producing the corresponding number of books.

[1]This example is adapted from Eugene F. Brigham and James L. Pappas, *Managerial Economics* (Hinsdale, Ill.: The Dryden Press, 1972), pp 224–225.

EXHIBIT 23.2
Breakeven chart
This breakeven chart is based on the data given in Exhibit 23.1. The slope of the total revenue line is equal to the book's price per copy. The slope of the total cost line is equal to the variable cost per unit of the book. The total cost line begins at a point on the vertical axis representing the total fixed cost of bringing out the book. The point where the total revenue and total cost lines intersect is the breakeven point. This point shows the minimum number of copies that must be sold in order to make it worthwhile to bring out the book.

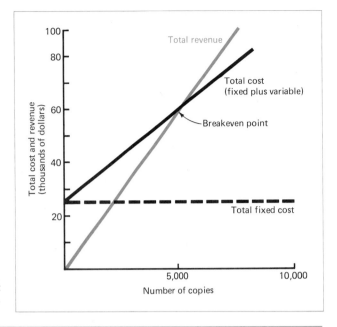

Once this chart is drawn, it is clear at a glance that the book ought to be brought out if the firm expects to sell at least 5,000 copies. The breakeven point is shown by the intersection of the two diagonal lines. To the left of this point, total costs exceed total revenue, and the firm would suffer a loss equal to the vertical distance between the diagonals. To the right of the breakeven point, the distance between the total revenue and total cost lines shows the profit to be earned if sales exceed the minimum.

This simple form of breakeven analysis can be applied to new product decisions in any firm where marginal costs are roughly constant. The empirical studies of short-run cost cited in the last chapter suggest that constant marginal costs are in fact often constant. Even if they are not, breakeven analysis is still possible. In the next chapter, we shall show how a form of breakeven analysis can be applied to the economist's traditional representative firm.

Linear Programming

Breakeven analysis is a useful tool when just one product is involved, and when all costs can be expressed in terms of money. Not all business problems are so simple. For one thing, many if not most firms produce more than one product. For another, money costs are not always the only kind of costs that must be kept in mind. The technique known as **linear programming** is a powerful tool often brought to bear on more complex business problems. The following very simple application, involving two products and three kinds of costs, will serve as an illustration of this useful technique.

Linear Programming A mathematical decision-making technique widely applicable in business decision making.

An Example

Acme Furniture is a small company that produces just two products, tables and chairs. When the costs of labor and raw materials are subtracted from the selling prices per unit of the two products, the firm earns a profit of $6 on each table produced, and $4 on each chair produced.

	Plane	Lathe	Wicker Machine
Table	15	10	. . .
Chair	5	20	30

EXHIBIT 23.3

Machine-time allocations for table and chair production at Acme Furniture Co. (figures are minutes per unit) Acme Furniture produces two products, tables and chairs. Output is constrained by the amount of time available on the firm's plane, lathe, and wicker machine. This table shows how much time on each machine is needed to produce one table or one chair.

Acme would like to expand its plant, but building new quarters and ordering new machinery will take time. In the short run, the firm's output of furniture is constrained by the fact that it owns just one lathe, one planing machine, and one machine for weaving chairseats. In the short run, then, opportunity costs of making tables and chairs are the amounts of machine time required for each type of furniture. Exhibit 23.3 shows how much time on each machine is required to manufacture one table and one chair. The exhibit shows that the table, which has many flat parts, takes relatively more plane time, and the chair, which has many round parts, takes relatively more lathe time. The table has no wicker parts at all, so that machine is used only for chairs.

Acme Furniture's problem, then, is this: In a 7½-hour working day there are just 450 minutes of each type of machine time available. Given the technology for tables and chairs, and given the relative profitability of the two, how many tables and how many chairs should be produced each day? (The chairs and tables are not the kind that go together to make a dining room set, so no particular ratio of tables to chairs need be observed.)

Solution

The situation facing Acme Furniture is a typical, if simple, linear programming problem. It can be solved as follows:

First, we construct Acme Furniture's production-possibility frontier for tables and chairs as shown in Exhibit 23.4. First we look at machine-time requirements for the plane. We see that if no chairs are produced, Acme can make 30 tables a day, while if no tables are produced, they can make 90 chairs a day. We draw a straight line from 30 on the table axis to 90 on the chair axis to show how the production possibilities for tables and chairs are constrained when only plane time is taken into account. This line is labeled "plane constraint." Using the same reasoning for the lathe, we draw a second diagonal from 45 on the tables axis to 22½ on the chair axis. This gets the label "lathe constraint." Because the wicker machine is used only for chairs, it does not constrain table production at all, but limits chair production to 15 per day. The "wicker constraint" is thus a vertical line in the figure.

The actual number of tables and chairs produced by Acme must stay within all three of these constraints. To produce 20 chairs and 5 tables, as at point A in the diagram, would be all right as far as the lathe and plane were concerned, but would use too much wicker machine time. To produce 15 chairs and 25 tables, as at B, would be within the wicker and plane constraints, but would take up too much lathe time. Only points along the line

EXHIBIT 23.4

Production possibilities for Acme Furniture
This exhibit shows how a production possibility frontier
for Acme Furniture can be constructed on the basis of
the data shown in Exhibit 23.3. Each machine imposes
a constraint on the quantity of output that can be
produced. In combination, the three constraints define
the production possibility frontier *CDEF.*

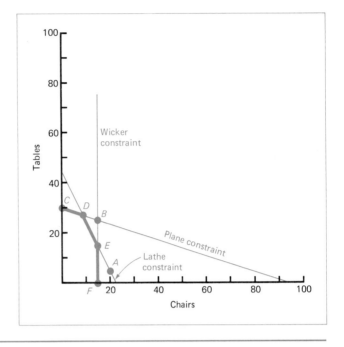

CDEF, which lies entirely on or below all three constraints, are points of
possible production. *CDEF* is thus Acme's production-possibility frontier.

The next step in solving the problem is to construct a grid showing
the profit that can be earned from producing various combinations of tables
and chairs. Exhibit 23.5 shows how to do this. A $60 profit can be earned
by producing 10 tables and no chairs, no tables and 15 chairs, or any combination of tables and chairs lying on a straight line between 10 on the
table axis and 15 on the chair axis. This line is labeled the "$60 profit line."

EXHIBIT 23.5

Graphical solution to Acme Furniture problem
This graph shows how to find the most profitable
combination of tables and chairs for Acme Furniture to
produce. First a grid of profit lines is constructed. Each
profit line shows various output combinations all
yielding a given level of profit. (Only a few such lines
are shown, but any number could be drawn to make
the grid as fine as was desired.) The most profitable
point of production is then the point where the production possibility frontier touches the highest profit line.

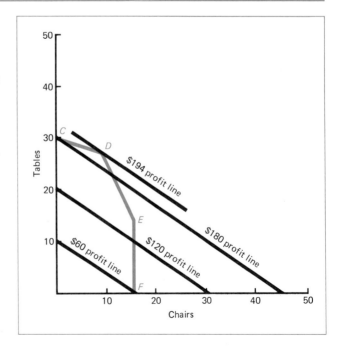

A $120 profit line can be constructed in the same way. It runs from 20 on the table axis to 30 on the chair axis. Any number of other profit lines can be drawn to make the grid as fine as one desires.

The stage is now set to complete the solution. First, superimpose the production-possibility frontier constructed in step 1 on the profit grid constructed in step 2. Then see which point on the production-possibility frontier reaches highest on the profit grid. That turns out to be point D, which represents a production of 9 chairs and 27 tables per day. This program earns the firm a profit of $194 per day. That is higher than any other production program that can be undertaken, given the constraints imposed by equipment limitations.

Practical Applications

The Acme Furniture problem is so simple that anyone could solve it in a few minutes by trial and error. The great value of linear programming is that it can be applied even when the number of process variables and constraints becomes very large. In such cases, the paper-and-pencil approach described above is replaced by computer techniques. Computerized linear programming can solve many highly complex, realistic, and important problems. Case 23.1 illustrates this.

CASE 23.1
Linear Programming in the Oil Industry[2]
In 1957, when interest in industrial applications of linear programming was just becoming widespread, a group of researchers for Standard Oil of California reported on a successful application of linear programming in oil refining. The problem was this. An oil refinery takes in crude oil, and through a process known as "cracking," separates it into a large variety of products, including gasoline, kerosene, diesel fuel, heavy fuel oil, and others. Crude oil coming from different fields varies considerably in the relative quantities of the various end products that can be extracted from it. In any given short-run period, a refinery must meet contract commitments to supply certain quantities of each product, at fixed prices. The refinery manager's problem is to buy the right mix of crude oils to minimize the total cost of meeting the contracts. The number of variables is so large that costly mistakes could be made if the refinery manager were to depend on trial and error. Put in mathematical form, the task becomes a routine linear programming problem. A solution can be found in a few minutes at a computer terminal.

[2]Based on W. W. Garvin, H. W. Crandall, J. B. John, and R. A. Spellman, "Applications of Linear Programming in the Oil Industry," *Management Science*, Vol. 3, No. 4 (July 1957).

Long-Run Decisions and Capital Budgeting
Let us turn now to some problems of long-run business decision making. In the short run, a firm must work within the constraints of its existing plant and equipment. In the long run, though, there are no fixed inputs. Plants can be expanded and new capital equipment purchased. In the world of pure theory, a firm expands its scale of production by moving out along a smooth, clearly defined long-run cost curve. In the real world, things are rarely so smooth. Expansion possibilities tend to come in the lumpy form of

Leonid Kantorovich, the Russian linear programming pioneer, became interested in economics somewhat by accident. In the late 1930s, when he was still a young professor of mathematics, he was approached by the director of a plywood mill. The director had a difficult problem of production scheduling. His plant had many different machines and received many different kinds of logs. The problem was how to match the right logs to the right machines. Kantorovich at first had to report that there was no known mathematical method for solving the problem, but he promised to work on it. Soon he worked out a version of what we now call linear programming, and the problem was solved. His 1939 paper, "Mathematical Methods for the Organization and Planning of Production," is the first published statement of linear programming.

During World War II, Kantorovich worked for a naval engineering school in Leningrad. He developed a brilliant reputation as a pure mathematician. In 1949, he received the Stalin Prize for work in a branch of mathematics known as functional analysis.

Leonid Vitalyevich Kantorovich (1912–   )

Meanwhile, a group of academicians working at a wartime research institute in the United States were wrestling with some problems concerning the optimal transportation pattern for military supplies. Among them were the mathematician George Dantzig and the Dutch-born economist Tjalling Koopmans. Neither of them had heard of Kantorovich or his work, but proceeding independently, they developed their own version of linear programming.

After the war, Kantorovich finally began to receive recognition for his work in economics. Under the relatively liberal regime of Nikita Krushchev, it finally became respectable for mathematicians to apply their talents to the politically sensitive area of economics. At the same time, increased intellectual exchange with the West had brought news of the Dantzig-Koopmans work. Soviet authorities belatedly discovered that one of their own citizens had a valid claim to priority of discovery in this important area. In 1958, Kantorovich was elected to the prestigious Soviet Academy of Sciences, and finally, in 1965, he shared a Lenin Prize for his work in mathematical economics.

The crowning mark of Kantorovich's international recognition was not to come for still another decade. Then, in 1975, he received the Nobel Prize in economics, jointly with Tjalling Koopmans, for his work in linear programming. Kantorovich now works in Moscow as the head of the high-level mathematical economics laboratory of the Soviet Institute of Economic Management. Koopmans, now Alfred Cowles Professor of Economics at Yale University, expressed delight at sharing the Nobel Prize with Kantorovich. He hoped that the award would provide a spur to the correspondence he had with his Soviet counterpart since the mid-1950s, and looked forward to a reinforcement of international cooperation in this important field.

specific investment projects that must be carried out all at once or not at all. The problem of deciding which investment projects to undertake is called the problem of **capital budgeting.**

Payback Period Analysis

The capital budgeting problem often takes the form of a choice among a number of alternative investment projects. When this is the case, any of a number of decision-making rules can be used. The simplest is called **payback period analysis.** We shall explain it by means of an example.

The Zeus Manufacturing Corporation is looking for ways to modernize its operations. Three departments have submitted proposals to the firm's manager. Project A is the installation of microfiche equipment to speed up order processing in the shipping department. This would cost

Capital Budgeting The area of business decision making that focuses on long-run investment decisions.

Payback Period Analysis A capital budgeting technique based on calculation of a project's payback period, that is, the length of time required for a project's net cash flows to repay the project's initial investment cost.

$30,000 and would save the firm $15,000 a year for the foreseeable future. Project B, turned in by the machine shop, asks for an overhaul of a large stamping machine that is reaching the end of its useful life. The overhaul will cost $15,000, and will extend the life of the machine for 3 years. It will save $6,000 per year on the rental of replacement equipment. Project C is to set up a plastic molding shop. This will allow Zeus to make certain small plastic parts for itself that it now buys from subcontractors. Setting up the shop will cost $100,000, and operating expenses for the shop will be $15,000 per year. Making the parts at Zeus will eliminate the $40,000 per year now spent for the parts purchased from outsiders. There will thus be a net improvement in cash flow, after operating expenses, of $25,000 per year. The equipment in the shop will last 5 years, and in the last year, there will be an extra $5,000 cost for taking out the worn-out equipment.

Exhibit 23.6 summarizes the three projects. The figure in the "net cash flow" column shows the net expense ($-$) or savings ($+$) in each year of the project. The initial investment cost is listed under year 0.

Let us see now how payback period analysis can be applied to the three projects. Project A will pay back $30,000 initial investment after 2 years of $15,000 per year improvement in net cash flow. The payback period for project B is $2\frac{1}{2}$ years, the length of time needed to recoup the initial $15,000 at $6,000 per year. Project C has a payback period of 4 years. On the principle that "time is money," Project A comes out on top. It returns the initial investment in the shortest time, so it gets top priority. Project B will get the next highest priority, and Project C will then be undertaken if enough funds are left ·after the first two are taken care of.

Year	Net Cash Flow	Comments
	Project A	
0	−30,000	Initial investment outlay
1	15,000	
2	15,000	
3	15,000	
4	15,000	
5	15,000	
6	15,000	Continues indefinitely
	Project B	
0	−15,000	Initial overhaul cost
1	6,000	
2	6,000	
3	6,000	
4	. . .	Machine scrapped
5	. . .	
6	. . .	
	Project C	
0	−100,000	Initial investment outlay
1	25,000	
2	25,000	
3	25,000	
4	25,000	
5	20,000	Includes scrapping cost
6	. . .	End of useful life

EXHIBIT 23.6
Payback period comparisons for three investment projects

This exhibit provides the data needed for a payback period analysis of three investment projects. Two years are required for project A to pay back its $30,000 initial investment. The payback period for project B is $2\frac{1}{2}$ years, and for project C it is 4 years.

Source: W. W. Garvin, H. W. Crandall, J. B. John, and R. A. Spellman, "Applications of Linear Programming in the Oil Industry," *Management Science*, Vol. 3, No. 4 (July 1957), pp. 407–430. Reprinted by permission.

Limitations

Payback period analysis is very easy to apply, and is widely used as a rough yardstick for ranking investment projects. Unfortunately, it has two drawbacks, which limit its accuracy. One is that it completely ignores what happens after the payback period is over. The other is that it is not sensitive to variations in the timing of net cash flows within the payback period itself. We can illustrate these drawbacks by extending our previous example.

Suppose that Zeus has modernized its shipping department and overhauled its stamping machine. Now it is ready to take on the plastics shop project. Three different suppliers sell the equipment needed. Supplier X will sell the equipment on the terms we gave earlier. Supplier Y will charge the same initial price, and its equipment will perform just as well. What is more, Y offers to repurchase the worn-out equipment for $15,000 at the end of the sixth year of the project. Supplier Z offers a slightly different type of equipment. The initial price is the same, but the annual operating cost is $20,000 rather than $15,000. Knowing that the added operating cost puts it at a disadvantage, supplier Z offers to sweeten the deal. It will pay the entire cost of operating the equipment for the first year and will match Y's offer to repurchase the equipment at the end of the sixth year. In addition, it agrees to send its own workers to handle the job of taking out the worn-out equipment during the fifth year.

The first and second columns of the table in Exhibit 23.7 summarize

EXHIBIT 23.7

Net present value analysis of three project variants
This exhibit gives the data needed to evaluate three investment project variants using the net present value approach. Note that the three project variants all have the same payback period, 4 years. They differ only in terms of net cash flows after the payback period and in terms of the timing of flows within the payback period. The project based on supplier Z is seen to be the most profitable, because it shows the highest net present value. A rate of interest of 10 percent per year is used in calculating the present values shown in the third column.

Year	Net Cash Flow	Discounted Net Cash Flow
	Supplier X	
0	−100,000	−100,000
1	25,000	22,750
2	25,000	20,750
3	25,000	18,750
4	25,000	17,000
5	20,000	12,400
6	. . .	. . .
Net present value		−8,350
	Supplier Y	
0	−100,000	−100,000
1	25,000	22,750
2	25,000	20,750
3	25,000	18,750
4	25,000	17,000
5	20,000	12,400
6	15,000	8,400
Net present value		+50
	Supplier Z	
0	−100,000	−100,000
1	40,000	36,400
2	20,000	16,600
3	20,000	15,000
4	20,000	13,600
5	20,000	12,400
6	15,000	8,400
Net present value		+2,400

Source: W. W. Garvin, H. W. Crandall, J. B. John, and R. A. Spellman, "Applications of Linear Programming in the Oil Industry," *Management Science*, Vol. 3, No. 4 (July 1957), pp. 407–430. Reprinted by permission.

the offers of X, Y, and Z in terms of net cash flows. Payback period analysis turns out not to work for comparing the three project alternatives. The payback period is exactly 4 years for all three suppliers. Clearly, though, supplier Y's offer is better than X's. It gives the same net cash flows during the payback period, and better cash flows thereafter. Z's offer seems even better than Y's. It pays back the same total amount during the first 4 years as the other two, but the distribution of the payments is weighted more heavily at the early end of the period, and "time is money."

Discounting

To make an accurate capital budgeting decision in a case like this, we need a way to compare payments that occur at different times. The method for doing this is known as **discounting.** Let us take a brief digression to explain how discounting works.

Discounting A method of comparing the value of receipts or outlays made at different points in time. See **Present Value.**

In a world where money can be invested at interest, it is always an advantage to receive a payment earlier rather than later. Consider, for example, the advantage of receiving $100 today rather than a year from now. If the $100 received today were invested at an interest rate of, say, 10 percent per year, we would have not $100, but $110 a year from now. With annual compounding of interest, $100 today would be worth as much as $110 a year from now, $121 two years from now, $133.10 three years from now, and so forth. The same thing can also be expressed in a different way. We can say that a dollar payable a year from now is worth only $.91 today, a dollar two years from now is worth $.83 today, a dollar three years from now is worth just $.75 and so forth, when the interest rate is 10 percent.

We can generalize this kind of example to any time period and any rate of interest. Let V_p be the sum of money that, if invested today at r percent per year interest, would grow to the sum V_t in t years. We say that V_p is the **present value** of the sum V_t *discounted* t years at r percent interest. The formula for calculating the present value of any future sum is

Present Value The present value V_p of a future sum of money V_t discounted for t years at r percent interest is the sum that, if invested today at r percent, would grow to the value V_t in t years. The formula for calculating present value is $V_p = V_t/(1 + r)^t$.

$$V_p = \frac{V_t}{(1 + r)^t}$$

Discounting and Capital Budgeting

Let us return now to the Zeus Manufacturing Company and its capital budgeting problem. Looking again at Exhibit 23.7, we recall that the problem was to evaluate three project variants that all had the same payback period. We can now compare the three project variants using what is called the **net present value approach** to capital budgeting. This approach is based on the discounting formula given above.

Net Present Value Approach A capital budgeting technique based on a comparison of the present values of the net cash flows generated by alternative projects.

The first step in applying the net present value approach is to find the interest rate that is to be used. This must reflect the opportunity cost of capital to the firm. If the firm plans to borrow money to finance the project, the interest rate used should be that which will be charged by the lender. If the firm plans to use its own funds to finance the project, the interest rate should be that which could have been earned had the funds been invested outside the firm. Let us suppose that, in this case, the proper interest rate is 10 percent.

COST AND PRODUCTION PROBLEMS OF BUSINESS MANAGEMENT

The second step is to calculate the present value of each year's net cash flow. These figures are shown in the third column of Exhibit 23.7. Finally, we add up the discounted net cash flows for each project, including the initial negative cash flow, which represents the project's initial cost. The sum for each project variant is called the net present value of that variant. Any project that shows a positive net present value will be profitable to undertake. The variant with the highest net present value is the most profitable.

Comparison of the net present values of the three variants shows why the payback period by itself is not always an adequate guide. If the equipment for the plastics shop is purchased from supplier X, the net present value of the project is negative. That means that if the cost of capital is 10 percent per year, it would be better to continue to buy plastic components from subcontractors at a cost of $40,000 per year than to set up an internal shop. With the deal offered by supplier Y, the added cash flow from selling the used equipment in year 6 is just enough to make the net present value positive. The company would be ahead by $50 if it buys equipment from Y and produces its own plastic components. Finally, the net present value approach shows how very attractive supplier Z's offer is. Simply by changing the time pattern of net cash flows within the payback period, the gain to Zeus from undertaking the project jumps from $50 to $2,400. The firm's final decision, then, is to build the shop, and buy the equipment from Z.

Conclusions

The examples in this chapter are just a light sampling of the techniques of modern business making, but they are enough to underline an important point. They show that in its broadest sense, the economic way of thinking does form the essential basis of managerial calculation. There are fundamental similarities in the treatment of fixed and variable cost, the use of marginal analysis, the calculation of opportunity cost and production possibilities, and the valuation of time as a scarce resource.

For the most part, the differences between the assumptions of economic theory and business administration are just matters of detail. Constant marginal costs are a good working assumption for business decision making, although economic theory is traditionally framed in terms of U-shaped cost curves. Most economic theory is formulated in terms of one-product firms, whereas multiproduct firms are actually common. Economic theory envisions the expansion of scale as a smooth, continuous process, while business managers encounter expansion possibilities as discrete "lumps" of specific investment projects. That the economic way of thinking can still be applied under these changed assumptions shows its versatility.

SUMMARY

1. A common business problem is whether or not to introduce some new product. The decision depends on the fixed cost of bringing the product out, the variable cost of producing it, and the revenue per unit that can be earned by selling it.

Breakeven analysis is a method for determining the minimum quantity of the product that must be sold in order for total revenue to cover total fixed plus variable cost. That minimum quantity is known as the project's breakeven point.

2. Many firms operate several processes or produce several products simultaneously, where input and output rates must be adjusted in order to minimize costs or maximize profits, and inputs and outputs are subject to certain constraints. Linear programming is a powerful method for dealing with problems of this form. With the aid of computers, practical problems involving quite large numbers of variables can be solved.

3. An important aspect of long-run business decision making is the problem of capital budgeting. Firms often must consider several projects or project variants, and decide which ones are most worthwhile to undertake. Payback period analysis is a simple, rough guide to capital budgeting decisions. Often, though, accurate capital budgeting decisions require more precise techniques, such as those used in the net present value approach.

DISCUSSION QUESTIONS

1. Turn to Exhibits 23.1 and 23.2. Imagine that you are the author of the book in question. When you take it to a certain publisher, the acquiring editor turns it down because she thinks it will only sell 4,000 copies. You have greater faith in the book than that and are sure it will sell at least 10,000 copies. You suggest a deal. The publisher will pay you no royalties at all on the first 4,000 copies sold, but will pay double royalties on all copies over 4,000. Redraw the breakeven chart to prove to the editor that the publisher will make money even if she is right about potential sales, and you both will make money if you are right.

2. Turn to Exhibit 23.5. Using the technique illustrated there, show that an increase in the price of chairs, with the price of tables unchanged, will induce Acme to produce more chairs and fewer tables. Will a gradually increasing chair price bring about smoothly increasing chair production, or will production increase all in a jump when some critical price is reached?

3. In the Stalin era, managers of Soviet firms were not allowed to use the net present value approach to capital budgeting. That method was considered "un-Marxist" because it made use of the concept of "interest," which was considered capitalistic nonsense. It was permissible, however, to use payback period analysis because that did not involve the explicit use of interest. What kinds of mistakes do you think Soviet managers made in their capital budgeting in those days? Are you surprised that eventually the ideological ban on the net present value approach was dropped?

4. You have two choices of where to live during your four years in college. You can rent an apartment, and pay $200 per month, which covers all expenses. Alternatively, you can buy a small house for $30,000, and live in that. (Your parents will loan you the money.) You think that you will be able to sell the house for the same price at which you bought it, and that you will have about $50 a month in expenses while you live there. Using the net present value approach, make a decision between buying and renting, first using an interest rate of 5 percent in your calculations, and then an interest rate of 10 percent.

CHAPTER 24
The Firm as Price Taker—Supply Under Perfect Competition

What You Will Learn in This Chapter
The theory of cost that we developed in Chapter 22 can provide the foundation for a theory of short-run and long-run supply. In making the step from a theory of cost to a theory of supply, we introduce the idea of a perfectly competitive market. Perfect competition allows us to separate the calculative and entrepreneurial elements of business decision making, and to concentrate on the former. As a by-product of our study of competitive supply, we shall obtain some interesting propositions about consumer sovereignty and the efficiency of resource allocation.

For Review
Here are some important terms and concepts that will be put to use in this chapter. Be certain that you understand them, or review them before proceeding.

Marginal utility and consumer equilibrium (Chapter 19)
Consumer sovereignty (Chapter 20)
Managerial calculation versus entrepreneurship (Chapter 21)
The theory of cost (Chapter 22)

In Chapter 21 we drew a distinction between two kinds of business decision making. The first we called managerial calculation. This meant business planning in a stable environment, where prices, demand conditions, technologies, and the like are known. The manager as calculator plans the best course of action for the firm, given these known conditions. Then we argued that businesspeople must be entrepreneurs as well as calculators. They must be alert to changing conditions, experiment with risky but promising changes in old routines, and try to outguess their competitors in the face of the unknown.

In the real world, of course, there is no sharp line between the two kinds of decision making. Some of our examples in the last chapter made this clear. We showed how formal methods of calculation can be applied to decisions such as bringing out a new product or making long-term investments, even though there are always uncertainties in such decisions that call for entrepreneurial judgment.

For textbook purposes, though, it is often useful to draw lines more sharply than they are drawn in reality. The present chapter is a case in point. We are going to study a problem of pure managerial calculation, as faced by the "typical firm" we introduced in Chapter 22. Let us proceed, then, to set the stage for our analysis by creating a carefully controlled environment for the firm.

The "Typical Firm" as Price Taker

The Price Taker

Price Taker   A firm that takes the prices at which it buys its inputs and sells its ouputs as fixed, determined entirely by forces outside its own control.

A **price taker** is a firm that takes the prices at which it buys its inputs and sells its outputs as fixed, determined entirely by forces outside its own control. If the firm makes widgets, and widgets sell for a $1.50 each, that is that. It makes all its decisions and all its plans as if nothing it could do would change that $1.50 price tag.

The price taker not only treats prices as fixed. It also treats them as the prices of markets in equilibrium. That means making certain assumptions about its competitors, customers, and suppliers. In particular, whenever the price-taking firm makes sales or production plans, it makes them on the assumptions that all *other* firms in the market have already fully adjusted to prevailing conditions. There is thus a strong "other things being equal" element in the world of the price taker. Whatever one firm does, it assumes that its decisions will not affect what other firms do. They are assumed to have made all of their decisions already.

All decisions that the price taker must make are, by their nature, purely calculative decisions. There is no room and no need in the world of the price taker for entrepreneurship. All the firm's management need do to earn maximum profits is to look at the given prices, organize internal operations so as to minimize costs, and then calculate what quantity of output to produce. Such things as advertising, introducing new products, or experimenting with new production techniques have no place.

The Structure of Pure Competition

Market Structure   The important structural characteristics of a market, including such things as the number of firms that operate there, the extent to which the products of different firms are diverse or homogeneous, and the ease of entry into and exit from the industry.

Perfect Competition   A market structure characterized by a large number of relatively small firms, a homogeneous product, good distribution of information among all market participants, and freedom of entry and exit.

Under what conditions might a firm actually *be* a price taker? Whether a firm is a price taker or not turns out to depend in large part on the structure of the markets in which it participates. When we speak of **market structure** in this sense, we have in mind such characteristics as the number of firms that operate in each industry, the extent to which the products of different firms are varied or all the same, and the ease or difficulty that firms face in getting into and out of the market. There are many possible structures that markets can assume. One of these is of particular interest to us now, because it makes firms behave as price takers. That is the market structure known as **perfect competition.**

Perfect competition, as a market structure, has four defining characteristics. First, there are many sellers and many buyers, each one of which sells or buys only a small fraction of the total market turnover. Second, the product traded in the market is entirely homogeneous; that is, the product sold by one firm is just like that sold by any other. Third, all participants in the market, buyers and sellers alike, are well informed about prices, sources of supply, and so forth. Finally, entry into and exit from the market must be very easy.

The first three of these characteristics, taken together, ensure that all firms will be price takers. Because each producer contributes only a small fraction of the total output, its individual actions will have no significant effect on the total quantity supplied in the market, and hence no effect on the market price. Because the product is homogeneous, a firm that tried to raise its price even a little above that of its competitors would find all its customers happy to shop elsewhere. Because all market participants are well informed, no one would be willing to pay or able to get a price higher than the prevailing one. No individual firm, then, has either the ability or the incentive to charge a different price than the market price for the goods it makes.

The fourth feature of perfect competition—easy entry and exit—is not strictly necessary to make firms price takers. It has particular importance for how perfectly competitive markets work in the long run. We shall discuss this matter later in the chapter.

Competition and Perfect Competition

We should go no further without mentioning a paradox associated with perfect competition. The paradox is this: Perfect competition, as we have defined it, is in many respects the exact opposite of competition as we see it in everyday business life.

When we think of business competition, we ordinarily think of rivalry and struggle. We think of Ford and General Motors battling for shares of the market. We think of advertising people talking up one product and putting down another. We think of Kodak working in secrecy to outflank Polaroid's technological supremacy. Perfect competition, though, is none of these things. In a perfectly competitive market, there is no reason to battle for market shares because there is plenty of room for each small firm to sell as much as it wants at the going price. There is no advertising in such a market, because buyers are already well informed, and goods are perfectly homogeneous—not only in fact, but in the eyes of their consumers as well. There is no need for secrecy about techniques or innovations, because all technological knowledge is widespread and there are no innovations. In short, the world of perfect competition is entirely free of all the ordinary signs of business rivalry.

With a bit of thinking, it is not hard to discover the reason for this paradox. All of the common aspects of competition we have mentioned—the battle for market shares, advertising, technological rivalry—have to do with competition among *entrepreneurs*. They are ploys used by business-people trying to beat their rivals in exploiting changed circumstances, or trying to disrupt an old market equilibrium to their advantage. In *perfect* competition, though, there is no entrepreneurship. The market environment is still competitive in the sense that any firms who fail to make their managerial calculations as accurately as their rivals may be forced out of the market. Firms are not sheltered from that kind of competition by any special privileges. Nonetheless, many more colorful or personalized aspects of competition are absent. Perfect competition must be thought of as an abstraction to be used in theory building, not as a description of business life.

Perfect Competition and Short-Run Supply

Our first use of perfect competition will be to build a theory of the short-run supply curve. To do this, we shall take the "typical firm" we introduced in Chapter 22, and place it in a perfectly competitive market. The firm now has no control over the price it will charge or over the nature of its product. It has only one "degree of freedom" left in its managerial calculations. That is to determine the quantity of output that will permit it to maximize profits.

Short-Run Profit Maximization

Exhibit 24.1 gives us a first look at the competitive firm's short-run profit-maximizing decision. Column (2) of the table shows the total cost associated with each level of output for the firm. The data are the same as those used in Chapter 22. The firm's total revenue for each level of output, assuming a price of $5 per unit, is shown in column (3). Total profit

EXHIBIT 24.1

Short-run costs, revenue, and profit for a price-taking firm

The data in this table can be used to find the profit-maximizing level of output for the typical perfectly competitive firm they represent. The profit-maximizing output (19 units) can be read directly from column (4). Alternatively, it can be found by following down columns (5) and (6) until the point is reached where marginal cost begins to exceed price.

(1) Quantity of Output	(2) Total Cost	(3) Total Revenue	(4) Total Profit	(5) Price per Unit	(6) Marginal Cost
0	$ 20.00	$ 0	$ −20.00	$5.00	
					3.80
1	23.80	5.00	−18.80	5.00	
					3.40
2	27.20	10.00	−17.20	5.00	
					3.05
3	30.25	15.00	−15.25	5.00	
					2.75
4	33.00	20.00	−13.00	5.00	
					2.50
5	35.50	25.00	−10.00	5.00	
					2.30
6	37.80	30.00	− 7.80	5.00	
					2.15
7	39.95	35.00	− 4.95	5.00	
					2.05
8	42.00	40.00	− 2.00	5.00	
					2.00
9	44.00	45.00	1.00	5.00	
					2.05
10	46.05	50.00	3.95	5.00	
					2.15
11	48.20	55.00	6.80	5.00	
					2.30
12	50.50	60.00	9.50	5.00	
					2.50
13	53.00	65.00	12.00	5.00	
					2.75
14	55.75	70.00	14.25	5.00	
					3.05
15	58.80	75.00	16.20	5.00	
					3.40
16	62.20	80.00	17.80	5.00	
					3.80
17	66.00	85.00	19.00	5.00	
					4.25
18	70.25	90.00	19.75	5.00	
					4.75
19	75.00	95.00	20.00	5.00	
					5.30
20	80.30	100.00	19.70	5.00	
					5.90
21	86.20	105.00	18.80	5.00	
					6.55
22	92.75	110.00	17.25	5.00	
					7.25
23	100.00	115.00	15.00	5.00	
					8.00
24	108.00	120.00	12.00	5.00	

(+) or loss (−) is simply the difference between total revenue and total cost; this difference is listed in column (4). We have only to read down the column to discover that 19 units is the profit-maximizing level of output. Any other output leads either to a smaller profit, or an actual loss.

Alternatively, we can use marginal analysis to identify the profit-maximizing level of output. Each additional unit of output sold adds $5 to the firm's revenue. The amount that production of each extra unit adds to total cost is shown by the marginal cost entries in column (6). [Note that these entries are equal to the differences between successive entries in column (2).] As long as producing one more unit adds more to revenue than it does to cost, total profit will rise. Comparing columns (4) and (5), we see that all units up to and including the 19th are profitable, judged by this standard. Producing the 20th unit, though, would add $.30 more to costs than to revenue. Profits would be less than at 19 units. The marginal approach, then, gives us the same answer for the profit-maximizing level of output.

A Graphical Approach

Our typical firm's profit-maximization problem can also be solved by a graphical method, similar to the breakeven analysis outlined in the last chapter. Consider Exhibit 24.2. In part *a* of this figure, we have drawn the firm's reverse-S total cost curve. The data for this curve are taken from

---

EXHIBIT 24.2

Short-run cost and revenue curves for a price-taking firm

The two diagrams drawn here are based on the data for the typical firm given in Exhibit 24.1. Part *a* of the exhibit uses a type of breakeven chart to identify the profit-maximizing output. In part *b*, the profit-maximizing output is found at the point where marginal cost is equal to the product price.

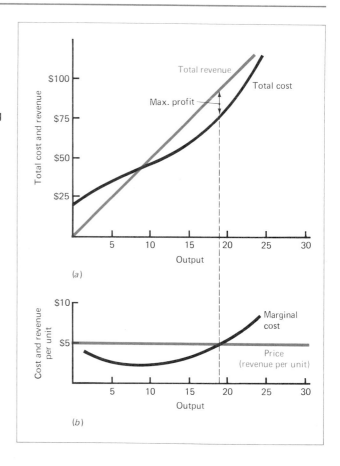

the table we have just been using. In the same figure, we have also drawn a total revenue curve for the firm. This is simply a straight line with a slope equal to the price of the product. The two curves intersect at approximately 9 units of output, which is the firm's breakeven level of operation. Now, though, our focus is not on the breakeven quantity of output, but on the profit-maximizing quantity. The total profit (total revenue minus total cost) for each level of output is equal to the vertical distance between the total revenue and total cost curves. That distance is greatest at 19 units of output. At that point, the upward-bending cost curve stops diverging from the revenue curve, becomes just parallel to it, and then begins to converge again.

The marginal approach can equally well be put in graphical form. Consider Exhibit 24.2b. There, we have drawn the firm's U-shaped marginal cost curve, and also a horizontal line at a height equal to product price, which shows revenue per unit. The point of profit maximization is the intersection of the marginal cost curve with the price line.

We can verify that profit is maximized at that intersection as follows: First, we note that at any point to the left of the intersection, marginal cost is less than the price of the product. Whenever this is the case, production of an additional unit of output will increase profit. (For example, if we begin from 12 units of output, we can add one additional unit at a marginal cost of $2.50 and sell it for $5.00, giving us a $2.50 increase in total profit.) Next we note that at any point to the right of the intersection of the marginal cost curve with the price line, marginal cost exceeds product price. This means that the firm can increase profit by reducing output. (For example, beginning from an output of 24 units, we see that elimination of the 24th unit saves $8.00 in costs and results in only $5.00 less revenue, thus giving $3.00 more profit.) Taken together, the conclusions that the firm can increase profits by increasing output at any point to the left of the intersection of price and marginal cost, and that it can increase profit by lowering output at any point to the right of this intersection, indicate that the marginal cost curve and the price line intersect at the profit-maximizing level of output.

Short-Run Supply Curve

Our analysis of the profit-maximizing decision gives us the key to the firm's short-run supply curve. We have just shown how to determine the quantity of output that a perfectly competitive profit-maximizing firm will produce given some particular price. All we need to do to get a supply curve for such a firm is to repeat the analysis for a whole range of prices. Exhibit 24.3 shows how this can be done.

Begin with a price of $5. As we saw before, the firm would choose to produce 19 units of output at this price. Point E_1 on the firm's short-run marginal cost curve must therefore be a point on the firm's supply curve. Suppose now that the price of the firm's product begins to fall, as a result of forces beyond its control. As it does, the point where price equals marginal cost moves down along the firm's marginal cost curve. Soon point E_2 is reached, where marginal cost and average total cost are equal. This

EXHIBIT 24.3

Derivation of the short-run supply curve for a price-taking firm.

In this diagram, we trace out the typical firm's short-run supply curve. When the price is $5, the firm will produce at point E_1. As the price falls, the firm moves down along its short-run marginal cost curve, as shown by points E_2 and E_3. The firm will continue to produce where price equals marginal cost until marginal cost falls below average variable cost. At that price, the firm will do just as well to shut down, that is, to produce at point E_4.

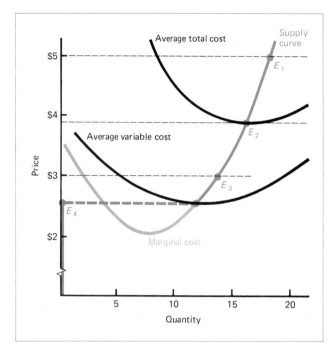

occurs at an output of approximately 17 units and a price of approximately $3.85. At this price, the best the firm can do is just to break even. Either a greater or a smaller output than the one that makes price equal to marginal cost would result in a loss for the firm.

If the product price falls still lower, the firm's problem becomes one of minimizing loss rather than maximizing profit. Consider a price of $3.00. We tentatively pick E_3, the point where marginal cost is equal to the price of $3.00 (about 15 units of output) as the point of loss minimization. Using the same reasoning as before, we can see that neither a small increase nor a small decrease in output would reduce the amount of loss. To cut back one unit would save less in costs than would be foregone in revenue, and to produce one more would add more to costs than would be gained. Because no profit can be earned, though, should the firm perhaps shut down altogether? Upon inspection, this turns out not to reduce losses. Shutting down reduces *variable* costs to zero, but *fixed* costs remain to be paid. At zero output, the total loss would be equal to total fixed costs, or to $20.00. In comparison, to produce 15 units of output costs $58.80 (see Exhibit 24.1). At $3.00 per unit, this output gives a revenue of $45.00 for a loss of only $13.80. We see that the price of $3.00, while not high enough to cover average total costs, is more than enough to cover average variable costs. After all production workers are paid, raw materials purchased, and other variable costs accounted for, there is a surplus remaining that helps pay at least part of the fixed costs.

If the price of the product were to decline still further, eventually a point would be reached where all such surplus disappeared. Below about $2.54, where marginal cost equals average variable cost, sale of the product would not cover even the bill for labor and raw materials. The loss-minimizing output would then be zero, point E_4 in the figure.

We have shown how we can find what quantity the firm will supply at any given price given the firm's cost curves. Points E_1 through E_4 are all on the firm's short-run supply curve.

The conclusions we have reached support an important generalization: *The short-run supply curve for a price-taking, profit-maximizing firm is that upward-sloping portion of the marginal cost curve lying above its intersection with average variable cost.*

The Short-Run Industry Supply Curve

Now that we have shown where the individual firm's supply curve comes from, let us move on to discuss the supply curve for a whole industry. As a first approximation, we can get an industry supply curve by horizontal addition of individual firm supply curves. This is shown in Exhibit 24.4. We must make one qualification, though. We have assumed that any individual firm can expand output without any change in input prices, but if all firms in an industry expand simultaneously, input prices will rise unless the input is available in perfectly elastic supply. If input prices rise as industry output expands, the result will be that the short-run industry supply curve will be somewhat steeper than the sum of the individual supply curves.

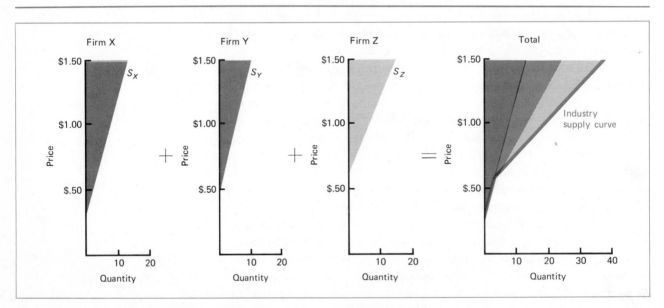

	Quantity Supplied			
Price	Firm X	Firm Y	Firm Z	Total
$ .40	1,500			1,500
$ .80	5,500	3,000	3,333	11,833
$1.20	9,500	7,000	10,000	26,500
$1.50	12,500	10,000	15,000	37,500

EXHIBIT 24.4

Approximate derivation of short-run industry supply curve

An approximation to the short-run industry supply curve can be obtained by horizontal summation of individual firm supply curves. Here the method of summation is shown for an industry with just three firms. If the prices of inputs vary as industry output varies, it will be necessary to make an adjustment in the industry supply curve.

Long-Run Supply
Under Perfect Competition

Exit and Entry

For the individual firm, the long run is distinguished from the short run by the fact that all, and not just some, inputs can be varied. In the long run, firms can go out of business entirely, disposing of all their fixed assets. New firms can come into existence, acquiring all the fixed and variable inputs they need from scratch. In some industries, special institutional factors may restrict the free entry and exit of firms. Public utility firms, for example, ordinarily need government permission either to set up as a new business or to shut down once they are in operation. Not so in a perfectly competitive industry. We recall that perfect freedom of entry and exit is a defining characteristic of perfect competition.

This assumption of free entry and exit plays a big role in our analysis of long-run supply in a competitive industry. Recall that in the short run, a price-taking firm may sometimes operate at a level of output below its breakeven point, in the interest of loss minimization. This is only a temporary strategy, though. In the long run, a firm must cover average total cost or shut down permanently, liquidating its fixed costs and leaving the industry.

If the demand for the output of a perfectly competitive industry suffers a permanent decline, and the product price falls below the average total cost of the representative firm in the industry, sooner or later some firms will voluntarily exit or will go bankrupt. As some firms leave the industry, the quantity of the product supplied to the market will decrease, and the market price will tend to recover. Eventually enough firms will leave to bring the price back up high enough to cover average total costs of the remaining firms. Then the exodus will stop, and equilibrium will be restored.

It follows, then, that a price-taking firm in a perfectly competitive industry cannot be in long-run equilibrium unless the price of the product it sells is at least as high as average total cost.

It also turns out that long-run equilibrium is not possible for such a firm when product price is above average total cost. Remember how we defined total private costs. To the economist, total costs include the implicit cost of a "normal" rate of return on the firm's capital. If price exceeds average total cost for the typical firm in a perfectly competitive industry, then firms must be earning profits in excess of the normal rate of return on capital. Such high profits act as a magnet, attracting new firms into the industry in question. As new firms enter, the quantity supplied to the market will increase, and the price will fall. As it does, the attraction for new entrants fades. When price declines to the level of average total cost, the industry and the firms within it return to equilibrium.

Long-Run Equilibrium

Long-run equilibrium for a firm in a perfectly competitive industry is not possible, then, when the price is either above or below long-run average total cost. It follows that in long-run equilibrium, price must be equal to long-run average cost. Two other important equalities must also hold. In long-run equilibrium, long-run average cost must equal short-run average total cost. (If short-run average total cost exceeds long-run average cost at a given level of output, that means that the firm's scale of operation is not ideally adjusted to that level of output. But long-run *equilibrium* means a state in which such adjustments in scale have in fact been carried out.) Furthermore, a firm cannot be in long-run equilibrium unless it is also in short-run equilibrium. That means that the product price must be equal to short-run marginal cost.

All this can be shortly stated as a four-part equation. For the price-taking firm in long-run equilibrium in a perfectly competitive industry,

$$\text{Price} = \begin{matrix}\text{Long-Run}\\\text{Average}\\\text{Cost}\end{matrix} = \begin{matrix}\text{Short-Run}\\\text{Average}\\\text{Total Cost}\end{matrix} = \begin{matrix}\text{Short-Run}\\\text{Marginal}\\\text{Cost}\end{matrix}$$

It is easy to construct a diagram showing what the long-run equilibrium position of such a firm looks like. This is done in Exhibit 24.5. There, we see four curves (one for each part of the above equation) all meeting at a single point. One final detail shows clearly in the diagram. That is the fact that in long-run equilibrium, the competitive firm's short-run and long-run average costs are at their minimums. It is easy to see that this must be the case. Price must be equal both to marginal and to average cost in long-run equilibrium, and marginal and average cost are equal only at the minimum point on the average cost curve.

The Long-Run Supply Curve

In the long run, expansion or contraction of a competitive industry's output occurs through the entry or exit of firms. The shape of the long-run supply curve for such an industry depends on how the entry or exit of firms affects input prices.

EXHIBIT 24.5

Long-run equilibrium for a perfectly competitive firm
In long-run equilibrium, the product price, long-run average cost, short-run average total cost, and short-run marginal cost of a perfectly competitive firm must all be equal. In this figure, the long-run equilibrium is found where the four curves come together at one point.

EXHIBIT 24.6

Three possible long-run supply curves

The shape of the long-run supply curve for a competitive industry depends on what happens to input prices as new firms enter and output expands. If input prices remain constant, the long-run industry supply curve will be perfectly elastic as in part *a* of this exhibit. If input prices are driven up as industry output expands, the curve will look like part *b*, and if they fall, it will look like *c*.

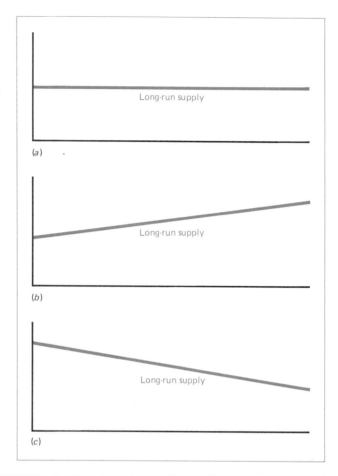

(a)

(b)

(c)

If the industry uses only unspecialized inputs of kinds that are used widely elsewhere in the economy, it is likely that expansion of the industry will not cause input prices to be bid up appreciably. (Here we are assuming that other things are equal, that is, that other industries are not trying to expand at the same time.) In that case, the entry of new firms into the industry will not cause the long-run minimum average cost of each firm to increase. The long-run industry supply curve will be perfectly elastic, as shown in Exhibit 24.6*a*. If the industry does use one or more specialized inputs not used elsewhere, expansion of the industry will substantially increase the demand for those inputs. This is likely to drive up their market price. The increase in the price of specialized inputs will cause the average cost curves of all firms in the industry to shift upward as industry output expands. The result will be an upward-sloping long-run industry supply curve, as in Exhibit 24.6*b*. Finally, it is possible under certain conditions that the price of some input might fall as demand for that input increases. This might happen, for example, if there were strong economies of scale in the industry supplying the input. If important inputs have downward-sloping long-run supply curves, the industry using those inputs may also have a downward-sloping long-run supply curve. This possibility is shown in Exhibit 24.6*c*.

Efficiency in Competitive Markets

We have not yet mentioned a major reason for economists' fascination with perfect competition—the proposition that perfectly competitive markets provide for consumers' wants and needs with perfect efficiency. This amounts to saying that competitive markets provide the ultimate in consumer sovereignty. In such markets, consumers not only get what they want—they get the greatest quantities and the best mix possible of the things they want. We have nowhere near enough room here to go into the topic of efficiency and competition fully, but we can give the general flavor of the argument with a simple example.

Shirts and Socks

Imagine an ultrasimple economy in which only two goods are produced, shirts and socks. Both the shirt and the sock industry are perfectly competitive. The short-run industry supply and demand curves for shirts and socks are shown in Exhibit 24.7. (These have been drawn as stair-step lines rather than smooth curves just so we can speak in terms of round numbers.)

Market equilibrium is achieved when the price of shirts is $7, with 10,000 shirts produced each month, and the price of socks is $3, with 13,000 pairs a month being produced. We wish to show that resources are efficiently allocated between the two industries when markets are in this equilibrium.

Demonstration of Efficiency

Our demonstration proceeds by showing that any allocation other than the equilibrium one is inefficient. Suppose that instead of the equilibrium allocation, production were set at 11,000 shirts and 9,000 pairs of socks per month. Using this as a starting point, consider what would happen if we shifted, say, $1,000 worth of resources from the production of shirts into the production of socks.

From the theory set forth in this chapter, we know that the height of the supply curve for a perfectly competitive industry is equal to marginal cost for each firm. Reading the diagram, then, we see that beginning from 11,000 shirts, each unit of output by which shirt production is reduced saves $8 worth of resources. Likewise, beginning from 9,000 pairs of socks, each additional pair of socks produced requires the use of $1 worth of resources. To shift $1,000 worth of resources from shirts to socks thus means that shirt production must be reduced by 125 units per month, and allows sock production to be increased by 1,000 pairs per month.

Now let us see how all this looks from the consumer's point of view. Recall the theory of consumer equilibrium we developed in Chapter 19. There we showed that the ratio of prices that consumers are willing to pay for any two goods is equal to the ratio of the marginal utilities of the two goods. In the range from 9,000 to 10,000 socks, it appears that consumers are willing to pay $6 per pair for socks. This is shown by the height of the sock demand curve. Similarly, in the range from 10,000 to 11,000 shirts, consumers are willing to pay $6 per shirt. It follows that in this range, the utility of a marginal pair of socks is equal to the utility of a marginal shirt.

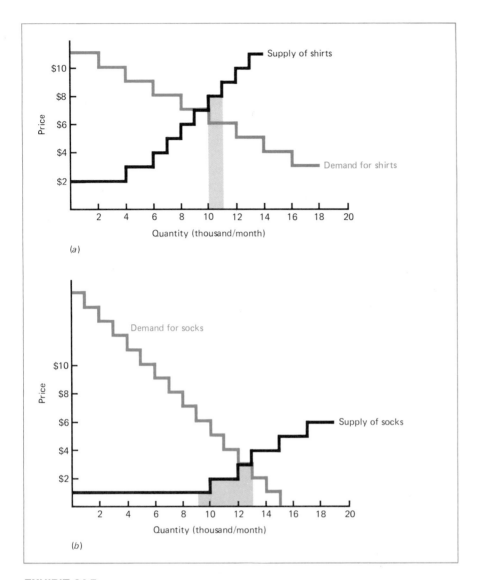

EXHIBIT 24.7

Resource allocation in a two-good economy

Perfectly competitive markets tend to allocate resources efficiently between industries. In this case, shifting $8 worth of resources from socks to shirts would produce an output mix less valued by consumers than the equilibrium mix.

Now we can see why producing 11,000 shirts and only 9,000 pairs of socks is inefficient. Starting from this point, a shift of $1,000 worth of resources from shirts to socks permits 1,000 more pairs of socks to be produced at an opportunity cost of only 125 shirts. Because in this range of output consumers value socks just as highly as shirts, this shift of production clearly makes consumers better off. The total quantity of resources used in production is not increased, so no one has to work any harder or be otherwise made worse off in their role as producer. (We assume that workers do not care whether they run the kind of machine that makes one product or the kind that makes the other.) Because consumers can be made better off without making producers worse off or using any more resources, to produce 11,000 shirts and 9,000 socks is inefficient.

The shift of resources from shirts to socks need not be limited to $1,000 worth. More and more resources can be pulled out of shirts and put into socks until the market equilibrium allocation of 10,000 shirts and 13,000 pairs of socks is reached. This requires a shift of $8,000 worth of resources in all. Any further shift of resources from shirts to socks beyond the equilibrium allocation would make consumers worse off. We can see from the figure that consumers would value the 13,001st pair of socks only two-sevenths as much as the 9,999th shirt ($2 versus $7, as shown by the demand curves). At the same time, the marginal pair of socks would cost four-sevenths as much as the marginal shirt ($4 versus $7, as shown by the supply curves). Extra socks would no longer be worth the sacrifice in shirts needed to produce them. We have demonstrated, then, that the competitive equilibrium allocation of resources is the only efficient allocation for this simple economy.

This example supplies us with some principles that we shall be able to apply later. Whenever we can identify situations where the market price of some good remains substantially higher than its marginal cost of production, we can be fairly sure that too few resources are being allocated to producing that good. Likewise, whenever we encounter a situation in which the price of a product is depressed substantially below its marginal cost, it is likely that its rate of production and use is higher than it ought to be. Applied on a case-by-case basis, and treated as being suggestive rather than conclusive, this line of argument has an important place in policy analysis.

Conclusions

It is tempting to draw a broader generalization from our last example. In an economy where all markets are perfectly competitive, would not all resources be allocated efficiently when all markets were in equilibrium? This proposition has a long history in economic thought, but it turns out to be of little practical significance. The trouble is that there are just too many qualifications to this generalization. One is that competitive markets allocate resources efficiently only if total private costs of production fully reflect opportunity costs. Where there is environmental pollution, taxation, regulation, or any of a number of other distorting factors, opportunity costs and private costs diverge. Also, the proposition requires that *all* markets in the economy be in competitive equilibrium if resources are to be allocated efficiently in any one of them. The proposition that competitive markets allocate resources efficiently cannot be applied to one market at a time. Either it holds for the whole economy, or it does not hold for any part of it.

Another, even more serious, limitation arises directly from the whole concept of perfect competition. All general propositions about the efficiency of perfect competition are based on an analysis that ignores the entrepreneurial element in business life. The theories set forth in this chapter tell us little about how efficiently resources are allocated in a world where change occurs, where knowledge is not perfectly distributed, and where markets are not always in equilibrium. Do markets with large numbers of small firms guarantee efficient entrepreneurial decision making in a world of change and uncertainty? Are such markets most productive of new and better ways to satisfy human wants? The theory of perfect competition says nothing one way or the other in answer to these questions. We shall return to them in later chapters, where we discuss market structures other than perfect competition.

When all is said and done, we must remember that perfect competition is one of the great abstractions of economics. As such, it produces many valuable insights. It helps us to think more clearly about what lies behind the law of supply and demand. It helps us to understand the calculative element in business decision making, which is an important part of the real world of business, if not all of it. It provides some insights into economic efficiency that, if not overgeneralized, can be of real use in comparing alternative economic policies. Finally, for some kinds of markets, it is not so very far from the mark in a descriptive sense. In the next chapter, we shall look at some markets that certainly fit the theory more closely than most.

SUMMARY

1. A firm is a price taker if it can do nothing to affect the prices of the inputs it buys or the outputs it sells. The characteristics of perfect competition are sufficient to make firms behave as price takers. Firms are too small to influence input or output prices by varying their own quantities supplied or demanded. The fact that consumers are indifferent between the products of different individual firms makes it impossible for those firms to raise their prices above the prevailing level without losing all their customers. The "other things being equal" assumption applies in a particularly strong way to the price-taking, perfectly competitive firm. It makes all of its managerial calculations as if whatever it did would not affect in any way what others did.

2. Perfect competition, as the technical name of a particular market structure, must be carefully distinguished from real-world business competition. Many common types of business rivalry amount to forms of competition among entrepreneurs. These forms of rivalry are absent in perfect competition, because there is no room there for entrepreneurship.

3. For the "typical firm" with U-shaped short-run cost curves, the short-run supply curve is that upward-sloping portion of the short-run marginal cost curve that lies above the average variable cost curve. If price falls below average variable cost in the short run, the firm will minimize its losses by temporarily shutting down. The short-run industry supply curve is approximated by the summation of the supply curves of individual firms. An adjustment must be made, though, for any change in input prices that might occur when all firms in the industry expand or contract simultaneously.

4. In long-run equilibrium, product price, long-run average cost, short-run average total cost, and short-run marginal cost must all be equal for the competitive firm. If price were to rise above long-run average cost, new firms would be attracted to the industry, driving the price back down. If price were below long-run average cost, some firms would leave the industry, allowing the price to rise again. In the long run, then, variations in industry output take place primarily through the entry or exit of firms, rather than variations in the quantity produced by each individual firm.

5. Competitive markets tend to allocate resources efficiently among various industries. The key to the efficiency of competitive markets is the fact that they keep prices equal to marginal costs. One must be wary, however, of drawing overly strong policy conclusions from propositions about the efficiency of perfect competition.

DISCUSSION QUESTIONS

1. Instead of saying that a perfectly competitive firm is a price taker, it is sometimes said that such a firm faces a perfectly elastic demand curve. Why are these two ways of putting the matter equivalent?

2. The concept of being a price taker can apply to consumers as well as producers. For which of the goods and services that you buy are you a price taker? Are there any goods or services you buy for which you are not a price taker?

3. If the government imposes a price ceiling on some product, does that make the firms that sell the product price takers, regardless of whether their industry fits the market structure of perfect competition?

4. Make a list of half a dozen products that you purchase frequently. Do you buy any of these things from firms that are perfect competitors? If the firms you bought from were not perfect competitors, did they compete in some other sense with rivals for your business?

5. Explain the role that the free entry and exit assumption plays in determining the nature of long-run equilibrium in a competitive industry.

6. Here is a definition of efficiency that economists often use: An economy is said to be operating efficiently if and only if there is no possible change that will make at least one person better off, and no person worse off. Show that the simple shirt-sock economy pictured in Exhibit 24.7 is efficient *in this sense* when and only when both markets are in competitive equilibrium.

CHAPTER 25
Agricultural Markets—Competition in Action

What You Will Learn in This Chapter
Agricultural markets fit the conditions of perfect competition much more closely than most. Major products are reasonably homogeneous, and are produced by large numbers of relatively small firms. Agricultural markets thus offer a good opportunity for applying supply and demand analysis. Agricultural markets are notoriously unstable. Low demand elasticities and the so-called cobweb effect contribute to this instability. From the 1930s until quite recently, the government pursued extensive price support programs to combat fluctuations in farm incomes. In the last few years, though, such controls have been all but abandoned.

For Review
Here is an important concept that will be put to use in this chapter. Be certain that you understand it, or review it before proceeding.
　　Elasticity of demand (Chapter 18)

The conditions of perfect competition never hold fully for any market in the real world. In some markets, though, the conditions are much more closely approximated than in others. If we want to see perfect competition, or something close to it, in action, we do best to turn to agriculture. Agricultural markets certainly meet the condition of a large number of small firms. As we learned in Chapter 21, 69 percent of all agricultural output is produced by sole proprietorships, and three-fifths of that output is produced by firms with sales of under $50,000 per year. Corporations with sales of over a million dollars a year, by contrast, account for only 13 percent of agricultural output. The conditions of product homogeneity and well-informed buyers and sellers also hold fairly closely for major agricultural markets.

What accounts for the strength of the small firm in agriculture? Perhaps the answer is better found by asking what accounts for the failure of the large corporation to meet with as much success there as in other industries. The history of the "agribusiness" boomlet of the late 1960s is instructive in this regard.

CASE 25.1
The Rise and Fall of Agribusiness[1]

It is not through lack of trying that the big corporations have failed to make a big impact on agriculture. During the late 1960s, scores of companies rushed into farming, attracted by the long-range prospect of food shortages, tax advantages, and the notion that a 10,000-acre farm would be ten times more efficient than a 1,000-acre farm. But the golden harvest never came.

For one thing, hoped-for economies of scale often just were not there. United Brands (famous for Chiquita bananas) tried to capture 25 percent of the national lettuce market in a $17 million acquisition program. By 1970, its operation was running an $8 million deficit, and it confessed, in a statement to the FTC, that "at the farm level, size does not bring with it any significant cost benefits." It added, "Farming has severe limitations on size in terms of economies of scale." S. S. Pierce, the big Boston food company, found out much the same. They tried to grow strawberries in 500-acre blocks where local farmers were growing them with intensive care on 25- to 50-acre sites. Pierce quickly ran into problems, and took a loss of $4.5 million on sales of $10 million.

The chronic instability of agricultural prices has been another enemy of agribusiness. Robert Di Giorgio of the half-billion-dollar Di Giorgio Corporation told reporter Baker that "If you want regularity of earnings over a period of five to ten years, it's hard to do that in farming. When you're in farming, you are subject to things beyond your control—weather, oversupplies, undersupplies, and market conditions." Di Giorgio has cut back to where agriculture represents only 2 percent of its business.

In other industries, the big corporations fight these kinds of instabilities with their high-powered marketing skills, but these skills too just do not seem to work out in agriculture. Purex, makers of a line of home-use products, thought its marketing power would give it a competitive edge in produce, grain, and cotton. By 1974 it was retrenching as fast as it could. United Brands tried a massive advertising campaign to build brand-identification of its lettuce, but still was not able to turn a profit.

Finally, the big corporations have had labor relations troubles which their size sometimes seems to have aggravated rather than alleviated. Purex and Tenneco both attributed part of their disappointing performance to disputes with Cesar Chavez' United Farm Workers of America.

Surveying the field, Baker reported that in addition to the companies mentioned above, CBK Agronomics Inc., the Gates Rubber Company, Multiponics Inc., and Gulf and Western had all pulled out entirely from agribusiness. Some corporate leaders, such as Robert Schramm of the Superior Farming Company (a subsidiary of the Superior Oil Company of Houston) think there can still be a place for the corporation in agriculture if management understands the cyclical and uncertain nature of farming. But he admits that his own venture hasn't turned a profit in five years and may not for fifteen more.

[1]Based on "No Keeping Them Down on the Farm," *The New York Times,* January 20, 1974, Section 3, p. 4. © 1974 by The New York Times Company. Reprinted by permission.

Supply and Demand in Agriculture

Because agricultural markets come so close to meeting the conditions for perfect competition, they give particularly good opportunities for applying supply and demand analysis. Let us begin by taking a look at the elasticity of demand for agricultural products.

EXHIBIT 25.1

Farm-level price elasticities of total demand for food products, 1955–1957

Farm Product	Demand Elasticity
Cattle	0.68
Calves	1.08
Hogs	0.46
Sheep and lambs	1.78
Turkeys	0.92
Eggs	0.23
Milk used for—	
Fluid milk and cream	0.14
Evaporated and condensed	0.26
Cheese	0.54
Ice cream	0.11
Butter	0.66
Other use	0.36
Soybean oil*	3.99
Cottonseed oil*	6.92
Other food oils*	7.04
Lard, total use*	0.54
Beverages[†]	0.36
Fruit and tree nuts	0.36
Vegetables	0.10
Sugar*	0.18
Potatoes, sweet potatoes	0.11
Dry beans, peas, peanuts	0.23
Wheat[†]	0.02
Rice (rough)[‡]	0.04
Rye[‡]	0.04
Corn[‡]	0.03
Oats[‡]	0.01
Barley	0.07

*Wholesale prices and quantities.
[†]Retail prices and quantities.
[‡]Does not include quantity demanded for export or for feed.

Source: G. E. Brandow, "Interrelations Among Demands for Farm Products and Implications for Control of Market Supply," Bulletin 680 (University Park, Pa.: Pennsylvania State University Agricultural Experiment Station, 1961), p. 59. Reprinted by permission.

Demand Elasticities

A few years ago, G. E. Brandow of the Pennsylvania State University Agricultural Experiment Station made a broad study of the demand for agricultural commodities.[2] We have reproduced his major results in Exhibit 25.1. The striking thing about this table is how low most of the elasticities are. With the exceptions of food oils, sheep, and calves, all the elasticities are less than one. Some of the elasticities are extremely low—the demand for wheat and oats for home use show virtually perfect inelasticity. (It should be noted, though, that the demand elasticities for these products would be somewhat greater if demand for use as feed grains and for export had been included in the estimates.)

The low demand elasticities contribute to the instability of agricultural income. Supply in agricultural markets can fluctuate sharply as a result of

[2]"Interrelations Among Demands for Farm Products and Implications for Control of Market Supply," Bulletin 680 (University Park, Pa.: Pennsylvania State University Agricultural Experiment Station), p. 59.

weather and other unpredictable factors. Inelastic demand means that prices move sharply when supplies change, and that farm earnings fall when supplies increase.

This is illustrated by Exhibit 25.2. Part *a* represents some agricultural commodity, say walnuts, and Part *b* some manufactured good, say widgets. An increase of 25 percent in the walnut crop sends prices plunging from $2 to $1, and causes walnut growers' revenues to fall from $200,000 to $125,000. Using the formula given in Chapter 18, this gives a demand elasticity of 0.33, not even particularly low as agricultural commodities go. In contrast, a 25 percent increase in the supply of widgets entails only a $.20 drop in price, at an elasticity of 1.9. Widget makers' revenues do not fall as the supply increases. Instead, they rise from $200,000 to $225,000.

The Cobweb Effect

The unpredictability of nature and low demand elasticity are not the only sources of price instability in agriculture. As early as the 1930s, economists trying to apply supply and demand analysis to agricultural markets noticed a phenomenon that has since become known as the **cobweb effect.**

The cobweb effect is a result of agricultural uncertainty plus the long period of agricultural production. It takes a whole year to grow most crops, and farmers must plant before they know what the harvest-time price will

Cobweb Effect A tendency for agricultural prices to rise above and then fall below the equilibrium level in alternate years, producing a pattern like a cobweb on a supply and demand diagram.

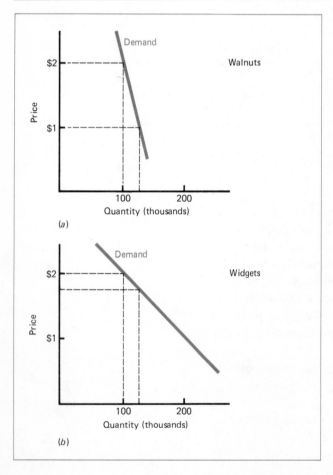

(a)

(b)

EXHIBIT 25.2
Markets with high and low demand elasticity
Low demand elasticity contributes to instability of farm prices and incomes. Here we show hypothetical demand curves for walnuts and widgets. A 25 percent increase in the walnut crop drives the price down by half, and cuts revenues from $200,000 to $125,000. By contrast, a 25 percent increase in widget output cuts the price by only $.25, and revenue rises.

EXHIBIT 25.3

The cobweb effect

The cobweb effect is another source of instability in agricultural markets. Here we suppose that in year 1, a bad crop pushes the wheat price up to $3.20. Expecting the high price to continue, farmers expand output the next year, and the price ends up below equilibrium, at point 2. High and low prices continue to alternate as equilibrium is approached in a cobweb pattern.

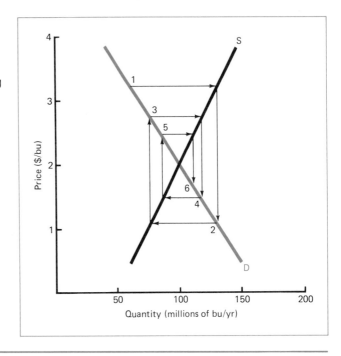

be. To a considerable extent, they tend to take this year's price as an indication of next year's price. That is all well and good, as long as the market is in equilibrium, so that the price is the same from one year to the next. If something such as a drought or a rash of hailstorms knocks the market out of equilibrium one year, though, peculiar things begin to happen.

Consider Exhibit 25.3, where we have drawn some hypothetical supply and demand curves for wheat. The equilibrium price of wheat, as shown, is $2.00 per bushel, and the equilibrium quantity produced is 100 million bushels per year. Suppose now that in some year (call it year 1) bad weather reduces the wheat crop to 60 million bushels. With the harvest so small, consumers bid up the price of wheat to $3.20—the price shown by the height of the demand curve at the point marked 1 in the diagram.

Farmers are very pleased by this price. They take it as an indication of good things to come, and plant the quantity that the supply curve indicates they will when the price is $3.20. This is 130 million bushels. If the weather is normal, then the harvest in year 2 is 130 million bushels, and the price drops to $1.06. Discouraged farmers cut back on their acreage, as shown by the supply curve, and plant only 78 million bushels the third year. This small crop drives the year 3 price up to $2.66, and in year 4, plantings are increased again. Gradually, the market heads back toward equilibrium. The pattern it makes on its way gives rise to the name of the cobweb effect.

This simple representation of the cobweb effect makes farmers sound quite naive. The first thing many people say when they see the cobweb diagram is, why has not some smart farmer figured out that the thing to do is to plant big acreages when the current price is low and cut back when it is high? In fact, farmers really are more sophisticated than to treat the future as a sure continuation of the immediate present, whatever the present happens to be. Nonetheless, they do take current prices, and the prices of other recent years, into account when they decide what to plant. Even if these present and recent past prices are only one group of factors among others that enter into the planting decision, some degree of cobweb effect can result.

Often cobwebs are complicated by the interaction of several crops. A case in point is the corn-hog cycle, in which future corn planting depends on this year's hog price. The result is an intricate pattern of fluctuation over a multiyear cycle.

Instability and Agricultural Policy

Parity Price Ratio The ratio of an index of prices that farmers receive to an index of prices that farmers pay, using the years 1910 –1914 as a base period.

The instability of agricultural prices is evident from Exhibit 25.4, which shows the historical record of the **parity price ratio.** This statistic is the ratio of an index of prices that farmers receive to an index of prices that farmers pay. The index uses the years 1910–1914 as a base period—years that have long been considered to represent the best period of peacetime farm prosperity in this century.

As the diagram shows, the parity price index has often had severe ups and downs. In the worst episode, from 1929 to 1932, the parity price ratio fell from 92 to 58 in just over 3 years. The collapse of domestic demand in

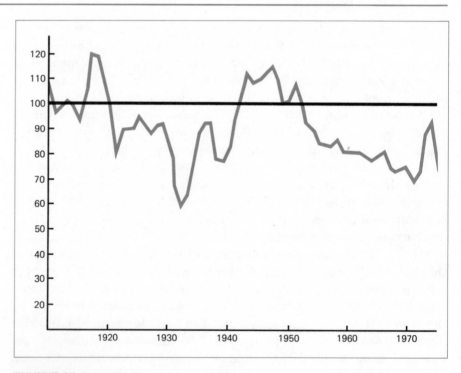

EXHIBIT 25.4

Parity price ratio

The parity price ratio is an index of prices received by farmers to prices paid by farmers. It has often fluctuated sharply from year to year. During the 1950s and 1960s, government policy helped stabilize the index, but did not prevent a steady decline. The end to most farm price supports brought renewed activity to the parity price ratio in the 1970s.

Source: Economic Report of the President (Washington, D.C.: U.S. Government Printing Office, 1976).

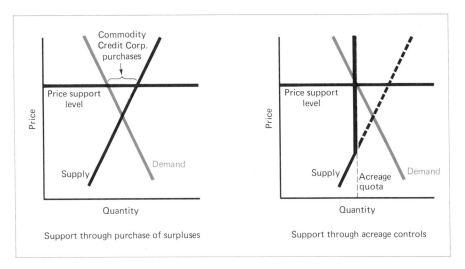

EXHIBIT 25.5
Two types of price support programs
Here we compare two types of farm price support programs. In part *a,* the support price is maintained by having the Commodity Credit Corporation purchase all market surpluses for storage or sale abroad. In part *b,* acreage controls are applied in an attempt to keep supply down to the level that will produce the desired price. The acreage quotas, in effect, put a "kink" in the supply curve.

these first years of the Great Depression pushed all prices down, but with agricultural demand so inelastic, farmers were hit worse than anyone else. The index of prices paid by farmers sank substantially, from 160 to 112 over this 4-year period, but the index of prices received fell catastrophically— from 149 to a mere 65. Mobs gathered in the nation's farm belt. The result was government action to stabilize farm prices.

Agricultural Stabilization Policy

The Agricultural Adjustment Act of 1933 was the first in a series of New Deal stabilization measures that culminated in the Agricultural Adjustment Act of 1938. Key features of these acts were a system of price support loans, handled through a Commodity Credit Corporation, and a system of quotas and soil conservation payments to reduce total acreage planted.

Exhibit 25.5 gives an idea of how these two kinds of stabilization measures work. The left-hand figure shows how Commodity Credit Corporation purchases try to absorb the surplus created when the support price is above the equilibrium level. The right-hand figure shows how production quotas and acreage limitations try to put a "kink" in the supply curve to make it intersect the demand curve at the desired price without any actual surpluses.

The years of World War II were good for farmers. After a brief dip to the 100 mark in 1949, the Korean war kept agricultural prices high until 1953. During the Eisenhower administration, however, the Department of Agriculture once again had its work cut out for it in the price stabilization field.

Now the problem became one of runaway technological advance on the farms. Between 1949 and 1959, output per worker hour in agriculture rose from an index of 56 to an index of 105, proportionately more than during the entire first half of the twentieth century. Farm employment fell, but not fast enough to prevent a 27 percent increase in total output over the decade. These developments put severe strains on price support programs. Acreage allotments were not working because every time acreage was cut back, farmers poured in fertilizers and machinery to grow more and more on less and less. The magnitude of agricultural surpluses became an acute political embarrassment. Public Law 480 of 1954 moved to dispose of agricultural surpluses by giving them away or selling them on "soft" terms abroad. The government even experimented with a technique to use surplus wheat in place of gravel to mix with asphalt for paving roads.

From Surpluses to a World Food Crisis

By 1973, farmers had received some $48 billion in federal subsidies under three Presidents, and subsidies were running at an annual rate of $3 billion. Taken strictly as stabilization measures, these subsidies can be said to have accomplished their purpose. Exhibit 25.4 shows a remarkable absence of year-to-year fluctuations in the 1950s and 1960s, although there was a steady downward trend in the parity price ratio.

In other terms, though, the price support programs came in for heavy criticism. It sometimes seemed almost to have been forgotten that the initial rationale for agricultural price stabilization had been to combat rural poverty. In the 1950s and 1960s, too many of the billions in price supports were going to the largest farmers who could afford thousands of acres on which to be paid *not* to grow crops, and too little money went to the smallest farmers. The real rural poor, agricultural laborers, were virtually untouched by conventional programs. What is more, consumers, whose interest is in low, not high, farm prices began to have an increasing voice in the political process. Things were ripe for a change.

As it was, supply and demand came to the rescue before policy makers took an independent initiative. In 1973, bad weather in much of the world (including the Soviet Union) sent U.S. food exports soaring to a record $17 billion. Prices rose rapidly, and in August 1973, the parity price ratio briefly touched the 100 mark for the first time in 21 years. Domestic consumer food costs went up 21 percent in 1973, and armies of housewives mobilized to march on Washington. The notorious American grain surpluses dwindled to nothing, probably never to return.

The response in Washington was a basic change in agricultural policy. Its chief features were the almost total lifting of acreage restrictions, and the replacement of support prices with a more flexible system of "target prices" that, for the time being at least, are *below* the market equilibrium for most commodities. American farmers were once again planting fence to fence and looking to the marketplace, not Washington, to learn what they would get for their crops.

Conclusions

Recent policy changes have made American agricultural markets an even better approximation to perfect competition than before. To give a final perspective on how these markets work, we give one more case study.

CASE 25.2
Down on the Farm, 1975[3]

Thomas, Okla., Aug. 29, 1975. A. O. Potter's hands are hard—half callouses, half ground-in dirt. He rides around in a dirty pickup truck, wears a faded baseball cap and always carries a wrench or two in the hip pocket of his blue jeans.

It is all something of a wheat farmer's disguise these days. The transformation from government-controlled to free-market grain dealing that began with the 1972 Soviet grain transaction turned Mr. Potter's pocket calculator into his most useful tool. And the sound of the commodity ticker in the McNeill Grain Company office is far more likely to command his attention than the sound of his tractor engine.

Mr. Potter, like the rest of the nation's wheat farmers, has become a sophisticated gambler. And between him and the foreigner who will eventually eat bread made out of his wheat are a host of other gamblers as well. They pile up gigantic telephone bills, making multimillion-dollar commitments with a simple long-distance O.K.

Mr. Potter grew 4,000 acres of wheat this year. It was ripe in mid-June. He paid professional harvesters—men with combines called "wheat gypsies" who follow the crop as it ripens from Texas to North Dakota—to pluck it out of his fields and truck it to the McNeill Grain Company's central elevator in Thomas. His harvest was about 80,000 bushels. He sold 10,000 bushels and began paying McNeill $1\frac{1}{2}$ cents per bushel per month to store the other 70,000 bushels.

Long before the harvest began, Ben Chambers, 34 years old, and Don McNeill, 24, who operate the elevator, began preparing to handle the crop. They knew the harvest would be big and that they did not have enough room in their storage bins to hold all the wheat their farmer customers would produce. So they phoned the nearest railroad and ordered hopper cars to stand by, and then hauled the excess wheat to large elevators in Enid, Okla., and Fort Worth.

During this time, the railroads and large grain companies—both of which own wheat-carrying hopper cars—were positioning their hoppers, using computer printouts close to local elevators throughout the Middle West.

During the June harvest, those cars hauled 200,000 bushels of wheat from McNeill's elevator in Thomas to Enid and Fort Worth elevators owned by the Continental Grain Company. Some of it probably was Mr. Potter's. Continental previously agreed to receive it and store it until McNeill decided to sell it.

That happened on August 26. Ben Chambers phoned Paul L. Krug, Jr., a 31-year-old Kansas City commodity manager for Continental, and asked what price he would pay. Mr. Krug's price was too low. So Mr. Chambers called several other grain companies and asked what they were paying. Two hours later he called Krug back, they argued over price briefly, and then settled on a compromise deal worth between one-half and three-quarters of a million dollars.

On August 26, Potter still owned 70,000 bushels. Ben Chambers was offering to buy it at $3.80 a bushel, for $266,000 in all. Mr. Potter was not selling. If the price hit $4, he could make $14,000 more than that. If the Soviet Union bought a lot more wheat, the price could go higher.

Like Mr. Potter, most wheat farmers that year were hanging on to their wheat as long as possible before selling. The price was rising steadily. Generally, the more wheat they hold, the higher the price. But there are dangers. If the steady flow of wheat is halted or slowed down by anything, large grain dealers slow down or stop buying it, and prices drop.

Four years earlier, when the federal government controlled wheat prices, farmers generally sold at harvest because there was little difference in price from one month to the next. That meant that farmers like Mr. Potter could spend their time worrying about the weather until harvest, then dash off to the county fair. Now, the simple task of growing the wheat is only half the farmer's work.

SUMMARY

1. Perfect competition requires markets that have large numbers of small firms, homogeneous products, well-informed buyers and sellers, and easy entry and exit. Agricultural markets fit these conditions rather closely, although no real-world markets can fit them perfectly. The agricultural sector of the economy thus makes a good place to find practical applications of supply and demand analysis.

2. Farm prices are subject to considerable instability. One of the reasons is that demand elasticities are quite low. That means that small changes in quantities supplied, brought on by such unpredictable factors as the weather, cause large changes in price. Low elasticity also means that farm incomes tend to fall when farm output rises. The cobweb effect is a further source of price instability. Farmers tend to take this year's price as an indication of next year's when deciding how much of each crop to plant. That makes prices and quantities first overshoot and undershoot their equilibrium levels.

3. Farmers suffered severely in the Great Depression. The government responded with a series of stabilization policies that aimed to steady prices by purchasing surpluses and restricting acreages. These policies continued through the 1950s and 1960s. The price support programs and rising productivity combined to create embarrassingly large surpluses. In the 1970s, conditions changed dramatically. A world food shortage developed that quickly eliminated the major agricultural surpluses, and sent farm prices to record highs. In the aftermath of the world food crisis, most acreage controls and price supports have been ended.

DISCUSSION QUESTIONS

1. Agriculture seems to fit the model of perfect competition more closely than most other industries, but does it really fit it perfectly? Are there any areas of agriculture in which a few large firms dominate the market? Are there some kinds of agricultural products for which the assumption of homogeneity does not really hold? Are there any significant barriers to entry and exit in agriculture?

2. From what you know of the determinants of demand elasticity, how can you explain the low elasticity of demand for farm products? Can you offer any explanation of the few exceptions to the pattern of low elasticities shown in Exhibit 25.1?

3. Redraw Exhibit 25.3, but make the demand curve fairly steep and the supply curve flatter than the demand curve. Now work through the cobweb effect again. What happens? Do you think this case has any real practical importance? Why or why not?

4. Other things being equal, we would expect that a policy of acreage quotas but no output quotas would cause an increase in output per acre. (Explain why.) Would this policy also be expected to cause an increase in output per worker hour? Why or why not? If not, how could you explain the sharp rise in productivity per worker hour in agriculture that took place during the 1950s?

5. Why were the acerage quotas and price supports of the 1950s and 1960s not a good way to help the poorest farmers? What would have been a more efficient way to accomplish that particular objective?

6. Is it really necessary for a farmer like A. O. Potter to be a gambler? If he wished, how could he make use of future markets (see Chapter 3) to sell at least part of his crop before he planted it, and thereby reduce his risk?

CHAPTER 26
Monopoly and Imperfect Competition

What You Will Learn in This Chapter
Outside the agricultural sector, few markets in the American economy fit the model of perfect competition very closely. In industries where there are only one or a few large firms, or where products are not homogeneous, firms are not price takers. They cannot be relied on to produce where price is equal to marginal cost. The behavior of firms in noncompetitive markets creates important problems for both theory and policy.

For Review
Here is an important concept that will be put to use in this chapter. Be certain that you understand it, or review it before proceeding.
  Perfect competition (Chapter 24)

Although the agricultural sector of the American economy roughly fits the pattern of perfect competition, much of the industrial sector does not. Markets with only one or a few firms, and markets with strongly differentiated products, are quite common. These noncompetitive market structures raise important questions for economic theory and policy, to which we now turn. In this chapter, we shall limit ourselves for the most part to questions of theory, saving policy issues for Chapter 27.

Industrial Concentration

Measuring Concentration
Large numbers of small firms are the hallmark of perfect competition. We measure how far the structure of some market departs from perfect competition by seeing how large a share of output is contributed by the largest firms. The most widely used measures of this kind are the four-firm and eight-firm **concentration ratios.** The four-firm concentration ratio is the percentage of all industry sales contributed by the four largest firms. The eight-firm ratio takes the eight largest firms into account.

Exhibit 26.1 shows four-firm and eight-firm concentration ratios for a selection of twenty-five American industries. The most concentrated in terms of the four-firm ratio is the production of telephone apparatus. The

Concentration Ratios The percentage of all industry sales contributed by the four or eight largest firms in an industry. Used as a measure of the competitiveness of a market.

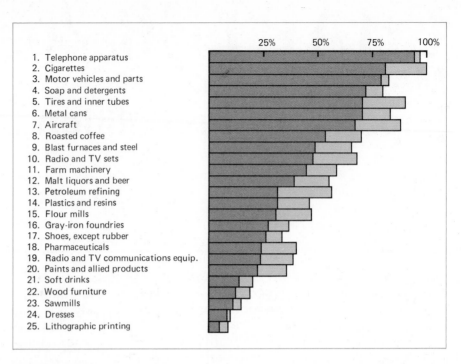

EXHIBIT 26.1

Four-firm and eight-firm concentration ratios for 1966—selected industries
Concentration ratios measure the percentage of industry output contributed
by the largest firms. This representative selection of twenty-five American
industries shows a wide range of concentration ratios. The figures given here
do not take into account foreign competition, or the fact that some industries
produce mainly for local markets.

Source: U.S. Bureau of the Census, *Statistical Abstract of the United States, 1970* (Washington,
D.C.: U.S. Government Printing Office, 1971), Tab. 1124.

eight-firm ratio puts the cigarette industry at the head of the list, with
100 percent of production accounted for by the eight largest firms. Motor
vehicles and parts come close behind. If just the production of completed
automobiles were counted, this industry would appear even more
concentrated.

At the bottom of the chart are a number of industries where even the
top eight firms account for less than a quarter of industry output. These
industries do not fit the perfectly competitive pattern as well as does agriculture, but they are clearly closer to it than the industries at the top of
our chart.

One qualifying consideration must be kept in mind when looking at
these concentration ratios. All the ratios are computed on the basis of total
sales by American firms, but the American economy as a whole is not the
relevant market for all industries. The markets for motor vehicles, tires,
aircraft, steel, and TV sets are world markets. International competition
in those markets means that the concentration of American firms is less
significant than in the case of, say, cigarettes, where foreign competition
is negligible. On the other hand, some other industries cater largely to local
markets. The concentration of sawmills within any local market, for example, is much greater than indicated by Exhibit 26.1.

Sources of Industrial Concentration

Economies of scale are one major source of industrial concentration. In Chapter 22, we saw that industries differ widely in terms of the size of firms necessary to achieve the minimum economic scale of production.[1] If economies of scale are strong enough that there is room in an industry for only a few firms of efficient size, perfect competition in that industry is impossible. Long-run competitive equilibrium requires each firm to be at the minimum point on its long-run average cost curve. If that minimum occurs at an output that is more than a small fraction of total industry output, the conditions for perfect competition will not be met.

There are other sources of industrial concentration as well. Some industries appear to be much more concentrated than economies of scale alone can explain. In many cases, government policies contribute to concentration. In other industries, concentration must be explained in terms of the past histories and business tactics of individual firms. We shall have more to say about these things in the next two chapters, in which we discuss government policy toward industrial concentration.

The Theory of Pure Monopoly

There is no single theory that can apply to all concentrated industries. Instead, there are a number of cases that must be treated separately. The first of these cases is **pure monopoly.**

A pure monopoly is a firm that accounts for 100 percent of the sales in its market. Such a firm has no competitors at all, and thus achieves the ultimate in industrial concentration. No industry listed in Exhibit 26.1 is a pure monopoly, but some cases do exist. Local utilities—gas, electricity, and water—often closely approximate pure monopoly. The U.S. Postal Service has a pure monopoly in the carriage of first class mail. Even such pure monopolies, though, are not absolutely free of competition. Pipeline gas and electricity each have monopolies, but they compete with one another in many uses. Water companies compete with the alternative of private wells. Even the Postal Service must compete with other forms of communication.

Pure Monopoly A market structure in which one firm accounts for 100 percent of industry sales.

The Monopolist Not a Price Taker

Our theory of perfect competition was designed to tell us the equilibrium price and quantity that would prevail in a market under given conditions of demand, resource availability, and technology. A theory of monopoly must do the same. The major difference between the two theories stems from the fact that the monopolist is not a price taker. The quantity of output that a monopolist decides to produce has a very definite effect on the price at which its product can be sold. In order to increase the quantity sold, a monopolist must move down along the demand curve for its product, lowering its price. If it wishes to raise its price, it must move up along its demand curve, reducing the quantity sold.

What happens to revenue when a monopolist varies its quantity of

[1]See Exhibit 22.5.

Price	Quantity	Total Revenue	Marginal Revenue
Marginal revenue with elastic demand			
$8.80	5	$44.00	
8.50	6	51.00	$7.00
8.20	7	57.40	6.40
7.90	8	63.20	5.80
Marginal revenue with inelastic demand			
$4.30	20	$86.00	
4.00	21	84.00	−$2.00
3.70	22	81.40	− 2.60
3.40	23	78.20	− 3.20

EXHIBIT 26.2
Calculation of marginal revenue
A firm's marginal revenue is the amount by which its total revenue changes when output is changed by one unit. When demand for the firm's product is elastic, revenue increases when output increases, so marginal revenue is positive. When demand is inelastic, revenue falls as output increases, so marginal revenue is negative.

Marginal Revenue The change in a firm's total revenue that results from a one-unit change in total output.

output depends on the elasticity of demand. If demand is elastic, the firm can earn more revenue by selling a greater quantity, even though the price is forced down. If demand is inelastic, it can earn greater revenue with a smaller output by charging a higher price. The change in total revenue that results from a one-unit change in output is known as the firm's **marginal revenue.** Exhibit 26.2 shows how marginal revenue is calculated. Notice that marginal revenue is positive when demand is elastic, and negative when demand is inelastic.

Profit Maximization

The idea of marginal revenue plays a key part in determining the profit-maximizing output for a pure monopolist. We can show this by way of an example. As a basis for our example, we use the same "typical" firm, with its U-shaped cost curves, as we used in Chapters 22 and 24. Now, though, we make this firm into a monopolist by placing it alone in a market, facing a downward-sloping demand curve.

Exhibit 26.3 gives total and marginal cost data for the firm. It also gives data on price, total revenue, and marginal revenue according to a hypothetical demand curve. The table makes it easy to find the profit-maximizing level of output. Reading down column (7), we see that profit is at its maximum when output is set at a level of 13 units. Total revenue increases beyond this point (reaching a maximum at 17 units of output) but total cost increases faster. From columns (4) and (5), we see that producing the 14th unit of output adds a marginal cost of $2.75, and earns a marginal revenue of only $2.20.

Alternatively, we can use a graphical approach for finding the monopolist's point of profit maximization. Consider Exhibit 26.4, which shows cost and revenue curves based on Exhibit 26.3. Part *a* shows total cost and total revenue curves for the firm. Because total revenue first increases and then falls as demand becomes inelastic, there are two breakeven points on the graph. Between them, at the point where the two curves are just parallel and the gap between them is at its widest, is the point of maximum profit.

Exhibit 26.4*b* shows the firm's marginal cost, marginal revenue, and demand curves. The profit-maximizing output level is found at the inter-

EXHIBIT 26.3

Total and per-unit cost, revenue, and profit data for a hypothetical pure monopolist

This table gives cost, revenue, and profit data for a hypothetical monopolist. By studying the table, we discover that profit rises with increased output as long as marginal cost remains below marginal revenue. The maximum profit is reached at 13 units of output. Beyond that point, marginal cost begins to exceed marginal revenue, and profit declines.

(1) Output	(2) Price	(3) Total Revenue	(4) Marginal Revenue	(5) Marginal Cost	(6) Total Cost	(7) Total Profit
1	$10.00	$10.00			$ 23.80	$ −13.80
			9.40	3.40		
2	9.70	19.40			27.20	− 7.80
			8.80	3.05		
3	9.40	28.20			30.25	2.05
			8.20	2.75		
4	9.10	36.40			33.00	3.40
			7.60	2.50		
5	8.80	44.00			35.50	8.50
			7.00	2.30		
6	8.50	51.00			37.80	13.20
			6.40	2.15		
7	8.20	57.40			39.95	17.45
			5.80	2.05		
8	7.90	63.20			42.00	21.20
			5.20	2.00		
9	7.60	68.40			44.00	24.40
			4.60	2.05		
10	7.30	73.00			46.05	26.95
			4.00	2.15		
11	7.00	77.00			48.20	28.80
			3.40	2.30		
12	6.70	80.40			50.50	29.90
			2.80	2.50		
13	6.40	83.20			53.00	30.20
			2.20	2.75		
14	6.10	85.40			55.75	29.65
			1.60	3.05		
15	5.80	87.00			58.80	28.20
			1.00	3.40		
16	5.50	88.00			62.20	25.80
			.40	3.80		
17	5.20	88.40			66.00	22.40
			− .20	4.25		
18	4.90	88.20			70.25	17.95
			− .80	4.75		
19	4.60	87.40			75.00	12.40
			−1.40	5.30		
20	4.30	86.00			80.30	5.70
			−2.00	5.90		
21	4.00	84.00			86.20	− 2.20
			−2.60	6.55		
22	3.70	81.40			92.75	−11.35
			−3.20	7.25		
23	3.40	78.20			100.00	−21.80
			−3.80	8.00		
24	3.10	74.40			108.00	−33.60
			−4.40	8.80		
25	2.80	70.00			116.80	−46.80

section of the marginal cost and marginal revenue curves. Beyond that point the cost of the marginal unit exceeds the increase in revenue earned by selling it, so profit falls. The profit-maximizing price is identified by the height of the demand curve directly above the intersection of the marginal cost and marginal revenue curves.

Monopoly and Competition Compared

It is instructive to compare the profit-maximizing equilibrium of a monopolist with that of a price taker. Profit-maximizing output for a price taker is the output that makes marginal cost equal to price. For a monopolist, the profit-maximizing output is the one that makes marginal cost equal to marginal revenue. Because a monopolist's marginal revenue is always less than the product price, the marginal cost of a monopolist's product is below its price when the firm is in equilibrium. If the monopolistic firm were to expand output until marginal cost were equal to price, it would

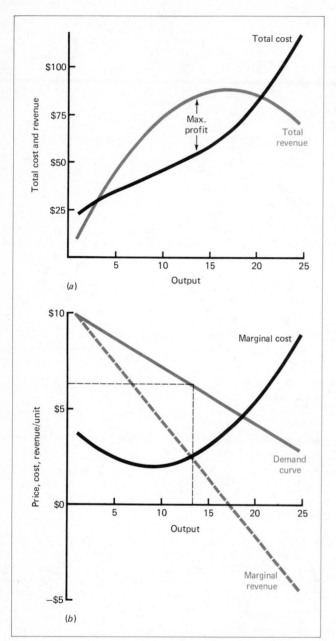

EXHIBIT 26.4

Profit maximization for a pure monopolist

In part *a*, the profit-maximizing level of output is the point of widest separation of the total cost and total revenue curves. In part *b*, the profit-maximizing quantity is found at the intersection of the marginal cost and marginal revenue curves. Note that the profit-maximizing price is given by the height of the demand curve directly above this intersection.

earn less than the maximum amount of profit possible for it. This can be verified from Exhibit 26.3. There we see that marginal cost and price are equal at about 19 units of output for the monopolist discussed in the example.

We saw in Chapter 24 that when the market equilibrium price of a product is above its marginal cost, resources are not being allocated efficiently. Applying this principle to monopolies, we get the result that monopolies produce inefficiently small quantities of output. We shall discuss the policy implications of this kind of inefficiency in Chapter 27.

Cartels

Sometimes an effective monopoly can be established by a group of firms acting cooperatively, rather than by a single firm. Such a group of firms is called a **cartel.** By studying cartels, we can learn more about how monopoly compares with perfect competition.

We shall proceed by means of a numerical example based on the imaginary product "snake oil." Snake oil is a folk medicine produced from a secret recipe shared by some 100 small family firms. For simplicity, we assume constant returns to scale, so that the long-run average cost curve for the industry is a horizontal line, as shown in Exhibit 26.5. The industry demand and marginal revenue curves are also shown in this exhibit.

Let us suppose initially that the 100 firms behave as perfect competitors. As we learned in Chapter 24, this will result in an equilibrium where price is equal to long-run average cost of $1 per bottle, and 400,000 bottles of snake oil are produced each month. Firms will earn the normal rate of return that economists always count as part of total private costs, but no more.

One day the heads of the 100 firms get together to form a cartel. It is their hope that by replacing competition with cooperation, they can advance their mutual interests. They elect one of their numbers as cartel manager. This manager is instructed to work out a production and marketing plan that will maximize total profits for the industry, and share these profits fairly among the 100 members.

The profit-maximizing problem faced by the cartel manager is exactly the same as that faced by a pure monopolist. Industry profits are maximized at the output where marginal revenue equals marginal cost, that is, 200,000 bottles per month for our example. By restricting output to that quantity, the price can be raised to $2 per bottle. Industry profits are increased by $200,000 per month. To share these profits fairly among all

Cartel   A group of firms that acts cooperatively to exercise monopoly power in a market.

EXHIBIT 26.5
The effects of a cartel in the snake oil industry
The snake oil industry is composed of 100 identical small firms. If these firms behave as perfect competitors, the industry will be in equilibrium where the demand curve and marginal cost curve intersect. If they combine into a cartel, they can increase their profits by restricting output to the point where marginal cost and marginal revenue are equal.

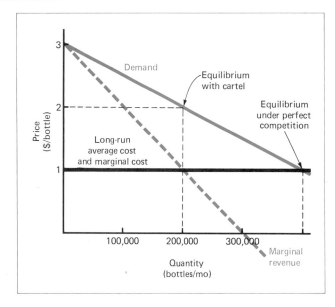

cartel members, each firm is given an output quota of just 2,000 bottles a month, half as much as before. By this arrangement the member firms reap the benefits of pure monopoly despite their small size and large numbers.

Problems of Cartels

Cartels are fine for their members, but not so good for their customers. Snake oil users end up spending the same amount of money on the product as under competition, and getting only half the quantity. Furthermore, the cartel is suspect on efficiency grounds because it raises price above marginal cost just as a monopoly does.

Cartels are very unpopular, except among the people who actually belong to them. Fortunately for the rest of us, cartels have two big built-in problems that prevent them from becoming very common, or very long-lived.

The first problem from which cartels suffer is control over entry to their industry. As long as competition in an industry keeps price down to the level of long-run average cost, membership in an industry tends to be stable. As soon as a cartel raises price above this level, however, the industry becomes a magnet for new entrants. The entry of new firms does not increase the total quantity that the cartel can sell at the profit-maximizing price. It only increases the number of members among which profits have to be shared. Unless there is a way for a cartel to control entry into its market, then, it cannot effectively serve the interests of its members.

The second, even more serious built-in problem of cartels is the enforcement of output quotas. In every cartel, each individual member always has an incentive to cheat on its quota by producing extra, unauthorized output. Take our snake oil cartel for example. The quota for each member was 2,000 bottles per month, just half of what each firm would produce under competitive conditions. What would happen if any one firm cheated on its quota by stepping up output to the precartel level, while the others continued to play by the rules?

The answer is simple. An extra 2,000 bottles per month by one firm would have a negligible effect on the market price, because it would represent only a 1 percent increase in industry output. By producing 4,000 bottles a month, the cheater would double its monthly profit—as long as others do not cheat too.

What if the others *do* cheat? What if all the other 99 firms stepped up output to 4,000 bottles per month, while one firm only stuck to its quota? With industry output at 398,000 bottles, the price would be forced down virtually all the way to the competitive level of $1 per bottle. The firm that played fair would gain nothing for its honesty.

Cartels and Government

The entry and cheating problems make purely voluntary cartels very unstable. A cartel with the power to force its members to play by the rules, however, is another story altogether. Here we are not just speaking of the racketeer who sends his thugs to keep a rival from muscling in on his territory. Much more commonly, cartels manage to survive and prosper by persuading legitimate government authorities to back them up with the force of law. In fact, it is difficult to think of a successful cartel in which government does not play a major role.

The best-known cartels are probably those whose members are themselves governments. OPEC, the Organization of Petroleum Exporting Countries, is a prominent example. OPEC's entry problem is kept under control by the fact that oil is not found just anywhere. The member governments of the cartel meet at the ministerial level to settle prices and quotas. The cartel is not entirely free from problems, and some members are less scrupulous than others about keeping to the letter of their agreements. Nonetheless, OPEC has proved more stable and long-lived than many observers believed it could be a few years ago.

Government-backed cartels are also found in the domestic economy, although they are usually called by some other name, The acreage quotas that the government used to keep farm prices up during the 1950s and 1960s were a classic example of a compulsory cartel. Many regulatory agencies, as we shall see in Chapter 28, enforce cartel-like practices for the industries they control. Licensed professions, such as law and medicine, restrict entry in cartel-like fashion through their tight control of professional education. In all these cases, it is against the law to break the cartel rules. Fines or jail sentences are imposed on those who grow cotton on unauthorized acreage, or sell airline tickets for a price lower than the Civil Aeronautics Board permits, or practice medicine without a license.

Not all industries are able to get the government backing needed to form a cartel, of course. There are many industries that are neither cartels nor monopolies, and yet do not fit the requirements of perfect competition either. Most of the industries listed in Exhibit 26.1 do not fit any of the theoretical boxes we have examined so far. More theories are needed to cover the middle ground between competition and monopoly.

The Theory of Oligopoly

Industries that have more than one firm but fewer than "many" firms are known as **oligopolies.** There is a sense in which oligopolies are more competitive than any of the kinds of industries we have discussed so far. What distinguishes oligopolies from perfect competition or monopolies is each firm's need to be constantly aware of its rivals' policies and market tactics. A wheat farmer does not have to worry about how many acres his neighbor plants, because he knows that they both supply such a small part of their perfectly competitive market that nothing they do will affect the prevailing price. A pure monopolist has no direct rivals to pay attention to. But oligopolists are competitive in the sense that the players of a game are competitive. Like game players, they must take their competitors' reactions into account in planning every move.

Because competition under oligopoly is like a game, it is difficult to represent oligopoly behavior in terms of simple rules. There are some theories, however, that explain parts of oligopoly behavior well enough to be worth looking at.

Oligopoly A market structure in which there are two or more firms each of which has a large share of total sales.

Kinked Demand Curve

One such attempt to explain how oligopolists interact with their rivals is the *theory of the kinked demand curve.* The kinked demand curve arises from a situation in which each individual firm makes two assumptions about the way its rivals will react to changes in its own policy. First, each firm assumes that if it lowers its price, the others will lower their prices too in order to keep their customers from being stolen. Second, each firm assumes that if it raises its price, the others will hold their prices constant and raid its customers.

Exhibit 26.6 shows how the market looks to an oligopolist who makes these two assumptions. Let *P* be the price ($1.70 in this case) that happens to prevail in the market at the moment. If the firm in question cuts its price below *P,* other firms will also lower theirs. Sales of the industry as a whole will then expand. This firm will keep about its same share of the market and will move down the lower slope of the demand curve. In contrast, if the firm raises its price, others will not follow. Instead of keeping its share of the market, it will lose customers to its rivals. As a result, the part of the firm's demand curve lying above the established price *P* is much more elastic than the part lying below.

Now let us bring marginal cost and marginal revenue into the picture. We give the firm a short-run marginal cost curve with the usual upward slope. The marginal revenue curve has a "step" in it that corresponds to the kink in the demand curve. To the left of the step, marginal revenue is very high, indicating that revenue will be lost very rapidly if the firm moves up the very elastic part of the demand curve. To the right of the step, marginal revenue is much lower, indicating that little extra revenue can be obtained by moving down the less elastic lower part of the demand curve. The marginal cost curve, as drawn, cuts the marginal revenue curve right at the step. The prevailing price is an equilibrium price for the firm, because it would be unprofitable to move in either one direction or the other.

The kinked demand curve equilibrium for an oligopolist is a particularly stable kind of equilibrium. Unlike a pure monopolist, the kinked

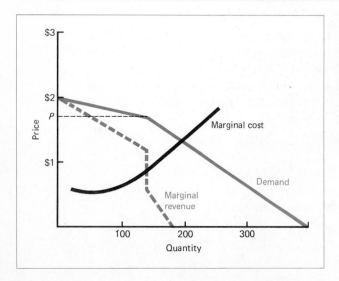

EXHIBIT 26.6

Oligopolist's kinked demand curve

An oligopolist will have a "kinked" demand curve if its rivals will follow any price reduction it makes, but not any price rise. There is a sharp step in the marginal revenue curve corresponding to the kink in the demand curve. Here, the marginal cost curve crosses the marginal revenue curve just at the step. That makes the equilibrium very stable.

demand curve oligopolist will not change price or output in response to small or medium-sized changes in cost. The level of marginal cost shown in Exhibit 26.6 could move up or down by as much as $.30 in either direction, and the firm would not change its price or output. The marginal cost curve would still cross the marginal revenue curve at the step. Only if cost changed by more than $.30 per unit would the firm break with the prevailing industry price.

Price Leadership

The kinked demand curve fails to explain one important aspect of oligopoly equilibrium. Why is the "established price" at one level rather than another in the first place? We can give no really general answer to this question, but one explanation that seems to apply in some industries is **price leadership.** The idea is that in some oligopolistic markets, one firm, the price leader, can count on the others to match its price changes whether they are up or down. To the extent that the price leader can count on being followed, it can adjust price and quantity to aim for equality of marginal cost and marginal revenue, much like a pure monopolist or a cartel manager. The basic steel industry in the United States is often cited as an example of the practice of price leadership, as the following case study relates.

Price Leadership   A situation in which one firm in an oligopolistic industry, the price leader, can count on the others to match its price changes whether they are up or down.

CASE 26.1
Price Leadership in Basic Steel

In the closing years of the nineteenth century, the great financier J. P. Morgan engineered one of the most remarkable series of mergers in American business history. The result was U.S. Steel, which by 1905 accounted for two-thirds of steel output in this country. Judge Elbert Gary was U.S. Steel's first chairman. In 1907, he inaugurated a famous series of "Gary dinners," to which he invited the other steel producers, none of whom accounted for more than 5 percent of the market. The result of the friendly discussions that took place at these dinners was the unchallenged price leadership of U.S. Steel.

In 1911, with the threat of an antitrust suit in the air, the Gary dinners were discontinued. Price leadership did not stop, however. Given the structure of the industry, no formal conspiracy was necessary to make the smaller producers realize that independent price increases would simply mean loss of business, and that the only safe time to raise prices was when the leader did so.

U.S. Steel's position as leader continued unchallenged for half a century, despite the fact that its share of the market shrank steadily. By the end of the 1950s, it was still the largest single firm, but had only a quarter of the market, and was less than twice as big as the runner up, Bethlehem Steel. During the 1960s the lead in pricing began to change hands once in a while. Price leadership did not entirely disappear, but U.S. Steel could no longer be certain that its lead would always be followed. Others found that they could sometimes initiate price changes and make them stick. The simple pattern that had prevailed so long was broken.

Limitations of Price Leadership

It would be wrong to think that an industry with strong price leadership is simply a cartel by another name. The powers of a price leader are much less than those of a cartel manager. For one thing, the price leader cannot set or enforce output quotas, so firms remain free to compete with one another for sales. The higher price is raised above marginal cost, the greater is the danger that this jockeying for market shares will break out into the open price warfare. Furthermore, the price leader exercises no control over entry into the industry. The bigger the gap between price and cost, the bigger the attraction for new entrants. These limitations on the power of price leadership, in comparison with the power of a formal cartel, no doubt contributed substantially to the decline in the market share of U.S. Steel during its period of price leadership.

The theories of the kinked demand curve and price leadership by no means exhaust the efforts of economists to analyze equilibrium under oligopoly. They do point to the only kind of conclusion that can safely be made about oligopoly behavior. That conclusion is that oligopolists have an interest in finding and maintaining a monopoly price for their product, but they lack the means to accomplish this objective to more than a partial degree.

Monopolistic Competition

There is still one important type of market structure to be considered. Some industries have the large number of firms necessary for perfect competition, but lack the homogeneity of product that perfect competition requires. Restaurants, drugstores, and barbershops are examples. Some of the manufacturing industries on the lower end of Exhibit 26.1, such as soft drinks, furniture, and dresses, also fit this pattern. The market structure of an industry with a large number of firms producing a differentiated product is known as **monopolistic competition.**

Monopolistic Competition A market structure in which there are many firms producing a strongly differentiated product.

Because each monopolistically competitive firm has a product a little different than the others, it is not, strictly speaking, a price taker. Each firm can raise its price at least a little, and still retain those of its customers who prefer the particular style or location or whatever the firm offers. This means that each monopolistic competitor faces a demand curve that is less than perfectly elastic. It must therefore base its managerial calculations on considerations of marginal cost and marginal revenue, just as a pure monopolist does.

Unlike pure monopolies, however, new firms may freely enter a monopolistically competitive industry. If the price in such an industry rises above average cost, permitting supernormal profits, new entrants will flock in. The quantity they add to total supply will depress price. Entry will stop only when the market reaches an equilibrium where price and average cost are equal.

Equilibrium Under Monopolistic Competition

Reasoning this way, we discover two necessary features of long-run equilibrium under monopolistic competition. First, marginal revenue must equal marginal cost for each firm, in order to meet the profit-maximizing criterion for a firm which is not a price taker. Second, long-run average cost must equal price, in order to meet the zero-profit criterion for equilibrium in an industry with free entry. These conditions are met when the cost, demand, and marginal revenue curves for the firm are arranged as in Exhibit 26.7. The firm represented by this figure produces an equi-

EXHIBIT 26.7

Long-run equilibrium of the firm under monopolistic competition

Two conditions must hold for a firm to be in long-run equilibrium in a monopolistically competitive industry. First, price must be equal to long-run average cost so that there will be no incentive for entry or exit. Second, marginal cost for the firm must equal marginal revenue. These conditions are met when the various curves are in the relative positions shown here.

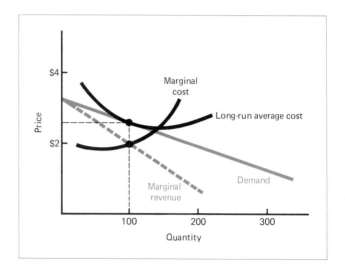

librium output of 100 units, and sells at a price of $2.60 per unit. It earns no profit in excess of the normal rate of return included in the measurement of costs.

Implications

Economists have long debated the implications of monopolistic competition for efficiency and consumer welfare. According to the traditional point of view, monopolistically competitive industries end up with too many firms, each of which produces too little output to be efficient. The basis for this view is evident from Exhibit 26.7. There we see that the firm's marginal cost is below its price, which is an indication that too few resources are devoted to production. Also, the firm is not producing at the minimum point on its average total cost curve, indicating that with fewer firms in the industry, each producing more, costs could be lowered. Economists who argue this way point to such things as two gas stations on each street corner, each of which has capacity enough to fill the tanks of all the cars that stop at that corner, as evidence of waste.

The trouble with criticism of monopolistic competition is that it implicitly assumes that product differentiation has no intrinsic value to consumers. All that the preceding argument establishes, in fact, is that prices would be a little lower if consumers were willing to settle for fewer supermarkets, each of which was a little more crowded, for fewer barbershops, each of which was a little less conveniently located, or for fewer flavors of ice cream. Each firm under monopolistic competition faces a trade-off between slightly lowering its product price, or spending a little more on marketing or product development to make its product a little more attractive to consumers. UCLA economist Harold Demsetz has argued that if the value to consumers of product differentiation is taken into account, there is no significant difference between monopolistic competition and perfect competition as far as economic efficiency or consumer satisfaction are concerned. The outcome of monopolistic competition, then, is an equilibrium where the degree of product diversification offered by the market is just that degree of product diversification that buyers are willing to pay for.

Joan V. Robinson
(1903–   )

When Joan Robinson was a young assistant lecturer at Cambridge University, she decided to stand the accepted procedures of economics on their head. "It is customary," she wrote, "in setting out the principles of economic theory, to open with the analysis of a perfectly competitive world, and to treat monopoly as a special case. . . . This process can with advantage be reversed. . . it is more proper to set out the analysis of monopoly, treating perfect competition as a special case." These words and the analysis to support them appeared in her *Economics of Imperfect Competition* in 1933. The book established her reputation immediately, and remains one of the basic pioneering contributions to this branch of economics. (As often happens in economics, a similar theory was developed independently and published in the same year by E. H. Chamberlin.)

Microeconomics was not Joan Robinson's only interest, however. She was a pioneer of macroeconomic thinking. Even as her work on imperfect competition came out, she was involved in the debate that preceded the publication of Keynes' *General Theory.* In fact, in much of her later macro work, she is critical of the very kind of "partial" analysis on which her theory of imperfect competition rests.

Joan Robinson has always been intensely interested in policy questions. In all her policy writings, she is a vehement critic of the market. In 1945, she wrote in *Private Enterprise and Public Control* that "the system of private property in its modern developments leads to great evils. Its inequality is not only an outrage on social justice, but also on common sense. It leads to large scale waste through unemployment, while the development of monopoly creates artificial scarcities and the dominance of the interests of property over the interests of human beings twists the whole system into a form for which it is impossible to find any reasonable justification." Her opposition to the market and her interest in broad normative questions also led her to write *An Essay on Marxian Economics* (1956), *Economic Philosophy* (1962), and *Freedom and Necessity* (1970). Now long past "retirement" age, Joan Robinson continues an active life as debater, social critic, and economic heretic.

Conclusions

The controversy over the welfare effects of monopolistic competition brings us up against a major problem that all of the theories set forth in this chapter share. The theories of monopoly, cartels, oligopoly, and monopolistic competition are all limited to analyzing managerial calculation for firms in different market structures. None of them explicitly discusses the effect of market structure on entrepreneurial decision making, or the effect of entrepreneurial competition on market structure.

Managerial calculation means effective exploitation of established techniques and widely available knowledge. Entrepreneurship is alertness to the economic value of new ideas and knowledge about changing circumstances. As soon as we begin to think in terms of entrepreneurship, and not exclusively in terms of managerial calculation, the relationship between monopoly and competition becomes much more complex. Here are three points in particular we need to take into account.

First, we need to recognize that monopoly is often the goal of entrepreneurial competition and the chief incentive to engage in it. The first firm to seize on new knowledge and put it to use is able to make profits in excess of the normal rate of return precisely because its new discovery establishes a temporary monopoly that it can exploit until its competitors successfully imitate or outflank it. If each new product had to be introduced at a price that just covered costs, or if each cost-reducing innovation had to be followed immediately by a matching reduction in price, there would be little reason to introduce such innovations at all. If the first firm to adjust to changing circumstances were not able to increase the gap between its costs and revenues by doing so, there would be no incentive to be first. Competition among entrepreneurs is competition for monopoly power of at least a temporary kind. In this sense, monopoly is not the opposite of competition, but a normal result of competition.

Second, we need to recognize that monopoly power, once achieved, acts as a spur to competition. This is not only true in the now familiar sense that an industry where monopoly profits are being made tends to attract new entrants. It also applies to competition among different industries and product groups for the consumer's dollar. The OPEC countries' exploitation of their oil monopoly has subjected oil to greatly intensified competition from other sources of energy. The rate of innovation in methods of energy production, and the rate of introduction of known energy-conserving technology, has been greatly speeded up. Even if the oil cartel were now to be broken up, world energy markets would not return to their former equilibrium pattern. In this sense, monopoly is not the opposite of competition, but a spur to competition.

Finally, when entrepreneurship as well as managerial calculation is taken into account, concentration ratios become poor measures of the competitiveness of markets. Instead of counting the number of firms in a market, other measures of competitiveness are needed. In particular, we need to ask to what extent is each firm's market share, whether large or small, protected by legal prohibitions against encroachment by other firms? To what extent is each firm's market share protected by exclusive ownership of unique productive resources? When market shares are so protected, competition is effectively thwarted, and established firms can engage in true monopolistic restriction. When market shares are not so protected, established firms, even if few in number, cut output and raise prices at their peril.

We have reviewed several theories of managerial calculation under different market structures in this chapter. All are products of an era in economic thought that stretched from the 1890s to World War II. They lend themselves well to the tools of graphical exposition and mathematical analysis worked out in those years. Theories of entrepreneurial competition have proved more difficult to put into simple graphs and formulas. They remain an important underdeveloped area of economics, and one that can be expected to receive increasing attention in years ahead.

SUMMARY

1. A pure monopoly accounts for 100 percent of the sales in its industry. Such a firm is not a price taker. As it expands output, it must lower its price in accordance with the demand curve for its product. The marginal revenue that such a firm earns by producing one more unit of output is less than the price at which that last unit of output is sold. To maximize profits, the monopoly produces up to the point where marginal cost and marginal revenue are equal. At that point, the price of the product must exceed its marginal cost.
2. Sometimes a group of firms act cooperatively to establish monopoly power

in a market by forming a cartel. The profit-maximizing conditions for a cartel are the same as those for a pure monopolist. Cartels suffer from two built-in weaknesses. The first is the need to control entry into their industry, and the second is the need to enforce output quotas on cartel members. The temptation to cheat on output quotas is a major source of instability for cartels. Usually, cartels cannot survive without using force to restrict entry and enforce quotas. Most long-lasting cartels are either backed by government power, or have governments themselves as members.

3. Oligopolies are competitive in a sense that neither monopolists nor perfect competitors are. Unlike firms in those other market structures, they must be constantly aware of their rivals' policies and market tactics. The gamelike nature of competition under oligopoly makes it particularly difficult to capture in any one simple theory. The theories of the kinked demand curve and of price leadership are two partially successful attempts to construct a theory of oligopoly.

4. Monopolistic competition is a market structure in which there are many firms, but also significant differences among the products of various firms. For a firm to be in long-run equilibrium in such a market, marginal cost must equal marginal revenue, and long-run average cost must equal price. Because price must be above marginal cost under those conditions, monopolistic competition is sometimes said to serve its customers inefficiently. Some economists argue, however, that monopolistic competition is just as efficient as perfect competition if one takes into account the value to customers of variety in the products that the market offers to them.

5. The standard theories of monopoly, oligopoly, and monopolistic competition are incomplete to the extent that they exclude entrepreneurial elements of competition. In the real world, the relationship between monopoly and competition is more complex than in these theories. When entrepreneurship is taken into account, monopoly turns out to be the goal of much competition, and at the same time, a spur to competition. The relationship between competition, entrepreneurship, and market structure remains an incompletely developed area of economics.

DISCUSSION QUESTIONS

1. Consider this statement: "The difference between a monopolist and a purely competitive firm is that the monopolist can charge any price it wants, while the competitor must take the market price as given." In what sense is it true that a monopolist can charge "any price it wants?" Can a perfect competitor also charge "any price it wants" in a sense?

2. Does the rule that profits are maximized where marginal cost equals marginal revenue apply only to monopolists, or does it apply also to competitors? Hint: What is the relationship between price and marginal revenue for a firm that is a price taker?

3. Is it a valid generalization to say that a profit-maximizing pure monopolist will always choose to operate at some point where its demand curve is inelastic? Why or why not?

4. If all the separate firms of a perfectly competitive industry were merged into a single monopolistic firm or organized into a cartel, we can be reasonably certain that consumers would end up paying a higher price than before and that efficiency would suffer. Can we be equally confident that breaking any existing monopoly or oligopoly up into a large number of small firms would result in lower prices and greater efficiency? Why or why not?

5. Can you see any similarity between a labor union and a cartel? Do labor unions need government support to survive? Think about this question briefly now, and then come back to it after you have read Chapters 29 and 30.

6. In what sense are oligopolies competitive industries? How does the competition of the "big three" automakers with one another differ from the competition of wheat farmers with one another?

7. It is sometimes remarked that an industry like gasoline retailing (service stations) has too many firms, many of which are not really profitable. Many marginal operators exist for a few years, and then shut down when they have exhausted their original capital and their sources of credit. Is this a predictable effect of monopolistic competition? Why or why not?

CHAPTER 27
Government Policy Toward Monopoly

What You Will Learn in This Chapter
Big business has long been a source of controversy in the American economy. In the last century, muckraking journalists did battle with business giants in oil, railroads, steel, and other fields. In 1890, public reaction resulted in passage of the Sherman Act, the first antitrust law. Other laws were passed later to further control monopolistic practices. Does big business really pose a serious threat to free enterprise and consumer welfare? Do our current antitrust laws do the right job and do it well? These and other questions are part of the continuing controversy over public policy toward monopoly.

For Review
Here are some important terms and concepts that will be put to use in this chapter. Be certain that you understand them, or review them before proceeding.
    Managerial calculation versus entrepreneurship (Chapter 21)
    Perfect competition and efficiency (Chapter 24)

In their attitudes toward the market economy, Americans have long drawn a distinction between big business and small business. To a certain extent, this distinction parallels the economist's distinction between concentrated and competitive market structures. In both the economist's and the popular view of the matter, big (monopolistic) and small (competitive) firms raise different kinds of policy issues. We shall devote this chapter to discussing some of the major policy issues raised by big business and monopoly. Because this is an area of economics where there is no universal agreement, we shall have to consider more than one viewpoint. We shall begin by reviewing the case against big business and the current state of government policy toward monopoly.

The Case Against Big Business and Antitrust Laws

Bigness in business, as George Stigler wrote some twenty-five years ago,[1] can have one of two meanings. It can mean that a firm is large relative to the market it serves, or large in absolute size. Some firms are big in one way,

---

[1]George J. Stigler, "The Case Against Big Business," first published in *Fortune,* May 1952, and widely reprinted since.

but not the other. Macy's department store is large in absolute size, but still accounts for only a tiny fraction of all retail sales in New York City. The Densmore Brick Co. of Lebanon, New Hampshire, has a huge share of the local brick market, but is a pigmy on an absolute scale. The serious problems of government policy toward big business do not arise for businesses like these. The case against big business is a case against those relatively few firms—General Motors, IBM, General Electric, U.S. Steel, and a short list of other famous names—that are both big relative to their market and big in absolute size.

The case against big business rests on two kinds of charges. First, the charge that big business is inefficient. This contention largely rests on the theory set forth in the last chapter. We saw that monopolies, and to some extent, oligopolies and monopolistic competitors too, are able to restrict output and raise prices above marginal costs. This, it is charged, results in inefficient resource allocation. Too few resources are devoted to producing the products of monopolized markets and too many are forced into competitive sectors of the economy.

The second part of the case against big business rests on the fear that bigness confers the power to break the rules of the free market economy. These rules call for open access to all markets, and the elimination of force and coercion from economic life. Sometimes big business breaks these rules through directly illegal acts. In the nineteenth century, some hired private armies to settle labor disputes. In our own time, many giant firms have been caught making huge bribes or illegal campaign contributions. But breaking the rules of the free market does not always mean stepping outside the law. Firms often operate within the political system to write new rules restricting competition and establishing further monopoly privileges for themselves. These actions of big business encourage countervailing political powerplays by labor and the general public. The result, it is often feared, is adrift toward a society of big business, big government, and big labor in which the individual counts for little, and big collective bodies count for everything.

The Antitrust Laws[2]

Since 1890, hostility toward big business has led to the passage of a series of laws aimed at controlling the abuse of monopoly power in the American economy. These laws have come to be known as **antitrust laws.** (The name comes from the fact that several large businesses in the late nineteenth century had adopted the *voting trust* as their legal form of organization. Under such a trust agreement, the voting rights to the stock of a number of competing firms were conveyed to a group of trustees, who managed the firms as a single profit-maximizing monopoly.)

Antitrust Laws A series of laws, beginning with the Sherman Act of 1890, which define government policy toward monopoly.

Sherman Act

The first national antitrust law was the Sherman Act of 1890. This act outlawed "every contract, combination in the form of a trust or otherwise, or conspiracy in restraint of commerce among the several States, or

[2]A more complete account of antitrust legislation, on which this section is partly based, can be found in James R. McGuigan and R. Charles Moyer, *Managerial Economics,* (Hinsdale, Ill.: The Dryden Press, 1975), chap. 17.

with foreign nations. . . ." It also declared that "every person who shall monopolize, or attempt to monopolize, or combine or conspire with any other person or persons, to monopolize any part of the trade or commerce among the several States, or with foreign nations, shall be deemed guilty of a misdemeanor."

Many firms have run afoul of the Sherman Act over the years. The following is the most famous early case.

CASE 27.1
The Breakup of Standard Oil[3]

"The Standard Oil Company of Ohio was incorporated in 1870, eleven years after Colonel Drake's historic oil strike in western Pennsylvania. Standard emerged triumphant from the competitive battles of the next decade, both through skilled management by John D. Rockefeller and his associates and through sharp competitive practices, including collection of rebates from the railroads. It produced very little crude, for it was unwilling to risk much capital in this speculative business, but was dominant in transportation and refining. In 1879 the shares of several Standard companies were transferred to the management of a small group of trustees in return for dividend-paying trust certificates. It was this expedient that gave the popular name "trust" to any big combination or even big corporation."

Public feeling against the oil monopoly was an important factor in causing passage of the Sherman Antitrust Act in 1890. The first legal blow against Standard was not struck under the Sherman Act, however, but under state law by an Ohio court. That suit led to the dissolution of the original trust, but other legal arrangements were soon worked out to maintain effective control of Standard Oil as a single unit.

In 1902–1904, a series of muckraking articles by the journalist Ida M. Tarbell focused new public attention on Standard Oil. A flow of state antitrust suits began, and also a federal investigation. The investigation finally led to a federal suit, filed by the Department of Justice in 1906. The government won the suit in trial court, and the defendants then appealed to the Supreme Court. In ruling on that appeal, Chief Justice White put forth the famous doctrine that the Sherman Act applied only to "unreasonable" restraints of trade, but that did not save Standard. The entire court agreed that the rule of reason did not shield the particular practices in which Standard had engaged. The combination was ordered dissolved into the thirty-three separate companies of which it had been formed, and recombination of any of the corporate units to create a new monopoly was forbidden.

[3]This account is condensed from Simon N. Whitney, *Antitrust Policies: American Experience in Twenty Industries*, Vol. 1, pp. 101–105. © 1958 by The Twentieth Century Fund, New York. Reprinted by permission.

Clayton Act

Despite the breakup of Standard Oil in 1911, and of American Tobacco in the same year, it was still felt that antitrust policy was not vigorous enough. In an effort to strengthen and clarify antitrust law, Congress passed the Clayton Act in 1914. This act has four major provisions as listed below.

1. It outlaws **price discrimination** among purchasers of goods, except when such discrimination is based on differences in grade, quality, and quantity of the product sold, or on tangible differences in selling costs. To discriminate otherwise is illegal if the effect is to lessen competition substantially or to tend to create a monopoly.

Price Discrimination A practice of offering different prices to different purchasers of the same good, when such price differences are not based on differences in grade, quality, and quantity of the product sold, or on tangible differences in selling costs.

Tying Contracts Contracts for the sale of a firm's products that include an agreement that the purchaser will not use or deal in the products of a competitor.

Interlocking Directorates Cases where the same person is on the board of directors of two or more firms.

2. The act forbids sellers from making **tying contracts,** when the effect of such contracts is to lessen competition. These are contracts for the sale of a firm's products that include an agreement that the purchaser will not use or deal in the products of a competitor.

3. An antimerger section of the act forbids any corporation engaged in commerce from acquiring the shares of a competing firm, or from purchasing the stocks of two or more competing firms. Again, the prohibition is not absolute, but applies only when the effect is to lessen competition substantially.

4. The one unconditional provision of the Clayton Act outlaws **interlocking directorates,** defined as cases where the same person is on the board of directors of two or more firms, if (a) the corporations are competitive, (b) if any one had a capital, surplus, and undivided profits of more than $1 million, and (c) where elimination of competition would violate the antitrust laws. Such interlocks are illegal whether or not proof of a reduction of competition can be found.

The Federal Trade Commission Act

In the same year as the Clayton Act, Congress passed the Federal Trade Commission Act, which supplements it. This act declares broadly that "unfair methods of competition in commerce are illegal." It leaves the determination of what constitutes unfair methods to the Federal Trade Commission, which the Act established as an independent government agency with the goal of attacking unfair practices. (The FTC was also given some regulatory functions in protecting the public against false and misleading advertisements for foods, drugs, cosmetics, and therapeutic devices.) The importance of the Federal Trade Commission Act lay not so much in broadening the scope of illegal business practices as in providing an independent antitrust agency with the power to initiate cases.

Other Antitrust Acts

Over the years, the original antitrust acts have been supplemented and modified by other laws. One of these was the Robinson-Patman Act of 1936. This act, sometimes called the "Chain Store Act," has the paradoxical aim of promoting competition by restricting it. Specifically, it strengthens the price discrimination provisions of the Clayton Act to protect small independent retailers from competition by chain stores, who would otherwise be able to use their large buying power to win big discounts from manufacturers. The act has not been entirely successful in this objective, as witnessed by the decline of independent grocers and retailers that has occurred since it was enacted. It has probably had some effect, though, in raising prices that consumers pay.

The Wheeler-Lea Act was passed in 1938 to strengthen both the antitrust and consumer protection sections of the Federal Trade Commission Act. Before its passage, the courts had weakened the FTC act by setting very strict standards for proof of damage to consumers or competitors in cases where unfair business practices were alleged. The Wheeler-Lea Act removed these restrictive interpretations, and made it possible to prosecute unfair competitive practices even where specific damage to competitors could not be proved.

Still another important amendment to the original antitrust acts was contained in the Celler-Kefauver Antimerger Act of 1950. This act extended the antimerger provisions of the Clayton Act in two respects. First, the act extends the scope of anitmerger law from **horizontal mergers,** the only ones originally outlawed, to **vertical mergers** and **conglomerate mergers** as well. Second, the original Clayton Act had dealt only with mergers made by buying competitors' stock. The Celler-Kefauver Act extends the prohibition to mergers via the acquisition of a competitor's assets (that is, its actual plant and equipment) as well, when the effect of such a merger is to lessen competition substantially.

Remedies

There are three major types of remedies that can be employed against companies engaging in illegal competitive practices.

First, the offending company can be broken up into several smaller companies, or forced to sell off some of its subsidiaries. The breakup of a company is called **dissolution.** This is the most drastic, and also the most controversial remedy. Despite some spectacular individual dissolutions, such as the Standard Oil and American Tobacco cases, it has been employed relatively rarely. But many economists who are advocates of a strong antitrust policy think that dissolution should be the usual remedy in antitrust cases. In their view, all corporate giants, including General Motors, IBM, U.S. Steel, and the rest, should be broken up.

Second, **injunctions** are frequently employed as a remedy in antitrust cases. Under an injunction, the offending company is left intact, but forbidden from carrying out specific acts or practices that have been found to lessen competition.

A third type of remedy in antitrust cases is the **consent decree.** Under a consent decree, the government and the offending company come to an agreement ending the anticompetitive practice in question without an actual court trial. The offender does not have to admit guilt, but does have to change its ways. Consent decrees have now become a very important instrument for the endorsement of antitrust laws.

Dissenting Opinion—The Case Against Antitrust Laws

American antitrust laws and the methods by which they are enforced are far from winning universal praise. Some economists and businesspeople object to specific features of the various antitrust acts. Others attack the whole idea of having an antitrust policy at all. Let us examine some elements of the case against antitrust laws.

Efficiency

The case against antitrust laws begins with a counterattack against the charge that big business is inefficient. The idea that big business is inefficient, it is said, arises from the one-sided emphasis that many economists place on theories of managerial calculation, to the exclusion of the entrepreneurial element in business decision making.

Horizontal Mergers Mergers between firms engaged in the same line of business, for example, a merger between two steel mills.

Vertical Mergers Mergers between two firms, one of which is a supplier or customer of the other, for example, a merger between a newspaper and a paper manufacturer.

Conglomerate Mergers Mergers between firms in unrelated lines of business, for example, between an aircraft maker and a sporting goods manufacturer.

Dissolution In antitrust cases, a remedy requiring the offending company to be broken up into several smaller companies, or to sell off some of its subsidiaries.

Injunction In antitrust cases, a remedy leaving the offending company intact, but forbidding it from carrying out specific anticompetitive acts or practices.

Consent Decree In antitrust cases, an agreement between the government and the offending company in which the latter is not brought to trial and does not admit guilt, but does have to modify its objectionable practices.

In Chapter 26, we analyzed the managerial calculation of a monopolist in an economy where there was perfect knowledge of prices, resources, and techniques, and where all markets were in equilibrium. On those assumptions, prices in monopolized sectors would be higher and the output of these sectors lower than efficiency requires. These distortions of prices and output result in waste of resources and loss of consumer welfare. How big are the losses, though? At least one widely cited attempt has been made to measure them. University of Chicago economist Arnold Harberger estimated that, in 1953, these losses amounted to only $225 million, or less than $1.50 per capita.[4] That is hardly enough to pay the salaries of government officials employed in prosecuting antitrust cases. Harberger's methods have been challenged by some, but even if his figures were wrong by a factor of ten, it would be hard to argue on pure efficiency grounds that monopoly ranked very high on America's scale of social problems.

Innovation

To many opponents of antitrust legislation, work like Harberger's only addresses a side issue. The main point, they say, is not the measurement of losses under hypothetical conditions of perfect knowledge and general equilibrium. What matters much more is knowing what kind of market structure best utilizes the nation's scarce resources of entrepreneurial talent. Over any extended period, the advancement of consumer welfare depends not so much on the efficient use of given resources as on a constant stream of new techniques and improved consumer products. A highly fragmented structure for industry, it is said, would not produce the most rapid progress. Large-scale firms are needed to develop and implement innovations as efficiently as possible.

This argument is often identified with Joseph Schumpeter. In his classic *Capitalism, Socialism, and Democracy,* he wrote:

> What we have got to accept is that big business has come to be the most powerful engine of progress and in particular of the long-run expansion of total output not only in spite of, but to a considerable extent through, strategy which looks so restrictive when viewed in the individual case and from the individual point of time. In this respect, perfect competition is not only impossible but inferior, and has no title to being set up as a model of ideal efficiency. It is hence a mistake to base the theory of government regulation of industry on the principle that big business should be made to work as the respective industry would work in perfect competition.[5]

Evidence

Schumpeter's criticism of antitrust policy has been pushed even further by some economists, who have suggested that the government should actually encourage mergers and the formation of industrial giants. This whole area is so controversial that many attempts have been made to bring evidence to bear on it. One recent attempt to bring together evidence from a number of sources reaches these conclusions:[6]

---

[4]A. C. Harberger, "Monopoly and Resource Allocation," *American Economic Review,* Vol. 44 (May 1954), pp. 77–87.

[5]Joseph A. Schumpeter, *Capitalism, Socialism, and Democracy.* (New York: Harper Torchbooks, 1950), p. 106.

[6]Richard Nelson, Merton Peck, and Edward Kalachek, *Technology, Economic Growth, and Public Policy* (Washington, D.C.: Brookings Institution, 1967).

Joseph Schumpeter was born in Trietsch, Moravia, then a part of Austria. He studied law at the University of Vienna, also attending the seminars of the leading economists of the Austrian school of the day. In 1906, he received a Doctor of Laws degree and briefly practiced law before turning to teaching as a career. He taught at several European universities, taking time out in 1919–1920 to serve as Austrian Minister of Finance. In 1932, he emigrated to the United States. There, he accepted a post at Harvard University, which he held until his death in 1950. In 1948, he was honored with the presidency of the American Economic Association.

Schumpeter's writings are characterized by a broad scope rare in twentieth-century economics. In his writings on economic development, business cycles, the history of economics, and economic systems, he attempted to portray the whole of the economic process. He had little use for the kind of economics that reduces everything to problems of managerial calculations, and then reduces those problems to an arid set of mathematical equations. To him, the crucial figure in economic life was the entrepreneur, not the clerk or manager. What is more, he saw the entrepreneur as operating in an environment shaped as much by history, politics, and religion as by simple forces of supply and demand.

Although his *History of Economic Thought* is probably Schumpeter's greatest scholarly achievement, it is *Capitalism, Socialism*, and *Democracy* that holds the greatest interest for the general student of economics. The book is, among other things, Schumpeter's reply to Karl Marx. The opening chapters of the book contain one of the most lucid and perceptive analyses of Marx's system ever written. Schumpeter then goes on to explain why he believes that capitalism will inevitably come to an end and be replaced by socialism. Unlike Marx, however, Schumpeter believed that capitalism would be killed not by its failures, but by its successes. In the process of explaining this paradoxical proposition, Schumpeter offers an analysis of the role of the entrepreneur in the market economy, and explains why, in the twentieth century, the entrepreneur has come to face an increasingly hostile intellectual environment. A minor but significant role in the downfall of capitalism, Schumpeter believed, would be played by the economic profession's myopic focus on the fairyland of perfect competition, and its blindness to the nature and importance of entrepreneurship.

Joseph Alois Schumpeter
(1883–1950)

First, overall evidence does show that industrial research and development spending is much more highly concentrated in large firms than employment or sales. In 1961, firms with more than 5,000 employees accounted for about 86 percent of such expenditures, compared with 41 percent of manufacturing employment, and 47 percent of sales. Larger firms also spend more on research and development as a fraction of sales.

These overall figures do not tell the whole story, however. For one thing, differences in research and development spending among firms of various sizes in a given industry are less pronounced than differences among industries. This reflects the fact that certain important industries, especially aircraft, have both huge firm size and huge research and development expenditures. Furthermore, although these expenditures rise rapidly up to the 10,000-employee size range, there is little evidence in most industries that the supergiants—those with 5,000 or more employees—spend proportionately more than the mere giants.

The authors of this study conclude that the evidence on firm size and innovation supports neither a policy of indiscriminate breakup of giants, nor a policy of indiscriminate encouragement of corporate mergers. Rather, they suggest that an optimum rate of innovation occurs when each industry has a mixed size distribution of firms. The optimum mix might well vary from industry to industry. They further conclude that a high rate of innovation requires a rate of turnover among firms in an industry that will bring in enough new firms to prevent excessive traditionalism.

Business Opinion

Antitrust laws, as might be expected, are not popular everywhere in the business community. It is true that some inefficient firms are protected by antitrust laws from competition that might otherwise drive them out of business. Many other firms, though—and not just those that are the most predatory or monopolistic—find it hard to look on federal antitrust officials as their benevolent protectors.

Business criticisms of antitrust tend to run along two lines. One line of argument accepts that there ought to be some type of antitrust law, but holds that the current law is too vague and too full of uncertainties. The trouble is that it is very bad for businesspeople to know in advance just which kinds of actions are illegal and which are not. The idea that mergers are illegal if they "substantially limit competition" can serve as an illustration. The law does not declare that all mergers are illegal *per se,* but just what percentage of the market must be involved in a merger before it is prohibited? In some cases, mergers involving firms with market shares of less than 3 percent have been found illegal. Other much larger mergers have been approved. As a result, even when two firms see perfectly sound business reasons for merging, it is very hard for them to know whether their action is legal or not. Such uncertainty is potentially a serious source of inefficiency.

One suggested cure is to replace current antitrust statutes with laws listing and defining specifically legal and illegal practices. The hope is that clearly stated laws against price discrimination, price fixing, mergers beyond a certain size, and so forth would be much easier to live with than the present uncertainty.

A somewhat different objection to antitrust laws also heard from the business community is that antitrust laws simply penalize business success. The very things that are marks of good management and superior service to customers—high profits, a rising market share, and rapid corporate growth—are the same things that bring a firm to the attention of antitrust officials. The Justice Department's current antitrust case against the IBM corporation is sometimes cited as a case in point. IBM's rise to dominance of the computer industry did not bring increased prices and reduced output of computers. Quite the opposite. But the reward of being a leader in growth and innovation has nonetheless been an antitrust suit that will drag on for years. Meanwhile, corporate funds and managerial talent will be diverted from the process of making computers to that of legal maneuvering.

Conclusions

When we back off from the specific arguments for and against antitrust legislation and look at the matter in perspective, we see one overriding problem. This problem is a basic shortcoming of economic theory. Economic theory purports to establish that under certain idealized conditions, the market structure of perfect competition leads to results superior to those achieved by monopoly. The great uncertainty, however, is which of all the market structures in between pure monopoly and perfect competition works best when, as is always really the case, ideal conditions do not hold. Because economic theory provides no clear guidelines, it is small wonder that the Justice Department, the Federal Trade Commission, Congress, and the courts have not come up with a more widely acceptable solution to the problem.

Perhaps the concepts of perfect competition and monopoly should be discarded altogether as guides to policy. As a middle ground, economists and policy makers could use the less precise but more useful concept of **workable competition.** As defined by Jesse Markham, "an industry may be judged to be workably competitive when, after the structural characteristics of its markets and the dynamic factors that shaped them have been thoroughly examined, there is no clearly indicated change that can be effected through public policy measures that would result in greater social gains than social losses."[7]

> **Workable Competition**   Any market structure in which, taking into account structural characteristics and the dynamic factors that shaped them, no clearly indicated change can be effected through public policy measures that would result in greater social gains than social losses.

Putting workable competition at the center of antitrust policy would change that policy in at least three respects.

First, it would move the concept of competition closer to the ordinary business meaning of rivalry, and away from the economist's idealization of perfect competition. In addition to considering concentration ratios within an industry, attention would have to be given to competition from rival products, and from potential competitors who might enter the market if an opportunity arose. Collusion, conspiracy, or excessive tacit cooperation among rivals would be the chief signs of uncompetitiveness to be watched for.

Second, workable competition would place a greater emphasis on innovation and entrepreneurship. In addition to counting the number of firms and measuring their market share, more attention would be paid to how the leading firms achieved their position. If the leading firms were those that had grown through success in introducing new methods and products, that would be taken as evidence of sufficient competition to guarantee good economic performance of the industry.

Third, if we follow Markham's definition, introducing the idea of workable competition to antitrust law would shift the burden of proof to antitrust prosecutors and away from industry. Before an industry could be proved not workably competitive, it would have to be shown beyond a reasonable doubt that antitrust measures would result in greater gains than losses.

Of course, the idea of workable competition leaves many questions to be answered and many controversies to be settled. Economists would still disagree on the size of efficiency losses from monopoly, and hence on the size of social gains from antitrust action. Arguments would continue over whether any particular firm's success was attributable to rapid technological innovation, or to questionable competitive tactics. Furthermore, those who rest their case for strong antitrust policy on the fear of big

---

[7]Jesse Markham, "An Alternative Approach to Workable Competition," *American Economic Review,* Vol. XI (1950), p. 349.

businesses as centers of political influence and extralegal power would remain ready to advocate the breakup of corporate giants, even if positive economic harm might be done. And so the debate goes on.

SUMMARY

1. The case against big business rests on two charges. One is that big business is inefficient. This charge stems from the idea that such businesses can restrict output and raise prices above marginal costs. The other major charge is that bigness confers the power to break the rules of the free market economy, which ·call for open access to all markets, and the elimination of force and coercion from economic life.
2. The first national antitrust law was the Sherman Act of 1890. This act outlawed combinations and conspiracies in restraint of commerce. It also outlawed attempts to monopolize any aspect of commerce. In 1914, this act was supplemented by the Clayton Act, which restricted mergers and identified certain specific anticompetitive practices. In that same year, the Federal Trade Commission was set up as an independent agency with power to bring anti- trust suits. Since that time, the Robinson-Patman Act (1936), the Wheeler-Lea Act (1938), and the Celler-Kefauver Act (1950) have modified and strengthened these earlier antitrust laws.
3. Not all economists and businesspeople accept the antitrust laws. It has been questioned that big business is really inefficient when entrepreneurial elements of competition are taken into account. Antitrust laws are further criticized for introducing unnecessary uncertainty into business decision making, and for penalizing business success.
4. The concept of "workable competition" offers a possible middle ground in the controversy over public policy toward big business. An industry is judged to be workably competitive when, after the structural characteristics of its markets and the dynamic factors that shaped them have been thoroughly examined, there is no clearly indicated change that can be effected through public policy measures that would result in greater social gains than social losses. Putting workable competition at the center of antitrust policy would move the idea of competition closer to the ordinary concept of business rivalry, place a greater emphasis on entrepreneurship, and shift the burden of proof from business to the government.

DISCUSSION QUESTIONS

1. Many people do not like big business. Do you think this is because they believe that big businesses are inefficient, or because they make too much money? Some big businesses do not make as much money as others, or even lose money. Do you think those businesses are better liked? Do you even know which big firms are profitable and which are not?
2. Have you read or seen any news items lately that featured big businesses "breaking the rules" of the free market? What rules were broken?
3. It has been proposed that all of our current complex antitrust laws could be replaced with a single law making it illegal for a firm to grow larger than a certain absolute size (defined in terms of assets or annual sales). In what way would such a law be better than the current antitrust laws? In what way might it be worse?
4. At the time this book was being written (mid-1976), the Justice Department was pursuing an antitrust suit against the IBM Corporation. Also, Congress was considering legislation that would break up the large oil companies. Has any action been taken against either IBM or the oil companies yet? Try to find out.

CHAPTER 28
Government as Regulator and Producer

What You Will Learn in This Chapter
Antitrust policy is far from the only way in which government intervenes in the market economy. Sometimes a private monopoly is left intact, but is subjected to regulation instead of to antitrust policy. Many inherently competitive industries are also regulated. As an alternative to regulating a private producer, government can itself become a producer of goods and services. In the American economy, most goods and services supplied by government are distributed free of charge. Government employs its powers as regulator and producer to accomplish distributional as well as allocational objectives.

For Review
Here are some important terms and concepts that will be put to use in this chapter. Be certain that you understand them, or review them before proceeding.
    Positive and normative economics (Chapter 1)
    Public goods (Chapter 4)
    Monopoly and efficiency (Chapter 26)

In Chapter 27 we discussed one important kind of government intervention in the market economy, antitrust policy. Now we turn to two others. If government is not willing to accept the outcome that the operation of the market produces in some industry, it does not need to limit itself to changing the market structure of that industry. One alternative is to leave the structure of the market untouched, but to subject producers to direct regulation. Another is for government itself to enter the market as a producer, either supplementing or supplanting the private firms operating there. Both of these alternatives are widely employed in the American economy. No discussion of *what, how, who,* and *for whom* would be complete that did not consider them at least briefly.

Government as Regulator

Natural Monopoly

Let us begin our discussion of regulation with a fairly simple case, that of utility regulation. Here, regulation presents itself as a direct al-

Natural Monopoly An industry in which total costs are minimized by having just one producer serve the entire market.

ternative to antitrust policy. For various technical reasons, public utilities tend to be **natural monopolies.** A natural monopoly is an industry in which total costs are minimized by having just one producer serve the entire market. Consider electricity, telephone service, water, or gas, to take the most common examples. It is easy for one utility to hook up extra customers in a neighborhood once it has run its basic lines, but wastefully expensive for separate companies to run duplicate sets of lines down each street. The problem is how to keep that one firm from restricting output and raising its price as a profit-maximizing pure monopolist would do.

A graphical example will help make the problem clear. Consider Exhibit 28.1. The firm represented there has roughly constant marginal costs and an L-shaped long-run average cost curve. The demand curve intersects the long-run average cost curve at a quantity Q_1, not far above the minimum economic scale of production. If this output were divided between even as many as two firms, each producing half the quantity Q_1, cost per unit would be substantially higher.

If a single firm operates in the market, it will tend to behave as a pure monopolist. Instead of producing Q_1, it will produce Q_2, which corresponds to the intersection between the firm's marginal revenue and marginal cost curves. The price corresponding to this output is P_2, far in excess of marginal cost. This would be a smaller output and higher price than efficient resource allocation requires.

Rate Regulation

In this analysis, then, competition by two or more firms is wasteful, and monopoly pricing by a single firm is wasteful too. The standard solution is to allow just one firm to operate, but to impose rate regulation on it. Instead of permitting the firm to charge the price P_2, the regulatory commission limits the price to no more than P_1, the price where the demand curve intersects the long-run average cost curve. The firm is forced to be a price taker, in effect, and chooses the quantity Q_1. Actually, maximum efficiency would require a price equal to *marginal* cost, and an output a

EXHIBIT 28.1
Cost and revenue curves for a natural monopoly
Because of the L-shaped average cost curve, one firm could supply the market with the quantity Q_1 more cheaply than could two firms, each producing half that much. A single unregulated firm, however, would behave as a monopolist, producing only Q_2 and selling at the price P_2. By imposing the price ceiling P_1, the firm is forced to act as a price taker and produces the desired quantity Q_1.

little greater than Q_1. The problem is that the firm would then suffer a loss and eventually go bankrupt unless it were paid a subsidy. Most economists would agree that the price P_1, which avoids the necessity of paying a subsidy, is close enough to the ideal for practical policy purposes.

Practical Problems

The argument for rate regulation of public utilities is based on the theories presented in Chapters 24 and 26. It is worth recalling the assumption on which those theories were based. For one thing, the theories assume that all participants in the market (including the regulators) possess accurate knowledge of cost and demand conditions. Second, they assume that when rate regulation is imposed on the monopoly, it will treat the rates as determined by forces beyond its own control, and will consequently behave as a price taker. Finally, they assume that underlying cost and demand conditions are stable and not subject to change.

In the real world, none of these conditions is wholly fulfilled. As a result, it is not quite so easy to make rate regulation work as Exhibit 28.1 suggests.

A major problem is that the regulators do not really know the shapes and positions of the firm's demand and cost curves. Not knowing these, they cannot directly identify the price and quantity where the demand and average cost curves intersect. They must use an indirect approach to finding the correct price instead, reasoning as follows: With the cost and demand curves shown in Exhibit 28.1, if the price were set above average cost, the firm would earn a higher rate of return than the average for other firms in the economy. If the price were set too low, the firm would earn a lower than average return. Therefore, if a price can be found that will allow the firm to earn just an average rate of return, that will be the price to charge.

Armed with this reasoning, the rate-setting process proceeds in five steps. First, the regulators measure the value of the firm's capital, which for our hypothetical firm is, say, $1,200,000. This is called the firm's *rate base*. Second, they measure the average rate of return for the economy, which, let us say, turns out to be 10 percent per year. (In practice, neither of these first two steps is quite as easy as it sounds, but we can afford to give the regulators the benefit of the doubt.) Third, they multiply the rate base by the permitted rate of return to figure out a total profit target for the firm. Step 4 is to ask the firm to propose a price or schedule of prices that it thinks will allow it to earn the target profit. Finally, as time goes by, the regulators monitor the firm's profits, cutting the price if profits rise too high and allowing the price to rise if profits fall below the target.

In an unchanging world where business decision makers behaved as price-taking managerial calculators, this approach might work fairly well. In a changing world, where business decision makers are entrepreneurs as well as calculators, rate regulation is less successful.

Cost Control

For one thing, the procedures of rate regulation tend to weaken the firm's incentive for cost reduction. The regulated firm is not really a price taker. Its managers know that if they let costs rise, they will be able to complain about low profits to the regulatory commission, which will be bound to grant a rate increase big enough to restore the target rate of return. Cost minimization, after all, is hard work for managers. Why not relax and take things easy? Why not take Wednesday mornings off for golf? Why not install new carpets on the boardroom floor, give a job to the president's incompetent nephew, and generally make life more pleasant at the expense of operating efficiency?

In addition to just slacking, a regulated firm is often tempted to over-expand its rate base. An unregulated firm will invest in additional capital only if the value of the extra output is sufficient to cover the cost of the investment. For a regulated firm, investment can be profitable whether it is productive or not. As an extreme case, imagine a regulated utility that spends $1 million on an investment project that adds absolutely nothing at all to output. The next time it goes before the regulatory commission, it can point to a million-dollar increase in its rate base, and legitimately ask for a corresponding increase in the profits it will be permitted to earn. Of course, because the new investment does not produce any new output, the only place the added profit can come from is a price rise. Not good for efficiency, but from the firm's point of view, profits from rate-base expansion are just as good as any other kind of profits.

Regulatory Lag

The tendency for regulated firms not to control costs is partly offset by a phenomenon known as **regulatory lag.** Regulatory commissions are not able to review a firm's performance as often as they might like. The investigations and hearings involved are quite time consuming. Often rates are changed only every few years. To the extent a firm thinks rates will not be changed often because of regulatory lag, it does have a short-run incentive to keep costs low. To be sure, cost cutting may eventually lead to a cut in the ceiling price for the product, but in the meantime, the firm may be able to earn several years of supernormal profits. In periods such as the 1950s and 1960s, when technological improvements permitted steady cost reductions for most American utilities, regulatory lag is believed to have speeded the rate of innovation.

In a period of rising costs, such as the 1970s, regulatory lag works against the interests of the firm. Costs rise faster than rates, and utilities lose money. Starved for funds, they find it hard to make the innovations for which changing circumstances call.

Putting all this together, we can see that regulatory commissions have plenty of difficulties to cope with. If costs and technology are stable, and if they are able to adjust rates frequently, regulation weakens the incentives to keep costs down and leads to wasteful capital investment. If regulatory lag is introduced, the incentive to cut costs is at least partly restored, but not without new ill effects. In periods of falling costs, rates will be too high, and in periods of rising costs, they will be too low. In the one case, monopoly profits reappear, and in the other, users of utility services are encouraged to be wasteful just when scarce resources most need to be economized. These problems have led increasing numbers of economists to be critical of the work of utility commissions. It has even led some researchers to doubt whether utility rate regulation has any beneficial effects at all.

Regulatory Lag The length of time, sometimes several years, that it takes a regulatory commission to review a firm's performance and react to changes in market conditions.

Regulating Competitive Industries

Regulation is by no means limited to industries that are natural monopolies, nor is it limited to setting maximum prices. Quite the opposite. Many industries are subjected to extensive regulation even though they appe₃ to be naturally competitive, and regulation often is concerned as mucĥ with setting minimum as maximum prices. Regulation of competitive issues raises some very complex issues of both theory and policy. To introduce some of these issues, let us begin with a case study.

CASE 28.1
Regulating the Airline Industry[1]

Since 1938, airlines in the United States have been closely regulated by the Civil Aeronautics Board (CAB). The initial mission of the CAB was to support and promote scheduled commercial air service in the early days before the industry became economically self-sustaining. But the CAB did not relax its grip on the industry when air travel reached self-sufficiency after World War II.

According to studies by William A. Jordan, the airline industry is inherently competitive. There are no large economies of scale, and entry into new markets is relatively easy. The CAB has had to work hard to counter this competitive tendency, but has succeeded in preventing a single new trunk carrier into the industry since it was set up in 1938. The CAB also controls competition on specific routes by saying which airlines can fly between which points. Its policy concerning the number of airlines allowed to compete on a single route has varied from time to time, and the result is a mixture of competitive and monopolized routes at present.

The CAB is the central force in fare setting for the industry. Technically, fares are changed on the basis of applications by airlines, but the power of the commissioners is very great. Once minimum fares are established, the CAB can enforce rules against competitive price cutting quite effectively.

The presence of entry control and minimum price regulation makes the airline industry sound like a classical cartel. As George W. Douglas points out, however, it is a cartel with some remarkable imperfections. The most important imperfection is the CAB's lack of power to control scheduling. As a result, on routes where two or more carriers compete, each airline tries to attract customers away from its rivals by adding flights up to the point where marginal cost is equal to marginal revenue. As more and more flights are added, the percentage of seats that are filled on each flight (the airlines call this the *load factor*) declines, and the average cost per passenger increases. In addition, airlines engage in other expensive types of "quality of service" competition, such as providing better meals or more beautiful stewardesses. This competition stops only when costs have risen so high that airlines are earning barely the average rate of return for the economy—or even less. Douglas reports that the airlines earned what the CAB considers a fair profit in only five of twenty recent years.

The combination of regulated price and entry, plus quality of service and scheduling competition, keeps the airline industry always on the verge of a vicious kind of disequilibrium. Each time the CAB lets fares rise, scheduling competition drives load factors down and costs up. The increased costs provide a justification for new fare increases to get profits back up to the target level, and the spiral goes higher and higher.

But, the reader might ask, is not all this really in the passengers' interest? After all, it is a great convenience to have flights so frequent and always to be sure of getting a seat. The answer to this is that yes, close

[1]Based on William A. Jordan, "If We're Going to Regulate the Airlines, Let's Do It Right," and George W. Douglas, "Regulation of the U.S. Airline Industry,: An Interpretation," in *Perspectives on Federal Transportation Policy*, James C. Miller III (ed.) (Washington, D.C.: American Enterprise Institute, 1975). © American Enterprise Institute for Public Policy Research (1975).

scheduling is good for the passengers, but so are low fares. Without regulation, airlines would compete partly by offering convenient service, but also partly by offering low fares. The result would be an equilibrium where the trade-off between fares and convenience suited consumer interests better than the present one.

The best evidence that fares would be lower without regulation is provided by the intrastate airlines that fly from point to point within Texas and California. Because they do not cross state lines, the CAB has no jurisdiction over them. These airlines offer comfortable and pleasant service, but they cut frills to a minimum. As a result, according to William Jordan's study, they are 60 to 100 percent more efficient than the regulated carriers, and offer fares that are 30 to 50 percent lower. The fact is that most people would rather pay $15 than $30 to fly from San Francisco to Los Angeles, even if the lower fare means giving up an in-flight snack and an empty seat to stretch out in.

The Distributive Function of Regulation

How can economic theory explain regulation in the airline industry? According to William Jordan, any valid explanation must take into account the *distributive* function of regulation. In Jordan's view, regulation of many industries, airlines included, has little to do with promoting efficiency. Instead, the main purpose of regulation is to split up the benefits of such industries in a different way than the market split them up under either competition or monopoly.

In Jordan's view, there are four main pressure groups that exercise some influence on the CAB. The airlines are one, airline passengers are a second, aircraft manufacturers a third, and the Airline Pilots Association (together with other industry labor unions) the fourth. The CAB hands out something to each of these. The airlines get their price fixing and entry restrictions. The passengers get convenient, high-quality service, although at a high price. The manufacturers get to sell a lot of airplanes, because of quality of service competition and low load factors. The airline workers get a lot of work—more flights mean more pilots and ground crews, whether there are any passengers or not.

The Future of Regulation

The regulatory branch of government in the United States is enormous, and still growing. The traditional "vertical" agencies, each regulating a single industry such as air transport, trucking, communications, or utilities, have been joined by a new group of "horizontal" regulators. The horizontal agencies are those such as the Occupational Safety and Health Administration, the Environmental Protection Agency, the Equal Employment Opportunity Commission, and the Consumer Product Safety Commission, whose powers extend across all industries in the economy.

Economists' faith in the beneficial effects of regulation, however, appears to decline in proportion to the growth of regulation itself. Economist George Eads, surveying much recent work in the economics of regulation, puts it this way: "The weight of economic evidence has become so great that any economist venturing to support regulation today is apt to find himself in a very lonely position. What only a short time ago was considered heresy now has assumed the status of conventional wisdom."[2]

---

[2]George Eads, "Economists vs. Regulators," in *Perspectives on Federal Transportation Policy,* ibid.

Perhaps most remarkable of all, there are critical voices here and there even within the regulatory establishment. In recent Congressional testimony, CAB Chairman John E. Robson said that regulation of the nation's airlines probably had forced air fares up unnecessarily. He urged Congress to cut back its control over air travel, giving greater freedom to airlines to raise and lower fares and start and stop service. Acknowledging the possible risks and disruptions of sudden deregulation, he contended that the risks and disruptions of continuing the present form of regulation would be even greater.[3]

Whether the immediate future will see any practical progress in the direction of deregulation, however, remains much in doubt. Robson's testimony in favor of deregulating the airlines was strongly opposed at the same Congressional hearings by airline unions, who of course benefit from the *status quo*. It is too early to forecast an outcome.

Government as Producer

If the government does not like the way resources are allocated or the way income is distributed by free markets, it can, as we have seen, regulate those markets. There is another alternative as well. Rather than leave production to private firms, regulated or unregulated, the government can itself become a producer.

What Kinds of Goods?

There is really no restriction on the kind of goods or services that government can supply. In communist countries, virtually all firms are government owned and all goods and services government supplied. In many Western European countries, the leading firms in such industries as steel, automobiles, shipbuilding, and aircraft are "nationalized," that is, owned and run by the government. Also in Western Europe, government ownership is widely used instead of regulation to accomplish political control of transportation, communications, and utilities.

In the United States, the role of government as a producer is somewhat more limited. Few goods or services are produced for direct sale to users. Instead, most government-produced goods and services are supplied to the public free of charge. These fall into two categories. First, the government supplies a certain number of public goods, national defense being perhaps the best example. As we saw in Chapter 4, the special properties of public goods make it difficult for private firms to produce and sell them at a profit. If they are provided to one citizen, their benefits are shared by all, so the problem arises of how to get would-be "free riders" to pay their share of costs. The government solves this free-rider problem by employing its power to tax.

In addition to public goods, the government also supplies a number of so-called **merit goods.** These include such things as education, police protection, and some kinds of medical services that are distributed free of charge on the ground that each citizen as a matter of human right merits his or her fair share.

Merit Goods Goods that are produced by government and supplied free of charge on the grounds that each citizen merits his or her fair share.

[3]Congressional testimony as reported in *The New York Times*, April 9, 1976.

How Much to Supply?

Once it is decided what kinds of goods the government will supply, one must ask how much of each ought to be supplied. We can approach this question either on a normative or a positive level. The normative approach enquires how much of each good the government ought to supply, and the positive approach asks how much of each good it actually does supply, given political institutions as they are. We shall begin with the normative approach.

Joint Marginal Benefit Curve A curve showing the dollar value of the total benefits that would be received by all members of a community as the result of a $1 increase in spending on a government-supplied good or service.

The first step in determining the optimal quantity of a public good or merit good is to construct a **joint marginal benefit curve.** Such a curve is shown in Exhibit 28.2. Its height at any point shows the dollar value of the total benefits that would be received by all members of the community as the result of a $1 increase in expenditure on the good in question. The curve in Exhibit 28.2 shows the joint marginal benefit of expenditures on, say, street lighting in an imaginary community consisting of just three people, Jones, Smith, and Brown. Suppose that with $100 already being spent on lighting, Jones feels that spending another dollar would give him the same added utility as he would get from spending an added $.50 on private goods. Smith equates the extra dollar of public expenditure with $.75 on private goods, and Brown puts the equivalent at only $.20. Adding these figures up, we determine that the height of the joint marginal benefit curve in the range of $100 to $101 is $.50 + $.75 + $.20 = $1.45.

The joint marginal benefit curve for each kind of public expenditure slopes downward because public goods and merit goods, like ordinary private goods, are subject to diminishing marginal utility. In this and many other respects, the joint marginal benefit curve closely resembles the market demand curve for a private good. Notice, though, that the units on the horizontal axis in Exhibit 28.2 are dollars' worth of expenditure rather than the physical units of quantity usually used in drawing demand curves.

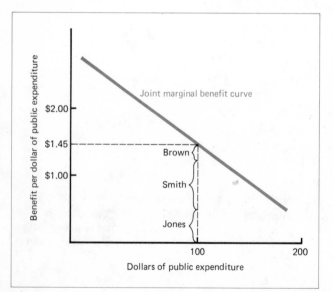

EXHIBIT 28.2
Joint marginal benefit curve for a public good or merit good
The height of the joint marginal benefit curve at each point indicates the dollar value of the total benefits that would be received by all members of the community as the result of a $1 increase in expenditure of the good in question. Here, for example, there are just three people in the community. Increasing expenditure from $100 to $101 would give Jones $.50 in added benefits, Smith $.75, and Brown $.20, for a joint marginal benefit at that point of $1.45.

Once the joint marginal benefit curve for a public good or merit good is constructed, it is easy to identify the optimal level of expenditure. The marginal cost of a dollar's worth of spending is $1. As long as the joint benefit of a marginal dollar of public expenditure on the particular good is greater than or equal to $1, added expenditure can be justified. When the joint marginal benefit drops below $1, members of the community would be better off to receive an extra dollar's worth of ordinary private goods, appropriately distributed among them. The optimal level of expenditure on the good represented in Exhibit 28.2 is thus $130.

Positive Theory of Public Spending

Let us move now from the normative theory of public spending to a positive theory. We can explain the purpose of a positive theory of public spending by analogy with the positive theories of supply that we developed

James Buchanan is a leader among the "new institutional economists" in applying the economic way of thinking to the political process. Buchanan completed his doctoral work at the University of Chicago in 1948 after receiving his bachelor's and master's degrees in his native Tennessee. He taught at Florida State University, the University of Virginia, and UCLA before going to the Virginia Polytechnic Institute in 1969. Since that time he has directed the Center for the Study of Public Choice, a research center largely devoted to exploring the common ground between economics and political science.

In 1962, Buchanan wrote *The Calculus of Consent* with his colleague Gordon Tullock. In this book, the authors explain how the new institutional economics approaches politics differently from much traditional political theory. Traditional analyses of political choice, they write, have

> often been grounded on the implicit assumption that the representative individual seeks not to maximize his own utility, but to find the "public interest" or "common good." Moreover, a significant factor in the popular support for socialism throughout the centuries has been the underlying faith that the shift of an activity from the realm of private to that of social choice involves the replacement of the motive of private gain by that of social good. . . .

James McGill Buchanan
(1919–   )

Buchanan and his colleagues, in contrast, believe that people do not change when they move from the market place into the realm of politics. In both realms, they seek to use existing institutions to their best advantage. Any analysis of political institutions that ignores the rational pursuit of self-interest on the part of individual citizens and government officials is liable to serious error.

In his *Demand and Supply of Public Goods* (1968), Buchanan made a pioneering contribution to the positive theory of public spending. Instead of asking how much of a public good the government ought to supply, as earlier writers on public goods had done, Buchanan sought to develop a theory of the political marketplace analogous to the theory of the economic market. He sought to learn who decides, and on what basis, how much of each good and service to provide, and how the costs are to be shared.

The new institutional economics and the positive theory of public spending are still relatively young fields within the economics profession, but both are growing rapidly and attracting new researchers. As the importance of government in the economy grows, it becomes more and more important to understand how government works. Merely understanding how it ought to work is not enough. By freeing the economics of government from past limitations, Buchanan and his colleagues have performed a major service.

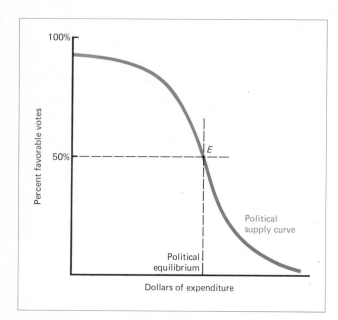

EXHIBIT 28.3
The political supply curve
The political supply curve summarizes the distribution of voter opinion on a public spending issue. The height of the curve at any point indicates the percentage of voters who support spending at least that amount on the good or service in question. The equilibrium quantity supplied under conditions of direct majority voting is that quantity where the political supply curve falls below the 50 percent line.

in Chapters 24 and 26. Those theories were designed to explain the quantity of output that a firm would tend to produce, given the institutional structure of the market in which it operates. Similarly, a positive theory of public spending seeks to explain how much a government will tend to spend on some good or service, given the structure of its political institutions.

The positive theory of public expenditure is a relatively young branch of economics, and one that is by no means perfected. Much promising work has been done in this area in recent years, however. Rather than attempt to survey this work as a whole, we shall try to convey something of its general flavor by a single example.

The Economics of Voting

An important part of the positive theory of public expenditure is concerned with the impact of democratic voting on public spending decisions. The economic theory of voting uses the assumption that voters try to maximize the net benefits that they reveive from government, that is, the difference between the value of benefits received and the value of taxes paid. This is a simplification of reality, of course. As in many areas of economics, however, simplifications are needed if progress is to be made.

At most levels of government in the American system, voters do not decide economic issues directly. Instead, they elect representatives, who in turn make decisions. Because this is only a very elementary discussion, however, we shall limit ourselves in this section to the exceptional case where voters do decide economic issues directly. The well-known New England town meetings provide the classic example.

Let us suppose, then, that a group of people operating under a system of direct majority vote is to consider supplying itself with a public good or merit good, say, elementary education. Naturally, there will be a wide variety of views on educational spending among members of the community. Exhibit 28.3 gives us a handy way of summarizing the pattern of voter opinion on the education question. The horizontal axis in this exhibit measures the amount of money to be spent on education, and the vertical axis measures percentage of voters holding a given opinion about expenditure. A curve, which we shall call the **political supply curve,** has been drawn in the space between the two axes in the figure. Its height above the horizontal axis at any point indicates the percentage of voters who would support *at least* that amount of expenditure on education.

Political Equilibrium

The point *E,* where the political supply curve drops below the 50 percent level, is the point of **political equilibrium.** It is the point toward which we can expect the actual level of expenditure determined by the voting process to tend. Clearly, no proposal to spend more than this amount can pass by simple majority vote. On the other hand, it is unlikely that the level of expenditure would long remain much below this level. If spending were less than the equilibrium amount, there would be a surplus of votes over and above what would be needed to pass that level of spending. Those who were particularly enthusiastic about spending on education would take this as a signal to submit proposals to increase the level, up to the point where they thought that any additional increase would lose them their majority.

How does the quantity of public good supplied, as determined by the political equilibrium, compare with the optimal amount? Exhibit 28.4 shows that the answer to this crucial question depends on the exact shape

Political Supply Curve A curve showing the distribution of voter opinion on a public spending issue. The height of the curve at any point indicates the percentage of voters who support spending at least that much on the good or service in question.

Political Equilibrium The quantity supplied of a public good or merit good at which political pressures for increased expenditure just balance pressures for decreased expenditure.

EXHIBIT 28.4

Equilibrium supply of a public good or merit good
The relationship between the quantity of a public good or merit good actually supplied under direct majority voting and the optimal quantity of that good depends on the exact shape of the political supply curve. If the curve has the shape p_2, too little will be spent; and if it has the shape p_3, too much will be spent. Only if it has the shape p_1 will the actual quantity supplied in political equilibrium equal the optimal quantity.

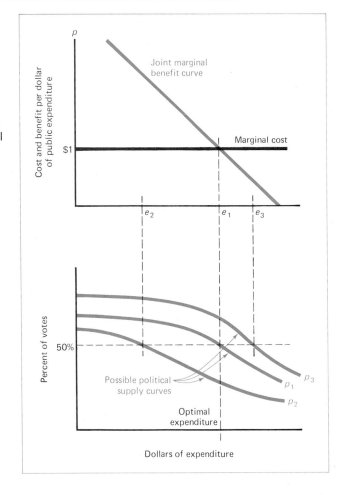

of the political supply curve. If the political supply curve had the shape of the curve labeled p_1, the political equilibrium level of expenditure would be e_1. As we can see from the joint marginal benefit curve in part a of the exhibit, this is exactly the optimal amount. If the political supply curve were instead to follow the pattern of p_2, expenditure would be confined to the level e_2, considerably less than the optimal amount. Finally, if the supply were like p_3, the point of political equilibrium would be reached only after expenditure exceeded the optimal level.

Burdens and Benefits

We appear to have answered one question only to raise another: What is it that determines the exact shape of the political supply curve? Its shape is determined by the manner in which the tax burden and the benefits of the public good or merit good are distributed among the voting public. Let us look at some general tendencies that might lead to over- or underexpenditure in a given case.

The level of expenditure preferred by a single individual is that level where his own share of the marginal benefit is equal to his own share of the marginal cost. The preferred supply for such an individual will be the same as the optimal supply for the community if and only if the percentage share of the total costs he receives is the same as the percentage share of the total costs he must bear. A person who receives a disproportionately large share of benefits will prefer that more than the optimal amount be supplied. A person who bears a disproportionately large share of the costs will want to see total expenditure fall short of the optimal point.

When expenditure decisions are made by voting, then, the relationship of the political equilibrium supply to the optimal supply will depend on which type of voter is more numerous. Consider a specific example. A certain country decides to maintain an army by means of the draft. Let us assume that the benefits of military protection are spread fairly evenly among the populace, but that a minority, those who are actually drafted, will bear a disproportionate share of the burden. Each draftee pays an implicit "tax" equal to the difference between the pay he actually receives in the military and the pay that would have been necessary to persuade him to leave civilian life and join voluntarily. The civilian majority will vote to maintain an inefficiently large army. If instead of using the draft, military personnel were paid enough to induce them to volunteer, with the extra expense being paid for out of a general income tax, this tendency toward excessive militarism would be reduced or eliminated.

Similar reasoning would lead us to conclude that if the costs of a project were spread evenly over the population, but a minority received disproportionately small benefits, there would again be overexpenditure. On the other hand, the benefits might be concentrated on a minority while the costs were evenly spread, or a minority might be exempt from taxation while the benefits were evenly spread. Under those conditions, direct majority voting would result in a level of expenditure below the optimal amount.

Out of all these various and conflicting possibilities, the only firm conclusion we can draw is that we can rely on the political equilibrium to give us the optimal supply of a public good only when the share of taxes paid by each voter to finance a given project is exactly proportional to the share of benefits he or she receives. If the political system were able to apportion taxes in this manner, it would, in effect, be imitating the market for ordinary private goods, where benefits received by individuals are also proportional to the expenditures they make. This actually happens very rarely, however.

Conclusions

In this chapter, as we have done more than once before, we have spent a few brief pages on a topic that is properly the subject of a whole book in itself. With no space to develop a complete theory, we have tried to use a few examples to suggest the sort of ground that an economic theory of government might be expected to cover. Let us try to tie these examples together now with three tentative conclusions about the role of government as regulator and producer.

Where to Intervene?

The government intervenes in many markets as regulator or supplier, but not in all. How is it determined where to intervene and where not to? As we have seen, this question can be approached on either a normative or a positive level.

Traditionally, the normative approach has emphasized that the government ought to intervene when, by doing so, it can improve the efficiency of resource allocation. Two kinds of intervention are most frequently prescribed on efficiency grounds. The first is the regulation of industries that are inherently monopolistic, in order to increase the quantities supplied by those industries and keep prices low. The second is the production of true public goods, in cases where private firms cannot be depended on to produce a dependable supply at any price. Economists who are concerned with efficiency tend to be skeptical about using government in its role as regulator or supplier for purely distributive purposes. The traditional view is that any desired redistribution of income should be carried out on a cash basis through tax and transfer policies. Transfers in kind or by manipulation of market prices are viewed as less desirable.

Positive theory is concerned not with where the government ought to intervene in the economy, but with where it does intervene. In contrast to the emphasis that normative theory places on efficiency, positive analysis points toward distribution as the main consideration behind much if not most intervention. As a case in point, we consider the regulation of competitive industries, such as air transport. As an example of the supply of a good for distributive purposes, we discussed the production of merit goods, such as education.

Self-interest and Government

A second point that our examples were intended to illustrate concerns the nature of an economic theory of government. In the theory of markets, we begin by assuming that individuals for the most part tend to act in their own economic self-interest. This means that, other things being equal, consumers try to get the most satisfaction from their limited budgets, firms try to maximize profit given the market conditions they face, and so forth. The assumption that individuals rationally pursue their economic self-interest is not, of course, realistic in every particular case. There is no doubt, however, that it is a stronger base for theory building than its opposite, the assumption that, for the most part, people act without regard for their economic self-interest.

Virtually all modern work in the positive economics of government also uses the self-interest assumption. Voters are portrayed as being more likely to vote for candidates who promise to provide them with greater benefits than for candidates who promise to impose greater burdens on them. Although we did not have time for examples in this chapter, other participants in the governmental process are treated similarly. Representatives are considered likely to favor legislation that will win them votes in the next election. Bureaucrats are portrayed as favoring policies that will enhance the power, size, and budgets of their particular bureaus or agencies. Theory building then proceeds by tracing the outcome of self-interested behavior, given the structure of government institutions.

One-Way and Two-Way Transactions

The third point we want to make concerns a fundamental difference between how governments and markets operate. Markets operate through a complex maze of two-way transactions. In each individual market exchange, a buyer and a seller must reach an agreement that leaves both better off than they would be if they had not made the exchange. That by itself is not enough to guarantee that markets will always allocate resources perfectly, but it helps. It establishes at least an underlying tendency: that when an exchange takes place, resources are moved from lower valued to higher valued uses. (By value here, we of course mean the subjective valuations of the individuals directly involved.)

When we look at how government works, this underlying tendency is missing. The basic unit of action for government is a one-way transaction. Government imposes taxes or regulations on private firms and individuals whether or not they wish voluntarily to submit to that taxation or regulation. It provides beneficial goods and services to people and firms free of charge, without asking if they would be willing to pay if it were necessary.

It is possible for resources to move from lower to higher valued uses in such one-way transactions, but it is equally possible for them to move from higher to lower valued uses. In a sense, we could say that government is a more powerful but less reliable mechanism of resource allocation than the market. Some things are easier for government to do than for the market to do, because government does not have to dicker, bargain, and negotiate until it gets the voluntary consent of everyone involved. It can act as soon as a bare majority, or sometimes even fewer, are in favor of an action. What we want, however, is not just activist government but good government. Unfortunately, the theories we have surveyed in this chapter cannot promise that that is what we shall always get.

SUMMARY

1. Natural monoplies, notably public utilities, are one kind of industry frequently subjected to government regulation. According to theory, regulating a natural monopoly can improve the efficiency of resource allocation if the regulator imposes a price ceiling close to or equal to marginal cost. In practice, regulators do not often succeed in achieving the theoretical ideal. For one thing, regulated firms may not behave as price takers, and as a result, regulation may remove incentives for cost minimization. Under other conditions, regulatory lag may make it impossible to adjust rates rapidly enough under changing economic conditions.

2. Regulation is not limited to industries that are natural monopolies. Air transport is one of several examples in which an industry that is inherently competitive is subjected to strict regulation. The regulation of competitive industries seems to have little to do with promoting efficiency. Instead, the purpose of regulation is to split up the benefits of an industry in a different way than either competition or monopoly would do. In the case of air transport, analysis suggests that the consumer bears a substantial burden of artificially high fares in order to benefit airlines, airline unions, and aircraft producers.

3. Sometimes government itself takes on the role of supplier of a good or service. Two major kinds of goods supplied by government in the United States are public goods and merit goods. Normative theory suggests that the quantity of a public good or merit good that government ought to supply is that quantity for which the joint marginal benefit of expenditure equals marginal cost. Positive analysis of voting and other political institutions indicates that this normative standard may often not be met, however.

4. Traditionally, normative economic theory has favored an active role for government as regulator or producer mainly in the cases of natural monopolies and public goods. Cash transfers and taxes are favored to accomplish distributive objectives. In practice, however, distributive considerations seem to dominate actual government decisions on where and how to intervene in the market economy. Much modern work in the economics of government is based on the assumption that people who make political decisions are no less concerned with their economic self-interest than are people who make market decisions. Analysis that proceeds on this assumption often reaches pessimistic conclusions about the ability of government intervention to achieve the goals of efficiency and equity that are identified by normative theory.

DISCUSSION QUESTIONS

1. Compare and contrast antitrust laws and regulation as alternative policies toward monopoly. Why is sometimes one and sometimes another used? In view of the criticisms of antitrust law we examined in Chapter 27, do you think that regulation should be used as a substitute for antitrust action in every case?

2. In the case of a true natural monopoly, do you think it would be best to have regulated private monopoly, public ownership of the monopoly, or an unregulated private monopoly? How do considerations of efficiency enter into your choice? Considerations of equity? Considerations of the actual, as opposed to the ideal operation of regulation and publicly owned producers?

3. Some government-produced goods seem to be partly merit goods and also partly public goods. For example, it is said that public health services are true public goods when they are devoted to the control of general epidemics, but merit goods when devoted to helping people to overcome individual health problems. Can you identify a public-goods component in police protection? Fire protection? Education?

4. Broadcast radio and television appear to be perfect examples of public goods. Once programs are broadcast to one member of the community, there is no way

for other members to be excluded from picking them up. Also, once a program is produced, the cost of adding one more listener is effectively zero. Nonetheless, radio and television in this country are not government produced. They are produced by private, profit-making firms. How do these firms avoid the free-rider problem?

5. Make as complete a list as you can of things you think are merit goods. What qualifies a good or service to be a merit good? If each person is entitled to a fair share of every merit good, is each person also obligated to supply merit goods to others? If the entitlement is universal but the obligation is not universal, how is it to be decided on whom the obligation should rest?

6. Turn to Exhibit 28.4. In that exhibit, we show that if the political supply curve has the wrong shape, direct majority voting will result in the wrong quantity of the good being supplied. Would we get better results in some cases if a two-thirds majority were needed to approve each public spending measure? If only one-third of the voters needed to approve expenditure? Could we always get the right amount of public spending by adjusting the voting rule differently for each different issue that came up? Would that approach be practical? Truly democratic?

PART FOUR
Factor Markets and Income Distribution

Factor markets are the markets in which the basic factors of production—labor, natural resources, and capital—are bought and sold. They perform two major functions in a market economy, helping to determine *how* and *for whom* output is produced.

Most goods and services can be produced in more than one way. Wheat, for example, can be grown by extensive cultivation of large areas of land using a lot of machinery and little labor, or by intensive cultivation of small areas with little machinery and much labor. The choice of production methods depends on the relative prices of the various factors. As those prices change, production methods can change too. Factors that are cheap are used intensively, while those that are expensive are used sparingly.

Factor markets also help determine *for whom* output is produced. Most people in the American economy earn their incomes by selling whatever factors of production they own. The greatest number sell their labor services. Many sell or rent land or capital that they own as well. Because markets determine factor prices, they determine how much of the total product will go to the owners of labor services, capital, and natural resources.

The distribution of income among factor owners is called the *functional distribution of income.* Functional distribution partly explains for whom output is produced, but it is not the whole story. It is also important to know which specific people actually receive what. This is called the *personal distribution of income.* The personal distribution of income depends both on the functional distribution of income and on the way that ownership of factors is distributed among persons.

Chapters 29 through 31 will be largely concerned with the functional distribution of income. In Chapter 29, we shall present the outlines of *marginal productivity* theory. In Chapter 30, this theory will be applied to labor markets, and used to help explain the nature and functions of labor unions. In Chapter 31, we shall turn to two other factor markets, those for natural resources and capital. We shall also discuss profits as a source of income. Finally, in Chapter 32, we shall take up the subject of the personal distribution of income, and in particular, the problem of poverty. We shall show how the operation of factor markets helps determine the incidence of poverty, and discuss various government policies aimed at reducing or eliminating poverty.

CHAPTER 29
Factor Markets and Marginal Productivity Theory

What You Will Learn in This Chapter
Factor markets play an important dual role in the economy, helping to determine both *how* and *for whom* goods are produced. Supply and demand analysis can be used to study factor markets just as it can be used to study product markets, but with a difference. In factor markets, it is firms that are the buyers and households that are the sellers, rather than the other way around. The theory of demand for factors of production is thus an extension of the theory of the firm, and the theory of factor supply an extension of the theory of consumer behavior. The study of factor markets gives rise to a theory of the functional distribution of income, which is the basis on which we shall later construct a theory of the personal distribution of income.

For Review
Here are some important terms and concepts that will be put to use in this chapter. Be certain that you understand them, or review them before proceeding.

The circular flow (Chapter 5)
Credit markets (Chapter 5)
Marginal utility and consumer equilibrium (Chapter 19)
The law of diminishing returns (Chapter 22)

In this chapter, we begin our discussion of factor markets by introducing some theoretical principles that apply to all of them.

The largest of the factor markets, measured by the value of transactions taking place there, is the labor market. In this market, workers exchange their services during specified periods of time for a wage or salary. Labor contracts may be informal spoken agreements between employers and individual workers, or they may be elaborately negotiated between a labor union and a huge corporation. A labor market based on such employment contracts is a specific feature of modern capitalist economies. In noncapitalist economies, different ways of allocating labor can be used. In times past, workers themselves were often bought and sold as slaves or serfs. In some kinds of socialist economies, the capitalist labor market is replaced by a system in which workers are not employees, but cooperative part-owners of the firms for which they work.

The market for natural resources takes in all exchanges involving land and the naturally occurring raw materials that can be extracted from the land. Resource markets sometimes operate through the outright sale of property, and sometimes through rental agreements. By convention, economists usually express natural resource prices in terms of rentals, even when discussing those resources for which outright sale is more common than rental.

Capital Market In the narrowest sense, the market in which manufactured means of production (capital) are bought, sold and rented. By extension, also those markets in which funds for the purchase of capital goods are borrowed and loaned, that is, credit markets.

The capital market, in its narrowest sense, is the market in which manufactured means of production—machinery, structures, and tangible productive equipment of all kinds—are bought, sold, and rented. The term capital market is also used in a second sense, meaning those markets in which funds for the purchase of physical capital equipment are borrowed and loaned. Those markets can also be termed *credit market* or *loanable funds* markets. Credit markets consist of all the firms and special organizations, including banks, savings and loan societies, the Wall Street stock and bond markets, and others, that act as intermediaries between savers and borrowers. The price paid for capital (or for the use of loanable funds) is the rate of interest.

The Demand for Factors of Production

The Firm in Factor Markets

In many ways, factor markets are much like product markets, which we have already studied. Our theories of supply and demand, and our tools of marginal analysis, apply to factor markets just as to product markets. But factor markets do differ from product markets in one major respect. In factor markets, it is firms that are the buyers, and *households* that are the sellers, rather than the other way around. A theory of the demand for factors of production must be based on the same considerations of price, revenue, and profit that determine the supply of products. A theory of factor supply, on the other hand, must be an extension of the theory of consumer choice.

Let us take the first steps, then, toward a theory of factor demand. We shall assume, as earlier, that firms aim to maximize profits. Each profit-maximizing firm must take three things into account when it makes its hiring decision. The first is the quantity of output produced by a unit of the factor in question. The second is the revenue derived from the sale of the output that will be produced, and the third is the cost of obtaining the factor.

Marginal Physical Product

Marginal Physical Product (of a factor) The increase in output resulting from a one-unit increase in the input of some factor of production, when the quantity of all other factors used remains unchanged.

The increase in output resulting from a one-unit increase in the input of some factor of production, when the quantity of all other factors used remains unchanged, is the **marginal physical product** of that factor. Suppose that employing one additional worker hour of labor in a lightbulb factory yields an added output of 5 lightbulbs, when no other inputs to the production process are increased. We then say that the marginal physical productivity of labor in that factory is 5 bulbs per hour. Or suppose that giving a farmer one more acre of land allows him to produce 20 more bushels of wheat per year, without increasing the amount of work he does, the amount of machinery he uses, or anything else. We then say that the marginal physical product of land on that farm is 20 bushels per acre. Finally, suppose that having one extra dollar of capital would allow a taxi company to carry one extra passenger one extra mile each year. That would put the marginal physical product of capital for that company at one passenger-mile per dollar.

It follows from the law of diminishing returns that the marginal physical product of each factor decreases as the quantity of the factor used increases. Let us use an imaginary "typical firm" to illustrate the principle of diminishing marginal physical product, much as we used such a firm to introduce the theory of cost. Exhibit 29.1 shows what happens to the total physical product and marginal physical product of one factor (it could be

(1) Quantity of Factor	(2) Total Physical Product	(3) Marginal Physical Product
1	20	
		19
2	39	
		18
3	57	
		17
4	74	
		16
5	90	
		15
6	105	
		14
7	119	
		13
8	132	
		12
9	144	
		11
10	155	
		10
11	165	
		9
12	174	
		8
13	182	
		7
14	189	
		6
15	195	
		5
16	200	
		4
17	204	
		3
18	207	
		2
19	209	
		1
20	210	

EXHIBIT 29.1
Total and marginal physical product of a factor of production
As the quantity of a factor increases with the quantity of other factors used remaining unchanged, total physical product increases, but at a decreasing rate. Marginal physical product, as part c of this exhibit and column (3) of the table in part a show, decreases as the quantity of the factor employed increases. This decrease in marginal physical product is a direct consequence of the law of diminishing returns.

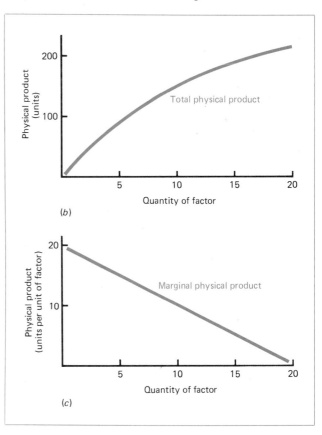

labor, natural resources, or capital) as the quantity of the factor employed increases, other things being equal. Throughout the range of factor input illustrated, total product increases each time the quantity of factor input is increased. Notice, though, that the rate of increase is less and less as each unit of input is added.

Marginal Revenue Product

To determine what quantity of each factor of production it should hire to maximize profit, a firm must take into account the *revenue* that will be earned from sale of the product of an added unit of factor input, as well as the size of the marginal physical product. We introduce a new term for this. The change in revenue resulting from the sale of the product produced by one additional unit of factor input is called the factor's **marginal revenue product.**

Marginal Revenue Product (of a factor) The change in revenue resulting from the sale of the product produced by one additional unit of factor input.

It is easy to calculate marginal revenue product for a perfectly competitive firm. Such a firm is a price taker. The price at which it sells its output does not change as the quantity of output it sells changes. The marginal revenue product of a factor employed by a competitive firm is simply equal to the factor's marginal physical product multiplied by the price per unit of the product. Exhibit 29.2 shows marginal revenue product for our typical firm when the firm is a price taker and the price of its output is $1 per unit.

Suppose, though, that the firm is not a price taker. Instead, let us say that it sells its output under conditions of monopoly or imperfect competition. When this happens, the calculation of a factor's marginal revenue product must take one additional variable into account. For a non-price-taking firm, output increases as the quantity of the factor used increases, and at the same time, the price of the product declines as the quantity of output sold increases. Under these conditions, the firm's marginal revenue is always less than the price of its product. Marginal revenue product must be calculated as marginal physical product times marginal revenue. Exhibit 29.3 shows marginal revenue product figures for our typical firm when it is not a price taker. The table assumes a straight-line demand curve, with the price falling from $1.50 per unit to $.50 per unit as output increases from 0 to 200 units.

Marginal Factor Cost

The third thing a firm must take into account to determine the profit-maximizing quantity of a factor is the cost of obtaining each additional unit of that factor. We call this the factor's **marginal factor cost.**

Marginal Factor Cost The amount by which a firm's total factor cost must increase in order for it to obtain an additional unit of that factor.

To keep things simple for the moment, let us consider only the case where a firm is a price taker in the market where it buys its factors of production. This will happen if the firm is only one among a large number of firms competing to hire that particular factor, and if the quantity of the factor that it uses is only a small fraction of the total used by all firms. For a firm that buys as a price taker, marginal factor cost is simply equal to the market price of the factor. If, for example, the market wage rate for typists is $3.50 per hour, then the marginal factor cost for this particular type of labor is $3.50 per hour for any firm that is a price taker in the market for typists.

EXHIBIT 29.2

Marginal revenue product for a typical price-taking firm
For a price-taking firm, the marginal revenue product of a factor is equal to the factor's marginal physical product times the price of the product. This table is constructed on the assumption that the product price is $1 per unit, and that marginal physical product is the same as in Exhibit 29.1.

(1) Quantity of Factor	(2) Total Physical Product	(3) Marginal Physical Product	(4) Revenue per Unit (Price)	(5) Marginal Revenue Product
1	20			
		19	$1.00	$19.00
2	39			
		18	1.00	18.00
3	57			
		17	1.00	17.00
4	74			
		16	1.00	16.00
5	90			
		15	1.00	15.00
6	105			
		14	1.00	14.00
7	119			
		13	1.00	13.00
8	132			
		12	1.00	12.00
9	144			
		11	1.00	11.00
10	155			
		10	1.00	10.00
11	165			
		9	1.00	9.00
12	174			
		8	1.00	8.00
13	182			
		7	1.00	7.00
14	189			
		6	1.00	6.00
15	198			
		5	1.00	5.00
16	200			
		4	1.00	4.00
17	204			
		3	1.00	3.00
18	207			
		2	1.00	2.00
19	209			
		1	1.00	1.00
20	210			

Profit Maximization

Profit maximization requires that a firm hire just enough of each factor of production to equalize marginal revenue product and marginal factor cost. If marginal revenue product exceeds marginal factor cost, hiring one more unit of the factor will add more to revenue than to cost, and hence increase profit. If marginal factor cost exceeds marginal revenue product, reducing input of the factor by one unit will reduce cost by more than revenue, and hence increase profit. Only when marginal revenue product and marginal factor cost are equal will it be impossible for any change in factor input to raise profit.

(1) Quantity of Factor	(2) Total Physical Product	(3) Marginal Physical Product	(4) Marginal Revenue per Unit	(5) Marginal Revenue Product
1	20			
		19	$1.35	$25.70
2	39			
		18	1.26	22.68
3	57			
		17	1.20	20.36
4	74			
		16	1.09	17.44
5	90			
		15	1.01	15.18
6	105			
		14	.94	13.16
7	119			
		13	.87	11.34
8	132			
		12	.81	9.72
9	144			
		11	.75	8.28
10	155			
		10	.70	7.00
11	165			
		9	.65	5.87
12	174			
		8	.61	4.88
13	182			
		7	.57	4.00
14	189			
		6	.54	3.25
15	195			
		5	.51	2.56
16	200			
		4	.49	1.96
17	204			
		3	.47	1.42
18	207			
		2	.46	.92
19	209			
		1	.45	.45
20	210			

EXHIBIT 29.3

Marginal revenue product for a firm with a downward-sloping demand curve

If a firm is not a price taker, marginal revenue declines as output increases. Marginal revenue product must be calculated as marginal physical product times marginal revenue. Here, we assume a straight-line demand curve with price falling from $1.50 per unit to $.50 per unit as output increases from 0 to 200 units. Marginal physical product data are the same as before.

Exhibit 29.4 illustrates the profit-maximization rule we have just given. The exhibit contains both a table and a corresponding diagram. They are constructed on the assumption that the firm is a price taker in the output market, selling its product at $1 per unit as in Exhibit 29.2. The firm is also assumed to be a price taker in the factor market, buying inputs of the factor at $5 per unit. Notice that profit rises as more of the factor is hired, up to the 15th unit of input. The firm just breaks even on the hiring of the 16th unit of input, and profit declines thereafter. It is between the 15th and 16th units of factor input that marginal revenue product becomes exactly equal to marginal factor cost.

Factor Demand Curves

We can draw an important conclusion from what we have just said: A firm's marginal revenue product curve for a factor is also that firm's

EXHIBIT 29.4

Profit maximization for a price-taking firm

Profit maximization requires that a firm hire just enough of each factor of production to equalize marginal revenue product and marginal factor cost. Here we assume that the firm is a price taker, as in Exhibit 29.2. The point of profit maximization falls between 15 and 16 units of output.

(1) Quantity of Factor	(2) Marginal Revenue Product	(3) Marginal Factor Cost	(4) Total Factor Cost	(5) Fixed Costs	(6) Total Revenue	(7) Total Profit
1			$ 5.00	$100.00	$ 20.00	−$85.00
	$19.00	$5.00				
2			10.00	100.00	39.00	− 71.00
	18.00	5.00				
3			15.00	100.00	57.00	− 58.00
	17.00	5.00				
4			20.00	100.00	74.00	− 46.00
	16.00	5.00				
5			25.00	100.00	90.00	− 35.00
	15.00	5.00				
6			30.00	100.00	105.00	− 25.00
	14.00	5.00				
7			35.00	100.00	119.00	− 16.00
	13.00	5.00				
8			40.00	100.00	132.00	− 8.00
	12.00	5.00				
9			45.00	100.00	144.00	− 1.00
	11.00	5.00				
10			50.00	100.00	155.00	5.00
	10.00	5.00				
11			55.00	100.00	165.00	10.00
	9.00	5.00				
12			60.00	100.00	174.00	14.00
	8.00	5.00				
13			65.00	100.00	182.00	17.00
	7.00	5.00				
14			70.00	100.00	189.00	19.00
	6.00	5.00				
15			75.00	100.00	195.00	20.00
	5.00	5.00				
16			80.00	100.00	200.00	20.00
	4.00	5.00				
17			85.00	100.00	204.00	19.00
	3.00	5.00				
18			90.00	100.00	207.00	17.00
	2.00	5.00				
19			95.00	100.00	209.00	14.00
	1.00	5.00				
20			100.00	100.00	210.00	10.00

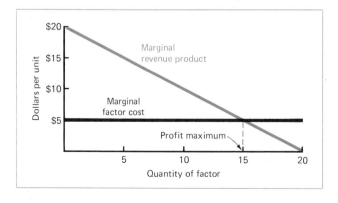

demand curve for that factor. A demand curve answers the question: What will be the quantity demanded at each price? The marginal revenue product curve gives the answer. That quantity of the factor will be demanded that makes the factor's price (more precisely, its marginal factor cost) equal to marginal revenue product.

We can add together individual firm demand curves for a factor of production to get a market demand curve for a factor of production. Such a market demand curve for a factor is a *derived demand curve*. The name is given because the demand for a factor of production does not arise from the usefulness of the factor services themselves. Instead it is derived indirectly from the usefulness of the products the factor can produce. The market demand for farmland is derived from the market demand for food, the market demand for printers from the market demand for books, and so forth.

Changes in Factor Demand

The demand for factors, like the demand for products, changes in response to changes in economic conditions. Consider Exhibit 29.5. Suppose that the demand curve D_0 is the market demand curve for some factor of production. A change in the market price of that factor will cause the quantity of the factor demanded to change by a movement *along* the demand curve. This is shown by the arrow drawn parallel to D_0. Changes in economic conditions other than a change in the factor's price can cause *shifts* in the factor demand curve, to positions like those labeled D_1 or D_2.

Three kinds of changes in particular are capable of causing shifts in the demand curve for a factor of production. First, an increase in demand for the product that the factor produces will shift the factor demand curve to the right. A decrease in demand for the product will cause the factor demand curve to shift to the left. Second, a change in the price of another factor of production used in combination with the given factor can also cause the demand curve for the given factor to shift. An increase in the

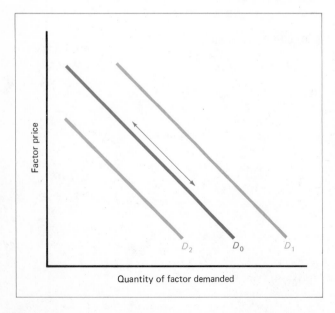

EXHIBIT 29.5
Movements along a factor demand curve and shifts in the curve
Changes in the price of a factor, other things being equal, will produce movements along a given factor demand curve as shown by the arrow. Other kinds of changes can shift the factor demand curve. An increase in demand for the product produced by the factor might shift the curve from D_0 to D_1. An increase in the price of another factor that is a complement to the given factor might shift the curve from D_0 to D_2.

Factor price

D_2 D_0 D_1

Quantity of factor demanded

price of a factor that is a substitute for the given factor will cause the demand curve for the given factor to shift to the right. An increase in the price of a factor that is a complement of the given factor will cause the demand curve of the given factor to shift to the left. Third, any change in technology that increases the marginal physical productivity of a factor will cause its demand curve to shift to the right, other things being equal.

Supply and Demand in the Labor Market

Up to this point, we have discussed marginal productivity and factor demand in completely general terms. Now we shall apply what we have learned to a specific factor market, the labor market. For the moment, we shall limit ourselves to the case in which labor is not organized, and individual workers compete with one another for jobs. In the next chapter we shall discuss organized labor. In the chapter following that, we shall look at the markets for capital and natural resources.

Individual Labor Supply Curve

We understand now how the demand for labor is determined. Next let us look at the determinants of labor supply. We shall begin by considering the labor supply of a single individual.

An individual person decides how much labor to supply to the market as part of the general problem of consumer choice. This decision can be analyzed in terms of the theory of consumer choice that we outlined in Chapter 19. Within the limits of a 24-hour day, we face certain alternatives. We can spend some time at work, in order to earn money with which to satisfy material wants. Alternatively, we can spend some time at leisure. This will allow us to consume what we are able to buy with what we have earned, to pursue such noneconomic goals as might interest us, and to rest up for the next day's efforts. We balance the relative advantage of these alternatives, to achieve a *consumer equilibrium*. We work just enough so that the marginal utility per hour of leisure exactly equals the marginal utility of the goods that we can buy with an hour's wage.

The wage rate affects our work-versus-leisure decision in two opposing ways. On the one hand, a higher wage rate tends to increase the amount of work we are willing to do, because greater material rewards compensate us for time taken away from other activities. On the other hand, a higher wage rate enables us to take more time off from work and still earn enough to enjoy a comfortable standard of living.

Taken together, the two effects of the wage rate on the willingness to work tend to give individual labor supply curves the sort of backward-bending shape shown in Exhibit 29.6. As that exhibit is drawn, rising wages at first induce the person in question to work more. Eventually, though, a point is reached where the person "spends" part of further wage increases on increased leisure.

Market Labor Supply Curves

In principle, we could get a labor supply curve for the economy as a whole by adding together the supply curves of all people for all kinds of labor. Such a curve might well have the same sort of backward-bending

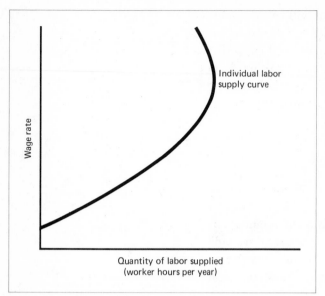

EXHIBIT 29.6
An individual's labor supply curve
On the one hand, a higher wage tends to increase the amount of work an individual is willing to do, because the extra money compensates for time taken away from leisure activities. On the other hand, a higher wage allows a person to take more time off from work and still enjoy a high standard of living. Taken together, the two effects tend to give the individual labor supply curve the backward-bending shape shown here.

shape as the individual supply curve. Practical problems of applied microeconomic analysis, however, do not usually focus on "the" labor market as a whole. Instead, we are more often interested in markets for particular kinds of labor, or labor markets in particular regions. The supply curves in these intermediate-sized labor markets are likely to be much more elastic than either individual labor supply curves or the economy-wide labor supply curve.

As an example, consider the market for typists in Chicago. Each individual typist may well have a backward-bending labor supply curve. Still, the quantity of typists supplied to this local market can be increased almost indefinitely by raising the wage rate. As wages of typists in Chicago increase, people are attracted into that labor market from other jobs, from other regions, or from outside the labor force. We thus expect this supply curve to have an ordinary upward-sloping shape as shown in Exhibit 29.7.

Competitive Equilibrium

Determining the wage rate in a labor market that is fully competitive on both sides is a straightforward exercise in supply and demand analysis. In Exhibit 29.8, for example, we have drawn a supply and demand curve representing the labor market for typists in Chicago. We assume that a large number of typists compete with one another for jobs, and a large number of employers compete with one another for typists, so that both are price takers. The demand curve for typists is the employers' combined marginal revenue curve. The supply curve is the one described in the last section.

It is easy to see that equilibrium in this market requires a wage rate of $3.50 per hour, with 200,000 typists employed. If the wage rate were lower, there would be a shortage of typists. Some firms, unable to fill all their job openings, would offer premium wages to workers from other jobs or other regions. The wage rate would be driven up to the equilibrium level. If, on

EXHIBIT 29.7

Hypothetical supply curve for typists

Although each individual typist may have a backward-bending supply curve, the supply curve for typists in any particular local market will have the usual upward-sloping shape. As the wage rises, people will be drawn into this occupation from other kinds of work or other localities.

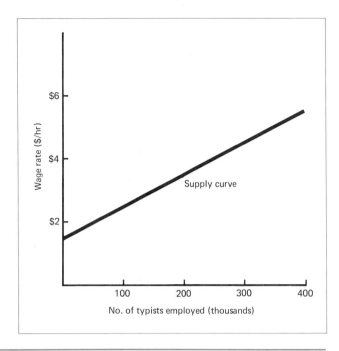

EXHIBIT 29.8

Determination of the equilibrium wage in a competitive labor market

When both employers and workers are price takers in the labor market, the point of equilibrium is found where the supply and demand curves intersect. Here, the equilibrium wage rate is $3.50 per hour and the equilibrium quantity of labor is 200,000 typists employed.

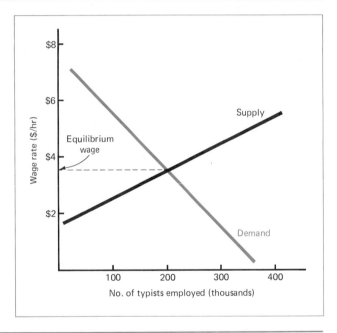

the other hand, the wage rate were above $3.50 per hour, there would be a surplus of typists. Many people would be looking for typing jobs who could not find them. After much fruitless search, some would become willing to accept work at lower than expected wages, thus pushing the wage rate down toward equilibrium. Others would drift away to other occupations or areas.

Note this important general point: In a labor market where both employers and employees are price takers, the equilibrium wage rate is equal to the marginal revenue product of labor. In the special case where all employers are price takers (perfect competitors) in the market where they sell their output as well as in the market where they purchase inputs, the equilibrium wage rate is equal to the marginal physical product of labor times the price per unit of output.

Monopsony

Monopsony A market in which there is only one buyer. (From Greek *mono*, single, plus *opsonia*, buying.)

Not every factor market has a large number of buyers competing with one another. The extreme situation, where there is only one buyer in a market, is called **monopsony.** Let us look at what happens in a labor market when there is a single monopsonistic buyer facing a large number of competing, unorganized workers.

There is an important difference between the case of competition and the case of monopsony. For a monopsonist, marginal factor cost is not equal to the price of the factor. Exhibit 29.9 shows why. The two parts of this exhibit represent the supply side of the market for typists in a small town where there is just one big employer (say, an insurance company), which employs all or almost all of the town's typists.

The supply schedule of typists shows us that no one will work in this occupation at all when the wage rate is $1.50 per hour or less. Above that wage, each extra one cent per hour will attract one more worker. Suppose now that our monopsonistic employer has hired 150 typists, paying them $3.00 per hour. Total labor cost for a labor force of this size is $450 per hour.

Exhibit 29.9(a)

(1) Quantity of Labor Supplied	(2) Wage Rate	(3) Total Factor Cost	(4) Marginal Factor Cost
1	$1.51	$ 1.51	
2	1.52	3.04	1.53
3	1.53	4.59	1.55
150	3.00	450.00	
151	3.01	454.51	4.51
152	3.02	459.04	4.53
200	3.50	700.00	
201	3.51	705.51	5.51
202	3.52	711.04	5.53

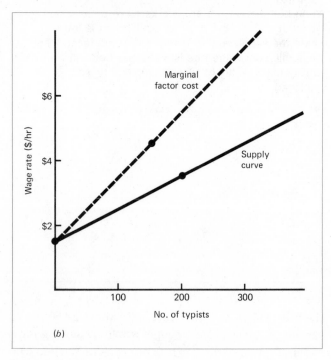

(b)

EXHIBIT 29.9

Marginal factor cost under monopsony

Under monopsony, marginal factor cost exceeds factor price. Consider an increase in quantity from 150 to 151 units of labor in this exhibit. The wage rate must be raised from $3.00 to $3.01 not just for the 151st employee, but for all the previous 150 as well. Marginal labor cost in this range is thus $4.51 per hour, not $3.01 per hour.

What will happen to the firm's total labor cost if it expands its labor force by one additional worker?

According to the supply curve, to hire 151 typists requires a wage of $3.01 per hour. That wage must be paid not just to the 151st worker, but to all workers. The total labor cost for a labor force of 151 typists, then, is $3.01 times 151, or $454.51. The addition of one more worker has raised total labor cost from $450.00 to $454.51, indicating a marginal factor cost of $4.51. Similar results are obtained if we choose other starting points from the table. *In every case, the marginal factor cost for the monopsonist is greater than the factor price* (wage rate).

In Exhibit 29.9*b*, we have drawn a marginal factor cost curve based on the marginal factor cost column of the table in part *a*. This curve is above the supply curve at every point. The relationship between the supply curve and marginal cost curve for a monopsonist, as shown in this figure, is analogous to the relationship between the demand and marginal revenue curves for a monopolist.

Monopsony Equilibrium

Once we know how to derive a monopsonist's marginal factor cost curve from the factor's market supply curve, determining the equilibrium level of employment for the firm is a matter of routine. In Exhibit 29.10, we have drawn the monopsonistic employer's labor demand curve (that is, its marginal revenue product curve) along with the labor supply and marginal factor cost curves from the preceding exhibit. We then follow the general rule that profit is maximized where marginal factor cost is equal to marginal revenue product. That means that in equilibrium, 150 typists are hired at a wage rate of $3.00 per hour.

EXHIBIT 29.10
Wage determination under monopsony
Here we have a monopsonist's labor demand curve, labor supply curve, and marginal factor cost curve. The quantity of labor required to maximize profits is found where the demand curve and marginal factor cost curves intersect. Note carefully that the equilibrium wage rate is *not* shown by the intersection of the marginal factor cost and demand curves. Instead, the equilibrium wage rate is equal to the height of the supply curve directly below that intersection.

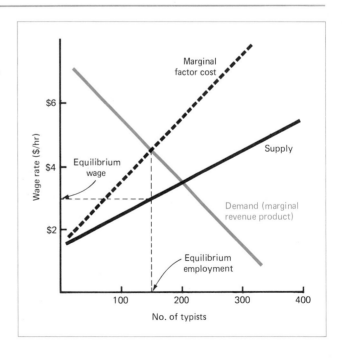

Note that when a labor market is in monopsony equilibrium, the wage rate is *lower* than the marginal revenue product of labor. In our example, the equilibrium wage rate is $3.00 per hour, while marginal revenue product is $4.50 per hour. Despite this discrepancy, increasing the quantity of labor hired would not increase revenue by enough to offset higher labor costs. The reason is that the cost of hiring another worker is not just the $3.51 per hour which must be paid to the 151st worker, but that sum plus the extra cent per hour by which the wages of all previously hired workers must be raised. This complete marginal factor cost is $4.51 per hour.

Conclusions

In the introduction to this chapter, we mentioned that factor markets not only determine how productive inputs are allocated among competing uses, but also how total output is divided among individual factor owners. Let us consider the case in which several factors of production are used by a firm, and factor markets are competitive. Profit maximization then requires that each factor be used up to the point where its marginal revenue product is equal to its price.

This tells us that each unit of each factor receives a reward that is equal to the contribution it makes to the firm's revenue. The idea that factors are rewarded according to their marginal productivity is known as the **marginal productivity theory of distribution.** The theory applies only to cases in which all factors are purchased in competitive input markets.

In an economy where all markets are perfectly competitive—not only input markets, but output markets as well—the marginal productivity theory would apply in an even stronger form. When output markets are competitive, it will be recalled, marginal revenue product is equal to output price times marginal physical product. In such an economy, the reward that each unit of each factor receives is exactly equal to the value of its marginal physical product. If an extra hour's labor in a widget factory produces two extra widgets, and each widget sells for $5, the wage rate must be $10 per hour, no more, no less.

Let us think for a moment about this principle of distribution, in which every factor receives a reward equal to the value of its marginal product. This appeals to many people as the most just principle of distribution possible. Everyone gets just what he or she contributes to the productive process. If a worker or factor owner were to decide to withhold a unit of productive services from the market, that person would suffer a loss of earnings exactly equal to the value of production that would be lost to the economy as a whole.

Not everyone favors distribution according to marginal productivity, however. Some people do not believe it leads to the best personal distribution of income. There are two main lines of criticism. Some critics argue that it is fine for factors to earn their marginal products, but that a just personal distribution of income also requires that the ownership of factors be justly distributed among persons. Others argue that productivity is completely irrelevant as a basis for distribution. Instead, distribution should

Marginal Productivity Theory of Distribution A theory of the functional distribution of income, according to which each factor receives a payment equal to its marginal revenue product.

be carried out on the principle of "to each according to his needs." These issues lie somewhat beyond the scope of this chapter, but we shall return to them in our later chapters on the problem of poverty, and on capitalism versus socialism.

SUMMARY

1. In factor markets, firms are the buyers and households are the sellers. The theory of demand for a factor of production is thus an extension of the theory of the firm. A profit-maximizing firm must take three things into account when it makes a hiring decision for any factor. These are (1) the quantity of output produced by a unit of the factor in question (marginal physical product); (2) the revenue derived from the sale of the output that will be produced by the extra unit of the factor (marginal revenue product); and (3) the cost of obtaining an extra unit of the factor (marginal factor cost).

2. A profit-maximizing firm will hire just enough of each factor of production to equalize marginal revenue product and marginal factor cost. In the special case where a firm is a price taker both in the market where it buys its inputs and in the market where it sells its outputs, profit maximization requires that each factor's price be equal to its marginal physical product times the product price. In either the general or the special case, the firm's demand curve for a factor of production is that factor's marginal revenue product curve.

3. The theory of labor supply for an individual household is an extension of the theory of consumer choice. Given the alternatives of work and leisure, each consumer works just enough so that the marginal utility per hour of leisure exactly equals the marginal utility of the goods that can be bought with an hour's wage. The labor supply curve for a single individual tends to have a backward-bending shape. The market labor supply curve for a particular occupation or locality, however, ordinarily has the conventional upward-sloping shape.

4. In a market where both workers and employers are price takers, the equilibrium wage rate and equilibrium quantity of labor are found at the intersection of the labor supply and labor demand curves. If workers are price takers but the employer is a monopsonist, the equilibrium quantity of labor is found at the intersection of the demand curve and marginal factor cost curve, and the equilibrium wage rate is determined by the height of the supply curve directly below this intersection.

5. In a competitive market where there are several factors of production, profit maximization requires that each factor be used up to the point where its marginal product is equal to its price. Each factor thus receives a reward equal to its marginal revenue product. This distribution is thought by some to be the most just distribution of income possible.

DISCUSSION QUESTIONS

1. What do we mean when we say that factor markets help determine *for whom* things are produced? Do we mean that workers consume exactly those things that they produce? Do they ever do this? When they don't, what other markets also help determine for whom things are produced?

2. In the text, we examined only factor markets where the buyers are firms. Are households ever the buyers of factors of production? Are you the direct purchaser of a factor of production when you hire someone to type a term paper for you? When you get your hair cut? When you buy or rent a plot of land for a vegetable garden? What changes would have to be made in our theory of factor markets to take into account the case where both buyers and sellers are households?

3. Have you ever wondered why European settlers in what is now the United States imported black slaves to do plantation work instead of just hiring workers from the native American population? One explanation runs like this: At first, the settlers did try to hire native workers. The trouble was that these people did not like to work long hours. The settlers raised the wages they offered, but to their surprise, the native workers then put in fewer hours, not more. Only then did the settlers give up and import slaves. Now, this story may be historical nonsense, but is it plausible from the point of view of factor market theory? Why or why not?

4. Review the *income* and *substitution effects*, which we introduced in Chapter 19. Can you explain the backward-bending individual labor supply curve in terms of the income and substitution effects?

5. Is a monopsonist necessarily a monopolist, and vice versa? Try to imagine a firm that is a monopolist in its product market, but not a monopsonist in its factor markets. Then try to imagine a firm that is a monopsonist, but not a monopolist.

6. Do you think there is any close connection between the value of what somebody produces and the amount he or she earns? Consider these specific examples: an auto worker; a real estate salesperson; a rock star; your economics professor; a member of the Civil Aeronautics Board; an owner of New York City municipal bonds. Why does the connection between earnings and product seem closer in some cases than in others?

7. Suppose you said to a friend or a friend said to you that it was just fine to let factor markets determine *how* things were produced, but the matter of *for whom* ought to be handled according to the principle of "to each according to his need." Sketch a reply to this remark that begins: "But that won't work. If you don't let markets determine *for whom,* they won't be able to determine the *how.* . . ."

CHAPTER 30
Labor Unions and Collective Bargaining

What You Will Learn in This Chapter
Although less than a third of all workers are unionized, unions play an important role in the economy. On a national scale, the union movement in the United States is only about a century old. Unions did not achieve their present strength until the 1930s, when favorable legislation was passed to aid their growth. Under the proper conditions, unions can raise the wages of their members relative to the wages of nonmembers. They do this by exercising monopoly control over the supply of labor, backing their power with the threat of a strike. Often, though, a union can win higher wages only at the cost of lost jobs.

For Review
Here are some important terms and concepts that will be put to use in this chapter. Be certain that you understand them, or review them before proceeding.
    Monopsony (Chapter 29)
    Sherman Antitrust Act (Chapter 27)
    Incomes policy (Chapter 17)
    Cost-push inflation (Chapter 14)

In 1972, 19,436,000 American workers belonged to labor unions—some 27 percent of all nonagricultural employees. These were distributed among 210 national unions, with a total of more than 54,000 local affiliates. The ten largest of these national unions, and their membership, are shown in Exhibit 30.1.

This union membership, although substantial, is not large by European standards. In Austria and Sweden, more than two-thirds of all workers belong to unions. In England, Germany, and the Netherlands, more than one-third are members. Only France among the major European countries has a comparably low level of unionization, with just 29 percent of the labor force unionized.

Who are the union members? Unionization is heaviest among blue collar workers. Eighty-four percent of union members are blue-collar workers. Less than 9 percent of all white-collar workers are unionized. Almost 80 percent of union members are men, although men make up only

Union	Members
Teamsters	1,855,000
Steel workers	1,400,000
Auto workers	1,394,000
Electrical workers (IBEW)	957,000
Carpenters	820,000
Machinists	758,000
Retail clerks	633,000
Laborers (INUA)	580,000
Meat cutters	529,000
Federal, state, county, and municipal employees	529,000

Source: U.S. Bureau of the Census, *Statistical Abstract of the United States, 1975,* (Washington, D.C.: U.S. Government Printing Office 1976), Table 606.

EXHIBIT 30.1

Membership of the ten largest American labor unions, 1972

Some 45 percent of all union members belong to these ten largest unions. Of the ten, the Teamsters and Auto Workers are independent. The others are all affiliated with the AFL-CIO.

62 percent of the labor force. Minority groups are represented in union ranks in about the same proportion as they are represented in the labor force. Workers with very high and very low incomes tend not to be found in unions—membership is concentrated in the middle ranges of income and education.

Union membership is rather unevenly distributed geographically. A band of states running from Illinois to New York have the highest level of unionization, in the 35–40 percent range. In the South, unionization is much less pervasive. North and South Carolina both reported less than 10 percent unionization of their labor force in 1972, and most other Southern states recorded less than 20 percent. What is more, unionization declined everywhere in the deep South between 1970 and 1972.

In Europe, union membership is associated with political support for socialist and communist political parties. In America, the popular image of unionists is somewhat the reverse. Union workers are often represented as more conservative on political and social questions than the nonunion public. In fact, survey data supports neither view. On a broad range of issues, including social programs, national defense, and foreign affairs, the opinions of union members differ very little from the opinions of the rest of the public.[1]

So much for generalities. These statistics are enough to show that unions, although not as strong as in some other countries, are large enough to play quite a significant role in the economy. Let us turn now to a more detailed look at their origins and functions.

The History of American Unionism

Earliest Beginnings

American unionism began toward the end of the eighteenth century. In the 1790s, craftsmen, including printers, shoemakers, and carpenters, formed local associations to further their economic interest. By the end

[1]See Derek C. Bok and John Dunlop, *Labor and the American Community* (New York: Simon & Schuster, 1970), pp. 58–63.

of the century, printers and shoemakers in Boston, Philadelphia, New York, and other cities of the eastern seaboard were bargaining collectively with employers.

These earliest labor groups followed the **craft union** pattern. This means that they were organizations of skilled workers, all in the same trade. Their skills and common interests made it relatively easy for them to work together in union activities, and gave their organizations some degree of monoply power in dealing with employers.

Craft Union A union of skilled workers all practicing the same trade.

The early local craft unions were usually short-lived. They faced many problems. It was not until 1842 that the courts recognized unions as being legal, and even after that date, the courts were often unfriendly. Furthermore, few of the early local unions were strong enough to survive the recurrent business depressions of the period. As soon as business fell off, they lost most of their bargaining power with employers. They then faded away, to be organized again in the next period of prosperity.

Knights of Labor

Unionism did not begin seriously on a national scale until after the Civil War. At that time, national unions began to appear, with local unions joining them as chapters. The most prominent of the national labor organizations in the post-Civil War period had the colorful name of the Noble Order of the Knights of Labor. This organization was founded as a secret society in 1869, but its growth began only after it abandoned secrecy in 1878. Membership reached a peak of more than 700,000 workers in 1886.

Many local unions of skilled craftsmen were affiliated with the Knights of Labor, but the Knights' principles went far beyond the narrow bounds of craft unionism. They welcomed anyone who worked for a living, including farmers, agricultural workers, and unskilled laborers. Only such "undesirables" as bankers, liquor dealers, Pinkerton detectives, and lawyers were excluded. The Knights' program was not limited to narrow economic concerns. It stressed workers' education and producer cooperatives, which would help counteract the "evil of wealth."

The breadth of organization and purpose of the Knights of Labor permitted rapid growth, but also led to the eventual decline of the group. After 1886, conflicts with craft unions increased. Public hostility, was aroused following the killing of a policeman during Chicago's Haymarket Riot of 1886, although no connection of the Knights with that event was ever proved. From that year on, the Knights of Labor were increasingly overshadowed by the emergent American Federation of Labor.

The AFL

The American Federation of Labor or AFL (first called the Federation of Organized Trades and Labor Unions) was founded in 1881. Its founders included some independent craft unions, and some local craft affiliates of the Knights of Labor who felt that the bargaining power of skilled craftsmen would be wasted in an attempt to win benefits for the unskilled. Since 1886, the AFL has played a dominant role in American union history.

The AFL found strong leadership under Samuel Gompers, its president for all but one year from 1886 until his death in 1924. Gompers sought to

Samuel Gompers
(1850–1924)

Samuel Gompers was born in a London tenement, the son of a skilled cigar maker. When he was 13, his family moved to America and settled on the East Side of New York. Gompers followed his father into the cigar trade.

Although his formal education ended at the age of 10, Gompers was very active in the workers' self-education movement of the time. In the cigar-making shops, work was organized on a piecework basis. A group of workers would have one of their members read to them while they worked, "paying" the reader by making his cigars for him. Gompers became acquainted with the works of Marx, Engels, and other European socialists in this way. Often he was chosen as the reader.

The cigar makers' union to which Gompers belonged fell apart in the depression of 1873. Gompers rebuilt it as a model of the craft unions he was later to unite under the American Federation of Labor. Key features of this union were high membership dues with central control of funds, national officers with control over local unions, and union-organized accident and unemployment benefits for members.

Gompers became disillusioned with radical socialism. The main role of unions, in his view, was to watch after the economic interests of their members. "Unions, pure and simple," he wrote, "are the natural organization of wage workers to secure their present material and practical improvement and to achieve their final emancipation. . . . The working people are in too great need of immediate improvements in their condition to allow them to forego them in the endeavour to devote their entire energies to an end however beautiful to contemplate. . . . The way out of the wage system is through higher wages."

During the 1890s, a socialist faction emerged within the AFL. They adopted a program calling for the collective ownership of all means of production, and other radical measures. Gompers opposed the group, and in the 1895 election for the AFL presidency, he was defeated. He fought back, however, and succeeded in regaining the presidency the next year, which he then held until his death.

Gompers was an ardent patriot throughout his career. During World War I, he opposed pacifism and supported the war effort. In 1918, he put his feelings in these words: "America is a symbol; it is an ideal; the hopes of the world can be expressed in the ideal—America."

avoid the mistakes that had led to the downfall of the Knights of Labor. The AFL owes its success largely to three features of its organization and philosophy that were prominent from its earliest years.

First, the AFL was based solidly on the principle of craft unionism. Its leaders thought that the dangers of economic depressions and employer opposition could be overcome only by relying on skilled workers who could not easily be replaced during strikes. The AFL itself was, in effect, an umbrella organization of national craft unions.

Second, the AFL emphasized "business unionism"; that is, it devoted most of its energies to bread-and-butter issues of pay and working conditions. Unlike many European labor unions, it was content to work within the capitalist system. It did not seek the overthrow of private property or the establishment of socialism.

Third, the AFL limited its political role to that of a lobbyist on labor's behalf. Again in contrast to European labor movements, it did not found a labor party. Gompers thought that excessive political involvement would lead to internal conflict within the labor movement, and would weaken its ability to achieve concrete economic objectives.

The AFL grew slowly at first, and then more rapidly. It reached 2 million members by 1904. Membership peaked at about 5 million in 1920, and thereafter declined to around 3 million in 1930.

Early Industrial Unions

Although the relatively conservative AFL dominated the union scene in the decades around the turn of the century, its principles were not universally followed. In places, there were notable early successes in organizing **industrial unions.** These included workers of all crafts and levels of skills within a given industry. The oldest major industrial union is the United Mine Workers, founded in 1890. After 1900, three successful industrial unions emerged in the clothing industry. The International Ladies' Garment Workers' Union was the strongest of these. Brewery workers also organized successfully. During the same years, though, industrial unionism suffered some spectacular failures. Strike efforts by steelworkers and railway workers were defeated after clashes involving Pinkerton detectives, state troopers, strikebreakers, and jailing of labor leaders.

On another front, the AFL was challenged by unionists who were unwilling to work within the capitalist system. The most notable of their organizations was the International Workers of the World (IWW), whose members were known as "Wobblies." The IWW campaigned for "one big union," which would embrace all workers of all skills and crafts, and for workers' management of industry. They were successful in organizing lumberjacks and agricultural workers, among whom conventional unionism had made few inroads. During World War I, the IWW opposed the American war effort, a stand that brought it under intense political attack. Many of its leaders and members were jailed, and the organization faded rapidly in importance.

Industrial Union A union of all workers in an industry, including both skilled and unskilled workers and workers practicing various trades.

The 1930s and the CIO

Unionism had declined in the 1920s, but during the Great Depression, the decline was reversed. In large part, the revival of organized labor was brought about by favorable legislation passed during the period. This legislation (discussed in some detail below) removed the major legal barriers to union organization, and crippled the antiunion efforts of employers.

In the improved legal climate, pressures grew for organizing the mass production industries—steel, rubber, automobiles, and others—which had resisted earlier attempts. This led to serious conflicts within the AFL. The AFL's old-line craft unionists did not believe that stable unions could be formed on the industrial principle. They also resented the efforts of industrial unions to recruit skilled workers in their industries. The AFL thought that these workers ought to join existing craft unions. As a result of this dispute, an opposition group formed within the AFL, led by John L. Lewis of the United Mine Workers. In 1938, the group was expelled from the AFL and formed the rival Congress of Industrial Organizations (CIO).

The CIO managed some major successes during the 1930s, the biggest being unionization of the steel industry. (The industry leader, U.S. Steel, agreed to collective bargaining in 1937.) Successful organization campaigns were carried out around the same time in the rubber, automobile, electrical, meat packing, and textile industries, to name just some.

The successes of the CIO demonstrated that craft unionism was not the only workable recipe for labor organization. They also contributed to a rapid growth in union membership—although the AFL itself grew rapidly too during the period. By 1939, union membership had risen to 29 percent of nonagricultural employment, more than double the figure of just four years earlier. By 1945, over a third of nonagricultural workers had been organized.

The AFL-CIO Merger

After the War, unions again faced difficulties. The political and legislative climate began to shift against them. Unionization drives in the South, expected to yield millions of new members, were relatively unsuccessful. During the 1950s, union membership stagnated. The CIO was more seriously affected, and it fell in membership to about half the size of the AFL.

Many union leaders felt that feuding between the AFL and the CIO accounted for a large part of labor's problems. At the same time, leadership of both unions passed into the hands of men who had not been so directly involved in the bitter disputes that had led to the original split. The distinction between craft and industrial unions seemed less important now that both types had proved to have their place. The outcome was an agreement to merge the two labor federations, signed in December 1955.

The Present and Future

Since the formation of the AFL-CIO, union membership has stabilized at around 25 percent of the labor force. Further efforts at unionization face serious difficulties. Chief among these is the fact that blue-collar workers, traditionally the easiest to organize, have become a declining fraction of the labor force. Major efforts now underway to organize government workers and agricultural laborers have met with some successes, though. If unionization becomes widespread in these occupations, membership figures will have considerable room to grow.

Collective Bargaining and Wage Rates

Union Goals

Labor unions have done many things for their members, and pursued many goals. They have bargained for shorter working hours and better health and safety conditions. They have founded pension funds for their members, promoted worker education, and engaged in party politics. For American unions, though, the number one goal has long been to achieve higher wages for their members. In this section, we shall look at the means that unions have to achieve higher wages. Later, we shall see how successful they have been.

The Union in a Competitive Market

We shall begin with the case where a union is formed in a previously competitive market, and seeks higher wages through the threat of a strike. Consider Exhibit 30.2. This figure shows a labor market in which the com-

EXHIBIT 30.2

The effect of unionization in a competitive labor market

A union formed in a previously competitive labor market can use a strike threat to bargain for higher wages. Here, the union threatens to strike unless the wage is raised from $1.33 per hour to $1.50 per hour. This puts a kink in the labor supply curve. If the union wins its wage demand, the quantity of labor hired will fall as the employers are pushed back up along their labor demand curves.

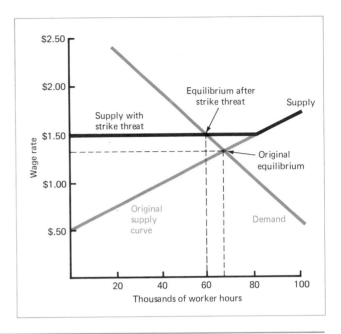

petitive equilibrium wage rate is $1.33 per hour. The equilibrium level of employment is 66,600 worker hours per year.

Suppose that the newly organized workers in this industry tell employers that they want $1.50 per hour, or else they will go on strike. The strike threat is shown in the diagram by a change in the shape of the supply curve. Originally, the supply curve had the usual shape. After the strike threat, employers face a supply curve with a kink in it. The horizontal left-hand branch of the new kinked supply curve indicates that if the employer does not pay at least $1.50 per hour, he will get no workers at all. Up to 80,000 worker hours can be engaged at $1.50 per hour. To hire more labor than that, the wage would have to be raised higher than the union is demanding.

Let us suppose that the employers decide they have no choice but to accept the union demand. They will react by shifting to a new equilibrium, in which they will hire 60,000 worker hours per year and pay the wage of $1.50.

Optimal Wage

This example brings out a problem faced by any union that bargains for higher wages with a competitive employer. The problem is that any increase in wages means reduced employment, because the higher wage will force the employer back up along his labor demand curve.

How far up along the labor demand curve should a union try to push? There is no easy answer, and no easy way to calculate an optimal wage demand. If the union wants to keep as many of its workers employed as possible, it may simply accept the competitive wage, and confine its bargaining to nonwage issues. Perhaps, though, the union wants to raise the total income of its members. If the demand curve is elastic in the region of the competitive wage, this can be done by pushing the wage up a bit. Although employment will fall, total labor income will increase.

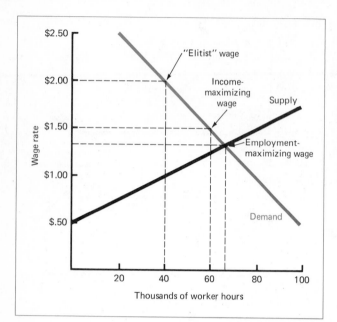

EXHIBIT 30.3
The wage-job trade-off
Unions facing employers who are price takers may choose various ways of dealing with the wage-job trade-off. If the union's objective is to maximize employment, it will not bargain for a wage higher than the competitive equilibrium. If the labor demand curve is elastic at the competitive equilibrium point, total income of union members can be increased by raising the wage to the point where the demand curve becomes unit elastic. If the union restricts membership to a limited elite group, it may push wages even higher.

In Exhibit 30.3, the labor demand curve is inelastic up to a wage of $1.50 per hour, unit elastic at that point, and elastic beyond. The $1.50 wage thus gives the largest possible total labor income, $90,000 per year. Unfortunately, keeping the wage at this level creates a surplus of labor. Workers will be willing to supply 80,000 hours per year, but only 60,000 will be demanded. The union could simply allow workers to compete for jobs on a first-come, first-serve basis, and not worry about those who could not get a job. Alternatively, it might try to share out the available work among all who wanted a job in the industry. Each worker would then be limited in the number of hours that could be put in. Whichever route is taken, a union that keeps the wage above the equilibrium level must be well enough organized to prevent nonunion workers from undercutting it.

Sometimes a strong union might ask for a wage even higher than the one that gives the maximum labor income. Suppose, for example, that the union took an elitist attitude, restricting membership to certain racial or ethnic groups, or to friends and relatives of current members. Look at Exhibit 30.3 again. An elite group of workers could push the wage up, say, to $2.00 per hour, if 40,000 hours per year were enough to satisfy them. To hold a card in such a union, needless to say, would be a jealously guarded privilege.

Featherbedding

Featherbedding The practice of insisting on purposely inefficient work rules, so that more workers will be needed to do a job.

Often powerful unions try to get around the trade-off between wages and jobs through the practice of **featherbedding.** Featherbedding means insisting on purposefully inefficient work rules, so that more workers will be needed to do a job. There have been some notorious examples of featherbedding in American industry. Rail unions have required firemen on diesel locomotives. In another case union printers have been required to set duplicate "dummy" type for newspapers when advertisers submitted copy in ready-to-print form. In still another industry, electricians had to tear apart and rewire on the job certain kinds of prewired electrical equipment.

If featherbedding simply meant that some workers stood idly by while others worked normally, it would just be another form of work-sharing. To the extent that featherbedding involves technical restrictions that lower productivity, though, it creates problems that simple work-sharing does not. Lowering productivity means shifting the labor demand curve to the left. In the end, total earnings for a group of featherbedding workers must be lower than earnings for an equal number of workers who practice a form of work-sharing that does not restrict productivity.

Union Versus Monopsonist

There is one exception to the trade-off between jobs and wages. That is the case in which a union faces a monopsonistic employer.

Consider Exhibit 30.4. This figure shows a labor market in which a monopsonistic employer faces a group of workers who are initially unorganized. The wage rate in equilibrium is $1.12 per hour, and only 50,000 hours of labor per year are hired.

Now consider what happens if a union confronts this monopsonist with a demand for a wage of $1.40 per hour, and backs the demand with a strike threat. As in Exhibit 30.2, this demand puts a kink in the labor supply curve. What is more important, along the horizontal part of the new labor supply curve, the monopsonist's marginal labor cost will be equal to the wage rate. The union says, in effect, that the firm can hire as many workers as it wishes at no more, and no less, than $1.40 per hour. That means that changes in the quantity of labor hired no longer require changes in the wage rate. One more worker hour raises total labor costs by no more and no less than $1.40.

EXHIBIT 30.4

The effects of unionization in a monopsony labor market

When a union faces a monopsonistic employer, it can sometimes both raise wages and gain more employment for its members. Here, the original monopsony equilibrium wage is just $1.12 per hour, and the monopsonist hires only 50,000 worker hours per year. A strike threat puts a kink in the monopsonist's marginal cost of labor curve. Marginal labor cost and marginal revenue product are not equal at a wage of $1.40, with 64,000 worker hours hired per year.

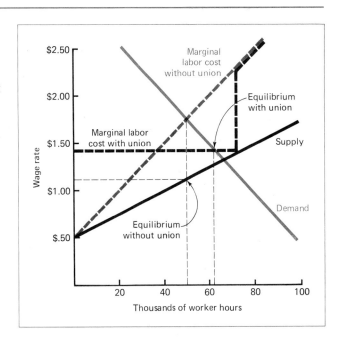

Let us suppose that the union is strong enough to make the monopsonist accept its wage demand on a take-it-or-leave-it basis. The new equilibrium will then be found where the new marginal labor cost curve intersects the demand curve. That means a wage rate of $1.40 per hour, and employment of 64,000 worker hours per year. Both the wage rate and employment are higher than in monopsonistic equilibrium.

Notice, however, that there is a limit on the power of a union facing a monopsonist to raise wages without losing jobs. This limit is set by the extent to which the original monopsony wage fell short of the competitive wage. Once the wage rate begins to exceed the level where the supply and demand curves intersect, further raises reduce employment. In fact, as Exhibit 30.4 is drawn, the wage of $1.40 per hour is already in the trade-off region. Maximum employment would be achieved with a wage rate of just $1.33 per hour. That, of course, is just equal to the competitive wage.

Bilateral Monopoly

Bilateral Monopoly A market in which both buyer and seller exercise monopoly power, and neither passively accepts the demands of the other.

Our last example assumes that the monopsonistic employer will accept the union demand on a take-it-or-leave-it basis. Not all employers need react this way. A strong employer might counter the union demand with the threat of a lockout, or some take-it-or-leave-it offer of its own. The kind of bargaining situation that develops when neither party to the labor contract acts competitively, and neither passively accepts the demands of the other, is called **bilateral monopoly.** The outcome of bargaining under bilateral monopoly is impossible to predict with the type of analysis used here. Economic theory can only specify a range of outcomes within which a settlement can take place. The actual outcome depends simply on the relative bargaining strength and skill of the two sides. The headline-making disputes in which "big labor" clashes with "big business" often fall into the category of bilateral monopoly.

Relative Wages

How successful unions are in raising the relative wages of their members depends on a number of things. First, it depends on whether the unions are strong enough to make a creditable strike threat. Second, it depends on how willing they are to sacrifice jobs in order to gain higher wages. Third, it depends on demand conditions in their sector of the labor market. No purely theoretical analysis can tell us which unions will be able to win higher relative wages and which will not. This is an empirical question that has drawn the attention of many economists. The following case reviews some of the results they have reached.

CASE 30.1
Labor Unions and Relative Wages[2]
In 1963, H. G. Lewis of the University of Chicago published a study of the effects of unionism on relative wages. As part of his work, he made an exhaustive survey of previous studies of individual industries. The main results of the earlier studies, as presented by Lewis, are shown in Exhibit 30.5.

[2]Based on H. G. Lewis, *Unionism and Relative Wages in the U.S.* (Chicago: University of Chicago Press, 1963).

EXHIBIT 30.5

Effects of unionization on relative wages in selected industries
Unions vary in their ability to win higher relative wages for their members. Cases where union wages are 25 percent higher or more than nonunion wages appear to be rare. Many unions gain only a very slight relative wage advantage for their members.

Author of Study	Industry	Years Covered	Effect of Unionization on Relative Wages
Rees	Steel	1945–1948	Zero or negative
Scherer	Hotels	1939–1948	Negligible 6–10%
Sobel	Tires	1936–1938	10–18%
		1945–1948	5–9%
Sobotka	Construction (skilled)	1939	25%
	Construction (unskilled)	1939	5%
Greenslade	Coal	1909–1957	Variable; 0–82%
Maher	Seven manufacturing industries	1950	0–7%
Craycroft	Barbers	1948	2%
		1954	19%
Rayaek	Men's clothing	1919	20%
		1926	12%
Sobotka	Airline pilots	1956	24–30%
Laurie	Local transit	1920s	15–20%
		1948	10%
Rapping	Seamen	1939–1957	6–35%

Source: Data from H. G. Lewis, *Unionism and Relative Wages in the U.S.* (Chicago: University of Chicago Press, 1963). © 1963 The University of Chicago Press. Reprinted by permission.

This table suggests that unions do have some measurable power over their members' relative wages. Often, however, this power is not great. Cases in which unions were found to raise relative wages more than 25 percent above the nonunion level are rare. Lower figures are common. In more than one instance, the relative wage power of unions declined over time. Their greatest impact was in the first years of organization.

Unions and Absolute Wages

It seems well established, then, that unions can affect relative wages. Are they also able to raise the average wages of all workers, as measured by the share of wages in national income? That is quite a separate question. This time, there is little theoretical basis for believing they can. Except in cases of true monopsony, which are likely to be temporary and purely localized, unions win their higher wages at the expense of fewer jobs. As the wage in unionized industries rises, the supply of labor to nonunionized sectors increases, keeping nonunion wages down.

National income statistics show labor's share of national income to be remarkably stable over time. Unadjusted figures show the proportion of wages in national income rising from about 60 percent in the 1920s to around 70 percent in the 1960s, but this change reflects factors other than unionization. It is largely explained by the relative growth of sectors of the economy that employ much labor (especially government and services), and the decline of those using less labor in proportion to other inputs. When an adjustment is made for this, labor's share of national income appears to have increased by only about 2 percent over the past half-century. This period coincides with the period of fastest union growth. We are left with the impression that the impact of unionization on average wages has been negligible.

Public Policy Toward Unions

The Problem

What should be the government's policy toward unions? This question has been a topic of impassioned political debate ever since unions began. Some have argued that all unions should be suppressed as illegal restraints on trade. Others have advocated government support for unions to promote industrial stability and high living standards for all. Still others have favored a laissez-faire policy, letting workers and management bargain without government interference. The debate has been clouded by disagreements about the true effect of unions on relative and absolute wages, and on industrial efficiency. Without taking a position, let us survey the changing course of government policy over time. As we shall see, first one and then another opinion has become dominant.

Early Court Hostility

Unions had trouble with the courts from their earliest days. Under precedents from English common law, they were often treated as illegal conspiracies in restraint of trade. *Commonwealth v. Hunt* was a landmark case decided in 1842 in Massachusetts. The court declared in that case that unions were not necessarily illegal in themselves, but it restricted the aims that unions could pursue and the means they could use to pursue them.

In the early twentieth century the legal climate grew, if anything, more hostile toward unions. In a series of cases from 1908 through the 1920s, the Sherman Antitrust Act was applied to unions. This happened in spite of considerable doubt as to whether Congress had originally intended the act to apply to unions.

In this period, the main legal weapon used against unions was the injunction. If a firm felt that union activities threatened it in any way, it could get an injunction barring unions from striking, picketing, publicizing labor disputes, assembling to promote their interest, and virtually anything else. Often such injunctions were issued without even hearing the union side of the case.

The Norris-La Guardia Act

As union membership sank to a low point in 1932, the legal climate was changed dramatically by the passage of the Norris-La Guardia Act. This act deprived antiunion employers of their biggest weapon, the injunction. The law declared, in effect, that the government should remain neutral in labor disputes. The courts could still intervene to protect tangible property and prevent the overt use of violence. As long as they remained nonviolent, however, unions would have the right to strike, picket, boycott, assemble, and persuade others to do these and other things.

The Wagner Act

The growing pro-labor climate of the New Deal era soon led to the passage of further labor legislation. The Wagner Act of 1935 came next. This act took government policy out of the neutral position where the Norris-La Guardia Act had left it, and put the government squarely on the side of the unions.

The Wagner Act declared that "employees shall have the right to self-organization, to form, join, or assist labor organizations, to bargain collectively through representatives of their own choosing, and to engage in concerted activities, for the purpose of collective bargaining or other mutual aid or protection." The law created its own enforcement machinery, in the form of a three-member National Labor Relations Board. This board was to oversee enforcement of the Act, arrange for representative elections, and act as judge and jury when the Act was violated.

The Wagner Act also outlawed a specific list of "unfair employer labor practices." Employers could no longer use lockouts, intimidation, blacklists, or spying. They could no longer force employees to sign contracts that made nonmembership in a union a condition of employment. In some cases, employers were even barred from speaking against unions.

The Taft-Hartley Act

The Wagner Act gave such a boost to labor unions that people began to worry whether it was working too well. Unions became strong and powerful. They could call strikes that could paralyze a region, and even threaten national welfare. After a series of particularly damaging strikes in 1946, a Republican Congress passed new legislation, amending the Wagner Act.

The Taft-Hartley Act (1947) tried to move public policy back toward a neutral position on labor issues. It modified the structure of the National Labor Relations Board and removed its powers as a prosecutor. It kept the list of unfair employer labor practices, but added a list of unfair union labor practices. These included restraint or coercion of employees by unions, strikes and boycotts aimed at forcing self-employed persons to join unions, and secondary boycotts. (These last are strikes or boycotts intended to force an employer to cease dealing in the product of another firm involved in a labor dispute.) The Act limited the closed shop, under which union membership is a condition of employment. It also provided machinery for federal intervention in strikes that threatened to create a national emergency.

The Landrum-Griffin Act

The last major piece of legislation defining government policy toward unions was passed in 1959. The Landrum-Griffin Act of that year put government in the business of policing internal union affairs for the first time. A series of scandals and Congressional hearings had brought several instances of corrupt or criminal practices of union officials to public attention. This legislation was an attempt to clean up unions.

A major provision of the act is a "bill of rights" for rank-and-file members. It guarantees their right of free speech, their right to vote in union elections, and so forth. The act also requires union reports on finances, regulates the term of office of union officials, specifies election procedures, and strengthens the Taft-Hartley Act's provisions against secondary boycotts.

Conclusions

For the moment, American legislation seems to have struck a balance that a majority can live with in the traditional policy areas. Most questions of organization, representation, and labor and employer bargaining practices are settled for the moment. In the 1970s, a new aspect of union activity has become a center of controversy. This is the role of unions in the process of inflation.

Earlier in this chapter, we argued that unions have a limited ability to raise their members' relative wages, but little power to raise the average wages of all workers, measured as a percentage of GNP. What about nominal wages, though? Can unions raise average wages measured in money terms, rather than as a share of national income? The theory of cost-push inflation, discussed in Chapter 14, says that unions can succeed in raising nominal wages. Rather than getting a bigger slice of the national income pie, though, their actions would only cause inflation, which erodes the purchasing power of their and everyone else's incomes.

Worries over cost-push inflation have led to pressure for a new form of government intervention in collective bargaining, namely, an *incomes policy*. Under an incomes policy, the government intervenes in collective bargaining not to strike a balance between labor and management, but rather in an attempt to contain an inflationary wage-price spiral. The United States experimented briefly with an incomes policy under President Nixon in 1971–1973. The policy was abandoned as a questionable success, but many people believe that it should be tried again. In countries like Britain, which have experienced even more severe inflation than the United States in recent years, incomes policy has become a major focus of national politics. Perhaps it will become so in this country as well.

SUMMARY

1. The first local craft unions in America were established toward the end of the eighteenth century. After the Civil War, a serious national union movement began, led at first by the Knights of Labor. The Knights were soon succeeded by the American Federation of Labor. The AFL emphasized craft unionism and concentrated on the bread-and-butter issue of higher wages. There were some early successes in industrial unionism toward the end of the nineteenth century, but industrial unionism became widespread only with the formation of the CIO in the 1930s. At first, the AFL and the CIO feuded bitterly, but in 1955, the two organizations merged. Today, about four-fifths of all union members belong to AFL-CIO affiliated unions.
2. The strike threat is a union's ultimate weapon in bargaining with employers for higher wages. A union wage demand backed up by a strike threat has the effect of bending the labor supply curve so that it becomes horizontal at the level of the wage demand. In a market where employers are price takers, a higher wage can usually be won only at the expense of jobs lost. Sometimes featherbedding or other kinds of work-sharing are used to spread available

work among all union members. Within certain limits, a union can win higher wages from a monopsonistic employer and gain higher employment at the same time.

3. Empirical studies show that many unions actually do succeed in raising the relative wages of their members. Often, though, the relative wage advantage of union members is only a few percent. It is doubtful that unions have a significant effect on the average wages of all workers, as measured in terms of the share of wages in national income.

4. Public policy toward unions has gone through several phases. Until the 1930s, courts were generally hostile toward unions. In the early part of this century, the Sherman Antitrust Act was applied to unions. Employers found it easy to obtain antiunion injunctions. During the Great Depression, the legislative climate changed. First the Norris-La Guardia Act abolished the injunction as an antiunion weapon, and made government a neutral party in labor disputes. Then the Wagner Act went even further, putting the government squarely on the side of unions. After World War II, policy moved back toward the neutral position with passage of the Taft-Hartley Act. The most recent major piece of labor legislation was the Landrum-Griffin Act of 1959. This put the government in the business of policing the internal affairs of unions for the first time. In the 1970s, the most controversial issues of labor legislation concern incomes policy and the role of unions in the process of inflation.

DISCUSSION QUESTIONS

1. Why do you think that unions are stronger in the Northeast than in the South? In what ways would workers in the Northeast gain if unionization became more widespread in the South? Would any workers lose if the South became more highly unionized?

2. Why do you think socialism has never been a strong political force in American unionism, even though the labor movements of almost every other country are strongly socialist or communist?

3. Is the nonteaching staff of your college or university unionized? If so, what union or unions represent them? Is the teaching faculty unionized? If not, do you know if there are any active attempts underway to unionize your faculty?

4. Why do you think some unions encourage wasteful featherbedding, rather than simple work-sharing, say, in the form of shorter hours or longer vacations?

5. In what ways do labor unions resemble cartels? Do you think labor unions deserve more public policy support than cartels of producers?

6. Do you think public employees should be allowed to form unions? Should they have the right to strike? What changes need to be made in our analysis of unions and labor markets in order for it to apply to unions of public employees? (Hint: What determines the labor demand curve of a unit of government?)

CHAPTER 31
Rent, Interest, and Profits

What You Will Learn in This Chapter
Wages and salaries account for about 75 percent of personal income in the United States, excluding transfers. The rest is made up of rent, interest, and profits. Although these items are less important than wages in quantitative terms, they play an important part both in income distribution and resource allocation. Pure economic rent is earned by any factor that is in perfectly inelastic supply. Interest plays two roles in the economy. It is the payment made by borrowers to lenders in credit markets, and at the same time, the return earned by capital as a factor of production. Just what is the true nature of profit is still a matter of some dispute. Various interpretations must be considered.

For Review
Here are some important terms and concepts that will be put to use in this chapter. Be certain that you understand them, or review them before proceeding.
    Entrepreneurship (Chapters 2 and 21)
    Elasticity of supply (Chapter 18)
    Explicit and implicit costs (Chapter 22)

In the last two chapters, we have looked closely at how labor markets work. Wages and salaries are a big part of the income distribution picture in the American economy. In 1975, they accounted for some three-quarters of all personal income. They are not the whole picture, however.

The remaining quarter of personal income is composed of rent, interest, and profits. These sources of income, although relatively small, deserve the same careful analysis we gave to wages and salaries. Rent, interest, and profits play a key role in the resource allocation process. They also play an important role in determining the overall distribution of income, as they are distributed somewhat less equally than labor income. Let us take the rest of this chapter, then, to look at these three income categories one by one.

Rent

Economic Rent

Pure economic rent is the income earned by a factor of production that is in completely inelastic supply. The classic example of a factor that earns rent is land. Land, in this context, means the natural productive powers of the earth and the locational advantages of particular sites. Artificial improvements are not taken into account. Neither are such matters as destruction of the soil through erosion, or creation of new land through reclamation.

Exhibit 31.1 shows how rent is determined by supply and demand in a competitive market. We consider some one particular category of land, say Kansas wheatland. The supply curve is a vertical line, because the quantity of land supplied does not vary as the rent that it earns varies. The demand curve for Kansas wheatland is the marginal revenue product curve for that sort of land as seen by Kansas wheat farmers. The marginal product of land falls as more land is used in combination with fixed quantities of labor and capital because of diminishing returns. The demand curve thus slopes downward to the right.

The rent the land earns is determined by the intersection of these supply and demand curves. If the rent is higher than the equilibrium we have shown, not all land will be put to use. The rent will then fall as land-owners compete with one another to find tenants. If the rent is lower than the equilibrium rate, farmers will not be able to find all the land they want. They will bid against one another for the limited available supply, and drive rents up.

Capitalization of Rents

We call the price of land a "rent," but much land, of course, is used by the person who owns it, and not rented by a tenant from a landlord. That does not change the way that supply and demand determine the value of land. It does mean, though, that we may sometimes want to speak of the price of land in terms of a lump-sum sales price rather than as a rent per month or per year.

There is a simple relationship between the value of a piece of land expressed as a rent and the price at which that piece can be sold in the market. We say that the market price of a piece of land is the **capitalized** value of its rent. By this we mean the sum that would earn an annual return equal to the annual rent if it was invested at the market rate of interest.[1]

Consider, for example, a piece of land with a perpetual rental value of $1,000 per year. If the prevailing rate of interest were 10 percent per year, a buyer would be willing to pay $10,000 for title to the land. If the rate of interest were 5 percent per year, the price of the land would rise to $20,000 and so forth.

Pure Economic Rent   The income earned by any factor of production that is in perfectly inelastic supply.

Capitalization (of a rent)   The capitalized value of a rent is equal to the value of that sum of money that would earn a periodic interest return equal to the rent if invested at the current market rate of interest.

---

[1]Alternatively, the capitalized value of a rent can be defined as the *present value* of that rent *discounted* at the market rate of interest. (See **Present Value** and **Discounting**, Chapter 24.)

EXHIBIT 31.1
Determination of rent by supply and demand
Pure economic rent is earned only by a factor that has a perfectly inelastic supply curve. Here, we show hypothetical supply and demand curves for Kansas wheatland. We take no account of any possibilities for creating or destroying such land, so the supply curve is vertical. The demand curve, as for other factors, is based on land's marginal revenue product.

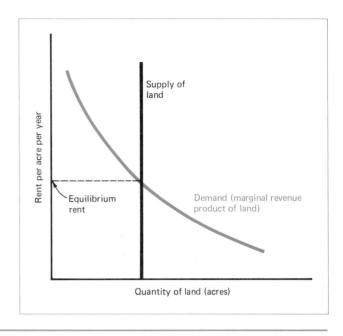

Other Rents

The term "rent" can refer to the market return earned by any factor of production that is unique or is in perfectly inelastic supply. Consider the very high incomes of people with unique talents such as singers, actors, and some professionals. These are more plausibly thought of as rents earned on their talents rather than as wages earned for the work they do. Artificially created legal privileges can be said to earn rents, too. For instance, part of the earnings of a New York taxicab could be counted as a rent earned from the "medallion" (license) that gives it the legal privilege to operate (because the supply of medallions is strictly limited by city authorities).

The hallmark of pure economic rent is inelasticity of supply. We must not confuse pure economic rent with what we loosely call the "rental" income earned by manufactured assets that are not in perfectly inelastic supply. Consider rental income of an apartment house owner, for example. It may partly be pure economic rent earned by some uniquely convenient site on which the building is located. In addition, though, the owner's income also includes implicit wages for any custodial work done in the building, implicit interest on money invested to build it, and so forth.

In part, what is pure economic rent and what is not depends on the time framework within which we are working. In the short run—say a period too short for new buildings to be constructed—we could make a case for considering the income earned from buildings as a rent. In the long run, when additional buildings can be supplied at a price, such "rental" income is clearly not a pure economic rent.[2]

[2]Turn back for a moment to Exhibit 6.2. Note that the national income accountant's "rental income of persons" is a mixed category not exclusively composed of pure economic rent. The items "net interest" and "corporate profits" also do not correspond perfectly to "interest" and "profits" as the terms are used in this chapter. "Proprietors' income" is a compound of interest from all sources, including implicit wages, earned by the owners of unincorporated businesses.

Interest and Capital

Two Aspects of Interest

The theory of capital and interest is in many ways the most complicated part of factor-market theory. We must be careful to understand the relationship between two different aspects of interest. We use the term *interest* to express both the price paid by borrowers to lenders for the use of loanable funds and the market return earned by capital as a factor of production. A person who loans $1,000 to another in return for a payment of $100 per year (plus eventual repayment of the principal) is said to earn 10 percent interest per year on his money. At the same time, a person who buys a machine for $1,000 and earns $100 a year by employing the productive services of that machine is said to earn 10 percent interest on his or her capital.

Consumption Loans

Let us begin our discussion with a look at how credit markets work. The suppliers of credit, that is, loanable funds, are savers. They are people who earn incomes now, but consume less than they earn in order to put something aside for expected future needs. In addition to savers, there are some people who want to consume more than their current income permits. These may be people who want to tide themselves over a temporary decrease in their incomes. They may be people with steady incomes who just do not want to wait to buy a car or take a vacation. These and other people who borrow for still other reasons are one source of demand for loanable funds. The loans they take out are called *consumption loans*.

Exhibit 31.2 shows how credit markets would look in an economy where consumption loans were the only source of demand for loanable funds. The willingness of savers to save, at various rates of interest, determines the shape and position of the supply curve. The eagerness of borrowers to bor-

EXHIBIT 31.2

Determination of the interest rate for consumption loans

If consumption loans were the only kind of loans ever made, the rate of interest would be determined as shown in this exhibit. The supply curve for loanable funds is determined by the willingness of savers to lend their money. The demand curve is determined by the eagerness of borrowers to consume now and pay later. The intersection of the two determines the interest rate.

row, at various rates of interest, determines the shape and position of the demand curve. The intersection of the two then determines the market rate of interest.

The Productivity of Capital

We have not yet said anything about production or capital. Opportunities to use capital as a factor of production are a second source of demand for loanable funds, in addition to the demand for pure consumption loans. To understand the demand for loans of this kind, we must understand why capital is productive.

Using capital means using a "roundabout" method of production rather than a direct method. A simple example will show what we mean by roundabout. Imagine a person whose business it is to make bricks. There are two available methods. The direct way of making bricks is to form them by hand out of raw clay scooped up from the ground, and bake them over an open fire. Let us suppose that by using this method, our worker can make 100 bricks per month. The alternative is a roundabout method. The brickmaker first spends a month making handmade bricks, and putting these together to make a kiln. When the kiln is completed, its hotter fire and lower fuel consumption make it possible to produce 110 bricks per month from then on. The roundabout method using capital (the kiln) lengthens the period between the time when work starts and the time that finished bricks begin to appear. In return, it increases the eventual rate of output. That is the sense in which capital is productive.

The brickmaker's experience is repeated in a more elaborate way whenever a firm makes a capital investment. Producing automobiles on an assembly line is a roundabout method of production compared to producing them one by one with hand tools. Constructing a building in which to hold economics classes is a roundabout method of education compared with holding classes in the woods under a tree. In every case, time is taken to construct synthetic aids to production in order later to produce more effectively.

Investment Loans

The brickmaker in our example invested directly, by actually building capital equipment that was needed. In a market economy, every firm does not need to build its own capital equipment. Anyone who sees an opportunity for increasing output by using a more capital-intensive (that is, a more roundabout) production process can borrow money and buy capital. The productivity of capital thus creates a source of demand for loanable funds in addition to the demand for consumption loans. We can call these investment loans.

Exhibit 31.3 shows how the rate of interest is determined when the demand for investment loans is added to the demand for consumption loans. The diagram shows that the rate of interest is higher when both types of loan demand are taken into account than it would be when only consumption loans were considered. In practice, the investment demand for loanable funds is much greater than the consumption demand. That means that the investment demand is the most important factor determining the rate of interest.

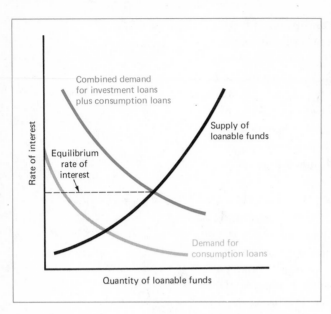

EXHIBIT 31.3
Determination of the interest rate with both consumption and investment loans
The demand for investment loans must be added to the demand for consumption loans to get the combined demand curve for loanable funds. Note that the equilibrium interest rate is higher in this exhibit than it would be if only consumption loans were taken into account.

Capital and Interest

To complete our discussion of capital and interest, let us look at the relationship between the demand for loanable funds and the demand for capital as a means of production. Exhibit 31.4 shows the short-run rental market for physical capital equipment—machines, buildings, and the like. In the short run, the supply curve is fixed by the existing stock of capital equipment. The demand curve is simply the marginal revenue product curve for capital equipment. The two determine the rental value of capital equipment.

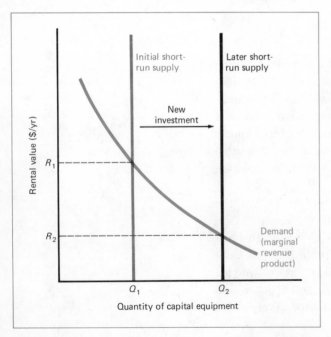

EXHIBIT 31.4
Short-run rental value of capital equipment and the long-run effect of investment
In the short run, the rental value of capital equipment is determined by the existing stock of capital and the demand (marginal revenue product) curve for capital. In the long run, new investment causes the supply curve to shift to the right. This would drive down the rental value, other things being equal. In practice, however, innovations continually shift the demand curve for capital to the right as well.

If the short-run rental price of capital equipment is high enough and the rate of interest is low enough, it will pay to build more such equipment. Suppose, for example, that the Avis corporation can buy a car for $4,000 with funds that it borrows at a 10 percent rate of interest. If it can earn $400 or more a year in rentals from the car, after operating expenses and depreciation, it will pay Avis to invest in expansion of its fleet.

Over time, as investment proceeds and capital accumulates, the short-run supply curve of capital shifts to the right. In the long run this would drive down the rental price of capital equipment and reduce the incentive to invest. The investment demand for loanable funds would thus diminish, and the rate of interest would fall. Theoretically, the economy could end up in a "steady-state" equilibrium. In this steady state, all worthwhile investment projects would have been completed, and consumption loans would provide the only remaining demand for loanable funds. In practice, the steady state never arrives. Technological innovation constantly pushes up the demand curve (marginal revenue product curve) for capital. The short-run rental value of capital equipment is thus kept high enough to justify substantial investment in new capital equipment year after year.

The Theory of Profit

Profit and Entrepreneurship

Entrepreneurship is sometimes called the "fourth factor of production," and profit the reward that this fourth factor earns. In a sense, entrepreneurship is a little like the three factors of production, labor, natural resources, and capital. First, entrepreneurship, like the others, is scarce. Not everyone possesses the ability to organize business undertakings and recognize new economic opportunities. Second, entrepreneurs do earn an income, in the form of the profit that remains after all the costs of their firms have been covered. Third, as is true for labor, natural resources, and capital, production cannot take place without entrepreneurship.

There is a limit, however, to how far we can push the parallel between entrepreneurship and other factors. The chief problem is that entrepreneurship is an intangible, not subject to measurement. There is no quantitative unit of entrepreneurship, and hence no way to determine a price per unit. Applying supply and demand analysis to this "fourth factor of production" just does not work. Understanding profit and entrepreneurship requires a different approach. Perhaps the best way to start is by clarifying what profit is *not*.

Profit and Net Revenue

When we first discussed the theory of the firm, we distinguished between what business accountants call profit and what economists call profit. To accountants, profit is the difference between a firm's revenue and its total explicit private costs. Economists, in contrast, subtract *implicit* costs of production as well as *explicit* costs of production from revenue when calculating profit.

In defining profit this way, we are distinguishing true profit from the implicit income of factors of production owned by a firm or its proprietor.

Consider, for example, a person who owns a fully equipped machine shop having a value of $100,000. Two hired workers operate the shop. Each is paid $10,000 per year. Suppose now that the firm's accounts show a revenue of $28,000, and a wage bill of $20,000. There is an accounting profit of $8,000, but this figure includes money that could have been earned even if the owner sold the machine shop and invested the $100,000 in stocks and bonds. If the average rate of interest on securities were 6 percent, $6,000 per year could have been earned in this way. An economist would thus compute the profits of the machine shop, in the strict sense, to be only $2,000 per year.

The value of any work performed in the shop by its owner ought also to be deducted from the $8,000 in computing true profits. This would represent wages that could have been earned from another employer. In addition, the rental value of the land the shop stood upon should be deducted too. This rent could have been realized had the shop been torn down and the property let to another tenant. After all these deductions, the business might even be seen to be operating at a loss.

Profit and Loot

There is something else beyond implicit factor income that is often confused with profits. This is money acquired not through production and voluntary exchange, as true profits are, but "earned" by coercive means, through involuntary expropriation of other people's property. Suppose that our machine shop owner, instead of paying the two workers the market wage of $10,000 per year, hires a gang of thugs to burn the workers' houses and molest their children unless they agree to work for $5,000. On paper, the firm's "profits" would then appear to be $10,000 greater than before. In reality, however, the owner would no longer be an entrepreneur, but a common crook. The money earned thereby ought not to be called profit, but something else. The vocabulary of economics lacks an accepted general term for the proceeds of coercive activity, but perhaps the word "loot" can serve as well as any. Our accounting of the machine shop owner's $30,000 revenue would then read as follows:

Total revenue	$28,000
Less: wages paid	10,000
Less: property income	6,000
Less: "loot"	10,000
True business profits	$ 2,000

"Looting" need not be so crude as in the example just given. If a firm earns money by misrepresenting its product and defrauding its consumers, that is loot, not profit. If it earns money by securing special privileges from the governmental agencies that eliminate honest competitors, that is loot, not profit. If it gets rid of industrial wastes by dumping them on unwilling bystanders, part of the firm's "profits" are really loot.

Why Are There Profits

We have now defined profit and distinguished it from implicit factor income and loot. This still leaves us with an important question: Why are there any profits at all? Why is the entire value of the product of all firms not divided up among the owners of the labor, natural resources, and capital used in the production process? These are subtle questions which have occupied the minds of many great economists. They have not yet received answers that everyone agrees upon. Still, it will be worth our while to look at some of the kinds of answers that have been suggested.

Risk and Profit

According to one theory, profits are a reward that the owners of businesses receive for bearing risk. Every business venture is subject to risk of failure. That is the nature of economic life in a world where the future is not known with certainty. People who merely hire out their factor services largely escape risk. A new business is usually expected to offer workers contractual guarantees that the payroll will be met even if the firm makes a loss. It is expected to offer banks or bondholders, who provide capital, security against default, and so forth. The owner or owners of the firm bear most of the risk of loss if the firm fails. In return, they get the privilege of keeping the profits if revenues turn out to be more than enough to pay off the obligations to hired factors. Why is it, though, that the profits earned by successful risk takers are not exactly offset by the losses of the unsuccessful? To answer this question, we must take a look at attitudes toward risk.

It is possible that some people are indifferent to risk. A person who was indifferent to risk would be indifferent between the opportunity to earn $10,000 per year with absolute certainty, or the opportunity to try for $20,000, subject to a 50–50 chance of failing and earning nothing. If everyone, or nearly everyone, were indifferent to risk, it is said, so many new businesses would be launched that failures would exactly outweigh successes, and on the average, business enterprise would earn no net profit.

In practice, though, most people seem to dislike risk. If they knew that they could earn a secure $10,000 per year, they would not launch a business with a 50–50 chance of failure unless that business, if successful, would pay *more* than $20,000. Because most people dislike risk, somewhat fewer business ventures are launched than would be otherwise. That makes opportunities a little more favorable, on the average, for those who *are* willing to bear a risk. As a result, the ventures they undertake succeed a little more often than they fail. When successes and failures are averaged out over the whole economy, profits more than offset losses. That excess of profits over losses is the reward that cautious factor owners are willing to pay the people who bear business risks, so that the owners can escape those risks themselves.

Profits and Disequilibrium

A second theory says that profits are the earnings of entrepreneurs who seize on the opportunities that exist when markets are in disequilibrium. Remember that market disequilibrium is a situation in which knowledge is not perfectly distributed. In disequilibrium, there are opportunities for alert entrepreneurs to catch the first signs of shifts in supply and demand conditions. Production and sales plans can be adjusted to the changed conditions before the conditions are fully reflected in market prices. Even more important, entrepreneurs seize on newly available methods of production or newly conceived products, and put the new ideas to use before anyone else. In all cases, the first people to put knowledge to use will find opportunities to "buy low and sell high." The difference between what they pay and what they receive is profit.

Entrepreneurial profits are, by their nature, always temporary. The first person who gets the idea of setting up a coin-operated automatic carwash is very likely to take in enough quarters to cover costs and still have something left over as profit. Later, when many competitors have entered the market, conditions will deteriorate a bit, and each operator will just barely cover costs. The carwash market will then be in equilibrium, and profit opportunities will have disappeared.

Any *particular* opportunity for entrepreneurial profit is temporary. It can exist only until everyone else catches on and the market reaches equilibrium. New opportunities always crop up to take the place of the old, however. Entrepreneurs who are alert enough can take advantage of one such opportunity after another. Profits are thus a permanent part of the distribution of income.

Monopoly Profits

Still a third theory identifies profits with the supernormal earnings of monopoly. In Chapter 27, we showed that a monopolist firm can restrict output and raise prices to bring in revenues that exceed all implicit and explicit costs. These monopoly profits are permanent at least in the sense that they exist in equilibrium, not just in the transition from one equilibrium to another.

Should monopoly profits really be considered a distinct category of income? Or can they in fact be accounted for in terms of other sources of income? The matter is open to conflicting interpretations. One view is that monopoly profit is distinct, because it results from "contrived" scarcity. By this it is meant that a monopoly purposely supplies less of its product or service than it conceivably could, in order to raise its price and operate where marginal revenue and marginal cost are equal.

Now the alternative point of view: If we look carefully at how a position monopoly is obtained and preserved, what appears to be monopoly profit often is seen really to be something else. Consider, for example, three sources of monopoly power: a monopoly based on ownership of some unique productive resource, one based on an artificial privilege, and one based on a technical innovation. In the first case, what appears to be monopoly profit might better be considered a rent. This rent is earned by the firm in its capacity as owner of the unique productive resource. In the second case, the monopoly profit might better be considered "loot." The loot is "earned" by the forceable exclusion of competitors. In the third case, what appear to be monopoly profits can be explained in terms of other kinds of earnings. There would appear to be no need to consider monopoly profit as a separate income source.

Conclusions

In this chapter we have discussed rent, interest, and profits purely in terms of positive economics. Many of the controversies about these kinds of income have little to do with positive economics, however. For some, the most important question is whether the particular people who receive nonlabor income *deserve* to receive it, in a normative sense. Questions like this raise the whole issue of poverty and the personal distribution of income. These questions are sufficiently important to deserve a chapter to themselves.

SUMMARY

1. Pure economic rent is the income earned by any factor of production that is in completely inelastic supply. Land is the classic example of a factor that earns a pure economic rent. Rent can be expressed either in terms of a periodic payment or as a lump-sum price paid when a piece of land is transferred from one owner to another. The market price of a piece of land is the capitalized value of the rent it can earn. Rent can also be said to be earned by other factors that are in perfectly inelastic supply. The special talents of uniquely gifted persons earn rents, and so do artificially created legal privileges.
2. We use the term *interest* both to express the price paid by borrowers to lenders in credit markets, and to express the income earned by capital as a factor of production. The rate of interest is determined in credit markets. The supply of credit depends on the willingness of savers to lend. The demand for credit is composed of the demand for consumption loans plus the demand for investment loans. There is a demand for investment loans because capital-using, roundabout methods of production are more productive than direct methods.
3. In the short run, supply and demand determine a rental price for capital equipment. If the rental value of newly produced capital equipment (expressed as a percentage of the cost of producing new capital equipment) is higher than the rate of interest, it will pay firms to expand their stocks of capital. As the stock of capital expands, the rental value of new capital, other things being equal, would tend to fall, thus reducing the investment demand for credit and driving down the rate of interest. In principle, these tendencies would eventually bring the economy to a "steady state" in which there was no new investment and the rate of interest was determined entirely by the supply and demand for consumption loans. In practice, technological innovation constantly pushes up the marginal productivity of capital, so there is always an incentive to invest.
4. Entrepreneurship is not a true factor of production, although it bears some resemblance to labor, natural resources, and capital. There are several theories about the true nature of profits. One theory holds that profit is the reward that entrepreneurs earn for performing the function of bearing risks. Another theory sees profits as earned primarily through buying low and selling high in situations of market disequilibrium. Still another theory considers monopoly profit to be a distinct type of income. It can be argued, however, that the profits earned by monopolies can all be traced to other sources.

DISCUSSION QUESTIONS

1. In 1974, American farmers earned a gross income of $101 billion. Part of this gross income went to cover explicit private costs of $74 billion, leaving farmers with $27 billion of net income. Would that net income best be thought of as wages, rent, interest, or profit? How might one go about making a rough breakdown of net farm income into these categories? Do you think that any farm income ought to be considered "loot?"
2. We have suggested that a part of the income of persons with exceptional talents might best be considered pure economic rent earned on those talents. Let us say that a certain opera singer makes $100,000 per year. How could you tell what part of his or her income is wages, and what part is rent? Here are three possible tests: (1) To find the rent, ask how big a pay cut the singer would take

before switching to a job where singing talent would be of no use. (2) To find the rent, measure the difference between this singer's income and the income of a singer with the same training but only average natural talent. (3) To find the rent, measure the difference between the singer's income in opera and the income he or she could earn in the next-best nonsinging job available. Which test is best? Would they all give about the same answer? Why or why not?

3. Turn back to Chapter 4 and Exhibit 4.6. Refresh your memory concerning the theory of tax incidence. How would the burden of a tax on pure economic rent be divided between resource owners and consumers? What about a tax on the "rental" income of apartment house owners?

4. Suppose that you decide to start a Christmas tree farm. You already own a suitable piece of land. You get seeds from pine cones picked up in the woods. You plant the seeds with your bare hands, using no tools or equipment of any kind. Five years later, you harvest the trees, breaking them off with your own hands, again rather than using any tools whatsoever. You sell the trees, and earn a handsome income. How should that revenue be divided into wages, rent, interest, and profit? Did you use any capital? If so, what form did your capital take? (Hint: Did you use a roundabout method of production?)

5. Suppose that a contractor places an ad in the newspaper for laborers. He offers to pay them $1 per cubic yard for removing rocks and dirt from a cellar hole. Four workers show up and start the job. Arnold is a person of average build. He uses a simple shovel and bucket for the job, and manages to earn $2 per day. Baker, a giant of a man, also uses a shovel and bucket but earns $5 a day. Charles brings a wheelbarrow with him, and earns $6 per day even though he is no stronger than Arnold. Davis uses a bucket and shovel, and like Arnold, earns only $2 per day at first. Not satisfied with this, he takes a month off to go through an intensive course in body building. When he comes back, he can earn $5 per day. Question: How should the income of each worker be categorized in terms of wages, rent, income, and profits?

6. By the term "loot," we mean income "earned" by someone through the use of coercion, fraud, theft, or intimidation. Is loot then a synonym for income earned illegally? What kinds of legally earned income ought perhaps to be counted as loot? What kinds of illegally earned income ought perhaps to be counted as ordinary wages, rent, interest, or profits?

CHAPTER 32
The Problem of Poverty

What You Will Learn in This Chapter

Factor markets do not distribute income equally among American families. Even in an economy that supplies families with a median income over $12,000, some 24 million Americans are officially classified as poor. Federal, state, and local governments have many ambitious antipoverty programs. These have somewhat reduced the inequality of income distribution over recent decades, but they have not eliminated the problem. Current programs are so expensive that there has been much discussion recently of streamlined transfer schemes such as the negative income tax. Not all economists think that transfers are the best answer to the poverty problem. Policies that aim to improve poor workers' chances in the job market also generate much current interest.

For Review

Here are some important terms and concepts that will be put to use in this chapter. Be certain that you understand them, or review them before proceeding.

Tax incidence (Chapter 4)

Human capital (Chapter 7)

Dual labor market (Chapter 15)

A Profile of Poverty in America

The Personal Distribution of Income

The factor markets that we have been studying distribute income far from equally among American families. Exhibit 32.1 gives an idea of who received how much, as of 1974. The table shows a median family income in 1974 of $12,836. Although this median was sufficient to provide a comfortable standard of living, it is worth noting that nearly a fifth of all families received less than half of that. It is the lower end of the income distribution profile that will particularly concern us in this chapter.

Exhibit 32.1, we should note, records only the distribution of before-tax money income, including cash transfers. To get a more accurate picture of the relative welfare of upper- and lower-income families, and of changes in

Income Bracket	Percent of Families in Each Bracket	Percent of Families in Each Bracket and below
Under $1,000	1.3	1.3
$1,000–$1,999	1.3	2.6
$2,000–$2,999	2.7	5.3
$3,000–$3,999	3.6	8.9
$4,000–4,999	4.1	13.0
$5,000–$5,999	4.4	17.4
$6,000–$6,999	4.4	21.8
$7,000–$9,999	13.8	35.6
$10,000–$14,999	24.3	59.9*
$15,000–$24,999	28.3	88.2
$25,000 and over	11.5	100.0

*Median family income $12,836.

Source: U.S. Bureau of the Census, *Statistical Abstract of the United States, 1975* (Washington, D.C.: U.S. Government Printing Office, 1976), Table 631.

EXHIBIT 32.1

Personal distribution of income in the United States, 1974

Income is not distributed equally among families in the United States. Almost a fifth of all families receive less than half the median income. A little more than half that number receive twice the median income or more.

the distribution of income over time, we must make certain adjustments. First, we have to correct for the different impact of direct personal taxes on families at different income levels. Second, we must adjust for differences in the average size of families in different income brackets. Third, we have to take into account the value of in-kind transfer payments taken. Exhibit 32.2 compares adjusted and unadjusted income distribution figures for selected years. The adjusted figures show income to be much more equally distributed than do the unadjusted figures.

Exhibit 32.2 also establishes an important point concerning the trend of income distribution over time. The adjusted data show that income

EXHIBIT 32.2

Changes in U.S. income distribution, adjusted and unadjusted data

In order to see what has happened to the distribution of income in the United States over the last two decades, certain adjustments must be made to the data on money income supplied by the federal government. When corrections are made for taxes, family size, and the value of in-kind transfers, we can see that income distribution has become significantly more equal since 1952.

Year	Lowest Quintile	Second Quintile	Third Quintile	Fourth Quintile	Highest Quintile
			Unadjusted Data		
1952	4.9	12.2	17.1	23.5	42.2
1962	5.0	12.1	17.6	24.0	41.3
1972	5.4	11.9	17.5	23.9	41.4
			Adjusted Data		
1952	8.1	14.2	17.8	23.2	36.7
1962	8.8	14.4	18.2	23.1	35.4
1972	11.7	15.0	18.2	22.3	32.8

Source: Unadjusted data from U.S. Bureau of the Census. Adjusted data from Edgar K. Browning, ''How Much More Equality Can We Afford?'' *The Public Interest* No. 43 (Spring 1976). Table III. Reprinted with permission of Edgar K. Browning. Copyright © by National Affairs, Inc.

distribution in the United States has become much more equal over the last twenty years. The unadjusted data do not show this change. Observers who have looked only at money income have often been misled into thinking that all the redistribution policies of the postwar period have had no effect on inequality. There is a simple explanation of the discrepancy between the two sets of figures. Government transfers in kind have grown much more rapidly than cash transfers. Much of the change has come in just the last ten years. In 1964, federal government transfers averaged $219 per poor person, of which $177 was in the form of cash and only $42 in kind. By 1973, federal transfers per poor person were up to $1,139. Cash transfers had grown by some two and a half times to $482, but in-kind transfers had grown more than fifteenfold to $657 per poor person.[1] The redistributional impact of these rapidly growing in-kind transfers shows up, of course, only in the adjusted data.

Poverty and Income Distribution

If we are to discuss poverty as a policy problem, we must know how income distribution and poverty are related. We might say, in a sense, that income distribution is a matter of numbers, while poverty is a matter of people. Measuring income distribution is just a routine task of positive economics. Measuring poverty, however, requires a normative judgment. It requires us to say how far down the income scale a family can fall before they have not enough or less than what they ought to have.

There is no single definition of poverty that everyone accepts. As a starting point, however, we can look at the method used by the federal government. The official method of distinguishing between the poor and the nonpoor is based on an "economy food plan" devised by the Department of Agriculture. This plan gives the minimum cost of obtaining a balanced, nutritive diet at prevailing market prices. The cost of the economy food plan varies, of course, according to the size of a family, the age of its members, and their place of residence. In 1974, the cost of a minimal diet was approximately $1,600 for an urban family of four.

By itself, a total income equal to the cost of the economy food plan would not be sufficient to keep a family well nourished. Families have other needs too. To take other needs into account, the government sets the **low-income level**—the dividing line between the poor and the nonpoor—at three times the cost of the economy food plan. Below that income level, the pressure of a family's needs for shelter, clothing, and other necessities tends to become so great that they will forego buying the food they need to get other things instead. Exhibit 32.3 shows low-income levels set for farm and nonfarm families of various sizes in 1974.

Low-Income Level The officially calculated dividing line between the poor and nonpoor, varying according to size of family, age of family members, and place of residence.

Problems with the Low-Income Level

The official approach to defining poverty is not without its critics. Some think that the level is simply too low. They point out that a "moderate" standard of living, as defined by the U.S. Bureau of Labor Statistics, costs nearly three times as much to maintain. Many families somewhat above the official poverty level, the critics say, still suffer the psycho-

---

[1]See Edgar K. Browning, "How Much More Equality Can We Afford?" *The Public Interest,* No. 43 (Spring 1976), Table 1.

No. of Family Members	Nonfarm	Farm
2	$3,211	$2,729
3	3,936	3,345
4	5,038	4,282
5	5,950	5,057
6	6,699	5,694
7 or more	8,253	7,015
Unrelated individuals	2,495	2,120

Source: U.S. Bureau of the Census, *Statistical Abstract of the United States, 1975* (Washington, D.C.: U.S. Government Printing Office, 1976), Table 651.

EXHIBIT 32.3
Official low-income levels for farm and nonfarm families, 1974
Official low-income levels are calculated on the basis of an economy food plan devised by the Department of Agriculture. The cost of this food plan is then multiplied by 3 to allow for purchase of other things than food. The low-income level for farm families is set at 85 percent of the level for nonfarm families.

logical effects of poverty because their living standard is so far below their expectations. Some go so far as to say that the idea of poverty is entirely relative, so that the poverty line ought to be defined as something like half the median income, rising as the general level of personal income rises.

Other critics complain that the official definition of poverty is too high, at least for many families. Compared to the kind of destitution from which millions suffered in the past and still suffer in two-thirds of the world, the standard of living that Americans call poverty is virtual luxury. It is certainly true that some facts about the American poor are remarkable by the standards of any other time or place. Consider those households that received $3,000–$5,000 income in 1973, an income bracket that straddles the low-income standard for three-and four-member urban families. Sixty-eight percent of such families owned one or more cars, and over 12 percent owned two or more. Seventy-one percent of families in this income bracket owned black-and-white televisions, and 37 percent had color sets. Fifty-five percent of these families had washing machines, 25 percent had clothes dryers, and 38 percent had air conditioners.[2]

Whatever the merit of these criticisms, the official definition of poverty at least gives a definite figure with which to work. We shall use it for the remainder of this chapter.

Who Are the Poor?

A few more summary statistics will give us an idea of who the poor Americans are. As of 1974, some 24 million Americans, or 11.6 percent of the population, were living below the official low-income level. The poor were not evenly distributed among the population, either demographically or geographically.

A substantial majority of poor people—67 percent—lived in metropolitan areas. However, a higher proportion of the rural population was poor. Only 9.7 percent of the population of metropolitan areas were poor, while 14 percent of people living outside cities were below the low-level. Remember, too, in this connection, that the official cutoff income is 15 percent lower for farm families.

[2]Data from *Statistical Abstract of the United States,* 96th ed. 1976, Table 665.
[3]All the data in this section consider only the money incomes of families. If the value of in-kind transfers received by poor families were taken into account, the number of families below the low-income level would be very greatly reduced.

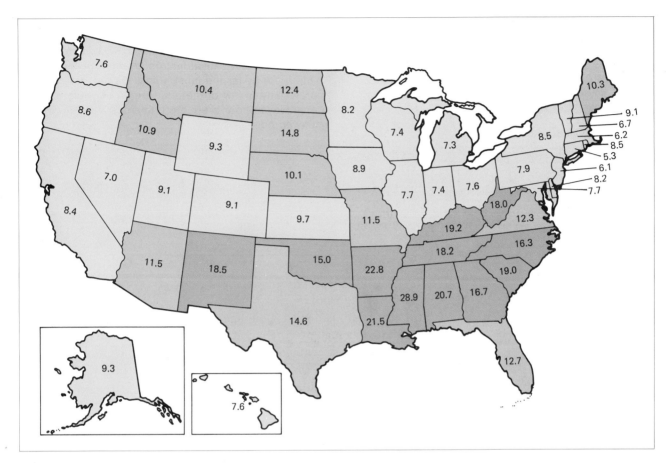

EXHIBIT 32.4

The geographical distribution of poverty in the United States, 1969

The data presented in this map show the percentage of families in each state which fell below the official low-income level in 1969. The data are not adjusted for differences in the cost of living from state to state. Such an adjustment would diminish extreme differences, but would not change the overall pattern.

Source: 1959, U.S. Office of Economic Opportunity, unpublished data, 1969, U.S. Bureau of the Census, *U.S. Census of Population: 1970* (Washington, D.C.: U.S. Government Printing Office, 1971), Vol. I.

The vast majority of the poor—some 72 percent—were whites. However, an even larger proportion of the nonpoor were whites. Only 8.9 percent of the entire white population were poor, but nearly 30 percent of the nonwhite population fell below the official poverty line. Among the rural black population, more than half were poor.

Poverty is also very unevenly distributed around the country. Exhibit 32.4 shows the percentage of families below the low-income level by states as of 1969. Connecticut had the lowest proportion of poor families, and Mississippi the highest—over five times more than Connecticut. Of the eleven states with more than 15 percent of families living in poverty, all but one (New Mexico) were in the South. (It should be noted, though, that the data on which the exhibit is based are not adjusted to take into account differences in the cost of living by states. To so adjust the data would not change the basic pattern, but would somewhat reduce the gap between North and South.)

Population Group	Percent of All Urban Poor
Elderly (65 and over)	18.3
Children (18 and under)	42.2
Adults in households headed by females	17.6
Adults in households headed by disabled males	3.0
Adults in households headed by unemployed males	7.0
Adults in households headed by employed males	11.9
Total	100.0

Source: Anthony Downs, *Who Are the Urban Poor?*, rev. ed. (New York: Committee for Economic Development, 1970), Table 6. Reprinted by permission.

EXHIBIT 32.5
Who are the urban poor? (1968)
These data were compiled by Anthony Downs to emphasize certain causal factors in urban poverty. Children are by far the most numerous category of the poor. Relatively few of the poor are employable adults. The employed poor are more numerous than the unemployed poor.

Why Are They Poor?

Still other data can shed some light on why persons and families fall below the low income cutoff. Exhibit 32.5 divides the urban poor of the United States into six categories devised by Anthony Downs. Although Downs' study was made several years ago, his data are still worth looking at, as they bring out causal factors of poverty.

Some 18 percent of the poor covered by Downs' study were aged 65 and older. Many of these were people who became poor only when they retired and their incomes dropped. Many were among the 15 percent of all elderly not eligible for social security payments, and others received social security checks too small to bring them over the poverty line. It should be mentioned that in one respect statistics on the elderly poor are hard to compare with those on other groups. A certain number of elderly persons have low money incomes, but still manage to live moderately well. Many have significant savings to draw on. Many also own homes and cars, fully paid for. The data given in the table do not take such considerations into account.

By far the largest number of poor persons in 1968 were persons under 18 years of age. The great number of poor children creates some of the most serious social problems associated with poverty. Most important, children from poverty-level families have poor ability to absorb education. This seems strongly attributable to a home environment of tension and conflict, with illiterate or alcoholic parents, where children's "belongingness" needs are poorly satisfied. Children from poor families are far more likely to grow up to be poor adults than children from nonpoor families.

Closely associated with the problem of poor children was the high percentage of poor families headed by women. The poverty rate for children was eight times higher in female-headed households than in male-headed households. Whether it is death, divorce, desertion, or illegitimacy that creates these female-headed households, women with dependent children find it very difficult to break out of poverty. Child care can be expensive or unavailable. Jobs for unskilled women workers tend to be low-paying. Work may lead to loss of important welfare benefits. There is often little incentive for poor female heads of families to enter the labor force.

Exhibit 32.5 divides poor households headed by males into three subgroups. Three percent of poor families were headed by disabled males. Almost 12 percent were headed by males who worked full time, but who did not earn enough to raise their families above poverty level. Only 7 percent of poor adults were in families headed by able-bodied males who were unemployed or working part time.

What Is to Be Done?

This profile of poverty in America gives us an idea of the dimensions and diversity of the problem. Next we shall look at what is being done to alleviate poverty, and what else might be done but is not. In the following section we shall look at antipoverty strategies based on income transfers, and in the final section, at strategies that operate through the labor market.

Helping the Poor: Transfer Strategies

Transfer Strategies

Transfer strategies are based on the idea that what the poor need to escape from poverty is money. Each poor person or family experiences an **income deficit** equal to the difference between that person or family's actual income and its low-income threshold. By adding together the income deficits of all families and unattached individuals, we can calculate an aggregate income deficit. This measures the minimum amount of money it would take in principle to eradicate poverty entirely. In 1973, the aggregate income deficit for the United States was approximately $11.9 billion.

Income Deficit The difference between a family's total money income from all sources and the official low-income level for that family.

The Social Security Act of 1935 is the heart of all transfer strategies for the elimination of poverty in the United States. This act, which has been amended many times, provides for a number of separate programs. Some of these are funded entirely by the federal government, and some are funded partly by the states. The various programs fall into two categories, social insurance and public charity. Let us look at each in turn.

Social Insurance

Social insurance programs are intended to protect all citizens against the financial hardships of old age, unemployment, disability, and ill health. They are supposed to be a form of mutual aid. Those who do not suffer from any of the listed risks pay into the social insurance schemes. The money they pay in is used to provide assistance to the old, the unemployed, the disabled, and the sick.

Although the alleviation of poverty is a major aim of social insurance programs, they are not considered to be charity. Contributions to the programs are compulsory, and the working poor contribute along with everyone else. Benefits of the programs are received as a matter of political right, not on a basis of need. The nonpoor benefit along with the poor. In 1974, only about 10 percent of social insurance benefits were received by poor families.

Problems of Social Security

The social security system has become the subject of increasing criticisms in recent years, as its current costs and projected future deficits have risen. Some of the major problems were built into the system from its beginning. New problems have resulted from a set of 1972 amendments to the original Social Security Act.

The biggest built-in problem with social security is the method used to finance it. As of 1976, funds for the system came from a payroll tax of 4.95 percent each on employers and employees for the first $15,000 of wages and salaries. Because the incidence of both halves of the tax is entirely on the worker, the effective rate is 9.9 percent. That does not include another 0.9 percent applied to Medicare. Because it is paid only on wages and salaries, and because no payroll tax is paid on incomes above $15,300, the tax is highly regressive. So long as such a large share of the burden of the program falls on low-income workers, it will remain relatively ineffective as an instrument of income redistribution.

The 1972 amendments placed new burdens on this regressive revenue base. First, benefits were increased 20 percent across the board. According to the demographic projections used by Congress, the system should have been able to absorb that increase without additional taxes. Unfortunately, those projections were already obsolete in 1972. They did not take into account the dramatic fall in the American birth rate that had taken place since 1964, and has continued since 1972. The declining birth rate means that, in the future, there will be more retired people for each member of the working-age population. At present, there are about 20 people aged 65 and over for each 100 persons aged 20 to 64. This ratio will remain stable for about the next three decades, but after that, it will begin to rise rapidly. By 2030, it will have risen to 30 retirees per 100 persons of working age. Inevitably, this demographic change means that social security taxes will have to rise or benefits will have to be cut in comparison with the levels foreseen in the 1972 ammendments.

The second problem with the 1972 amendments concerns inflation. The authors of the proposals quite properly decided that retired workers should be protected against having their social security benefits eroded by inflation that occurred after they reached retirement age. Unfortunately, the formula chosen by Congress to protect against inflation actually overcompensates. Inflation now causes social security benefits to rise in real terms, rather than merely to keep pace with prices. In fact, given the nature of the formula and current rates of inflation, retiring workers will soon begin receiving social security benefits that are actually higher than their most recent earnings. These higher benefits further burden the system.

None of the problems of the Social Security System have yet been resolved. It appears certain, however, that resolving them will increase the tax burden of the program. It is very likely that the tax burden will as much as double. As that happens, there will surely be a major battle over the role that the regressive payroll tax should play in raising increased revenues for the system.

Public Charity

Public charity is the second major category of government transfer program. As the name implies, public charity is more directly targeted at the poor than is social insurance. Public charity programs come in a wide variety of forms. Some provide direct cash benefits to the poor. The best known of these is the federally sponsored program of Aid to Families with Dependent Children. Many state governments also have programs providing public assistance in cash form. Some programs provide aid "in kind," that is, in the form of specific goods or services, or in the form of funds earmarked for certain types of expenditure. The federal government's food stamp program, commodity distribution scheme, rent subsidies, and school lunch subsidies fall into this category. So does Medicaid, which covers healthcare expenditures for poor families. Finally a variety of more specialized services are provided through public charity, including counseling and rehabilitation services, for the poor, and care in orphanages and other institutions. As we mentioned above, in-kind transfers have grown more rapidly than cash transfers in recent years.

Critics of Public Charity

Public charity programs collect an even more vociferous group of critics than do social insurance schemes. A great variety of specific complaints are heard. The most important of these fall into three groups.

First, public charity programs are criticized for dispensing aid in ways that increase dependency rather than encouraging self-help. A "poverty trap" can be created in which each dollar earned by a poor family results in the loss of a dollar's worth of benefits. Under these conditions, the transition from welfare to self-supporting status may simply not be worth the effort. One HEW report, for example, found that in 1969 more than 70 percent of mothers who were heads of poor families could not earn more by working than they could receive from Aid to Families with Dependent Children, even when jobs were available. On a broader level, one hears criticisms of the whole client-benefactor relationship that exists between the poor family and the welfare bureaucracy. This can engender a psychology of dependence that in some cases keeps one generation of a family after another on the public assistance rolls.

A second complaint frequently heard—sometimes but not always from a different set of critics is that the welfare system is open to cheating and abuse. There is little overall data on welfare cheating, but everyone has favorite anecdotes. Some report welfare mothers driving up in Cadillacs to collect checks for nonexistent children. Some concern the sons of wealthy professionals living on food stamps while their parents put them through law school. Whatever the total dollar magnitude of these abuses, they point unmistakably to one thing: The very complexity of the welfare system can be a barrier to meeting the needs of the honest, and an invitation to the ingenuity of the unscrupulous.

Perhaps the most telling criticism of the combined social insurance and public charity programs is that they have not eliminated poverty. The magnitude of the aggregate income gap—just $12 billion in 1973—seems tiny in comparison with the $90 billion in federal transfer spending in that same year. Is there not perhaps some way to eliminate measured poverty while reducing the cost of transfer programs to the taxpayer? Let us look at how the federal transfer strategy might be simplified and overhauled.

Filling the Income Gap

The aggregate income deficit amounts to less than 1 percent of gross national product. Could not poverty be eliminated altogether simply by giving each poor family a cash grant equal to its own income deficit, and collecting the necessary $12 billion from the general taxpayer? The answer

Marginal Tax Rate   The net increase in taxes paid or decrease in transfers received by a family for each $1 increase in the family's earned income.

to this question is *not necessarily*. The problem is that a program such as we have described would subject poor families to an effective **marginal tax rate** of 100 percent. For each $1 more of income they earned, they would lose $1 in federal transfers. For each $1 less of income they earned, they would gain $1 in federal transfers. Poor families would have no economic incentive to work at all. Such a program would also distort the incentives of workers with incomes just above the poverty line. They would see that all their efforts were getting them only slightly greater rewards than those received by people who did not work at all. As disincentives cut into earned incomes, the aggregate income deficit would increase. In the end, much more than the originally estimated $12 billion transfer would be needed to eradicate poverty.

Negative Income Tax

Is there any way to carry out massive income transfers without encountering the disincentive effects of a 100 percent marginal tax rate? Yes, say backers of the **negative income tax.** Under a positive income tax—the kind we have now—individuals pay the government an amount that varies according to how much they earn. A negative income tax puts the same principle to work in reverse. It makes the government pay individuals an amount that varies in proportion to their earnings.

Negative Income Tax   A general term for any of a number of transfer programs that would pay benefits or collect taxes from families according to a schedule based on earnings, while keeping marginal tax rates low enough to avoid serious disincentive effects.

Exhibit 32.6 shows how a negative income tax could be set up. The horizontal axis of the figure measures the income a household earns. The vertical axis measures what it actually receives after payments from or to the government. The 45-degree line represents the amount of disposable income that households would have if there were no tax of any kind. The negative and positive income tax schedules show the disposable income of families with the negative income tax program in force.

As the exhibit is drawn, the benefit received by a family with no income at all is just equal to the average low-income level. That is necessary if the scheme is to eliminate officially measured poverty entirely. Starting from zero earnings, benefits are reduced by $.50 for each $1 earned. When

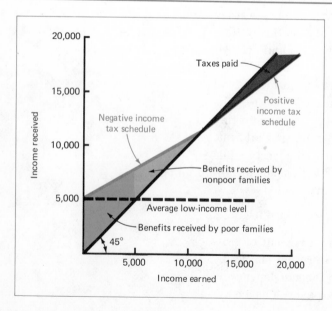

EXHIBIT 32.6
Possible schedules for a negative income tax
A negative income tax redistributes income without imposing extremely high marginal tax rates on either taxpayers or beneficiaries. In order to maintain low marginal tax rates, some benefits are given to nonpoor families, and some poor families are given more than they need to reach the low-income level. The cost of a negative income tax scheme must thus always be greater than the aggregate income deficit.

earned incomes reach a level equal to twice the low-income level, a break-even point is reached where no taxes are paid and no benefits received. Beyond that point, a positive income tax schedule of the kind we are familiar with takes over.

The negative income tax has the great advantage of maintaining work incentives for all beneficiaries. The marginal tax rate for poor families is only 50 percent as the exhibit is drawn. This is presumably low enough to prevent widespread withdrawal of effort. Note, however, that the cost of the program is still much greater than the initial size of the aggregate income deficit. All but the very poorest families receive more than the minimum they need to reach the low-income cutoff. What is more, many non-poor families—those with earned incomes in the $5,000–$10,000 range—also receive benefits.

Many practical questions about the cost and workability of a negative income tax cannot be answered by armchair economics. They can be answered only on the basis of actual experience with running such a program. Some significant experiments have already been carried out, one of which is described in the following case study.

CASE 32.1
The New Jersey Graduated Work Incentive Experiment[4]

From 1968 to 1972, a negative income tax experiment involving 1,300 low-income families was carried out in four eastern cities. The program was called the New Jersey Graduated Work Incentive Experiment. A variety of different benefit schedules were used with different groups of subjects. The level of guaranteed minimum income ranged from 50 to 100 percent of the poverty-level income, and the marginal tax rate for the beneficiaries varied from 30 to 70 percent. Only households headed by a male were included in the experimental group.

The central objective of the experiment was to investigate the effect of the negative income tax on work incentives and labor supply. Results of the experiment indicated strongly that the labor supply effects of such a program are small. Over all, it appeared that there might be a 5 to 10 percent reduction in the amount of work done by participants in the program. Somewhat surprisingly, no statistically measurable differences in labor supply response were observed within the range of 30 to 70 percent marginal tax rates. Some experimenters tentatively took this to indicate that marginal tax rates of at least 50 percent could be used without seriously eroding work incentives.

A detailed study of the labor supply response of beneficiaries revealed some further items of interest. In particular, it appeared that the 5–10 percent overall reduction in hours worked did not take the form of total withdrawal from the labor force of any significant number of workers. Rather, reductions came from fewer hours worked, fewer dual jobs and, in some cases, longer periods of job search between jobs. Reductions in labor supply appeared to be more pronounced for secondary than for primary workers. They were also more pronounced for whites than for blacks or Spanish-speaking workers.

A secondary purpose of the experiment was to test the administrative feasibility of a negative income tax. Results were encouraging in this respect also. Despite problems of interpreting some of the data, and lack of clearcut statistical results in some areas, it was felt that, as an experiment in experimentation, the New Jersey program had been a success. It has encouraged further investigation of the negative income tax as a practical policy alternative.

[4]Joseph A. Pechman and Michael Timpane (eds.), *Work Incentives and Income Guarantees. The New Jersey Negative Income Tax Experiment,* (Washington, D.C.: Brookings Institution, 1975).

Political Problems

In addition to problems posed by the need for more practical information on cost and effects, the negative income tax scheme faces a number of political problems. One such problem is posed by the diversity of living standards in different parts of the country. The business of setting benefits would be greatly complicated by the need to reconcile regional interests. A further problem is how the negative income tax should relate to other programs. Many economists believe that it would make great sense to use a comprehensive negative income tax to replace all existing social insurance and public charity programs. Existing programs are not easy to eliminate, however. Each has its own army of lobbyists among beneficiaries, politicians, and public officials. Yet simply to tack a negative income tax onto the existing welter of programs would increase rather than diminish the total cost of all transfer programs. It would increase rather than diminish the complexity, overlaps, and conflicting incentives that characterize the current system. For the moment, it appears that political realities will keep the negative income tax in the textbooks, but interest in the scheme has become so widespread that it may not stay there forever.

Helping the Poor: Job Market Strategies

Transfer strategies for helping the poor are based on the diagnosis that people are poor because they do not have enough money. The implied cure is to give them additional resources in cash or in kind. Now we turn to a second, rather different approach to the problem of poverty. This approach is based on the diagnosis that poverty results from a failure of factor markets to allocate human resources properly. By implication, putting wasted manpower to work would make many poor households self-supporting.

The diagnosis that poverty is a matter of factor market failure must be broadly interpreted if it is to have any credibility at all. The data presented in Exhibit 32.5 suggested that very few of the poor are adults in households headed by unemployed, able-bodied males aged 18 to 65. A narrowly conceived jobs-for-the-poor approach that focused just on this group would not make much of a dent on the overall poverty picture. In a broader sense, though, much more poverty is attributable to job-related sources. The number of elderly poor and working poor would be reduced if the market provided higher-paying jobs. The number of families headed by women, where the highest proportion of poor children are concentrated, would be less if it were not for the destructive effect on family life of men's inability to get good jobs. In the long run, job market strategies for alleviating poverty could benefit all the poor.

The Dual Labor Market Theory

Job market failure as a source of poverty is not just a matter of unemployment. According to one theory, the problem lies in the existence of a *dual labor market*. One sector of the labor market contains high-wage jobs with profitable firms. These not only pay more, but are more likely to be unionized, offer more opportunities for advancement, and are less affected by macroeconomic fluctuations. The secondary job market, in contrast, contains low-paying jobs with marginal firms. These are held by unorganized workers with unstable work patterns. They are largely "dead-end" jobs with few opportunities for advancement, and are heavily hit by cyclical swings in unemployment.

According to proponents of the dual labor market theory, the two parts of the job market are kept separate by a complex of interacting factors. Discrimination, attitudes, motivation, and work habits determine which sector a worker is in. Once in the secondary sector, a worker develops attitudes and work habits that make discrimination more likely. The dual labor market theory has clear implications for antipoverty policy, namely, that such a policy must aim at breaking down the barriers between the two market sectors. In what follows, we shall look at some possible means of doing this.

Education

Economists like to view education as an investment in human capital. By spending money and taking time away from current employment, people can improve their skills and productivity. Later they can sell their services at higher wages in the labor market. One antipoverty strategy, then, is to make good-quality education available to poor and children of the poor, in the hope that this education will make them self-supporting.

There are actually two different ways in which education might have an impact on the problem of poverty. On the one hand, education benefits the particular individuals who are educated, thus taking people one by one out of poverty. On the other hand, improved education has a general impact on the equality of income distribution. By increasing the supply of highly educated workers, it lowers their relative wages. Both kinds of effects are slow, however, and far from foolproof.

Let us look first at elementary education. Here we encounter the problem of an uncertain relationship between the quantity of educational inputs and the quality of educational outputs. Despite numerous studies, it is by no means clear that spending more on schools improves the performance of the pupils who go to them. To a considerable extent, home and community environment may be more powerful than formal education in transmitting those crucial attitudes, motivations, and work habits that decide which sector of the labor market a person will end up in.

Increased spending on higher education appears to be an even less certain method for combating poverty. It is true that a college education gives upward mobility for many individuals from impoverished backgrounds. Those who succeed in college, however, are likely to be those with the attitudes and abilities that would bring them success in any event, even if they never had the chance to go to college. There is some evidence that in the early 1970s, salaries for college-trained workers began to fall in response to an increased supply of graduates. This may be having some effect on the inequality of income distribution. There are probably other better ways to achieve the same effect, though. It would seem better to bring up the income of the poor rather than to push down the income of college graduates by encouraging their oversupply.

One thing remains to be said in favor of education as an antipoverty measure. Although the economic effects of subsidizing education may be difficult to measure, a good education is something that most disadvantaged parents want for their children. Improvements in education thus fill a perceived need. This may be important in itself.

Discrimination

Many economists believe that discrimination plays an important role in separating the two sectors of the labor market. During the 1960s, there was considerable occupational upgrading among blacks. Yet blacks are still less than proportionately represented in high-paying jobs, and more than proportionately represented in secondary-sector jobs. The level of black family income rose during the 1960s from 55 to 64 percent of white family income. During the early 1970s, however, it slipped back. Wages for blacks continued to rise, but this was more than offset in terms of family incomes by rising black unemployment, falling black labor force participation, and increases in the percentage of black families headed by women.

Since the Civil Rights Act of 1964, discrimination in employment has been illegal under federal law. The Equal Employment Opportunity Commission has broad powers to enforce this act. Enforcement in the form of "affirmative action" to encourage minority employment has probably gone about as far as it can without introducing compulsory racial quotas for employers. Under present law, these would themselves be a form of illegal discrimination against white male workers.

Antidiscrimination laws have had some effect, but there are economic limits to what can be expected from them. The market contains built-in antidiscrimination incentives of its own. Suppose it were true that the low-paid secondary sector of the labor market contained substantial numbers of workers who were there only because of their race. Suppose that these workers had the same skills, motivations, and work habits as everyone else. If this were the case, there would be potential profit opportunities in employing those workers. Not all entrepreneurs could be expected to pass them up. True, there would be some employers who because of prejudice, tradition, or community pressure would rather hire less competent whites than more competent blacks to do a job, or who would pay whites more than equally skilled blacks. Nonetheless, other employers who ignored tradition or community pressure could cut their labor costs and gain a competitive edge. In fact, that may be why tradition-minded communities in the South, in the days before civil rights legislation, felt it necessary to enforce segregation with specific "Jim Crow" laws. If they had not, market forces might have brought about a degree of integration unacceptable to them.

No one would claim that these antidiscriminatory market incentives operate so quickly or thoroughly that they entirely eliminate all labor market discrimination. It is likely, though, that they do operate well enough to ensure that the residue of discrimination left by the market is relatively small. Removing that small residue is really all that can be hoped for from equal opportunity legislation.

Other Demand-Side Strategies

Elimination of discrimination is an antipoverty strategy that works from the "demand side" of the market. Such a program differs from programs of training and education, which try to benefit the poor by enabling them to supply more attractive services to the factor market. Instead, demand-side strategies aim to increase the demand for the services that poor people are already equipped to offer. There is a feeling among some dual labor market theorists that an effective antipoverty program must emphasize demand-side strategies. These economists hope that demand-side strategies can operate more quickly and certainly than education and job training, although the latter might still have a job to do in the long-run.

Besides antidiscrimination legislation, there are two other widely discussed demand-side strategies. One is the concept of public employment. In its most ambitious form, a public employment program would make the government an "employer of last resort," so that all poor people, no matter how meager their skills or training, would be able to get jobs and become self-supporting.

In Chapter 15, we discussed public employment in the context of the macroeconomic problem of unemployment. There we raised one difficulty potentially encountered by public employment. That is the problem that the jobs the government sector can most easily create—service jobs requiring little capital investment, and producing nonmarketed outputs—tend not to be as productive as jobs in the private sector. That means that there is a danger that an employer-of-last-resort program would transfer large quantities of labor from the high-productivity private sector to the low-productivity public sector. To avoid this danger, wage subsidies have been proposed as an alternative demand-side strategy. Wage subsidies would raise the demand for labor in the private sector by paying private firms to hire impoverished workers whom they otherwise would not employ. In recent years Britain has experimented with wage subsidies as an alternative to public employment, and some success is reported.

Conclusions

The economics of poverty is, in many ways, the most discouraging branch of economics to study. When we first look at statistics on income distribution, the problem looks so small. Just shifting 1 percent of gross national product down to the lowest quintile of the population seems to be all that is required. Then we begin to look at all of the efforts already being made in the name of equality and distributive justice. Expenditures on social insurance, public charity, education, job training, and all the rest are enormous compared with the size of the aggregate income deficit. Somehow, all this money just does not seem to hit the target.

Economists, of course, have plenty of simple and elegant solutions. If we really want to eliminate poverty, what we need to do is abolish all existing programs and replace them with a single, streamlined negative income tax, or something like it. But our political system is not built to pursue a goal such as eliminating poverty in a straightforward, single-minded way. It is a system of give and take that responds to many opposing interests, and the current array of poverty programs is the natural outcome.

SUMMARY

1. In 1974, some 24 million Americans were officially classified as poor, according to the federal government's low-income levels. The low-income levels are based on the cost of an economy food plan calculated by the Department of Agriculture. In classifying families as poor or nonpoor, only before-tax money incomes are taken into account. This practice leads to an overstatement of the number of poor families. If the effects of taxes and in-kind transfers are taken into account, the distribution of income in the United States appears to have become significantly more equal over the last two decades.

2. The Social Security Act of 1935 is the heart of the federal income transfer effort. The act provides social insurance benefits to almost all Americans, poor and nonpoor, paying for these benefits with a payroll tax. At the present, the social security system is entering a difficult period. Projected future benefits far exceed projected future revenues. Raising the payroll tax would be unpopular, partly because the tax is so regressive. Reforms are clearly needed, but it is far from certain when they will come or what form they will take.

3. Public charity benefits are paid to families on the basis of need, in contrast to social insurance benefits, which are paid as a matter of right. Public charity includes both cash and in-kind transfers. Public charity programs have many critics. In some cases, benefits are given out in forms that increase rather than reduce dependence on public charity. The very complexity of the many programs makes them open to abuse. Worst of all, they have not succeeded in eliminating poverty despite the vast sums of money spent.

4. The negative income tax is a simplified transfer scheme often suggested as an alternative to current antipoverty efforts. A key feature of the negative income tax is a relatively low marginal tax rate for families at all income levels. Limited local experiments tentatively confirm the practicality of the negative income tax. The idea is not yet as popular in Congress, however, as it is among economists.

5. Job market strategies for aiding the poor approach poverty as a problem of factor market failure. More is involved than just unemployment. One theory states that antipoverty efforts must aim at breaking down a dual labor market. Some think that the government should approach the problem from the supply side with education and job training programs. Others emphasize demand-side programs including antidiscrimination measures and public employment.

DISCUSSION QUESTIONS

1. It is sometimes said that poverty is not the fault of individuals, but the fault of society. Do you agree? What do you think the statement means? Because "society" is itself composed of individuals, does it mean that certain nonpoor individuals are responsible for the poverty of poor individuals? If so, which individuals are responsible? Do you think that any of your own actions may be at fault in causing someone else to be poor?

2. According to the logic of the federal government's low-income standard, an officially poor family is likely not to be able to afford an adequate diet. Do you think it odd that so many poverty-level families, who cannot afford adequate nutrition, do seem able to afford cars, television sets, clothes dryers, and air conditioners? Is it natural and reasonable that a poor family should own such things? Would you favor legislation that attempted to force poor families to spend more on food and less on seemingly unnecessary appliances? Could the data on appliances indicate a defect in the official method of measuring poverty?

3. What are the relative merits of cash versus in-kind transfers? Review Chapter 19, paying particular attention to the concepts of marginal utility and consumer equilibrium. Suppose that program A gives a family a $1,000 cash benefit, and program B gives the family $1,000 worth of goods in kind, in proportions not selected by the family itself. Which program do you think would be likely to give the family greater utility? To make the question easier to answer, assume a simplified economy where there are only two goods, food and clothing. What if the two goods were food and whiskey?

4. Suppose that there were a universally effective negative income tax in force, so that measured poverty was entirely eliminated. Would you then be willing to see other social insurance programs, including social security (retirement), unemployment insurance, and medicare abolished? Why or why not?

5. What are the relative merits of job market versus transfer strategies for combatting poverty? Do you think either one could ever entirely replace the other? Why or why not?

PART FIVE
The Economics of Life on a Small Planet

In recent years, economists have devoted increasing attention to the interrelated questions of pollution, population, and resource depletion. These questions take on an increased urgency as our planet Earth seems to shrink year by year. Each year there seem to be fewer clean and unpolluted areas remaining. Each year the ratio of the Earth's surface area to its population declines. And each year we burrow deeper into our planet's mines and wells to extract scarce resources that can never be replaced. What does the future hold in store?

Economics, as the "science of scarcity," has much to say about pollution, population, and resource depletion. The more scarcity presses upon us, the more important it is to use what we have wisely. Economics can help in three ways. First, it can help us formulate realistic standards of wise use against which to measure the actual allocation of resources. Second, economics can help identify the sources of past and present errors in resource use. And third, economics can help us to formulate improved policies that will allow us to meet the challenge of the future successfully.

We shall begin in Chapter 33 with the problem of pollution. Here we shall be able to put our familiar tools of supply and demand to work in a novel way to analyze the supply and demand for pollution opportunities. This will give us a framework for comparing several different strategies of pollution control.

Next, in Chapter 34, we shall turn to the problems of population and resource depletion. The problem of population, in particular, has a long history in economic thought. The classical economists of the eighteenth and early nineteenth centuries were, in a sense, pessimists on the question of population. They foretold imminent economic stagnation as population outran food supplies. For a century or more thereafter, such fears seemed groundless. Now, when our world supports more billions of people than the classical economists would ever have dreamed possible, population pessimism is returning.

In both Chapters 33 and 34, we discuss the problems of our shrinking planet largely from the perspective of the United States and other industrialized countries. It is in the countries of the third world, though, that these problems are the most pressing. In Chapter 35, we examine the problems and prospects of less developed economies.

CHAPTER 33
The Economics of Pollution

What You Will Learn in This Chapter
The problem of pollution can be considered from many points of view, but to the economist, it is simply a problem in resource allocation. Disposal of waste products always involves opportunity costs. Either we must suffer a deterioration of the environment, or we must reduce our consumption of material goods, or we must use scarce factors of production in costly efforts at pollution abatement. Our familiar tools of economic analysis, including supply and demand, can help us understand why there is a pollution problem in the first place, and help us to compare alternative policies for controlling pollution.

For Review
Here are some important terms and concepts that will be put to use in this chapter. Be certain that you understand them, or review them before proceeding.

  Opportunity cost (Chapter 1)
  The margin, marginal (Chapter 1)
  Market justice and distributive justice (Chapter 1)

Pollution as an Economic Problem

Pollution and Scarcity

Everyone has something to say about pollution. There are as many different ways of looking at the problem as there are people. Ecologists look at pollution in terms of the disruption of complex systems of plant and animal life. Politicians look at pollution in terms of votes. Moralists look at it in terms of good and evil. Economists also have their own point of view.

From the economic point of view, pollution is a problem of scarcity. The critical scarce resource is the waste disposal capacity of the environment. That capacity is not unlimited. Air, water, and land areas can absorb human wastes to a certain extent without adverse effects. Some production by-products can be incorporated into natural cycles. Small amounts of pollutants can be diluted to imperceptible concentration. However, these capacities for natural recycling and dilution are smaller than the waste output of our economic system in many areas now. Once we have identified pollution as an economic problem, we can apply familiar tools of economic analysis to it. In the discussion that follows, we shall show how such economic ideas as opportunity cost, marginalism, and supply and demand can help us understand the problem of pollution, and find ways to deal with it.

Opportunity Costs

Economists think of environmental issues in terms of *trade-offs* and *opportunity costs*. Some trade-offs involve converting wastes from one form into another. Most methods of pollution abatement do not really *get rid* of wastes, but merely change their physical form. Production and consumption are, after all, subject to the law of the conservation of matter. Scrubbing systems on factory smokestacks convert airborne wastes into waterborne wastes, but they do not reduce the total tonnage of wastes. Sewage treatment systems convert waterborne wastes into solid wastes, but some place must still be found to dump the sludge. Incineration gets rid of solid wastes, but creates airborne wastes.

Recycling

Recycling is often pictured as a way out of these trade-offs. Recycling converts wastes into useful substances rather than other wastes. Yet even recycling involves opportunity costs. To gather bottles and cans and remelt them, or to remove sulfur from the smoke of burning coal and oil requires a lot of energy. Using energy produces waste heat. Ultimately, recycling means trading off *material* pollution for *energy* pollution.

Of course, this does not mean that waste treatment and recycling are futile. It is just *because* wastes cannot be made to vanish that it is very important to release them into the environment in the least destructive way. Changing wastes from one form into another allows us to make the maximum use of scarce environmental waste disposal capacities under a variety of local conditions.

Product Trade-Offs

There is also a second important set of trade-offs bearing on the pollution problem. Pollution can sometimes be reduced by substituting one *product* for another. We can, for example, substitute unleaded for leaded gasoline. We can produce fewer material goods and more services. We can reduce pollution still further by giving up marketable goods and services in favor of such nonmarket goods as increased leisure and the direct enjoyment of nature through outdoor recreation.

The Marginal Principle

All these trade-offs mean a lot of decisions. We cannot make these pollution control decisions without some general standards. To economists, it seems natural to express many of the important standards in *marginal* terms. As an example, let us consider the decision of *how much* pollution should be tolerated. This decision, we can show, requires us to find a balance between two margins.

EXHIBIT 33.1

The marginal social cost of pollution

The marginal social cost of pollution is the total cost to all members of society that results from a one-unit increase in pollution. At low levels of pollution, within the natural absorptive capacity of the environment, the marginal social cost of pollution may be zero. As the quantity of pollution increases, the marginal social cost of pollution probably tends to increase for most pollutants.

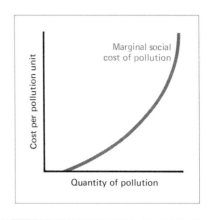

Social Cost

The first margin is the **marginal social cost of pollution.** For a given type of pollution, this means the total cost to all members of society of an additional unit of pollution. Suppose, for example, that in a community of 1,000 people, each additional pound of sulfur dioxide emitted cost *each* person 0.003 cent in the form of damage to painted surfaces, and 0.004 cent in terms of personal discomfort. The marginal social cost of sulfur dioxide pollution in this community could thus be $1,000 \times (0.003 + 0.004)$ = 7 cents per pound.

Marginal Social Cost of Pollution The total cost to all members of society of an additional unit of pollution.

For most kinds of pollution, it is likely that the marginal social cost of pollution increases as its quantity increases. A graph of the marginal cost of pollution would thus have the form shown in Exhibit 33.1. Marginal social cost begins at zero for pollution within the natural absorptive capacity of the environment. As pollution concentrations become first unpleasant and then dangerous, marginal social cost rises to a high level.

Abatement Cost

The second margin is the **marginal cost of pollution abatement.** This means the economic cost of reducing pollution of a given kind by one unit. Other things being equal, the marginal cost of pollution abatement tends to rise as the level of pollution decreases. For example, in controlling automobile exhaust emissions, relatively cheap devices can cut pollution by half. Somewhat more complicated and expensive devices are required to cut it in half again, to the level of 75 percent abatement. Very elaborate and costly methods must be installed to cut it in half a third time, to 87.5 percent abatement, and so forth. With such examples in mind, we draw marginal abatement cost curves with downward slopes, as in Exhibit 33.2.

Marginal Cost of Pollution Abatement The cost of reducing a given kind of pollution by one unit.

Optimum

In Exhibit 33.3, now, we draw both schedules in one diagram. This allows us to identify the point where the marginal cost of abatement is equal to the marginal social cost of pollution. That happens at the point where the two curves intersect. As far as economics is concerned, this is the *optimal quantity of pollution.* Pollution in excess of this amount represents a misallocation of resources. The damage done by additional pollution then exceeds the cost of eliminating it. Excessive abatement, which means oper-

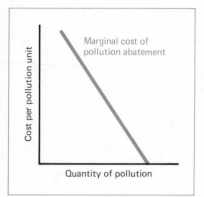

EXHIBIT 33.2
The marginal cost of pollution abatement
The marginal cost of pollution abatement is the cost of reducing pollution by
one unit. The cost of eliminating pollution tends to increase as the percentage
of all pollution eliminated increases. That gives the marginal cost of pollution
abatement a downward slope.

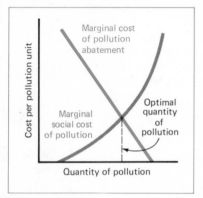

EXHIBIT 33.3
The optimal quantity of pollution
The optimal quantity of pollution is determined by the intersection of the
marginal cost of pollution abatement curve and the marginal social cost of
pollution curve. To the left of that point, the benefits of further reductions in
pollution do not justify the high cost of abatement. To the right of the intersection, the cost of abatement is less than the cost imposed on society by
additional pollution.

ating to the left of the intersection point, is also wasteful. It also represents
an unnecessary reduction in human welfare. If the marginal cost of pollution abatement exceeds the marginal social cost of pollution, we can gain by
trading a small reduction in environmental quality for a relatively large
increase in material production.

Measurement Problems

This marginal analysis gives a simple theoretical standard for pollution
control. The standard is not so easy to apply in practice, however. There
are severe problems of measurement, especially on the side of social cost.
Attempts to measure the social cost of pollution usually concentrate on
such things as damage to property, health cost measured in terms of medical expenses and time lost from work, and the value of wildlife and crops
killed. Actual estimates suffer from several defects.

First, data on the costs of pollution are at best fragmentary. There are
many gaps, which must be filled by pure guesswork. Second, it is difficult
to account for purely subjective costs. These include offenses to aesthetic
sensibilities and discomforts not actually resulting in damage to the health.
Yet these subjective costs have a very real economic value. The fact that
many people spend hard-earned money to avoid the effects of pollution by
leaving polluted areas shows such costs to be real. Finally, estimates of
the social cost of pollution rarely give more than the average cost figures.
Yet it is marginal cost data, much more difficult to obtain, that are really
relevant to pollution policy decisions.

There are problems too in estimating the costs of pollution abatement. One major problem is that calculations must take into account not only the direct costs of getting rid of one form of pollution, but also the social costs of any different forms of pollution produced as a result. Measuring these is subject to all the problems of measuring the social cost of any kind of pollution. We shall have to keep these practical difficulties in mind when we consider policy alternatives.

Economic Strategies for Pollution Control

Supply and Demand

Controlling pollution is a problem of economic policy. As in many other cases, we can use our old friends supply and demand to explain where the problem comes from, and to compare alternative solutions. Let us see how supply and demand analysis can be applied to pollution.

Look at Exhibit 33.4. We have drawn the marginal cost of pollution abatement curve again there, but now we have given it a new name: the *demand curve for pollution opportunities*. It is very easy to understand why the same schedule serves both purposes. Simply ask how much a firm would be willing to pay, if necessary, for the opportunity to dump an additional unit of untreated waste directly into the environment. The answer is that it would pay any sum smaller, but never any sum larger, than the cost of pollution-free waste disposal.

So much for the demand curve. In Exhibit 33.4 we have drawn the supply curve for pollution opportunities as a straight line lying right along the horizontal axis. That indicates that unlimited pollution opportunities are available without paying any price at all. The equilibrium quantity of pollution is found where the two curves intersect. Unless the social cost of pollution is also zero, which is not the case, this equilbrium is not where we want to be. What can be done?

EXHIBIT 33.4
Supply and demand for pollution opportunities
The marginal cost of pollution abatement curve can also be called the demand curve for pollution opportunities. The position of the supply curve for pollution opportunities depends on how much firms must pay in order to discharge wastes into the environment. If they do not have to pay at all, the supply curve will coincide with the horizontal axis as shown here, and the equilibrium quantity of pollution will be greater than the optimum quantity.

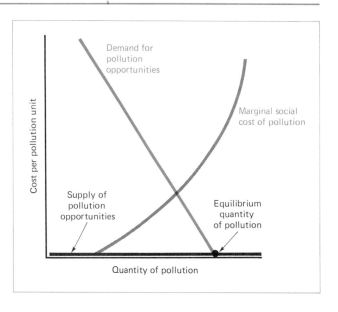

The Regulatory Approach

Most current government policies for controlling pollution take a regulatory approach. Congress sets up some agency with authority to control pollution of particular types or in particular areas. Sometimes the regulators simply set a maximum amount of pollution permitted from each source, and leave the choice of abatement method up to the polluter. In other cases, regulators specify that certain abatement procedures must be followed. Regulation such as this has the effect of rationing pollution opportunities. It can prevent the economic system from ending up on an equilibrium like that shown in Exhibit 33.4, where there is too much pollution.

Although the regulatory approach has in many cases been effective, economists often find fault with it. For one thing, regulations can be written too rigidly, so that they do not give polluters enough incentive to search for the least-cost method of cleaning up their wastes. For another, regulation does not always ensure that the burden of cleaning up will be efficiently allocated among various pollution sources. Critics of the regulatory approach have suggested some alternative strategies for pollution control that more directly make use of supply and demand. Let us examine some of these alternatives.

Residual Charges

Residual Charges Charges of a fixed amount per unit of waste imposed on all sources that discharge a given kind of waste into the environment.

One nonregulatory strategy for controlling pollution works by shifting the pollution opportunity supply curve with **residual charges.** Residual charges, are, in effect, waste disposal taxes. There are charges of a fixed amount per unit of waste, imposed on all sources of a given kind of waste. As an example, consider a residual charge on sulfur dioxide emissions. Suppose that all sources of this type of pollution had to pay a fee of $.05 per pound for all sulfur emitted into the atmosphere.

Exhibit 33.5 shows the effect of such a residual charge. The charge

EXHIBIT 33.5
The effect of a residual charge
A residual charge makes it necessary for polluters to pay for the opportunity to discharge wastes into the environment. Here, the charge is set at $.05 per unit. The residual charge moves the pollution opportunity supply curve upward to the position shown, and forces polluters up and to the left along their demand curve, thus reducing the equilibrium quantity of pollution.

EXHIBIT 33.6

An optimal residual charge

Ideally, a residual charge could be set just high enough to reduce pollution by the optimal amount. Here, the supply curve for pollution opportunities cuts the demand and marginal social cost curves just at their point of intersection. In practice, such fine tuning of residual charges is quite difficult.

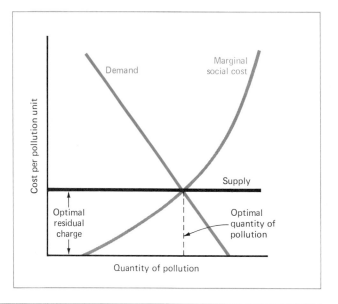

shifts the pollution opportunity supply curve up from its position along the horizontal axis to a position $.05 higher. Polluters would react to the tax by moving back along their demand curve to a new equilibrium where there is less pollution. They will do this because it will pay them to use all pollution abatement methods that can remove a pound of sulfur from stack gases for $.05 or less.

By raising or lowering the amount of charge, any desired degree of pollution control can be achieved. Ideally, the charge would be set so that the pollution opportunity supply curve passes exactly through the intersection of the marginal abatement cost curve (demand curve) and the marginal social cost curve. This ideal situation is shown in Exhibit 33.6. Unfortunately, there is no easy way to determine just where this intersection is, and hence just what the charge should be. The agency responsible for setting the rate of the residual charge is faced with the measurement difficulties we mentioned above.

Objections to Residual Charges

Pollution taxes and residual charges are likely to figure prominently in future policy debates. Let us take a moment to look at some objections one often hears to residual charges. The objections come from three principal sources: industry, consumers, and environmentalists. Industrialists sometimes say that residual charges would impose an "unfair double burden" on industry. They would have to pay the charge at the same time that they are undergoing the expense of installing pollution abatement equipment. Consumers object that industry would be able to pass the burden of the charge along in the form of higher product prices. Environmentalists protest that residual charges mean granting a "license to pollute." They fear that industry would just put up the money and keep right on despoiling the environment as before. Let us take up each of these objections in turn.

Double Burden

The "double burden" objection is the weakest of the three. No industry is ever forced by a residual charge to pay a double burden. Any polluter always has the option of paying the charge and making no effort to reduce pollution at all. In this case, it bears just one burden, that of the charge itself. Any money it spends on pollution abatement equipment will be spent for one reason only. That will be if it is *cheaper* to install the equipment than to pay to pollute. Far from being a second burden added on top of the tax, abatement expenditures represent a way to escape from the tax and hence reduce the total burden.

Passing the Burden

The argument that residual charges can be shifted to consumers has more of an element of truth in it. Exhibit 33.7 shows why. Let D represent the demand curve for a commodity and S the market supply curve, before there is any pollution control policy. These conditions give an equilibrium at E, with a price p and a quantity of output q. A residual charge will raise the marginal cost of production. The increase will be either the amount of tax paid per unit of production or the cost of the abatement equipment needed to avoid payment, whichever is smaller. This will shift the whole supply curve up to the new position S'. The vertical distance between the old and new supply curves is equal to the per unit burden of the charge. With the new supply curve S', equilibrium is at E' with price and quantity p' and q', respectively. The difference between the new price and the old one shows the share of the burden passed along to the consumer. As the figure is drawn, this is about half the burden of the tax. The exact share passed on will vary from product to product, depending on the shapes of the supply and demand curves.

We see, then, that at least part of the burden of a residual charge can be passed along to consumers. But does this really constitute a valid criticism of the policy? A strong argument can be made that it does not. We must remember that *someone* always pays the price of pollution. Different

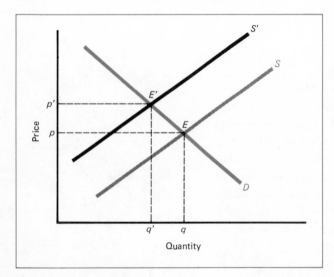

EXHIBIT 33.7
Effect of a residual charge on product price
Here we see the effects of a residual charge in terms of the supply and demand for a product produced by a firm that must pay the charge. The product supply curve is shifted up from S to S'. This causes the equilibrium price of the product to rise from p to p'. Part, but not all, of the cost increase is thus passed along to the consumer.

policies only change *who* pays for it. Under current conditions, producers and consumers of pollution-intensive goods both get a free ride. They shift the burden to innocent third parties. If we want to lift the burden from these third parties, why should consumers expect to be able to continue their free ride?

Higher prices for high-pollution products would actually be beneficial. They would stimulate consumers to make the trade-offs that must be made if the environment is to be protected. If the prices of relatively "dirty" products rise compared to relatively "clean" products and services, consumers would shift their spending patterns accordingly. If firms could not pass along to consumers a part of the pollution taxes imposed upon them, it is not easy to see how the necessary change in consumption habits would come about.

License

The third objection, that residual charges are just a "license to pollute," is open to more than one interpretation. Depending on how it is interpreted, it may be wholly invalid or partially valid.

Sometimes the argument is made to imply that residual charges would have no effect on pollution. It is said that businesses would just pay the charge and carry on as before. But this is flatly incorrect, unless one is going to deny that supply and demand applies to waste disposal as it does to other business activities. At other times, the "license to pollute" argument is meant as an objection to the fact that the taxes would eliminate only a part, and not all of pollution output. In this application, too, the argument violates good economic reasoning. To eliminate *all* pollution regardless of cost, as some environmentalists advocate, would involve greater sacrifices of material welfare than we could justify in terms of consumer satisfaction. Instead we have argued that pollution control should proceed only up to the point where the marginal cost of pollution abatement begins to exceed the marginal social cost of pollution.

A third interpretation of the "license to pollute" argument makes more economic sense. The problem is that no direct compensation is offered to those downwind or downstream of any pollution sources that do continue polluting even after imposition of the charges. To these remaining victims, it seems unjust that a firm can legally continue to make life miserable just by paying a fee to the government. Polluters, it is argued, should pay compensation to their victims, not taxes to the government.

Pollution Control and Property Rights

The question of who should be compensated for pollution damage raises the whole issue of pollution and property rights. The basic idea is this: From the point of view of property rights, pollution is *theft*. If you use the airspace in and around my home as a dumping ground for your unwanted combustion products, you are stealing waste disposal services from me. If you use my living room as a reverberation chamber for noise from your truck or motorcycle, you are robbing me of my right to peace and quiet. As owner, I ought to have the right to prevent you from using my property in these ways, unless you negotiate with me in advance to buy my permission. If you do not, I should be able to bring civil or criminal action against you in a court of law.

Unfortunately, the law, as it now stands, is stacked against property owners and in favor of polluters. Certain changes could be made, however, to redress the balance. It could, for example, be made easier for private citizens to initiate lawsuits when their property is attacked by pollution. At present, property owners often must wait for local governments to take legal action on their behalf. If the polluters have more "pull" in the statehouse or city hall than their victims do, the victims may wait in vain. Also, it could be made easier for large groups of citizens to act jointly, through class action suits or other means, to gain legal redress for damages done to them.

What would be the economic effect of laws permitting property owners to protect themselves from pollution? One possible effect would be the creation of a private market for pollution rights. In this market, people would sell pollution opportunities to firms in return for a price high enough to compensate for the damage done. If all individuals sold pollution rights at prices equal to the marginal cost to them of pollution damage, the pollution market would look as it does in Exhibit 33.8. The pollution opportunity supply curve would follow exactly along the marginal social cost curve. The equilibrium quantity of pollution would be exactly the economically optimal amount.

Objections

Of course, the legal protection of private property rights as a method of pollution control is open to certain practical objections, just like all other methods. One objection is that not all environmental resources that are open to pollution damage are privately owned. Would this mean that polluters would retain unlimited opportunities to dump their wastes in public waterways, world oceans, publicly owned wilderness areas, and the like? One way to overcome the problem would be to auction off all rivers, oceans, national parks, and the like to private owners. The private owners

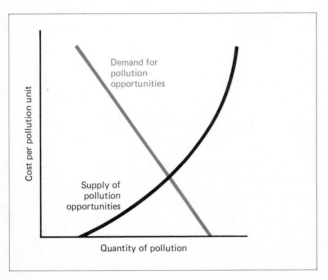

EXHIBIT 33.8
Pollution opportunities with perfect protection of private property
If all property were privately owned and if polluters always had to compensate victims for damage to persons or property, a private market in pollution opportunities would be created. Ideally, the supply curve in this market would exactly coincide with the marginal social cost of pollution curve. The equilibrium quantity of pollution would then equal the optimal quantity.

could then protect them from damage. Short of this radical proposal, taxes and user charges could be used to protect such public resources, while private law protected privately owned resources.

There is a second objection to giving private owners blanket rights to protect their property against pollution. Such a policy might result in excessive reduction in pollution levels. A potential polluter located in a densely populated area might have to negotiate pollution opportunity contracts with tens of thousands of individual small property owners before emitting even a single puff of smoke. The expense of doing this would be prohibitive, even if the actual charges paid to each owner were in themselves reasonable. To avoid these expenses a firm might spend far more than the economically optimal amount on pollution abatement. Perhaps, of course, we have suffered from too much pollution for so long that it would be a pleasant novelty to suffer from too little. Speaking more practically, though, we might concede that the property-rights approach probably works best when the impact of pollution is relatively concentrated. Some type of residual charge scheme may be a better answer when damages are very widely dispersed.

Conclusions

The main objective of pollution control, as we have discussed it in this chapter, has been to improve the efficiency of resource allocation. A complete analysis of environmental policy should look at the normative implications of these policies as well. In concluding our discussion, let us look at pollution control policies in terms of market justice and distributive justice.

By the standard of market justice, the effects of pollution control policies of almost any kind appear to be beneficial. Pollution is theft. It is a form of coercion through which producers enjoy unjustifiably high profits, and consumers of high-pollution products enjoy unjustifiably low prices. Third parties, as victims of pollution, are unwillingly forced to bear the costs without sharing in the benefits. Policies that put a price tag on pollution help to correct these injustices by making everyone pay the full cost of the things produced and consumed.

Strictly speaking, according to the standard of market justice, a policy should not only impose penalties on polluters, but should also provide compensation to its victims. Policies based on enforcement of private property rights, including the right of pollution victims to sue for damages, do this, while residual charges do not.

From the point of view of distributive justice, the effects of pollution control policies are more problematical. If one's notion of distributive justice is simply increased equality of real incomes, antipollution measures may well make things worse. We would have to study carefully the exact distribution of the costs and benefits of various alternative policies in order to be certain on this point. Without such study, we can only make some conjectures. These conjectures suggest, however, that low-income groups might not fare well. They might bear a disproportionately large share of the costs of pollution control policies, and receive a disproportionately small share of the benefits.

One result of effective pollution control policies, as we have seen, must be to raise the prices of goods to consumers. Low-income groups spend a larger portion of their budget on material goods and devote a smaller portion to consumption of services and to savings. The burden of pollution taxes might thus be expected to rest more heavily on them in proportion to their incomes.

At the same time, it seems likely that the benefits of pollution control policies are less valuable to the poor than to the rich. Suppose that the benefits of pollution control were equally distributed in *physical* terms. For example, suppose that the level of air pollution were lowered just as much in low-income as in high-income neighborhoods. This does not mean that the benefit would be equally distributed in *economic* terms. Clean air and other environmental amenities are to a considerable extent "luxury goods." They have a high value to those who already have a generous supply of material goods, and a relatively low value to those who do not. How many pounds of beef, or pairs of shoes, or dollars, would poor people be willing to give up in order to reduce by half the sulfur dioxide content of the air they breathe? How much would wealthy people be willing to sacrifice for the same purpose? It is easy to see that, at least beyond a certain point, pollution control policies may reflect the tastes only of the relatively well-to-do.

SUMMARY

1. Pollution can be viewed as a problem in the allocation of scarce resources. In this case, the scarce resource is the waste-absorption capacity of the environment. Once this capacity is exceeded, further waste disposal must incur opportunity costs of one kind or another. If wastes are discharged untreated into the environment, the opportunity costs take the form of a less healthy and pleasant world in which to live. If costly pollution abatement techniques are used, scarce factors of production must be diverted from other uses. No policy can help us avoid these trade-offs altogether. The economic problem of pollution is how to balance the social cost of pollution against the economic cost of pollution abatement.

2. Supply and demand analysis can be applied to the problem of pollution control. The marginal cost of pollution abatement curve can be thought of as a demand curve for pollution. If there are no pollution controls of any kind, the supply curve for pollution opportunities is a horizontal line at zero height. The equilibrium quantity of pollution will be too high when the supply curve has that shape. All pollution control policies aim in one way or another to limit the supply of pollution opportunities.

3. The regulatory approach to pollution abatement is, in effect, a form of administrative rationing for pollution opportunities. It has been effective in some cases, but economists often criticize it as inefficient. Residual charges are an alternative pollution control method. Under a residual charge scheme, the supply curve for pollution opportunities becomes a horizontal line at a height equal to the charge per unit of waste. Still another approach to pollution control is through the enforcement of private property rights. Ideally, if all property were privately owned, and polluters had to compensate owners for all damage to persons and property, the supply of pollution opportunities curve would coincide with the marginal social cost of pollution curve. Each approach has its advantages and its practical difficulties. For the moment, it seems worthwhile to experiment with all methods.

4. Pollution raises normative as well as positive issues. One such issue is that of compensating victims of pollution. The regulatory and residual charge approaches to pollution control do not compensate victims. Pollution control via defense of private property rights appears to be superior in this respect. Another normative question concerns the distributive impact of pollution control. In the absence of firm evidence to the contrary, it seems plausible to think that the costs of pollution control may be borne more than proportionately by the poor, and the benefits of pollution control may accrue more proportionately to the well-to-do.

DISCUSSION QUESTIONS

1. Why has pollution become a major national policy issue only recently? Is pollution worse that it used to be? Do the cars of New York City today discharge more waste each day than the horses of New York City did in 1901? Has our high standard of living actually caused more pollution, or has it made us less willing to tolerate it than we used to, or has it done both?
2. Can you think of circumstances in which the marginal social cost of waste disposal for a firm is also a part of its explicit private costs of production? Of its implicit private costs? Of neither its implicit nor its explicit costs?
3. When does "waste disposal" become "pollution"? How do you distinguish between the two? Is the distinction a matter of positive economics or of normative economics?
4. Many environmentalists are uncomfortable with the concept of an economically optimal amount of pollution. They tend to think that less pollution is always better. Do you agree? Do you think that the difference between these environmentalists' viewpoint and the viewpoint set forth in this chapter is one of values or of analysis?
5. Suppose that you are a member of Congress when a bill comes up to abolish all specific pollution control regulations for automobile exhausts. In place of the present regulations, there would be a residual charge of $.01 per mile placed on all driving. The rate of charge would be reduced appropriately for those drivers who could prove that their cars were equipped with effective emission control devices. Would you favor this measure? Why or why not? If your only objection is that you think $.01 per mile is too low a charge, how high do you think the rate should be?
6. Many of the Great Lakes have become seriously polluted. Among the people damaged by this are the owners of lakefront property. Do you think that these owners ought to be permitted to bring suit against any company polluting the lake where their property is located? If such suits were permitted, do you think many would be brought? Should property owners who win their cases against polluters be able to obtain a cease-and-desist order stopping all further pollution, or should they simply be awarded monetary damages?

CHAPTER 34
Population, Resources, and the Economic Future

What You Will Learn in This Chapter
In recent years the economic future has become a subject of increasing public concern. Certain problems must be overcome in order to ensure continued long-term economic growth. The problem of pollution is one of them. Other problems are population growth and the depletion of nonrenewable resources. These problems are at least partly economic in nature. A study of population movements in the past, and their relation to economic development, can help us assess our prospects for the future. We also need to understand how markets allocate nonrenewable resources over time, and how they respond to the increasing scarcity of such resources.

For Review
Here are some important terms and concepts that will be put to use in this chapter. Be certain that you understand them, or review them before proceeding.
    Resource allocation (Chapter 2)
    Diminishing returns (Chapter 22)

We have spent many chapters in this book discussing the questions of *what, how, who,* and *for whom.* In recent years, increasing attention has been drawn to a fifth great economic question: *how long?* How long will scarce resources last? How long can economic growth continue? How long will we be able to continue feeding ourselves? The question of *how long* brings kinds of scarcities to our attention that we have not paid much attention to up to now. These are scarcities that arise from the limited size of the planet Earth itself. There is room on our planet for only a finite number of human beings. The mineral resources of the planet can last only a finite length of time at present rates of consumption. The economic future cannot simply be an endless extrapolation of past economic trends.

In part, our economic future depends on whether we learn to deal successfully with the problem of pollution, discussed in the last chapter. If pollution does not do us in, there remain two other major problem areas, population growth and resource depletion. We shall discuss these two in what follows.

The Economics of Population

Population Arithmetic

We can begin by reviewing some of the simple arithmetic of population growth. For a population to increase, it is obvious that more people must be born than die each year. (In saying this and in what follows, we ignore immigration and emigration.) The number of people born into a population per 1,000 per year is the **crude birth rate** for that population. The number who die per 1,000 per year is the **crude death rate.** The difference between the two is called the **rate of natural increase.**

Exhibit 34.1 shows crude birth rates, crude death rates, and rates of natural increase for a selection of countries, according to the latest available data. In interpreting data such as these, it sometimes helps to translate rates of natural increase into population doubling times. We have done this in the last column of the table. The faster the rate of natural increase, the shorter the period of time required for the population to double in size.

Growth Curves

A population that grew indefinitely at a constant rate of natural increase would double each time a fixed number of years elapsed. It would reach 2, 4, 8, 16, 32, 64 (and so forth) times its original size, following the

Crude Birth Rate   The number of people born into a population per 1,000 per year.

Crude Death Rate   The number of people in a population who die per 1,000 per year.

Rate of Natural Increase   The current rate of growth of a population calculated as the crude birth rate minus the crude death rate.

EXHIBIT 34.1
Birth rates, death rates, and natural increase of population for selected countries, 1969–1970
The current rate of population growth for a country can be found by subtracting the crude death rate from the crude birth rate. The faster the rate of population growth, the shorter the time period required for the population to double.

Country	Crude Birth Rate	Crude Death Rate	Rate of Natural Increase	Approximate Doubling Time of Population (years)
Ecuador	44.9	11.4	33.5	21
Mexico	43.2	9.7	33.5	21
Pakistan	50.9	18.4	32.5	21
Algeria	49.1	16.9	32.2	22
Kenya	47.8	17.5	30.3	23
Zambia	49.8	20.7	21.9	24
India	42.8	16.7	26.1	27
Afghanistan	50.5	26.5	24.0	29
Egypt	36.8	14.4	22.4	31
Cuba	29.6	7.5	19.1	37
Argentina	22.5	8.6	13.9	50
Japan	18.8	6.9	11.9	59
Australia	20.4	8.7	11.7	60
USSR	17.0	8.1	8.9	79
United States	17.9	9.5	8.4	83
Italy	17.5	10.1	7.4	95
France	16.7	11.4	5.3	132
United Kingdom	16.7	11.9	4.8	148
Czechoslovakia	15.5	11.2	4.3	163

Source: UN Statistical Yearbook, 1973.

EXHIBIT 34.2

Typical S-shaped curve of population growth

A living population cannot grow indefinitely in a finite environment. Under laboratory conditions, populations of bacteria or fruitflies or other organisms tend to follow S-shaped growth curves such as the one shown here. In the long run, it seems inevitable that the growth curve of human population will also begin to decrease.

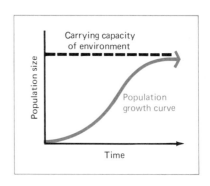

same sort of growth path as that followed by the value of a sum of money invested at compound interest. Normally, however, living populations are not able to grow exponentially without limit. Suppose that bacteria are allowed to multiply in a jar of nutrient, or a population of fruitflies is allowed to grow in a glass cage or a room of fixed size, or a breeding pair of dogs is introduced on an island previously inhabited only by rabbits. Under such conditions, the growth of the population of bacteria, fruitflies, or dogs typically follows the kind of S-shaped growth curve shown in Exhibit 34.2. At first, the population will expand at an exponential rate. The biological characteristics of the species in question determine the population doubling time under optimal conditions. Sooner or later, though, the population will begin to fill up its jar or cage or island or whatever. Then, under more crowded conditions, the time needed to double the population will increase. Eventually, overcrowding will bring population growth to a halt.

Must the growth of human population also be subject to this S-curve pattern? In the long run, it surely must. Estimates of the maximum human population of earth vary widely, but no one doubts that there is some finite ceiling. (One admittedly fanciful estimate places the limit as high as 20 million times the present world population. This would require people to live 120 to the square meter in a 2,000-story building covering the entire earth. Even that limit would take only 890 years to reach at the present rate of growth of world population!)

In the short run, though, the growth of human population has not followed the simple S-curve pattern. In fact, over as long a period as any kind of population estimates can be made, the world rate of natural increase has been accelerating, not slowing down. World population has doubled in about the last 45 years, and will double again in the next 35, if the current rate of growth continues. The last preceding doubling of population took about 80 years, from 1850 to 1930. The doubling before that took some 200 years. It is hard to imagine that this trend will continue. We must be living at present very close to the bend in the world population curve, after which the rate of population will begin to decline.

Population Equilibrium

There is really no doubt whatever that the level of human population is headed for an equilibrium state in which births will just balance deaths. The really interesting question is what will that equilibrium look like? Let us explore some possibilities.

First, imagine a market economy in which people earn money to buy the necessities of life only by selling factor services. The population begins to approach some fixed limit to population growth, defined, for example, by the food supply. Income is distributed unequally in this society. As population nears the ceiling, the price of food will rise relative to the wage rate. The lowest-income groups will find their standard of living reduced, and this will eventually affect their birth and death rates. At some point there will begin to be an excess of deaths over births among the poorest classes. This will be accompanied by a balance between births and deaths for those living just at the margin of subsistence. An excess of births will be possible only among the well-to-do. When enough people have finally been pushed down to or below the margin of subsistence, population growth as a whole will cease. We can call the result a *marginal subsistence equilibrium* for population.

A marginal subsistence equilibrium assumes great inequality. It implies affluence for a few against the backdrop of destitute masses, whose members are continuously replenished by the excess children of the rich driven down into poverty. If we remove the assumption of inequality, the result is a second type of population equilibrium, which we can call the *absolute subsistence equilibrium.* Under this solution, as crowding begins to lower the living standards of a population, taxes and transfers are used to share the burden equally among all. This equality permits population growth to go on longer; no one is starved or crowded to the point that they cannot reproduce until everyone is starved or crowded to that point. The total number of people living in poverty in the absolute subsistence equilibrium is greater than in the marginal subsistence equilibrium.

Dismal Economics

Population projections like these were what once caused economics to be called the "dismal science." As long ago as 1798, Thomas Malthus forecast a marginal subsistence population equilibrium for humanity. This would come about through the operation of the law of diminishing returns, as a growing population caught up with a fixed supply of agricultural land. According to Malthus' theory, only the landlords who owned the means of producing precious food would escape eventual poverty. Even the capitalists would eventually be ground down and their profits reduced to zero.

Malthus' prophecy has not come true for Great Britain, the United States, or other advanced industrial countries. These countries have instead achieved, or nearly achieved, a nonsubsistence population equilibrium with low birth rates, low death rates, and high living standards. The process by which this has been achieved is a good illustration of how economic and demographic processes interact.

The Demographic Transition

In a preindustrial society, birth rates and death rates are both very high, and the rate of natural increase of population is low. With industrialization and economic development, per capita incomes begin to rise. The first demographic effect of rising income is a reduction in the death rate. This is brought about by better nutrition, better hygiene, and better medical care. With the birth rate remaining high, the drop in the death

Thomas Robert Malthus was born in England in 1766, and received what was, for his time, a radical upbringing. His father was an admirer of Rousseau and Condorcet. One of his tutors was imprisoned for expressing the wish that the French revolutionaries would invade and liberate England. He studied at Cambridge, took holy orders, and became a curate.

In 1793 a book appeared that had a great impact on the circles in which young Malthus moved. The book was *Enquiry Concerning Political Justice and Its Influence on Morals and Happiness* by the anarchist and socialist William Godwin. As a result of many lively debates over this book and subsequent essays by Godwin, Malthus decided to write down his own view that population growth constituted an insurmountable barrier to a society of absolute equality and abundance. This writing appeared as *An Essay on the Principle of Population* in 1798.

The heart of Malthus' argument was the doctrine that population tended to grow in geometric progression (2, 4, 8, 16, and so forth) while the means of subsistence grew only in arithmetic progression (2, 4, 6, 8, and so forth). As population increased, increasingly less-fertile land would have to be brought into cultivation. Population would outstrip food production, and wages would be driven down to the subsistence level.

Famine, vice, misery, and war could be avoided only if people engaged in "moral restraint," that is, later marriages with fewer children per family. Schemes such as the Poor Laws or subsidized housing for the poor were worse than useless. They simply encouraged population growth, and hence led to an actual deterioration of conditions.

Malthus' views influenced Darwin in developing his "survival of the fittest" doctrine in the nineteenth century. More than anyone else, it was Malthus who was responsible for earning political economy the name of the "dismal science." Not everyone has interpreted Malthus in such a negative light, however. John Maynard Keynes placed Malthus firmly in "the English tradition of humane science . . . a tradition marked by a love of truth and a most noble lucidity, . . . and by an immense disinterestedness and public spirit."

Thomas Robert Malthus (1766–1834)

rate increases the rate of natural increase. Population enters a phase of very rapid growth.

If there are sufficient natural resources, and if there is enough investment in new capital, economic growth can outstrip population growth. Per capita income then rises. This has happened in all the major industrialized countries of the world. In these countries, rising per capita incomes have eventually caused the birth rate to fall. Population growth has then slowed, and population equilibrium has been approached.

The whole cycle, from falling death rates to rapid population growth to falling birth rates and equilibrium, is called the **demographic transition.** Exhibit 34.3 provides a graphical representation of the demographic transition. Part *a* of this exhibit represents the course of the crude birth rate and death rate over time. Part *b* shows what happens to the rate of natural increase as it first rises and then falls. Part *c* shows the familiar S-curve pattern of population growth that results from the demographic transition. The human population growth curve shown there differs in an important respect from that of flies in a cage or dogs on an island. The difference is that it levels off at an equilibrium population below the biologically maximum level set by subsistence requirements.

The crucial part of the demographic transition is the fall in birth rates produced by rapid economic development. Demographers do not completely

Demographic Transition A population cycle that accompanies economic development, beginning with a fall in the death rate, continuing with a phase of rapid population growth, and concluding with a decline in the birth rate.

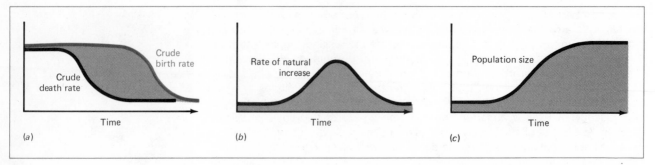

EXHIBIT 34.3
The demographic transition
In a preindustrial society, both birth rates and death rates are high, so that population growth is slow. The first effect of economic development is a drop in the death rate. This brings on a period of rapid population growth. As economic development continues, the birth rate begins to fall. Population growth decelerates and eventually may fall to zero.

understand the mechanisms that bring about this decline in birth rates. In large part, the decline is probably caused by increasing urbanization. Traditionally, a large number of children is an economic asset to a farm family, because children can contribute to production from an early age. In the city, children tend to be an economic burden. There is no guarantee of remunerative jobs for them, and their food, clothing, and housing cannot be produced at home. More subtle changes in life styles and attitudes toward family life, which occur as income rises, also seem to be involved in the demographic transition.

Net Reproduction

To complete the demographic transition and approach an equilibrium population takes many decades. To understand why the transition takes so long, we need to know more about population growth than crude birth rates and crude death rates alone can tell us.

Crude birth rates and death rates can be misleading because they depend on both the underlying reproductive behavior of a population and its age structure. A more direct measure of reproductive behavior is the **net reproduction rate** for a population. The net reproduction rate is the average number of daughters born to each female child in the population over her lifetime. If the net reproduction rate is equal to one, then the population is, in the long run, just replacing itself. If it is greater than one, then the population has a long-run tendency to grow. If it is less than one, it has a long-run tendency to shrink.

In the short run, the rate of natural increase in a population may be positive even when the net reproduction rate is one or less. In particular, this will happen when population growth has been slowing in the recent past. The present population of the United States provides a case in point. The net reproduction rate in the United States is now very close to one, but it has fallen to that level only recently. The elderly people now in high mortality brackets are members of the relatively small generation born around the turn of the century. Those in the high fertility range are mem-

Net Reproduction Rate The inherent long-term rate of growth of a population, measured as the average number of daughters born to each female child over her lifetime.

bers of the much larger generation who were born immediately after World War II. The disproportion in the size of the generations causes the crude death rate to be lower than it will eventually be in the long-run equilibrium, and the crude birth rate to be higher. If there is no further change in reproductive behavior, and the net reproductive rate remains approximately equal to one, it will take some 40 to 60 years for the rate of natural increase to fall to zero. Only at that date will the demographic transition in this country be altogether complete.

Population Policy

In a country where the net reproduction rate is as low as it is in the United States, there is really no pressing problem of population policy. True, some people who think the country is already overcrowded would prefer immediate zero population growth. As an immediate objective, however, zero population growth would require fairly drastic policies, such as licensing of motherhood or compulsory contraception. Most people would probably prefer gradually coasting to a halt as we now appear to be doing.

Population growth *is* a serious problem for economic policy, though, in all those countries that have not completed the demographic transition. That includes most of the world outside the advanced industrial economies of the Northern Hemisphere. We shall return to a discussion of the particular problems of population and economic development in the next chapter.

The Economics of Running Out

Let us turn now to another aspect of the question *how long?* This is the scarcity of resources that are limited primarily in terms of their stocks rather than their flows. Using up these resources means eventually running out of them.

Sources and Sinks

The things we are running out of can be classified as **sources** and **sinks.**[1] Sources are naturally occurring stocks of useful productive inputs. Sinks are naturally occurring means of disposing of useless or harmful by-products and consumption. Both are scarce.

The sources whose scarcity is of greatest concern are those of metals and fossil fuels. The currently usable sources of some of these things appear to be in startlingly short supply relative to current rates of use. Charts like the one shown in Exhibit 34.4 have received wide publicity. This chart shows that currently exploitable sources of at least eleven vital raw materials will not last out the lifetime of students now in college. A number of important sources, it appears, will not even last out the lifetime of those students' dogs and cats!

Comparable figures for the most important natural sinks are more difficult to come by. Some natural sinks—the capacity of lakes and rivers

Sources Naturally occurring stocks of useful productive inputs.

Sinks Naturally occurring means of disposing of useless or harmful by-products of production and consumption.

---

[1]The theory we are about to look at applies only to sources and sinks that are privately owned. Many sources, including mines, oil wells, and the like are in fact privately owned. Many sinks, in contrast, are not. The problem of intelligent use of such natural sinks as the air and large bodies of water, when these are not private property, were discussed in the chapter on pollution.

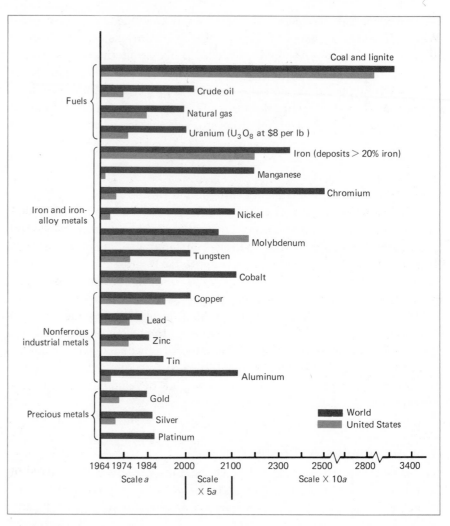

EXHIBIT 34.4

Estimated lifetimes of recoverable mineral resources

This exhibit shows lifetimes of estimated recoverable reserves of mineral resources. Reserves are those that are of high enough grade to be mined with today's techniques. Increasing population and consumption rates, unknown deposits, and future use of presently submarginal ores, are not considered.

Source: From p. 71 of *Population, Resources, Environment: Issues in Human Ecology,* 2nd ed., by Paul R. Ehrlich and Anne H. Ehrlich. W. H. Freeman and Company. Copyright © 1972. First appeared in Preston E. Cloud, Jr., "Realities of Mineral Distribution," *Texas Quarterly,* Vol. 11 (1968), pp. 103–126. Reprinted by permission.

to bear human and industrial wastes, for example—have already been exhausted in places. They must be replaced by costly artificial means of disposal. Of more concern for the long run are three sinks for which no known artificial substitutes are available.

The first of these is the earth's capacity to absorb waste heat from energy-using economic activities. At present rates of growth of energy use, the production of waste heat is estimated to reach the danger level in about 100 years. If drastic climatic effects are to be avoided, we shall have to begin before that point to rely on so-called invariant energy sources. These are sources like solar, wind, wave and geothermal power, which only redirect energy naturally present in the environment, unlike fossil fuels, nuclear fission, and nuclear fusion, which make net additions to the earth's energy balance.

The second sink that is a long-run concern is the ability of the atmosphere to absorb carbon dioxide. Since 1880, the carbon dioxide content of the atmosphere appears to have increased by about 12 percent. A significant part of this increase is believed to have been caused by combustion of fossil fuels. Beyond some point, excessive carbon dioxide in the air would have serious climatic effects, because atmospheric carbon dioxide limits the rate at which the earth can radiate excess energy into space.

There is a third troublesome kind of sink that no one quite knows what to do about. This is the kind of sink needed to dispose of the radioactive by-products of nuclear power production. Many nuclear by-products are so toxic that they will have to be kept sealed away from contact with the environment for 1,000 years or more. That is why nuclear engineers sometimes call the disposal of radioactive wastes the "thousand-year problem." Engineers are hoping that they will be able to solve the thousand-year problem sooner or later, but for now, many radioactive wastes are being stored in temporary facilities.

Market Allocation over Time

The main economic problem that arises in connection with depletable sources and sinks is how to allocate them over time. Should they be used up as fast as possible, in the hope that something will be there to replace them when they run out? Should they be severely rationed so that they will last as long as possible? Should their rate of use be gradually tapered off year by year? As a starting point for answering these questions, let us look at how the market allocates resources over time.

Suppose that there is some resource that exists in a known, limited quantity and costs very little to extract from the sources where it is found. Let us use natural gas, just for the sake of example. The owners of natural gas wells can either sell their gas now, or conserve it to sell in the future. Each alternative has its advantages. If they sell their gas now, they can use the revenue they take in to invest in stocks or bonds, to provide them an interest income after their gas supplies are exhausted. On the other hand, if some resource owners conserve their gas while others sell now, the owners who hold back may be able to sell at a higher price later. Gas will then be even scarcer than it is at present. Which should owners do: sell now, or wait?

It is not hard to figure out what will happen if this decision is left to the market. Enough gas will be sold now to ensure that the price will be pushed up in the future, as less and less is left. Enough gas will be conserved, however, so that the *expected rate of increase in price will not exceed the market rate of interest*. To confirm this, suppose for a moment that it were not true. Let us say that the price next year is expected to be 15 percent higher than this year, but that the market rate of interest is only 10 percent. Any one resource owner can hold back $1,000 worth of gas, and sell it next year for $1,150. His alternative would be to sell now, and invest the $1,000 in securities that will be worth $1,100 next year, including accumulated interest.

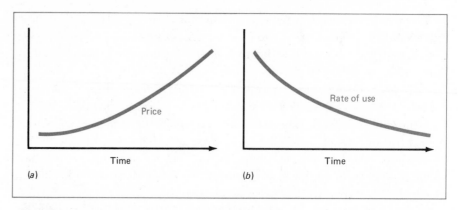

EXHIBIT 34.5
Market allocation over time of a nonrenewable resource
The market price of a nonrenewable resource tends to rise over time. Supply
and demand conditions limit the rate of depletion, so the price will not rise
at a rate faster than the rate of interest. As the price rises, the rate of use
falls, other things being equal.

The alternative of holding back is clearly the more profitable. As some
producers begin to turn off their production valves, though, the quantity
of gas currently supplied will decrease. That will cause the current price
to be bid up by supply and demand. At the same time, the larger quantity
of gas left in reserve will tend to depress the expected price next year. Only
when the spread between this year's and next year's price has diminished
to 10 percent will owners stop switching from current production to
conservation.

In short, when there is a resource that exists in a known, fixed quantity,
and whose cost of extraction is low, the market will allocate that resource
over time as shown in Exhibit 34.5. The price will rise over time at a rate
equal to the rate of interest. Other things being equal, the rate of use will
fall as the price rises.[2]

Qualifications

The preceding argument puts a maximum on the rate at which the
price of a scarce resource will increase and the rate at which it will be used
up. There are circumstances under which the rate of use and of price increase would be less rapid than the rate of interest. In particular, this would
be the case if the resource were costly to extract, or if high prices stimulated
a search for new reserves or for substitutes. Let us consider some examples.

First, suppose that the current price of a resource is equal to the current marginal cost of extracting it. In that case, the quantity supplied will
be limited by the quantity demanded at the current price rather than by
the expected effect of current use on future prices. The quantity demanded
may very well not be high enough to deplete the resource fast enough to
push its future price up at a rate equal to the interest rate.

[2]If economic growth or population growth cause the demand curve for the resource
to shift steadily to the right as time goes by, this pattern may be somewhat modified. The
rate of price rise will still not exceed the rate of interest, but the rate of use could, for a time,
increase before it begins to taper off.

Second, consider the possibility that there are reserves of a resource that cannot be profitably exploited now, but that can be used if the price rises a little. The presence of those reserves may limit the rate of price increase, because they will increase expected future supply. In practice, the usable reserves of many important resources do appear to increase quite elastically as demand and prices rise. Partly this is because higher prices make it worthwhile to spend more money on exploration, and partly because they make it worthwhile to exploit known low-grade reserves. The tendency of reserves to expand and prices to increase makes data like those given in Exhibit 34.4 of little use for serious planning of resource policy. Oil reserves are a case in point. Between 1950 and 1968, oil production expanded by 280 percent, but proved reserves increased by 420 percent. It would have been an error to have based policy in the early 1950s on the assumption that the world's reserves of oil would be exhausted by the early 1960s.

Finally, we must consider the possibility that high prices for natural resources will stimulate the production of substitutes. The following case study describes how this can happen.

CASE 34.1
Commercial Development of Alternative Energy Sources

As oil prices increased during the 1970s, a great interest in alternative energy sources developed. Congress voted funds for long-range studies of wind power, solar power, geothermal power, and even wave power. The price increase did more than just stimulate activity in Congressional committee rooms, however. It brought a response from the market as well. Entrepreneurs, some operating on a large scale and others working in their own basements, moved to exploit the new price conditions. The American Solar Heat Corporation (AMSOLHEAT) of Danbury, Connecticut, is a typical example of this kind of entrepreneurship.

Note the emphasis on relative price changes in the AMSOLHEAT advertisement reproduced in Exhibit 34.6. The firm offers nothing really new in the way of technology. It uses techniques that were already in use during the 1940s and 1950s, before cheap energy made them uneconomical. Now, at current prices for oil and gas, solar hot water heat is again economical. It can be sold not as a plaything, but as a practical way for homeowners to save money on their energy bills.

None of what we have said guarantees, of course, that we shall always have unlimited supplies of all resources we want. The point is rather that, in a market economy, we do not have to worry about just "running out" some day, like falling off a cliff. As natural resources reserves are depleted, prices will rise. The price rise will slow the rate of growth of consumption. This interaction between reserves and current prices is the market's way of looking ahead, and can be counted on to produce a smooth transition to changing circumstances.

Conclusions

Can we conclude that we live in the "best of all possible worlds," in which we do not need to worry about a population explosion or the depletion of scarce natural resources? Unfortunately, we cannot. Two worries remain.

EXHIBIT 34.6

A market response to the energy crisis
When the oil embargo pushed the cost of energy up, entrepreneur Joseph Heyman of Ridgefield, Connecticut, responded by founding the American Solar Heat Corporation (AMSOLHEAT). His product uses technology that has long been known, but was uneconomical while conventional fuels were cheap.
Source: American Solar Heat Corp., Danbury, Conn.

One worry is that resource owners will be stupid and short sighted, and will allow their resources to be depleted at a rate faster than the rate that will give them the highest possible income in the long run. Anecdotal evidence suggests that in years past, especially in the frontier era when people thought that natural resources were altogether unlimited and would never run out, this kind of private short sightedness may sometimes have occurred. Today we presumably have less to fear from the failure of resource owners to pursue their own self-interest.

A second, more serious worry arises from the fact that not all natural resources are under the control of private owners. In the last chapter, we saw how scarce natural sinks could sometimes be polluted up to and beyond their absorption capacity when those sinks were publicly owned and left free for every user. Much the same thing can happen when depletable sources of minerals or fossil fuels are controlled by political rather than market forces.

The American government's policy on oil and natural gas is a clear case in which political forces have operated more short sightedly than market forces. For years, the Federal Power Commission, which regulates natural gas prices, acted in the short-run interest of powerful consumer groups by forcing gas producers to sell at a regulated price below the market equilibrium price. As a result, natural gas has been used extremely wastefully. It has even been used for electric power generation, where more efficient substitutes are available. Natural gas reserves are now far below what they would be if control of pricing and production had been left to the market. More recently, the same mistake has been repeated with oil prices. Fearing political repercussions, Congress has legislated artificially low prices for petroleum products. Again, the result is predictable. Depletion of scarce known reserves will be accelerated, existing supplies will be used wastefully, and research on alternative energy sources will be retarded.

We must conclude with a final warning about a possible misinterpretation of the economic theory of resource markets. Economic theory tells us that the market can reasonably be relied on to guarantee efficient use of depletable natural resources. That does not mean, however, that the scarcity of natural resources imposes no limit to economic growth. Even if resources were used with perfect efficiency, the world could eventually face a decline in output and living standards as things run out.

There is no doubt that the depletion of natural resources puts a drag on economic growth. Up to now, that drag has been more than compensated for by advances in technology and the accumulation of capital, both of which permit higher levels of output per unit of natural resource input. However, no purely theoretical consideration can guarantee that technology and capital accumulation will always advance fast enough to save us. A sufficient rate of capital accumulation is a particularly important requirement for continued growth. It takes more investment per unit of output to build solar power stations than oil-fired power stations. It takes more investment per unit of output to build nonpolluting factories than to use natural sinks for waste disposal. It takes more capital per unit of resources to extract metals from low-grade than from high-grade ores. Economists can only hope that capital accumulation and technological progress will win the race against depletion. No promises can be made.

SUMMARY

1. A population grows whenever its crude birth rate exceeds its crude death rate. In a finite environment, living populations cannot grow indefinitely. If the birth rate does not fall to the death rate, overcrowding will force the death rate up to the birth rate.

2. Population growth in developed countries has undergone a process known as the demographic transition. In preindustrial society, both birth and death rates were high. As industrialization began, death rates fell, and a period of rapid population growth began. Economic growth was even more rapid than population growth, however, so per capita incomes rose. This brought death rates down and reduced the rate of population growth.

3. In a market economy, the forces of supply and demand limit the rate at which nonrenewable natural resources are depleted. Too rapid depletion would drive current prices down and push expected future prices up so that the expected rate of price increase would exceed the rate of interest. Resource owners would then find it to their advantage to reduce current supply in order to sell later when the price was higher. The rate of price increase for a nonrenewable resource in a market economy thus tends to be equal to or less than the rate of interest. This encourages a proper balance between capital accumulation and resource conservation as alternative ways of preparing for the economic future.

DISCUSSION QUESTIONS

1. Do you agree that we must be near the bend in an S-shaped world population curve, even though every bit of evidence from the past points to continuous acceleration of world population growth? If so, why? If not, explain how you think continued acceleration of population growth can continue.

2. In early phases of industrialization, urbanization seems to be a major factor in bringing birth rates down. Today, birth rates are still falling in the United States, even though the degree of urbanization is no longer changing rapidly. What other factors do you think are at work causing the continued decline in birth rates?

3. One method to limit population growth in the United States works like this. Each person, when born, would be given one birth permit allowing him or her to have a child. Each couple could then have two children if they wanted. If they wanted fewer than two children, they could sell their excess certificate or certificates to couples who wanted more than two. Would you favor such a proposal under current conditions? Would you favor such a proposal in comparison to other population control policies if changing circumstances seemed to make overpopulation a much greater danger for this country than it is now? Assume now that the proposal were implemented, and that the net reproduction rate in this country remained below one. What would you expect to happen to the market price of birth permits?

4. Suppose that you are due to inherit $1 million when you graduate from college. You take a course in environmental studies, and your professor convinces you that short-sighted capitalists are using up mineral and energy resources at far too fast a rate, so that we shall soon run out of many important ores and minerals altogether. Would this give you any ideas about profitable ways to invest your million? Do you think your professor believes firmly enough in his predictions to invest his own savings the same way?

5. Review the AMSOLHEAT advertisement reproduced in Exhibit 34.6. How much is your hot water bill each year? (If you do not pay your own hot water bill, ask your parents or your professor what a typical family in your town pays for hot water.) If you could cut this bill by 70 percent, would it pay you to spend $1,260 on a solar hot water heater? (Assume that you can finance the project with a 12 percent home improvement loan from your local bank.) If your answer is no, how low would the interest rate have to be to make the solar heater pay, given the size of your hot water bill? How big would your water bill have to be, given a 12 percent rate of interest?

CHAPTER 35
Economic Development in a World of Scarcity

What You Will Learn in This Chapter

Less developed countries face even more serious problems of population, resources, and environment than do developed countries. They are also less well equipped to surmount them. For one thing, these countries have not yet gone through the demographic transition. Many of them are in danger of being caught in a "population trap" that could bring economic growth to a halt. The capital resources of less developed countries are also very limited. They cannot do everything at once, and face a difficult choice between a development strategy emphasizing industry and one emphasizing rural development.

For Review

Here are some important terms and concepts that will be put to use in this chapter. Be certain that you understand them, or review them before proceeding.

Sources of economic growth (Chapter 7)
Demographic transition (Chapter 34)

For two chapters now, we have looked at the problems of pollution, population, and resources that cloud the economic future for the world's advanced industrial countries. These problems pose some serious challenges for economic policy. Mistakes have been made in the past that must not be repeated in the future. Nonetheless, the picture is not entirely one of gloom. The developed countries face the future with some big advantages. Most of them have completed the demographic transition and left acute population problems behind. They also have the potential for capital formation that they will need to replace natural resources with synthetic substitutes.

In the less developed countries of the world, things are going to be more difficult. These countries must deal with the same problems of pollution, population, and resources, plus some others of their own, and are less well equipped to do so. Let us turn now to an examination of the problems and prospects for the economic future of the "third world." We begin with an attempt to understand just what economic development is.

Three Faces of Development

Economic Development as Growth

The less developed countries that constitute what we call the third world have many differences, but also many things in common. The most conspicuous thing they have in common is low per capita income. No magic number divides the developed from the less developed countries, but development economics tends to focus on those with per capita gross national products of less than $500 per year. In Asia, China, India, and Bangladesh, with their vast populations, all fall in this poorest group. On the African continent, only Libya and South Africa escape unqualified less developed status. In South America, many countries, including Brazil, Bolivia, Haiti, Guatemala, and several others remain below the $500 mark. (Others, including Argentina, Chile, Venezuela, and Mexico are enough above the line to be counted as members of an intermediate group.) All in all, the less developed countries contain some two-thirds of the world's population.

To draw these distinctions in terms of per capita incomes is to say that economic development equals economic growth. That is the traditional view of the matter, and it is a view that still has much truth to it. Economic growth can occur without bringing a better life to everyone, but it is hard to see how a better life for all can come without at least some growth. This is especially true for those least developed countries that have less than $100 of gross national product per capita.

Much of development economics, then, focuses on ways to enable a country to grow. Growth-oriented development studies usually emphasize capital accumulation as the great key. Capital accumulation has accounted for only about 15 percent of economic growth in the United States in recent years, but it is more important for less developed countries. In such countries there is a great shortage of capital. Typically, saving and investment are only 5–7 percent of gross national product. This compares with over 15 percent in the United States, and 35 percent in Japan and the Soviet-type economies. Without capital accumulation, it is difficult to put unemployed and underemployed people to work. Without capital it is equally difficult to improve the level of education, or to take advantage of imported technology. Yet although capital accumulation and growth are important, they are not the whole story of economic development. Development has other faces too.

Development as Industrialization

The developed countries are not only richer than the less developed countries, they are also more highly industrialized. Developed countries typically have between a fifth and a quarter of their populations engaged in manufacturing industry. In the less developed countries, the proportion is likely to be 10 percent or less. A second interpretation of economic development, then, is that it means industrializing just as the advanced countries have done in the past.

The view that development means industrialization, like the view that development means economic growth, has much truth to it. The less developed countries have large and growing urban populations. Only industrialization offers these much hope of employment. As incomes rise in a developing country, the demand for manufactured goods increases rapidly. It makes sense to meet many of these needs with domestic sources of supply. Many less developed countries have valuable raw materials that they now export for processing. These could be processed domestically instead. Still, despite all this, the importance of industrialization to development should not be exaggerated.

For one thing, an overemphasis on industrialization may cause resources to be wasted on ill-conceived "showcase" projects. Not every less developed country needs a steel mill and an automobile works. Even small-scale industrial projects may be inappropriate if they mean building an exact replica of some plant originally designed for Manchester or Milwaukee, where relative factor scarcities and other market conditions are completely different.

What is more, an overemphasis on industrialization can lead to the neglect of other development objectives. To see why, let us take a look at a third face of economic development.

Development as Depauperization

It is a widely shared opinion that a major goal of economic development should be a better life for the poorest of the poor. These are the people at the low end of the income distribution in the poorest countries. They are the true paupers. They lack adequate food, often lack all access to medical care, and not infrequently lack even the most primitive shelter.

Development economists once were confident that the benefits of growth and industrialization would automatically "trickle down" to the poorest of the poor. Unfortunately, this optimism may not be justified, as

---

Irma Adelman was born in Cernowitz, Roumania. After coming to the United States, she studied at the University of California at Berkeley, receiving a Ph.D. in economics in 1955. She taught at Stanford, Johns Hopkins, and Northwestern University, before moving to the University of Maryland in 1972.

Professor Adelman has earned a reputation as one of the foremost writers on the subject of development economics. In all of her writings, she stresses the extreme complexity and interrelatedness of the phenomena of economic development. There is no simple explanation for underdevelopment, such as a deficiency of capital, or a lack of entrepreneurial talent, or an adverse ratio of population to natural resources, or a hostile international environment.

Because of the complex nature of underdevelopment, there can be no single key to development. Gradualist approaches to development policy are likely to fail. Instead, what is needed is some large shock that will significantly change the way the people of a less developed society behave. Adelman believes that the government must play a large role in administering these critical shocks.

Irma Adelman has employed quantitative methods widely in her studies of development. These quantitative studies led her to the disturbing discovery that very often in the early stages of development, the poorest 60 percent of the population become even poorer, both in relative and absolute terms, as the economy grows. Rather than the "trickle down" effect that earlier writers hoped for, there can instead be a "trickle up." She concludes that governments are choosing the wrong goals in economic development. There is a trade-off between sheer growth of GNP, on the one hand, and depauperization, on the other. For moral as much as for economic reasons, Adelman believes that governments ought to adopt depauperization as their primary development goal.

Irma Adelman (1930–)

recent research of Irma Adelman and C. T. Morris has shown.[1] Their recent work focuses on the range of development from sub-Saharan Africa to the poorest countries of South America, that is, from about $100 to $500 per capita income. In these countries, development tends to bring both relative and absolute impoverishment to the poorest 60 percent of the population. At very low levels of development, there appears to be no "trickling down" at all. The poor begin to benefit only after an intermediate level of development has been reached.

Adelman and Morris have concluded that the policies needed to benefit the poor are different than those needed to maximize growth rates. The ideas of development as growth or industrialization, they say, should be replaced with the idea of **depauperization.** Depauperization means not only providing the necessary material basis for life, but also access to education, status, security, self-expression, and power. Depauperization stresses the removal of social, political, and spiritual deprivation as much as physical deprivation. It has as much to do with equity as with growth.

Depauperization Economic development of a kind that benefits the poorest of the poor, providing them not only with the material necessities of life, but also with access to education, status, security, self-expression, and power.

Two Strategies

The choice of development goals strongly influences the strategy that can best promote the development process. The Soviet Union represents one extreme. For Soviet planners, development meant industrialization above all else. Through high rates of saving, they sacrificed consumption to achieve rapid growth. Through collectivization, they sacrificed the growth of agriculture to achieve the growth of industry. Eventually, the benefits of successful industrialization began to trickle down to the population at large. Initially, though, living standards declined, and the overall distribution of income shifted in favor of industrial workers and against peasants.

Even where industrialization as an end in itself is not made a higher priority than overall growth, the benefits of development may be spread very unevenly. Many less developed countries suffer from what is called a **dual economy.** In such an economy, a modern, Westernized industrial sector provides high wages for better educated workers and a tax base to pay a middle class of civil servants. Meanwhile a secondary, traditional sector remains largely untouched. Sometimes, the overall growth rate of GNP can be maximized by concentrating available development resources on the modern sector, at least in the short run. Often also foreign aid and the investments of multinational corporations are concentrated on the modern sector of dual economies.

Dual Economy A less developed economy that is sharply divided into a modern, Westernized industrial sector capable of rapid growth, and a traditional rural sector that remains stagnant.

There is a second kind of development strategy that contrasts with the industry-first approach. Instead, it emphasizes redistribution and mass education first, and growth later. Redistribution in the context of less developed countries means most importantly the redistribution of land ownership. Education means mass education in literacy and general knowledge, rather than just specialized training for participation in the modern sector. If this strategy works, redistribution can provide the basis for rural development and education can provide the basis for the growth of

[1]Irma Adelman and C. T. Morris, *Society, Politics, and Economic Development,* (Baltimore: Johns Hopkins, 1967).

broadly based, labor-intensive industry. Adelman and Morris cite Israel, Japan, South Korea, Singapore, and Taiwan as countries that have successfully followed this strategy. China should probably be added to the list. In the last century, American economic development followed this strategy much more nearly than did economic development in Europe.

Population and Development

Death Control and Birth Control

Whatever development strategy they choose, all less developed countries face certain common problems that they must somehow overcome. None are more serious than the closely related problems of death control, birth control, and population growth. In Chapter 34 we introduced some basic concepts of population economics. Now let us see how these apply specifically to less developed countries.

Traditional societies of the past had high birth rates, high death rates, and relatively stable populations. In developed economies, both deaths and births are controlled by the techniques of modern medical science, and population growth rates are also low. Today's less developed countries lie between these two demographic patterns. They have successfully imported modern methods of death control, especially the control of epidemic disease, but birth control has not fully taken hold. As a result, population growth rates are very high.

Turn back for a moment to Exhibit 34.4, which gives population growth data for a selected group of developed and less developed countries. The countries are ranked in order of their rates of population growth. Near the middle of the table we find Afghanistan which, with both the highest crude birth rate and crude death rate of all listed countries, most closely fits the traditional pattern. Even there, though, modern medicine has had an effect on the death rate. The rate of natural increase of population is very substantial, at 22.4 per 1,000 per year. At the bottom of the table are the United Kingdom and Czechoslovakia, where birth rates and death rates are very nearly in equilibrium. At the top are Ecuador and Mexico—by no means the poorest of less developed countries—where death rates are as low as those in the United States or Great Britain, but birth rates are nearly as high as in the poorest parts of Africa. These are the countries where, to use the popular phrase, the "population bomb" is ticking away.

The Population Trap

Birth rates, death rates, economic growth, and income levels are in very delicate balance during economic development. We explained in Chapter 34 that countries that develop successfully undergo a process called the demographic transition. During the demographic transition, rising income levels first depress death rates, causing population growth rates to accelerate, and then depress birth rates, causing population growth to slow.

Exhibit 35.1 shows what happens to per capita income and population growth, assuming steady economic growth during the demographic transition. In part *a,* the vertical axis measures the level of per capita income. We suppose that when income is below the level *A,* people are so poor that

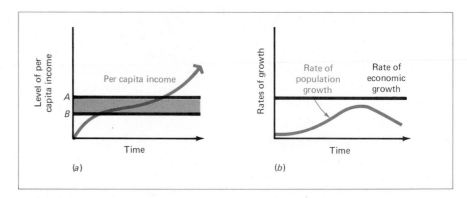

EXHIBIT 35.1

The demographic transition

Here we show the effects of the demographic transition in terms of economic growth and population growth. We assume that death rates begin to fall once per capita reaches the level *A,* and that birth rates begin to fall once per capita reaches the level *B.* During the transition, the growth of population speeds up and that of per capita income slows. Economic growth always stays above population growth, however.

death rates are high, and when it is above *B,* people are prosperous enough that birth rates are low. (Of course, things are really more complicated than this. There are not really any sharp cutoff levels of income, but our simple assumption will serve to make the point.) In part *b,* the vertical axis measures growth rates of total GNP and of population. Note that population growth never exceeds the growth of GNP. The curve of per capita income in part *a* always moves upward, although it rises less rapidly in the zone between *A* and *B* while the demographic transition is under way.

Can today's less developed countries complete this process as the developed countries have done? It is to be hoped that they can, but it is by no means certain. There is a real danger that they will get caught in a **population trap,** and their attempt to make it through the demographic transition will abort.

Population Trap A situation in which the rate of population growth rises above the rate of economic growth, halting the growth of per capita income and aborting the demographic transition.

Exhibit 35.2 shows schematically how a country could fall foul of the population trap. Suppose that such a country begins development normally, as did the country represented in Exhibit 35.1. This time, though, either population growth is more rapid or economic growth slower. At time *T,* the growth of population begins to exceed the growth of income, and per capita income starts to fall. Instead of completing the demographic transition, the country falls back into a subsistence equilibrium with birth and death rates both high and per capita income stagnant.

Escape

In the nineteenth century, when Western Europe and North America were industrializing, death rates fell only slowly, and only after living standards had already begun to improve. Population growth rates did not rise above 1 percent per year in most cases. Today, modern death control techniques have reached almost every corner of the globe, no matter how poor. That makes it more difficult for today's less developed countries to

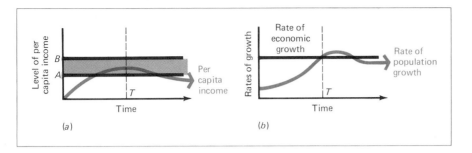

EXHIBIT 35.2
The population trap
If at some point during the demographic transition the rate of population growth exceeds the rate of economic growth, a country may be caught in a "population trap." As this exhibit is drawn, the country enters the trap at time *T*. At that point, per capita income begins to fall, and the demographic transition is absorbed.

escape the population trap. During the nineteenth century, the American economy experienced growth rates of GNP in the range of 3.5 to 4.5 percent per year. Rates of growth in that range are no longer good enough for less developed countries, where population itself can grow as fast as 3.5 percent per year. Any growth rate for GNP slower than 6 to 7 percent per year gives little hope for escaping the population trap just by outrunning it. Countries like South Korea or Taiwan may make it, but those like Haiti, Chad, or Dahomey, where per capita incomes are already falling, will not.

The only other way to escape the population trap is to bring down the birth rate while incomes are still low. There is some evidence that in countries where the benefits of growth have been widely shared among the population, birth rates have begun to fall at per capita income levels as low as $200. In other countries, highly publicized birth control campaigns have had little if any effect. India is one country where voluntary programs of birth control have consistently fallen short of targets. As India now retreats from democracy, the government there seems to be moving toward a get-tough policy. In some cases subsidized housing and other social benefits are withdrawn from families that have a third child. In other cases, the government is threatening compulsory sterilization. It remains to be seen whether such programs will have an effect, and whether they will be copied in other less developed countries.

Food and Development[2]

Hunger

We now turn to the aspect of economic development that causes the greatest concern of all. That is the problem of hunger.

Hunger comes in varying degrees. People are said to be undernourished if they suffer from a quantitative lack of calories. They are said to suffer

[2]This section draws at many points on the useful survey *World of Hunger*, by Jonathan Power and Anne-Marie Holenstein (London: Temple Smith, 1976).

from malnutrition if the food they do get contains insufficient protein and other nutrients, even if energy requirements are met. Undernourishment leads to actual starvation. In recent years it has been a major problem in the countries just south of the Sahara in Africa, India, Bangladesh, and Sri Lanka in Asia, and in Bolivia, Haiti, and El Salvador in the Americas, to list only a few. Malnutrition is much more widespread, and has long-run effects that are hardly less devastating. A protein insufficiency in the diets of young children and breast-feeding women is especially dangerous, because it retards brain development. People who survive a malnourished childhood are likely to suffer from lethargy and lack of productive ability in later life. These are hardly the traits required for the labor forces of poor countries struggling to achieve development.

Accurate statistics on world hunger are hard to come by. Definitions vary, and the governments of some of the worst-hit countries are reluctant to supply information. Some who have studied the problem believe that as many as two-thirds of the world's population may suffer from undernourishment or malnutrition in some form. The data in Exhibit 35.3 are based on much more conservative methods of estimation, but they still show an appallingly serious problem.

Hunger and Population

The relationship between hunger and population is complex. It is natural to think of overpopulation causing hunger, with a Malthusian growth of numbers of people outstripping food production. Hunger can be a spur to population growth, too, however. Malnutrition leads to high infant mortality. High infant mortality, in turn, leads to the desire to have a large family, so that at least some children will survive. Perhaps the relationship between malnutrition and desired family size is part of the reason why birth rates have fallen earliest in those countries that have distributed the benefits of development widely among their populations.

When the world food problem is presented as a race between production and the growth of demand, the results are sobering. Information presented at the World Food Conference in 1974[3] placed 71 less developed countries in three groups according to food and population trends during the period 1953–1971. In 24 of these countries, the rate of increase in food production fell short of population growth. In an additional 17, the rate of increase of food production exceeded the rate of growth of population, but fell short of the rate of growth of domestic demand. Because rising incomes permitted people to eat more, these countries had to increase food imports (or in some cases, decrease food exports), thus making things harder yet for the countries in the first group. In the 30 remaining countries, the rate of growth of food output exceeded the rate of growth of demand, but even some of these countries experienced regional problems because of maldistribution within their borders.

What can be done about the world food problem? In the remainder of this section, we shall examine some possible approaches.

[3]Preliminary Assessment of the World Food Situation, World Food Conference, 1974, UNIE/Conf. 65/Prep./6. Data also presented as Table 7 in Power and Holenstein, *World of Hunger.*

EXHIBIT 35.3

Estimated numbers of people with insufficient protein/energy supply, by regions, 1970

According to the relatively conservative estimates reported in this table, some 388 million people had less than minimum standards of nutrition in 1970. Some observers think that nearly two-thirds of the world's population may suffer from malnutrition to some extent.

Region	Population (billions)	Percentage Below Lower Limit (percent)	Number Below Lower Limit (millions)
Developed regions	1.07	3	28
Developing regions excluding Asian centrally planned economies	1.75	20	360
Latin America	0.28	13	37
Far East	1.02	22	221
Near East	0.17	20	34
Africa	0.28	25	68
World (excluding Asian centrally planned economies)	2.83	14	388

Source: Jonathan Power and Anne-Marie Holenstein, *World of Hunger* (London: Temple Smith, 1976). Reprinted by permission.

Food Aid

In 1954, the American Congress passed the Agricultural Trade Development and Assistance Act, commonly known as PL480. This act has been the heart of world food aid efforts. During the 1960s, the United States gave up to 84 percent of all world food aid. The less developed countries were able to rely on food aid for 30 to 45 percent of their food imports.

Under Title 1 of PL480, food was sold on favorable terms to governments. Under Title 2, food went free to governments and to the United Nations World Food Program. Title 2 food aid was aimed at the especially underprivileged, and at disaster relief. At the same time the populations of less developed countries were benefitting from PL480, American farmers were benefitting. The program was thus a combination of idealism and self-interest, but the combination for a long time seemed to work well.

Problems of Food Aid

Despite the very substantial benefits to countries receiving food aid, PL480 and the food aid programs of other governments have had their critics. It is important to realize why food aid alone is not likely to provide a long-run answer to the world food problem.

First of all, because American food aid is based on a mixture of charity and self-interest, it is liable to disruption from the self-interest side. When American farmers were producing huge grain surpluses, voters and consumers were happy to see the surpluses given away. Now that the chronic surpluses have disappeared, giving food hurts more than it used to. For one thing, there are now plenty of paying customers for American grain exports.

Also, grain prices have risen so high that further increases in exports put serious pressure on domestic food prices. Such exports thus now meet opposition from consumer groups. Since 1972, the total volume of American food aid has declined. In 1974, the amount of food delivered under aid programs fell to a third of the 1972 level. PL480 has thus proved least reliable just when it has been needed most.

There is a second serious problem in the tendency of some receiver governments to rely on food aid as a substitute for domestic agricultural development. In some cases, the motivation has been political. Necessary agricultural reforms would have threatened the privileges of entrenched ruling classes, so that getting American aid seemed like an easier way out. In other cases, food aid has disrupted domestic markets. Food aid kept prices low in the less developed countries. This was fine for the landless poor, but it greatly reduced incentives to farmers. Sometimes, the effect of food aid on relative prices made nonfood cash crops more attractive to grow than food crops.

Finally, many critics of food aid are unhappy about the standards by which recipients have been selected. The countries receiving greatest aid in recent years have been those such as South Vietnam, Chile, South Korea, Jordan, Syria, and Israel that have been crucial to American foreign policy. India, Bangladesh, and Sri Lanka, where need has been greatest, have gotten only something like a fifth of the total. The power that food exports give to the American government is certain to grow in coming years. Soon perhaps this food power will exceed even the power wielded by oil exporters. It is small wonder that the less developed nations are looking for ways to reduce their dependence.

Need for Rural Development

Throughout the world, less developed countries are urbanizing rapidly—far more rapidly than today's developed countries did at comparable stages of their own growth. The reasons for this urbanization are complex. Partly the modernity and the promise of a better life in the city attracts new population. Partly the problem is education systems that do not emphasize agricultural topics. Whatever the causes, cities are not able to meet the aspirations of all those who arrive in them. Urban unemployment rates are very high. Many of those who are employed work in tertiary services, from shining shoes to hustling, that contribute little to economic development or to the development of those individuals. Huge shanty towns surrounding third world cities are the rule rather than the exception.

Current rates of urbanization far exceed the potential for industrial development in most poor countries. A recent OECD study[4] calculated that, just to keep urban unemployment from rising in a typical less developed country, industrial output would have to grow at 18 percent per year. Even in Brazil, which has had outstanding success with industrialization and urban development, industrial growth has run at only 15 percent per year. To get rid of the 20 to 25 percent unemployment common in cities of less developed countries, industry would have to grow at something like 30 to 35 percent per year for a decade.

[4]David Turnham, *The Employment Problem in Less Developed Countries,* (Paris: Organization for Economic Cooperation and Development, 1971), as cited by Power and Holenstein, *World of Hunger,* pp. 74–75.

When urban unemployment and the food problem are considered together, it is not surprising that many development economists believe that the real hope for the less developed countries lies in the countryside. The hope is to hold people on the land, and make them productive there within a meaningful community structure. If the third world nations can do that, they may be able to feed themselves, distribute what little they have more equitably, meet the nonmaterial aspirations of their populations, and retain their independence. That, at least, is what the advocates of rural development say. They all recognize that there are problems, though.

Technological Problems

Rural development does not mean just the introduction of new agricultural methods. It also means the growth of small-scale industry in villages and towns. These are necessary to meet local needs and provide employment for those whom even the most ambitious land reform program would leave landless. Is the technological basis for such development available?

In some respects, technological progress has been remarkable. The most talked-about development is the appearance of new, high-yield varieties of wheat and rice. Under laboratory conditions, these new varieties can triple food output per acre. They provide the best hope for less developed countries to escape from the sheer shortage of land.

Unfortunately, high-yield wheat, rice, and other grains cannot just be stuck in the ground and expected to do their magic. The secret of their success lies in their ability to absorb huge quantities of fertilizers. If ordinary varieties of grain are overfertilized, they produce only luxuriant growth of stems and leaves, or seedheads so heavy that they break the stalk of the plant. With high-yield varieties, extra fertilization produces growth where it is needed. Without such fertilization, the new varieties actually produce less than traditional crops. (In many cases, heavy use of pesticides and irrigation are needed as well.)

As the use of high-yield varieties has spread, less developed countries have become more dependent on imported fertilizers. They now produce barely half their own fertilizer needs. What is worse, fertilizer production depends critically on oil. This is particularly true of nitrogen fertilizers, which make up half the total used. These are made almost entirely from natural gas and petroleum products. The "green revolution" has been extremely hard hit by high oil prices, because outside the Middle East, few less developed countries have their own oil supplies.

Rural industrial development faces technological problems that are, if anything, greater than those faced by agricultural development. Western industrial research has developed technology designed to use cheap capital and save expensive labor. The opposite conditions prevail in rural areas of the third world. Very little research has gone into the development of simple but sophisticated labor-intensive ways of doing things.

Institutional Problems

A number of institutional problems also threaten rural development. Chief among these are the problem of land reform and the problem of supplying credit to rural areas.

Advocates of rural development support land reform. Land reform means buying (or sometimes confiscating) the large holdings of absentee landlords, and distributing the land in the smallest feasible parcels among those who actually till the soil. The effects of land reform, if it works, are threefold. First, a small landowner has a greater incentive than a tenant farmer to improve the land and introduce better production techniques. Second, wide distribution of ownership means wider distribution of the product, with all the benefits this is believed to bring. Third, land reform can lead to more stable rural community structures. This helps stop the rush to the city. It also helps provide the dignity and sense of personal worth that are part of the process of depauperization.

Many countries have carried out thorough land reforms, but many others have not. Two problems hold back further land reform. One major problem is political. The land-owning classes often dominate the political structures of less developed countries, and are reluctant to relinquish this hold. The second is economic. Under some circumstances, technological considerations may make it more productive to consolidate land holdings into bigger farms to realize economies of scale. To some extent, land reform can involve a trade-off between growth and depauperization.

The other major institutional weakness that holds back small-scale rural development is a weakness of credit markets. In many less developed countries, small farmers have no access to banks and other modern credit facilities. They must rely on local money lenders or merchants, who charge extremely high rates of interest.

High-yield crops have made the credit problem more serious than ever. The green revolution can actually work against the small farmer. Higher yields drive land rents up, and put downward pressure on output prices. The new varieties cannot be used without expensive fertilizers and pesticides, but buying these only puts the small farmer more at the mercy of the money lender. Thus if land reform is carried out without credit reform, land reform can in fact retard the introduction of new techniques.

Conclusions

The tone of much of this chapter has been pessimistic. There is no doubt that the problems of the less developed countries will be very difficult to surmount, and that some countries will fail. There is every doubt of the ability and the will of the industrialized countries to carry the burden of development. Nonetheless, there are places where things are going right rather than wrong. It is fitting to end this chapter with one of these success stories.

CASE 35.1
The Fondo Negro Project[5]
In the Dominican Republic, a fascinating experiment is attempting to get around the barriers to credit distribution in the rural areas of less developed countries. Convinced that small farmers could make use of credit if given proper backup with agricultural expertise, the Dominican Development Foundation (a private, nongovernment organization) has tried to find a way that is nonbureaucratic, simple, and above all, appealing to small farmers. They have done this by working through groups of farmers rather than individuals.

[5]Based on Jonathan Power and Anne-Marie Holenstein, *World of Hunger* (London: Temple Smith, 1976). Reprinted by permission.

Farmers who want to receive credit must set up an association. They receive money in the name of the group and agree to be responsible as a group for the repayments of individual members. Banks have found that 10 percent or more of small farmers default on their loans. The Foundation has got the default rate down to 4.2 percent. The social pressure of not letting the group down works astonishingly effectively.

The groups vary enormously. Some of them are quite loosely knit. Individual members operate independently and get together only to receive the loan. In others the collective system works at nearly every level of production. For example, a tomato farm is worked by a group of thirty families. They share the land and the cost of a large pump to bring water up from the river. They organize the planting, weeding, and reaping operations so that everyone takes an equal part of the load. This project—the community of Fondo Negro—has established itself in one of the driest and most impoverished parts of the Dominican Republic. The annual rainfall is only 650 mm, and average monthly temperatures vary from 25 to 30°C. Yet these peasant farmers have cultivated 115 hectares of land and have made in the first year a net profit of $263 per hectare. That is some $1,052 per family! Before they were set up in business by the Foundation and given the credit to prime their operations, the yearly income had been about $100 per family.

Here is a detailed breakdown of the economics of the project: The project consisted of putting 115 hectares of land into the cultivation of tomatoes. A yield of 546 cwt (hundredweight) per hectare was obtained. The total crop was 62,790 cwt. Sold at $1.50 per cwt, this brought in the sum of $94,185 in the first agricultural year.

Costs per hectare were $557.20. Direct costs of cultivation totalled $66,389. Out of this, $4,320 was paid to the 30 agricultural workers participating as a labor force, at the rate of $2 per day during 24 days per month over a period of 3 months and $62,050 was spent on other operational costs and agricultural expenses.

The capital investment reached $18,292.77, of which $3,060.00 related to enclosures and piping and $15,232.77 to irrigation and plant. There was a depreciation for this period of $1,829.28, taking 10 years as the time of use for the capital investment. Hence the direct profits from the cultivation were $25,997.72, or $225.89 per hectare. The economic surplus for the group was $30,297.72, if we add profit and the amount they obtained as payment for their labor. This gives an average profit of $263.46 per hectare.

The Foundation's more advanced groups are now having their loan applications transferred to commercial banks. Convinced that these small farmers will not default after all, the big banks have been persuaded to take them on as normal customers. So far 105 groups are receiving loans in this way, and the default rate is down to 1 percent.

SUMMARY

1. Economic development is a complex phenomenon. A major part of development is sheer economic growth—increasing the size of GNP as a whole. Development also means industrialization. In countries that have developed in the past, industry has grown more rapidly than agriculture. In extreme cases, such as that of the Soviet Union, the agricultural sector has actually been stripped of resources to aid the more rapid growth of industry. A third aspect of economic development is depauperization. This means not only growing, but distributing the benefits of growth to the poorest classes. An industry-first growth strategy may hamper depauperization.

2. Virtually all less developed countries face serious population pressures. Modern death control techniques have been introduced to all corners of the globe, no matter how poor. Where birth rates are still high, population growth rates are more rapid than they ever were during the demographic transition in developed

countries. If the growth rate of GNP does not keep up with the growth of population, a country may be caught in a population trap. In order to complete the demographic transition successfully, many countries will have to find a way of lowering birth rates while per capita incomes are still at a very low level.

3. Some observers believe that as many as two-thirds of the world's population suffer from undernourishment or malnutrition in some form. In many developing countries, population growth is outstripping food production, making the problem worse. In the past, food aid has provided an important stopgap, but food aid alone is not a long-run solution. Rural development is needed if less developed countries are to be able to feed themselves. Technological advances, including high-yield grains, provide a potential basis for rural development. Economic and institutional problems remain, however. Some way must be found to provide the fertilizers, pesticides, and capital needed to make the best use of high-yield grains. Land reform and credit reform are also necessary parts of successful rural development.

DISCUSSION QUESTIONS

1. In what ways are the problems faced by the less developed countries similar to the problems faced by the United States 100 or 200 years ago? In what ways are they different? Will today's less developed countries follow a similar path to economic development, or is a different route more promising?

2. Less developed countries are short on capital. Foreign firms are often willing to invest in such countries. Is foreign investment a good way for them to solve their capital shortage? What would you think might be the advantages and disadvantages of such foreign investment?

3. Less developed countries tend to have less equally distributed incomes than do developed countries. Why do you think this is so? Why do you think development sometimes increases rather than reduces inequality?

4. Do you see any similarity between the "dual economy" of some less developed countries, and the "dual labor market" that some economists believe exists in this country?

5. Americans eat huge quantities of meat. Each pound of meat requires up to 10 pounds of grain to produce. It is sometimes said that Americans could help the world food problem simply by eating less meat. Suppose that this advice were taken to heart, and Americans cut their meat consumption in half, eating more bread instead. Would the grain that was thus saved ever actually reach the hungry poor in the developing countries? If so, explain how shifts in market prices and changes in supply and demand conditions would operate to get it there. If not, explain why the market would fail to move the grain in the desired direction.

6. It is sometimes said that it is pointless just to give money to developing countries to buy food, because this money will just end up lining the pockets of Kansas farmers without doing the less developed countries themselves any real good. Is this concern wholly justified, partly justified, or wholly unjustified? Why?

PART SIX
International Economics

U p to this point, we have studied micro- and macroeconomics solely within the context of a single national economy. We have not yet mentioned a whole area of economic theory, the theory of international trade.

The first question that we need to ask about this area of economics is why a separate theory of international trade is necessary. Does it really make that much difference that buyers and sellers in certain markets live on opposite sides of national boundaries? The differences between international and national markets are small enough so that most of our familiar tools of analysis apply to both, but there are enough differences to require that these tools be applied in new ways and to new problems. A separate body of theory is thus justified.

From a microeconomic point of view, the most significant feature of international markets is that finished products tend to move more easily in them than do factors of production. Land, with its natural resource deposits and associated climate factors, is the most immobile of factors. Labor also tends to be fairly immobile because of cultural, political, and linguistic barriers. Capital tends to be the most internationally mobile factor of production, but even it does not move as unrestrictedly between countries as within.

Factor immobility is significant because it causes persistent differences in relative and absolute costs of production between nations. With factors immobile, goods that make intense use of labor tend to be cheaper in countries where labor is relatively abundant, agricultural commodities tend to be cheaper in countries with good climates, and so forth. Were factors more mobile, countries with high labor costs would hire more foreign workers until their costs for labor-intensive products had fallen. Countries with bad growing conditions would import soil and sunlight to equalize the costs of agricultural production. In general, internation differences in production costs would be minimized. The microeconomic part of international trade theory will be discussed in Chapter 36.

From a macroeconomic point of view, the main point distinguishing international from national economics is the fact that different countries have different currencies. These fluctuate in value relative to one another. Different currencies make it possible for countries to pursue independent macroeconomic policies. This can mean inflation in one place and deflation across the border, differences in economic growth rates, and a variety of other things. When it comes to studying problems of international currency markets and the balance of payments, these differences become crucial. These macroeconomic issues are discussed in Chapter 37.

CHAPTER 36
International Trade and Comparative Advantages

What You Will Learn in This Chapter

The principle of comparative advantage lies at the heart of the theory of international trade. A country is said to have a comparative advantage in producing a good whenever it can produce that good at a lower opportunity cost than its trading partners. A country can hold a comparative advantage in production of a good even though its absolute production costs, measured in terms of factor inputs, may be higher than costs elsewhere. International specialization according to comparative advantage brings mutual gains to trading countries. Despite the promised benefits of free trade, however, many arguments are heard in favor of protecting domestic industry against foreign competition.

For Review

Here are some important terms and concepts that will be put to use in this chapter. Be certain that you understand them, or review them before proceeding.

    Monopoly (Chapter 26)
    Monopsony (Chapter 30)
    Distributive justice (Chapter 1)

The Theory of Comparative Advantage

If we are to study international trade from a microeconomic point of view, we must begin with the theory of comparative advantage. In a sense, international trade theory starts here historically as well as logically. The theory was first clearly set forth by David Ricardo early in the nineteenth century. Ricardo wanted to show why it would be to England's advantage to maintain active trade with other countries. To do so, he used an example very much like the following.

An Example

Let us imagine two countries, which we shall call "Norway" and "Spain." Both countries have farms and offshore fishing beds, but the moderate climate of Spain makes both the farms and the fishing beds more productive. The number of labor hours required to produce a ton of each product in the two countries is shown in Exhibit 36.1. For simplicity, we

	Spain	Norway
Fish	4	5
Grain	2	5

EXHIBIT 36.1

Labor hours per ton of output in Spain and Norway
The figures in this table show the number of labor hours required to produce each ton of fish and grain in Spain and Norway. Spain has an absolute advantage in the production of both goods. Norway has a comparative advantage in fish and Spain has a comparative advantage in grain.

shall consider only labor costs in this example. We shall think of other costs as proportional to labor costs. Also, we shall assume per-unit labor costs to be constant for all levels of output.

This table reveals two kinds of differences in the cost structure of the two countries. First, we notice that *both* fish and grain require fewer labor hours to produce in Spain. Spain is said to have an **absolute advantage** in the production of both goods. Second, we notice that there are differences in the opportunity costs between the two countries. Let us look at the cost of each good in each country, not in terms of labor hours, but in terms of the other good. In Norway, producing a ton of fish means foregoing the opportunity to use 5 labor hours in the fields. A ton of fish thus has an opportunity cost of 1 ton of grain there. In Spain, producing a ton of fish means giving up the opportunity to produce 2 tons of grain. In terms of opportunity costs, then, fish is cheaper in Norway than in Spain, and grain is cheaper in Spain than in Norway. The country in which the opportunity cost of a good is lower is said to have **comparative advantage** in producing that good.

Absolute Advantage In international trade theory, the ability of a country to produce a good at absolutely lower cost, measured in terms of factor inputs, than its trading partners.

Comparative Advantage In international trade theory, the ability of a country to produce a good at a lower opportunity cost, in terms of other goods, than its trading partners.

Pretrade Equilibrium

If no trade takes place between Norway and Spain, equilibrium in fish and grain markets in the two countries will be established independently. We have simplified things by ignoring all costs but labor costs, and assuming these to be constant. In pretrade equilibrium, the ratio of the price of fish to the price of grain in each country will thus be equal to the ratio of labor inputs needed to produce the goods. In Norway, where a ton of grain and a ton of fish both take the same labor to produce, the price of fish will be equal to the price of grain. In Spain, where a ton of fish takes twice as much labor to produce as a ton of grain, the equilibrium price of fish will be twice the price of grain.

Suppose that each country has 1,000 labor hours available for production of fish and grain. The way this will be divided between the two products in each country will depend on demand and consumer tastes. Let us suppose that demand conditions are such that in Norway, 100 tons of grain and 100 tons of fish are produced, while in Spain, 350 tons of grain are grown and 75 tons of fish are caught. The quantities produced and consumed in pretrade equilibrium are noted in Exhibit 36.2.

The Possibility of Trade

The stage is now set to consider the possibilities for trade between Norway and Spain. A superficial look at labor costs in the two countries might make us think there were no possibilities for trade. Norwegians might

David Ricardo, the greatest of the classical economists, was born in 1772. His father was a Jewish immigrant and a member of the London stock exchange. Ricardo's education was rather haphazard, and he entered his father's business at the age of 14. In 1793 he married, abandoned strict Jewish orthodoxy, and went into business on his own. These were years of war and financial disturbance. The young Ricardo developed a reputation for remarkable astuteness, and quickly made a large fortune.

In 1799, Ricardo read the *Wealth of Nations,* and first developed an interest in questions of political economy. In 1809, his first writings on economics appeared. These were a series of newspaper articles on "The High Price of Bullion," which appeared the next year as an influential pamphlet. Several other short works added to his reputation in this area. In 1814, he retired from business to devote full time to political economy.

Ricardo's major work was *Principles of Political Economy and Taxation,* first published in 1817. This work contains, among other things, a pioneering statement of the principle of comparative advantage, as applied to international trade. With a lucid numerical example, Ricardo shows why it is to the mutual advantage of both countries for England to export wool to Portugal and import wine in return, even though both products can be produced at absolutely lower costs in Portugal.

But international trade is only a sidelight of Ricardo's *Principles.* The book covers the whole of economics as then known, beginning with value theory, and progressing to a theory of economic growth and evolution. Ricardo, like his friend Malthus and later follower John Stuart Mill, held that the economy was growing toward a future "steady state." In this steady state, economic growth would come to a halt, and the wage rate would be depressed to the subsistence level.

Ricardo's book was extraordinarily influential. For more than half a century thereafter, much of economics as written in England was an elaboration of or commentary on Ricardo's work. The most famous of all economists to fall under the influence of Ricardo's theory and method was Karl Marx. Although Marx eventually reached revolutionary conclusions that differed radically from any views Ricardo held, his starting point was Ricardo's labor theory of value, and Ricardo's method of analyzing economic growth.

David Ricardo (1772–1823)

like to get their hands on some of those cheap Spanish goods, but why should the Spanish be interested? After all, can they not produce everything at home more cheaply than it can be produced abroad? If so, how could they gain from trade? A closer analysis shows us that this superficial view is incorrect. Absolute advantage turns out to be unimportant in determining patterns of trade. Only comparative advantage matters.

EXHIBIT 36.2

Pretrade equilibrium outputs of fish and grain in Spain and Norway

If Spain and Norway do not engage in trade, each country will have to meet all its needs from its own resources. The quantities of goods produced in each country depends on the strength of domestic demand. The relative prices of the two goods in each country will be determined by their labor costs, as shown in Exhibit 36.1.

	Spain	Norway	World Total
Fish	75	100	175
Grain	350	100	450

It is not hard to show that possibilities for trade exist. Imagine that an enterprising Norwegian fishing party decides to sail into a Spanish port with a ton of their catch. Spanish merchants in the port where they arrive will have been used to giving 2 tons of grain, or its equivalent, for a ton of fish. The Norwegians will have been accustomed to getting only an equal weight of grain for each ton of fish. Any exchange ratio between 1 and 2 tons of grain per ton of fish will seem more than normally attractive to both parties. For instance, a trade of $1\frac{1}{2}$ tons of grain for a ton of fish will make both the Spanish merchants and the Norwegian fishing party better off than they would have been had they traded only with others from their own country.

Gains from Specialization

The opening of trade between Spain and Norway will soon begin to have an effect on patterns of production in the two countries. In Norway, farmers will discover that instead of working 5 hours to raise a ton of grain from their own rocky soil, they can fish for 5 hours instead, and trade their catch to the Spaniards for $7\frac{1}{2}$ tons of grain. In Spain, people will find that it is no longer worth their while to spend 4 hours to catch a ton of fish. Instead, they can work just 3 hours in the fields. The $1\frac{1}{2}$ tons of grain that they grow will get them a ton of fish from the Norwegians. In short, the Norwegians will find it worth their while to specialize in fish and the Spanish will find it worth their while to specialize in grain.

Suppose now that trade continues at the ratio of $1\frac{1}{2}$ tons of grain per ton of fish until both countries have become completely specialized. Spain no longer produces any fish, and Norway no longer produces any grain. Norwegians catch 200 tons of fish, half of which is exported to Spain. The Spanish grow 500 tons of grain, 150 of which are exported to Norway. Exhibit 36.3 summarizes this posttrade situation.

A comparison of this table with Exhibit 36.2 reveals three noteworthy things. First, it shows that Norwegians are better off than before. They have just as much fish to eat, and 50 tons more grain than in the pretrade equilibrium. Second, it shows that Spaniards are better off. They have just as much grain to consume as ever, and more fish. Finally, comparing the last columns of the tables shows that total world output of both grain and fish has risen as a result of trade. Everyone is better off, and no one is worse off.

		Spain	Norway	World Total
Fish	Production	0	200	200
	Consumption	100	100	200
Grain	Production	500	0	500
	Consumption	350	150	500

EXHIBIT 36.3
Posttrade production and consumption of fish and grain in Spain and Norway
In this table, we assume that Spain and Norway have traded fish for grain at a ratio of 1½ tons of grain per ton of fish. Both countries have become entirely specialized. Comparing this table with that in Exhibit 36.2, we see that consumers in both countries have more of both products than they did in the absence of trade. We note also that total world production of fish has risen from 175 to 200 tons, and total world production of grain from 450 to 500 tons.

Generalized Mutual Advantage

The principle of mutual advantage from international trade is perfectly general. It applies to any situation where one country has a comparative advantage over another in producing some good. Wherever there is a comparative advantage, international specialization can increase consumption in each trading country, and world output as a whole.

A complete analysis of international trade would add many details. We would have to allow for cases in which only one country became fully specialized, and for cases in which our constant cost assumption did not hold. No part of the more detailed theory, however, would undermine our basic conclusion: International trade and specialization promote world economic efficiency and generate mutual advantages to all trading nations.

Protectionism and Trade Policy

Free Trade Challenged

There is a strong theoretical case that free international trade promotes world efficiency and consumer welfare. Nonetheless, many nations pursue policies that actively thwart such trade. We refer to policies that interfere with international trade by the general term **protectionism.** The most common protectionist policies are the imposition of **tariffs,** which are taxes levied on imported goods, and **import quotas,** which are limitations on quantities imported. The American government imposes tariffs and quotas on a number of goods.

In what follows, we shall look at some of the more commonly heard arguments in favor of protectionism. Some of them, as we shall see, are altogether false. Others are partly valid in terms of positive economics. Still others focus primarily on normative considerations.

Protectionism A policy of shielding domestic industry from foreign competition.

Tariff A tax levied on imported goods.

Import Quota A limitation on the quantity of a good that can be imported in a given time period.

Cheap Foreign Labor

One common argument against free trade sees a threat in imports from countries where wages are lower than in the United States. At the same time, though, workers in those countries fear competition from American workers backed by heavy capital investment. If one argument were true, both ought to be. If both were true, then trade must be making everyone worse off.

Fortunately, both arguments are false. It is exactly such differences in factor supplies and comparative costs that create opportunities for mutual advantage. The fallacious "cheap foreign labor" argument implies that trade is *best* conducted with countries differing as little as possible from our own. The theory of comparative advantage suggests, in contrast, that trade with such countries is likely to offer the *least* benefit. There is sometimes (but not always) an element of truth in the "cheap foreign labor" argument if it is applied to specific groups of workers, as we shall see below. But applied to average standards of living, as it often is, it is false.

Infant Industries

The famous "infant industry" argument is a second weapon in the protectionist arsenal. It runs like this: Suppose that a certain country has a comparative disadvantage in the production of tacos, but wishes to establish a domestic taco industry. To do so, it prohibits imports. This permits the domestic taco industry to expand and mature. Production costs fall and efficiency increases. Eventually, the country achieves a true comparative advantage in tacos. At that time, consumers will recoup the losses they must suffer in the meantime while the industry "grows up."

This sequence of events is not, in fact, wholly impossible. Nonetheless, it does not justify protection. If the present value of future gains to consumers more than offsets near-term losses, the taco industry ought to be able to grow without protection. It can borrow money to cover short-term operating losses while it competes with cheap foreign tacos. Eventually, when the industry matures and gains its comparative advantage, it can pay off the loans and have some left over. No special protection is needed to ensure the emergence of a domestic taco industry.

Suppose, though, that such borrowing would not be profitable for the taco industry. That, then, would be a sign that the future gains are so small, or so distant, that they do not offset current losses. In that case, to protect the industry would be to promote misallocation of resources over time. Sometimes it is suggested that imperfections in the credit market might make it difficult for an "infant industry" to borrow the funds it needs to finance expansion. But if true, this would at most create a case for government-sponsored loans to the infant industry. It would still not constitute a case for tariffs.

Terms of Trade

A third well-known protectionist theory is the "terms-of-trade" argument. This has some respectable basis in positive economics. The argument applies to a country that exercises monopoly or monopsony power in the international market. For example, suppose that America is the world's largest exporter of wheat and the largest importer of textiles. Restricting wheat exports and textile imports would then drive the world market price of wheat up and the world market price of textiles down. If the price movement were great enough, the improved terms of trade would more than compensate for the decrease in the volume of trade.

The terms-of-trade argument is valid (at least as a possibility) as it stands. Two things should be noted about it, however. First of all, it does not quite challenge the doctrine of comparative advantage head-on. What it really says is that by clever market manipulation, a country may be able to get a larger share of the gains from trade than it would if international markets operated unrestrictedly. Second, it cannot be applied to both sides of a market at once. If all countries try to play the terms-of-trade game, all of them lose. For one to play it openly invites mutually self-defeating retaliation.

Macroeconomics

Another partially valid protectionist argument suggests that trade may not be beneficial in times of macroeconomic disequilibrium. The basic idea is this. When a country is experiencing widespread unemployment, cutting off imports in a key sector may increase domestic employment. This may "prime the pump," and put the economy on the road to macroeconomic recovery at the expense of only small microeconomic losses. The best rejoinder to this argument is that there are more sophisticated tools of macroeconomic policy that can do the same job with less microeconomic damage.

Multiple Factors

Our discussion up to this point has been limited to an economy in which there is only one factor of production, labor. Removing this assumption has some interesting implications. To see what these are, let us modify our earlier Spain-Norway example. We shall assume from now on that fishing requires a relatively large capital investment per worker, and farming a relatively small one. In the accepted terminology, fishing is said to be *capital intensive* and farming *labor intensive.*

We shall still assume that in the absence of trade, the opportunity cost of fish would be higher in Spain than in Norway. The theory of comparative advantage still applies, regardless of the number of factors of production with which we deal. International trade will still make it possible for total world production of both fish and grain to increase. It will still enable the quantities of both goods available for consumption in both countries to increase. Now, a new question arises concerning the gains from trade. How will they be distributed internally within each country?

Internal Distribution

To answer this question, we need to look at what happens in factor markets as trade brings about increasing specialization in each country. In Norway, production shifts from farming to fishing. As grain production is phased out, large quantities of labor and relatively small quantities of capital will be released. The shift in production will thus create a surplus of labor and a shortage of capital. Factor markets can return to equilibrium only when wages fall relative to the rate of return on capital. Only then will fisheries adopt relatively more labor-using methods of production. Meanwhile, in Spain, an opposite process occurs. The shift from fishing to farming depresses the rate of return on capital, and increases the wage rate. This causes Spanish farmers to use more capital per worker than before.

These changes in relative factor prices determine how the gains from trade are distributed among the people of each country. Spanish workers and Norwegian ship owners will gain doubly from trade. They will gain first because trade increases the size of the pie (that is, the total available quantity of goods), and second because the factor price shifts give them a relatively larger slice of the larger pie. For Norwegian workers and Spanish farm owners, in contrast, one of these effects works against the other. They still benefit from the growth of the pie, but they get a relatively smaller piece of it than before. They may or may not end up better off on balance as a result of trade. Suppose that the comparative advantage in the pretrade situation were large, and that the difference in factor intensity between the two countries were small. Norwegian workers and Spanish farm owners would then still gain from trade in an *absolute* sense, even though they would lose ground *relative* to others in their own country. If conditions were not so favorable, however, they could end up absolutely worse off than before trade began.

Mobility

In the preceding section, we considered only two broadly defined factors of production, labor and capital. What we said there applies even more forcefully when we turn our attention to narrowly defined factors of production. Suppose that we think not in terms of labor in general, but in terms of farmers and fishermen, and not in terms of capital in general, but in terms of boat owners and tractor owners. Then it becomes even more likely that trade will have a strongly uneven impact on incomes. The more specialized and less mobile factors of production are, the more relative factor prices will shift as a result of trade. The more likely it then will be that some specific groups will be harmed by trade.

Let us take an example nearer to home than that of Norwegian farmers and Spanish fishermen. Consider instead the effects on the American economy of increased imports of Japanese textiles. We can divide the impact of increased textile imports into three parts. First, all consumers in the country will benefit because textiles will be cheaper than before. Second, the Japanese will increase their purchases of American goods. This will benefit Americans who work in export-oriented industries. Finally, American textile workers and manufacturers will suffer a decreased demand for their products. Those with relatively mobile skills or assets can escape most of the impact by moving to other industries. For example, a truck driver working for a textile firm could switch to hauling peaches, or a plant making shirt boxes could switch to making shoe boxes. Some workers, however, would be less mobile because of their personal circumstances or the specialization of their skills. They would be likely to suffer a loss of income that would more than offset the benefits they would receive as consumers from cheaper textiles. Imagine a middle-aged, highly specialized spinning machine operator, with all his savings tied up in a house in a small textile town. He would derive slim consolation from being able to buy a cheap Japanese raincoat to wear on his weekly visits to the unemployment office.

In aggregate terms, the loss to the group adversely affected is more than offset by the gains to others in the economy. But this fact is not likely to make much practical impression on unemployed textile workers. They will see free trade as a threat, and will campaign for protection. The government will then have a hard political decision to make. Which group of interests should it look after? How much weight should it place on the widespread gains from trade, and how much on the complaints of particular people who do not share in those gains? Is there any way to reconcile these conflicting interests?

Distributive Justice

These are questions of normative economics. If the people who lose from free trade are more deserving than those who gain, then the principle of distributive justice might call for protection. Protection will not necessarily advance distributive justice, however. The immediate impact points in that direction, but a number of things must be taken into account before we can make a balanced judgment.

First, to protect textiles would benefit textile workers. Suppose that these workers were relatively low paid and had lower than average mobility. If one's idea of distributive justice emphasized support for the incomes of low-paid workers, the impact of a protectionist policy would be beneficial.

Second, the tariff or quota would also benefit the owners of other factors used in the textile industry. These would include stockholders, other investors, executives, and owners of real estate in textile communities. On the average, ownership of nonlabor resources tends to be concentrated in the hands of people with relatively high incomes. It is hard to say that with these other factors owners would gain more or less from protection than workers would. That could be discovered only by empirical study. It is very likely that this part of the impact, considered separately, would tend to increase inequality.

Third, protecting textiles would hurt consumers at large by raising textile prices. Again, it is hard to be sure about the distributional impact of this without detailed study. We would have to know whether high-or low-income groups tend to spend the greater share of their incomes on textile products. A seat-of-the-pants guess is that the pinch of higher textile prices would be felt more keenly by low-income groups.

Finally, even if we determined that the benefits of protection were concentrated on groups meriting special consideration, and adverse effects on less meritorious groups, one difficulty remains. We know that the losses to those harmed by protection will be greater in aggregate than the benefits to those helped. Does the gain in equality, if any, more than offset this loss in efficiency? In short, protecting a certain industry *might* improve things from the point of view of distributive justice, but this result is far from certain.

Alternative Policies

Let us suppose, for the sake of argument, that we were happy with the distributional impact of protecting textiles. Suppose even that we judge this favorable result to outweigh the necessary loss in efficiency. Would this make us support protectionism? Not yet. Before we come to any definite conclusion, we should compare the policy of protection with any alternative policies that might have the same beneficial distributive effects. One such alternative might be to subsidize the retraining and relocation of textile workers who lose their jobs. Another would simply be to pay these workers cash compensation.

How would these alternatives rate? In the terms of efficiency, they are not perfect, but probably they are better than tariffs or quotas. In terms of distributive justice, they seem to offer two advantages. One is that benefits are more precisely concentrated on the people we want to get them. The other is that the tax burden required to fund the alternative programs is likely to be distributed more equitably than the burden of high textile prices would be.

Conclusions

The debate over the merits of free trade versus protectionism has gone on for centuries. Adam Smith himself was one of the early spokesmen for free trade, with his doctrine that a highly developed division of labor depended on the widest possible market. Since his time, protectionism has never been widely popular in the economics profession. Among politicians, however, the pendulum has swung back and forth several times. There have been great eras of free trade, alternating with severe tariff wars. Today, it is hard to think of a major industrial country that does not have politically strong protectionist sentiment. Still, protectionists have not really had their way. Grudgingly, and against strong opposition, the world has moved toward freer trade in many ways in recent years. Trade policy will continue to be a source of political controversy in years to come. That is the only safe prediction.

SUMMARY

1. A country is said to have a comparative advantage in the production of any good that it can produce at a lower opportunity cost than its trading partners. Trading nations can realize mutual benefits if each specializes in products for which it has a comparative advantage. Such specialization can give consumers in each country more of all goods than they would have without international trade.

2. Some arguments against free trade are based on considerations of positive economics. Of these, the "cheap foreign labor" and "infant industry" arguments have little merit. The "terms of trade" argument establishes that a country with monopoly or monopsony power in international markets can gain by imposing tariffs on imported goods—but only if its trading partners do not retaliate. Trade restrictions are sometimes used to combat domestic unemployment in periods of macroeconomic disturbance, but conventional tools of macro policy are likely to be superior for such a purpose.

3. Other protectionist arguments emphasize normative considerations. In a world of multiple factors of production, many of which may be highly specialized, certain groups of workers or capitalists can gain by the exclusion of foreign competition. Their gains are more than offset, however, by losses to others of their fellow citizens.

DISCUSSION QUESTIONS

1. Suppose you learned that Vladimir Horowitz, the great pianist, was also an amazingly proficient typist. Knowing this, would it surprise you to learn also that he hired a secretary to type his correspondence, even though he could do the job better and faster himself? What does this have to do with comparative advantage?

2. Turn to Exhibit 36.1. Suppose that new, high-yield grains were introduced in Norway, so that the number of labor hours needed to grow a ton of grain there were cut from 5 hours to $2\frac{1}{2}$ hours. What would happen to trade between Norway and Spain? Would it still pay for Norwegians to import their grain from Spain? If the labor hours per ton of grain in Norway fell all the way to 2, what would happen to the pattern of trade?

3. A few years ago, President Nixon announced something called "Project Independence" that was intended to free this country from dependence on imported oil through development of domestic energy resources. What would be the benefits of that policy? Would everyone in the country potentially benefit from such a policy, or only some groups? What disadvantages would Project Independence have, compared with continued dependence on foreign oil?

4. Suppose that you became President of the United States, and that you were a convinced advocate of free trade. Would your policy be to cut out all U.S. tariffs and quotas at once, or would you bargain with your trading partners, saying that you would cut U.S. tariffs only if they cut their own tariffs? Why would a mutual reduction be better than a one-sided reduction?

5. Simple trade theory suggests that countries will export goods in which they have a comparative advantage and import goods in which they have a comparative disadvantage. In fact, countries often import the same kinds of goods they export. For example, most countries that are big exporters of automobiles are also big importers of automobiles. Why do you think that happens?

CHAPTER 37
The Balance of Payments and the International Monetary System

What You Will Learn in This Chapter

The macroeconomic branch of international trade theory focuses on problems of the balance of international payments. A country runs a balance of payments deficit if it pays out more to foreigners than it takes in from them. If the situation is reversed, the country runs a balance of payments surplus. Because there are many different kinds of international transactions, there are several different ways of measuring a country's balance of payments. The effects of a payments imbalance on exchange rates and on the domestic economy depend on the rules of international monetary institutions. In recent years there have been dramatic changes in the structures of these institutions. The future of the international monetary system is still uncertain.

For Review

Here are some important terms and concepts that will be put to use in this chapter. Be certain that you understand them, or review them before proceeding.

Money and national income determination (Chapter 13)
Elasticity (Chapter 18)
Tariffs and quotas (Chapter 36)

Of all the economic news that makes the headlines, that involving the balance of payments is probably the least well understood. Even well-informed people, who read news reports of inflation and unemployment with at least a basic understanding of what is going on, may have only the haziest idea of how the international monetary system works. This makes our job in this chapter in some ways a hard one. In a few short pages, we must try to deal with an area of economics that is properly the subject of a specialized course itself. At the same time, we cannot fairly assume that the reader has much of a head start. We shall try to meet these difficulties by limiting our objectives, concentrating on the basics, and omitting all but a bare minimum of technicalities.

The Balance of Payments

Domestic Trade and Payments

We shall begin by presenting some basic terms and concepts relating to the balance of payments. To get a better understanding of the balance of payments among nations, we shall first look at the balance of payments among states.

Suppose that two states, say Illinois and Wisconsin, trade only with each other. Wisconsin sells food to Illinois and acts as a vacationland for Illinois residents. Illinois sells manufactured goods to Wisconsin. If the dollar value of Illinois imports (Wisconsin exports) equals the value of Illinois exports (Wisconsin imports), the quantity of money in each state will remain unchanged. The amount spent on food and travel by Illinois residents will be offset by the amount earned by other Illinois residents who sell manufactured goods. The same will be true in Wisconsin. Bank deposits in both states will remain unchanged. Payments will be in balance.

Deficit and Surplus

Balance of Trade Deficit (Surplus) A country runs a balance of trade deficit (surplus) if the value of goods and services that it imports exceeds (falls short of) the value of goods and services that it exports.

Next, suppose that people living in Illinois buy more from Wisconsin than they sell. This creates a **balance of trade deficit** for Illinois and a **balance of trade surplus** for Wisconsin. Initially, Illinois residents can make up the deficit by running down their dollar holdings. Banks in Illinois will notice that deposits are declining, and banks in Wisconsin will notice that deposits are increasing. If the deficit persists, people and banks in Illinois will find themselves low on dollars. They may borrow from Wisconsin banks or merchants in order to continue their purchases. Illinois banks that are short on dollars may borrow from Wisconsin banks that have excess dollars. These funds in turn may be lent by Illinois banks to customers planning to buy goods from Wisconsin or planning to vacation there. In sum, a deficit state can finance a balance of trade deficit either by running down its stocks of currency or by short-term borrowing. If such borrowing is used, it is referred to as a **short-term capital flow.**

Short-Term Capital Flows Loans to or from foreigners, payable within one year or less.

Long-Term Capital Flows Long-term loans to or from foreigners, or transactions with foreigners involving capital assets.

Capital Account Deficit (Surplus) A country runs a capital account deficit (surplus) if the value of long-term capital flow to foreigners exceeds (falls short of) the value of long-term capital flows from foreigners.

Suppose now that the balance of trade in goods and services is corrected. Let us consider some different kinds of transactions. Suppose that Wisconsin residents buy stock in Illinois firms, and wealthy Illinois doctors buy farms in Wisconsin. These transactions are called **long-term capital flows.** If Illinois doctors spend less on farms than Wisconsin residents spend on stocks, we say that Illinois has a **capital account surplus** and Wisconsin a **capital account deficit.** A capital account deficit can be financed in much the same way as a trade deficit is financed. Wisconsin residents can draw down their holdings of dollars. They can also borrow from individuals or banks in Illinois, or they can borrow from their own banks which, in turn, borrow from banks in Illinois.

International Trade and Payments

Now let us turn to trade and payments between countries. We shall replace the state of Illinois in our example by the United States, and the state of Wisconsin by Mexico. All the movements of goods and services and capital assets that were possible between states are also possible between nations. There is just one major difference. *Each country has its own cur-*

rency. Mexico has the peso and the United States has the dollar. At the outset, let us assume that $1 is worth 12 pesos, without asking for the moment just why.

When Mexican goods are sold to foreigners, Mexican merchants will want to be paid in pesos. That is how they must meet their payrolls and pay their other expenses. Likewise, Americans doing business with Mexico will want to be paid in dollars. Each international transaction will thus require an intermediate step not necessary in trade between states: a visit to the **foreign exchange market.** By the foreign exchange market, we mean the whole family of institutions (including Mexican and American banks, specialized foreign exchange dealers, and official agencies of both governments) through which dollars may be exchanged for pesos and pesos for dollars.

Suppose that trade between the two countries is in balance, and there are no movements of long-term capital. The value of dollars brought to the foreign exchange market by Americans wanting to do business in Mexico will then be the same as the value of pesos brought by Mexicans wanting to do business in the United States. Trade is not always in balance, however. If the United States runs a trade deficit with Mexico, the value of dollars brought to the market will exceed the value of pesos taken there. In that case, any of a variety of things may happen. For a time, Americans may be able to finance the deficit by running down any stocks of pesos they have accumulated in the past. If that is not possible, Americans may ask Mexican exporters to accept deferred payments. That is the same as asking them for a loan. It is a type of short-term capital flow. Alternatively, American importers or their banks may get loans of pesos from Mexican banks. That is another type of short-term capital flow.

Goods Balance

The first line of Exhibit 37.1 gives the **goods** or **merchandise trade balance.** It is the difference between exports and imports of tangible goods. We can see from the table that the United States exported more than it imported in the years 1961 and 1966. By 1971, the situation was reversed. For the first time in the postwar period, we imported more than we ex-

Foreign Exchange Market The whole group of institutions, including banks, specialized foreign exchange dealers, and official government agencies through which the currency of one country may be exchanged for the currency of another.

Merchandise Trade Balance (Goods Balance) The difference between exports and imports of tangible goods.

EXHIBIT 37.1

U.S. balance of payments (billions of dollars)

Because there are so many different kinds of international transactions, there are many different ways of measuring a country's balance of payments surplus or deficit. Here are six common measures for the United States for selected recent years.

	1961	1966	1971	1974
Goods (merchandise trade balance)	5.6	3.8	−2.7	−5.3
Goods and services	5.6	5.2	0.7	3.8
Current account	3.1	2.3	−2.8	−3.3
Current account and long term capital (basic balance)	0	−1.7	−9.4	−10.7
Net liquidity balance	−2.3	−2.2	−22.0	−18.9
Official settlements balance	−1.3	0.2	−29.8	−8.4

Balance of Goods and Services
The merchandise trade balance plus the balance of services.

ported. (This caused great alarm in U.S. government circles.) The second item in Exhibit 37.1 includes services as well as goods. It is called the **balance of goods and services.** Services, or "invisibles" as they are sometimes called, include tourist expenditures, shipping, insurance, and income from foreign investments. All of these are "net"; that is, they are the difference between foreign purchases of American services and American purchases of foreign services. Investment income is the difference between the income received by Americans from their overseas investments and the income received by foreigners from their investments in the United States. By comparing lines 1 and 2 of the exhibit, we see that the service balance was zero in 1961 and positive in 1966, 1971, and 1974. The change was due primarily to a growth in income from direct American investments abroad.

Current Account Balance

Current Account Balance   The balance of goods and services plus net private and government transfers.

The third item in Exhibit 37.1 is the **current account balance.** It includes goods and services, plus net private and government transfers. When an American sends a check to a relative or charitable organization abroad, that is a private transfer. When the American government extends foreign aid, a government transfer occurs. As one would expect, the United States transfers more abroad than foreigners transfer to Americans.

Other Balances

Basic Balance   The current account balance plus long-term capital flows.

The fourth line of Exhibit 37.1 adds long-term capital flows to the current account balance. This item is called the **basic balance.** The table indicates that American investment abroad has exceeded investment by foreigners in the United States. This difference has been getting larger over time. Private short-term capital flows and government actions must offset any positive or negative basic balance.

Net Liquidity Balance   The basic balance plus short-term capital flows.

The fifth item is the **net liquidity balance.** This balance is frequently used as an overall indicator of our balance of payments position. The net liquidity balance adds short-term capital flows to the basic balance. (An "errors and omissions" item is also included.) Short-term capital, for accounting purposes, is anything maturing in less than a year. As we saw earlier, short-term capital flows can balance a payments deficit or surplus. Short-term capital transactions can also arise because of interest rate differentials between countries. In each of the years examined in Exhibit 37.1, the short-term capital account (net) contributed to a further imbalance in the balance of payments. The "errors and omissions" item is normally small, usually $1 billion or less. However, in 1971 it jumped to nearly $11 billion and is the factor most responsible for the large disparity between the basic balance and the net liquidity balance.

Official Settlements Balance
The net liquidity balance plus private liquid capital flows.

The final entry in Exhibit 37.1 is the **official settlements balance.** It differs from the liquidity balance mainly by including private liquid capital flows. Normally, if foreigners are financing a U.S. deficit by acquiring dollars, this item is positive. However, in 1971, this item was negative. The reason was that foreigners expected a fall in the value of the dollar. In order to profit by the change, they reduced their holding of dollars. More will be said about this later.

The official settlements balance, as its name implies, must be offset by government actions. The government of a deficit country can finance the remaining imbalance by encouraging governments of surplus countries to accumulate its currency. It can also run down its holdings of currency of the surplus country. In the past, the dollar was sought by many governments as a reserve asset, so the United States had little trouble persuading surplus countries to hold dollars. In recent years, things have changed. By 1971 it took a great deal of arm twisting, and ultimately some corrective action by the United States, to get foreign governments to hold dollars.

Foreign Exchange Markets and Exchange Rates

Foreign Exchange Markets

We are now ready to take up a question we previously had set aside. What is it that determines the rate at which one currency exchanges for another? Why is a dollar worth 12 pesos, rather than 10 or 14 or some other number of pesos? To arrive at an answer, we must first take a closer look at the foreign exchange market, to which we have previously referred only casually. Following this, we shall discuss alternative international monetary systems. Each of these is characterized by a different set of rules that governments pursue in intervening in the foreign exchange markets.

Foreign exchange markets, like so many other markets, can be analyzed in terms of supply and demand. To illustrate, let us return to the foreign exchange market in which pesos are bought and sold. The supply and demand curves for this market are shown in Exhibit 37.2.

Demand

We have drawn the demand curve for pesos with a negative slope. In practice, the slope depends on what happens to the demand by foreigners for Mexican goods when the exchange rate changes. Consider, for example, a piece of leather luggage made in Mexico that carries a domestic price of 500 pesos. If the rate of exchange were $1 per peso, an American would have

---

EXHIBIT 37.2
The foreign exchange market for pesos and dollars
The foreign exchange market for pesos and dollars is the whole complex of institutions, including banks, foreign exchange dealers, and official government agencies, through which pesos may be exchanged for dollars and dollars for pesos. The equilibrium rate is determined by the intersection of the supply and demand curves for a currency in the foreign exchange market.

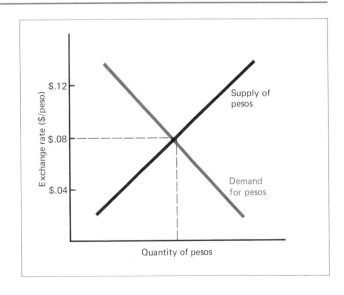

to put up $500 to obtain the luggage. Not much luggage would be sold, which means that not very many people would need to buy pesos. On the other hand, if a peso costs only $.10, the luggage would carry a price tag of only $50 to a U.S. buyer. Many such buyers would rush to exchange their dollars for pesos to take advantage of the bargain.

Supply

We have drawn the supply curve for pesos with an upward slope for similar reasons. Imagine that Mexicans are interested in buying American cars. If a peso is worth only $.10, a Mexican buyer would have to put up 30,000 of them to buy a car costing $3,000 in the United States and might think twice about the matter. But if a peso were worth $1, a car would cost only 3,000 pesos, and many more Mexican citizens could afford one.[1]

Shifts

Now let us consider some factors that can shift the demand and supply schedules. First, demand. Two important factors affecting demand are the price level in Mexico and Mexican interest rates. Should the price level in Mexico rise, say, by 10 percent, the Mexican luggage, which previously sold for 500 pesos, would now sell for 550 pesos. At each exchange rate, foreigners would need 10 percent more dollars to buy Mexican goods. They thus would demand fewer pesos at each rate of exchange, and the demand curve would shift to the left.[2] Alternatively, an increase in Mexican interest rates would increase the yield on investments made in Mexico and make Mexican assets more attractive to foreigners. This would increase the demand for pesos at any given exchange rate, and shift the demand schedule to the right. The demand curve for pesos can thus be shifted either by factors affecting Mexico's trade account or by factors affecting its capital account. In addition, the demand curve for pesos can be influenced by economic events outside Mexico's borders. If there is a sharp upturn in the American economy, for example, American consumers' demand for all goods and services will rise. This includes their demand for Mexican luggage, Acapulco vacations, and other Mexican exports. To get these things, they must trade in more dollars for pesos, and the peso demand curve will once again shift to the right.

From what we have said about demand, it is not hard to guess what factors might shift the supply curve of pesos. Only the names of the two countries need to be exchanged. A fall in the price level or a rise in the interest rate in the United States could induce Mexicans to bring more pesos to the market to offer for dollars. So will an upturn in nominal incomes in Mexico. These things would shift the supply curve rightward. On the other hand, inflation in the United States, a fall in American interest rates, or a recession in Mexico would all cause the supply curve of pesos to shift to the left.

---

[1]To be precise in this matter, an upward-sloping supply curve for pesos requires that Mexicans have an *elastic* demand for American goods. In a more detailed treatment of foreign exchange markets, we would have to consider also the possibility of an inelastic Mexican demand for American goods, and thus a backward-bending supply curve for pesos.

[2]Here we assume the American demand for Mexican goods also to be elastic. See footnote 1 above.

What happens when supply and demand curves shift around in the foreign exchange market? That depends on the rules of the game, as determined by international monetary institutions. Before describing the actual rules that have governed the international monetary system in recent years, let us examine two theoretically possible "pure" systems. These will teach us some important elements of theory, and provide a framework of reference from which to discuss the real systems.

The Gold Standard

The first international monetary system we shall look at is one in which the exchange rates of one currency for another are rigidly fixed. This would be the case if both Mexico and the United States were on a strict **gold standard.** For the two countries to be on a gold standard means that "peso" and "dollar" are really just terms for differing quantities of gold, that is, local names for gold coins of different sizes with pictures honoring different sets of dictators and colonial slaveowners. Suppose that 12½ of the coins called "peso" weigh the same as one of those called "dollar." The value of a peso would then be $.08.

Gold Standard An international monetary system in which the currencies of different countries are simply names for differing quantities of gold.

With these circumstances in mind, let us look at the foreign exchange market. Turn to Exhibit 37.3. Suppose that initially the market is in equilibrium with the supply curve in the position S, and the demand curve in the position D_1. Then suppose that for some reason, say, an increase in American incomes, the demand curve for pesos shifts to the right to the position D_2. This creates a surplus of pesos, as shown by the horizontal gap between the supply and demand curves at the exchange rate of $.08 per peso. American citizens are bringing more dollars to the exchange markets than Mexican citizens are willing to sell.

Imbalance

Since both countries are on the gold standard, it is easy for the Mexican government to deal with the imbalance. It buys the excess dollars, melts them down, remints them as pesos, and sells them to Americans wanting to

---

EXHIBIT 37.3
Foreign exchange market adjustments under a gold standard
An increase in American demand for Mexican goods shifts the demand curve for pesos from D_1 to D_2. This creates a balance of payments surplus in Mexico. Under a gold standard, this surplus leads to an increase in the Mexican money supply. That pushes up Mexican prices and cuts Mexican interest rates, shifting the demand curve back to D_3. It also stimulates Mexican demand for American goods and assets, shifting the peso supply to S_2. These demand and supply curve shifts restore equilibrium at the original exchange rate.

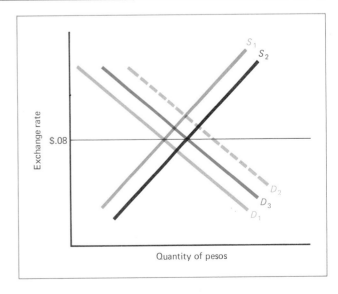

do business in Mexico. This action by the Mexican authorities has immediate repercussions. The newly minted pesos increase the Mexican money supply. As we learned in earlier chapters, an increase in the money supply tends to (1) raise prices, (2) lower interest rates, and (3) stimulate economic activity. Higher prices and lower interest rates in Mexico shift the demand curve for pesos to the left, because Mexican goods and securities become less attractive to American buyers. At the same time, rising nominal incomes in Mexico shift the supply curve of pesos to the right, as Mexicans buy more imports from the United States.

Meanwhile, the U.S. money supply falls as dollars flow into the Mexican mint. The resulting macroeconomic events north of the border reinforce the movements of the supply and demand curves. Sooner or later the curves will shift to positions like S_2 and D_3, where supply and demand are once again equal at the fixed exchange rate. When this happens, money supplies in both countries are once again stabilized, and equilibrium is reestablished.

Restoration of Equilibrium

We see, then, that a gold standard system contains a built-in mechanism that restores equilibrium automatically in the event of changes in supply and demand. This mechanism works in three steps. First, imbalance in the foreign exchange market causes changes in the money supplies of the trading countries. Next, changes in domestic money supplies cause changes in prices, interest rates, and nominal incomes in the domestic economics. Finally, these changes in turn cause corrective shifts in supply and demand curves in the foreign exchange market.

Flexible Rates

The second possible international monetary system we shall consider is one based on completely flexible exchange rates. "Peso" and "dollar" are now no longer names for differing quantities of gold. They are the names of two completely independent paper currencies issued by the Mexican and U.S. governments. Let us see how this system operates in the face of changing conditions in international markets.

Suppose once again that the foreign exchange market is initially in equilibrium and that payments in both countries are in balance. The demand curve is at D_1, the supply curve is at S_1, and the equilibrium price of pesos at $.08 as shown in Exhibit 37.4. Once more an increase in nominal incomes in the United States causes the demand curve to shift to D_2. What happens? This time the excess demand for pesos meets with no action on the part of either government. American importers bid against one another for the limited supply of pesos that Mexican citizens are willing to sell and drive the price of the peso upward to an equilibrium level around $.12. As the exchange rate rises, Mexicans are encouraged to buy more American goods, moving up along the peso supply curve in the process. At the same time, Americans are partially discouraged from buying more Mexican goods. They move up and to the left along their new demand curve. These movements restore payments to balance on both sides, with no action taken by government and no changes in the domestic money supply in either country.

EXHIBIT 37.4

Foreign exchange market adjustments under flexible rates

An increase in American demand for Mexican goods shifts the demand curve for pesos from D_1 to D_2. That creates a balance of payments surplus for Mexico. Under a system of flexible exchange rates, the surplus is corrected by a movement along the supply curve to a new equilibrium exchange rate where S_1 and D_2 intersect. No changes in the Mexican money supply need occur.

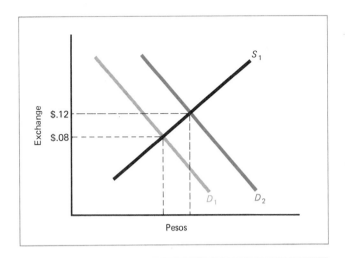

The Postwar International Monetary System

Bretton Woods

After World War II, the major trading nations of the world favored neither a rigid gold standard nor a perfectly flexible system of exchange rates. Instead, meeting under United Nations auspices at Bretton Woods, New Hampshire, in 1944, they established a mixed system. The International Monetary Fund (IMF), with headquarters in Washington, D.C., was established to administer the new system. At the present time, 124 nations are members of the IMF.

Adjustable Peg

The system established at Bretton Woods was based on the idea of an "adjustable peg." Let us look in brief at the rules of the international monetary game as it was played under the watchful eye of the IMF from 1944 until early 1973. So-called **par values** were established for each currency in terms of the U.S. dollar. Exchange rates were "pegged" at the par values. This means that they were allowed to fluctuate under the influence of supply and demand within a narrow band ranging from 2.25 percent above par to 2.25 percent below par. (The limits were only 1 percent until December 1971.) When the value of a currency rose to the upper limit or fell to the lower one, the government of the country in question was obligated under IMF rules to intervene and prevent further movement. A government faced with an excess demand for its currency at the limit rate had to sell enough of its own currency in exchange for dollars to soak up the excess demand. A government faced with an excess supply of its currency had to buy it in exchange for dollars if necessary to keep its price from slipping below the limit.

If the government of a deficit or surplus country got tired of intervening in the exchange market, it had another option under the rules of the game. It could "adjust the peg," that is, change the par value of its currency. This might be done in either of two slightly different ways. One was

Par Values Under the monetary system run by the International Monetary Fund from 1944 to 1973, the par value for a currency was the official exchange rate around which the actual exchange rate was permitted to fluctuate only within a narrow band.

immediately to declare a new par value above or below the initial value. The other was temporarily to *float* the currency. That means letting it find a new equilibrium value under the influence of supply and demand without government intervention. A new par value would later be fixed at the market-determined rate when things seemed to have settled down. (A few countries, notably Canada, let their currencies float for years at a time in the postwar period. This, however, was considered to be a violation of at least the spirit, if not the letter, of IMF rules.)

Adjustable Peg in Action

Let us look at the IMF system in action using our example of the United States and Mexico once again. Exhibit 37.5 shows the initial position, with supply at S_1 and demand at D_1. Equilibrium is achieved at an exchange rate of $.10 per peso. We shall assume this to be the par value. The upper and lower limits of permissible fluctuation are indicated by the shaded band from $.1025 to $.0975. (The width of the band has been exaggerated in the exhibit to make it easier to read.)

Now suppose that persistent inflation in Mexico begins to shift the demand curve for pesos to the left. Until the demand curve reaches the position D_2, the exchange rate floats downward as in a system of fully flexible rates. If inflation persists, however, and the demand curve shifts as far as position D_3, the Mexican government must do something. Its first recourse is to draw on its reserve of dollars in order to soak up the excess supply of pesos. This action tends to decrease the domestic money supply. The excess pesos put into the exchange market now go to the Mexican government treasury rather than going to American importers or tourists, who would buy Mexican goods from Mexican merchants, who would redeposit the pesos in Mexican banks. As in the case of the gold standard, this fall in the Mexican money supply would have a deflationary effect on the Mexican economy. The demand and supply curves would shift back to a point where they would intersect within the permissible exchange rate band.

What if the Mexican government does not have any reserves of dollars with which to buy pesos and support their price? Or what if after a period of supporting the peso, it runs out of dollars? As a stopgap measure, it had the right, under the rules set up at Bretton Woods, to borrow dollars from the IMF and continue its support efforts. If it did not want to do this, or if it borrowed up to the limit without eliminating the excess supply of pesos, it could devalue. That would mean letting the par value of the peso fall to the intersections of S_1 and D_3 in Exhibit 37.5. New limits of fluctuation would then be set up around that value.

Avoiding Adjustment

Under the postwar adjustable peg system, adjustments were not entirely automatic, even when exchange rates reached their permissible limits of fluctuations. The two possible mechanisms for restoring equilibrium in the foreign exchange markets—changes in the domestic money supply, or changes in par values—could both be short-circuited. Let us see how this could be done.

EXHIBIT 37.5

The foreign exchange market with an adjustable peg
Under the adjustable peg system, small shifts in supply or demand simply cause exchange rates to fluctuate within a narrow band around the par value of a currency. A shift in the demand curve for pesos from D_1 to D_2 would thus cause the value of the peso to fall from its par value to its lower limit, $2\frac{1}{2}$ percent below the par value. If there were a larger shift in demand, such as from D_1 to D_3, the Mexican government would have to intervene in the foreign exchange market, buying enough pesos to keep their value from falling below $.0975.

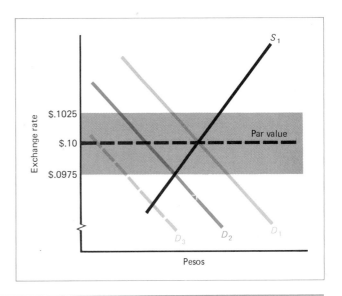

Refer once again to Exhibit 37.5. Suppose that when the demand curve shifts to the position D_3, the Mexican authorities do not want to float or devalue the peso. For domestic political or economic reasons, however, they do not want the deflationary consequences of a decrease in the domestic money supply either. For the time being, they could avoid both devaluation and deflation by an operation known as **sterilization.** For each peso taken out of circulation by their support actions, they could put a brand new peso back into circulation by any of the usual tools of domestic monetary policy. This action "sterilizes" or short-circuits any effect of the exchange markets on the domestic economy. (Sterilization, of course, could also be used by surplus countries wanting to avoid increases in the domestic money supply.)

Sterilization A policy of using domestic monetary policy to offset the effect of a balance of payments deficit or surplus on the domestic money supply.

Sterilization, unfortunately, has one serious drawback. Because it thwarts the automatic mechanism that would restore payments balance to an economy, there is no assurance that a country will not have to keep supporting and sterilizing forever once it starts! This unappealing prospect often drives governments to desperate measures.

Trade Restrictions

Suppose that a government is faced with a persistent balance of payments deficit, and does not want either to deflate or devalue. When it begins to run out of foreign reserves and IMF borrowing rights, it can reduce the excess supply of its currency by imposing direct restrictions on foreign trade. Such restrictions come in several kinds and varieties. Among the most commonly employed are the following:

1. Tariffs, which we discussed in the last chapter, are special taxes levied on imports at their point of entry. They accomplish their objective by raising the price of foreign goods to domestic buyers. If Mexico imposes tariffs on American goods, the supply curve for pesos will shift to the left.

2. Quotas, which we also encountered in Chapter 36, are legal limits on the quantity of particular types of goods that can be brought into a country in a given period of time. If Mexico imposes quotas on American goods, the supply curve of pesos will shift to the left.

3. Exchange controls are another type of trade restriction. One common form of exchange control is for the government to assume a legal monopoly on buying and selling foreign exchange. Importers and tourists must then apply to the government for foreign exchange rather than buying in the international market. The government can ration the available quantity of foreign currency as it sees fit. (In diagrammatic terms, a government that adopts exchange controls in effect replaces the supply curve of its currency with a vertical line that can be moved about at will.)

4. A final type of trade restriction is the use of export subsidies. Subsidies to exports make it possible for domestic firms to sell their goods at prices more attractive to foreigners. In our example, if Mexico were to adopt export subsidies, the demand curve for pesos would shift to the right.

The trouble with all these policies is that they invite retaliation by foreign countries. Such retaliation can cancel out any beneficial effects on the balance of payments. The end effect of a general imposition of trade restrictions is a decline in the total volume of international trade, and a decline in the efficiency and prosperity of the world economy as a whole.

Weaknesses of the System

Although the adjustable peg system established at Bretton Woods lasted nearly thirty years, it suffered from some elemental weaknesses that led eventually to its downfall. The main weakness of the system was that it was crisis-prone. Because adjustments were never fully automatic, governments often resisted making small adjustments when they would have been only slightly painful. Instead, they waited for pressures to build up that eventually tore the system apart.

In outline, here is the scenario for the kind of international monetary crisis that repeatedly occurred under the Bretton Woods rules. Some country, let us say the United Kingdom, runs a persistent balance of payments deficit. A chronic excess supply of British pounds sterling appears on the world's exchange markets. The British government is forced to support the pound. It does not want to deflate, so it sterilizes. (Or else it does deflate, but not enough to do any lasting good.) Gradually dollar reserves are run dangerously low, and the British government is forced to borrow from the IMF or the U.S. Treasury. It may try imposing exchange controls or other trade restrictions, but these meet with threats of retaliation and domestic political resistence. It becomes harder and harder to keep the pound from breaking through the floor.

Speculation

At this point *speculation* enters the picture. Let us interrupt our scenario for a brief digression on speculation. Speculators are active all the time in international currency markets. Their game works like this: Suppose the pound is floating around happily between its upper limit of

$2.45 and its lower limit of $2.35, changing a bit from day to day. If I buy £100,000 today at $2.40, and tomorrow the vagaries of supply and demand carry the rate up to $2.41, I can change them back into dollars and pocket a clear profit of $1,000. The problem is that in normal times no one can quite be sure whether the pound is on its way up or its way down. I might just as easily lose $1,000. Heads you win, tails you lose. Speculators are professional risk takers who perform a number of useful economic functions. In normal times, though, they do not play a very big role in the international payments picture.

Now back to our scenario where the British government is hanging desperately on the brink of a forced devaluation. At this point, speculators are faced with the kind of situation they are always looking for, but are rarely lucky enough to find. That is a situation in which it is *heads you win, tails you break even.* The question of the day is, will the pound hold at $2.35, or will it be devalued? Suppose that I sell all the pounds I can get my hands on, borrowing them if necessary. If the pound is devalued to $2.10 tomorrow, I can buy pounds back to pay off the loans and make a huge profit. If the British government somehow muddles through, and the pound holds, I lose practically nothing. At the very worst, the pound will rise a cent or two off its floor and I will have to pay a few days' or weeks' interest on the loans.

The final scene in the sterling crisis is set when speculators start to pour hundreds of millions of pounds into the foreign exchange market. The excess supply of sterling becomes overwhelming, and the last straw forcing an *actual* devaluation is the speculative pressure occurring in *anticipation* of the devaluation.

Crisis and Reform

In early 1973, an especially severe crisis occurred, involving the U.S. dollar, the German mark, and the Japanese yen. In response to this crisis, the major trading nations took the bold step of abandoning the adjustable peg, and allowing their currencies to float vis-à-vis one another. The relative value of the yen, the dollar, and the mark were allowed to find their own levels under the influence of supply and demand.

The international monetary system that emerged from the crisis of 1973 is still a mixed system. It contains a number of features that do not conform exactly to a pure flexible rate system. It usually is referred to as a flexible rate system because it is so much more flexible than the adjustable peg, but two important restrictions must be kept in mind.

First, not every currency floats against every other currency. Rather, the system is one in which major blocks of currencies float against one another. A major group of countries of Western Europe tried pegging their currencies against one another in an arrangement colorfully known as "the snake." Countries with strong trading ties with the United States have pegged their currencies to the dollar. Those with strong ties to Britain have pegged theirs to the pound. Movements between blocks have been substantial, though. Because increased flexibility has been introduced, several currencies have swung by as much as 20–30 percent. Occasionally there have been swings of 2 or 3 percent in a single day.

Second, movements of exchange rates have been characterized by the active but largely uncoordinated intervention of central banks. Movements in exchange rates are often resisted, either because of their possible effects on domestic inflation or because of their possible impact on particular politically sensitive sectors of the domestic economy. A float of a currency with sporadic central bank intervention is sometimes called a "dirty float." This term aptly distinguishes the current system from the perfectly flexible system of economic theory.

Conclusions[3]

The new world of the "dirty float" has not been with us long enough to allow any really conclusive evaluation. Enough has been learned, though, to be able to say that flexibility has worked much better than its opponents feared, although not as well as its strongest advocates had hoped. Here are some tentative conclusions that can be drawn from the first two years of experience with the new system.

First, it does appear that flexible rates have permitted countries to correct payments balances. In the days of the adjustable peg, critics of flexible rates often argued that demand elasticities for goods traded internationally might be so low that changes in exchange rates would have hardly any effect on nations' balance of payments. Not all the evidence is in, but what there is seems not to confirm the worst fears of these "elasticity pessimists."

Second, flexible rate advocates are disappointed that the new system has not led to a reduction in the use of trade restrictions. Critics of the adjustable peg used to argue that trade restrictions were desperation measures forced on governments by the inflexibility of the old system. Unfortunately, no tendency toward a withering away of trade restrictions can yet be seen.

Third, the new system has not been as effective as some thought it would be in freeing domestic macroeconomic policy from the influence of world monetary effects. This can be seen as either a good or a bad thing, depending on one's point of view. Under the old system, governments often damaged their domestic economies by deflationary policies aimed at maintaining unrealistic parity values for their currencies. Now they are a little less likely to do so, although they remain under some pressure in that direction. On the other hand, under the old system international pressures sometimes restrained governments from pursuing recklessly inflationary policies. That was seen as a plus. It is probably fortunate that the new system has not led to complete autonomy of domestic policy from international effects, so that exchange rates still provide some degree of anti-inflationary discipline.

Finally, some observers of the new system have been surprised at the size of the impact that exchange rate movements have had on domestic inflation. When devaluation of a country's currency leads to domestic inflation, the effectiveness of that devaluation is reduced. The problem of

---

[3]This section draws on a useful paper by Marina V. N. Whitman, "The Payments Adjustment Process and the Exchange Rate Regime: What Have We Learned?" *American Economic Review*, May 1975.

transmitting inflationary problems from one country to another is at the same time made worse. In theory, it should be possible for exchange rate movements to take place with no significant effect on domestic price levels. Things have not worked out this way in practice.

There is no point in even pretending to forecast what the future will bring. A return to an adjustable peg system, or some slightly more flexible variant of it, is by no means out of the question. The European "snake" is an example of a movement in that direction.

There is also a small but vocal group of economists who favor a return to a strict gold standard. They see the inflationary effects of either floating rates or an adjustable peg as a great danger. They view the prospect of taking the weapon of discretionary monetary policy away from national governments as beneficial to the world economy. But gold standard advocates are a definite minority.

A recent survey of experience with flexible rates concluded modestly that "flexible rates are a second best in a world where the efficiency advantages of integration and a single international money must yield place to nations' insistence on individual sovereignty in the determination of domestic targets and policy instruments."[4] The writer added that it is hard to imagine any workable alternative to flexible rates in a world where nations experience high and widely varying rates of inflation. At the moment, the betting must be that flexible rates will be with us for some time to come, but nothing is certain. Readers of this chapter are advised to pay attention to the newspapers.

SUMMARY

1. If a country imports a greater value of goods and services than it exports, it runs a balance of trade deficit. Such a deficit can be financed by drawing down domestic holdings of foreign currency, or by short-term borrowing from foreigners. A capital account deficit occurs if purchases of capital assets from foreigners exceed sales of capital assets to foreigners. Such a deficit can be financed in the same way as a balance of trade deficit.

2. The exchange rates between different currencies are determined in foreign exchange markets. Changes in incomes or prices or interest rates in a country will affect the demand for that country's currency. Changes in foreign incomes or price levels or interest rates will affect the supply of a country's currency.

3. Under a gold standard, an automatic mechanism restores equilibrium whenever a country runs a payments deficit or surplus. Such an imbalance causes the money supply of a deficit country to fall. That leads to lower prices, higher interest rates, and lower nominal incomes in the deficit country. Those effects stimulate the demand for and reduce the supply of the country's currency on foreign exchange markets, thus restoring equilibrium. Opposite effects are felt in a surplus country.

4. Under a system of flexible exchange rates, a balance of payments deficit or surplus is corrected entirely by movements in exchange rates. No government action need be taken, and no changes in domestic money supplies need occur.

5. The postwar international monetary system established at Bretton Woods in 1944 was neither a gold standard nor a purely flexible system. It featured an "adjustable peg," that is, an official par value for each currency around which fluctuations were permitted within a narrow range. Temporary payment surpluses or deficits could be corrected by government intervention in foreign

[4]*Ibid.*

exchange markets. Persistent payments imbalances could be corrected by changes in par values. The system worked tolerably well for many years, but it was always crisis-prone. The adjustable peg was abandoned in 1973 after a particularly severe series of crises.

6. Under the current international monetary system, major currencies or blocs of currencies float against one another in a system of essentially flexible exchange markets. The system does not work perfectly, but it seems to work better than the critics of flexible rates feared prior to 1973.

DISCUSSION QUESTIONS

1. Have you seen any news items lately that concern the balance of payments surplus or deficit between your state and neighboring states? Why is the balance of payments between states of less interest than the balance of payments between nations?

2. A country that runs a trade deficit is often said to have an "unfavorable" balance of payments. What is unfavorable about such a situation? Are not the citizens of a country better off if they are able to consume many foreign goods without having to give up an equivalent value of goods in export?

3. Trace the effects of each of these kinds of transactions in terms of the balance of payments accounts given in Exhibit 37.1:
    a. A London businessman buys $1 million in stock in General Motors through the New York Stock Exchange.
    b. A woman in Cleveland sends $100 as a Christmas gift to her aunt in Poland.
    c. You fly to Japan on an American carrier, and spend $1,000 on photographic equipment while you are there. You bring the goods back with you when you return.
    d. While you are on vacation in Mexico, the owner of a local movie house hires you to distribute advertising leaflets to your fellow American tourists. He pays you 100 pesos. You save the money, and change it into U.S. dollars when you return home.

4. Suppose that the British demand for foreign goods is unit elastic and the foreign demand for British goods is perfectly inelastic. (Check these terms in the glossary or review Chapter 18 if you are not certain of them.) Could the British government then correct a balance of trade deficit by devaluing the pound? If not, is there any other way for it to correct a balance of trade deficit?

5. If a government wishes to "peg" its exchange rate, what does it have to do? Does it just announce the par value it wants to maintain, or does it have to back up its announcement with actions? What kind of actions?

PART SEVEN
Economic Systems
Compared

When we speak of an economic system, we mean the whole pattern of economic institutions that determine the way resources are allocated in a society. In most branches of economics, systems and institutions are among the "givens" of our analysis. For example, in macroeconomics, we develop theories concerning how an increase in the money supply will affect prices and interest rates, on the assumption of a given institutional structure of the banking system and credit markets. Sometimes we examine the effects of the change in one particular institution, while assuming that others do not change. An example would be a study of the effects of fixed versus flexible exchange rates on world trade. In the branch of economics we call comparative economic systems, though, the scope of our analysis is much broader. Institutions and whole systems of institutions become the variables rather than the givens of analysis.

Economic systems can be grouped into broad categories on the basis of certain common traits. One way to classify economic systems is on the basis of property rights. Property can be owned privately, owned cooperatively by voluntary associations of individuals, or owned by the government. In practice, examples of each kind of ownership can be found in almost every economic system, but often one form or another predominates. In those economies that we call capitalist, for example, there is widespread private ownership of nonlabor factors of production. In socialist economies, cooperative or government ownership prevails.

Economic systems can also be classified in terms of their organizational structure. In Chapter 21, we learned that there are two general principles by which the division of labor in an economy may be coordinated. One is the managerial principle, which depends on centralized decision making, with coordination accomplished by means of orders passed from superiors to subordinates within a hierarchical organization. The other is the market principle, which depends on decentralized decision making and the use of the price system as a means of coordination. In capitalist economies, there is a tendency for managerial coordination to be confined to the internal business of individual firms. Relationships between firms are coordinated on a market basis. In socialist economies, in contrast, there is usually an attempt to introduce managerial coordination on a larger scale, in the form of national economic planning.

In Chapter 38, we shall see how these two bases of classifications can be used in various combination to identify a variety of different subtypes of capitalist and socialist economies. We shall also enter briefly into the general debate on the relative merits of the various systems. In Chapter 39, then, we shall take a more detailed look at one of the largest socialist economies, that of the Soviet Union.

CHAPTER 38
Capitalism Versus Socialism

What You Will Learn in This Chapter
Beyond all particular issues of economic policy lies the wider issue of capitalism versus socialism. In the course of more than a century of debate on this topic, several distinct schools of capitalism have emerged. Socialism is supposed to replace the ''anarchy of the market'' with the ''planning principle,'' and ''production for profit'' with ''production for use.'' Economists attempt to move the debate on capitalism versus socialism from the plane of such generalities to specifics of economic efficiency and economic justice.

For Review
Here are some important terms and concepts that will be put to use in this chapter. Be certain that you understand them, or review them before proceeding.

Market justice and distributive justice (Chapter 1)
The market as a mechanism for using knowledge (Chapter 2)
Functional distribution of income (Chapter 29)
Managerial and market coordination (Chapter 21)
The nature of the firm (Chapter 21)
Efficiency and perfect competition (Chapter 24)

At many points in this book, we have debated the merits of one policy or another. Most of these policy alternatives, though, have concerned relatively small changes within our market economy, or relatively small shifts of responsibility between government and the market. Now we come to a debate that transcends all discussions of particular policies. This is the debate over capitalism versus socialism as the organizing principle for the economy as a whole. We shall begin by attempting to clarify just what "capitalism" and "socialism" mean, and then move on to a comparison of the two types of systems.

Capitalism
Capitalism is an economic system based on private ownership of all factors of production. Individual business firms make use of managerial coordination internally, but relationships among firms are coordinated by means of

prices and markets. Capitalism can be called a system of "free enterprise," because all production and consumption is carried out on the basis of free contracts and voluntary exchanges. The "rules of the game" under which capitalism operates prohibit the use of force, violence, threats, or fraud in economic relationships at all levels.

Capitalism gets its name from the fact that, by and large, it is owners of capital who play the role of entrepreneurs. When new firms are started, people with capital usually take the initiative, and hire the labor and natural resources they need to carry out their plans. In ongoing firms, it is usually the people who supply capital to the firm who control its policies and share its profits. Other factor owners make their contributions on a contract basis without acquiring any direct control over policy.

The term capitalism has been applied to such a broad variety of economic systems that it becomes necessary to distinguish several different varieties. Here, we shall distinguish three kinds of capitalism that differ from one another in terms of the economic role played by government. This role can range from nothing at all to very substantial, as we shall now show.

Classical Liberal Capitalism

Classical Liberal Capitalism A capitalist system in which the economic role of the state is limited to protecting private property rights and providing a court system to resolve private disputes.

Under the tenets of **classical liberal capitalism** the government has an important, but strictly limited role in the economy. In the classical liberal conception, government is a referee who enforces the rules of the game. Government has just two functions. The first is to maintain a police force, a system of courts, and if necessary a military establishment to protect property rights against criminal activity and foreign aggression. The second is to provide a court system for the peaceable settlement of disputes that arise over the terms of private contracts. Marxist opponents of capitalism say that this means that the government simply acts as the "executive committee" of the capitalist class, and settles all disputes in favor of the owners of capital. Classical liberals deny this "executive committee" doctrine. Their ideal is a government that would be impartial—a government that would be as vigilant in protecting the property rights of consumers and workers as in protecting those of capitalists.

Under classical liberal capitalism, the government has a monopoly on the legitimate use of force, but it uses its coercive powers only against those who violate the property rights of others. The sole exception is that the government may force private citizens to pay whatever minimal taxes are needed to finance its defense and law enforcement agencies.

Anarcho-Capitalism

Some pro-capitalists are even more strongly opposed to the use of force in economic affairs, and even more strongly in favor of the free market than are the classical liberals. They believe that even the limited government of classical liberalism is too much. If it is right to protect private property, then the government need have no monopoly in this field. Furthermore, if it is wrong to use force in economic life, then the use of force by the government to collect taxes is also wrong. Following this reasoning, society should dispense with the institution of government altogether. This combination of a radical attack on government (anarchism) with a defense of private property (capitalism) is called **anarcho-capitalism,** or alternatively, **radical libertarianism.**

Radical libertarians believe that in an anarcho-capitalistic society, profit-seeking private firms would take over all of the legitimate functions now performed by government. Like classical liberals, they believe that private firms could deliver the mail, dispose of garbage, and collect tolls from motorists to pay for the construction and repair of highways. Unlike classical liberals, they believe that private arbitration firms could settle disputes between parties to business contracts, that private insurance companies could provide protection against criminal activity, and that the criminals themselves could be tracked down by private detectives (hired by the insurance companies) and locked up in privately run jails. A few hours spent with a radical libertarian tract such as Murray Rothbard's *For a New Liberty*[1] have convinced many a sceptic that the principles of private enterprise are much more widely applicable than they ever imagined.

Anarcho-Capitalism (Radical Libertarianism) A capitalist system in which no state exists at all, with all goods and services, including defense, police, and court services, supplied by private firms.

State Capitalism

Let us look now at the opposite end of the capitalist spectrum from radical libertarianism. There we find systems that are basically capitalist, but in which government plays a much larger role than just enforcing the rules of the game. We shall use the term **state capitalism** to describe these systems.

Under state capitalism, government provides an alternative to the market as a means by which individuals and firms can win control over resources. If a firm wishes to increase its profits, it can cut costs and improve its product. Alternatively, it can lobby the government for regulations that will drive its competitors out of business and permit it to charge monopoly prices. If homeowners want to improve the value of their houses, they can buy larger lots to build on. Alternatively, they can persuade local zoning officials to force their neighbors to buy larger lots for their houses. If people want to live comfortably in retirement, they can save from their own wages during their working lifetimes. Alternatively, they can arrange that other people's wages be taxed to pay them social security.

In effect, in every sphere of economic life under state capitalism, the government and the market provide parallel structures for determining *Who, What, How,* and *For Whom.* To the extent that most factors of production continue to be privately owned, such a system can still legitimately be called capitalist. Clearly, though, it is a rather different form of capitalism than that envisioned by classical liberals.

State Capitalism A capitalist system in which government intervenes widely in the market, and provides an alternative to the market as a means by which individuals and firms can win control over resources.

Socialism

Any difficulties we might have with defining capitalism are small in comparison with the problems raised by socialism. The doctrines and systems that have been called "socialist" are so diverse that any short definition is bound to offend at least some people who call themselves socialists. If we keep these cautionary words in mind, however, there would seem to be no reason

---

[1] Murray N. Rothbard, *For a New Liberty* (New York: Macmillan, 1972).

Socialism Any of a number of doctrines that include the tenets that: (1) some major share of non-labor factors of production ought to be owned in common or by the state; and (2) that justice requires incomes to be distributed at least somewhat more equally than under classical liberal capitalism.

Centralized Socialism A socialist system in which all capital and natural resources are owned by the government, which plans all production as if the economy were one big firm.

not at least to try a definition. As we shall use the term here, **socialism** will mean any of a number of doctrines that include two tenets: first, that some major share of nonlabor factors of production ought to be owned in common or owned by the state; and second, that justice requires incomes to be distributed at least somewhat more equally than under classical liberal capitalism. We shall say no more about socialism in general. Instead, we shall turn to a number of particular types of socialism.

Centralized Socialism

Perhaps the most widely discussed variety of socialism, and to many, the only "pure" variety, is **centralized socialism.** In such a system, all capital and natural resources are government-owned. The government sets up some kind of central planning board that coordinates all production according to strict managerial principles. This board issues plans that have binding force on all individual units where production is actually carried out. In a literal sense, the entire economy is one big firm.

In the most commonly described form of centralized socialism, planning is carried out in physical terms. The plans drawn up by the central planning board specify the number of tons of steel or number of yards of cloth or whatever to be made in each factory. The plans also specify the number of tons of coal or pounds of yarn or whatever to be used up in producing the output. Labor is the only factor of production not directly owned by the state. Workers are free to choose their own jobs within the framework of the plan. (Forms of centralized socialism in which workers are assigned to specific jobs are by no means unknown, however.) Governments that have espoused centralized socialism have generally tried to bring agriculture as well as industry under the sway of central planning.

Although Karl Marx was notoriously reluctant to draw up blueprints for the socialist future he foresaw, careful study of his writings suggests that he thought of the socialist economy in centralized terms. As we shall see in the next chapter, that has certainly been the interpretation placed on Marxism by ideological authorities in the Soviet Union. Today, however, one often encounters people who think of themselves as Marxian socialists without being strict centralists on economic matters. Many Eastern European reformers and Western Marxist radicals are noncentralists.

Lange's "Market Socialism"

From the early days of this century, one aspect of centralized socialism has been consistently criticized by economists. That is the principle of planning in physical terms. Opponents of socialism argued that it would be beyond the capacity of central planners to specify the physical quantities of the millions of inputs and outputs required for thousands of firms. Even if workable sets of plans could be drawn up, planners could not guarantee that they had found the most efficient possible combination of inputs for production of the given outputs, and the most efficient pattern of outputs to satisfy consumer demands. During the 1930s, the economist Oskar Lange issued a justly famous reply to these critics. He set forth his ideas in a series of articles entitled "On the Economic Theory of Socialism."

Lange claimed that central planning in physical terms was neither the only nor the best way of running a socialist economy. Instead, he proposed

In his 61 years, Oskar Lange achieved not one, but two distinguished careers as an economist. Born in Tomaszow, Poland, he came to the United States to study at the University of California and Stanford University. He then remained in America to teach at the University of Michigan, Stanford University, and the University of Chicago. His famous "On the Economic Theory of Socialism" appeared in the *Review of Economic Studies* in 1937, and gave him an international reputation.

Lange's interests as an economist went beyond the question of the economics of socialism. He was a pioneer in econometrics, and did important early work in macroeconomics as well. In 1944, he wrote *Price Flexibility and Full Employment,* in which he attempted to establish Keynes' employment theory as a special case within a general equilibrium theory.

By this time, Lange had acquired U.S. citizenship, but in 1945, he renounced this to become the Polish ambassador to the United States. After serving as ambassador, he next became Poland's delegate to the United Nations. Finally, in 1947, he returned to Poland to begin the second phase of his career as an economist. He held various positions in the Communist Party and government, and in 1957, became the Chairman of the Polish Economic Council.

As a leading economist in Communist Poland, Lange turned to electronic computers and cybernetics to reconcile his earlier views on market socialism with Soviet-type central planning. He described the market as a cumbersome and slow-working servo-mechanism, the best available in the days before computers, but now obsolete. Without repudiating his earlier work, he characterized its proposed trial-and-error system as quaintly out of date. He continued to write on econometrics and economic cybernetics until his death in 1965.

Oskar Lange (1904–1965)

a system in which the socialist managers of individual firms would mimic the behavior of managers under perfectly competitive capitalism. A central planning board would exist, but its major function would no longer be to issue commands. Instead, their main function would be to set prices for goods and factors of production. Managers would take these prices into account, and conduct the actual operation of their firms according to two rules. First, quantity of output produced by each firm would be that quantity that would make the marginal cost of production equal to the assigned price of the product. Second, a combination of factor inputs would be chosen to produce each product that would make the marginal physical product of each factor equal to the marginal physical product of any other factor.

Managers would requisition whatever quantities of factors of production they needed to produce according to these rules. They would produce whatever quantities of outputs the rules required. In any particular period, it might happen that the uncoordinated actions of individual firms would result in a surplus or shortage of some goods or factors. If this were to occur, the function of the central planning board would be to correct any imbalances. They would assign the price of any factors or goods of which there was a shortage, thus discouraging their use. Similarly, they would lower the prices of any goods or factors of which there was a surplus, thus encouraging greater use. In this way, production and use would be brought into equilibrium, and the plans of individual firms coordinated.

Lange's system, of which this is only the barest sketch, immediately caught the imagination of his readers. The system appeared to offer two major advantages over centralized socialism with physical planning. First, the burden of work on central planners would be lessened, because they would be responsible only for prices. Individual managers would do their own planning of physical input and output requirements. Second, Lange's rules for managers closely resembled the rules of managerial calculation under perfect competition. That made it seem likely that inputs and outputs would be chosen more efficiently than under a regime of physical planning. We shall return to these points later in this chapter.

Participatory Socialism

Participatory Socialism is the third socialist system we shall look at. Under participatory socialism, the means of production belong neither to the state nor to private capitalists. Instead, they are owned in common by the workers who actually operate them. The workers of each firm participate democratically in management, hence the name "participatory" socialism. Relationships among firms, and between firms and consumers, are coordinated by markets as in a capitalist economy. The government may intervene in the operation of this socialist market, but its intervention need not be greater than under state capitalism.

Under participatory socialism, workers, rather than capital owners, are the entrepreneurs. If successful, they share in the profits. The functional distribution of income is determined by marginal productivity principles much as under capitalism, but the principles that govern the personal distribution of income are quite different. The ownership of nonlabor factors of production is not highly concentrated as it is under capitalism, but instead is widely shared by all workers. As a result, workers receive in addition to their wages a bonus or "social dividend" that represents their share of profits and of the product of resources owned in common. To the extent necessary, of course, this principle of distribution can be supplemented by social insurance to meet the needs of the elderly, the disabled, and the nonworkers.

Participatory socialism is not just a creature of abstract theory. An entire national economy, that of Yugoslavia, has operated under a system of workers' management since the early 1950s. In the Yugoslav economy, a new firm can be created by central or local government, by an existing firm, or by a group of individuals. Once it comes into being, it takes on an independent life of its own, entering into market relationship with its customers and suppliers. The basic governing unit of a Yugoslav firm is the workers' council in which all workers participate. This council directly reviews and approves basic long-run policy decisions, including the important decision regarding distribution of the income of the firm. The council also elects a smaller executive council, and a director to handle the day-to-day business of the firm. Although Yugoslavia's communist government claims to find authority in Marx's writings for this brand of socialism, the system could hardly be in greater contrast to the centralized blueprint of official Soviet doctrine.

By most general measures, participatory socialism has worked well in Yugoslavia. Although Yugoslavia was very nearly the poorest country in Europe at the end of World War II it grew faster over the next two decades than any other European country. Furthermore, Yugoslavs have enjoyed a far greater degree of political and personal freedom than their comrades in other Eastern European countries. This fact is by no means

Participatory Socialism   A socialist system in which the means of production are owned collectively by the workers of individual firms, who participate democratically in the process of management, and share the profits of their firms.

unrelated to the difference in economic systems. Yugoslavia has its share of economic problems, which range from high inflation and regional disparities in incomes to complaints that workers spend too much time at factory meetings and not enough on the production line. Nonetheless, it is a system from which there is much to be learned in both the East and the West.[2]

European Social Democracy

The fourth kind of socialism we shall look at is European social democracy. Social democratic parties have either held power or been a strong opposition party in most countries of Western Europe and Scandinavia since World War II. Although there are important differences among the parties of various countries, we can illustrate the main principles of social democracy with the example of the British Labor Party. The defining characteristics of British social democracy are an overriding concern for the poor, and a belief in equality. By equality, in the words of a leading labor Party spokesman, "we mean more than a simple redistribution of income. We want a wider social equality embracing the distribution of property, the educational system, social class relationships, power and privilege in industry—indeed, all that is enshrined in the age-old socialist dream of a classless society,"[3] In pursuit of this goal of equality, the Labor Party, like its counterparts on the continent of Europe, has instituted wide-ranging "welfare state" policies. These are supposed to guarantee to every citizen, as a matter of political right, minimum standards of health care, education, food, and housing. On the other end of the scale, people with inherited wealth (or even simply high earned incomes) pay confiscatory rates of taxation. The Labor government has also made strong efforts to reduce selectivity in education, in an attempt to eliminate an important source of class distinction.

On the matter of ownership of the means of production, at least the more moderate Labor Party leaders are not dogmatists. The same spokesman we just quoted writes that a "mixed economy is essential to social democracy. For while a substantial public sector is clearly needed to give us the necessary control over the economy, complete state collectivism is without question incompatible with liberty and democracy."[4] Britain's public sector is indeed substantial by American standards. There is extensive nationalization of steel, coal, railroads, shipbuilding, aircraft, automobiles, and several other important industries. Still, a very large private sector remains. British nationalized industries are supposed to be run on competitive business principles, and are supposed to turn a profit to help finance the government's welfare state policies. In practice, though, the managers of nationalized industry complain of capricious political interference in their affairs. Many of the largest nationalized industries operate at enormous losses, requiring heavy subsidies from the taxpayer.

As economic systems, social democracy and state capitalism are not

---

[2]The best popular treatment of participatory socialism in Yugoslavia and elsewhere is Jaroslav Vanek's *The Participatory Economy* (Ithaca, N.Y.: Cornell University Press, 1971).

[3]Anthony Crosland, *Social Democracy in Europe* (London: Fabian Tract 438, 1975), p. 1.

[4]*Ibid.*

far apart. In fact, political power has passed back and forth several times between the British Labor Party and their opponents, the Conservatives (who are typical state capitalists) with surprisingly few shifts of economic policy. Although they lie to the "left" of any major American political grouping, the European social democrats represent the "right" within the broad spectrum of possible socialisms.

Socialism: Pro and Con

Our catalog of capitalist and socialist economic systems is now complete. In the remainder of this chapter, let us turn to a brief survey of the ongoing debate over the relative merits of various systems. Socialist slogans have long proclaimed the superiority of socialism over capitalism. Socialism, it has been said, replaces the "anarchy of the market" with the "planning principle." It also replaces "production for profit" with "production for use," and replaces capitalist exploitation of the working classes with a system in which the whole product goes to the real producers. Such slogans are impressive to hear, but difficult to evaluate. What exactly is "the planning principle"? What is the difference between production for profit and producing for "use"? And what exactly is meant by "exploitation"? Let us see if a discussion in terms of mundane economic standards can shed some light on the merits of socialism.

Static Efficiency

The first standard we shall use for comparing economic systems is that of static efficiency. In comparative economics, this term means the efficiency of resource allocation as it would be under conditions of universal equilibrium, in which resources, production technologies, and consumer tastes were known to everyone and forever changing.

Under perfect competition, a capitalist economy could, in principle, operate with complete static efficiency. If claims are to be made for socialism on grounds of static efficiency, then, it must be shown that it could do at least as well as capitalism under the same ideal conditions. That was what Oskar Lange set out to prove. He accepted that any kind of socialism that relied on central planning in physical terms would score poorly in terms of static efficiency. In his own system, however, efficiency would be guaranteed. Managers would be instructed to make the proper adjustments in marginal costs and marginal products, while central planners would be instructed to adjust prices to market-clearing, equilibrium levels.

That was only a starting point. It was not enough for Lange to show that under ideal circumstances, his socialist system could function at least as efficiently as capitalism. He went on to argue that under the circumstances that actually prevailed in the real world, his system would do better. First, he claimed that his system solved the problem of monopoly. Under capitalism, in an industry with only one or a few firms, managers tend to equate marginal cost with marginal revenue rather than with price. That violates static efficiency conditions. In Lange's own system, in contrast, managers would be instructed to follow the same rule (marginal cost = price) no matter how few firms there were in a market.

Furthermore, Lange pointed out that even competitive markets would not operate efficiently when pollution or other distorting factors caused private costs to deviate from opportunity costs. Under his own system, central planners could automatically correct for such things. They would simply build the appropriate incentives or penalties into the prices that they set.

Counterclaims

Lange's claims for the superior static efficiency of his system have brought forth three kinds of counterclaims. First, some critics have attacked the system directly in Lange's own terms. It has been suggested, for example, that the trial-and-error pricing system that Lange's central planners are to use would be too time-consuming, and might even be unstable. Also, it is not clear how the trial-and-error method for finding market-clearing prices could be applied to goods that were custom made, as much important industrial equipment is. Finally, it has been argued that Lange's system would do poorly where considerations of time and risk played an important role in the pricing process.

A second, rather different kind of criticism comes from advocates of state capitalism and moderate social democrats. These argue that a full transition to socialism is not necessary to achieve the desired gains in static efficiency. Instead, it would make more sense to keep a market economy and introduce *ad hoc* corrections to deal with problems such as monopoly and pollution where necessary.

Finally, the most telling of all criticisms of Lange's system simply rejects static efficiency as an important standard of evaluation. Any gains in static efficiency from his system would be offset by other disadvantages. This raises the issues of dynamic efficiency and growth, to which we now turn.

Dynamic Efficiency and Growth

Dynamic efficiency and economic growth are standards for evaluating economic systems that accept the world as it is, with changing technologies, resource availabilities, and consumer preferences. Dynamic efficiency and growth are closely related. Economic growth measures the overall rate of expansion of the output of goods and services. Part of any increases in economic growth that occurs may be attributable to increased supplies of factors of production. More capital is accumulated through saving, more labor through population growth or more hours of work per capita, and more natural resources through mineral discoveries or territorial expansion. When we speak of *dynamic efficiency,* we are referring to the rate of growth it can sustain with a given rate of expansion of factor supplies. High dynamic efficiency depends partly on the ability of a system to generate scientific and technical advances. It depends even more on the ability of its entrepreneurs to take advantage of opportunities quickly and effectively as they emerge.

Some claims have been made for socialism on the grounds of dynamic efficiency. One is that the absence of private patent rights would speed the spread of innovations under socialism. Another is that monopolistic firms under capitalism consciously obstruct technological progress because they have vested interests in traditional products and methods of production. More commonly, though, the emphasis of socialist writers has been on the ability of their systems to raise the rate of economic growth through better mobilization of the factors of production.

One way for socialist planners to increase the rate of economic growth is for them to divert a larger share of national product into saving and investment than would be forthcoming under a free market system. It was once popular to claim that individual consumers had a "faulty telescopic facility." Thus people underrated the value of increased future incomes that could be earned by saving more now, and overrated the value of present consumption. Paternalistic socialist planners could feel justified in cutting present consumption to increase investment, because whether consumers realized it or not, such policies would make them better off in the long run. Socialist planners have pursued other policies as well to increase factor supplies. These have included encouragement of long work hours, increased labor force participation by women, mobilization of surplus rural labor for work in industry, and intensified exploitation of new agricultural land and mineral resources. Socialists of almost every variety have advocated some policies to accelerate economic growth. Lange thought that his socialist planners should opt for more investment. The Yugoslav government has taken a variety of steps to ensure that the country's labor-managed enterprises do not distribute too large a share of their revenues among workers for current consumption. As we shall see in the next chapter, though, it is the advocates of centralized socialism who have placed the greatest emphasis on growth. In fact, the ability of centralized socialism to mobilize massive factor supplies is sometimes said to more than outweigh the inferior static and dynamic efficiency of such a system. Factor mobilization is alleged to give centralized socialism an edge over all alternatives in terms of economic growth.

Counterclaims

Critics have long claimed that dynamic efficiency is the area of socialism's greatest economic weakness. This was brought out very clearly in the protracted "socialist controversy," to which Lange's famous papers were a contribution. The beginning of the socialist controversy is usually given as 1922, the year the Austrian economist Ludwig von Mises published a paper in German entitled "Economic Calculation in the Socialist Commonwealth."[5] In this paper, Mises attacked socialism for what he saw as its inability, in the absence of markets and a price system, to put collectively owned means of production to efficient use in pursuing the socialist planners' chosen ends. Lange began his own defense of socialism by acknowledging that Mises had identified an important weakness in the writings of socialists of his day. He went so far as to suggest that in the future socialist commonwealth, a statue should be erected in Mises' honor, so that no one would forget that prices and markets would be essential under socialism too. Lange then set forth his own proposals as we have described above.

[5]Translated in F. A. Hayek (Ed.), *Collectivist Economic Planning*, 6th ed. (London: Routledge & Kegan Paul, 1963).

Ludwig von Mises was born when the "marginal revolution" that established modern economics was just getting under way, and lived to celebrate the centenary of that revolution. In the meantime, he became one of the foremost economists of the twentieth century.

Mises was born in Lemberg, Austria, and educated at the University of Vienna. He taught at the University of Vienna until the Nazis arrived, and then moved to Switzerland. In 1940, he came to the United States, where he became a citizen in 1946. In 1945, he joined the faculty of New York University, where he remained until his retirement in 1969, at the age of 88.

Mises' most original theoretical work was his *Theory of Money and Credit,* published in German in 1912. In that work, he became the first to apply the general principle of consumer choice to explain the demand for cash balances. He went on to apply this theory as an explanation of expansions and contractions in economic activity. This pioneering insight, that macroeconomic fluctuations have their roots in microeconomic behavior, was lost sight of by mainstream economics during the Keynesian era. Today, however, the importance of the phenomena about which von Mises wrote is widely recognized.

In 1922, Mises set forth his famous critique of socialism. This work had a major influence on socialist writers of the day. Oskar Lange in the United States and Abba Lerner in England took Mises' criticism very seriously, and set out to create a new "market socialism" that would solve the allocation problem as elegantly and accurately as any capitalist market. Mises, however, was unimpressed. To him, it was impossible to separate the market as an allocational mechanism from the real-world striving of owners after rents and entrepreneurs after profits. He dismissed Lange's and Lerner's work as that of "men playing at markets as boys play at trains."

Ludwig von Mises (1881–1973)

In 1949, Mises published his monumental *Human Action.* This work is a treatise on all of economics, a grand work on the scale of Smith's *Wealth of Nations* or the *Principles* of John Stuart Mill. In *Human Action* Mises developed all of his views on theory, methodology, and policy at great length. Throughout the book, and indeed, throughout his whole career, Mises championed the libertarian doctrine that all government intervention in the economy is to be regarded with intense suspicion. Mises was a great teacher, and his influence lives on through the many students he taught over the years.

Mises and his Austrian colleague Friedrich von Hayek were by no means satisfied with Lange's solution to the problem of resource allocation under socialism. What Lange had done, they said in effect, was only to solve the problem of managerial calculation under socialism. But Lange completely neglected to deal with the even more important problem of entrepreneurship. As Mises put it,

> The cardinal fallacy implied in this and all kindred proposals is that they look at the economic problem from the perspective of the subaltern clerk whose intellectual horizon does not extend beyond subordinate tasks. They consider the structure of industrial production and the allocation of capital to the various branches and production aggregates as rigid, and do not take into account the necessity of altering this structure in order to adjust it to changes in conditions. What they have in mind is a world in which no further changes occur and economic history has reached its final stage.[6]

Hayek added to the force of Mises' criticism with his insights into the role of the market as a mechanism for using knowledge. Effective entrepreneurship requires making use of particular knowledge of time and place

---

[6]Ludwig von Mises, *Human Action* (New Haven: Yale University Press, 1949), p. 703.

as well as general knowledge of the opportunity cost of widely marketed goods. The existence of a price system makes the general information on opportunity costs available to people on the spot. Perhaps Lange's artificial price system would also be able to serve this purpose. To make use of the equally important particular knowledge of time and place, though, the people on the spot need independence of action and adequate incentives. Under capitalism the necessary independence is provided by private ownership of the means of production. The necessary incentives are provided by the opportunity to earn profits when decisions are taken correctly, and the responsibility for bearing losses when things go wrong. Under socialism, the person on the spot is inevitably an economic civil servant. Such a person's independence in the economic hierarchy is limited. Furthermore, the civil servant's incentives operate in the direction of playing it safe, and not rocking the boat.

The critics do not deny, for the most part, that a socialist economy can achieve a high rate of economic growth despite low dynamic efficiency, by means of forced savings and in some cases forced labor mobilization. Such growth, however, may be growth at too high a price. This point is underlined by the fact that high saving and growth rates can, if desired, be achieved under state capitalism (as in Japan) without any substantial sacrifice of dynamic efficiency.

Conclusions

It would be very misleading to think that socialism owes its widespread support solely to its purportedly superior economic performance. There are many socialists for whom the problems of production are secondary to the problems of economic justice. Economic justice, of course, means different things to different people, but here are at least some of the things it means to socialists:

First, the socialist conception of economic justice means equality. In the time-honored phrase, it means "from each according to his ability, to each according to his need." Some socialists are willing to accept the degree of inequality of labor income that would result from wage payments proportional to marginal productivity. Even these advocate supplementing wages with some kind of equalizing "social dividend" or "social wage" to be paid for with the interest, rent, and profits earned by collectively owned nonlabor factors.

Second, socialist economic justice is supposed to mean an end to exploitation. In this view, the profits, rents, and interests earned by non-workers under capitalism do not truly reflect any real productive contribution of inanimate factors of production. They are instead unfairly deducted from the just earnings of labor. Socialists thus often oppose the nonwage earnings even of small-scale shopkeepers, landlords, or moneylenders, despite the fact that these earnings may not raise their recipients very high up the ladder of income distribution.

Finally, many socialists hold that economic justice requires not only that workers get a fair share of the product, but also that they have some voice in the actual management of business affairs. Some socialists pay only lip service to this principle. They promote systems in which workers end up as remote from the functionaries of the central planning bureaucracies as they are from boardroom management under capitalism. Others, the participatory socialists, make this the first and foremost element of economic justice.

Whatever the specific content given to the concept of economic justice, any argument that a socialist economy is inefficient can always, in the last resort, be met by the reply that one can afford to tolerate inefficiency in the name of equity.

Two kinds of counterclaims are advanced against the contention that socialism is necessary to achieve economic justice. One comes from left-wing state capitalists of the kind widely represented among "liberal" Democrats and Republicans in the United States. These people are basically in sympathy with the egalitarian aims of socialism. They simply argue that the government of a capitalist country can, if it has the will do to so, use tax and transfer policies to distribute income however one would want. As we mentioned earlier, this variety of opinion merges imperceptably at some point with the position taken by moderate European social democrats.

The less moderate view on capitalism, socialism, and economic justice is heard from classical liberals and radical libertarians. These conceive of economic justice primarily in terms of what we have called "market justice." What economic justice requires, they say, is a system in which all people are able to devote their own energies and abilities exclusively to the pursuit of their own chosen objectives, without coercive intervention by anyone. In this view, the first requirement is a free market in which workers, consumers, and resource owners can participate on a purely voluntary basis. In such a system, no person has a right to demand another to turn over a part of his or her property or produce without offering a fair exchange. Nationalization of the means of production or redistributive taxation are thus unjust *per se,* and equality has nothing to do with the matter.

SUMMARY

1. Any market economy in which all factors of production are privately owned, and in which the owners of capital, for the most part, play the role of entrepreneurs, can be called a capitalist economy. In both theory and practice, there is a broad range of different kinds of capitalism. The American economy is a form of state capitalism, in which government intervenes widely in the affairs of the market. Classical liberals advocate limiting the role of government to the provision of police, defense, and court services. Anarcho-capitalists favor reducing the role of government all the way to zero, with even the minimal functions of the classical liberal state being performed by private firms.

2. Any system can be called socialist in which at least some substantial part of nonlabor factors of production are collectively owned, and in which an attempt is made to distribute incomes more equally than under classical liberal capitalism. Socialist systems differ widely from one another in the role they assign to the market. Centralized socialism envisions an economy run as one big firm, in which the market plays no role at all. Lange's socialist economy, participatory socialism, and European-style social democracy all depend heavily on the market as a mechanism of resource allocation, but use redistribution policies to modify the personal distribution of income.

3. The static efficiency of an economy means its theoretical efficiency under idealized conditions in which resources, production technologies, and consumer tastes are completely known and unchanging. A capitalist economy could achieve complete static efficiency under perfect competition. Centralized social-

ism is widely thought to score poorly in terms of static efficiency. Lange built the case for his own brand of socialism largely on consideration of static efficiency. He argued that, under ideal conditions, his system would operate as well as a capitalist market economy, and that in real-world conditions, it could achieve higher static efficiency.

4. Dynamic efficiency and growth are additional standards by which to judge the performance of an economic system. Centralized socialism claims a superior growth potential because of its ability to mobilize resources of capital and labor and focus them on the task of economic expansion. Questionable dynamic efficiency is seen as a major weakness of Lange's system.

5. Socialists claim that their systems provide greater economic justice than does capitalism. By economic justice, they mean distributive justice. Some state capitalists claim that the welfare state can achieve distributive justice without socialism. Other critics of socialism emphasize the standard of market justice, and see capitalism as superior to socialism according to that standard.

DISCUSSION QUESTIONS

1. Why do you think it is that owners of capital so often perform the entrepreneurial function in an economy where factors of production are privately owned? Why should land owners not play this role? Why not workers? Why not people who own no resources at all, but hire everything they need on a contract basis? Can you think of exceptions to the rule that entrepreneurs are also owners of capital?

2. What position do you think an advocate of classical liberal capitalism would take on each of these issues, discussed in earlier chapters: antitrust policy, regulation, poverty, pollution, and protectionism? How, if at all, do you think the classical liberal position on these issues would differ from the anarcho-capitalist position?

3. Of all the kinds of economic systems discussed in this chapter, which kind would you expect American "big businesses" to favor? Why? On what evidence do you base your answer?

4. Explain just what it means to say that under centralized socialism, the whole economy is run as "one big firm." In an anarcho-capitalist economy, which would entirely lack any government antitrust policy, do you think private businesses would grow and merge with one another to the point that the whole economy were one big private firm? Why or why not?

5. Review the "cobweb effect" (Chapter 25). In Lange's system, central authorities periodically review each market to see if there is a shortage or surplus. If there is a surplus they cut prices, and if there is a shortage they raise prices. Firms and consumers respond to these price changes in accordance with their supply and demand schedules. Do you think that the price adjustment procedure in Lange's economy could ever fall victim to the cobweb effect? Why or why not?

6. There are no serious legal barriers to the emergence of participatory socialist firms in the American economy. If the workers in a private firm pooled all their resources (perhaps making temporary sacrifices to increase their rate of savings), they could buy up the firm's stock share by share until they owned a controlling interest. They would then be in more or less the same position as the worker-owners of a Yugoslav firm. Why do you think workers so rarely do this in our economy? Do you know of any example of worker-owned and operated firms in the American economy?

CHAPTER 39
The Soviet Economy

What You Will Learn in This Chapter
The Soviet economy is a huge experiment in centralized socialism. Since the end of the 1920s, both agriculture and industry have been brought into a comprehensive system of central planning. Individual enterprises and collective farms are, in theory, the subdivisions of a single firm. The origins, structure, and performance of this system tell us much of interest about socialist economics in particular, and the problem of resource allocation in general.

For Review
Here are some important terms and concepts that will be put to use in this chapter. Be certain that you understand them, or review them before proceeding.
    Price indexes (Chapter 6)
    Sources of economic growth (Chapter 7)
    Capital budgeting (Chapter 23)
    Centralized socialism (Chapter 38)

In the last chapter we discussed many different kinds of economics systems, including several varieties of socialism. In this chapter we turn from theoretical comparisons to an extended case study of one kind of socialism. That is the centralized socialism of the Soviet Union. In a sense, the very size of the Soviet Union as an industrial, political, and military power makes the Soviet economic system worth taking a closer look at. There is another reason for studying it as well. That is to learn more about the general problem of resource allocation and what must be done to solve it successfully. Let us turn, then, to a survey of the origins, structure, and performance of the Soviet economy.

Origins

Marxism-Leninism

We shall begin our discussion of the Soviet economy with a word on its ideological origins as a system founded on the principles of Marxism-Leninism. The voluminous writings of Karl Marx are largely devoted to the evolution and structure of capitalism. Marx wanted to pave the way for revolution by demonstrating that capitalism was headed for a breakdown, but he did not attempt to lay down a detailed blueprint for the coming socialist economy. There is little doubt, though, that he envisioned the socialist economy in highly centralized terms. Private ownership of non-labor factors of production would be abolished, and planning would replace the market as the primary means of resource allocation.

V. I. Lenin, the leader of the Russian Revolution, was if anything more of a centralist than Marx himself. The secret of Lenin's political success in Russia was the highly centralized, disciplined structure of the Bolshevik Communist Party he led. It was natural for him to apply the same methods of administration to the economy. In a book written just before he came to power, Lenin likened the task of running the economy to that of running the post office, or any other bureaucratic administrative agency. The important thing would be a strong party leadership to define economic goals clearly and to provide the discipline and the will necessary to carry them out.

War Communism

Within months of the revolution of October 1917, the Bolsheviks were engaged in a Civil war with their White Russian opponents. From the beginning of the civil war, the market economy was altogether abandoned. Trade between the city and countryside was replaced with forced requisitioning of agricultural products. Virtually all industry was nationalized, including many small-scale businesses. Retail trade was also nationalized, although a substantial black market soon emerged. Industrial labor was put under semimilitary discipline, with workers sent to jobs wherever the need was most pressing. As a final blow to the market, a massive outpouring of paper currency from the new government sent inflation spiraling so high that money became useless. Workers in essential positions were paid in kind. Party ideologists proudly proclaimed that socialism had come to the Russian economy.

Either the civil war or the government's radical policies taken one at a time would have produced economic chaos. In combination, they were a disaster. Militarily, the Bolsheviks scraped through against the odd assortment of White Russians and Western armies of intervention who opposed them. By 1921, however, with the war over, the economy was in sad shape. Agricultural production was down by one-third and industrial production down to less than a quarter of its 1913 level. Half the urban population had fled to the countryside in search of food. It was time for a change of direction.

The NEP

With the threat of war removed, Lenin launched his New Economic Policy, known as the NEP. It was a step backward, taken, as he put it, in order to prepare for two steps forward. Lenin had endorsed the centralist and antimarket policies of War Communism, which fitted closely the views he had expressed before the revolution.[1] Now he set those policies aside in

---

[1] On Lenin's attitude toward War Communism, see Paul Craig Roberts, *Alienation and the Soviet Economy* (Albuquerque, N.M.: The University of New Mexico Press, 1971), Chap 2.

order to get production back on its feet. Trade and small industry went back to private hands. Buying replaced forced requisitioning in agriculture. The peasants once again found it worth their while to sow the fields they had let go fallow. Currency reform put the brake on inflation, and the money economy reappeared. The "commanding heights"—heavy industry, transportation, banking, and foreign trade—remained in government hands, while the rest of the economy followed its own course. Planning was reduced to the issuing of "control figures," which were not directives but merely forecasts intended to help guide investment decisions.

As an instrument for economic recovery, the NEP was a great success. By 1928, prewar production levels had been surpassed in both industry and agriculture. Lenin had died in 1924, and Stalin was busy consolidating his power in the party. It was time to take the "two steps forward" that Lenin had promised.

Collectivization and the Five-Year Plan

The two steps forward taken in 1928 were the First Five-Year Plan for industry, and the policy of collectivization in agriculture. These two steps were designed to overcome two features of the NEP that Stalin saw as serious defects. First, as long as the NEP was in force, central authorities were altogether unable to control the direction of a market economy. Events went their own way while the nominal "planners" sat on the side and collected statistics after the fact. Second, the NEP provided no mechanism for transferring resources from agriculture to industry. The party needed such a transfer in order to pursue its favored "industry first" development strategy. Higher taxes, lower agricultural prices, or worst of all forced requisitioning of grain, would only result in a withdrawal of effort by the peasants, as during the civil war.

In industry, the Five-Year Plan was, for the first time, supposed to set the course of development in advance. Annual operational plans were to be drawn up in accordance with it. The annual plans were to include assignments of the necessary raw materials to producers on a nonmarket basis. Above all, the Five-Year Plan envisioned a massive program of capital investment.

Industrial growth was to be financed by obtaining more agricultural produce. Collectivization was the technique used to make sure that the needed grain moved from the country to the city. Between 1928 and 1932, some 15 million peasant households—about two-thirds of the rural population—were formed into 211,000 collective farms. On the collectives, land and livestock were owned in common, while agricultural machinery was supplied by independent machine-tractor stations. Land was worked in common too, and a complex system of payment to collective farmers was introduced. Party control over the peasantry was immeasurably strengthened. Party policy could be imposed on the collectives in a way that had never been possible while argiculture was in private hands.

Collectivization was at least a qualified success. The policy wreaked havoc with agricultural production. The number of livestock fell nearly by half, as peasants slaughtered them rather than turn them over to the collectives. Grain output also fell sharply, both because of the general chaos accompanying collectivization, and because the incentive structure of the collectives themselves discouraged effort. Despite the disruption of production, though, the flow of goods from the countryside to the city increased. That, after all, had been a major objective of the policy.

Partly, the increased flow to the cities occurred because collectivization put the grain where party authorities could get their hands on the first share, before the remainder was distributed to the peasants. Partly, more grain went to the cities because there were fewer livestock left to eat it in the countryside. There were fewer people there too. Several millions died in the initial turmoil of collectivization and the subsequent famine of 1932–1934.

Emerging Outlines

Out of the disorder of the early 1930s, an economic system emerged that displayed most of the major features of the Soviet economy today. Industry, trade, banking, transportation, and foreign commerce were all completely nationalized, with only the most trivial exceptions. Agriculture was almost entirely collectivized. At the top of the system sat Gosplan, the state planning agency which undertook central planning in physical terms. This agency and the ruling party guided the economy with a development strategy emphasizing centralization and planning in physical terms.

In the next section of this chapter, we shall look at some details of the structure and functioning of this system. Then, in the final section, we shall attempt an evaluation of its performance.

Structure

Central Hierarchy

According to the official party handbook, *Fundamentals of Marxism-Leninism,* the Soviet economy functions as a single enterprise, directed by a single will. At the top of the economic hierarchy are the highest political organs of the Soviet government, the Supreme Soviet and its Council of Ministers. Under the Council of Ministers come a number of specialized agencies, including Gosplan, the Central Statistical Administration, and the State Bank. Also under the Council of Ministers are a long list of ministries with specific industrial responsibilities, such as coal, railroads, and ferrous metallurgy. Subordinate to these are numerous regional agencies that act as intermediaries between the central government and the individual firms that stand at the bottom of the hierarchy.

Parallel to the government administrative structure is a Communist Party hierarchy. This also has important economic responsibilities. One of these is to observe, check, and report to the Party leadership what is going on in firms and administrative agencies throughout the economy. A second party responsibility is to control appointments to administrative and managerial posts at all levels. A third party responsibility is to mobilize effort and exhort the labor force to greater efforts in service of the plan. In addition to these specific responsibilities, local party officials consult and participate in many kinds of managerial decision making at the enterprise level.

Enterprise Status

Operation of the individual Soviet enterprise is governed by a so-called technical-industrial-financial plan. This plan is issued annually and broken down into quarterly and monthly segments. The most important part of the plan is the production plan, which specifies how much output is to be produced, what assortment of products is to be included in total output, and when output is to be delivered. Other parts of the plan specify the quantities of labor and material inputs allotted to the firm. A financial section gives targets for costs, wage bills, profits, use of short-term credit, and so forth. In all, the plan may contain two dozen or more specific physical and financial targets that the firm is to meet.

The plan has the binding force of law on enterprise management. In principle, criminal penalties can be imposed for failure to fulfill the plan, although administrative penalities such as demotion or transfer to less desirable jobs are more commonly used. Positive incentives are also provided. Very substantial bonuses are given to managers who successfully fulfill or overfulfill the various parts of their plans.

Planning Procedures

The heart of the planning process is a set of *material balances* drawn up by Gosplan. These are summaries of the sources and uses of 200 or 300 of the most important industrial commodities. The purpose of each balance is to ensure that the sources (supply) and uses (demands) for each good are equal, and that there will be no shortages or surpluses.

In a simplified form, the process by which material balances are drawn up works something like this. As soon as Gosplan receives directives from the political authorities, indicating the general rate of projected development and the most important priorities, work begins on a preliminary set of balances called control figures. These show roughly how much of each good must be produced and how much must be used in each sector of the economy if the overall goals are to be met. The next step is to pass these control figures down through the planning hierarchy. There the main balances are broken down into requirements for each region of the country, and finally for each enterprise.

When enterprise managers receive these preliminary control figures, they are supposed to suggest ways they can increase outputs or reduce inputs to achieve more ambitious targets. They also have an opportunity to complain if they think the plans exceed their capacity for output or do not provide sufficient inputs. Enterprise responses to the control figures are then sent back up through the hierarchy to Gosplan at the center.

When the original control figures are corrected in the light of information collected from below, it is likely that the sources and uses of materials will no longer balance. People actually responsible for carrying out the plans will often have tried to make their jobs easier by asking for reduced output targets or increased supplies of inputs. A complex procedure of adjustment and bargaining follows in which Gosplan tries to eliminate threatened material shortages without sacrificing overall targets. In some cases, shortages may be covered by imports, or by drawing down reserve inventories. More commonly, Gosplan responds by tightening the plan.

That means putting pressure on producers to accomplish more with less. If the tightening process goes too far, what results will be a balance "on paper only." The plan will contain concealed shortages that will emerge during its execution.

The final balances are now broken down again. In addition to the crucial 200 or 300 materials subject to central balancing, individual ministries or regional authorities will in the meanwhile have prepared balances on thousands of other goods that are not of economywide significance. These material balances together eventually become the technical-industrial-financial plans for all firms through the economy. All of this is a very time-consuming process. Often the final plans are not completed until the planned year is several weeks or even months under way.

Labor Planning

The planning process for one important resource needs special treatment. Allocating labor is partly a matter of *how* goods are to be produced and partly a matter of *who* is to do any particular job. Indirectly, the decisions made on the hows and whos also affect income distribution, the resource allocation.

Roughly speaking, the *how* is decided by central planners. Gosplan draws up labor balances for various kinds of work in much the same way that material balances are drawn up. Basic policy on how much labor each enterprise is to use to accomplish the tasks are specified in the technical-industrial-financial plan.

The *who* of labor allocation, in contrast, is largely handled by markets. For the most part, individual workers are free to choose their occupation and place of work. Two methods are used by the central authorities to ensure that the right number of workers are available in each sector of the economy. One is to offer substantial wage differentials, paying premiums for skilled work or for work that is unattractive. The other is the manipulation of labor supply through education and manpower training programs.

Individual enterprises are able to excercise some degree of control over the wages they pay. They can do this both by adding bonus payments to standard wages and by exercising discretion in deciding the skill bracket to which any particular worker is assigned. The overall result is a system where variations in wages are used to ensure balance between the supply and demand for labor. This is the single most important instance of the use of the market for resource allocation in the Soviet economy.

Informal Structure

Our description of the formal administrative structure of the Soviet economy exactly fits the model of centralized socialism. Communications follow vertical paths up and down the planning hierarchy. The messages passed to enterprise management have the binding force of law. Managers are rewarded or reprimanded in accordance with their degree of obedience to the plan. Only the method of assigning particular workers to particular jobs provides a major exception.

A close study of the *informal* structure of the Soviet economy, however, shows that central control is not absolute. A good deal of informal "horizontal" communication and exchange occurs between firms. Plans are not always treated as binding, but as only one among a number of factors influencing management behavior. And the attainment of a comfortable and prosperous life for a Soviet manager is not always just a matter of obeying commands to the letter. Let us turn now to an examination of informal independence within the Soviet system.

The Safety Factor

Soviet managers do not passively wait for plans to arrive from above, and then do the best they can to fulfill them. Instead, they direct considerable efforts to making sure that they have a "safety factor" that will cushion them against the danger of being assigned impossible tasks and then being punished for failing to achieve them.

Safety factors often take the form of large inventories of inputs or semi-finished products. Inventories have always been a problem in the Soviet Union. Sometimes when there are shortages, inventories get squeezed so low that any break in deliveries disrupts production. Other times, when an enterprise manages to get its hands on more of some essential material than it needs, it hoards the scarce material as a safety factor against future shortages.

A rather different form of safety factor takes the form of deliberately concealed productive capacity. By hiding its true capacity, an enterprise hopes to get an easy plan. Suppose that when provisional control figures come down to some textile mill, they call for an output of, say, 100,000 yards of fabric in the next year. The manager knows that this is just about what he can squeeze out, given the inputs the control figures say will be given him. It does not pay him to let Gosplan know that, however. Instead, he complains that he cannot possibly do more than 90,000 yards unless his labor force is substantially increased and he gets a bigger allotment of synthetic yarn. If he can get the easy 90,000 yard plan, he will have achieved his safety factor. He will not fall short of the target even if something goes wrong during the year.

Of course, the people in Gosplan know that managers always try to develop a safety factor of some kind. They act on that knowledge when they are juggling their material balances to make them come out even. They do not hesitate to tighten up the plan even when told from below that it cannot be done. The whole thing develops into a sort of game. This greatly increases the degree of uncertainty involved in the planning process.

Procurement

According to the formal structure of the Soviet economic system, individual enterprise managers are not responsible for procuring their own raw materials, energy supplies, equipment, or other inputs. As part of the plan, each user of, say, copper tubing is given a schedule of deliveries he can expect. At the same time, some supplier is given a corresponding schedule of deliveries that he is to make. The user and supplier do not even need to communicate directly with one another. The necessary plans are all supposed to be set up on the basis of information passed vertically to higher authorities.

In practice, however, managers who simply sit passively waiting for carloads of copper tubing to roll up to their factory gate are likely to be in trouble. Instead, they must be concerned that either their assigned supplies may be behind schedule on their production plan, or that the suppliers may be trying to tuck away a hoard of tubing as a safety factor against future demand. Managers of the user enterprises must take appropriate measures to deal with this problem. For one thing, they keep on their payrolls people colorfully known as "pushers." The pushers' job is to go around wining and dining and wheedling suppliers, much as the salespeople of a capitalist firm go after potential buyers. Of course, technical-industrial-financial plans do not allow for funds to hire pushers. They have to be worked in under the title of consulting engineer, or something of the sort.

Sometimes all pushers have to do to get supplies moving on time is to twist a few arms. Other times they may have to pay outright bribes. On still other occasions, pushers may work out a black market barter deal under which one firm will come up with a hoarded carload of copper tubing in exchange for a desperately needed crate of ball bearings. All in all, the telephone lines are always busy, despite the fact that such things are theoretically unneccessary in a centrally planned economy.

Selective Fulfillment

The plan specifies not one, but many targets for each enterprise. There are targets for total production, for assortment of production, for cost reduction, for technological improvements, and for numerous other things. Sometimes the end result of issuing so many different targets is to give managers more rather than less freedom to maneuver. This happens when it becomes impossible to fulfill all targets at once, so that managers must decide which part of the plan will be most impressive to fulfill. The following much-repeated anecdote illustrates the nature of the problem.

CASE 39.1
Fulfilling the Plan in a Soviet Nail Factory

There was once a factory whose business it was to manufacture nails for use in the construction trade. In a certain year, the plant was assigned the task of producing *x* tons of nails, which were to be distributed among a variety of sizes according to the needs of Soviet carpenters. Before the planned year was far underway, the unfortunate manager of the enterprise realized that he could not achieve his target for total output if he kept to the planned assortment. His past experience had taught him that the authorities were much more interested in the total output than in the assortment plan, so he decided on an ingenious strategy. He gave up making little nails, which were a bother to produce and weighed hardly anything, and concentrated on enormous spikes. In that year he turned out far more than *x* tons of output. He was gloriously rewarded for overfulfilling the plan.

Naturally, the long-suffering Soviet carpenters complained. They had no way of fastening together anything smaller than two railroad ties! An ingenious Gosplan official hit on a solution. The next year, when the plan was issued, the total output target for our enterprise was not stated in tons, but in number of nails, by count. The reader can guess how the enterprise manager responded. He gave up entirely on huge spikes. These took altogether too much hard-to-procure steel. Instead, he concentrated on production of the tiniest pins and brads, which used hardly any metal and counted millions to the ton.

Naturally, the long-suffering Soviet carpenters. . . .

Perhaps this anecdote has become exaggerated with the telling, but not by much. In real-life Soviet stores, one finds the assortment of shoe sizes out of step with the assortment of feet, because big sizes take too much leather, while bonuses are based on the number of pairs produced. One finds paint mixed so thinly that two coats are needed instead of one, because bonuses are paid on the basis of number of gallons. One finds new models and styles very rarely, because the innovation plan is less important than the output plan. All in all, the very multiplicity of plan targets reduces the real degree of control the planners achieve over what is actually produced.

Selective Toleration

Naturally, the central authorities are not unaware of the games managers play. They know that the letter of the law is sometimes broken, that reserves are hidden, and that some parts of the plan are less important than others. They could crack down severely on managerial independence, but they do not. They know that the economy could not function if they did. Planners know that the best plans they can make are full of inconsistencies and contradictions. They have to rely on local initiative and ingenuity to overcome these defects in the plan, even if the local initiative involves breaking the law. As a result, the authorities take a pragmatic attitude of selective toleration toward the independent, polycentric behavior of enterprise managers. If a manager acts on his or her own initiative, and by doing so, manages to fulfill the plan, nothing is said. Bonuses are paid and all is well. Only if illegal methods are used and the plan still is not fulfilled is the manager responsible, and liable to be called on the carpet. In short, it is recognized that the pushers, the bribes, and the safety factors are the grease that keep an imperfectly fashioned machine running.

Performance

Growth Record

Soviet leaders, and indeed ordinary Soviet citizens, are extremely proud of one aspect of their economy's performance. That is its growth record. Within the lifetimes of millions, Russia has been transformed from an economic backwater into one of the world's leading industrial powers. In 1917, Russia had achieved only something like the level of economic development of today's Brazil. It had only a small industrial sector, set against a backdrop of vast rural poverty. Today Soviet living standards are comparable to those of Italy. Soviet industrial capacity exceeds that of West Germany, and in certain particular fields, such as steel output and military technology, the Soviet Union equals or surpasses the United States.

Exhibit 39.1 presents the Soviet growth record and compares it to growth in the United States. In the upper figure, representing economic growth in the USSR, two sets of data are presented.

The official Soviet statistics show an enormous surge of growth during the 1930s, interrupted by the devastation of World War II, and continuing at very high but gradually declining rates thereafter. On the same chart, a Western estimate of Soviet growth is also given. This also shows very respectable growth rates, but by no means so spectacular as the official Soviet figures.

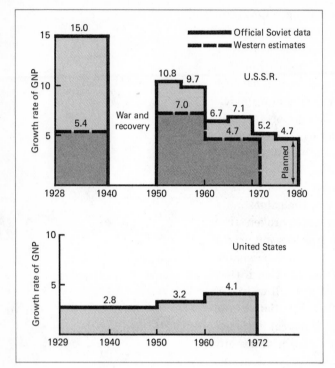

EXHIBIT 39.1
Growth rates of GNP: USSR and United States
The Soviet Union has a very impressive record of economic growth. Western and Soviet estimates of this growth use different methods and arrive at different numbers, but even by Western measures, growth has consistently been more rapid in the Soviet Union than in the United States. Since World War II, Soviet rates of economic growth have gradually declined.

Source: From Paul R. Gregory and Robert C. Stuart, Soviet Economic Structure and Performance (New York: Harper & Row, 1974), p. 378 (Soviet data recomputed from Abram Bergson and from Stanley Cohn). Reprinted by permission. Also from "Breznehev's Russia," The Economist (London, 14 February 1976), p. 63. Reprinted by permission. All Soviet official data from published sources; Western estimates from Abram Bergson, Real National Income of Soviet Russia since 1928 (Cambridge, Mass.: Harvard University Press, 1961), pp. 180, 210, 261. Used by permission of the publisher. Also from Stanley Cohn, "General Growth Performance of the Soviet Economy," U.S. Joint Economics Committee, Economic Performance and the Military Burden in the Soviet Union (Washington, D.C.: U.S. Government Printing Office, 1970).

Why do Western and official Soviet estimates differ so much? The answer is largely a matter of the accounting conventions used. Real GNP statistics are always derived by using some index of prices to adjust nominal GNP data in a way that will make it possible to compare data for different years. It turns out to make a great deal of difference which base year is chosen for the index. Choice of an early base year gives rise to numbers that exaggerate the rate of growth, especially for an economy that is undergoing rapid structural changes. Soviet statisticians like to use the earliest possible year. The 15 percent growth rates of the 1930s reflect the use of 1928 prices as a basis for calculations. Western practice makes use of a later base year. Soviet accounting practices differ from Western ones in other ways as well, including the way output of services is measured, the way introduction of new kinds of products are taken into account, the way agricultural harvests are computed, and so forth.

In many cases, it is not a matter of Soviet statistics being wrong and Western calculations of Soviet performance being right, but merely a matter of arbitrary choices of accounting convention. What is important for comparative purposes is to express the growth performance of different countries by using conventions that are as nearly the same as possible. It is the Western estimates of Soviet growth that ought to be compared with the figures given for the United States in the lower part of Exhibit 39.1.

Sources of Soviet Growth

If we ask why the Soviet economy has grown faster than the American economy, the answer comes clearly through all the imperfections in the statistical material. The major source of the Soviet success in achieving rapid economic growth has been the ability of the centrally planned economy to mobilize vast new supplies of factor inputs. In the decades immediately before and after World War II, the number of labor hours employed in the Soviet economy increased at a rate of 2.2 percent per year, while increasing at only 0.5 percent per year in the United States. Even more impressive, the Soviet capital stock grew at a rate of 7.4 percent per year, compared with just 1 percent per year in the American economy. These very rapid rates of growth of factor supplies have more than compensated for the inferior dynamic efficiency of centralized socialism. The type of growth experienced by the Soviet Union, based primarily on expansion of inputs, is often called **extensive growth,** as compared to the American **intensive growth** based on better utilization of inputs.

Extensive growth is just as effective as intensive growth in adding to the economic power and prestige of a nation as a political unit, but it has certain disadvantages for individual citizens. Most important, a much larger share of GNP has been diverted from consumption into investment in the USSR than in the United States. The figures for 1964 were 35 percent versus 17 percent. As a result, Soviet consumption per capita is only something like a third that of the United States, even though GNP per capita is nearly half. It is also worth noting that Japan, the only noncommunist industrial nation to invest as high a fraction of GNP as the Soviet Union, has grown twice as fast in recent years. The Japanese experience shows what can be accomplished when rapid growth of inputs is combined with high dynamic efficiency, rather than employed as a substitute for it.

There is major concern among Soviet planners that the strategy of extensive growth will not continue to work in the future. As Exhibit 39.1 showed, Soviet growth rates have fallen steadily in the postwar period. Whether the cumbersome institutions of central planning can be reformed in a way that will permit a new era of technological dynamism and socialist entrepreneurial initiative remains very much open to question.

Extensive Growth Growth based predominantly on the mobilization of increasing quantities of factor inputs.

Intensive Growth Growth based predominantly on improvements in the quality of factor inputs and in the efficiency with which they are utilized.

Pricing and Efficiency

As nearly as it can be measured (which is in fact only very roughly), the Soviet economy is as inefficient in static terms as it is in dynamic terms. Western estimates indicate that the Soviet economy gets only about half as much output per unit of input as does the American economy. There are a number of reasons for this. In part it may have to do with the structure of managerial incentives. In part it may have to do with the motivation and work attitudes of Soviet workers in industry and agriculture. But it is likely that the major source of poor static efficiency of the Soviet economy is the lack of a price system capable of communicating information on opportunity cost to economic decision makers.

Consider two functions performed by the price system in a capitalist economy. The first is an accounting function. Prices make it possible to add apples and oranges and come up with a total expressed in dollars' worth of fruit. The second is an allocative function. The prices of inputs provide a measure of the opportunity of doing a thing or doing it a certain way, and the prices of outputs measure the value of doing it.

In the Soviet economy, the price system performs the first of these functions, but not the second. Industrial goods and consumer goods are all given prices, so that industrial accountants can turn in reports on the number of rubles' worth of output produced. The prices, however, are based on custom and arbitrary accounting conventions that have little relationship to opportunity costs. Without knowledge of opportunity costs as reflected in a price system, Soviet planners often have difficulties deciding what to produce and how to produce it. Exact economic calculations are in fact impossible. In their place, Soviet planners can use one of three methods of deciding the what and how of resource allocation. First, they can give up calculations in terms of prices altogether, and employ rough rules-of-thumb based strictly on engineering considerations. Second, they can do profit-and-loss calculations in terms of their own imperfect prices, even though the answers will at best be only approximately right. Third, they can imitate Western practice. As the following case study shows, though, none of these methods is foolproof.

CASE 39.2
The Great Dieselization Blunder[2]

During the 1950s, Soviet planners were faced with a classic problem in resource allocation. The problem was to decide what proportion of truck and tractor engines should be diesel-powered, and what proportion gasoline-powered. The decision taken was in favor of massive dieselization. It is revealing to look at the considerations that influenced this important decision.

First, from a strictly engineering point of view, diesels seemed quite attractive. They offer substantially higher mechanical efficiency, and are in many ways more elegant and technically sophisticated devices than gasoline engines. Second, the price of diesel fuel in the Soviet economy was low relative to gasoline—about 30 rubles a ton for diesel compared with 60 to 100 rubles for gasoline in the late 1950s. Finally, an examination of Western experience showed extensive dieselization of transportation equipment and heavy tractors.

Far from being a wise piece of economic calculation, though, the dieselization program turned out to be a great blunder. For one thing, diesels require greater initial costs. In part, then, the diesel versus gasoline decision is a matter of proper capital budgeting, in which higher initial costs must be balanced against discounted future gains. One defect in the Soviet price system happens to be that the discount rate used by planners in such decisions is too low. Because the discount rate is, in effect, the "price" of future gains in terms of present costs, there is a bias in favor of techniques involving inefficiently large initial costs. This no doubt played a part in the dieselization blunder.

What is more, available evidence indicates that the official Soviet price for diesel oil was too low in comparison to gasoline in the 1950s. Thus, the price far underestimated the relative opportunity cost of the heavier fuel. In the United States, the refinery price of diesel is only a very little less than that of gasoline. (Different rates of road-use taxation make for a greater price difference at the pump.)

Finally, imitation of Western experience failed to take into account the special circumstances of the Soviet economy. It turns out that the kinds of crude oil available in the Soviet Union are less suitable for making diesel fuel than those available in the United States. In order to provide fuel for all the new diesel engines, refineries were given plans that they could fulfill only by letting the quality of diesel fuel decline. They used oil to make diesel that should have been made into kerosene or furnace oil. Even worse, they al-

[2]Based on Robert W. Campbell, *The Economics of Soviet Oil and Gas* (Baltimore: Johns Hopkins University Press, for Resources for the Future, 1968), pp. 164–167.

lowed the sulfur content of diesel fuel to rise substantially. Cylinders and pistons wore out quickly when fed a diet of inferior fuel. Under these circumstances, the operating cost of diesel engines turned out to be higher, not lower than that of gasoline engines.

In the 1960s, planners realized their mistake and reversed their earlier decision. A program of de-dieselization began, and perhaps the right ratio of the two kinds of engines has now been reached. If so, the discovery is one made not as a result of rational economic calculation, but as a result of an enormously expensive process of trial and error.

Soviet Agriculture

If rapid industrial growth is the Soviet Union's proudest accomplishment, agriculture is its most distressing failure. While Soviet industry grew at a rate of 6.5 percent per year in the first half of the 1970s, agriculture crept ahead at only 2.0 percent (both official figures). In 1961, then-Premier Nikita Khrushchev set a target of 302 million tons of grain for 1980. In 1975, with three-quarters of Khrushchev's time span elapsed, output was a mere 140 million tons. That was an exceptionally bad year, to be sure, but even the official 1980 target has been scaled down to 218 million tons.

The roots of Soviet agricultural problems date from the earliest days of collectivization. In the Stalin area, agriculture was a cow to be milked for the benefit of industrial development. Now that it has become a serious constraint on industrial development, it is proving difficult to reverse the effects of decades of neglect.

The heart of the Soviet agricultural system is the collective farm, or **kolkhoz.** On paper, the kolkhoz is a cooperative, not very different from such participatory socialist institutions as the Yugoslav worker-managed firm or the Israeli kibbutz. In practice, the collective farm is a far cry from the ideal. Three institutions exercise close control over it from outside. First, the Party controls the selection of collective farm management, and directs internal decision making. Second, the kolkhoz, like the industrial enterprise, is subject to a plan specifying inputs, outputs, production methods, capital investment projects, and dozens of other details. Third, until 1958, collective farms did not own their own agricultural machinery, but instead, depended on rural "machine-tractor stations." These were able to use their monopoly on equipment to control the collective's affairs even further.

In the 1930s, the whole structure of agricultural administration was aimed at one purpose only: moving the indispensable minimum of grain from farm to city. To that end, delivery targets for the kolkhoz were set not as percentage of output, but at a fixed rate per acre sown. If bad weather brought yields down, the collective farmers bore the entire burden of the shortfall. The state and industry were guaranteed their share. Although it would seem that this would create strong incentives for the collective to work hard to avoid shortfalls, the effect was blunted by a complex and inefficient system of distributing collective income among individual kolkhoz members. Individuals were left with few individual incentives to contribute to the common effort.

Khrushchev must be credited with recognizing that the agricultural problem needed a solution. He abolished the hated machine-tractor

Kolkhoz The Soviet collective farm, formally organized as a producer cooperative.

stations and made important changes in internal work organization and management systems. Unfortunately, he diverted much energy and resources into ill-conceived crusades that soaked up resources with few long-term results. One was the famous "virgin lands" campaign. (This put millions of acres of semidesert to the plow for the first time ever.) Another was the attempt to introduce the growing of corn, which followed his trip to America in 1955. Even more than dieselization (which was also touted as a boon to agriculture), the corn campaign was a naive imitation of foreign practice with little attention paid to radical differences in local conditions.

Agricultural policy in the last decade, like so much else under the Brezhnev leadership, has been characterized by caution mixed with sober determination. Agricultural investment has risen from 14 percent of all investment in 1960 to 31 percent in 1976. In the next five years, the farms are to be flooded with some 2 million new tractors and a half million harvesters. Unfortunately, this investment has not been accompanied by the further radical institutional reforms that would seem to be needed to raise the appallingly low level of agricultural productivity. Nearly a quarter of the entire Soviet labor force still works in agriculture. Productivity per worker is only about a fifth of the U.S. level.

Conclusions

What sort of future does the Soviet economy face? Since the early 1960s, there has been a great amount of talk, both in the Soviet Union and in the West, about economic reform. To many, the declining Soviet growth rate indicates a necessity to switch from an extensive to an intensive growth strategy, and that cannot be done within current economic institutions. These were designed to mobilize resources and to implement vast structural changes, not to use scarce resources as efficiently as possible.

Reform proposals have centered on three areas. First, there is a need to reform managerial incentives so that, in the Soviet phrase, "the interests of management will coincide with the interests of the national economy." The most important part of reforming incentives must be to make *profit* the primary performance indicator for the enterprise. Profit alone would replace the dozens of indicators of output, assortment, cost, and productivity. Second, there must be a radical price reform. Profit cannot be used as an indicator of economic performance unless industrial prices reflect opportunity costs. Third, there is a need for decentralizing some decision making, and establishing direct links between firms, bypassing the cumbersome planning bureaucracy.

The Soviet government has responded to these reform proposals by encouraging discussion, but it has done very little else. Compared to the radical changes envisioned by some reformers, what has actually been accomplished is very, very little. Two official sets of reforms have been attempted. In 1965, Premier Aleksei Kosygin announced one set of reforms. Those were to reduce the number of plan targets for each enterprise from two dozen or more to about eight, and place profit high among these eight as a source of managerial bonuses. In a related group of reforms, there was an attempt to restructure industrial prices during the years 1966 and 1967.

These reforms have eliminated some of the worst previous abuses. The old practice under which plants were rewarded for their achievements in "gross output" regardless of whether the output could be sold or not has been replaced by an emphasis of "realized output," or actual sales. This helps reduce problems such as firms that produce shoes all of one size, which then rot in a warehouse for lack of users. Price reform did make some progress in bringing prices in line with average costs of production. This eliminated the need to pay enormous subsidies to some firms whose output had always been undervalued. For the most part, though, the reforms have been very limited. A system with eight separate and often conflicting plan targets is a long way from introduction of profits as a single indicator. Furthermore, since 1971, the direction of change has shifted, with the number of plan indicators increasing again. By the same token, making prices equal to average cost is by no means the same as making them equal to opportunity cost.

Explanations for the slow pace of reform vary. Some blame the extreme political conservatism of the Brezhnev regime and the opposition of vested interests within the economic bureaucracy. Others say there is a fear that if economic reforms are introduced, political reforms will have to follow. The Soviet leadership still lives in terror of the Czechoslovak experience, in which economic reform played a role. Still others point out that reform is just not easy. You cannot reform incentives until you have reformed prices, you cannot reform prices until you have greater managerial independence, and you cannot give managers greater independence until you have rationalized their incentives. But, then, you cannot do everything at once either, so you end up doing nothing and hoping for the best!

What the future will bring is a matter of speculation. The most hopeful sign is the great amount of reform and experimentation that is being carried out in Eastern Europe. Every country in Eastern Europe except Albania has introduced reforms that go far beyond anything tried in the Soviet Union. Each set of reforms is different from the others. Perhaps when a new, more daring leadership comes on the scene in the Soviet Union, they will find in some one or other of these experiments a path worth following.

SUMMARY

1. The origins of the Soviet economic system are found, first, in the Marxist-Leninist ideology, and second, in the practical experience of the first years of Soviet rule. After the 1917 revolution, an overambitious attempt to abolish the market economy all at a blow (War Communism) was followed by a temporary restoration of the market (the New Economic Policy). The main features of what we now know as the Soviet-type economy, central planning in physical terms plus collectivization of agriculture, were established around 1928. These were designed to serve the government's objectives of complete political control of the economy and extensive, industry-first economic growth. The combination of planning plus collectivization was effective in achieving those objectives.

2. In its formal structure, the Soviet economy is a fully centralized hierarchy. Individual firms receive plans that specify both inputs and outputs in physical terms, as well as many other targets. These plans are legally binding on firms. In practice, managers of Soviet firms have considerable room for maneuver in

fulfilling their plans. They bargain for safety factors, exercise initiative in procuring scarce inputs, and fulfill plans selectively. Central authorities tend to tolerate a certain degree of managerial independence as long as independent action results in fulfillment of the most important plan objectives.

3. The outstanding feature of Soviet economic performance has been rapid economic growth. The rate of growth, has, however, slowed in recent years. The need to switch from a strategy of extensive growth to one of intensive growth has focused attention on the inefficiency of the Soviet system. Soviet economic efficiency is hampered by inadequate managerial incentives and a price system that does not reflect opportunity costs. Many proposals have been put forward for reforming the system, but there has been little practical progress with reform in the Soviet Union. In the Soviet-type economies of Eastern Eurpoe, however, a number of interesting and far-reaching reform experiments have been carried out.

DISCUSSION QUESTIONS

1. During the early War Communism period in the Soviet Union, many leading economists seriously proposed the complete abolition of money as part of the transition to a centralized socialist system. Money was restored during the NEP, however, and no further attempt was made to abolish it after central planning began in earnest in the 1930s. Why do you think even a centrally planned socialist economy finds it difficult to get along without money?

2. Any economist who has studied the Soviet economy closely can supply dozens of "horror stories" like that of the famous nail factory (Case 39.1). What kind of horror stories involving flagrant misallocation of resources do you know for the American economy? Would you look for such horror stories in independent private enterprise? In regulated industries? In government itself? Explain.

3. How can we be certain that the right proportion of gasoline and diesel engines are used in the American economy? Or can we?

4. In the Soviet Union, market mechanisms are used to match workers jobs, and wage differentials between jobs and regions are largely determined by supply and demand considerations. Do you think that this means labor resources are likely to be more efficiently allocated than other factors of production in the Soviet Union? Why or why not? In answering this question, you may wish to compare the determinants of labor demand curves in the American and Soviet economies.

5. In reforming a Soviet-type economy, why is it difficult to introduce profit as the major success indicator for management before there has been a thoroughgoing price reform? Why is it difficult to reform prices before managerial incentives have been reformed?

6. In what ways do you think a centralized socialist economy of the Soviet type might be better equipped than a capitalist economy to deal with problems of population, resources, and pollution? In what ways is it less well equipped?

Glossary

Absolute Advantage In international trade theory, the ability of a country to produce a good at absolutely lower cost, measured in terms of factor inputs, than its trading partners.

Accelerator Effect The tendency of increases in national income to induce new investments, which in turn fuel further increases in national income.

Accommodating Monetary Policy A policy under which the Federal Reserve expands the money supply in an attempt to keep interest rates from rising when the Treasury sells bonds to cover a budget deficit.

Aggregate In economics, an adjective used to describe any quantity that is a grand total for the whole economy.

Aggregate Demand The total value of all planned expenditures of all buyers in the economy.

Aggregate Demand Schedule A schedule showing what the nominal level of total planned expenditure (aggregate demand) will be at each possible level of nominal national income.

Aggregate Supply The total value of all goods and services supplied in the economy; identical to national product.

Aggregate Supply Schedule A table or graph showing the level of nominal national product (aggregate supply) associated with each level of nominal national income.

Allocation The distribution or assignment of things to specific uses. In economics, the term *resource allocation* means determining what will be produced, how it will be produced, who will produce it, and for whom it will be produced.

Anarcho-Capitalism (Radical Libertarianism) A capitalist system in which no state exists at all, with all goods and services, including defense, police, and court services, supplied by private firms.

Antitrust Laws A series of laws, beginning with the Sherman Act of 1890, which define government policy toward monopoly.

Ascetics People who try to achieve happiness by purposely limiting their desires.

Autonomous Consumption The level of consumption shown by a consumption schedule for a zero disposable income level.

Balance of Goods and Services The merchandise trade balance plus the balance of services.

Balance of Trade Deficit (Surplus) A country runs a balance of trade deficit (surplus) if the value of goods and services that it imports exceeds (falls short of) the value of goods and services that it exports.

Balanced Budget Multiplier A multiplier showing how much equilibrium nominal national income will change in response to a change in government purchases matched dollar for dollar by an offsetting change in net taxes. The value of the balanced budget multiplier is always exactly 1.

Base Year For measurement of real GNP, the year from which prices are used in evaluating both base year and current year outputs.

Basic Balance The current account balance plus long-term capital flows.

Bilateral Monopoly A market in which both buyer and seller exercise monopoly power, and neither passively accepts the demands of the other.

Bonds Certificates issued by a borrower that entitle the lender (called the bondholder) to receive fixed periodic payments of interest, plus a larger final payment when the bond "matures" after a set number of years.

Breakeven Analysis A business decision-making technique that relates fixed and variable costs to revenue per unit in order to identify the minimum level of output needed to break even on a project.

Capital As a factor of production, all manufactured productive resources such as tools, industrial equipment, structures, and artificial improvements to land.

Capital Account Deficit (Surplus) A country runs a capital account deficit (surplus) if the value of long-term capital flows to foreigners exceeds (falls short of) the value of long-term capital flows from foreigners.

Capital Budgeting   The area of business decision making that focuses on long-run investment decisions.

Capital Market   In the narrowest sense, the market in which manufactured means of production (capital) are bought, sold and rented. By extension, also those markets in which funds for the purchase of capital goods are borrowed and loaned, that is, credit markets.

Capitalism   An economic system based on private ownership of all factors of production, receiving its name from the fact that, by and large, it is owners of capital who act as entrepreneurs in such an economy.

Capitalization (of a rent)   The capitalized value of a rent is equal to the value of that sum of money that would earn a periodic interest return equal to the rent if invested at the current market rate of interest.

Cartel   A group of firms that acts cooperatively to exercise monopoly power in a market.

Centralized Socialism   A socialist system in which all capital and natural resources are owned by the government, which plans all production as if the economy were one big firm.

Circular Flow of Income and Product   The flow of goods from firms to households and factor services from households to firms, counterbalanced by the flow of expenditures from households to firms and factor payments from firms to households.

Civilian Labor Force   All civilians aged 16 or over, who are either (a) employed, (b) actively looking for a job, (c) laid off from a job to which they expect to be recalled, or (d) waiting to start a new job that will begin within 30 days.

Classical Liberal Capitalism   A capitalist system in which the economic role of the state is limited to protecting private property rights and providing a court system to resolve private disputes.

Cobweb Effect   A tendency for agricultural prices to rise above and then fall below the equilibrium level in alternate years, producing a pattern like a cobweb on a supply and demand diagram.

Commodity   (1) In a general sense, any good or service produced to be sold in any market; (2) in a more particular sense, any of a number of basic industrial raw materials and agricultural products, such as gold, silver, wheat, corn, cattle, or hogs, that are traded in organized future markets.

Commodity Inflation   A variety of cost-push inflation in which a spontaneous increase in commodity prices is the initial source of general price increases.

Comparative Advantage   In international trade theory, the ability of a country to produce a good at a lower opportunity cost, in terms of other goods, than its trading partners.

Complements   A pair of goods for which an increase in the price of one good causes a decrease in the quantity demanded of the other, other things being equal.

Concentration Ratios   The percentage of all industry sales contributed by the four or eight largest firms in an industry. Used as a measure of the competitiveness of a market.

Conglomerate Mergers   Mergers between firms in unrelated lines of business, for example, between an aircraft maker and a sporting goods manufacturer.

Consent Decree   In antitrust cases, an agreement between the government and the offending company in which the latter is not brought to trial and does not admit guilt, but does have to modify its objectionable practices.

Constant Returns to Scale   Said to be experienced when there are neither economies nor diseconomies of scale.

Consumer Equilibrium   A state of affairs in which consumers cannot increase the total utility they obtain from a given budget by shifting expenditure from one kind of good to another. In consumer equilibrium, the marginal utility of dollar's worth of one good must be equal to the marginal utility of a dollar's worth of any other.

Consumer Price Index   A price index based on a "representative market basket" of about 400 goods and services purchased by urban wage earners and clerical workers. This index is calculated using base year quantities.

Consumption Opportunity Line (Budget Line)   A line showing the various combinations of goods that can be purchased at given prices with a given budget.

Consumption Schedule   A graphical or numerical representation of the way in which nominal consumption expenditure varies as nominal income varies, other things being equal.

Contractionary Gap   The gap between planned expenditures and the national product at the target level of national income when aggregate supply exceeds aggregate demand at that level.

Corporation   A firm in which the ownership is divided into equal parts called shares, with each shareholder's liability limited to the amount of his or her investment in the firm.

Cost-Push Inflation   Inflation that is initially touched off by a spontaneous rise in wages, profit margins, commodity prices, or other elements of cost during a period of slack aggregate demand.

Cost-Push Illusion   The phenomenon that demand-pull inflation often looks like cost-push inflation to those caught up in it, because inventories cushion the immediate impact of demand on prices at each link in the chain of distribution from producers to retailers.

Craft Union   A union of skilled workers all practicing the same trade.

Credit Markets   A general term of the complex of financial institutions, including commercial banks, savings and loan associations, the stock and bond markets, insurance companies, and others that act as intermediaries between households which save and firms which invest.

Crowding Out Effect   The tendency of expansionary fiscal policy to cause a drop in private planned investment expenditure as a result of a rise in the interest rate.

Crude Birth Rate   The number of people born into a population per 1,000 per year.

Crude Death Rate The number of people in a population who die per 1,000 per year.

Crude Quantity Theory of Prices (Quantity Theory) The theory that the price level in an economy is simply proportional to the quantity of money in circulation.

Current Account Balance The balance of goods and services plus net private and government transfers.

Currency Coins and paper money.

Deficit (of the government budget) An excess of government purchases over net taxes.

Deficit Spending A policy of purposely allowing government purchases to exceed net taxes, with the difference being made up by borrowing from the public or creating new money.

Demand Curve A graphical representation of the relationship between the price of a good and the quantity of that good demanded.

Demand Deposits Deposits at commercial banks that permit the depositor to make payments to others by writing a check against the deposit. Demand deposits are what we commonly call checking accounts.

Demand Management A general term for the fiscal and monetary policies used to control aggregate demand for purposes of economic stabilization.

Demand Schedule A table showing the quantity of a good demanded at various prices.

Demand-Pull Inflation Inflation that is initially touched off by an increase in aggregate demand.

Demographic Transition A population cycle that accompanies economic development, beginning with a fall in the death rate, continuing with a phase of rapid population growth, and concluding with a decline in the birth rate.

Depauperization Economic development of a kind that benefits the poorest of the poor, providing them not only with the material necessities of life, but also with access to education, status, security, self-expression, and power.

Diminishing Marginal Utility (Principle of) The greater our rate of consumption of some good, the smaller the increase in utility we get from a unit increase in our rate of consumption.

Diminishing Returns (Law of) If the output of some good is increased by increasing the quantity of one variable input while the quantity of other inputs used remains fixed, then a point will eventually be reached beyond which the quantity of output produced by each additional unit of the variable input will diminish.

Discount Rate (in the Banking System) The interest rate paid by commercial banks to borrow reserve funds from the Fed.

Discounting A method of comparing the value of recipts or outlays made at different points in time. See **Present Value.**

Diseconomies of Scale Said to be experienced whenever long-run average cost increases as output increases.

Disposable Personal Income (disposable income) Personal income minus personal income taxes.

Dissaving Negative saving; the difference between disposable income and consumption expenditure when consumption exceeds disposable income.

Dissolution In antitrust cases, a remedy requiring the offending company to be broken up into several smaller companies, or to sell off some of its subsidiaries.

Distributive Justice The principle of distribution according to innate merit or, roughly, the principle of "from each according to his abilities, to each according to his needs."

Dual Economy A less developed economy that is sharply divided into a modern, Westernized industrial sector capable of rapid growth, and a traditional rural sector that remains stagnant.

Dual Labor Market The division of the labor market into a primary sector, containing good jobs with established firms, and a secondary sector, containing low-paid, unstable jobs with marginal firms.

Econometrician An expert in the statistical analysis of economic data.

Economic Ideology A set of judgments and beliefs concerning efficiency, market justice, and distributive justice as goals of economic policy, together with a set of prejudices or beliefs concerning matters of positive economics.

Economies of Scale Said to be experienced whenever long-run average cost decreases as output increases.

Efficiency The property of producing or acting with a minimum of expense, waste, and effort.

Effective Demand The quantity of a good that purchasers are willing and able to buy at a particular price.

Egalitarianism The principle that economic goods should be distributed equally among all members of society.

Elastic (Demand or Supply) An elasticity numerically greater than 1.

Employed According to the official Bureau of Labor Statistics definition, a person who (a) works at least one hour a week for pay or at least fifteen hours per week as an unpaid worker in a family business, or (b) normally works the required number of hours, but is temporarily not working because of bad weather, illness, vacation, or a labor dispute.

Entrepreneur In general, anyone who is alert to opportunities for buying low and selling high in order to make a profit. More particularly, someone who undertakes to buy factors of production and organizes them for the production of useful goods or services in the hope that those goods or services can be sold at a profit.

Excess Quantity Demanded The amount by which the quantity demanded of a good exceeds the quantity supplied, when the price of the good is below the equilibrium level.

Excess Quantity Supplied The amount by which the

quantity supplied of a good exceeds the quantity demanded when the price of the good is above the equilibrium level.

Excess Reserves   Commercial bank reserves in excess of the minimum legally required levels.

Expansionary Gap   The gap between planned expenditures and national product at the target level of national income when aggregate demand exceeds aggregate supply at that level.

Expected Rate of Return   The annual net improvement in a firm's cost or revenue that it expects to obtain by making an investment expressed as a percentage of the sum invested.

Expenditure Approach   A method of estimating aggregate economic activity by adding together the nominal expenditure of all economic units on newly produced final goods and services.

Explicit Private Costs   All costs that a firm must cover by explicit payments to outsiders.

Extensive Growth   Growth based predominantly on the mobilization of increasing quantities of factor inputs.

Factors of Production   The basic inputs of natural resources, labor, and capital used in the production of all goods.

Featherbedding   The practice of insisting on purposely inefficient work rules, so that more workers will be needed to do a job.

Federal Reserve System (Fed)   The central banking system of the United States, which provides banking services to government and commercial banks, and regulates the activities of commercial banks.

Fiscal Policy   The policies that determine the levels of government purchases and taxes.

Fixed Inputs   Those inputs whose quantities cannot be varied in response to short-run changes in output.

Fixed Investment   Purchases by firms of newly produced capital goods, such as production machinery, newly built structures, office equipment, and so forth.

Flows   Processes occurring continuously through time, measured in units per time period.

Foreign Exchange Market   The whole group of institutions, including banks, specialized foreign exchange dealers, and official government agencies through which the currency of one country may be exchanged for the currency of another.

Frictional Unemployment   That portion of unemployment accounted for by people spending relatively short periods between jobs.

Full Employment Balanced Budget   A rule under which tax and spending policy would be adjusted so that the federal budget would be in balance if the economy were at full employment.

Future Markets   A market in which buyers and sellers agree to deliver or take delivery of some commodity at a specified future date and at a price currently agreed on.

General Equilibrium Analysis   An approach to the study of markets in which we say "if such-and-such an event occurs, the effect on the market for good X will be so-and-so, provided that other markets also adjust fully to the event in question."

Gold Standard   An international monetary system in which the currencies of different countries are simply names for differing quantities of gold.

Government Purchases of Goods and Services (government purchases)   Expenditures made by federal, state, and local governments to purchase goods from private firms and to hire the services of government employees.

Gross National Product (GNP)   The dollar value at current market prices of all final goods and services produced annually by the nation's economy.

Homogeneous   Having the property that every unit is just like every other unit.

Horizontal Mergers   Mergers between firms engaged in the same line of business, for example, a merger between two steel mills.

Human Capital   A name for the productive potential of an individual person. The term calls attention to the fact that this productive potential can be increased by "investing" in education or job training.

Hyperinflation   Very rapid inflation, on the order of 1 percent per week or more increase in prices.

Implicit Private Costs   The opportunity to a firm of using resources that the firm itself owns.

Import Quota   A limitation on the quantity of a good that can be imported in a given time period.

Income Approach   A method of estimating aggregate economic activity by adding together the incomes earned by all households.

Income Deficit   The difference between a family's total money income from all sources and the official low-income level for that family.

Income Effect   That part of the change in quantity demanded of a good whose price has fallen that can be traced directly to the change in real incomes resulting from the price change.

Income Velocity of Money (Velocity)   The ratio of nominal GNP to the quantity of money, hence, the average number of times per year each dollar of the money supply is used for income-generating purposes.

Incomes Policy   A policy of directly controlling wages, salaries, earnings, and prices in order to fight inflation.

Indexing   A policy under which wages, interest payments, taxes, and other things expressed in nominal terms are revalued upward to keep pace with inflation.

Indifference Curve   A graphical representation of an indifference set.

Indifference Set   A set of consumption alternatives each yielding the same utility, so that no member of the set is preferred to any other.

Industrial Union A union of all workers in an industry, including both skilled and unskilled workers and workers practicing various trades.

Inelastic (Demand or Supply) An elasticity numerically less than 1.

Inferior Good A good for which an increase in the income of buyers causes a leftward shift in the demand curve.

Inflationary Pressure Curve A graph, derived from Okun's law and the definition of the price level, that shows the amount of inflation associated with each rate of unemployment, given an initial unemployment rate and a rate of growth of nominal output.

Inflationary Recession A period of rising unemployment during which the rate of inflation remains high, or even continues to rise.

Injunction In antitrust cases, a remedy leaving the offending company intact, but forbidding it from carrying out specific anticompetitive acts or practices.

Inside Lag The delay between the time a policy action is needed and the time policy action is taken.

Intensive Growth Growth based predominantly on improvements in the quality of factor inputs and in the efficiency with which they are utilized.

Interlocking Directorates Cases where the same person is on the board of directors of two or more firms.

Inventory Investment Changes in the stocks of finished products and raw materials firms keep on hand. If stocks are increasing, inventory investment is positive; if they are decreasing, it is negative.

Investment The sum of fixed investment and inventory investment.

Joint Marginal Benefit Curve A curve showing the dollar value of the total benefits that would be received by all members of a community as the result of a $1 increase in spending on a government-supplied good or service.

Keynesian Cross A graph that shows how the equilibrium level of nominal national income is determined. The "cross" is formed by the intersection of the aggregate demand and aggregate supply schedules.

Kolkhoz The Soviet collective farm, formally organized as a producer cooperative.

Labor As a factor of production, the contributions to production made by people working with their minds and their muscles.

Law of Demand The quantity of a good demanded by buyers tends to increase as the price of the good decreases, and tends to increase as the price decreases, other things being equal.

Linear Programming A mathematical decision-making technique widely applicable in business decision making.

Liquidity A property that an asset is said to have if it can be acquired and disposed of quickly and easily without the danger of a loss in nominal value.

Long-Run Average Cost The cost per unit of producing a given output when the quantities of all inputs have been adjusted to reduce that cost to a minimum.

Long-Run Perspective Any time perspective long enough that the quantities of all of a firm's inputs can be varied.

Long-Term Capital Flows Long-term loans to or from foreigners, or transactions with foreigners involving capital assets.

Low-Income Level The officially calculated dividing line between the poor and nonpoor, varying according to size of family, age of family members, and place of residence.

Lump Sum Taxes Taxes that do not vary as income varies.

M_1 The money supply defined as currency plus demand deposits.

M_2 The money supply defined as M_1 plus time deposits at commercial banks.

Managerial Calculation The kind of decision making needed by a firm operating in markets that are in equilibrium, with given production methods, prices, and demand conditions.

Margin, Marginal Terms referring to the effects of making a small increase in any economic activity. See specific glossary entries under *marginal cost, marginal product,* etc.

Marginal Average Rule The rule that marginal cost must be equal to average cost when average cost is at its minimum.

Marginal Cost The rate at which total cost increases as output increases. Alternately, the cost of producing one additional unit of output.

Marginal Cost of Pollution Abatement The cost of reducing a given kind of pollution by one unit.

Marginal Factor Cost The amount by which a firm's total factor cost must increase in order for it to obtain an additional unit of that factor.

Marginal Physical Product (of a factor) The increase in output resulting from a one-unit increase in the input of some factor of production, when the quantity of all other factors used remains unchanged.

Marginal Productivity Theory of Distribution A theory of the functional distribution of income, according to which each factor receives a payment equal to its marginal revenue product.

Marginal Propensity to Consume The fraction of each added dollar of disposable income that goes to added consumption.

Marginal Propensity to Save The fraction of each added dollar of disposable income that is not consumed.

Marginal Rate of Substitution The rate at which one good can be substituted for another without gain or loss in satisfaction. Equal to the slope of an indifference curve at any point.

Marginal Revenue   The change in a firm's total revenue that results from a one-unit change in total output.

Marginal Revenue Product (of a factor)   The change in revenue resulting from the sale of the product produced by one additional unit of factor input.

Marginal Tax Rate   The net increase in taxes paid or decrease in transfers received by a family for each $1 increase in the family's earned income.

Marginal Social Cost of Pollution   The total cost to all members of society of an additional unit of pollution.

Markets   A general term referring to all of the various arrangements that people have for trading with one another.

Market Equilibrium   A condition in which the separately formulated plans of buyers and sellers of some good exactly mesh when tested in the marketplace, so that the quantity supplied is exactly equal to the quantity demanded at the prevailing price.

Market Justice   The principle of distribution according to acquired merit. The observance of property rights and the honoring of contracts. Roughly, the principle of "value for value."

Market Structure   The important structural characteristics of a market, including such things as the number of firms that operate there, the extent to which the products of different firms are diverse or homogeneous, and the ease of entry into and exit from the industry.

Merchandise Trade Balance (Goods Balance)   The difference between exports and imports of tangible goods.

Merit Goods   Goods that are produced by government and supplied free of charge on the grounds that each citizen merits his or her fair share.

Monetarists   Economists who believe that movements in the money supply are the primary causes of "ups" and "downs" in business activity.

Money Demand Schedule   A schedule showing the quantity of money that people desire to hold in their portfolios given various values for the interest rate and the level of nominal income.

Money Multiplier   The ratio of the money supply (M_1) to total reserves.

Monopolistic Competition   A market structure in which there are many firms producing a strongly differentiated product.

Monopoly Power   A seller's power to raise the price of a product without losing all, or nearly all of his or her customers.

Monopsony   A market in which there is only one buyer. (From Greek *mono*, single, plus *opsonia*, buying.)

Multiplier Effect   The ability of a $1 shift in the aggregate demand schedule to induce more than a $1 change in the equilibrium level of nominal national income.

Multiplier (Simple)   The ratio of an induced change in the equilibrium level of national income to an initial change in planned expenditure. Also known as the simple multiplier, to distinguish it from other specialized terms. The value of the multiplier is given by the formula $M = 1/(1 - \text{MPC})$.

National Income   The total of all incomes, including wages, rents, interest payments, and profits, received by households.

National Product   The total value of all goods and services supplied in the economy.

Natural Monopoly   An industry in which total costs are minimized by having just one producer serve the entire market.

Natural Rate of Unemployment   That rate of unemployment that would prevail if the expected rate of inflation were equal to the actual rate of inflation.

Natural Resources   As a factor of production, land with its original fertility and mineral deposits.

Negative Income Tax   A general term for any of a number of transfer programs that would pay benefits or collect taxes from families according to a schedule based on earnings, while keeping marginal tax rates low enough to avoid serious disincentive effects.

Net Exports   The value of all domestically produced goods and services sold to foreigners less the value of all goods and services bought from foreigners; exports minus imports.

Net Liquidity Balance   The basic balance plus short-term capital flows.

Net National Product (NNP)   A measure of national product adjusted to exclude the value of investment expenditures that merely replace worn out or obsolete capital goods. Officially, NNP equals GNP minus the capital consumption allowance.

Net Present Value Approach   A capital budgeting technique based on a comparison of the present values of the net cash flows generated by alternative projects.

Net Reproduction Rate   The inherent long-term rate of growth of a population, measured as the average number of daughters born to each female child over her lifetime.

Net Tax Multiplier   A multiplier showing how much equilibrium nominal national income will change in response to a change in net taxes. The formula for the net tax multiplier is $M_T = \text{MPC}/\text{MPS}$.

Net Taxes   Total tax revenues collected by government at all levels minus total transfer payments disbursed.

Nominal Values   Measurements of economic values made in terms of actual market prices at which goods are sold.

Normal Good   A good for which an increase in the income of buyers causes a rightward shift in the demand curve.

Normative Economics   That part of economics that is devoted to making value judgments about what economic policies or conditions are good or bad.

NOW Accounts   Accounts that permit checks to be written on interest-bearing time deposits. NOW stands for "negotiable orders of withdrawal."

Official Settlements Balance The net liquidity balance plus private liquid capital flows.

Okun's Law A rule of thumb that says that for each percentage point by which the unemployment rate rises above the "full employment" benchmark (traditionally taken to be 4 percent measured unemployment), actual output will fall below potential output by about 3 percent.

Oligopoly A market structure in which there are two or more firms each of which has a large share of total sales.

Open Market Operations Purchases or sales of government securities between the Fed and the public, used as an instrument of monetary policy.

Opportunity Cost The cost of doing something as measured by the loss of the opportunity to do the next best thing instead with the same amount of time or resources.

Output Gap The difference between actual real GNP and potential real GNP in any year.

Outside Lag The delay between the time policy action is taken and the time its effects on the economy are felt.

Par Values Under the monetary system run by the International Monetary Fund from 1944 to 1973, the par value for a currency was the official exchange rate around which the actual exchange rate was permitted to fluctuate only within a narrow band.

Parity Price Ratio The ratio of an index of prices that farmers receive to an index of prices that farmers pay, using the years 1910–1914 as a base period.

Partial Equilibrium Analysis An approach to the study of markets in which we say "if such-and-such an event occurs, the effect on the market for good X will be so-and-so, provided that other markets are not disturbed from equilibrium."

Participatory Socialism A socialist system in which the means of production are owned collectively by the workers of individual firms, who participate democratically in the process of management, and share the profits of their firms.

Partnership A firm formed by two or more persons to carry on a business as co-owners. Each partner bears full legal liability for the debts of the firm.

Payback Period Analysis A capital budgeting technique based on calculation of a project's payback period, that is, the length of time required for a project's net cash flows to repay the project's initial investment cost.

Perfect Competition A market structure characterized by a large number of relatively small firms, a homogeneous product, good distribution of information among all market participants, and freedom of entry and exit.

Perfectly Elastic (Demand or Supply) The situation where the quantity demanded or supplied can vary without a change in price. Corresponds to a hori-

zontal demand or supply curve. Elasticity undefined numerically.

Perfectly Inelastic (Demand or Supply) An elasticity numerically equal to 0. No quantity change in response to a price change.

Permanent Income Hypothesis A hypothesis that reconciles a high, long-run marginal propensity to consume with a low, short-run marginal propensity to consume, by saying that people are likely to consume less out of transitory increases in income than out of those increases that they consider to be permanent.

Personal Income The total of all income, including transfer payments, actually received by households before payment of personal income taxes.

Phillips Curve A curve showing the relationship between the rate of inflation and the level of unemployment. Inflation, usually placed on the vertical axis of such a figure, may be measured either in terms of the rate of change in wages or the rate of change in a price index.

Planned Investment Schedule A graphical representation of the way in which the rate of planned investment for the economy as a whole varies as the rate of interest varies, other things being equal.

Policy Variable Those elements of the economy that are under the direct control of the government.

Political Equilibrium The quantity supplied of a public good or merit good at which political pressures for increased expenditure just balance pressures for decreased expenditure.

Political Supply Curve A curve showing the distribution of voter opinion on a public spending issue. The height of the curve at any point indicates the percentage of voters who support spending at least that much on the good or service in question.

Population Trap A situation in which the rate of population growth rises above the rate of economic growth, halting the growth of per capita income and and aborting the demographic transition.

Portfolio Balance The idea that people try to maintain a balance among the various kinds of assets they own, including money, consumer durables, stocks, and bonds, shifting from one kind of asset to another as economic conditions change.

Positive Economics That part of economics that is limited to making scientific predictions and purely descriptive statements.

Potential Output (potential real GNP) The level of output that the economy could in principle achieve if it were operating on the production possibilities frontier. Potential output can be estimated from actual real output using Okun's law.

Present Value The present value V_p of a future sum of money V_t discounted for t years at r percent interest is the sum that, if invested today at r percent, would grow to the value V_t in t years. The formula for calculating present value is $V_p = V_t/(1 + r)^t$.

Price Discrimination A practice of offering different

prices to different purchasers of the same good, when such price differences are not based on differences in grade, quality, and quantity of the same product, or on tangible differences in selling costs.

Price Elasticity of Demand (Elasticity of Demand) The percentage change in the quantity of a good demanded, divided by the percentage in the price of the good.

Price Elasticity of Supply (Elasticity of Supply) The percentage change in the quantity of a good supplied, divided by the percentage change in the price of the good.

Price Leadership A situation in which one firm in an oligopolistic industry, the price leader, can count on the others to match its price changes whether they are up or down.

Price Index In the most general sense, the ratio of current-year nominal GNP to current-year real GNP. See also *consumer* and *wholesale price indexes*.

Price Taker A firm that takes the prices at which it buys its inputs and sells its outputs as fixed, determined entirely by forces outside its own control.

Production Possibility Frontier A curve showing the possible combinations of goods that can be produced by an economy, given the quantity and quality of factors of production available.

Profit Income earned by buying low and selling high. Includes the case in which an entrepreneur buys factors of production and uses them to make something that can then be sold for more than the cost of obtaining the factor inputs.

Profit-Push Inflation A variety of cost-push inflation in which a spontaneous increase in profit margins is the initial source of price increases.

Progressive Tax One that takes a larger percentage of income from people whose incomes are high.

Protectionism A policy of shielding domestic industry from foreign competition.

Public Goods Goods or services having the two properties that (1) they cannot be provided to one citizen without being supplied also to his neighbors, and (2) once provided for one citizen, the cost of providing them to others is zero.

Pure Economic rent The income earned by any factor of production that is in perfectly inelastic supply.

Pure Monopoly A market structure in which one firm accounts for 100 percent of industry sales.

Rate of Natural Increase The current rate of growth of a population calculated as the crude birth rate minus the crude death rate.

Real GNP A measure of aggregate economic activity obtained by evaluating current-year quantities in terms of the prices of some base year.

Real Values Measurements of economic values that include adjustments for changes in prices between one year and another.

Reflation An expansion of aggregate demand after a period of high unemployment and decelerating inflation. Reflation brings substantial short-term gains in employment with little or no inflationary penalty.

Regressive Tax One which takes a larger percentage of income from people whose income is low.

Regulatory Lag The length of time, sometimes several years, that it takes a regulatory commission to review a firm's performance and react to changes in market conditions.

Required Reserve Ratios Legally required minimum quantities of reserves, expressed as ratios of reserves to various types of deposits.

Reservation Wage The wage (adjusted for nonmonetary advantages and disadvantages of a job) below which a person will not accept a job offer.

Reserves (of Commercial Banks) Money held by commercial banks as cash or non-interest-bearing deposits with the Federal Reserve.

Residual Charges Charges of a fixed amount per unit of waste imposed on all sources that discharge a given kind of waste into the environment.

Saving Schedule A graphical or numerical representation of the way in which nominal saving varies as nominal income varies, other things being equal.

Scarcity As used in economics, not having enough to fill all subjective wants.

Scientific Prediction A conditional prediction having the form "if *A*, then *B*, other things being equal."

Shortage In technical economic terminology, an excess quantity demanded.

Short-Run Perspective Any time perspective short enough that the quantities of at least some of a firm's inputs cannot be varied.

Short-Term Capital Flows Loans to or from foreigners, payable within one year or less.

Sinks Naturally occurring means of disposing of useless or harmful by-products of production and consumption.

Socialism Any of a number of doctrines that include the tenets that: (1) some major share of nonlabor factors of production ought to be owned in common or by the state; and (2) that justice requires incomes to be distributed at least somewhat more equally than under classical liberal capitalism.

Sole Proprietorship A firm owned and usually managed by a single person, who receives all profits of the firm and who personally bears all of the firm's liabilities.

Sources Naturally occurring stocks of useful productive inputs.

Speculative Demand (for Money) The part of money demand arising from the advantages of money as an asset with a fixed nominal value, which offers protection against the danger of capital loss in periods when it is feared that the prices of other assets may fall.

Speculator A person who buys something now at a low price, hoping to be able to sell it later at a high price.

State Capitalism   A capitalist system in which government intervenes widely in the market, and provides an alternative to the market as a means by which individuals and firms can win control over resources.

Sterilization   A policy of using domestic monetary policy to offset the effect of a balance of payments deficit or surplus on the domestic money supply.

Stocks   Accumulated quantities existing at a particular time, measured in terms of simple units.

Stop-Go-Policy   A cycle of acceleration, inflationary recession, deceleration, and reflation brought about by alternating political pressures to "do something" first about inflation and then about unemployment.

Substitutes   A pair of goods for which an increase in the price of one good causes an increase in the quantity demanded of the other, other things being equal.

Substitution Effect   That part of the increase in quantity demanded of a good whose price has fallen that can be traced directly to the principle of diminishing marginal utility, not taking into account the change in real income resulting from the change in price.

Supply Curve   A graphical representation of the relationship between the price of a good and the quantity of that good supplied.

Supply Schedule   A table showing the quantity of a good supplied at various prices.

Surplus   In technical economic terminology, an excess quantity supplied.

Surplus (of the government budget)   An excess of net taxes over government purchases.

Survivorship Principle   The principle that business decisions are more often made by people with good judgment, because those with good judgment make profits and survive, whereas the incompetents soon loose their decision-making positions.

Target Level of National Income   The level of nominal national income that policy makers think will permit their main economic goals (full employment, price stability, economic growth, or whatever) to be best realized.

Tariff   A tax levied on imported goods.

Tax Incidence   The matter of who bears the economic burden of taxation.

Time Deposits   Interest-paying accounts at commercial banks against which it is not ordinarily possible to write checks. Both passbook savings accounts and certificates of deposits are included, except for certain very large certificates of deposit used by corporate depositors.

Total Private Costs   Explicit plus implicit private costs.

Transactions Demand (for Money)   The part of money demand arising from the usefulness of money as a generally acceptable medium of exchange.

Transitivity   The principle that tells us that if A is preferred to B, and B is preferred to C, then A must be preferred to C.

Transfer Payments   All payments made by government to individuals that are not made in return for goods or factor services currently supplied. Social security benefits, welfare payments, and unemployment compensation are major forms of transfers.

Transmission Mechanism   The whole set of ways in which monetary policy exerts an impact on the economy.

Tying Contracts   Contracts for the sale of a firm's products that include an agreement that the purchaser will not use or deal in the products of a competitor.

Unemployment Rate   The percentage of the civilian labor force who are not employed.

Unit Elastic (Demand or Supply)   An elasticity numerically equal to 1.

Utility   The economist's term for the pleasure, satisfaction, and need fulfillment that we get from the consumption of material goods and services.

Variable Inputs   Those inputs whose quantities can be varied in response to short-run changes in output.

Vertical Mergers   Mergers between two firms, one of which is a supplier or customer of the other, for example, a merger between a newspaper and a paper manufacturer.

Wage-Push Inflation   A variety of cost-push inflation in which a spontaneous increase in nominal wage rates is the initial source of price increases.

Wholesale Price Index   A price index based on a sample of about 2,500 goods purchased in large quantities in transactions between firms. This index is calculated using base-year quantities.

Workable Competition   Any market structure in which, taking into account structural characteristics and the dynamic factors that shaped them, no clearly indicated change can be effected through public policy measures that would result in greater social gains than social losses.

Suggestions for Further Reading

Introduction

Boulding, Kenneth E., *Economics as a Science* (New York: McGraw-Hill, 1970).

Bowen, William G., "Econometrics," in *Perspectives in Economics,* Alan A. Brown, Egon Neuberger, and Malcolm Palmatier, eds. (New York: McGraw-Hill, 1971).

Brown, Alan A., and John E. Elliot, "Scope and Method of Economic Analysis," in *Perspectives in Economics,* Alan A. Brown, Egon Neuberger, and Malcolm Palmatier, eds. (New York: McGraw-Hill, 1971).

Ebenstein, William, *Today's Isms: Communism, Fascism, Capitalism, Socialism,* 6th ed. (Englewood Cliffs, N.J.: Prentice-Hall, 1970).

Kirzner, Israel M., *The Economic Point of View: An Essay in the History of Economic Thought* (Princeton, N.J.: Van Nostrand, 1960).

Olson, Mancur, Jr.; "Economics, Sociology, and the Best of All Possible Worlds," *The Public Interest,* Vol. 12, (1968).

Robbins, Lionel C., *An Essay on the Nature and Significance of Economic Science,* 2d rev. ed. (London: MacMillan, 1935).

Part One

Economic Report of the President, transmitted to the Congress of the United States, 1966. Section on twenty years of policy experience with the Full Employment Act, pp. 170–186.

Phelps, Edmund S., ed., *Private Wants and Public Needs: Issues Surrounding the Size and Scope of Government Expenditure,* rev. ed. (New York: Norton, 1965).

Posner, Richard A., *Economic Analysis of Law* (Boston: Little, Brown, 1972).

Smithies, Arthur, "Economic Analysis of the Public Sector," in *Perspectives in Economics,* Alan A. Brown, Egon Neuberger, and Malcolm Palmatier, eds. (New York: McGraw-Hill, 1971).

Part Two Chapters 5–7

Abraham, William I., *National Income and Economic Accounting* (Englewood Cliffs, N.J.: Prentice-Hall, 1969).

Beckerman, Wilfred, *Two Cheers for the Affluent Society* (New York: St. Martin's 1974).

Cole, H. S. D., et al., eds., *Models of Doom: A Critique of the Limits to Growth* (New York: Universe Books, 1973).

Kuznets, Simon S., "Problems of Interpretation of National Income Accounts," in *National Income: A Summary of Findings* (New York: National Bureau of Economic Research, 1946).

Meadows, Dennis L., et al., *The Limits to Growth* (Washington, D.C.: Potomac Associates, 1972).

Part Two, Chapters 8–10

Heilbroner, Robert L., and Peter Bernstein, *A Primer on Government Spending* (New York: Random House, 1963).

Heller, Walter W., *New Dimensions of Political Economy* (Cambridge: Harvard University Press, 1966).

Part Two, Chapters 11–13

Board of Governors of the Federal Reserve System, *The Federal Reserve System: Purposes and Functions,* 6th ed. (Washington, D.C.: Board of Governors of the Federal Reserve System, 1974).

Campbell, Colin, and Rosemary Campbell, *An Introduction to Money and Banking,* 2d ed. (Hinsdale, Ill.: Dryden Press, 1975).

Friedman, Milton, and Walter W. Heller, *Monetary versus Fiscal Policy* (New York: Norton, 1969).

Friedman, Milton, and Anna Schwartz, *A Monetary History of the United States, 1867–1960* (Princeton, N.J.: Princeton University Press, 1963).

Samuelson, Paul A., "Monetarism Objectively Evaluated," in *Readings in Introductory Economics,* John R. McKean and Ronald A. Wykstra, eds. (New York: Harper & Row, 1971), pp. 120–132.

Smith, Warren L., "Monetary Institutions and Policies," in *Perspectives in Economics,* Alan A. Brown, Egon Neuberger, and Malcolm Palmatier, eds. (New York: McGraw-Hill, 1971).

Part Two, Chapters 14–17

Friedman, Milton, *Monetary Correction,* Occasional Paper No. 41 (London: Institute for Economic Affairs, 1974).

Friedman, Milton, *Unemployment versus Inflation? An Evaluation of the Phillips Curve* (London: Institute for Economic Affairs, 1975).

Gurley, John G., "Have Fiscal and Monetary Policies Failed?" *American Economic Review,* Vol. LXII (1972).

Stigler, George, "The Economics of Minimum Wage Legislation," *American Economic Review,* Vol. 36 (1946).

Part Three, Chapters 18–20

Galbraith, John Kenneth, *The Affluent Society* (Boston: Houghton Mifflin, 1958).

Hayek, Frederick August von, "The Non-Sequitur of the Dependence Effect," *Southern Economic Journal* (April 1961).

Henderson, James M., and Richard E. Quandt, *Microeconomic Theory: A Mathematical Approach,* 2d ed. (New York: McGraw-Hill, 1971), Chap. 2.

Holloway, Robert J., Robert A. Mittelstaedt, and M. Venkatesan, eds., *Consumer Behavior: Contemporary Research in Action* (Boston: Houghton Mifflin, 1971).

Leftwich, Richard H., *The Price System and Resource Allocation,* 5th ed. (Hinsdale, Ill.: Dryden Press, 1975).

Murray, Barbara B., ed., *Consumerism, the Eternal Triangle: Business, Government and Consumers* (Pacific Palisades, Calif.: Goodyear Publishing Co., 1973).

Sackrin, S. M., "Factors Affecting the Demand for Cigarettes," U.S. Department of Agriculture *Agricultural Economics Research* (July 1962).

Simon, Julian A., *Issues in the Economics of Advertising* (Urbana, Ill.: University of Illinois Press, 1970).

Part Three, Chapters 21–23

Baumol, William., *Economic Theory and Operations Analysis.,* 2d ed. (Englewood Cliffs, N.J.: Prentice-Hall, 1965), Chaps. 5, 6, 13, and 19.

Brigham, Eugene F., and James L. Pappas, *Managerial Economics* (Hinsdale, Ill.: Dryden Press, 1972).

Galbraith, John Kenneth, *The New Industrial State* Boston: Houghton Mifflin, 1969).

Henderson, James M., and Richard E. Quandt, *Microeconomic Theory: A Mathematical Approach,* 2d ed. (New York: McGraw-Hill, 1971), Chap. 3, Chap. 8, pp. 312–329, and Chap. 9.

Kirzner, Israel M., *Competition and Entrepreneurship* (Chicago: University of Chicago Press, 1973).

Marris, Robin, "Galbraith, Solow, and the Truth about Corporations," *The Public Interest,* No. 11 (1968).

Part Three, Chapters 24–28

Andreano, Ralph L., Superconcentration/Supercorporation (Andover, Mass.: Warner Modular Publications, 1973).

Armentano, D. T., *The Myths of Antitrust:* Economic Theory and Legal Cases (New Rochelle, N.Y.: Arlington House Publishers, 1972).

Brozen, Yale, "Competition, Efficiency and Antitrust," *Journal of World Trade Law,* Vol. 3 (1969).

Brozen, Yale, ed., *The Competitive Economy: Selected Readings* (Morristown, N.J.: General Learning Press, 1975).

Buchanan, James, and Gordon Tullock, *The Calculus of Consent* (Ann Arbor, Mich.: University of Michigan Press, 1962).

Demsetz, Harold, "Why Regulate Utilities?" *Journal of Law and Economics,* Vol. 2 (1968).

Heady, Earl O., *A Primer on Food, Agriculture, and Public Policy* (New York: Random House, 1967).

Henderson, James M., and Richard E. Quandt, *Microeconomic Theory: A Mathematical Approach,* 2d ed. (New York: McGraw-Hill, 1971), Chap. 4 and 6.

MacAvoy, Paul W., ed., *Crisis of the Regulatory Commissions* (Problems of the Modern Economy Series) (New York: Norton, 1970).

Stigler, George J., "The Case Against Big Business," *Fortune* (May 1952).

Stigler, George J., *The Citizen and the State: Essays on Regulation* (Chicago: University of Chicago Press, 1975).

Weiss, Leonard, "Pure Competition and Agriculture," *Case Studies in American Industry* (New York: Wiley, 1967).

Weston, John Frederick, and Sam Peltzman, *Public Policy Toward Mergers* (Pacific Palisades, Calif.: Goodyear Publishing Co., 1969).

Part Four

Böhm-Bawerk, Eugen von, "The Nature of Roundabout Production," in *Contemporary Economics, Selected Readings,* 2d ed., Reuben E. Slesinger, Mark Perlman, and Asher Isaacs, eds. (Boston: Allyn and Bacon, 1967).

Franklin, Raymond S., and Solomon Resnik, *The Political Economy of Racism* (New York: Holt, 1973).

Reynolds, Lloyd G., *Labor Economics and Labor Relations,* 6th ed. (Englewood Cliffs, N.J.: Prentice-Hall, 1974).

Ricardo, David, *The Principles of Political Economy and Taxation* (Hammondsworth, Middlesex: Penguin Books, 1971), Chap. 2.

Rossi, Peter H., and Katherine C. Lyall, *Reforming Public Welfare* (New York: Russell Sage Foundation, 1976).

Tabb, William K., *The Political Economy of the Black Ghetto* (New York: Norton, 1970).

Wachtel, Howard M, "Looking at Poverty from a Radical Perspective," in *Modern Political Economy,* James H. Weaver, ed. (Boston: Allyn and Bacon, 1973).

Part Five

Bauer, Peter T., *Dissent on Development: Studies and Debates in Development Economics* (London: Weidenfeld and Nicolson, 1971).

Beckerman, Wilfred, *Pricing for Pollution* (to be published).

Dolan, Edwin G., *TANSTAAFL, The Economic Strategy for Environmental Crisis* (New York: Holt, 1971).

England, Richard, and Barry Bluestone, "Ecology and Class Conflict," *Review of Radical Political Economics,* (Fall/Winter, 1971).

Freeman, Myrick A., Robert H. Hareman, and Allan V. Kneese, *The Economics of Environmental Policy* (New York: Wiley, 1973).

Malthus, Thomas Robert, *An Essay on the Principle of Population; Text, Background, Contemporary Opinion, Essays,* Philip Appelman, ed. (New York: Norton, 1976).

Mills, Edwin S., "Economic Incentives in Air Pollution Control," in *The Economics of Air Pollution,* Harold Wuluzin, ed. (New York: Norton, 1966).

Power, Jonathan, and Anne-Marie Holenstein, *World of Hunger* (London: Temple Smith, 1976).

Weisskopf, Thomas E., "Capitalism, Underdevelopment, and the Future of the Poor Countries," in *Economics and World Order.* Jagdish Bhagwati, ed. (New York: Macmillan, 1972).

Part Six

Morgner, Aurelius, "International Economics: Theory and Policy," in *Perspectives in Economics,* Alan A. Brown, Egon Neuberger, and Malcolm Palmatier, eds. (New York: McGraw-Hill, 1971).

Pen, Jan, *A Primer on International Trade* (New York: Random House, 1967).

Stevens, Robert Warren, *A Primer on the Dollar in the World Economy* (New York: Random House, 1972).

Triffin, Robert, "International Economics, Monetary Reform," in *Perspectives in Economics,* Alan A. Brown, Egon Neuberger, and Malcolm Palmatier, eds. (New York: McGraw-Hill, 1971).

"The United States Balance of Payments: Exchange Rates—How Flexible Should They Be?" *Hearings before the Joint Economic Committee,* 88th Cong. 1st sess., 1963. Especially testimony by Henry Wallich (pp. 495–499) and Milton Friedman (pp. 451–456).

Part Seven

Berliner, Joseph S., "Managerial Incentives and Decision Making: A Comparison of the United States and the Soviet Union," in *Comparisons of the United States and Soviet Economies,* Joint Economic Committee, U.S. Congress Part I, pp. 349–376, 1959.

Crosland, Anthony, *Social Democracy in Europe* (London: The Fabian Society, 1975), (Fabian Tract 438).

Friedman, Milton, *Capitalism and Freedom* (Chicago: University of Chicago Press, 1962).

Gregory, Paul R., and Robert C. Stuart, *Soviet Economic Structure and Performance* (New York: Harper & Row, 1974).

Lange, Oskar, and Fred M. Taylor, *On The Economic Theory of Socialism* (New York: McGraw-Hill, 1964).

Mandel, Ernest, *An Introduction to Marxist Economic Theory* (New York: Pathfinder Press, 1970).

Mises, Ludwig von, *Socialism: An Economic and Sociological Analysis* (New Haven: Yale University Press, 1951).

Nove, Alec, "Soviet Agriculture under Brezhnev," *Slavic Review,* Vol. 29 (1970).

Rothbard, Murray N., *For a New Liberty* (New York: Macmillan, 1973).

Vanek, Jaroslav, *The Participatory Economy.* (Ithaca, N.Y.: Cornell University Press, 1971).

Index